Easements and Servitudes

A Treatise
on the
American Law
of
Easements and Servitudes

By

EMORY WASHBURN, LL.D.

Second Edition

BeardBooks

Washington, D.C.

HON. HORACE BINNEY, LL.D.

In dedicating this work to you, without first asking permission, I may have presumed too far upon the acquaintance which I share with the profession and your fellow-citizens generally, through your distinguished learning as a jurist, your practical wisdom as a statesman, and the fruits of a long life of usefulness and honor.

In this hour of peril to all we hold dear, it is grateful to recall that a few remain who, like you, stood by the nation's cradle at its birth, and have watched over its wonderful growth as it rose and expanded under the protection of wise laws, and the invigorating influences of beneficent institutions.

It is impossible to contemplate even so minute a department of the law as that to which the following pages are devoted, without perceiving something of the all-pervading spirit of progress and improvement which has hitherto vitalized the jurisprudence of our country. And of no State can this be more truly said than of Pennsylvania, within which your labors have been chiefly employed.

You have borne your full share, as a minister of the law, in giving form and consistency to that jurisprudence which, we trust, will carry it safely through the ordeal of a civil war, again to bless a prosperous and a united people.

In the hope that the light of returning harmony and prosperity over our common country, under the protection of Law, may yet gild the declining hours of so active and useful a life, permit me to subscribe myself, with high respect,

Your obedient servant,

EMORY WASHBURN.

CAMBRIDGE, February, 1863.

ERRATA.

On page 97, 23d line, *for* covenantor *read* covenantee.
" 133, last line, *for* judgment *read* enjoyment.
" 271 note, *for* § 16, *read* Section 6.

PREFACE

THE manner in which the first edition of this work has
been received, is a gratifying evidence not only of a want in
the profession to be supplied, but that the attempt to meet it
has been reasonably successful. It has encouraged the author to a renewed effort to render the work still more satisfactory and complete. In the present edition he has incorporated about a hundred pages into the text of the work,
and has endeavored to collect for reference every case to
which he had access, which had been decided, upon the subjects of which it treats, before the volume went to press.
The subjects upon which the text has been chiefly enlarged,
have been the doctrine of Easements created by implication,
upon the division of heritages, and the interesting, modern
doctrine of mutual easements and servitudes between parts
of a once common estate, growing out of their relation to
each other in the orderly arrangement of buildings, &c.,
upon streets, squares, and open areas in cities and villages.
Other subjects also have been more fully developed, and in a
few instances the text has been changed to conform to the
changed condition of the law.

A reference to the numerous cases which have been decided by the courts since the publication of the former
edition, would serve to indicate the growing interest and
importance of the subjects of which it treats. Indeed it
could hardly be otherwise, in view of the growing wants of

a busy, thriving community, who are constantly building up towns and villages, and calling into exercise the privileges and conveniences which a successful prosecution of industry and the arts demands. While the law is continually making progress in this direction, it is rather by the application by courts of known and familiar principles to new cases as they arise, than by any action of the law-making power in the State. It is for this reason, that a somewhat liberal reference has been made, in this as in the former edition, to elementary treatises of foreign jurists.

The author would be doing injustice to his own feelings if he failed to acknowledge a grateful sense of the expressions of favor with which his attempt to supply an American work upon the Law of Easements and Servitudes, has been received. And he can only add the hope that the present volume may be found equally acceptable, at least, with that whose place it has been prepared to supply.

CAMBRIDGE, June, 1867.

PREFACE

THE following work was undertaken at the suggestion of various gentlemen of large experience, that something of the kind was needed by the profession. This conviction has been strengthened in my own mind, at every step of the progress of its preparation. There were, it is true, treatises extant upon some of the topics embraced in it, and one upon the general subject of Easements had attained a high rank as a work of merit. But an American lawyer need not be reminded that the treatise of Messrs. Gale and Whatley, or that of Mr. Gale, as it appears in the third edition, was in all respects English in its character, and in the authorities which one finds there cited. If here and there this rule has been departed from, it has been too infrequent to detract from its character as a purely English work.

It appeared in 1839, and in 1840 was republished in New York, with notes " by E. Hammond, Counsellor at Law." In 1848, a second edition of the English work was published, and in its Preface the authors explain, in half apologetic terms, why they had presumed to admit into it the few American cases which it contained. " In Acton *v.* Blundel," they remark, " the Court of Exchequer Chamber cited American authority as at least proper to be weighed and examined in deciding a case upon principle. In the present edition, two cases have been inserted, decided in the courts of the United States, upon a question very bare of authority, — the legal relation of owners of several stages of a building. They have been taken from an edition of this work published at New York." A third edition, bearing also the name of Mr. Willes, was published in 1862, which not only sustained the high character which the work had previously held, but did not detract from its exclusive nationality, so far as the United States were concerned.

While, however, no one has any right to object that the authors of that work chose to confine their references to such cases as were of authority in the English courts, it is not to be lost sight of, that there were scattered through the volumes of American reports, at the times when it appeared, literally hundreds of cases, bearing directly upon the subjects of which it treated, many of which, for research and ability, would not have suffered in comparison with the ablest judgment to be found, upon a like subject, on the records of the English courts.

It was not, therefore, strange that a sentiment prevailed, that the American Bar needed a convenient medium of reference, where the learning of the American courts, upon a subject of such general interest as is here treated of, might be found by the side of that of the Queen's Bench and Exchequer Chamber.

Another reason why a treatise upon the English law alone, however perfect, could not but be inadequate to the wants of the profession in the United States, grows out of the difference there is in the condition of the two countries, and the fact that the jurisprudence of a people must conform to their peculiar wants and circumstances. It is the difference between a community where everything has become settled and compact by age, and tradition and prescription have fixed, in the national mind, notions and ideas which render all but inflexible the canons of property and right; and a people who, while sharing in these traditionary habits of legal thought, have been busy in ingrafting upon an existing system laws adapted to the wants and condition of a new and growing body politic, in a country with essentially different physical capacities from that from which they had borrowed their jurisprudence, and requiring its rules of property to conform to the genius of its institutions and the forms of its government.

In order, however, to be able to trace and understand wherein this complex system of the American common law is coincident with or differs from that of England, its rules are to be sought and studied in the multiplied and constantly increasing volumes of reported cases of the English, as well as our own national and State courts; while the difficulty of doing this, from their very multiplicity, is to many, if not most of the profession, well-nigh insurmountable.

These are among the considerations to which the present work owes its conception and execution. And while for the arrangement of its parts, as well as the collection of most of its materials, I have been obliged to content myself with the unaided results of my own reflection and research, I have not hesitated to avail myself of works like those of Messrs. Tudor, and Woolrych, and Angell, which treat more or less in detail upon the subjects which make up the body of this.

It has been my aim to examine, for myself, every reported case which bore sufficiently upon the topic under consideration to warrant a reference to it as an authority. The cases thus examined considerably exceed a thousand in number, and the fact is alluded to only that, if effort in that direction shall be found less successful than I could have wished, it may not seem to have failed from the want of reasonable diligence.

In one respect, I may add, I found much embarrassment in the preparation of the work.

No lawyer need be told that many of the principles of the common law of Easements are derived directly from the

Civil law, and may be found in the Scotch and Continental systems of jurisprudence. The question early arose in this preparation, how far it was desirable to collect and compare the analogies that exist between these systems and that of the common law. While such a reference might have given to the work an air of learning and research disproportioned to the actual labor it would have cost, it could not have failed to swell it to an inconvenient size, and, what seemed to be far more objectionable, it could at best have been of but doubtful utility. So far as the courts of common law had, in their reported cases, adopted principles which were common to both systems, it was unnecessary to restate them in the language of the original sources from which they had been derived. And so far as there were parts of these systems which had never been recognized by the courts, a discussion of them could be little better than speculative in its character, and would require careful and extended explanations and limitations, that they might not mislead.

After considerable reflection, therefore, it was concluded to omit, with a few exceptions, references to works upon the Civil and Continental law, except for purposes of explanation and definition. And so far as this rule has been departed from, the exceptions have been limited to topics upon which the common law seemed to be especially defective and unsatisfactory. Such was the case, for instance, in the matter of "party walls." And where this has been done, the citations are made to furnish their own explanation, and are in little danger of misleading even the casual reader.

If it should seem to any one that the citations of authorities in the work are unnecessarily numerous, it is due to the subject to remind such, by way of explanation, that not a little of the law of Easements, as it is now understood in the courts of common law, has been progressive in its character and recent in its development.

The rule, for instance, which regulates the rights of respective mill-owners upon the same stream to the use of the water thereof, was settled in England as late as 1805. And the rights of adjacent owners of land in respect to subterranean waters percolating from the one into the other, it is believed, were for the first time adjudged by any court of common law in that of Massachusetts in 1836, but were not finally settled by the House of Lords, in England, until 1859. And because these decisions have been so recent and progressive, one would hardly feel at liberty to assume that any proposition to which they relate has become sufficiently familiar law to be stated without its accompanying authority. For the same reason, if a point has been raised and settled or discussed in more than one court, the profession would have a right to expect that, if a reference is made to reported cases at all, it should be extended to all that bore upon the subject they were examining. When to this it is added that the questions which have come under the cognizance of the courts were many of them so far original in their character as to require a recourse to analogies and general principles rather than settled authorities, it will be seen why the judges, in their opinions, have taken a wider range of discussion than the particular matters before them, and why the reasoning and analogies which have been made use of under one state of facts, have been resorted to for illustration in their application to others. The same case may therefore be found a subject of reference, not only upon different propositions, under different phases, upon the same subject, but upon different subjects themselves, as they have come up in the course of the work. Another reason for collecting and citing, in some instances, many cases upon a single point, has been the desirableness of bringing together the related decisions of the courts of the different States, in order, so far as might be, to work out something like a homogeneous system of American law upon a subject of such common interest. If to this is added the circumstance of the great number of these individual cases, which has been spoken of in another connection, it is hoped that the multiplication of these citations will be accounted for without supposing it to be the result of carelessness or a desire of unnecessary display.

Aside from the want of an American treatise upon the subject of Easements and Servitudes, there is something in the importance and wide application of the subject itself, in its practical bearings, which seemed to call for the means of understanding it more familiarly. The interests with which it is connected are not only various and multiform, but they concern the comfort and convenience of men in their relations to one another, as well as in that of members of the broader associations of neighborhoods and civil communities. Its laws are found adequate to determine rights which are too minute to be measured by any scale of value, at the same time that they embrace within their care interests as vast as those involved in the business and enterprise of a whole people. They serve to trace out the footpath from the cottage to the spring that supplies the daily wants of its inmates, and to define the line of eaves' drip along the few inches of soil upon which it falls, at the same time that they reach and limit the rights and relations of property between the citizen and the public in the banks and waters of the broad rivers which form the highways of commerce, and guide and regulate the application of the elements in ministering to the industry and arts which sustain and enrich a nation.

In carrying out a work designed to embody the elements of such a system into a practical and convenient form, no reasonable endeavor has been spared to make it what it was supposed the profession desired; but for its success, its reliance must be upon their indulgence.

CAMBRIDGE, February, 1863.

CONTENTS.

CHAPTER I.

OF THE NATURE, CHARACTER, AND MODE OF ACQUIRING EASE-
MENTS AND SERVITUDES.

CHAPTER II.

EASEMENTS AND SERVITUDES OF WAY.

CHAPTER III.

OF EASEMENTS AND SERVITUDES OF WATER.

CHAPTER VI.

REPAIRS OF EASEMENTS AND REMEDY FOR INJURIES.

TABLE OF CASES CITED.

THE LAW

OF

EASEMENTS AND SERVITUDES.

CHAPTER I.

OF THE NATURE, CHARACTER, AND MODE OF ACQUIRING EASEMENTS AND SERVITUDES.

SECTION I.

NATURE, CLASSIFICATION, AND QUALITIES OF EASEMENTS, ETC.

1

1. From the various modes of use and enjoyment to which lands may be subjected, there results an idea of property in these distinct from that of actual possession, with which the feudal doctrine of real property is chiefly associated. Almost every shade of interest or right of control over corporeal hereditaments may exist, from the absolute dominion of the allodial proprietor to the briefest and most qualified use which may be made of them, by mere license and indulgence, which necessarily leads to a classification of rights, in treating of Real Property as a general system.

It is of one only of these classes that this work proposes to treat, and, although somewhat comprehensive in its character, it is embraced under the generic term of *Easements* or *Servitudes*.

2. Various forms of definition have been applied in describing this class of interests in real property, which are more or less comprehensive, as the court or writer was contemplating the subject as an entire system, or in its more limited and restricted sense.

Thus the definition adopted by Bayley, J., from " Termes de la Ley," which he calls " a book of great antiquity and accuracy," is " a privilege that one neighbor hath of another by charter or prescription, without profit "; and it is illustrated " as a way or sink through his land, or such like." [1] And, in another case, the court, in giving illustrations of what are easements, speak of " rights of way, rights to water, right to pollute water, and rights of common," as being " well defined as easements, to be exercised

[1] Hewlins v. Shippam, 5 Barnew. & C. 221 ; Cowel, Interp. " Easement."

by one person over the land of another," and add: "The right acquired by time to send noxious vapors over another's land is another instance."[1]

The essential qualities of easements are these : 1st, they are incorporeal ; 2d, they are imposed on corporeal property, and not upon the owner thereof; 3d, they confer no right to a participation in the profits arising from such property ; 4th, they are imposed for the benefit of corporeal property ; and 5th, there must be two distinct tenements, — the dominant, to which the right belongs, and the servient, upon which the obligation rests.[2] But it is not necessary that the dominant and servient estates should be in contiguity with each other.[3] A contract for a right to pass over the lands of another is an easement extending only to a temporary disturbance of the owner's possession. The grantee of such an easement is not the owner or occupant of the estate over which the way is used.[4]

3. These definitions, it will be perceived, exclude the right of taking profits in another's land, commonly called *profits à prendre*, although the court, in Rowbotham v. Wilson, embrace rights of common as expressly within the term *easement*, and although, as will appear hereafter, such rights were included in those of *servitude* under the civil law, with which easements are understood to be in most, if not all respects, identical.

Mr. Burton speaks of them thus : " Rights of accommodation in another's land, as distinguished from those which are directly profitable, are properly called easements."[5]

[1] Rowbotham v. Wilson, 8 Ellis & B. 123. " All easements are things incorporeal, mere rights invisible and intangible." Bowen v. Team, 6 Rich. 298. A servitude is thus defined by the Code Nap., § 637: " Une charge imposée sur héritage pour l'usage et l'utilité d'un héritage appartenant à un autre propriétaire." The civil law recognized a servitude which was due from one person to another, which was not recognized by the laws of France or England. Inst. L. 1, tit. 3, § 2. 1 Lepage Desgodets, 4. Gütter. Brac. 98.

[2] Wolfe v. Frost, 4 Sandf. Ch. 72 ; Tud. Lead. Cas. 107.

[3] Perrin v. Garfield, 37 Vt. 312.

[4] Cook Co. v. C. B. & Q. R. R., 35 Ill. 464.

[5] Burt. Real. Prop., § 1165.

Nor does the last definition embrace the class of rights which one may have in another's land, like a right of way or of common, without its being exercised in connection with the occupancy of other lands, and therefore called a right *in gross*. Mr. Burton says, " Such a right (of way), if in gross, seems to be not properly a tenement." [1] *Servitus* presupposes a relation existing between two pieces of land. Rights granted to the person only, were not held to be *servitudes*.[2] But, after all, it partakes so much of the character of an easement, that, like the rights which the inhabitants in certain localities may acquire by *custom*, or the public by *dedication*, to pass over the land of an indi-
[*4] vidual, for instance, it *would be difficult to treat of easements and servitudes, without embracing these rights, as well as that of taking profits in another's land which one may enjoy in connection with the occupancy of the estate to which such right is united. An illustration of what constitutes an easement, as distinguished from a *profit à prendre*, would be this. All rights of way are easements. So is the right to enter upon another's land, and to erect booths thereon on public days, or to dance and play at lawful sports. So are aquatic rights of whatever kind when enjoyed by those who do not own the soil, such as a right to take water from a spring or a well upon another's land for domestic use. But a right to take and carry away sea-weed is a *profit à prendre*, and not a technical easement. Nor can it be prescribed for as a personal right, or a right by custom.[3]

Indeed, the latter branch of the subject is expressly included in the definition given by the court in Ritger *v.* Parker, viz.: " An easement or servitude is a right which one proprietor has to some profit, benefit, or lawful use, out of, or over, the estate of another proprietor." [4]

[1] Burt. Real. Prop., § 1166.

[2] Gütter. Brac., c. 15, p. 122.

[3] Hill *v.* Lord, 48 Maine, 99. *Post*, *78, *79.

[4] Ritger *v.* Parker, 8 Cush. 145. In treating of the subject in this broader sense of the term, it is believed we are fully sustained by the following, among other

4. The term which is applied to interests in land, such as have been above referred to, by the civil law, is "Servitudes." Nor can the doctrines of the common law upon the subject be fully understood or explained, without occasionally referring to those systems from which the common law has borrowed many of its rules. A "servitude" is defined to be "a right, whereby one thing is subject to another thing or person, for use or convenience contrary to common right." "Services," it is further said, "may be divided into *real* and *personal*. Real, which are also called '*prædial* services,' are such as one estate owes unto another estate, as, because I am the owner of such a ground, I have the right of a way through the ground of another person, or, because I am possessed of this house, my neighbor cannot beat out a light or window out of his own house towards mine, or build his house higher without my leave." [1]

It is the nature of servitudes not to constrain any one to do, but to suffer something, "ut aliquid patiatur aut non faciat." [2]

*" Hence," says Mr. Erskine, " it may be perceived [*5] that he whose tenement may be subject to a servitude is not, in the common case, bound to perform any act for the benefit of the person or tenement to which it is due. His whole burden consists either in being restrained from doing, or in being obliged to suffer something to be done upon his property by another. In the first case, in which the proprietor is barely restrained from acting, the servitude is called *negative*, in the last *positive*." [3]

Both terms, *Easements* and *Servitudes*, are used by common-law writers, and often indiscriminately. The former,

authorities : Brakely *v.* Sharp, 1 Stockt. 9; Doe *v.* Wood, 2 Barnew. & Ald. 724; Kieffer *v.* Imhoff, 26 Penn. St. 438; Shelf. R. P. Stat. 6; 1 Lomax, Dig. 614; Tud. Lead. Cas. 107; Karmuller *v.* Kratz, 18 Iowa, 357.

[1] Ayl. Pand. 306; Ersk. Inst. 354.

[2] 2 Fournel, Traité du Voisinage, 361; D. 8, 1, 15; 5 Duranton, Cours de Droit Français, 498, ed. 1834; Lalaure, Traité des Servitudes, 9.

[3] Ersk. Inst. 352.

however, is more generally applied to the right enjoyed, the latter to the burden imposed. The right of way which one man has, as the owner of an estate, over the land of another, is an easement in the one estate and a servitude upon the other.

As both terms may, at times, be employed in this work, this explanation seemed to be necessary in order to prevent confusion in the forms of expression that may be made use of.

5. There is an important distinction to be observed between an Easement and a License, lest the apparent similarity in their mode of enjoyment should mislead the inquirer, at times, as to their character. An Easement always implies an interest in the land, in or over which it is to be enjoyed. A License carries no such interest. The interest of an easement may be a freehold or a chattel one, according to its duration; whereas, whatever right one has in another's land by license may, as a general proposition, be said to be revocable at will by the owner of the land in which it is to be enjoyed.[1]

Thus it is said, " An easement must be an interest in or over the soil." [2] " It lies not in livery, but in grant, [*6] and a *freehold interest in it cannot be created or passed, (even if a chattel interest may, which I think it cannot,) otherwise than by deed." [3]

And where a right of way was set off to a widow as appurtenant to her dower land, it was held to continue only during the continuance of her life estate.[4]

The foregoing distinction between a license and an easement may be illustrated by the effect given to a conveyance of the land in or over which it is to be enjoyed. A conveyance of land by the grantor, who has given a parol license to

---

[1] *Ex parte* Coburn, 1 Cow. 568 ; Wolfe v. Frost, 4 Sandf. Ch. 72 ; Foster v. Browning, 4 R. I. 47 ; *post*, p. *7.

[2] Per *Cresswell*, J., Rowbotham v. Wilson, 8 Ellis & B. 123.

[3] Hewlins v. Shippam, 5 Barnew. & C. 221, per *Bayley*, J.

[4] Hoffman v. Savage, 15 Mass. 131. See Symmes v. Drew, 21 Pick. 278 ; Grant v. Chase, 17 Mass. 446.

another to enjoy a right in the nature of an easement in it, *ipso facto*, determines the license ; whereas whoever takes an estate upon which a servitude has been imposed, holds it subject to the same servitude, and in the same manner as it was held by his grantor.[1]

6. It may be further remarked, by way of preliminary explanation, that, while in acquiring an easement by grant or prescription, which is deemed to be evidence of a grant, a grantor and a grantee are always implied, there is a class of easements which the residents of vills or particular localities may acquire by what is called *custom*, although not claimed by them as personal rights, nor as rights belonging to a body politic, nor by any right or claim as grantees.[2]

And in further explanation of the distinction there is between an easement or servitude, properly so called, and a right by custom, it may be stated, that among the rights which have been held to be gained by custom, are those of the people of a particular vill coming together to dance upon a particular close, or drawing water for their use from *a certain well or spring of water. But these rights do [*7] not extend to the taking of profits in the land of another, such as catching fish in his waters, or taking sand from his soil or herbage from his close. This can only be acquired by grant or prescription, and implies a person or body politic *in esse*, competent to take by deed.[3] If the grant be a personal license of pleasure, it extends only to the individual, and is not to be exercised by or with servants ; but if it be a license of profit and not for pleasure, it may. The case referred to was of a license to hunt, and as it included the right to kill

[1] Wallis v. Harrison, 4 Mees. & W. 538 , Hills v Miller, 3 Paige, 254, 257.

[2] Brakely v. Sharp, 1 Stockt. 9 ; Lockwood v. Wood, 6 Q. B. 31, 66 , Day v Savadge, Hob 85 ; Gateward's case, 6 Rep. 60 ; 1 Lomax, Dig 614 ; Smith v Gatewood, Cro. Jac. 152.

[3] Bland v. Lipscombe, 4 Ellis & B. 714, note; Grimstead v. Marlowe, 4 T. R. 717; Abbot v Weckly, 1 Lev. 176 ; Waters v. Lilley, 4 Pick. 145 ; Race v. Ward, 7 Ellis & B. 384 , Wickham v. Hawker, 7 Mees & W. 63. See *post*, sect 4, pl. 12, 13, 18 , chap. 3, sect. 10.

and take with him the deer at his pleasure, it was held a license to go on with his servants, or send them to hunt; whereas, if it was a mere license to hunt at his pleasure, he cannot take away the game, nor go with servants, nor assign his license to another.[1]

7. This right of *profit à prendre*, if enjoyed by reason of holding a certain other estate, is regarded in the light of an easement appurtenant to such estate; whereas, if it belongs to an individual, distinct from any ownership of other lands, it takes the character of an interest or estate in the land itself, rather than that of a proper easement in or out of the same.[2] Where, in the grant of one parcel of land, it was agreed that the grantee should " have the use of the timber" on another parcel, belonging to the grantor, it was held that the right granted was one " *in alieno solo*, like common of turbary, or the right to take coal or ore in another's land, and was when assignable not properly an easement but a *profit à prendre* which may be acquired by grant or prescription, and a covenant by the owner of the soil that it shall exist, amounts to a grant of it." And if not assignable, but a mere personal privilege, the covenant gives an irrevocable license for its exercise. But the court, though they hold it an incorporeal right, do not decide whether, in this case, the right to use the timber was a personal one in gross, or a right appurtenant to the granted estate.[3]

8. It will be necessary to refer to these distinctions again. And they have been noticed at this stage of the work chiefly for the purpose of defining the meaning of certain terms and phrases which will often occur in the progress of it. And the following citations are added for the same purpose, — the first as showing the sense in which the term easement is used in its connection with the civil law, the others as pre-

[1] Duchess of Norfolk *v.* Wiseman, cited 7 M. & W. 77, from the Y. Books. *Post,* p. *28. See Manwood, 108.

[2] Per *Walworth,* Ch., Post *v.* Pearsall, 22 Wend. 425; Grimstead *v.* Marlowe, 4 T. R. 717; *post,* sect. 4, pl. 20.

[3] Clark *v.* Way, 11 Rich. (Law), 621; *post,* p. *11.

senting what is believed to be its use, at this day, in courts of common law.

" In the Civil Law, a servitude which is but a single right of property, and is called in our law an Easement, is a burden affecting lands, by which the proprietor is restrained from the full use of his property, or is obliged to suffer another to do certain acts upon it, which, were it not for the burden, would be competent solely to the owner." [1] " The right of making use of the land of others, whether it be that of the public or individuals, for a precise and definite *purpose, not inconsistent with a general right [*8] of property in the owner, especially where it is for the public use, is, in legal contemplation, an easement or franchise, and not a grant of the soil or general property." [2]   In the words of Bramwell, B., an easement is " something additional to the ordinary rights of property "; and in those of Williams, J., it is " a right accessorial to the ordinary rights of property." [3]

9. The ownership of an easement, and that of the fee in the same estate, are in different persons.   Nor does the interest of the one affect that of the other, so but that each may have his proper remedy for an injury to his right, independent of the other.   Thus the owner of the fee may recover his seisin by a proper action in his own name, and the owner of the easement, if disturbed in the enjoyment of it, may sue for such disturbance in his own name. [4]

10. It is hardly necessary, after the above definitions, to add, that the existence of two distinct and separate estates or tenements is implied in the existence of an easement; the one in favor or for the benefit of which it exists, and is called *dominant,* and the other, over or upon which it is exercised, and is called *servient;* and, as will be seen

---

[1] Laumier v. Francis, 23 Mo. 181.

[2] Boston Water Power Co. v. Boston & Worcester R. R., 16 Pick. 512, 522.

[3] Rowbotham v. Wilson, 8 Ellis & B. 123, 152.   See also Harback v. City of Boston, 10 Cush. 295; Shelf. R. P. Stat. 6.   Dubuque v. Maloney, 9 Iowa, 450.

[4] Hancock v. Wentworth, 5 Metc. 446 ; Morgan v. Moore, 3 Gray, 319.

hereafter, if at any time these estates are united under one ownership and possession, the easement is at once extinguished.[1]

11. A man may have a way, *in gross*, over another's land, but it must, from its nature, be a personal right, not assignable nor inheritable ; nor can it be made so by any terms in the grant, any more than a collateral and independent covenant can be made to run with land.

And if one has a right of way appendant or appurtenant to an estate, he cannot grant it separate and distinct from the land to which it belongs.

[*9]   *So where there was a grant of a right of way *for all purposes*, though it might authorize the grantee to use the way for purposes not connected with the use of the land granted therewith, yet if land was in fact granted therewith, so far as the use exceeded the purposes which were properly connected with the enjoyment of the land, it would be a personal right, and not assignable. When, therefore, the grantee conveyed the dominant estate " with all ways," &c., it did not convey any right of way as being appurtenant, under that grant, except such as was connected with the use and enjoyment of the land to which it was annexed. " It is not," say the court, " in the power of a vendor to create any rights, not connected with the use and enjoyment of the land, and annex them to it ; nor can the owner of land render it subject to a new species of burden, so as to bind it in the hands of an assignee.[2]

The language of the court in White v. Crawford,[3] might seem to conflict with what is said above : " As to ways in gross, that they may be granted or may accrue in various forms to one and his heirs and assigns, there can be no doubt. There is a strong example of such a grant in the case of

[1] Tud. Lead Cas 108   Mabie v Matteson, 17 Wis. 1 ; 1 Desgodets, ch. 2, art. 1.

[2] Ackroyd v Smith, 10 C. B. 164, 167, 188; Garrison v. Rudd, 19 Ill. 558; Woolr. Ways, 16 ; *post*, sect 2, pl 16.

[3] White v. Crawford, 10 Mass. 188.

Senhouse *v.* Christian,[1] upon which the defendants justified as heirs of the original grantee."

12. But the language of Walworth, Ch., in Post *v.* Pearsall,[2] would seem to furnish a clew by which these cases may be reconciled with the above doctrine of Ackroyd *v.* Smith. The distinction seems to be this : If the easement consists in a right of *profit à prendre*, such as taking soil, gravel, minerals, and the like, from another's land, it is so far of the character of an estate or interest in the land itself, *that, if granted to one in gross, it is treated as an [*10] estate, and may, therefore, be one for life or inheritance. But if it is an easement proper, such as a right of way and the like, and is granted in gross, it is a mere personal interest, and not inheritable. The case of Senhouse *v.* Christian was one where there was a grant of a way, and the question was, chiefly, as to the mode and extent of using it, and the point of its being inheritable does not seem to have arisen in the hearing. But the very terms of the grant implied an occupancy of the grantor's land to a certain extent, as, for instance, to "make and lay causeways," &c., and it was held to be the grant of a right to lay a framed wagon-way across the grantor's land.

12 *a*. In a very recent case in Massachusetts,[3] Foster, J. examines the question of a grant of a right to draw water from a spring by means of an aqueduct, and how far it was itself a subject of grant independent of the ownership of any estate to which it was appurtenant, in a full and elaborate opinion, in which it is clearly shown that such a right is the subject of grant and inheritance, although not accompanied by the grant of an estate in land. The right was created by a reservation by the original owner of the estate upon which the spring was situated when granting the same, the reser-

---

[1] Senhouse *v* Christian, 1 T. R 560.

[2] Post *v* Pearsall, 22 Wend 425 ; Perley *v.* Langley, 7 N H 233 , *post*, sect 4, pl. 20   See also 2 Blackst Comm 33, the case of Common , Welcome *v.* Upton, 6 Mees & W. 536, case of Pasturage

[3] Goodrich *v* Burbank, Allen, not yet reported.

vation being to the grantor, his heirs and assigns, without any reference to any estate with which it was to be used ; and the injury complained of was cutting the aqueduct by the owner of the soil. He cites, with approbation, the language of Curtis, J : [1] " If I have a spring, I may sell the right to take water from it by pipes to one who does not own the land across which the pipes are to be carried, and I may restrict the use to a particular house, or not, as I please." " Incorporeal hereditaments may be inseparably annexed to a particular messuage or tract of land by the grant which creates them and makes them incapable of separate existence. But they may also be granted in gross, and, afterwards, for purposes of enjoyment, be annexed to a messuage or land without the right, or a conveyance of the right without the land."

Although, in the cases above cited from both the New York and Massachusetts courts, there is a distinction made between the grant of water and of a *profit à prendre*, where water is, as it may be, a subject of sale in gross as a thing of value, it does not seem to be violating any principle of law to regard it as a species of *profit à prendre*, and therefore a subject of separate grant. Thus in Chatfield v. Wilson, the court, speaking of water in the earth or percolating under its surface, say : " Such water is to be regarded as part of the land itself, to be enjoyed absolutely by the proprietor within whose territory it is." [2] And in giving judgment in Acton v. Blundell, Tindal, C. J. remarks : " It (the case) falls within that principle which gives to the owner of the soil all that lies beneath his surface ; the land immediately below is his property, whether it is solid rock or porous ground or venous earth, or part soil, part water. The person who owns the surface may dig therein and apply all that is there found to his own purposes, at his free will and pleasure." [3]

---

[1] Lonsdale Co. v. Moies, 21 Law Rep. 664 ; see De Witt v. Harvey, 4 Gray, 489 ; Buffum v. Harris, 5 R. I. 243 ; Borst v. Empie, 1 Seld. 40.

[2] Chatfield v. Wilson, 28 Verm. 49.

[3] Acton v. Blundell, 12 M. & Wels. 354. See Buffum v. Harris, 5 R. I. 253.

And though it might be difficult to raise a prescriptive right of inheritance in the privilege of an aqueduct by a personal enjoyment, independent of its user in connection with some estate, and although a right to the enjoyment of water from a well or spring or river may be gained by custom, since no part of the soil or freehold, proper, is thus carried away any faster than it is ordinarily supplied from natural sources, yet, after all, it is an interest in land ; and as the judge in Goodrich v. Burbank very properly and forcibly remarks, " we are unable to distinguish between the right to take water by a canal from a pond for the purposes of power and the right to take it from a spring in a pipe for domestic purposes." [1]

If the grant of a right to take water in or from the grantor's estate can be regarded as " taking a profit in the soil," the cases seem clear that it may be to one and his heirs, independent of the ownership of any estate to which the right is to be appurtenant. Thus a right " to search and get " minerals,[2] or to hunt in a man's park and carry away the deer,[3] are subjects of grant, and may pass to assigns.

And the court in Hill v. Lord say, " that the right to water in wells or cisterns would be an interest in the land or a *profit à prendre*." [4]   And though, if the action were against a stranger for taking water from a spring of running water, the distinction might be a valid one between water in a stream and water in a well or cistern, it would not seem to lie in the mouth of the grantor to justify cutting off the supply which is enjoyed by means of a pipe laid through his land from a spring that rises within the same, the right to take and enjoy which, by maintaining such pipe, he or those under whom he claims title had conveyed by deed.

13. The owner of an easement in another's land has nei-

---

[1] See *post*, *79, *80. Hurd v. Curtis, 7 Met. 114.

[2] Muskett v. Hill, 5 Bing. N. C. 694.

[3] Thomas v. Lovell, Vaughn, 351 ; Bailey v. Stephens, 12 C. B., N. S. 108.

[4] Hill v. Lord, 48 Maine, 100.

ther the general property in nor seisin of the servient estate, though he may, by holding a fee in the estate to which such easement is appurtenant, have an estate of inheritance in the easement. And from being something impalpable, of which a seisin cannot be predicated, easements are classed with incorporeal hereditaments, and are so designated in the definitions thereof.[1]

14. If one claims a prescriptive right to an easement in another's land, by reason of owning or occupying land to which such right is appurtenant, he is said to claim in a *que estate*, and it is only in this form that a claim of a *profit à prendre*, by prescription, can be sustained.[2]

15. The case of Doe *v*. Wood illustrates the distinction between the grant of a specific portion or share of soil, and that of a right or privilege to acquire something by acts done upon the soil of another. In that case, the grant was of a right to search for metals in the grantor's land, and to [*11] raise and dispose of the same when found there, *during the time. It was held to be, not a specific grant of the metals in the land, but a right of property only as to such part thereof as, under the liberties granted, should be dug and got; that the grantee had no estate as property in the land itself, or any particular portion thereof, or in any part of the ore ungot therein, and that it was very different from a grant or demise of the mines or metals in the land. The right to obtain the minerals is spoken of as an "incorporeal privilege." [3] If, however, the grant be of a mine with mining privileges, it is not an easement, but a part of the freehold.[4]

16. In classifying servitudes, the civil law recognized a much more minute subdivision of the various forms they as-

[1] Winslow *v*. King, 14 Gray, 321; Ayl. Pand. 306; Baer *v*. Martin, 8 Blackf. 317; Pitkin *v*. Long Island R. R. Co., 2 Barb. Ch. 221; Orleans Navigation Co. *v*. Mayor of New Orleans, 2 Mart. 214.

[2] Grimstead *v*. Marlowe, 4 T. R. 717; Abbot *v*. Weekly, 1 Lev. 176.

[3] Doe *v*. Wood, 2 Barnew. & Ald. 724.

[4] Caldwell *v*. Fulton, 31 Penn. 475; Zinc Co. *v*. Franklinite, 13 N. J. 341; Grubb *v*. Bayard, 2 Wallace, Jr. 81; *ante*, p. *7.

sumed, than those in use in the common law, although, as already remarked, the latter has borrowed so liberally from the former. And though, in treating of the subject, the more general classification of the common law will be observed, it seems proper to mention some, at least, of the divisions, and their designation, which were known to the civil law in its practical application. For though it is said by Martin B., that the civil law has no binding authority in the administration of the common law in England, the cases are numerous in the American courts, where the doctrines of the civil law are referred to, in determining the rights of parties in respect to easements and servitudes.[1]

That class of servitudes which are chiefly treated of in this work were called *Predial*, from *Prædia*, lands and tenements, being such services as one estate owes to another. These were again divided into *rural* and *urban*, the one relating to land not occupied by buildings, the other affecting buildings, whether in a city proper, a vill, or in the country.[2]

Among the *rural services* was the right of passing over the land of another, which took various names of *Iter, Actus*, and *Via* or *Aditus*, according to the extent and mode of using the same ; the right of bringing water through another's land, called *Aquæ ductus*, when done by pipe or rivulet ; the right of drawing water, of watering cattle, of pasturage, hunting, hawking, fishing, making lime and digging gravel, chalk, stone, or sand, for the use of the dominant estate, though not for other uses, such as the manufacture of earthenware. All these were what were called *affirmative* services.

*The *urban services* were either *affirmative* or *nega-* [*12] *tive*. Among the *affirmative* urban services were the right to rest the wall of a house for its support against that of another, and to require the owner of the latter to keep the same in repair ; the right to fix and rest a beam or timber or

---

[1] Dodd *v.* Burchell, 1 H. & Colt. 121.
[2] Güterb. Brac., c. 15 ; 1 Desgodets, ch. 1, art. 2.

stone in the wall of another's house, in which case the latter was not bound to keep his wall in repair; the right to extend a balcony over the land of another, or to excavate a vault beneath it ; the right to extend the eaves of one's house over the land of another, to turn the droppings of his eaves upon the house or ground of another, or to receive the droppings from another's eaves upon one's own land, for his·own use and benefit ; a right to have a sink or *gutter* through a neighbor's house, to construct what lights or windows he chooses against the estate of another, and to have a clear and pleasant prospect from one's house over another's court or yard, or to have a passage-way through another's house or yard to one's own.

Among the *negative* services of an urban character were, that one's neighbor should not turn the droppings of the eaves of his house upon the house or ground of him who has the servitude ; that he should not darken his windows, or hinder his prospect by building, or by planting trees; that he should not make windows overlooking his premises; and a right to restrain another from building his house above a prescribed height.[1]

The 637th to the 701st articles of the Code Napoleon describe and enumerate the servitudes known to the French law, and include, — 1st, such as arise from the situation of places, as the respective rights of the owners of adjacent lands in respect to the waters upon the one passing upon or across the other, the boundaries of adjacent lands, [*13] and *the like ; 2d, such as are created by law, among which are towing-paths upon banks of rivers and highways, and party walls and ditches between two estates, and party or division hedges dividing lands, servitudes of views over a neighbor's property, and those of eaves of roofs and of ways answering to ways of necessity at common law;

---

[1] Ayl. Pand. 306 – 310 , Wood, Inst Civ. Law, 147; 1 Brown, Civ Law, 182, 183 , 1 Kauff Mackeldey, 335 – 347 ; 2 Fournal, Traité du Voisinage, 400 ; D. 8, 2, 2 and 3 ; Ibid. 8, 3, 1. See Shelf. R. P. Stat. 6 ; *post*, chap. 3, sect. 12.

3d, servitudes created by the act of man, which are divided
into *urban* and *rural*, answering to a like division in the civil
law, servitudes *continual* and *continuable*, and servitudes *apparent* and *non-apparent*. Another division of the subject is,
1st, how servitudes are created, and 2d, what are the rights
of the owner of the property to which the servitude is due.[1]

The Civil Code of Louisiana follows substantially the Code
Napoleon, in relation to servitudes predial or landed, though
somewhat more minute in their subdivision, and the rules by
which they are created or regulated, extending from Articles
642 to 818 inclusive, beginning at p. 96 of Upton and Jennings's edition of that work.

But it has not been thought advisable to occupy space in
transcribing any of these codes, any further than it may be
found of use by way of illustrating corresponding parts of the
common law upon the subject.

The same may be said of the Scotch law of servitudes,
which substantially follows the civil law, and may be found
embodied in Erskine's Institutes.[2]

17. Many of the classifications of easements in the Code
of France are recognized by the courts of common law, as,
for instance, that of *continuous* and *discontinuous*, which are
thus defined: " Continuous are those of which the enjoyment is or may be continual, without the necessity of any
actual interference by man, as a waterspout or a right of light
light or air. Discontinuous are those the enjoyment
*of which can be had only by the interference of man, [*14]
as rights of way, or a right to draw water." [3]

---

[1] 2 Code Nap , Barrett's transl., Art. 637 – 689   See 2 Fournel, Traité du Voisinage, 400 – 407. The doctrines of the civil code, relating to the easements and
servitudes of buildings, were borrowed principally from the *coutume* of Paris,
while those affecting other property than buildings were derived from the Roman
law. 2 Law Mag. & Rev. 8

[2] Ersk. Inst , fol ed 352 – 370   See also 3 Burge, Col & F. Law, 400 , *post*,
chap 3, sect. 12.

[3] Lampman *v* Milks, 21 N Y. 505 , Durel *v.* Boisblanc, 1 La. Ann. 407 ;
Pheysey *v* Vicary, 16 Mees. & W 484 , Polden *v* Bastard, 4 B. & S. 258 ; Suffield
v. Brown, 10 Jur N S 111 ; Kerr *v* Kerr, 14 Louis, 177

2

It may be further added, that in affirmative easements the servient tenement must permit some act to be done thereon by the owner of the dominant estate, such as passing over it as a way, discharging water upon it from a channel or spout or eaves of his house.   In negative easements, the owner of the servient estate is prohibited from doing something upon his own land which he otherwise might do, such as not building upon the same, when by so doing he obstructs the light and air from reaching the dominant estate, or not digging in his soil so as to weaken the foundations of the house standing on the dominant estate, and the like.[1]

18. An instance of a negative easement or servitude is found in Pitkin v. Long Island R. R. Company, in the obligation which the respondents entered into with a land-owner, to stop their cars at a particular place adjoining his property. The court held it, in substance, an easement or servitude, binding upon the property of the company, and an interest in their land in favor of the land-owner.   The land proprietor in such case had a negative easement in the property of the railroad company, whereby he might restrict them, as owners of a servient tenement, in the exercise of general and natural rights of property, so as to compel them to use it in a particular way, by keeping certain erections thereon, and stopping with their trains of cars at a particular place for his use and benefit as the owner of the adjacent land, which thus became the dominant tenement. It was, therefore, held to be an incorporeal hereditament, the right or title to which could only be acquired by a grant or deed under seal, or by prescription.[2]

19.   The instance given in a reported case, illustrat-
[*15] ing the *distinction between natural, legal, and conventional easements, in respect to their origin, is that of the natural servitude to which a lower field is subject, to

---

[1] Tud. Lead. Cas. 107.

[2] Pitkin v. Long Island R. R. Co., 2 Barb. Ch. 221, 231. See also Day v. New York Central R. R. Co., 31 Barb. 548. Greene v. Creighton, 7 R. I. 1 ; post, pp. *63, *508.

receive the surface water which flows on to a lower level from a higher one.[1] Though this is treated of more at length in a later stage of the work, it may be remarked that such a servitude is only regarded as a natural one, in respect to the water which is naturally upon the higher field, and not as to such as is created by the industry of man. While the owner below may not do anything to prevent the water naturally thereon from flowing from the upper field upon his own, the upper one has no right to do anything upon his land to increase the burden upon the field below, beyond what may arise from a proper cultivation of the same for agricultural purposes. And even in so doing he may not dig ditches to discharge water, that naturally stands stagnant upon his own land, on to that of a lower proprietor.[2]

20. The term "natural easements," as applicable, especially, to the case of flowing water, is often made use of by courts of common law, and is not likely to mislead the reader, inasmuch as the context usually shows in what sense the term is employed. But as it will appear hereafter that an easement, when technically considered, is an interest which one man has in another's estate by grant, or its equivalent, prescription, it seems, at first thought, to be inconsistent to characterize what belongs to an estate as inseparably incident thereto, and forming a part and parcel

---

[1] Laumier *v.* Francis, 23 Mo. 181. See Ersk. Inst., fol. ed. 352; Orleans Navigation Co. *v.* Mayor of New Orleans, 2 Mart. 214; 2 Fournel, Traité du Voisinage, 400.

The French law reckons five *natural* servitudes, viz.: 1. The flowing of water from higher to lower land. 2. The right to a spring or fountain of water on the part of the owner in whose land it rises. 3. The right of a land-owner to a watercourse flowing through or forming a boundary of his land. 4. The fixing and maintaining boundaries between lands of adjacent owners; and 5. Building and maintaining fences for separating the lands of different owners. 1. Lapage Desgodets, 15.

[2] Martin *v.* Jett, 12 La. 501; La. Civ. Code, Art. 656; Sowers *v.* Shiff, 15 La. An. 301; Duranton, Cours de Droit Français, 159; Delahoussaye *v.* Judice, 13 La. An. 587; Orleans Navigation Co. *v.* Mayor of New Orleans, 3 Mart. 214; *post*, chap. 3, sect. 1, pl. 19.

thereof, by the name of easement or servitude. It may be in many and perhaps most respects like an easement, and may be treated of accordingly, and yet will hardly come within the requisites of what constitutes an easement at common law. And Erle, J., in Stokoe v. Singers, [*16] *accordingly says: "The right to the natural flow of water is not an easement, but a natural right."[1]

21. By the French law, there may be such an arrangement of the parts of two estates belonging to the same person, that, for fancy or convenience, the use of the one is made available to the enjoyment of the other. Thus, for instance, the one may enjoy the advantage of a look-out or prospect across the other, and for this purpose windows may have been opened in the latter; or doors may have been opened through the walls separating the estates, by which communication may be had with the street; or water may be conducted by an aqueduct from a pond or a fountain which belongs to the owner of one estate into a meadow which he may wish to water. And these may be mutual, each estate having for this purpose an advantage in the other, reciprocally, or the arrangement may be such that only one of the two estates enjoys a benefit from the other. The arranging and adapting the two estates in this way to each other is called *Destination du père de famille*. But this does not extend to discontinuous easements like rights of way.[2]

So long as both estates belong to the same person, though the uses thus made of one estate for the benefit of the other may, in some sense, be a service, it cannot be a servitude in the eye of the law, for *nemini res sua servit jure servitutis*.[3] But if the owner convey one of these estates to one, and another to another, or they come to different heirs by his death, this service, so far as it is continuous and apparent in

[1] Stokoe v. Singers, 8 Ellis & B. 36; 2 Fournel, Traité du Voisinage, 400.
[2] Cleris v. Tieman, 15 La. An. 316; Fisk v. Huber, 7 La. An. 323.
[3] Cary v. Daniels, 8 Met. 466; Mabie v. Matteson, 17 Wis. 10.

its character, becomes a servitude in favor of the one over and upon the other estate.   And among these may be mentioned the servitude of light and air, of supplying water, of drain, and the like.

Though artificial in their creation, they have some of the qualities of natural easements, as they pass with the separate estates in the manner of natural easements, without being mentioned in the deed.   That what had been a simple use or service, while the estates belonged to the same proprietor, is by the law changed into a servitude at the moment *of their separation, is founded upon the presumption [*17] which the law raises of an agreement by both parties to leave things in the same state into which they have been put, if there is no stipulation for changing it.   The law on this subject, which will be found to be very analogous to that which prevails in England and this country upon the division of heritages, where one part has had the use and enjoyment of the other,[1] is declared in the Code, though it was borrowed from the early *coutumes* of several of the provinces of France. Articles 692 and 694 of the Code are the text upon which several commentators have treated, when considering this subject, among whom are Pardessus, Toullier, and Merlin. The language of Art. 692 is : " An appointment by the father of a family has the effect of writing in regard of continual and apparent servitudes."   Art. 694 : " If the owner of two heritages, between which there exists an apparent mark of servitude, dispose of one of the two heritages without the contract containing any agreement relative to the servitude, it continues to exist actively or passively in favor of the property aliened, or upon the property aliened." [2]

---

[1] *Post*, sect. 3, pl. 26.

[2] Code Nap., Barrett's transl., Art. 692, 694 ; Lalaure, Traité des Servitudes Réelles, liv. 3, ch. 9 ; Pardessus, Traité des Servitudes, 430, ed. 1829 ; 3 Toullier, Droit Civil Français, 447 *et seq. ;* Merlin, Repertoire de Jurisprudence, tit. *Servitude*, §§ 17 – 19 ; 3 Burge, Col. & F. Law, 439 ; 1 Fournel, Traité du Voisinage, § 110 ; La. Civ. Code, § 763 ; Lavillebeuvre *v.* Cosgrove, 13 La. Ann. 323 ; Seymour *v.* Lewis, 13 N. J. 443.

Though the subject will be resumed in another part of the work, it may be well to remark here that this doctrine of the French law has obtained a place in the English Common law, rather by way of illustration and analogy, than as a governing principle. In one case the Lord Chancellor took occasion to say : " This comparison of the disposition of the owners of two tenements to the *destination du père de famille* is a mere fanciful analogy, from which rules of law ought not to be derived." [1]

That servitude known to the civil law under the name of " Non officiendi luminibus vel prospectui," was practically acknowledged as one known to the common law, and as binding upon the owners of an estate, by the courts of New York, in a case where the owner of several house-lots lying together sold one of them, and at the same time covenanted with his vendee that the other land belonging to him in front of that sold should be kept open for public use.[2]

[*18]   *SECTION II.

INCIDENTS TO ACQUIRING RIGHTS OF EASEMENT, ETC.

1. Before proceeding to examine the characteristics of the

---

[1] Suffield *v.* Brown, 10 Jur. N. S. 111.

[2] D. 8, 2, 15 ; Hills *v.* Miller, 3 Paige, 254, 257 ; Barrow *v.* Richards, 8 Paige, 351 ; Ersk. Inst., fol. ed. 356.

several kinds of easements known to the common law, and the rules applicable to these, it seems proper to consider certain general principles which are common to all, in order to save the necessity of repetition. And first, as to the mode of their acquisition.

These, being interests in land, can only be acquired by grant, and ordinarily by deed, or what is deemed to be equivalent thereto, a parol license being insufficient for the purpose.[1]

2. A parol license to erect a dam upon another's land, for *instance,[2] or to cut and maintain a ditch [*19] thereon for drawing water to the licensee's land, is revocable at will at common law, and in one case was held to be so after an enjoyment of eighteen years.[3]

The law of the several States will be found, it is believed, to be the same as that just stated, so far as it applies to unexecuted licenses. But there is an exception in some of them, in the case of executed licenses, when the licensee has incurred expense in the execution of the same, equity in such case holding, for purposes of remedy, that such shall be deemed an executed contract. But in most of the States, the doctrine that no permanent estate in lands can be created by parol, prevails; and it is accordingly held, that a licensee holds his privilege of using or occupying the licenser's land, whatever it is, strictly at the will of the licenser, who may

---

[1] Morse v. Copeland, 2 Gray, 302; Bryan v. Whistler, 8 Barnew. & C. 288; Cook v. Stearns, 11 Mass. 533; Dyer v. Sanford, 9 Metc. 395; Hewlins v. Shippam, 5 Barnew. & C. 221; Miller v. Aûburn & Syracuse R. R. Co., 6 Hill, 61; Fentiman v. Smith, 4 East, 107; Nichols v. Luce, 24 Pick. 102; Mumford v. Whitney, 15 Wend. 380; Middleton v. Gregorie, 2 Rich. 637; Pitkin v. Long Island R. R. Co., 2 Barb. Ch. 221; Kenyon v. Nichols, 1 R. I. 411; Collam v. Hocker, 1 Rawle, 108; Fuhr v. Dean, 26 Mo. 116; Orleans Navigation Co. v. Mayor of New Orleans, 2 Mart. 214, 229, 236; Cocker v. Cowper, 1 Crompt. M. & R. 418; Wood v. Leadbitter, 13 Mees. & W. 838; Adams v. Andrews, 15 Q. B. 284; Thompson v. Gregory, 4 Johns. 81; Bird v. Higginson, 2 Adolph & E. 696; Somerset v. Fogwell, 5 Barnew. & C. 875. Sedden v. Del. & H. Canal, 29 N. Y. 639.

[2] Mumford v. Whitney, 15 Wend. 380; Cook v. Stearns, 11 Mass. 533.

[3] Cocker v. Cowper, 1 Crompt. M. & R. 418.

at his pleasure revoke the same. The subject is fully examined in 2 Am. Lead. Cases, 682 – 706. The States which
adopt the rule of equity above stated are Pennsylvania, Indiana, and Iowa.[1] Those which retain the doctrine of the
common law are, among others, the following: New York,
Massachusetts, Connecticut, North Carolina, South Carolina,
Rhode Island, Wisconsin, Illinois,[2] and New Hampshire;[3]
while in Vermont the question is left undecided in the case
cited below.[4] But the distinction which will hereafter be
more fully considered, between a license to do an act upon
the licenser's land, and that to do it upon the land of the
licensee, should not be overlooked, since the last, when executed, is not revocable.[5]

3. The grant by which an easement is created may be evidenced in several ways. It may always be done by the production of an existing deed. So it may be by prescription,
or a long enjoyment of the easement claimed, under circumstances which raise an implication of title originally acquired
by grant.

So the law often regards the enjoyment of an easement as
evidence that a deed once existed, though now lost, and gives
to this presumption the same effect in establishing a title as
if the deed were produced.

4. The latter mode of treating the enjoyment of an easement as evidence of a title to the same by deed, has taken
the place, in modern practice, of the ancient doctrine of prescription. The chief difference between them consists mere-

[1] Rerick v. Kern, 14 S. & R. 267 ; Lacy v. Arnett, 33 Penn. 169 ; *post*, p. *318 ;
Snowden v. Wilas, 19 Ind. 14 ; Stephens v. Benson, 19 Ind. 369 ; Wickersham
v. Orr, 9 Iowa, 260 ; Beatty v. Gregory, 17 Iowa, 114.

[2] Selden v. Del. & Hud. Canal, 29 N. Y. 639 ; Wolfe v. Frost, 4 Sand. ch. 72 ;
Drake v. Wells, 11 Allen, 141, 144 ; Foot v. N. H. & N. Co., 23 Conn. 223 ;
Bridges v. Purcell, 1 Dee. & Bat. (Law) 492, 497 ; Trammell v. Trammell, 11
Rich. (Law) 471 ; Foster v. Browning, 4 R. I. 47 ; Hazleton v. Putnam, 3
Chand. (Wis.) 117 ; French v. Owen, 2 Wis. 250 ; Woodward v. Suly, 11 Ill.
157 ; 1 Wash. R. P. 411.

[3] Carleton v. Redington, 1 Foster, 308.

[4] Hall v. Choffer, 13 Verm. 150, 157.

[5] *Post*, p. *560.

ly in this.   To constitute what was, technically, considered
a prescription, the use and enjoyment by which the same was
established were required to be beyond the memory of man.
So that it might always be rebutted by showing by testimony,
if such was the case, when the enjoyment of the right claimed
had its origin or beginning.   Whereas, by raising a presumption from a user and enjoyment, that a deed, now assumed
to be lost, was once given to the claimant granting the easement claimed, the effect originally given to a prescription is
gained, after such enjoyment shall have been continued for
a length of time answering to the period of limitation beyond which one dispossessed of lands is not at liberty to re-
gain his seisin by making entry for that purpose.[1]   In
such cases, in the language of Lord Mansfield, *" not [*20]
that the court really thinks a grant has been made,"
but they presume the fact for the purpose, and from the
principle of quieting the possession.[2]   And it may be remarked, that practically, in modern use, the distinction between the ancient doctrine of technical prescription, and the
modern one of a presumed grant, where the deed has been
lost, is not observed when speaking of titles acquired by
long-continued user and enjoyment ; the terms *prescription*
and *prescriptive rights* being now used to express the whole
class of titles, the evidence of which depends upon such user
and enjoyment.

Cases may arise where the owner of a parcel of land depends for a right of way to the same, for instance, upon both
an implied grant and a grant of a prescriptive right.   Thus,
where there were three lots of land, A, B, and C ; A, adjoining the highway, belonged to the same one who owned C, to
which he had a prescriptive right of way from A over B.
The owner of A and C sold the latter to a stranger, who

---

[1] Morse *v.* Copeland, 2 Gray, 302 ; Gayetty *v.* Bethune, 14 Mass. 49 ; 1 Greenl.
Ev., § 17, note ; Sherwood *v.* Burr, 4 Day, 244 ; Rooker *v.* Perkins, 14 Wis. 82 ;
post, sect. 4, pl. 2.

[2] Eldridge *v.* Knott, Cowp. 214 ; Campbell *v.* Smith, 3 Halst. 141.

had no access to the same except over A and B. It was held that he thereby acquired a right of way by an implied grant as one of necessity over A, and a prescriptive right over B, as being appurtenant to C.[1]

5. In treating of acquiring an easement, like a right of way *in alieno solo*, by grant, it is common to couple with it a like acquisition by reservation, although it is said not to be technically true that a way can be created for the first time by exception or reservation, since it is neither a parcel of the thing granted, nor does it issue out of the thing granted. A way, therefore, *reserved*, as the word is used in a popular sense, is strictly an easement newly created by way of a grant from the grantee in the deed of the estate to the grantor; and the same is true of hawking, fishing, fowling, and the like.[2]

[*21]   *And it is said that "what will pass by words in a grant will be excepted by like words in an exception."[3]

Still, it is competent for a party who is the grantor of an estate to create a right of way over the same, in his own favor, either in gross or annexed to his other land, by a reservation thereof inserted in his deed of the estate; or it may be done, though in terms it be an exception. The court say: "We consider it immaterial whether the easement for the way intended to be established is technically considered as founded on an exception, a reservation, or an implied grant."[4]

If created by reservation, it must be to the grantor himself. And the case cited below, while it illustrates the distinction between an exception and a reservation in a grant, will serve to show the construction which courts give to reservations when of an easement. A granted to B a parcel of

---

[1] Leonard *v.* Leonard, 2 Allen, 543.

[2] Durham & Sund. R. R. Co. *v.* Walker, 2 Q. B. 940; Wickham *v.* Hawker, 7 Mees. & W. 76; Doe *v.* Lock, 2 Adolph. & E. 705. See Dyer *v.* Sanford, 9 Metc. 395.

[3] Shepp. Touchst. 100.   [4] Bowen *v.* Conner, 6 Cush. 132.

land, excepting one acre at a certain corner, " on which there is a tannery," and reserved to himself and his use " a certain well and water-works laid down for the purpose of supplying the tannery aforesaid with water." It was held to create an easement in the granted land in favor of the part excepted, to which it became appurtenant, and it passed with the acre through successive grantors as incident or appurtenant to the same. Nor was the use of the water restricted to the tannery, but was a general reservation of the right of water.[1]

But easements often pass by construction, by grant which the law would not reserve by implication. As where one granted land which was flowed by a dam on his own land, it was held that he did not impliedly reserve a right to flow it. Whereas, if he granted or devised the mill or land on which the dam stood, he would grant the right to flow the land as then flowed by the dam.[2]

In respect to whether the reservation is of a perpetual interest, like a fee, in the easement reserved, the question seems to turn upon whether it is a personal right, an easement in gross, or one for the benefit of the principal estate and its enjoyment, whoever may be the owner. In the latter case, it is held to be permanent right appurtenant to the principal estate in the hands of successors or assigns, without words of limitation. The courts of Maine treat such a reservation as an exception, to obviate the objection.[3]

6. So where tenants in common divided their estates, and in the deed of one part the grantor reserved a right of way over the granted part for the benefit of the other part, it was held to create an easement in favor of the latter, which ran with it into whosever hands it should come.[4]

---

[1] Borst v. Empie, 1 Seld. 33.

[2] Burr v. Mills, 21 Wend. 272, 274.

[3] Karmuller v. Krotz, 18 Iowa, 359; Winthrop v. Fairbanks, 41 Maine, 312; Smith v. Ladd, 41 Maine, 320; Bowen v. Connor, 6 Cush. 132. In Borst v. Empie, sup., the reserve was to the grantor and his use without the word "heirs."

[4] Mendell v. Delano, 7 Metc. 176; Smith v. Higbee, 12 Vt. 113; Karmuller v. Krotz, 18 Iowa, 359.

So where one granted land to another, which adjoined other lands which belonged to him, and reserved in his deed a right of way across the parcel. granted, in favor of his other lands, and at the same time gave to the parcel granted a right of way across these other lands of the grantor, it was held that he thereby created rights of way appurtenant to both the parcels, which passed with these parcels in the subsequent conveyances thereof, whether mentioned or not in the deeds as existing easements.[1]

7. And this case is put by Shaw, C. J., in Dyer v. Sanford, above cited, by way of illustration. There are three adjoining tenements. Two of them, the first and third, belong to A ; the middle one to B. B grants to A the right by deed to drain No. 1, through No. 2, into and through No. 3, into a common sewer ; and inserts in the deed, that he, B, is to have a right to enter his drain into the drain of [*22] A, *and thereby to drain No. 2 through No. 3, into the common sewer. If A accepts this deed, and constructs a drain from No. 1 to and through No. 3, B thereby acquires a right to enter his drain into the same, though it cannot technically be regarded as a reservation.[2]

So, in an early case, where the owner of land " granted and agreed with A. B., his heirs and assigns, that it should be lawful for them at all times afterwards to have and to use a way by and through a close," &c., it was held to be an actual grant of a way, and not a covenant only, for the enjoyment of such right.[3]

8. It is held in Maryland, that, while a right of way de novo could be created by a deed of grant or lease, it could not be by deed of bargain and sale, though an existing right of way could be passed or transferred by a deed of bargain and sale, and required all the solemnities necessary to pass estates by such deeds.[4]

---

[1] Brown v. Thissell, 6 Cush. 254.   [2] Dyer v. Sanford, 9 Metc. 395, 405.

[3] Holmes v. Seller, 3 Lev. 305 ; Gibert v. Peteler, 38 Barb. 514.

[4] Hays v. Richardson, 1 Gill & J. 366.

9. If now these two modes of acquiring easements, by grant and prescription, are considered separately, the subject of a title by grant also divides itself into express grants, and grants by implication or construction of law.

Before, however, pursuing the subject under these several heads, it may be well to state, that, when an easement has been acquired by either of these modes in favor of a dominant over a servient estate, it passes to the respective owners of these estates as an easement in favor of the one, and a servitude or burden upon the other, into whosever hands the respective estates may come. The easement, in such case, becomes *appendant* or *appurtenant,* as it is called, to the estate in whose favor it has been created or acquired, and, as the law expresses it, *runs with it.* The terms *appendant* and *appurtenant* are defined in the Termes de la Ley as " things that by term of prescription have belonged, *appertained, and are joined to another prin- [*23] cipal thing, by which they pass and go as accessory to the same principal thing," &c. And it is said that, " to make a thing appendant or appurtenant, it must agree in quality and nature to the thing whereunto it is appendant or appurtenant, as a thing corporeal cannot properly be appendant to a thing incorporeal, nor a thing incorporeal to a thing corporeal." But it is not true that the term is applicable only to things acquired by term of prescription. Thus, in the cases above cited, in the first, one sold a house-lot in front of which was an open area belonging to him, upon which he covenanted that no house should be erected, but that the same should be always kept open as public property. Being a part of the transaction of the purchase and sale, and a consideration for the same, it was held to create an easement in favor of the lot thus sold, and that the first grantee thereof, having conveyed the same to another, could not release it to the vendor or his assigns, or authorize them to erect buildings upon this open space. Nor would the easement be destroyed by a division of the estate to which the easement belonged.[1] In the other, A granted to B twenty acres of land, and also a right to dig ore in another parcel of ten acres. And the question was whether the conveyance of the twenty acres carried with it a right to dig ore in the other parcel. And it was held that it did not, but that the right to dig ore was an incorporeal hereditament and a servitude in and upon the ten acres, but not appendant to the twenty acres, since the enjoyment of the one was in no wise necessary to the enjoyment of the other.[2]

10. A recent case in Massachusetts will serve, also, to illustrate what is requisite to create an easement, and render the same appurtenant to an estate, and to show that a [*24] right *does not necessarily become appurtenant to an estate, although affecting the same, and granted to or reserved by the tenant thereof. In that case, A owned two estates adjoining each other, upon one of which was a dwelling-house having a projecting part in the rear of one story in height. He sold the latter, subject to a restriction that the owner thereof should never raise the projection any higher than its then present condition. After that he sold the other estate to the plaintiff, and then executed a release to the first purchaser of the restriction upon his parcel, and the latter proceeded to raise the projecting part of his house another story. The plaintiff brought a bill in equity to restrain him, on the ground that the right of enjoying his estate free from such an obstruction, which originally belonged to his grantor, passed as an easement therewith when he purchased it. But the court held that there was nothing in the deed of the first estate which showed that the restriction was intended to enure to the benefit of the estate now owned by the plaintiff, nor could he, therefore, as the owner thereof, avail himself of a right which his grantor had se-

---

[1] Hills v. Miller, 3 Paige, 254 ; Ayl. Pand. 312 ; D. 8, 4, 12 ; Whitney v. Lee, 1 Allen, 198 ; Whitney v. Union, 11 Gray, 359 ; Brouwer v. Jones, 23 Barb. 160 ; Parker v. Nightingale, 6 Allen, 341.

[2] Grubb v. Guildford, 4 Watts, 223, 244, 246.

cured to himself without rendering it appurtenant to the estate.[1]

Under the civil law, services did not admit of a division, and therefore a way or a road through a man's estate cannot be bequeathed in part nor taken away in part, for a service is total, *in toto fundo*, and total in every part thereof.[2]

11. There is, moreover, a kind of appendency or appurtenancy of one easement to and upon another easement, in some cases, which is sometimes called a secondary easement. It passes with the principal easement as being necessary or convenient to the enjoyment of the same.

Thus in Stenhouse *v.* Christian, where there was a grant of a way for the purpose of carrying coals across a *certain parcel of land with wagons, wains, and other [*25] carriages; it was held that the grantee, as an incident to the grant, had a right to make a framed wagon-track along the course of the way indicated in the grant.[3]

So in Prescott *v.* Williams, the right to enter upon the land of another, and clear out obstructions in a watercourse which a mill-owner above had a right to enjoy through such land, was held to be an incident to such natural easement in the nature of a secondary easement.[4]

So the grant of a right of pasturage carries the right of way to and from the pasture. So that of drawing water, or of fishing or hunting, gives a right of access and egress to and from the estate in which it is to be enjoyed.[5]

But after all, instead of these ancillary rights being some-

---

[1] Badger *v.* Boardman, 24 Law Rep. 303; Parker *v.* Nightingale, 6 Allen, 348.

[2] Ayl. Pand. 311; Dig. 8, 1, 6.

[3] Senhouse *v.* Christian, 1 T. R. 560; D. 8, 2, 19; Ibid. 8, 4, 11, 1; *post*, chap. 3, sect. 1, pl. 19; 2 Fournel, Traité du Voisinage, 404; 3 Toullier, Droit Civil Français, 500.

[4] Prescott *v.* Williams, 5 Metc. 429; Prescott *v.* White, 21 Pick. 341; Bract., fol. 232.

[5] Bract., fol. 232 *a;* Code Nap., Art. 696; 2 Fournel, Traité du Voisinage 404.

thing appurtenant to easements, they seem rather to constitute an essential part or element of the principal easement
itself, and will be further treated of when the subject of incidents of grants, and what is embraced therein, comes to be
considered.[1]

12. It may also be stated in this connection, in order to
save repetition, that if an easement, like a right of way over
another's land, becomes appurtenant to an estate, it passes
with the grant of the principal thing, whether such grant, in
terms, embraces privileges and appurtenances or not; and
this, whether it is necessary to the enjoyment of the granted
estate or not.[2]

[*26]   *13. Where, therefore, one grants or reserves a
right of easement over one parcel of land in favor of
another, such easement, by such act of creation or annexation,
would become incident and appurtenant to such estates respectively, and pass as appurtenant in after conveyances, by,
or even without, the word *appurtenances,* so long as such
estates should subsist as distinct estates in different proprietors. Nor could the easement be separated from the principal estate, except by him who has a disposing power over
the estate.[3]

But this rule does not apply where there is a conveyance of a specific parcel of land carved out of a larger one
held by the grantor, and described by metes and bounds.
In such case, nothing would pass as parcel of the granted
premises which was a matter of ease and convenience only,
except what is included within the boundaries expressed

[1] *Post,* sect. 3, pl. 5.

[2] Kent *v.* Waite, 10 Pick. 138; Atkins *v.* Bordman, 2 Metc. 457; Beaudely *v.*
Brook, Cro. Jac. 189; Jackson *v.* Hathaway, 15 Johns. 447; Brown *v.* Thissell,
6 Cush. 254; Underwood *v.* Carney, 1 Cush. 285; Smith *v.* Higbee, 12 Vt. 123;
Staple *v.* Heydon, 6 Mod. 1; Grant *v.* Chase, 17 Mass. 443; Lawton *v.* Rivers,
2 M'Cord, 445; Pickering *v.* Stapler, 5 Serg. & R. 107; United States *v.* Appleton, 1 Sumn. 402; Morgan *v.* Mason, 20 Ohio, 401; Harris *v.* Elliott, 10 Peters,
54; Karmuller *v.* Krotz, 18 Iowa, 360.

[3] Ritger *v.* Parker, 8 Cush. 145; French *v.* Braintree Manufacturing Co. 23
Pick. 216.

in the deed.[1] Nor does it apply to any but existing easements.[2]

14. And though a man may acquire an easement in gross, like a right of way over another's land, separate and distinct from the ownership of any other estate to which it is appendant, yet if his right to such way result from his ownership of a parcel of land to which it is appendant, he cannot by grant separate the easement from the principal estate to which it is appendant, so as to turn it into a way in gross, in the hands of his grantee.[3]

15. It may, accordingly, be stated as a general principle, that if an easement has become appurtenant to an estate, it follows every part of the estate into whosoever hands the *same may come by purchase or descent; " *qua-* [*27] *cunque servitus fundo debitur, omnibus, ejus partibus debitur,*" provided the burden upon the servient estate is not thereby increased.[4]

SECTION III.

OF ACQUIRING EASEMENTS BY GRANT.

1. How Easements may be created by grant.
2. Easements never presumed to be in gross.
3. No one but the owner of the soil can grant an Easement.
4. No tenant in common can create Easements in Estates in common.
5. Implied grants of Easements.
6. Easements of necessity result from grants or reservations.
7. Nichols v. Luce. All Easements the result of grants.
8. Easements by grant implied from having been used.
9. Cases of Easements implied, as forming a part of the thing granted.

[1] Grant v. Chase, 17 Mass. 443.

[2] Russell v. Scott, 9 Cow. 279.

[3] Acroyd v. Smith, 10 C. B. 164; Year B. 5 Hen. VII., fol. 7, pl. 15, per *Fairfax*, J.; Woolr. Ways, 16; Garrison v. Rudd, 19 Ill. 558.

[4] Orleans Navigation Co. v. Mayor of New Orleans, 2 Mart. 233; Lewis v. Carstairs, 6 Whart. 193; Watson v. Bioren, 1 Serg. & R. 227; Case of a Private Road, 1 Ashm. 417; Lansing v. Wiswall, 5 Denio, 213; Garrison v. Rudd, 19 Ill. 558; *post*, sect. 3, pl. 38; 3 Toullier, Droit Civil Français, 494; D. 8, 3, 23, 3.

1. IF now we recur to the mode of creating an easement by grant, it may be by deed in express terms, as where one owning an estate grants to the owner of another estate a right to enjoy certain privileges in or out of the grantor's estate, which does not give the grantee a right to enjoy the estate itself by exclusive or permanent occupation. So it may be created by a covenant of the owner of one estate with the owner of another estate, that he should have a right to

enjoy certain profits or privileges out of the former, as has already been stated.[1]   And Pollock, C. B. says: "It cannot be denied, that if a man builds a house, and there is actually a way used or obviously and manifestly intended to be used by the occupiers of the house, the mere lease of the house would carry with it the right to use the way, as forming part of its construction.   And so if there were publicly exhibited, prior to a bill of sale of it, a model of the house and its appurtenances describing the right of way, that would have the same effect.   So if a plan were thus exhibited describing the right of way, and a contract of purchase or lease were entered into with reference to that plan, that might have the same effect."[2]   Or this may be done by a grant of one parcel of the grantor's land to another, and reserving similar privileges in and out of the grantor's premises to himself as owner of the remaining parcel, or by granting such privileges with the granted parcel, out of the parcel so retained.   A grant of a license to one and his heirs to hunt upon the licenser's land must, in order to be effectual, be by deed.   But a license for a single time may be good, though by parol only.[3]   And where an easement is granted or reserved in express terms by deed, the only question ordinarily open for consideration concerns the proper construction of the language of the deed.[4]   Nothing, however, passes as incident to the grant of an easement, but what is requisite to a free enjoyment of the privilege granted.[5]   An easement may be created subject to a condition subsequent, and whether it is so, depends, of course, upon the construction of the deed.   But if so created in connection with and appurtenant to land granted, and the condition be broken, it

[1] Clark v. Way, 11 Rich. Law, 624; ante, p. *7; Gibert v. Peteler, 38 Barb. 484, 514; Parker v. Nightingale, 6 Allen, 341; Brouwer v. Jones, 23 Barb. 153; post, p. *63; Green v. Creighton, 7 R. I. 1.

[2] Glave v. Harding, 3 H. & Norm. 944.

[3] Wickham v. Hawker, 7 M. & W. 79; post, p. *8.

[4] Shepp. Touchst. 88.

[5] Bean v. Coleman, 44 N. H. 544; Lyman v. Arnold, 5 Mason, 198; Maxwell v. M'Atee, 9 B. Mon. 20; 3 Kent, 419, 420.

does not form the ground of forfeiture of the land, nor can the easement be recovered from the grantee by a writ of entry, independent of the land to which it is incident.[1]

The concurrence as well of the owner of the heritage which it is wished to charge with the servitude, as of him in favor of whose heritage it is desired to create it, is necessary in order to impose a servitude upon one in favor of the other. And he only can thus impose a servitude who is of a capacity to act freely, and has a full right of disposal of the estate itself. Neither a minor, therefore, nor a married woman, while under the control of her husband, can impose a servitude upon a heritage.[2] Nor can a wife by her admissions make evidence that it exists.[3] The acquisition of easements, moreover, whether with or without the will of the owner of the servient estate, followed the analogy of the acquisition of corporeal things. It required in the first place, the owner's voluntary act of creating or imposing the servitude, and in the next place something answering to the " traditio " of the civil law of a corporeal thing. Servitudes, however, might be acquired without the consent of the owner of the servient land, by prescription.[4]

2. Though an easement, like a right of way, may be created by grant in gross, as it is called, or attached to
[*29] the *person of the grantee, this is never presumed when it can fairly be construed to be appurtenant to some other estate; and if it is in gross, it cannot extend beyond the life of the grantee.[5] Nor can it be granted over, being attached to the person of the grantee alone. Whether the thing granted be an easement in land or the land itself, may depend upon the nature and use of the thing

---

[1] Chapin v. Harris, 8 Allen, 594. See Watkins v. Peck, 13 N. H. 375 ; Gray's case, 5 Co., 78.

[2] Lalaure, Traité des Servitudes Réelles, 34 ; post, sect. 4, pl. 69.

[3] M'Gregor v. Wait, 10 Gray, 74.

[4] Güter, Brac. c. 15.

[5] Case of Private Road, 1 Ashm. 417 ; Acroyd v. Smith, 10 C. B. 164 ; Garrison v. Rudd, 19 Ill. 558 ; Woolr. Ways, 16.

granted. If it be non-continuous, or to be used only occasionally, like a way, the grant creates only an incorporeal hereditament, an easement and not the land.[1]

So an easement like that, for instance, of drawing water from another's well, may be limited to certain hours, or a right of way may be confined to a part of the day, or to a certain place.[2]

3. An important principle is to be remembered, that no one can grant an easement out of land in favor of another, unless he has the entire interest in the soil. If, for instance, there are tenants in common of land, or several persons having a common interest in an estate, neither of them can, by grant, create an easement therein in favor of a stranger. Thus where a number of persons were proprietors of the channel of a river as trustees, under an act of Parliament, and a major part of the sharers in the profits of the river granted to another a right to construct and use a channel through the bank thereof, the court say: "The concurrence of all the proprietors of the river is necessary to the transfer of any right or interest in it. . . . . The grantee, under his lease, might at any moment be ousted by any one of the other proprietors, and therefore he was in fact invested with no definite, permanent, or assignable right under it. . . . . The grant is merely the license of two out of many co-proprietors to do certain acts, and enjoy certain privileges, and that cannot be considered as a hereditament which would pass, either as respects its privileges or its liabilities, to the assignee of the grantee. . . . . Where there is not an entire interest in the soil vested in the grantor, he cannot grant an easement arising out of it to another." [3]

*4. Notwithstanding the strong language of the [*30] court in the above case, it perhaps might leave some little doubt whether, from the peculiarity of the joint owner-

[1] Jamaica Pond v. Chandler, 9 Allen, 164.
[2] 3 Kent, Comm. 436.
[3] Portmore v. Bunn, 3 Dowl. & R. 145.

ship of the property in that case, the doctrine would apply with full force in the common case of tenants in common. And the court in Mendell *v.* Delano[1] seem disposed to waive the question whether one tenant in common can grant a right of way over the common estate to a stranger. But it seems to be settled, elsewhere, that he cannot.[2] And this is consistent with the well-settled doctrine that one tenant in common cannot properly convey a distinct part of the land held in common to a stranger by metes and bounds.[3] One tenant in common has no right to flow the common land though by a dam erected upon his own several estate.[4]

And in the Civil Code of Louisiana there is an express declaration, that " the co-proprietor of an undivided estate cannot impose a servitude thereon without the consent of his co-proprietor." [5]

But it seems that one tenant in common of an estate may acquire an easement in respect to it which will enure in favor of his co-tenants as well as himself.[6]

So minors through their guardians, and wives through their husbands, may acquire easements in favor of their estates.[7]

5. The subject of acquiring easements by implied grant opens a wide field of inquiry, in which it would be necessary to refer to a great variety of decided cases. But, for the present, a general statement of principles only will be attempted, which apply to easements as interests in [*31] lands, *leaving their application, in detail, to their connection with the several classes into which easements divide themselves.

---

[1] Mendell *v.* Delano, 7 Metc. 176.

[2] Lalaure, Traité des Servitudes Réelles, 38 ; Collins *v.* Prentice, 15 Conn. 423 ; Marshall *v.* Trumbull, 28 Conn. 183 ; Watkins *v.* Peck, 13 N. H. 360 – 381 ; *post,* sect. 4, pl. 76.

[3] Bartlet *v.* Harlow, 12 Mass. 348 ; Varnum *v.* Abbot, 12 Mass. 474.

[4] Great Falls *v.* Worster, 15 N. H. 460.

[5] La. Civ. Code, Art. 734. See D. 8, 1, 2 ; Ibid. 8, 2, 26 ; 3 Toullier, Droit Civil Français, 418, 420.

[6] 3 Toullier, Droit Civil Français, 424 ; Lalaure, Traité des Servitudes Réelles, 40.

[7] 3 Toullier, Droit Civil Français, 423.

The broad principle upon which such easements are created, or pass, by implication, by the grants of the estates to
'which they are or are made appurtenant, rests upon the familiar maxim, *Cuicunque aliquis quid concedit, concedere videtur et id, sine quo res ipsa esse non potuit.*[1]

But nothing except what is properly appurtenant to an estate passes with it, unless forming a parcel of the granted
premises. And where, therefore, a mill was granted with its
appurtenances, it did not convey the soil of a way which had
been immemorially used with it, because land cannot be appurtenant to land. But it did pass the easement of a way as
being properly an appurtenant to the mill.[2]

The grant or reservation of a " way " or " road," without
other words of description, carries an easement only, and not
the fee in the soil.[3]

Nor does the grant of a right to dig a canal through one's
land, carry with it a right of property in the materials excavated, unless such material may be used in constructing the
canal. How far it may belong to the grantee in such case is
not decided in the case cited.[4]

The doctrine is a general one, that the grant of a thing
carries all things as included, without which the thing granted cannot be enjoyed. By which are to be understood things
incident and directly necessary to the thing granted. The
case stated by Plowden, as illustrating this, is the grant of
one's trees standing upon his own land. The grantee may,
as a part of the grant, enter upon the land and cut them
down and carry them away. And Twisden, J., in Pomfret
v. Ricroft, says : " When the use of a thing is granted, every thing is granted by which the grantee may have and enjoy

---

[1] Broom, Max. 362 ; Liford's case, 11 Rep. 52 ; Shepp. Touchst. 89 ; Thompson *v.* Banks, 43 N. H. 540

[2] Leonard *v.* White, 7 Mass 6. See Tabor *v.* Bradley, 18 N. Y. 109 , *post,*
pl 25, *a.*

[3] Jamaica Pond *v.* Chandler, sup. , Graves *v.* Amoskeag Co., 44 N. H 465
Leavitt *v.* Towle, 8 N H 97.

[4] Lyman *v* Arnold, 5 Mason, 197.

such use, as if a man gives me a license to lay pipes in his land to convey water to my cistern, I may afterwards enter and dig the land to mend the pipes, though the soil belongs to another and not to me." [1]

6. It is upon this principle that ways of necessity pass with lands when granted, and although ordinarily treated of as a class distinct from those created by grant, they are, in fact, acquired in that way, as being incident to the principal thing granted.[2] And the same principle applies to cases of devises of lands. One devisee, if necessary, may pass over land devised to another, in order to gain access to that which has been devised to himself.[3]

So if one grant a parcel of land which is so connected with another parcel belonging to him that he can [*32] have *access to the latter only over the granted parcel, the law reserves to him a right to pass over the same, as a way of necessity. But it must be strictly a way of necessity, and great convenience will not be sufficient.[4]

This principle, however, is subject to this limitation, that if the purposes for which the land is granted are inconsistent with the exercise of such reserved way, no such right of way will be raised by implication in favor of the grantor, on the idea of necessity.[5]

[1] Plowd. 16 a; Pomfret v. Ricroft, 1 Saund. 321; Hinchcliffe v. Kinnoul, 5 Bing. n. c. 1; Darcy v. Askwith, Hob. 234.

[2] Bullard v. Harrison, 4 Maule & S. 387; Gayetty v. Bethune, 14 Mass. 49; Lawton v. Rivers, 2 M'Cord, 445; Turnbull v. Rivers, 3 Ibid. 131; Cooper v. Maupin, 6 Mo. 624; 3 Kent, Comm. 423; 1 Wms. Saund. 323 a; Atkins v. Bordman, 2 Metc. 457; Beaudely v. Brook, Cro. Jac. 189; Staple v. Heydon, 6 Mod. 1; Nichols v. Luce, 24 Pick. 102; Kimball v. Cocheco R. R. Co., 7 Fost. 448; Williams v. Sanford, 7 Barb. 312.

[3] Pearson v. Spencer, 1 B. & S. 580; s. c., 3 B. & S. 761; Tracy v. Atherton, 35 Verm. 53.

[4] Brigham v. Smith, 4 Gray, 297; Collins v. Prentice, 15 Conn. 39; Pierce v. Sellech, 18 Conn. 321; Lawton v. Rivers, 2 M'Cord, 445; Cooper v. Maupin, 6 Mo. 624; Clark v. Cogge, Cro. Jac. 170; Smith v. Kinard, 2 Hill, So. C. 642; Packer v. Welsted, 2 Sid. 39, 111; 3 Kent, Comm. 422; Woolr. Ways, 20; Pinnington v. Galland, 9 Exch. 1; Dutton v. Tayler, 2 Lutw. 1487; Chichester v. Lethbridge, Willes, 71, note; Staple v. Heydon, 6 Mod. 1; Leonard v. Leonard, 2 Allen, 543; Howton v. Frearson, 8 T. R. 50.

[5] Seeley v. Bishop, 19 Conn. 128.

So where one owns two estates, like dwelling-houses, and a drain or way, for instance, is made and used from one over or through the other, and the same is necessary for the proper enjoyment of the first, and the owner convey the first to a stranger, he thereby grants a right to maintain such drain, or to use such way, in connection with the granted premises; which is but a single illustration of a pretty widely extended principle applicable to cases of easements passing with one of two parts of an inheritance, where the same has been divided by grant or partition.[1]

And in anticipation of what will be said in another connection, it may be remarked that the principle here stated does not apply to easements which are not in their nature continuous, unless they are ways of necessity.[2] Nor, in the absence of express words, does it extend to such easements as are separable from the principal thing granted or reserved. It applies to cases where one tenement is necessarily dependent upon another, like two houses dependent on each other for support.[3]

7. The law upon this subject is fully considered and explained in Nichols *v.* Luce, above cited, and may be thus summarily stated. All easements are, in fact, gained by grant, the only difference in this respect being the mode of proof. Thus prescription presupposes and is evidence of a previous grant. While what is called necessity is only a circumstance resorted to in order to show and explain the *intention of the parties, in raising an implica- [*33] tion of a grant. The deed of the grantor creates the way, when it is one of necessity, as much as it does where it creates it by express grant. One is by implication, the other is a grant in terms.[4]

---

[1] Hills *v.* Miller, 3 Paige, 254; 2 Washb. Real. Prop. 32; Alston *v.* Grant, 3 Ellis & B. 128; Thayer *v.* Payne, 2 Cush. 327; Pyer *v.* Carter, 1 Hurlst. & N. 916.

[2] Polden *v.* Bastard, 4 B. & S. 257; Pearson *v.* Spencer, 1 B. & S. 580; s. c., 3 B. & S. 761; Dodd *v.* Burchell, 1 H. & Colt. 113.

[3] Suffield *v.* Brown, 10 Jur. N. S. 111.

[4] Nichols *v.* Luce, 24 Pick. 102; Collins *v.* Prentice, 15 Conn. 39; Atkins *v.* Bordman, 2 Metc. 457.

8. On the other hand, easements often pass by implication, from the manner in which the grantor of the premises may have used the same, if reference is made to such use in his deed. Thus, if having two parcels, he shall have used a way over one in a definite and accustomed manner, and shall grant the parcel with which such way has been used to a third person, with " all ways," it would carry a right to use this way across the grantor's other land. The use, when proved, defines what " way" it is that was intended by the deed.[1]

It may be remarked, however, that the same rule of construction is applied in the case of the grant of a house " with the lights," as of land "with the ways." One who should sell his house in that form, would not have a right to obscure the windows by building on his adjacent vacant land. Whereas, if he had such a lot, and conveyed it before he did his house, without reserving the right of light to the windows to the same, the vendee might build upon such lot, though he thereby wholly obscured the light of these windows.[2]

9. A few cases may be referred to by way of illus-
[*34] tration * of what may pass by implication by a grant,
as part of, or appurtenant or incident to, the principal thing granted. Thus, the grant of a mill carries the head of water by which it is carried;[3] so it carries a right to flow the grantor's land,[4] and the whole right of water which had been previously used with it by the grantor;[5] so it carries the flow of the water in the race-way.[6] And if it draws its principal supply of water from a reservoir upon the same stream, at a

---

[1] Staple v. Heydon, 6 Mod. 1; Atkins v. Bordman, 2 Metc. 457; Kooystra v. Lucas, 5 Barnew. & Ald. 830; Com. Dig. *Chimin*, D. 3; Plant v. James, 5 Barnew. & Ad. 791; Oakley v. Adamson, 8 Bing. 356; Hinchcliffe v. Kinnoul, 5 Bing. N. C. 1; Gayetty v. Bethune, 14 Mass. 49.

[2] Tenant v. Goldwin, 2 Ld. Raym. 1089.

[3] Rackley v. Sprague, 17 Me. 281.

[4] Hathorn v. Stinson, 10 Me. 224.

[5] Strickler v. Todd, 10 Serg. & R. 63; Vickerie v. Buswell, 13 Me. 289.

[6] Wetmore v. White, 2 Caines, Cas. 87.

distance above the mill, a conveyance of the mill carries also the upper dam and reservoir as incidents, inasmuch as the grant of the mill would be practically inoperative without these.[1] So when one granted to another a right to have the washings of ore from his ore bed pass into the stream which ran through the grantor's meadow and be deposited upon the meadow, and the effect in time was to raise the meadow so much that the dirt washed from the ore passed off the meadow on to an adjoining pasture of the grantor, it was held to come within the incidents of the grant, and therefore no violation of the grantor's right, although the grant specified only the meadow.[2] So the devise of a mill carries buildings, land, and privileges necessary to its use.[3] So the exception from the grant of a larger estate, of " the brick factory," was held to include with such factory the land on which it stood, and the water privilege belonging to the same.[4] The grant of half a dam conveys with it half the water-power;[5] so the reservation of a " mill-site " embraces not only the land of such site, but also a right of flowage of a pond for the use of the mill.[6] So, in several cases, the grant of a house carries with it the right to enjoy the unobstructed use of light therewith.[7]

10. But the grant of a mill-site, with the right to erect and maintain a mill thereon, is a grant of land, and not an easement in land.[8] And the grant of " a mill " would not only pass the land on which it stands, but it may embrace the free use of the head of water existing at the time of the grant, and the rights of way and all other easements which

---

[1] Perrin *v.* Garfield, 37 Verm. 312.   See *post*, p. *42, and Brace *v.* Yale, there cited.

[2] Bushnell *v.* Proprietors, &c., 31 Conn. 150.

[3] Whitney *v.* Olney, 3 Mason, 280.

[4] Allen *v.* Scott, 21 Pick. 25.

[5] Runnels *v.* Bullen, 2 N. H. 532.

[6] Oakley *v.* Stanley, 5 Wend. 523 ; Lampman *v.* Milks, 21 N. Y. 505 ; Stackpole *v.* Curtis, 32 Me. 383.

[7] Swansborough *v.* Coventry, 9 Bing. 305 ; Durel *v.* Boisblanc, 1 La. Ann. 407.

[8] Farrar *v.* Cooper, 34 Me. 394.

have been used with the mill, and which are necessary to the enjoyment of it.   And it was held that the use of a mill-yard, so long as the mill continued to be occupied, [*35] *passed as an easement thereto by the assignment of the mill.[1]   So the devise of a mill was held to carry the appurtenances used by the testator in his lifetime, such as the dam, water, and race, and the land before the mill used for loading and unloading grain, &c., with teams.[2]

The grant or reservation of a " mill-privilege " or a " mill-site " is understood to carry the land itself, and not a mere easement in the land.   But with it would pass the right to the use of the water, with the use of the appendages belonging to the mill ; and it was left to the jury to determine the extent of the mill-yard, the use of which passed as incident to the mill standing on the privilege.[3]

In the grant of a parcel of land, part of a larger estate, the grantor excepted out of his grant what was then a tan-yard, and reserved " a well " upon the granted premises, " and waterworks laid down for the purpose of supplying the tannery aforesaid with water."   It was held to be a general reservation of an easement to draw water thereby for any purposes, and not limited to the use of the tan-yard.[4]

The devise of a mill-privilege with privileges and appurtenances, passes all the privileges and easements which had before become attached to the same, such as the right to build and maintain a dam, erect mills, all rights of flowage of lands of the lessor or others, all rights of ways, of laying logs or lumber, and of mill-yard, whether the same may have been acquired by grant or prescription.[5]

---

[1] Blake v. Clark, 7 Me. 436 ; Atkins v. Bordman, 2 Metc. 463.

[2] Blain's Lessee v. Chambers, 1 Serg. & R. 169.   See also Gibson v. Brockway, 8 N. H. 465 ; Maddox v. Goddard, 15 Md. 218 ; Swartz v. Swartz, 4 Penn. St. 353 ; M'Tavish v. Carroll, 7 Md. 352.

[3] Moore v. Fletcher, 16 Me. 63 ; Crosby v. Bradbury, 20 Me. 61 ; Jackson v. Vermilyea, 6 Cow. 677.

[4] Borst v. Empie, 1 Seld. 40.

[5] Thompson v. Banks, 43 N. H. 540 ; Dunklee v. Wilton R. R., 24 N. H. 495 ; Seavey v. Jones, 43 N. H. 441.

But where a tract of land was granted " with A. D.'s mill-seat excepted," it was held to be an exception of a right to flow a pond on the land for the mill, and not of the land itself on which the pond was raised.[1]

11. And the grant of land bounding on or near a pond or stream of water, reserving to the grantor the mill and water-privilege connected with such pond or stream, is a reservation of the right to flow the land granted, so far as is necessary or convenient, or so far as it has been usual to flow it for that purpose.[2] But a different rule has at times been insisted on, in respect to a right to flow lands being raised by implication, where the mill is the subject of grant, from that which is applied in case of a reservation of a mill. If the mill-owner sells his mill and dam, but retains the lands which had been flowed thereby, he conveys, as an essential part of the grant, the right of flowage of these lands, so far *as the same is necessary. But if he sell the [*36] lands, retaining the mill, it has been held that he would not have a right to flow the land, unless he expressly reserved the right so to do.[3]

But the above doctrine is controverted as to the distinction between a grant and reservation ; and it was held, that, if one having land, on which are a mill, a mill-dam, and pond of water, sell the land on which the dam stands, and the head of water is raised, without any express reservation, the purchaser takes it subject to the easement of these, as incident to the mill retained by him.[4]

So where the owner of a spring lot and of a paper-mill on another tract, by an artificial arrangement conveyed the

[1] Everett v. Dockery, 7 Jones, No. C. 390 ; Whitehead v. Garris, 3 Ibid. 171.

[2] Pettee v. Hawes, 13 Pick. 323.

[3] Preble v. Reed, 17 Me. 169 ; Hathorn v. Stinson, 10 Me. 224 ; Rackley v. Sprague, 17 Me. 281 ; Burr v. Mills, 21 Wend. 290 ; M'Tavish v. Carroll, 7 Md. 352 ; Johnson v. Jordan, 2 Metc. 234 ; Carbrey v. Willis, 7 Allen, 370 ; Suffield v. Brown, 10 Jur. N. S. 111 ; Tenant v. Goldwin, 2 Ld. Raym. 1093 ; White v. Bass, 7 H. & Norm. 731.

[4] Seibert v. Levan, 8 Penn. St. 383. See also Harwood v. Benton, 32 Vt. 724. Nicholas v. Chamberlain, Cro. Jur. 121.

water from the spring to the mill for the use of the mill, in
the manufacture of paper, and sold the spring lot by itself,
the purchaser took it subject to the burden of this easement
of water for the mill, although the latter was retained by the
grantor.[1]

12. But whether any and what privileges pass by a grant
of a thing, as well as the measure or limits of what is
granted, often depends upon the circumstances and condition of the property, and the language of the grant construed
in the light of these circumstances. One general test is, how
far the incidents claimed are necessary to the reasonable enjoyment of what is expressly granted.

Thus where land was granted across which a public highway had been laid out, and was in use, and the owner conveyed it with covenants, and in his deed reserved or excepted
the roads across the premises, it was held not to be a reservation or exception of the land itself included in this way,
but an exception of the easement from the covenants in his
deed.[2]

So a grant of land running &c. to a passage-way, which
was reserved to the grantor to be used as such, and to be
used by the grantee and his assigns in common with the
grantor and others claiming under him, was held to be that
of an easement in and not the soil of the way. But its use
was limited to the land granted, and did not extend to any
acquired afterwards.[3]

And where the grant was of a right of way "over my land
where it is necessary," it was held to extend only to such
lands as the grantee owned when the grant was made.[4]

13. In the first place, in order to have a right of easement
in or over one piece of land pass by the grant of another parcel, it must be an existing easement, actually appurtenant
by use and enjoyment, and by having been exercised with

[1] Seymour v. Lewis, 13 N. J. 439 ; *post*, sect. 3, pl. 25 & 25 *a*.
[2] Leavitt v. Towle, 8 N. H. 96.
[3] Stearns v. Mullen, 4 Gray, 155.
[4] Smith v. Porter, 10 Gray, 67.

the occupation of the latter parcel. It is not enough that the grantor, when he made his deed, had a right, in the nature of an incorporeal hereditament, to an easement in the other land which he had never exercised or applied. Thus A sold a parcel of land through which a stream of water flowed to B, and reserved the streams and soil under the same, with a right to erect dams and mills, and to overflow the land for the use of the mills. B sold a part of these lands to C, subject to these reservations. C, by verbal permission and agreement of A, erected a dam *on [*37] his land, thereby overflowing a part of B's land. It was held, that, until A had exercised the reserved right to flow, the reservation was inoperative, since it would not until then be ascertained what lands were thereby to be flowed, the reservation being of a right only to use these lands for a specific purpose, while the direct interest in the soil was in the grantee; and that this right, so reserved, was an incorporeal hereditament which could be granted by deed only, and therefore the verbal license of A to C to flow B's land was of no avail.[1]

So where one made a lease *in fee* of a farm, " excepting seven acres, and saving and reserving to the lessor all watercourses suitable for the erection of mills, with the right of erecting mills, edth three acres of land adjoining thereto, and also saving and reserving the right to erect dams and cut ditches for the use of such water-works." The lessor leased these seven acres in fee to S., who erected a mill thereon, and flowed a part of the three acres. But it was held, that, though by the conveyance of the seven acres he acquired a right in the same manner as his lessor had to erect mills thereon, he did not thereby acquire a right to flow the three acres, although his lessor had this, because it was not appurtenant or annexed to the parcel of seven acres. It was an incorporeal hereditament in the lessor, which would only pass by express grant; nor did it change the rights of the

---

[1] Thompson *v.* Gregory, 4 Johns. 81.

parties, that the lessor, after the commencement of the action, indorsed on the lease that it was the intention of the same to convey the right to flow the three acres.[1]

The case of Morgan v. Mason may be referred to as an illustration of rendering an easement in one parcel of land appurtenant to another, so as afterwards to pass with the latter. J. M. bought of Polluck fifteen acres of land lying upon one side of a stream, in 1834. At that time, May [*38] *owned land above this parcel upon both sides of the stream, and upon the side of the stream opposite to the fifteen acres. In 1837 he conveyed to J. M. one acre of the land opposite the fifteen acres, and extending as far up the stream as that did, and by the same deed conveyed to J. M. a right to build a dam across the stream at the upper line of the fifteen-acre and one-acre lots, far enough and high enough to raise the water in the stream to a certain height, and to go upon May's land, at all times, to repair it. The dam was erected, and a race made upon the fifteen-acre lot, by which the water of the pond was conducted and discharged into the stream below the one-acre lot, and upon this race within the fifteen-acre lot a mill was standing in 1837, which was operated by the water of the same, and continued to be up to 1845. At that time the fifteen-acre lot was sold on execution against J. M. by metes and bounds, with the privileges and appurtenances thereto belonging. All J. M.'s other lands were sold under a mortgage to another creditor, and the question was, whether this water-right upon another tract of land, and acquired at a different point of time, had become so appurtenant to the fifteen-acre lot as to pass with it, without being expressly named. And it was held that it did, being necessary to the enjoyment of the mill standing on the fifteen-acre lot, and used with it; and that it passed as incident to it, without requiring that it should be mentioned in the deed.[2]

1 Russell v. Scott, 9 Cow. 279.

2 Morgan v. Mason, 20 Ohio, 401, 414. See Underwood v. Carney, 1 Cush. 285.

14. *Appurtenant,* as applied to easements, which pass by
grant of the principal thing, is confined " to an old existing
right." It is not enough that the same man may own one
piece of land, and a right to use another piece of land, in
a qualified manner, in connection with it. If he conveys
the first parcel independent of the right in the second, it
passes no claim to his grantee beyond what is expressly
granted, unless he has so united them, by a practical
*application of the one for the benefit of the other, [*39]
as to have given thereby a value and advantage to the
principal estate which is presumed to enter into the consideration which he receives upon conveying the same. It is for
this reason, among others, that if one owns two parcels of
land, over one of which he has a convenient way to the other,
which he uses, it is not supposed he intends to enhance the
value of the one at the expense of the other; and when he
sells either of these parcels, it is not presumed that he attaches to such parcel a burden or privilege in respect to the
other, unless he expressly so declares in his deed. Such
way would not pass as appurtenant, unless made so expressly
by the deed, although the estate " with its appurtenances "
is granted.[1]

15. But if, in a case like that supposed, the owner of two
parcels of land, over one of which there was a defined and
ascertained way used by him in connection with the other
parcel, were to convey the latter parcel, with " the ways, or
all the ways, now used " therewith, such way would become
appurtenant to the parcel by the act of the owner, evidenced
by the language of his deed.[2]

So if one own White Acre and Black Acre, and uses a way
from White Acre over Black Acre to a mill, a river, or the

---

[1] Barlow v. Rhodes, 1 Crompt. & M. 439 ; Whalley v. Tompson, 1 Bos. &
P. 371 ; Grant v. Chase, 17 Mass. 443. *Bayley,* J., in Barlow v. Rhodes, says of
Morris v. Edgington, 3 Taunt. 24 : " I consider that merely as a case of a way of
necessity." Plant v. James, 5 Barnew. & Ad. 791.

[2] Whalley v. Tompson, 1 Bos. & P. 371 ; Barlow v. Rhodes, 1 Crompt. & M.
430 ; Kooystra v. Lucas, 5 Barnew. & Ald. 830 ; Com. Dig. *Chimin,* D. 3.

like, and conveys White Acre to a stranger, " with all ways,"
it will pass a right of way with it over Black Acre to the mill,
&c.[1]

16. But though, where there is an existing easement, like
a way belonging to an estate, it will pass with the estate, if
granted " with the privileges and appurtenances," or, by
later cases, without adding these words, the use of these
words will not create a new easement, nor give a
[*40] right to *use a way which has been used with one
part of an estate over another part, while both parts
belonged to the same owner. But if the words in the grant
of the principal estate be " with all ways therewith used, or
heretofore used," the ways actually in use at the time of
the conveyance would pass.[2] And in James v. Plant,[3] the
court held that " appurtenances " in the habendum of the
deed under consideration was not confined to that which
is, in legal strictness, an appurtenant, such as an easement, the enjoyment whereof has never been interrupted
by unity of possession or extinguished by unity of seisin,
but that it would let in and comprehend a right of way
which had been usually held, used, and occupied or enjoyed with the principal estate conveyed. But the ground
upon which this was so held was, that " ways, paths, and
passages" had been mentioned in the deed among the premises granted. Otherwise the word "appurtenances" in the
habendum would only pass a way legally incident to the enjoyment of the property.[4]

Thus it is said by Crompton, J., in respect to the claim of
an easement of a pump upon one estate in favor of another,
both of which estates were claimed under the same devisor :
" This is not a *continuous* easement, nor an easement belonging to the cottage, but a mere enjoyment for two years by

---

[1] Staple v. Heydon, 6 Mod. 1.

[2] Gayetty v. Bethune, 14 Mass. 49 ; Grant v. Chase, 17 Mass. 443 ; *ante*, sect.
1, pl. 11.

[3] 4 A. & Ellis, 749.

[4] Worthington v. Gimson, 2 E. & Ellis, 624.

the tenant, of the privilege of using the pump.   If this had been an old easement attached to the cottage, it would pass by the words "appertaining and belonging." But to create a new easement which did not exist before, the will must have devised the cottage with the pump therewith enjoyed.[1]

17. So where, upon partition made of an estate by mutual deeds of release, upon one part of the estate there was a mill which was assigned to one cotenant, and a part of the land which was flowed by the mill was assigned to another, and in the deed the expression was contained, " the brook to remain for the mills as heretofore," it was held that the mill-owner had a right to flow the land of the other, and that the extent to which this might be done was to the height to which the dam of the mill, in its original state, was designed and was of a capacity to raise it, although when the deed was made the dam had become depressed in the centre, and incapable, in that state, of flowing water to its original height.[2]

18. Where one conveyed land with a water-privilege, by metes and bounds, on which one end of a dam across the stream rested, and reserved to himself the privilege of drawing so much water from the pond for fulling so much cloth, but there was no existing mill, the grantor insisted that, by implication, he had a right to erect such mill upon the land, in order to enjoy the reserved right of water-power. But it appearing that there was other land in the neighborhood which he could obtain suitable for erecting such mill, which might be operated by a canal to be cut across the granted premises, it was held that the right to erect the mill upon the premises, not being a necessary one in order to enjoy the reservation, did not pass thereby.[3]

19. Upon a like principle, where one made a grant or

---

[1] Polden v. Bastard, 4 B. & Smith, 264.
[2] Vickerie v. Buswell, 13 Me. 289.
[3] Cocheco Mg. Co. v. Whittier, 10 N. H. 305.

[*41] *lease of a tan-yard, with a right to take sufficient
water from a stream upon the grantor's land for the
use of the tan-yard and to carry a bark-mill, it did not give
the grantor a right to foul the water by discharging the con-
tents of the tan-yard into the water thus used. It not being
necessary to its enjoyment, the right to do this did not pass
with the principal thing granted, however convenient it
might be.[1]

20. The case of Hull v. Fuller may serve to show how far
courts are sometimes obliged to refer to the state and condition of the premises, as well as the purpose of the grant, in
order to fix and define the limits of a grant of an easement.
The terms of the grant, in that case, were of a definite parcel of land, " and the whole of a mill-pond which may be
raised by a dam on said falls to a road," &c. As this neither
fixed the dimensions of the pond, nor the height of the dam,
the grant was held to be of a right to erect such a dam as
would afford a reasonable use of the mill-privilege, and when
a dam should be built, and a pond thereby should be raised,
such as would effect that purpose, the boundaries of the
grant would thereby become fixed and ascertained. By that
grant the purchaser had a right to build such a dam as
could be constructed at the falls, and of such a height as
would well answer the purposes of mills contemplated to be
built there.[2]

21. While it is true that the grant of a principal thing
carries whatever is necessary to its enjoyment, this is limited
by what the grantor had, at the time, the power to convey.[3]
So it might be limited by the effect which the construction
to be given might have upon other interests and estates connected with the one granted. Thus, though if one
[*42] had a single saw-mill for instance, upon a stream, *and
were to convey the same by deed, it would carry, by

---

[1] Howell v. M'Coy, 3 Rawle, 256.

[2] Hull v. Fuller, 4 Vt. 199.

[3] Tourtellot v. Phelps, 4 Gray, 370 ; Lampman v. Milks, 21 N. Y. 505 ; United
States v. Appleton, 1 Sumn. 492.

implication, the dam and water-privilege belonging to the same ; yet if he owned several mills standing upon the same privilege, and were to convey one of them by the same distinctive term of " saw-mill," " grist-mill," or the like, it would only pass the particular mill thus designated, and sufficient water only to carry it. The law would not extend the constructive grant to the destruction of the other mills standing on the same privilege.[1]

In one case there were two mills upon a stream, and a reservoir above them both, the water from which came, successively, to these mills. The owner of them sold the lower mill, conveying it by metes and bounds, without mentioning the reservoir. The other mill and reservoir afterwards came into the plaintiff's hands, and upon the owner of the lower mill undertaking to exercise the right to draw water from the reservoir, it was held that he acquired no right, by implication, to do this against the consent of the owner of the upper works, although it so happened that between the upper and lower mills there was no place where the owner of the latter could erect a dam, and raise a head of water by a pond.[2]

22. Where an easement, like an artificial drain, for instance, has been created and granted for a particular use and purpose, it cannot be changed by the grantee to another though like use, nor can the grantee increase the amount or extent of such use beyond what was originally intended and embraced in the grant. Thus, A granted to B a right to construct and maintain an artificial trench across A's land, to drain the water from a certain cleared parcel of land by ditches made thereon discharging into this trench. The grantee afterwards drained the specific parcel by ditches running in a direction other than to this trench, but cleared an-

[1] Crittenden v. Field, 8 Gray, 621 ; Vickerie v. Buswell, 13 Me. 289 ; Stackpole v. Curtis, 32 Me. 383.

[2] Brace v. Yale, 4 Allen, 393 ; 2 Wash. R. P. 664. See ante, p. *34, for distinction between this and the case of Perrin v. Garfield there cited.

other parcel, and drained the water from that by ditches running into this trench. It was held that he had no right,
under such grant, to increase the quantity of water intended
to be thereby discharged through the trench, and that he had
no right to discharge water coming from other sources than
that specified in the grant, although it might not exceed in
quantity that which was contemplated to flow through the
trench, even though, while doing it, the grantee forbore to
use it for discharging the water originally intended to flow
through it.[1]

23. Although, as has more than once been said, no easement in one parcel can be said to be appurtenant to another
           by reason of any use made of the two, so long as they
[*43] both *belong to the same person, the cases are nu-
           merous where, upon dividing the heritage, as it is
called, — that is, by the owner of two or more estates or
parts of an estate selling one of them by itself, and retaining
the other, or conveying it to some third person, — privileges
in favor of the one have been held to pass as incident to the
same, and a corresponding burden imposed upon the other,
from the nature of the estate, the arrangement of the parts
of the estate, and the degree of necessity there is of giving
such a construction to the conveyance, in order to give it a
reasonable effect. This is not intended to embrace that class
of cases already referred to, where, as in the case of a way,
an estate is conveyed granting therewith " all ways " or
" ways in use," the ways actually used in connection with
the part granted have been held to pass by the terms of the
deed.

The ground upon which this doctrine both of the French
and the common law rests seems to be, that, where the owner
of two heritages, or of one heritage consisting of several
parts, has arranged and adapted these so that one derives a
benefit or advantage from the other of a continuous and
obvious character, and he sells one of them without making

---

[1] Carter v. Page, 8 Ired. 190.

mention of those incidental advantages or burdens of one in respect to the other, there is in the silence of the parties an implied understanding and agreement that these advantages and burdens, respectively, shall continue as before the separation of the title.[1]

Thus where two parcels lay, one in front and the other in rear, in relation to a highway, and there was a private way used over the front lot from the rear one to the highway, and the owner of the two conveyed the front lot to a stranger, it was held that he took it subject to the use of this private way from the rear lot to the highway. It became, at once, a way appurtenant to the rear lot.[2] So where a parcel of land was conveyed to which the owner had been accustomed to have access by a way across another open parcel to the highway, it was held that his grantee might use this way, though not one of absolute necessity, if another way could not be constructed by him at a reasonable expense, having reference to the value of the land.[3]

*24. Questions of this kind have often arisen in [*44] cases of one or more houses erected in a block belonging to the same owner, where one is dependent upon another for its lateral support, or the water collecting in the one has been discharged by a drain through another, and the like, and in some cases in respect to lights in houses which have been conveyed.

Thus in Richards v. Rose, the proprietor of a parcel of land erected a number of dwelling-houses upon the same in one block, each supporting the other, and each obviously needing the support of the other. It was held that, if he conveyed one of these, he created an easement of support in its favor as against the adjoining house, and a servitude

---

[1] See ante, sect. 1, pl. 21, as to *Destination du père de famille. Post,* p. *53 ; Penn. R. R. *v.* Jones, 50 Penn. 424.

[2] M'Tavish *v.* Carroll, 7 Md. 352.   See Brakely *v.* Sharp, 1 Stockt. 9 ; McCarty *v.* Kitchenman, 47 Penn. 239.

[3] Pettingell *v.* Porter, 8 Allen, 1.

upon the adjoining tenement of support to the one which
he had granted.[1]

25. So many questions, especially of late, have turned
upon the construction and effect of conveying part or parts
of one or more heritages, which the owner had so adapted
or arranged as to make certain uses of one part convenient
or necessary for the enjoyment of the other, that a special
reference to decided cases becomes proper, in order to
ascertain, if possible, the rule or test by which to determine
whether and how far an easement or servitude may thereby be
granted or reserved by implication.

Under the French law, this is provided for by the code.
What is there called *la destination du père de famille* " has
the effect of writing in regard of *continued* and *apparent* servitudes." And " if the owner of two heritages, between
which there exists an apparent mark of servitude, dispose of
one of the two heritages without the contract containing any
agreement relative to the servitude, it continues to exist,
actively or passively, in favor of the property aliened, or
upon the property aliened." [2]   This, it will be perceived, is a
positive inference of law from the act of the parties, rather
than the constructive terms of an agreement between them.
And yet, according to Pardessus, it is not in consequence of
the principle that servitudes follow the estates to which they
belong, into whosesoever hands they come, since no one can
owe a servitude to himself, but by a just and legitimate
presumption of intention with which they were created, and
the silence of the one who makes a disposition of the estate,
and the good faith which is due to him who, seeing the
condition of the estates, has a right, naturally, to conclude
that they were thus transmitted by the vendor.[3]

The same principle has been adopted, by analogy, to a
greater or less extent, by different courts, as a basis of con-

[1] Richards *v.* Rose, 9 Exch. 218 ; *ante*, sect. 1, pl. 21.
[2] Barrett's Cod. Nap. §§ 692, 694.
[3] Pardes. Serv. 447.

struing grants, though it is believed that the common law, in order to give this effect, requires that what is thus claimed as a servitude or easement should be reasonably, and in some cases absolutely, *necessary* as well as *continuous* and *apparent*. This analogy to the French law is expressly recognized by the Court of Pennsylvania, in the case of a way which was claimed by the devisee of one part of an estate over another part of the same estate in the hands of another devisee. The testator had, in his lifetime, divided his estate among his sons in distinct occupancy, retaining one part in his own possession, but gave them no title to the same during his lifetime. One of the sons in occupying his part made use of a way which the father had constructed before the division over that in possession of the father, which, a part of the distance, was fenced out as such, and over this the son had passed to mill and to meeting and a neighboring village, the same being his most convenient way to and from these. After the father's death, the one to whom he devised the homestead part, denied to the devisee of the other part the right to pass over this way. But the court, though they say that such easements were commonly those of water, like drains, water-pipes &c., yet being a distinct and notorious way fenced out, it passed as a permanent disposition as appurtenant or perhaps as parcel of the property devised, placing it upon the intention of the testator and not upon any necessity there was for such way.[1]

The case of Ewart *v.* Cockrane is often quoted as a leading one upon this subject. The premises were a dwelling-house, garden, and tan-yard, the tan-yard being owned by one, and the house and garden by another, from 1788 to 1806. They then were owned by the same person until 1819. In 1819 the owner conveyed the tan-yard, and it came, at last, to the defendant. In 1822 he conveyed the house and garden, and

[1] Phillips *v.* Phillips, 48 Penn. 178; Penn. R. R. *v.* Jones, 50 Penn. 424; Keiffer *v.* Imhoff, 26 Penn. 438. See Huttemeier *v.* Albro, 18 N. Y. 48; *post,* p. *46; McCarty *v.* Kitchenman, 47 Penn. 239.

they came to the plaintiff. There had been a drain in use from the tan-yard into a cesspool or tank in the garden, from 1788, and was continued till 1853, when the defendant stopped it. The Chancellor, Ld. Campbell, said, " I consider the law of Scotland as well as the law of England to be, that when two properties are so possessed by the same owner, and there has been a severance made of part from the other, anything which was used and was necessary for the comfortable enjoyment of that part of the property which is granted, shall be considered to follow from the grant, if there be the usual words in the conveyance. I do not know whether the usual words are essentially necessary, but when there are the usual words, I cannot doubt that that is the law." Both he and Lord Chelmsford held that the easement passed with the tan-yard, because it was " necessary for the convenient and comfortable enjoyment of the property, as it existed before the grant." [1]

In Worthington v. Gimson, two farms and two parcels adjoining belonging to two persons in common, partition was made between them, giving one farm and the two parcels to one, and the other farm to. the other, and in the deeds were included " their and every of their rights, members, easements, and appurtenances." A way had previously been in use across the two parcels for the accommodation of the farm set to the other owner, who now claimed it as an easement. But the court held that it did not pass, as it did not appear to be *necessary* for the enjoyment of the premises. " It would not pass under the term ' appurtenances,' because the way is not within the strict legal sense of that word." There may be a class of easements like drains or sewers, which must necessarily be intended to remain after the severance of the property, and in such case the necessity of the easement may be ascertained. [2]

---

[1] Ewart v. Cockrane, 4 McQueen, 117. See also Hall v. Lund, 1 H. & Colt, 676 ; Shaw v. Etheridge, 3 Jones, N. C. 300.

[2] Worthington v. Gimson, 29 L. Jour. Q. B. 116 ; 2 E. & Ellis, 618.

The rule of the French law is also referred to by the court of N. Jersey, in the case of an aqueduct which was held to be *reserved* to the grantor, although not in express terms, upon the principle that where the owner of two parcels so arranges one in reference to the other as to derive an apparent and continuous benefit from what is of the nature of an easement in the other, and he conveys one of the parcels, it carries with it or is subject to the enjoyment of this as an easement in fact. In that case, the owner of a paper-mill and a lot with a spring in it, laid an aqueduct from the spring to his mill for the use of the latter. He subsequently conveyed the spring, but without reserving the easement of the aqueduct, and it was held that the grant was subject to this easement, it being open, apparent, and continuous in its character; nor is the idea of supplying water, elsewhere, raised in the discussion of the case.[1]

But where the thing to be used is disconnected from the estate to which it is claimed as appurtenant, and its use is not *continuous*, the right of enjoyment of it will not pass as an incidental easement upon dividing the heritage.[2]

A case where a right of way was held to pass upon granting one of two parcels belonging to the same person, although not a way of necessity, but because the parcels had been so used in relation to each other by the owner, was this. There were three parcels of land, the first and third belonged to A, who had a prescriptive right of way from 1 to 3 across 2, and in going from 3 to a public way, A used to pass across 2 and 1. A sold 3 to a third person, and it was held that the right of way across 2 passed as appurtenant to that lot, and that a right to pass across 1 to the public way passed also as an easement, although the purchaser could have access to it by a less convenient way.[3]

---

[1] Seymour *v.* Lewis, 13 N. J. 439.

[2] Polden *v.* Bastard, 4 B. & Smith, 258.

[3] Leonard *v.* Leonard, 7 Allen, 277, 283. See also Pearson *v.* Spencer, 1 B. & Smith, 580; s. c., 3 B. & Smith, 761.

And another case, where the condition and use of the
property granted, in case of several parcels owned by one
person and conveyed separately by him, serve to fix the
rights of the purchasers, was this : A owned, upon a stream,
two mills, and B owned an intermediate mill upon the same
stream. A opened a sluice from above the dam of B, along
the bank of the stream to his lower mill, thereby drawing a
part of the water in B's pond to the pond of the lower mill.
In this state of the property, A purchased B's mill, thereby
owning the three estates, and subsequently sold them to
three distinct purchasers. And it was held that the purchaser of the middle mill took it subject to the right in the
lower one to draw the water from the pond of that mill in
the manner in which it was done when the conveyance was
made.[1]

In Louisiana, when a party grants an estate to which an
apparent easement belongs, he is considered as warranting
that he will do nothing to prevent its full enjoyment, though
no mention is made of it in the grant.[2]

The latest English case which has come to hand bearing upon this subject is Russell v. Harford, decided in
1866.[3] In that case the defendant was, originally, the owner
of two adjoining parcels with dwelling-houses thereon, which
he had let to two different tenants. On lot A was a well,
from which the tenant of lot B by permission drew water
for his premises, by a pipe laid from B to the well. In this
condition of things, the lots were sold by the defendant at
auction, A being first bid off by the tenant thereof, and then
B, by the tenant of that lot. The plaintiff bid off A, and the
defendant, the vendor, declined delivering any deed of the
estate unless it contained a reservation or exception of the
right of the owner of B to draw water from the well, and
the right to repair and renew the pipe aforesaid.

[1] Elliott v. Sallee, 14 Ohio St. 10 ; Morgan v. Mason, 20 Ohio, 401.

[2] Bruning v. N. Orleans Canal, &c., 12 Louis. An. 541.

[3] Russell v. Harford, L. R. 2 Eq. 507.

The suit was in equity to compel the defendant to give an unrestricted deed. One of the conditions of sale stated that the premises were sold " subject — to rights of way and water, and other easements (if any) charged or subsisting thereon."

The purchaser of B, had been tenant from year to year of the premises which he bid off. The plaintiff insisted that the facts did not establish a right of easement to water in B over A, but that the quasi servitude to which the latter had been subjected by the owner, was discharged by his absolute sale thereof to a purchaser by the vendor of both parcels while he owned them both, and he cited Suffield v. Brown as an authority. The defendant insisted that the easement passéd because lot B would be useless without the right to water, and cited Wardle v. Brocklehurst,[1] but did not refer to Pyer v. Carter. The Vice-Chancellor, Kindersley, without citing any authority, held that this right could not have been embraced in the expressions used in the conditions of sale, as the only right of the tenant of B to draw water was by license from the owner, that the two purchasers of the lots made their contracts upon the basis of the conditions of sale, and that if it had intended to create a right or liability as between the purchasers of the different lots, it should have been clearly expressed in the terms of the sale, and in the absence of any such restriction or limitation, the plaintiff was entitled to a deed without other exception or reservation of the servitude claimed.

The case therefore seems to have turned upon the construction given to the contract of the parties, rather than upon any implied grant or reservation of a right growing out of the sale of one of two heritages. And another circumstance in the case distinguishes it from those where the parts of the heritage have been arranged and adapted to each other by the owner thereof, since, in the case under consideration, the laying of the pipe from the well in one parcel to the house on the other, was done by the tenants

---

[1] Wardle v. Brocklehurst, 29 L. J. (Q. B.), 145.

thereof, independent, for aught that appears, of any act or intention on the part of the owner of the estate.

25 *a.* In several, especially of the more recent, cases which have been cited, that of Pyer *v.* Carter has been referred to, and an importance given to it which renders it desirable to ascertain to what extent it is to be regarded as a statement of what the law is upon the subject of which it treats.

The case is repeatedly cited in the present work, and was received, at the time of the preparation of the former edition, as the law of the English courts. It is reported in 1 H. & Norm. 916, and the facts, as stated, were these : The plaintiff's and defendant's houses adjoined each other. They had formerly been one house, and were converted into two by the owner of the whole property. Subsequently the defendant's house was conveyed to him, he knowing the existence of this drain ; and after that the plaintiff took a conveyance of his house from the same grantor. At the time of the respective conveyances, the drain ran under the plaintiff's house and then under the defendant's house, and discharged itself into the common sewer. The plaintiff's house was drained through this drain ; but he might have stopped it, and made a new one over his own land into the sewer, for six pounds. The court held that, under these circumstances, the plaintiff had an easement of drain through the defendant's premises by an implied grant, and that the defendant was liable for stopping it. The Chancellor, in giving an opinion in the case of Suffield *v.* Brown,[1] seems to have gone out of his record to attack and endeavor to overrule this case of Pyer *v.* Carter. The case before him was one where a man, owning a dock and wharf, with a strip of land adjoining it, sold the wharf and strip of land, without making any reserve in favor of the dock. He had been accustomed, when using the dock for vessels, to have their bowsprits extend over some part of the wharf, and, from the size of the dock, this was necessary in order to have vessels lie there. He attempted to enforce

---

[1] 10 Jur. N. s. 111.

this right against his grantee, but the court refused him the relief which he claimed. The easement claimed was, obviously, a non-continuous one, nor was there anything to render it apparent beyond the fact of the size and dimensions of the dock. The connection between such an easement as this and the case of a drain, as in Pyer *v.* Carter, is far from being obvious. But the Chancellor takes occasion to go much at length into the doctrine of easements by implied grants. He cites from Mr. Gale's work his remarks upon this subject, and adds: " But I cannot agree that the grantor can derogate from his own absolute grant, so as to claim rights over the thing granted, even if they were, at the time of the grant, continuous and apparent easements enjoyed by an adjoining tenement which remains the property of him, the grantor." He next proceeds to comment upon the doctrine of *destination du père de famille*, in the manner already stated,[1] and then notices " the fallacy in the judgment of the Court of Exchequer in the case of Pyer *v.* Carter "; and concludes, " I cannot look upon the case as rightly decided, and must wholly refuse to accept it as an authority." He approves of the doctrine of Nicholas *v.* Chamberlain,[2] and Sury *v.* Pigott,[3] which are also repeatedly referred to in the present work, and admits that there may be two adjoining houses so constructed as to be mutually subservient to and dependent on each other, neither being capable of standing or being enjoyed without the support it derives from its neighbor, in which case the alienation of the one house by the owner of both, would not estop him from claiming, in respect of the house he retains, that support from the house sold which is, at the same time, afforded in return by the former to the latter tenement, as in Richards *v.* Rose.[4] But where the right is separable, it is severed, and either passed or extinguished by the grant. If it were not for what is said by him of Nicholas *v.* Chamberlain, it might, perhaps, be assumed, that he made

---

[1] *Ante*, p. *17.   [3] Palmer, 444.
[2] Cro. Jac. 121.   [4] 9 Exch. 218.

a distinction between granted and reserved rights. But that case expressly disregards such a distinction. Some of the Chancellor's positions certainly seem to be opposed to opinions which more than one of the American courts have expressed, and as to the point ruled by the court in Pyer *v.* Carter, the weight of authority, so far as numbers are concerned, seems to be against his opinion.

Thus, in one case, Martin B. says Pyer *v.* Carter " was no more than an implied grant of a right analogous to that of flowing water," and " went to the utmost extent of the law ; but, if considered, that decision cannot be complained of; for if a man have two fields drained by an artificial ditch cut through both, and he grants to another one of these fields, neither he nor the grantee can stop up the drain in it. I agree with the law as laid down in that case, and I think it may be supported without extending the doctrine of the right of way." [1]

Channel B. in Hall *v.* Lund says : " In Ewart *v.* Cochrane, the House of Lords confirmed the principle of the decision in Pyer *v.* Carter," and adds, " the case of Pyer *v.* Carter, which was confirmed, and its principle explained by the House of Lords, compels me to come to this conclusion," that is, the judgment which he rendered in that case.[2]

The doctrine of Pyer *v.* Carter is recognized more or less directly and authoritatively, in the cases following, viz. : By the Chancellor in Ewart *v.* Cochrane, by Wightman J. in Worthington *v.* Gimson,[3] and Polden *v.* Bastard,[4] by the New York court in Huttemeier *v.* Albro,[5] by the reporter in Glave *v.* Harding,[6] and by the court of Pennsylvania in McCarty *v.* Kitchenman,[7] in which the opinion of the Chancellor in Suffield *v.* Brown, is referred to, with the remark that the easement in that case was neither continuous nor

---

1 Dodd *v.* Burchell, 1 H. & Colt, 121.
2 1 H. & Colt. 681, 685. See also 105 Eng. C. Law Rep. 626 ; note Am. Ed.
3 2 E. & Ellis, 618.
4 4 B. & Smith, 258.   6 3 H. & Norm. 944 note.
5 18 N. Y. 52.   7 47 Penn. St. 243.

apparent, and it does not seem to have been regarded as an authority in deciding the case then before them.

In Crossley v. Lightowler, in 1866, the counsel on both sides refer to Pyer v. Carter, and Suffield v. Brown, and the Vice-Chancellor Wood states what the decision in the former established, without any suggestion that it is not a reliable authority, and one of the counsel insists that Suffield v. Brown does not overrule it.[1]

The case is also cited by Chapman J., in Leonard v. Leonard,[2] and by Hoar, J., in Carbrey v. Willis,[3] but without comment or objection. Nor has any case except Suffield v. Brown been found which militates with the doctrine of that case, unless that of Randall v. McLaughlin [4] is to be so regarded.

In the latter case, Hoar, J., in giving the opinion of the court, says: " The authority of Pyer v. Carter, the leading English case on which the plaintiff relies, was wholly denied by the Chancellor of England in the opinion given in Suffield v. Brown, which contains an elaborate review of the whole doctrine, resulting in conclusions substantially like those to which we came in Carbrey v. Willis." The facts and judgment in the last-mentioned case were these. A drain was an ancient one constructed by the owner of two or more houses, passing from one under the other to the place of discharge. One of these houses he sold to one person, and the other to another, but the drain was not apparent, and neither of the purchasers knew of its existence for many years after such purchase by them, when it was discovered by becoming obstructed. As the lower of the two houses was first sold, if the drain could be claimed for the benefit of the upper one, it must be by way of implied *reservation*, as in the case of Pyer v. Carter, as it was not mentioned in the deed. The court, with obvious propriety, held " that no easement can be taken as reserved by implication unless it is *de facto* an-

[1] L. R. 3 Eq. 286.
[2] 7 Allen, 283.
[3] 7 Allen, 369.
[4] 10 Allen, 366.

nexed and in use, at the time of the grant, and is necessary to the enjoyment of the estate which the grantor retains." " Where there is a grant of land by metes and bounds without express reservation, and with full covenants of warranty against encumbrances, there is no just cause for holding that there can be any reservation by implication, unless the easement is strictly one of necessity."

The case of Randall v. McLaughlin was in many respects like that of Carbrey v. Willis. There was a drain passing from one house under the other, both of which, originally, belonged to one man who conveyed the lower house, with covenants of warranty, to one, and subsequently the upper house to another. But the Court held that this drain did not attach as an easement to the upper house, because the requisite necessity " does not exist, in the view of the law, where an equally beneficial drain could be built on the plaintiff's land with reasonable labor and expense." Reference is also made to Johnson v. Jordan[1] and Thayer v. Payne.[2]

Both these cases have also been repeatedly referred to in this work, and they are now recalled only so far as they are supposed to bear upon the point under consideration. In the first of these, which was the case of a drain passing under two or more houses originally belonging to one person, who had sold and granted them separately at auction on the same day, to distinct owners, no mention was made of the drain in the conveyance. The judge instructed the jury that if, with reasonable labor and expense, a drain could be made without going through the plaintiff's (the lower) house, the owner of the other house had no right to enter and open the drain on the plaintiff's premises, and the jury found that such drain could be made. The court put the question of right of easement upon the construction to be given to the deed, in which the intention of the parties was not expressed in terms. They distinguish between an artificial drain and

[1] Post, p. 82; 2 Metc. 234.   [2] 2 Cush. 327.

a watercourse, the latter of which no proprietor has a right to obstruct or divert, nor is it affected by any unity of ownership of two estates over which it flows. In case of an artificial drain passing from one parcel through another, and the owner grant the first, "such drain may be construed to be *de facto* annexed as an appurtenance and pass with it." Whereas, if the grant be of the second or lower parcel, while the grantor owns the first, "it might reasonably be considered that, as the right of drainage was not reserved in terms, when it naturally would be if so intended, it could not be claimed by the grantor. The grantee of the lower tenement, taking the language of the deed most strongly in his favor and against the grantor, might reasonably claim to hold his granted estate free of the encumbrance." This, however, was *obiter* reasoning on the part of the court, for they add, " but neither of these rules will apply to the present case," the conveyances of the two parcels being simultaneous, and being like a partition between two tenants in common, " where each party takes his estate with the rights, privileges, and incidents inherently attached to it," rather than the case of grantor and grantee, where the grantor conveys a part of his land by metes and bounds, and retains another part to his own use. In the case of Johnson *v.* Jordan, certain easements and servitudes were attached to the parcels granted, and were described in the conveyances. But as this right of drain was not mentioned, " and as it was not necessary to the enjoyment of the estate, and had not been *de facto* annexed so as to pass by general words as *parcel* of the estate, it did not pass by force of the deed."

In Thayer *v.* Payne, the grant was of the upper of two parcels, the grantor retaining the lower one. It was held, that if the use of the drain was necessary to the beneficial enjoyment of the premises granted, the right to use it would pass. But the court add, " the settlement of this question will, of course, involve the inquiry, whether or not a drain could be conveniently made with reasonable labor and expense, without going through the plaintiff's land. Because, if the defendant can furnish his house with a drain, it cannot be necessary to the enjoyment of his estate that he should have a drain through the land of the plaintiff." And the language of the court, in Carbrey v. Willis, bearing upon the point of substituting a new drain, in determining how far the one in use is to be regarded as necessary, is, " this necessity cannot be deemed to exist if a similar privilege can be secured by reasonable trouble and expense." " Where the easement is only one of existing use and great convenience, but for which a substitute can be furnished by reasonable labor and expense, the grantor may, certainly, cut himself off from it by his deed, if such is the intention of the parties. And it is difficult to see how such an intention could be more clearly and distinctly intimated than by such a deed of warranty." And this doctrine is reaffirmed in Randall v. McLaughlin.

The English doctrine of Pyer and Carter seems to be, that if one owns two houses, and, what is true of most houses, a drain of some kind is necessary for them, and the owner makes this a common drain for both by its passing from the upper under the lower house, and this arrangement of its parts is obvious and apparent to any observer; and he conveys one of these to another who sees and knows the condition of the two estates, the drain is to be regarded as it were a parcel of the thing granted, an easement or servitude, as it was the upper or lower house which was granted, and that all covenants and grants in his deed would have reference to this state of things, and be construed accordingly. He would by his covenant warrant the premises as they were, instead of extinguishing and abandoning the enjoyment of what had been obviously provided and intended as a means of what was necessary to the enjoying of the upper premises, merely because he warranted the lower one to be free of encumbrances. This view of the law treats such a drain as if it were a permanent watercourse, without distinguishing between its flowing from a spring upon the surface of the soil, or a variety of smaller springs opened by digging the cellar upon the upper lot, the water of which must be disposed of by an artificial watercourse, as much as that from a surface spring by its natural course.

The cases of Johnson v. Jordan and Carbrey v. Willis, seem to concede the doctrine of an easement being granted or reserved by implication in a grant in all cases where "the easement is strictly one of necessity." But, ordinarily, deeds are construed by the language in which they are expressed, if there is no reference made to extraneous circumstances. And, inasmuch as it is just as competent for the owner of premises, if he so intends, to extinguish a necessary easement as it is to extinguish a convenient one, to fill up his cellar or abandon its use as to dig a new drain, it is not easy to see why a mere covenant of warranty against encumbrances should be held to be any more an abandonment of the easement in the one case, in the absence of any words to indicate it, than in the other. The cases are numerous where the extent of the covenants in a deed are limited by what " the deed in its descriptive part purports to convey." [1]

And the question naturally arises, why, so far as words go, the same covenant in one case should be held to intend to relinquish an easement, and not to do it in another. And as to the policy of the two rules, the English must be regarded as the more definite and easy of application, since what is " reasonable labor and expense " in providing a new drain, in any given case, is a mere relative term, depending upon the circumstances of each particular case. What is reasonable in the country might not be in the city, and what is, by that standard, necessary for a cheap, poor house, would not be for a costly or expensive one.

It may not aid, perhaps, in settling a question like this, to refer to other decided cases, but there are some which seem to bear upon the general principles involved in this distinc-

---

[1] Miller v. Ewing, 6 Cush. 40; Adams v. Ross, 1 Vroom, 509.

tion between the cases of Pyer *v.* Carter and Carbrey *v.*
Willis. In a case in Pennsylvania, where the question was
whether an existing highway was an encumbrance, within
the meaning of covenants in a deed, the court say, "if there
be a public road or highway, open and in use upon it (the
granted estate), he must be taken to have seen it, and to
have fixed, in his own mind, the price that he was willing to
give for the land with a reference to the road, either making
the price less or more as he conceived the road to be injurious or advantageous to the occupation and enjoyment of
the land." [1]

In New Ipswich Co. *v.* Batchelder, the right to use an
artificial canal passed with a grant of the mill, although it
extended beyond the parcel as granted by metes and bounds.[2]

And in Nicholas *v.* Chamberlain, as already said, the court
held that an artificial aqueduct would pass or be reserved by
implication, upon a grant of the house to which it was appurtenant, or the land in which it was laid, as the case
might be, though it was not named.[3]

Parke B., in Pheysey *v.* Vicary, says: "If it is necessary
to the safety of a house that the water should flow down a
drain, the right of watercourse through it is reserved by implication in every grant of the house." [4]

And in Hurd *v.* Curtis, where one had a certain privilege
of water for a mill, which used to flow from the dam to his
mill in an artificial trench, across an intervening piece of
land which he conveyed to another person while so used, the
court suggest whether he did not, by implication, reserve a
right to have the trench kept open, as it was the open and visible mode of operating the mill, though of this they did not
give any decided opinion.[5]

And the case of Seymour *v.* Lewis, above referred to, is a
case of a reserve of the water of a spring by implication, in

---

[1] Patterson *v.* Arthurs, 9 Watts, 154.   See also Lampman *v.* Milks, 21 N. Y.
505 ; *post*, p. *48.

[2] 3 N. H. 190.   [4] 16 M. & Welsb. 489.

[3] Cro. Jac. 121.   [5] 7 Metc. 115.

land granted, in which no mention of such easement was made.[1]

The American annotator of 1 B. & Smith's Reports, in a note to Pearson v. Spencer, says: "It may be considered as settled in the United States, that, on the conveyance of one of several parcels of land belonging to the same owner, there is an implied grant or reservation, as the case may be, of all apparent and continuous easements or incidents of property, which have been created or used by him during the unity of possession, though they could then have had no legal existence apart from his general ownership." And he cites numerous cases as tending to establish that general proposition.[2]

But while this would seem to sustain and be fully sustained by the case of Pyer v. Carter, the inference to be drawn from Carbrey v. Willis and Randall v. McLaughlin, seems to be, that though this would be true where the dominant estate is conveyed and the servient estate reserved, it would not be so where the servient estate is granted and the dominant reserved, unless the easement claimed is one strictly of necessity and another cannot be substituted at reasonable labor and expense.[3]

But to bring a case within the principle of Pyer v. Carter, there must be a knowledge on the part of the grantor, as well as the grantee, that that which is claimed as an easement in favor of the estate granted, existed and had been enjoyed. Thus, where a land company conveyed to a purchaser a parcel of land designated by metes and bounds, on which the grantee, without their knowledge, had erected and was then using a mill, the dam of which flowed other lands of the grantor's than those conveyed, it was held that the purchaser did not, thereby, acquire any right to flow those lands as an easement appurtenant to an existing mill.[4]

26. The doctrine is broadly stated, that, upon the sever-

[1] 13 N. J. 439; ante, pl. 25.
[2] Post, pp. 73, 76, 77; 101 Eng. C. L. 586.
[3] See post, p. *529.
[4] Tabor v. Bradley, 18 N. Y. 109.

ance of a heritage by a grant of a parcel of it, it will, by implication, pass all those continuous and apparent easements which have in fact been used by the owner during the unity of ownership and possession, though they have no legal existence as proper technical easements. And in applying this doctrine, it is competent to show, by parol, [*45] what * had been used and were in use as appurtenances of the estate, at the time of its conveyance, but not to show what the parties intended to embrace in the deed as easements.[1]

Where a deed poll of an estate recited that the grantor *or* his heirs was to have a right of way over the granted premises to the grantor's other lands, it was construed to be a reservation of a way to the grantor, and to secure to him the way, not merely in gross, but as appurtenant to his estate. And it was further held by the court, that, had the way been fenced out and in use, such a recital in the deed would have been, in effect, an exception from the grant, and the way would thereby have become appurtenant to the grantor's other land.[2]

In Durel *v.* Boisblanc, where two houses standing upon two lots, with an alley between them, were sold, and it was obvious that the only access to one of these was through this alley, and they were sold at the same time, but nothing was said in the deeds of any right of passing over this alley to the premises, it was held that as to one of the houses an easement, and as to the other a servitude of way over this alley, were created by the grant of the parcels standing in such relation to each other.[3]

The right in such cases, it will be perceived, is not simply that of a way of necessity, which is limited in its duration

---

[1] Kenyon *v.* Nichols, 1 R. I. 411.   See Elliott *v.* Rhett, 5 Rich. 405 ; Glave *v.* Harding, 3 Hurlst. & N., Am. ed. 937 ; 2 Washb. Real Prop. 38, 54, 56 ; Harwood *v.* Benton, 32 Vt. 24 ; Code Nap., Art. 694 ; *ante*, sect. 1, pl. 21 ; M'Carty *v.* Kitchenman, 47 Penn. 243 ; Evans *v.* Dana, 7 R. I. 310.
[2] White *v.* Crawford, 10 Mass. 183, 188.
[3] Durel *v.* Boisblanc, 1 La. Ann. 407.

by the necessity, but becomes permanently appurtenant to the principal estate by the force and effect of the deed itself.

27. The case of Elliott *v.* Rhett was that of a rice-swamp, in which ditches regulating the flooding and draining of the same had been dug and were in use, and the same was sold in separate parcels. The court say : " Those *benefits or inconveniences which, according to the [*46] scheme of culture that was adopted by the owner of the whole body of land, were enjoyed or suffered by a parcel thereof that he has sold, provided they are of an unintermitting character, and are shown by external works, pass with the parcel as necessary incidents of the land. They are like the natural easements of running water and supporting soil." Accordingly it was held, that if, when conveyed in parcels, an artificial embankment upon one parcel regulated the flow of the water, and prevented its flooding other parts, it would be regarded like a natural embankment. And a temporary break in the same, existing at the time of the conveyance, would make no difference, unless the owner had thereby introduced and adopted a new and permanent system of management of the estate, or an abandonment, at least, of the former one. The court add : " The natural easement, if any existed, was once superseded by the disposition of the owner of the two tenements; the artificial easement which he created, whatever may have been its extent, existed at the time of the sale, and is in no respect entitled to less consideration than if it existed by nature." [1]

A recent case in New York was decided in accordance with the general doctrine above stated, though the facts were not identical with those of the cases cited. In that case a man died having several lots of land with buildings thereon in the city, situate at the intersection of D. and E. streets, three fronting on D. Street, running back to an alley

---

[1] Elliott *v.* Rhett, 5 Rich. 405, 415, 419.

which runs from E. Street along in the rear of them all, and along the side of the lot which fronted on E. Street. This alley had been used for the accommodation of these front lots on D. and E. streets for forty years, by the owner of the entire estate. After his death his heirs conveyed one of the [*47] lots on D. Street, "together with all tenements, *hereditaments and appurtenances thereto belonging," and described it by a line running so and so, " to the southerly side of an alley-way," and " thence along the said alley-way," so many feet. In their deed of the estate on E. Street, the alley is excluded by the boundaries and description of the premises, though no reference is made to it in the deed. Without specifying the terms of the deeds of the other parcels, the question was whether the right of way through and over this alley from E. Street to the first-mentioned lot was conveyed. It was held that it could not pass under the term " appurtenances," for the owner could not be said to have a right of way over his own land appurtenant to another parcel of his own land. But it having been in open use for the accommodation of the lot at the time of its conveyance, it was held that it passed as incident to the grant of the principal estate. " It is," say the court, " a general rule that, upon a conveyance of land, whatever is in use for it as an incident or appurtenance passes with it. The law gives such a construction to the conveyance, in view of what is thus used for the land as an incident or appurtenance, that the latter is included in it. Whether a right of way or other easement is embraced in a deed, is always a question of construction of the deed, having reference to its terms, and the practical incidents belonging to the grantor of the land at the time of the conveyance."

It will be perceived that the easement in this case was not spoken of as one of necessity. The principal estate fronted upon a public street, and was therefore accessible otherwise than by this alley. The existence of a known and continuous use of the thing claimed in connection with the thing granted, at and prior to the time of the grant made, raises the implication of an intent to embrace it in the grant.[1]

In accordance with this principle, where one sold lots fronting upon an open space which had once been occupied by a railroad, but, afterwards, upon a surrender of that, as a highway, it was held that the use of the highway as a means of access to these lots became annexed to them by the grant, and could not be defeated by the grantor, as owner of the soil of the highway, upon the same being discontinued, since the grantor could not take away what he had once granted by force of his deed.[2]

So where the owner of a block or square of city land made partition thereof, by deeds, among several persons, *and in each deed bounded the lot by an alley running [*48] through the block, each proprietor of a lot became entitled to a private way in the alley.[3]

28. The recent case of Lampman v. Milks presents an elaborate examination and discussion of the effect of granting an estate with which the grantor had been accustomed to use certain privileges in the nature of easements, though not naturally belonging to them, nor properly appurtenant to the same, nor granted by deed, with the principal estate, in express terms.

C, owning forty acres of land through which a natural watercourse ran, flooding half an acre of the same, changed the natural course of the stream by an artificial channel which he dug, leaving this half-acre thereby dry and fit for a building lot. After the water had flowed in this channel for several months, he sold the half-acre to the plaintiff, and continued for near ten years to own and occupy the remainder of the land. He then sold it to the defendant, who soon after stopped the artificial channel, and diverted the stream into its original course. In an action for the injury thereby occasioned, the question arose whether the purchaser of the

[1] Huttemeier v. Albro, 2 Bosw. 546 ; s. c., 18 N. Y. 48.
[2] Plitt v. Cox, 43 Penn. 488.   [3] Carlin v. Paul, 11 Mo. 32.

remainder of the forty acres took it as it was when granted to him, or took it with a right to have the natural flow of the stream restored to its original watercourse ; or, in the language of the court, " Whether an owner who, by such artificial arrangements of the material properties of his estate, has added to the advantages and enhanced the value of one portion, can, after selling that portion with those advantages openly and visibly attached, voluntarily break up the arrangement, and thus destroy or materially diminish the value of the portion sold ? "

So long as both parts belonged to the same owner, there could be no easement in favor of one part or servitude [*49] upon *another.   But the doctrine of the court was, that when the owner of two tenements sells one of them, or the owner of an entire estate sells a portion of the same, the purchaser takes the tenement, or the portion sold, with all the benefits and burdens which appear, at the time of sale, to belong to it, as between it and the property which the vendor retains.   Nor is this a rule in favor of purchasers alone ; and if, instead of a benefit conferred, a burden be imposed upon the portion sold, the purchaser, provided the marks of the burden be open and visible, takes the property with the servitude upon it.   The parties are presumed to contract in reference to the condition of the property at the time of the sale.   The court, accordingly, held that the purchaser, in this case, took his estate discharged of the original servitude of the overflow by the waters of the stream.

In the course of his opinion, the judge refers to and reviews several of the earlier and later leading cases, in which the questions above suggested were more or less directly considered.   Among them was William Copie's case,[1] where one having two tenements, and a gutter from one of them ran over or across the other, sold one tenement to one and

---

[1] Copie's case, Year B. 11 Hen. VII. 25 ; Dodd v. Burchell, 1 H. & Colt, 121, per Martin B.

the other to another ; and it was held that the easement
and servitude of the gutter passed with the respective estates
by the form of the grant.   He also cited the case of Nicholas *v.* Chamberlain, where the owner of an estate constructed an aqueduct from a spring on the same to the
dwelling-house standing thereon, and then granted the dwelling-house.   It was held to carry with it the easement of the
aqueduct.[1]   Also the cases [2] which are found more at length
in another part of this work, remarking that neither of these
came within that class of grants where easements have
been held to pass under broad and *comprehensive [*50]
terms, such as " a mill," " a messuage," " a farm,"
and the like, under which the same were virtually included
as a part of the thing thereby described, as has already been
explained.[3]

   29. The court, in the principal case above cited, in order
to carry out their illustration of the circumstances under
which an easement will pass by a grant of the estate with
which it is to be enjoyed, state the case of one owning a
dwelling-house opening upon a vacant piece of land belonging to him, over which it receives light and air.   If he conveys the house by itself, neither he nor his grantee may afterwards build upon the vacant lot so as to obstruct the windows
of the house ; and they refer to Palmer *v.* Fletcher,[4] Riviere
v. Bowers,[5] Compton *v.* Richards,[6] Coutts *v.* Gorham,[7] and
Story *v.* Odin,[8] which will be again referred to in connection
with easements of light and air.[9]

   [1] Nicholas *v.* Chamberlain, Cro. Jac. 121.

   [2] Robins *v.* Barnes, Hob. 131 ; United States *v.* Appleton, 1 Sumn. 492 ; New
Ipswich W. L. Factory *v.* Batchelder, 3 N. H. 190 ; Dunklee *v.* Wilton R. R., 4
Fost. 489.

   [3] Lampman *v.* Milks, 21 N. Y. 505.   See White *v.* Chapin.   Allen, not yet
reported.   *Post,* p. 129.

   [4] Palmer *v.* Fletcher, 1 Lev. 122.

   [5] Riviere *v.* Bowers, Ry. & M. 24.

   [6] Compton *v.* Richards, 1 Price, 27.

   [7] Coutts *v.* Gorham, 1 Mood. & M. 396.

   [8] Story *v.* Odin, 12 Mass. 157.   See also Swansborough *v.* Coventry, 9 Bing.
305.

   [9] See White *v.* Bass, 7 H. & Norm. 722.

30. The court also refer to another class of easements, by way of illustration, which are treated of in this work, and that is the right which one man has, under certain circumstances, to a support of his dwelling-house by the land of another, or by the walls of an adjoining tenement. Thus, for instance, if one owning a dwelling-house with the adjoining land convey the house, neither he nor his assigns could lawfully excavate the adjoining land, so near to the foundation of the house as essentially to impair its security, as was settled in the case of Lasala v. Holbrook.[1]

So if the owner of two lots erect a house upon one whose eaves discharge the water upon the other, and sell the [*51] house *in that state, the right thus to discharge the water passes with the house as an easement, and a servitude upon the adjacent lot.[2]

31. The case of Thayer v. Payne[3] was also cited in the same case. But it seems to rest rather upon the doctrine, that what is necessary to enjoy a thing granted passes by a grant of the principal thing, than that of an implied easement, growing out of the principal estate, having been used in a particular manner by the grantor. The subject of inquiry in that case was a drain connected with two tenements, one of which had been granted to the defendant by the plaintiff. The drain led from the defendant's tenement through the plaintiff's, and was held to pass, as an easement, with the defendant's tenement, although not granted in terms, because the jury found it necessary to the enjoyment of the same. Had it been otherwise, though existing at the time of the conveyance, it would not have passed.[4]

32. The general subject may be further illustrated by the case of Hinchliffe v. Kinnoul, where there had been a long

---

[1] Lasala v. Holbrook, 4 Paige, 169; *post*, chap. 4 sect. 1, pl. 7.

[2] Alexander v. Boghel, 4 La. 312.

[3] Thayer v. Payne, 2 Cush. 327. See also Brakely v. Sharp, 1 Stockt. 9, 17; Johnson v. Jordan, 2 Metc. 234, 240; Ferguson v. Witsell, 5 Rich. 280; Pyer v. Carter, 1 Hurlst. & N. 916.

[4] *Ante,* p. 67.

lease of land, during which houses had been erected thereon
by the lessee or his assigns, and a sub-lessee of one of the
tenements had made use of a passage-way along the side of
it, through which a " coal-shoot " had been used by him for
supplying the house with coal, and water-pipes had been laid
along this passage-way for supplying the house with water,
and in making repairs to the house this passage-way had been
used as a means of access thereto.   A few years before the
expiration of the general lease of the premises, the reversioner of the entire estate made a reversionary lease of the tenement above mentioned, in which he described it with
great exactness, and added, " together with *all and [*52]
singular the appurtenances unto the said piece or
parcel of ground, messuage, or tenement, erections, buildings, and premises belonging or anywise appertaining." The
question was, if the right of passage, &c. passed under this
lease, inasmuch as they never could have become appurtenant as against the reversioner, and he only granted such estate as he had.   It was held, that, being in existence, and necessary to the enjoyment of the leased premises, they passed
therewith as necessarily incident thereto, although not specially named in the lease.   The court, however, waived the
question whether these were properly appurtenant to the
thing granted, and held that it was enough that the lease
was made by a party who was entitled to the reversion both
of the house and the soil of the passage-way, and had a right
to grant or continue the existence of such right at the time
the lease was to come into operation and effect, and the words
of the lease would admit of that construction.[1]

33. The case of Pheysey v. Vicary may also be referred
to as a further illustration of what passes by way of easement
upon the severance of one or more tenements.   In that case
the owner of two dwelling-houses, standing near each other,

---

[1] Hinchliffe v. Kinnoul, 5 Bing. N. C. 1. See *post*, chap. 5, sect. 1, pl. 7,
where this case is again referred to, upon the question of the effect of unity of
title of two estates upon an existing easement. See also Osborn v. Wise, 7
Carr. & P. 751.

devised one to the plaintiff, and the other, " and the appurtenances thereto belonging," to the defendant. There was a
wrought track from the street along in front of the defendant's house continued on in front of the plaintiff's, which,
passing around a circular plat, returned into the street over
the same track as that by which it commenced; and this
track had been used as the means of access to the two
houses, although there was a means of access from the street
        to each of the houses from the rear of the land on
[*53] which the houses stood. The question was, *whether
        the plaintiff had a right to use this wrought track as
a means of access to his house. It was claimed, not as a
way of necessity, but as appurtenant to the estate devised
to him by reason of having been thus used.

It was contended that the way in this case came within
the principle of a *destination du père de famille* of the civil
law, which Pardessus defines, " La disposition ou l'arrangement que le proprietaire de plusieurs fonds a fait pour leur
usage respectif"; and which, by the Code Napoleon, " has
the effect of writing in regard of continual and apparent servitudes." The Code of Louisiana declares such use as the
owner has intentionally established on a particular part of
his property in favor of another part, to be equal to a title
with respect to perpetual and apparent servitudes thereon.
But the court, Parke B., held that " the way can only pass
in one of two modes, viz. either under the word ' appurtenances' in the will, or as of necessity. A right of way to
one of two houses, though of necessity, may be extinguished
by unity of ownership or possession, though, when either
house is regranted singly, it would pass by implication as
necessarily incident to that grant." That all that passed in
this case, under the term *appurtenant*, was a way of necessity, which does not come under the class of continuous or
permanent easements, but was one to be exercised only from
time to time, and only while the necessity continued. " If
it is necessary to the safety of a house that water should flow

down a drain, the right of watercourse through it is reserved by implication in every grant of the house." [1]

But if the drain of one house be so badly construct-ed as *to be a nuisance to the house through which it [*54] passes, and the owner of both lease the latter, retaining the former, he will be liable for suffering it to remain so, though in the same condition as when leased. The law does not, in such case, reserve to him anything more than a reasonable use of such drain.[2]

34. In determining whether a right like that of a drain or other easement shall pass, by implication, with premises under a grant, though not mentioned, much stress is laid upon its being of an apparent and continuous character, and in one case the objection was taken, that, when the pur-chaser of one of two tenements acquired his title, he did not know of the existence of the drain, the same being under ground. But the court held that he must have known that the tenement claiming the drain must have some drainage, and he was therefore bound to examine and as-certain its existence, and that no actually "apparent signs" were necessary to charge him with notice of the same.[3]

But still, in order that an easement should thus pass, by implication, under the grant of an estate, it must be one that is apparent as well as continuous, and such as is indicated by the condition of the premises at the time of the grant. And where there were skeletons of buildings standing to-gether, with openings in them, but apparently uncertain whether for doors or windows, a right of a particular way as belonging to the premises would not pass as one of its appur-tenances by a conveyance of one of the houses in that state.[4]

---

[1] See ante, sect. 1, pl. 21 ; Pheysey v. Vicary, 16 Mees. & W. 484 ; White v. Leeson, 5 Hurlst. & N. 53 ; Pardessus, Traité des Servitudes, 430, 431 ; Glave v. Harding, 3 Hurlst. & N., Am. ed. 937 ; Code Nap., Art. 692 ; La. Civ. Code, Art. 763 ; ante, p. *44.

[2] Alston v. Grant, 3 Ellis & B. 128. .

[3] Pyer v. Carter, 1 Hurlst. & N. 922.

[4] Glave v. Harding, 3 Hurlst. & An., Am. ed. 937, 945.

6

35. This subject is more fully examined in Johnson *v.* Jordan, already cited. That was also a case of a drain from one tenement through another, which had been used [*55] by the *owner of both tenements when they belonged to one and the same person. So long as he owned the two, he could convey the one with or without the encumbrance or advantage of the drain, as he might elect, depending, of course, upon his intent as expressed in his deed. In the absence of anything relative to the drain in a deed of one of the parcels, the question was, what construction did the law give to such deed in respect to such drain? An important circumstance appeared in the examination of the case, which was, that the slope of the ground was such as not to require that the drain from the one tenement should run through the other, but admitted of constructing a new drain for the upper tenement, at no disproportionate expense, without interfering with the lower one, although the drain in its present form was a convenient one, and had been in use before the conveyance. The court held that such rights of water-way or drain as would be easements under the ownership of the two estates by different persons, and were necessary to the enjoyment of the thing granted, and had been previously used with the estate, would pass as appurtenant to the same. If, therefore, one owning two tenements have a drain from the one over or through the other, and he sell the first with its *appurtenances*, it would pass the right of drain as being *de facto* annexed as an appurtenance. But if he were to convey the lower tenement, making no mention of the drain in his deed, he would not be considered as reserving a right of drain from his remaining tenement through the one granted. In that case, however, the owners of the several tenements acquired their titles to the same by simultaneous conveyances from the original owner, and it was held that they were to be considered in the light of tenants in common, who had made partition of their estates, when each party takes his estate with the rights, privileges, and incidents in-

herently attached to it, rather than as grantors and grantees. It was held, that, as no mention was made of the drain in the deed, and as it was not *necessary* to the [*56] enjoyment of the upper tenement, the right to use it did not pass by the conveyance.[1]

36. Thus where the owner of a parcel of land made a ditch therein, whereby the upper part of it was drained, and subsequently conveyed this part of it with a part of the ditch, retaining the part with the ditch through which the part so conveyed was drained, it was held that he could not afterwards stop the ditch so as to prevent the water being drained from the vendee's land.[2]

So where one owning two estates near each other, through one of which flowed a stream of water, leased the other parcel, and authorized the tenant to divert the water from the one on to and through the other, and while in that condition sold the latter with all watercourses and appurtenances, it was held that he was not, after such sale, at liberty to stop the water from flowing through the granted premises, and thereby restore the stream to its original state.[3]

It is stated in Jenkins's Centuries : " A way is extinguished by unity of possession, and is revivable afterwards, upon a descent to two daughters, where the land through. which, &c. is allotted to one ; and the other land, to which the way belonged, is allotted to the other sister ; and this allotment, without specialty to have the way anciently used, is sufficient to revive it." [4]

One owning lands upon both sides of a stream raised a dike along one bank to prevent the water from overflowing the land on that side, the effect of which was to throw more water than had before been done upon the opposite bank.

---

[1] Johnson v. Jordan, 2 Metc. 234. See Nichols v. Luce, 24 Pick. 102 ; Goddard v. Dakin, 10 Metc. 94 ; New Ipswich W. L. Factory v. Batchelder, 3 N. H. 190 ; Nicholas v. Chamberlain, Cro. Jac. 121 ; *ante*, p. 66.

[2] Shaw v. Etheridge, 3 Jones, No. C. 300.

[3] Wardle v. Brocklehurst, 1 E. & Ellis, 1058.

[4] Jenk., case 37. See also James v. Plant, 4 Adolph. & E. 749.

'After his death his estate was divided among his heirs, one heir taking the land upon one side, and another that upon the other side of the stream. The latter heir then erected a dike upon his side of the stream, the effect of which was to protect his own land, and throw an increased amount of water upon the opposite bank, which had in the mean time been conveyed by the first heir to a stranger. The court held that the heirs took the estate in the condition in which the same was at the father's death, subject, of course, to the dike which he had constructed, in the same way as if it had

been a natural one, and therefore that the new dike [*57] was a *nuisance to the land upon the opposite side of

the stream. The same would have been the law if the ancestor had conveyed the land with the dike upon it; he would not have had a right to erect one on his own side of the stream.[1]

So where the estate of a deceased was divided between two heirs by metes and bounds. Upon one of the parts was a mill, but the dividing line of the estates cut off a part of the dam, leaving it within the limits of the other part of the estate. It was held that the owner of the mill had a right to keep up and maintain that part of the dam which was cut off by the dividing line, the same being necessary to the enjoyment of the mill which had been set to him.[2]

37. The case of Brakely v. Sharp was one where this doctrine of an easement passing, or otherwise, with part of an estate upon the division of a heritage, was twice considered, and may be regarded as a leading one upon the subject. In that case, the intestate owned two farms at his death, with a house on each, and had constructed an aqueduct from a spring upon one of them to both these houses. Upon his death, the farm upon which was the spring, was set to the

[1] Burwell v. Hobson, 12 Gratt. 322.

[2] Kilgour v. Ashcom, 5 Harr. & J. 62 ; Tyrringham's case, 4 Rep. 36. Seymour v. Lewis, 13 N. J. 439 ; Elliott v Sallee, 14 Ohio St. 10.

widow and one heir, and the other farm to the other heir.
The question arose as to the effect of this partition upon the
right which the owner of the second farm had to share, in
connection with his house, in the benefit of this aqueduct.
The Chancellor held, that if the ancestor, while owning both
farms, had conveyed to a stranger the one which was set to
the widow, he would have lost all benefit of the aqueduct as
an easement, if he had not expressly reserved it in his deed.
It would have been derogating from his own grant to have
claimed it, unless expressly reserved.   In this respect there
was an essential difference between a natural and an artificial watercourse, as the former, when it passes, passes as
a right *ex natura ;* and for this the Chancellor cited
*Hazard v. Robinson. But in the present case the [*58]
widow and heir did not stand in the light of purchasers
from the ancestor.   All the heirs came in with equal rights,
and no preference arose from mere priority of assignment.
It became, therefore, a question, whether this aqueduct was
necessary for the enjoyment of the farm set to the other heir.
If it was, it would pass like a right of way of necessity, and
as it appeared that it was the only way by which the house
was supplied with water, it was held that it passed with the
farm with which it had been enjoyed.[1]

38. Where an easement is secured to a dominant estate,
and is designed to benefit the same in whosoever hands it may
be, it will, as a general proposition, enure to the benefit of
the owner of any part of the same into which it may be
divided, provided the burden upon the servient estate intended to be created is not thereby enhanced.   Thus, where
one sold a parcel of land for building purposes, which
opened upon a vacant area which was to be kept open for
air and prospect, the plaintiff, having become the owner of
a part of this estate, was held entitled to an injunction
against the owner of the open area to prevent his building
thereon, although he held under a grant from the original

---

[1] Brakely *v.* Sharp, 2 Stockt. 206 ; Hazard *v.* Robinson, 5 Mason, 272.

grantor, and the original grantee had consented to his building upon the vacant land.[1]

And it is often stated, that a way appurtenant to a close is appurtenant to every parcel into which this close may be divided. But it should be limited, however, it would seem, so that no additional burden is thereby created upon the servient estate.[2]

[*59]   *Thus, in the case of Underwood v. Carney, a grantor owned a passage-way with an estate upon the east and one upon the west side of it. He sold the estate on the east side with a right of way over this passage-way, reserving a right to erect a fence along the west side of it which should not narrow it more than so many inches. He afterwards divided his estate upon the west side by conveying parts of it to two different individuals, and the question was whether each of these had a right of way over this passage-way. The court held that they had, that the right of way was appurtenant to the whole and to every part of this estate, and that the owner of each part took it with this right of way attached to it, although it was not named in the deed.[3]

So in Watson v. Bioren, where the parcel granted was a lot in a city, ten feet in width, bounded by an alley three feet wide, and the grantee divided this parcel into two, the court held that the right of way belonged to both parcels: "When land is conveyed with a right to the grantee, his heirs and assigns, to pass over other land, this right is appurtenant to all and every part of the land so conveyed, and,

---

[1] Hills v. Miller, 3 Paige, 254, 257 ; 2 Washb. Real Prop. 32 ; 3 Kent, Comm. 420 ; Barrow v. Richard, 8 Paige, 351. See Maxwell v. East River Bank, 3 Bosw. 124. Brouwer v. Jones, 23 Barb. 160 ; Gibert v. Peteler, 38 Barb. 513, 514 ; Easter v. L. M. R. Road, 14 Ohio St. 54 ; post, p. *63.

[2] Whitney v. Lee, 1 Allen, 198 ; Underwood v. Carney, 1 Cush. 285 ; Watson v. Bioren, 1 Serg. & R. 227 ; Staple v. Heydon, 6 Mod. 1 ; Codling v. Johnson, 9 Barnew. & C. 933 ; Hills v. Miller, 3 Paige, 254 ; post, chap. 2, sect. 3, pl. 18.

[3] Underwood v. Carney, 1 Cush. 85.

consequently, every person to whom any part is so conveyed is to enjoy the right of passage." [1]

But this doctrine would seem to be limited to cases where the easement annexed to the land was a general one, intended to accommodate one part of the granted parcel equally with another, and not to be enjoyed with some particular part of it, or for special and limited purposes. Thus, where the owner of a public house near a river had a right of passage by boats, by the river, for himself and his servants to bring corn for the use of the house, and brick, tile, and materials for repairing the same, and to land them upon the frontage of the establishment, it was held that no occupant of this frontage could claim to exercise the *same right unless he was also occupant of the public [*60] house.[2]

39. And the proposition is universally true, that if one acquires a right of way to one lot or parcel of land, he cannot use it to gain access first to that parcel, and thence over his own land to other lands belonging to him. So far as he should use it for access to or accommodation of other parcels than the specific one to which it is appurtenant, he would be a trespasser.[3] So when the owner of a well granted to the owner of an adjacent estate a right to take water from it, and the owner of the latter lot conveyed his estate to the owner of another estate adjacent to his, with appurtenances, &c., it was held that the latter did not thereby acquire any right to take water for the use of the estate which originally belonged to him by virtue of his having purchased the other estate.[4]

---

[1] Watson v. Bioren, 1 Serg. & R. 227.

[2] Bower v. Hill, 2 Bing. N. C. 339. See Allan v. Gomme, 11 Adolph. & E. 759 ; So. Metrop. Cemetery Co. v. Eden, 16 C. B. 42 ; *post*, chap. 2, sect. 3, pl. 18 ; Lewis v. Carstairs, 6 Whart. 193 ; 3 Toullier, Droit Civil Français, 496.

[3] Lawton v. Ward, 1 Ld. Raym. 75 ; Watson v. Bioren, 1 Serg. & R. 227 ; Davenport v. Lamson, 21 Pick. 72 ; Case of Private Road, 1 Ashm. 424 ; Jamison v. M'Credy, 5 Watts & S. 129, 140 ; Viner, Abr. *Chimin Private*, A. 2 ; French v. Marstin, 4 Fost. 440, 451 ; 1 Rolle, Abr. 391 ; Howell v. King, 1 Mod. 190 ; Kirkham v. Sharp, 1 Whart. 323 ; Colchester v. Roberts, 4 Mees. & W. 769.

[4] Evans v. Dana, 7 R. I. 306.

40. The effect to be given to the division of an estate to which an easement has attached, is provided for by the Civil Code of Louisiana. And it was held, in a case where the owner of an estate divided it by a wall which he erected and in which a window was inserted, and he then sold the separate parcels in this condition, that the easement of light attached to the parcels, so that, though the owner of one parcel had boarded up the window upon his side of the wall, and it was in that condition when the defendant bought the other parcel, the latter was justified in removing these boards in order to enjoy the right of the light.[1]

41. But where a way, for instance, is created in favor of an estate for one purpose, or in reference to a particular use to be made of such estate, it ceases to be appurtenant, if the estate is essentially changed in its mode of occupation. Thus, where a way belonged to an open parcel of land for the use of it as an open parcel, and the owner of the [*61] same *erected a cottage thereon, covering the entire space, it was held that by such change in the premises the right of way was extinguished.[2] But a way which has been gained by prescription is not lost by its ceasing to be an important right to the owner.[3]

42. Although it might, perhaps, be difficult to embody the leading doctrines of the foregoing cases into any general proposition, it would seem that, in case of a division of an estate consisting of two or more heritages, whether an ease or convenience which may have been used in favor of one, in or over the other, by the common owner of both, shall become attached to the one or charged upon the other, in the hands of separate owners, by a grant of one or both of those parts, or upon a partition thereof, must depend, where there are no words limiting or defining what is intended to be embraced in such deed or partition, upon whether such

---

[1] La. Civ. Code, Art. 763 – 765 ; Lavillebeuvre v. Cosgrove, 13 La. Ann. 323.
[2] Allan v. Gomme, 11 Adolph. & E. 759.
[3] Crounse v. Wemple, 29 N. Y. 543.

easement is necessary for the reasonable enjoyment of the part of such heritage as claims it as an appurtenance. It must be reasonably necessary to the enjoyment of the part which claims it, and where that is not the case, it requires descriptive words of grant or reservation in the deed, to create an easement in favor of one part of a heritage over another.

In Archer v. Bennett, there was a mill and a kiln designed for the use of the mill, but separate buildings. A grant of the mill with its appurtenances was made, and the question was if the kiln passed. It was held that it did not pass as an appurtenant to the mill, being in itself land. But if it was necessary to the use and enjoyment of the mill, it passed as a part of the mill, " as by grant of a messuage the conduits and water-pipes pass as parcel though they are remote." [1]

43. It has sometimes been attempted to create an easement in favor of a dominant estate over a servient one by estoppel, from the fact of the owner of the latter standing by and witnessing the expenditure of money by the owner * of the former, in reference to an enjoyment [*62] of what would be an important easement to the same, and acquiescing in the same without notice or objection. Questions of this kind have arisen in cases of the erection of costly dwelling-houses whose windows open upon the adjacent unoccupied premises of another, who has suffered the expenses of such structures to be incurred without objection or notice of any intent to exercise a right to disturb the enjoyment of the same. In one case this was done while the servient estate was in the possession of a tenant having a particular estate, the reversioner being cognizant of such expenditure. The court say, " The fullest knowledge with entire, but mere acquiescence, cannot bind a party who has no means of resistance." And the court go further, and seem to cover the whole ground, that no such estoppel can be set up in fa-

[1] Archer v. Bennett, 1 Lev. 131.

vor of the dominant estate. "There may appear to be some hardship in holding that the owner of a close, who has stood by without notice or remonstrance while his neighbor has incurred great expense in building upon his own adjacent land, should be at liberty, by subsequent erections, to darken the windows, and so destroy the comfort of such building. Yet there can be no doubt of his right to do so at any time before the expiration of twenty years from their erection." [1]

But the ordinary doctrine of estoppel by deed applies in case of a grant of an easement, so that if a person without title profess to convey an estate, or to grant an easement, his conveyance operates by way of estoppel, if at a subsequent period he acquires the fee, and the subsequently acquired estate is bound thereby, or, as it is termed, the newly acquired estate feeds the estoppel.[2]

And where the owner of an estate has stood by and [*63] seen *another expend money upon an adjacent estate, relying upon an existing right of easement in the first-mentioned estate, and without which such expenditure would be wholly useless and wasted, and has not interposed to forbid or prevent it, equity has enjoined him from interrupting the enjoyment of such easement. So where he has by parol granted a right to such easement in his land, upon the faith of which the other party has expended moneys which will be lost and valueless if the right to enjoy such easement is revoked, equity has enjoined the owner of the first estate from preventing the use of the easement.[3]

44. This seems a proper place in which to notice a class of easements which may be called equitable because chiefly within the cognizance of courts of equity, to which brief

[1] Blanchard v. Bridges, 4 Adolph. & E. 176; see post, chap. 5, sect 7, pl. 7.

[2] Per Watson, B., Rowbotham v. Wilson, 8 Ellis & B. 145, cites Weale v. Lower, Poll. 54, 68; Rawlyn's case, 4 Rep. 52 a.

[3] Tud. Lead. Cas. 109; Anonymous, 2 Eq. Cas. Abr. 522; Short v. Taylor, Ibid.; 2 Story, Eq. Jurisp. 388; Tarrant v. Terry, 1 Bay, 239; Powell v. Thomas, 6 Hare, 300; Clavering's case, cited in last case, p. 304; Williams v. Jersey, Craig & P. 91; Devonshire v. Eglin, 14 Beav. 530; post, chap. 3, sect. 4, pl. 23.

reference has been made, *ante*, pl. 38.   They are also mentioned in other parts of the work.   But the number and importance of the cases involving such interests which have recently been decided, demand a more direct and connected notice of the present state of the law upon the subject.   The principal cases noticed in the first edition of this work were Barrow *v.* Richards, Hills *v.* Miller, and Whitney *v.* Union R. Co., nor will it be necessary to refer to these again, except in their connection with the cases of a more recent date, which are here collected.

An example of the class of easements here intended may be found in Parker *v.* Nightingale,[1] the facts in which case were briefly these.   The estates in question were situate upon a " court " or " place " in Boston, and consisted of several dwelling-houses erected upon each side of a *cul de sac*, or a street open only at one end.   The land on which these had been erected, originally belonged to several heirs, who agreed between themselves that it should be laid out into a court, to be occupied, exclusively, by dwelling-houses, and that in conveying the lots the grantees should be laid under obligation by way of condition or limitation of the use thereof, " that no other building except one of brick or stone, of not less than three stories in height, and for a dwelling-house only," should be erected by them.   The deeds of the lots were accordingly respectively made upon this condition, and the same was referred to or repeated in the subsequent conveyances.   One of the tenants of one of the houses erected under this arrangement, was about to open a restaurant in the house which he occupied, and the proprietors of the other houses in the court prayed an injunction to restrain him from so doing.

The original grantors had ceased to have any interest in the court, and it will be perceived that whatever there was of covenant or condition in the original deeds, was between the grantors and grantees severally, and not between the

[1] Parker *v.* Nightingale, 6 Allen, 341.

several grantees, and that, consequently, there was an entire
want of privity between them. And the question was if the
several proprietors, holding by independent titles, could enforce against any one of them the negative easement of not
using the premises except as a dwelling-house. The importance of the principle involved in this inquiry can hardly be
overestimated in a country where new villages and streets
are being built up, and it is often desirable to define and
limit the character and condition of the buildings to be
erected or the purposes for which they may be occupied.
Bigelow, C. J., in giving the opinion of the court in this case,
sustaining and enforcing this easement, and enjoining the defendant from using his house as a restaurant, goes fully, and
with great clearness, into a discussion of the grounds upon
which it rests. " A covenant, though in gross at law, may
nevertheless be binding in equity, even to the extent of fastening a servitude or easement on real property, or of secur-
ing to the owner of one parcel of land a privilege, or, as it is
sometimes called, " a right to an amenity " in the use of an
adjoining parcel, by which his own estate may be enhanced
in value or rendered more agreeable as a place of residence."
" So long as he " (the original purchaser) " retains the title
in himself, his covenants and agreements respecting the use
and enjoyment of his estate will be binding on him personally, and can be specifically enforced in equity." " A purchaser
of land, with notice of a right or interest in it existing only
by agreement with his vendor, is bound to do that which his
grantor had agreed to perform, because it would be unconsci-
entious and inequitable for him to violate or disregard the
valid agreements of the vendor in regard to the estate of
which he had notice when he became the purchaser. In
such cases it is true, that the aggrieved party can often have
no remedy at law. There may be neither privity of estate
nor privity of contract between himself and those who attempt to appropriate property in contravention of the use or
mode of enjoyment impressed upon it by the agreement of

their grantor, and with notice of which they took the estate from him." He goes on to show that the purpose of the restriction inserted in the deeds was for the benefit and advantage of other owners of lots situated on the same street or court. " Thus, a right or privilege or amenity in each lot was permanently secured to the owners of all the other lots." Nor would it change the result, though the original owners still retained some of the lots in their own hands. " The effect of such restriction inserted in contemporaneous conveyances of the several parcels, under the circumstances alleged, was to confer on each owner a right or 'interest in the nature of a servitude in all the lots situated on the same street, which were conveyed subject to the restriction." And the bill in behalf of the other proprietors was sustained.

The court had occasion to reaffirm the general doctrine above expressed, in the subsequent case of Hubbell v. Warren,[1] where the defendant conveyed one of several house-lots upon a public square to the plaintiff, and stipulated in the deed that the houses to be erected on these lots should not be set within ten feet of the line of the street ; and it was alleged in the bill which was to restrain the defendant from building within less than twelve feet of the line of the street, that, when plaintiff took his deed, the defendant orally agreed that the houses should not be built within that distance from the street, and that he the plaintiff had erected his house accordingly. The court say : " That an agreement between owners of adjacent parcels of land, restricting the mode of its use and enjoyment, although not entered into in the form of a covenant or condition, or so framed as to be binding upon heirs or assigns by virtue of privity of estate, may nevertheless create a right in the nature of a servitude or easement in the land to which it relates which can be enforced in equity, is now well settled in this Commonwealth. But, to establish such quasi-servitude or easement, it must appear, either by express stipulation or necessary and unavoidable implica-

---

[1] Hubbell v. Warren, 8 Allen, 173.   See Wolfe v. Frost, 4 Sandf. c. 72.

tion, that the parties intended to impose a *permanent* restraint on the use or mode of occupation of their respective estates." This might be done by a condition or reservation incorporated into a grant, or appended to it as a covenant real, or so inserted as to carry notice to all persons that the use of the premises is, to a certain extent, qualified or limited, and the intent to create a servitude or privilege, in its nature perpetual, manifested. But where it rests in parol, or in form of a covenant in gross, or by a separate independent agreement, it must contain a stipulation in express terms that the right or privilege is to be a permanent restriction on the land, or such as leads to the conclusion that that is the intention of the parties. And the case turned upon the nature of the agreement in this respect as to the two feet in question, which in terms related to the first erection of the houses only, and not to subsequent changes.

The above citations serve to show the nature and limitations of easements and servitudes growing out of agreements over which equity exercises cognizance, and it will not be necessary to refer so fully to other cases of a like character in which a similar doctrine has been maintained.

The case of Tallmadge *v.* E. River Bank,[1] was in many respects like that of Hubbell *v.* Warren, except that the parol agreement under which the parties had acted, was made in reference to a permanent arrangement between several estates as to their occupation. These were upon a street in New York, which was originally laid out upon a plan, and a space eight feet in width, on each side of the street and outside of the lines thereof, was platted and laid down upon the plan which the owner of the land declared, to the first purchasers of the lot, was to be kept open in front of the houses to be erected thereon. He built several houses himself in conformity to this line, occupying this strip by doorsteps and enclosed areas, and when he sold them he stated to the purchasers that this space was always to remain so,

[1] Tallmadge *v.* E. River Bank, 26 N. Y. 105.

but he put no restrictions in his deeds, and bounded the lots by the line of the street. One of the purchasers of lots to whom this restriction was stated, built his house accordingly. But a purchaser under him was beginning to build upon this eight feet in front of his house, when the other proprietors in the street sued out a bill to enjoin him. One ground upon which they did it, was that this space had been dedicated to the public as a street. The court held that there had been no such dedication, but that the representations and circumstances under which the sales were made, bound the original vendor in equity to have the terms kept and fulfilled upon which the first purchasers acquired and paid for their estates, and attached to his other lots, and to all who purchased with knowledge. And the injunction was granted.

As an example of the extent to which courts are disposed to carry the doctrine of constructive negative easements, even in favor of third parties, reference is made to the cases of Greene v. Creighton and Gibert v. Peteler. In the first of these, several owners of a lot of land in the city of P, proposing to open a street across it, and to dedicate it to the city, joined in a deed poll to the city of P, of the land of the street for the purposes of a highway, and in it recited that it was " understood, covenanted, and agreed by the grantors for themselves, their heirs and assigns," that no building should be built within so many feet of the line of the street. Although the deed was to the city, the court held that in view of the common benefit for which the deed proposes to impose a restriction upon the heirs and assigns of the covenantors, it was " to be construed as a grant in fee to each of a negative easement in the lands of all, and, as such, capable of being enforced by the appropriate remedies at law and in equity." [1]

In the case of Gibert v. Peteler,[2] one G, who, owning premises, the view from which he wished to be kept open, bought

---

[1] Greene v. Creighton, 7 R. I. 1.

[2] Gibert v. Peteler, 38 Barb. 488, 514 ; Brouwer v. Jones, 23 Barb. 153; Seymour v. M'Donald, 4 Sandf. c. 502; Clash v. Martin, 49 Penn. 289.

an estate, the building upon which would obstruct this view, but had the deed made to a third person without any trust being declared in his favor. At G's request, this latter estate was then sold to F, who covenanted with his grantor, his heirs and assigns, that they should not erect anything upon the premises to obstruct the view from G's house. There were several successive conveyances of this parcel in which the covenant of restriction was noticed, and G made a qualified release to one of the owners of the restriction as to a part of the premises. But several of the later conveyances made no reference to this restriction. The court held that there was a negative easement or servitude upon this estate in favor of G, which could be enforced in equity if not at law. " The action of courts of equity in such cases is not limited by rules of legal liability, and does not depend upon legal privity of estate, or require that the party invoking the aid of the court should come in under and after the covenant. A covenant or agreement, restricting the use of any lands or tenements in favor of or on account of other lands, creates an easement, and makes one tenement, in the language of the civil law, servient, and the other dominant, and this without regard to any privity or connection of title or estate in the two parcels or their owners. All that is necessary is a clear manifestation of the intention of the person who is the source of title to subject one parcel of land to a restriction in its use, for the benefit of another, *whether that other belong at the time to himself or to third persons, and sufficient language to make that restriction perpetual.*"

The case of Badger *v.* Boardman is not in conflict with the above doctrines, because, though there was originally a restriction upon the estate of the defendant, it was not created in favor of that belonging to the plaintiff.[1]

A reference to the cases cited below, will show that the

---

[1] Badger *v.* Boardman, 16 Gray; Parker *v.* Nightingale, 6 Allen, 348. See also Wolfe *v.* Frost, 4 Sandf. c. 72, for the grounds on which an alleged similar parol agreement was not held to create an easement.

English Courts of Chancery hold, substantially, the same
doctrines as those above adopted by the American courts.[1]

Without stopping to notice these cases in detail, it may be
proper to refer to the fact that in Tulk v. Moxhay, the court,
in enforcing the servitude, do not regard the covenant which
originally created it as running with the land ; " that the
question does not depend upon whether the covenant runs
with the land is evident from this, that if there was a mere
agreement and no covenant, this court would enforce it
against a party purchasing with notice of it, for if an equity
is attached to the property by the owner, no one purchasing,
with notice of that equity, can stand in a different situation
from the party from whom he purchased." Another fact
which appeared upon the hearing was, that the character of
the occupants and condition of the tenements for whose
convenience the square in question had been left open by
contract, as well as that of the square itself, had essentially
changed, without affecting the easement in their favor.   And
in the case of Piggott v. Stratton it was held, that after an
easement had once attached in favor of one estate over
another by a covenant made by the original purchaser of the
servient estate with his vendor, it was not competent for the
covenantor to affect this right, while the dominant estate
was in another's hands, by releasing the owner of the servient estate from the obligation of the covenant.

But in order to give to a conveyance the incidents of an
equitable servitude or easement in the parcel granted, there
must be an intention to do this shown on the part of those
who make the conveyance.   Thus, where one conveyed a
parcel of land by metes and bounds, and referred to a plan
as having the lot laid down upon it, it was held not to convey
any rights in other lots on the same plan which did not

[1] Tulk v. Moxhay, 1 H. & Twells, 105 ; s. c., 11 Beavan, 571 ; 2 Phillips, 774 ;
Piggott v. Stratton, 1 De G. F. & Jones, 33 ; Coles v. Sims, 5 De G. M'N. & Gord.
1 ; s. c., 1 Kay, 56 ; Rankin v. Huskisson, 4 Sim. Ch. 13 ; Whitman v. Gibson,
9 Sim. 196 ; Mann v. Stephens, 15 Sim, 377.

adjoin the granted premises, although on the plan these were
called " ornamental grounds " and " play-ground." [1]

SECTION IV.

OF ACQUIRING EASEMENTS BY USER AND PRESCRIPTION.

[1] Light *v.* Goddard, 11 Allen, 5.

1. The doctrine of user and enjoyment as evidence of the grant of an easement, under which a title may be claimed, involves an inquiry into the rules applicable to what the law denominates *Prescription*.

Anciently, as already stated, prescription implied a claim to an incorporeal hereditament arising from the same having been enjoyed for so long a time that there was no existing evidence as to when such user and enjoyment commenced. Its origin must have been, in the quaint language of the law, at a time " whereof the memory of man runneth not to the contrary." At one time this was fixed at the commencement of the reign of Richard I. But it was always sufficient, if no evidence existed of a time at which it had not begun, and subsequent to which it must have had its origin, though it was open to be rebutted by proof that the use did begin within the period of memory.[1]

And *prescription*, when properly used, is still applied to incorporeal hereditaments, and not to lands.[2]

The common law, in this respect, corresponds with the distinction made by the civil law between *Usucapion* and *Prescription;* the former being a mode of acquiring title to a thing itself by the effect given to a long possession or enjoyment of it, the latter being applied to the manner of acquiring or losing the various kinds of right by the effect of the lapse of time. And the reader should bear in mind that it is in this limited sense of the term, that prescription is to be regarded in treating of the present subject.[3]

Under the Roman law, where a *bonâ fide* possessor had acquired a *res mancipi*, something corporeal in its nature, by tradition or any other inappropriate form of transfer, and had possessed the same for two years in the case of immovables, or for one year in the case of movables, what was called *Quiritarian* ownership was the result. The office which *Usucapion* performed for *res mancipi* was, in a measure, performed for *res nec mancipi*, or things incorporeal in their nature, by *prescription*, though the period required was a longer one, and the ownership took the name of *Bonitarian*.[4]

[1] 1 Lomax, Dig. 614, 615 ; Litt., § 170; Co. Litt. 115 *a* ; 2 Tuck. Blackst. 31 ; Mayor of Hull *v.* Homer, Cowp. 109.

[2] Ferris *v.* Brown, 3 Barb. 105 ; Caldwell *v.* Copeland, 37 Penn. 431 ; Ayliff, 326 ; Güter, Bracton, c. 15.

[3] Merlin, Repertoire de Jurisprudence, tit. *Prescription*, sect. 1, § 1 ; D. 8, 1, 14.

[4] 11 Law Mag. & Rev. 109.

*2. To obviate the uncertainty of title arising from [*66]
a user and enjoyment, however long in time, the
courts, in accordance with the idea of quieting titles to lands
after a certain prescribed period of enjoyment, which is regulated by local statutes of limitation interposing a bar to
claims of priority of right after a certain limit of time, adopted the notion of presuming an ancient grant by deed which
had been lost.

The presumption of a grant from long-continued enjoyment arises only where the person, against whom the right is
claimed, might have interrupted or prevented the exercise of
the subject of the supposed grant.[1]

In the words of Mr. Tudor : " Amidst these difficulties, it
became usual, for the purpose of supporting a right which
had been long enjoyed, but which could be shown to have
originated within time of legal memory, or to have at one
time been extinguished by unity of possession, to resort to
the clumsy fiction of a lost grant, which was pleaded to have
been made by some person seized in fee of the servient, to
another seized in fee of the dominant tenement, and, upon
enjoyment being proved for twenty years, the judges held, or
rather directed juries to believe, that a presumption arose
that there had been a grant made of the easement which had
been subsequently lost." [2]

The fiction of presuming a grant from twenty years possession or use, was invented by the English courts in the
eighteenth century, to avoid the absurdities of their rule of
legal memory, and was derived by analogy from the limitation prescribed by the Statute of 21 Jac. 1, c. 21, for actions
of ejectment, not upon a belief that a grant in any particular case has been made, but on general presumptions.[3]

The doctrine was originally adopted for the purpose of
quieting titles, and giving effect to long-continued posses-

[1] Webb v. Bird, 13 C. B. N. Y. 843 ; Chasemore v. Richards, 7 H. L. Cases,
349.

[2] Tud. Lead. Cas., 114.

[3] Edson v. Munsell, 10 Allen, 568.

sions. Until a comparatively recent period, no deed could be pleaded without a profert. But when grants came to be presumed from long-continued possession and enjoyment, it was held that the profert might be dispensed with, on suggestion that the deed was lost by time or accident.[1]

3. This period, unless other provision was made in the local statutes of the State in which the questions have arisen, has been assumed to be the term of twenty years. So that now an enjoyment of an easement for the term of twenty years raises a legal presumption that the right was originally acquired by title. And this, though the jury should not find, as a fact, that any deed had ever been made. And although the user began in fact as an act of trespass.[2]

4. The result has therefore been, that the modern doctrine of prescription requires merely a user and enjoyment of at least twenty years, instead of the former requirement of immemorial enjoyment. But there seems to be one distinction between ancient and modern prescriptions which has not always been regarded by courts or writers, and that is, while under the ancient doctrine of prescription such an enjoyment was regarded as conclusive evidence of title, [*67] *prescription, as used at this day, only raises a legal presumption of such title, which may be rebutted by other evidence.[3]

And speaking of length of enjoyment as the basis of a presumed grant, the court, in Cooper v. Smith, say : " Length of time cannot be said to be an absolute bar like the statute of limitations, but is only a presumptive bar to be left to a jury. This presumption of grant from long usage, is for the

---

[1] Valentine v. Piper, 22 Pick. 93 ; Melvin v. Lock, &c., 17 Pick. 255; Emans v. Turnbull, 2 Johns. 313.

[2] Sibley v. Ellis, 11 Gray, 417.

[3] 1 Report Eng. Comm. 51 ; 1 Greenl. Ev., § 17 ; Sargent v. Ballard, 9 Pick. 251, 255; Campbell v. Wilson, 3 East, 294, overruling in part Holcroft v. Heel, 1 Bos. & P. 400; Livett v. Wilson, 3 Bing. 115; Tyler v. Wilkinson, 4 Mason, 397 – 402, and the comments thereon in Lamb v. Crossland, 4 Rich. 536, 543 ; Best, Presumpt. 103 ; Cooper v. Smith, 9 Serg. & R. 26 ; Corning v. Gould, 16 Wend. 531.

sake of peace and furtherance of justice. It cannot be supposed, where there has been a long exercise and possession
of such right, that any person would suffer his neighbor to
obstruct the light of his windows or render his house uncomfortable, or to use a way for so long a time, with carts or carriages, unless there had been some agreement between the
parties to that effect. But this principle must always be
taken with this qualification, that the possession, from which
a party would presume a grant or easement, must be with
the knowledge of the person seized of the inheritance." [1]

And the language of the court, in Ricard v. Williams, is :
" Presumptions of this nature are adopted from the general
infirmity of human nature, the difficulty of preserving muni-
ments of title, and the public policy of supporting long and
uninterrupted possessions. They are founded upon the consideration, that the facts are such as could not, according to
the ordinary course of human affairs, occur, unless there was
a transmutation of title to, or an admission of, an existing
adverse title in the party in possession."

*5. But, in the language of Lord Mansfield, in [*68]
Mayor of Hull v. Horner: " There is a great difference between length of time which operates as a bar to a
claim, and that which is only used by way of evidence. A
jury is concluded by length of time that operates as a bar.
So in the case of a prescription, if it be time out of mind, a
jury is bound to conclude the right from that prescription, if
there could be a legal commencement of the right. . . . .
But length of time, used merely by way of evidence, may be
left to the consideration of the jury, to be credited or not,
and to draw their inference one way or the other, according
to circumstances." [2] The language of Eyre, C. J., in Hol-

---

[1] Cooper v. Smith, 9 Serg. & R. 26.   See also Yard v. Ford, 2 Wms. Saund.,
5 ed. 175, note; Tinkham v. Arnold, 3 Me. 120; Ricard v. Williams, 7 Wheat.
59, 109; post, pl. 29, 66; Cooper v. Barber, 3 Taunt. 99; Merlin, Repertoire de
Jurisprudence, tit. Prescription, sect. 1, § 1; Valentine v. Piper, 22 Pick. 95; Edson v. Munsell, 10 Allen, 568; Stevens v. Taft, 11 Gray, 33.

[2] Cowp. 108, 109; Parker v. Foote, 19 Wend. 309, 315; Livett v. Wilson, 3
Bing. 115; Darwin v. Upton, 2 Saund. 175 c; Campbell v. Wilson, 3 East, 294.

croft *v.* Heel, as to twenty years being an actual bar, is therefore too strong.[1]

Of the many American cases that might be selected sustaining the above view, that of Wilson *v.* Wilson may be cited, where the court of North Carolina say: "The presumption of a grant arising from the use of an easement for more than twenty years, and acquiescence by the owners of the land, might be repelled by other evidence, and if the presumption was not repelled, they (the jury) ought to find for the defendants," who claimed the easement. And they cite, with approbation, 2 Stark. Ev. 669, upon the same subject.[2]

6. An instance of an adoption in full of the ancient doctrine of prescription in speaking of the modern notion of prescriptive rights, is the language of Duncan, J., in Strickler *v.* Todd: "I begin to think that the country has been long enough settled to allow of the time necessary to prove a prescription. . . . . It is well settled, that if there has [*69] been an *uninterrupted exclusive enjoyment above twenty-one years (the period of limitation in Pennsylvania) of water in any particular way, this affords a *conclusive* prescription of right in the party so enjoying it, and that is equal to a right by prescription."[3] And Parsons, J., in Rust *v.* Low, says: "The country has been settled long enough to allow of the time necessary to prove a prescription."[4]

7. But as to the effect to be given to the use of a way across another's land for twenty years, it was held by the English courts to be the rule, not that a jury *must*, but that they *may* presume a grant, and that they are at liberty to infer a grant and to treat the user as an adverse possession or enjoyment, unless the owner of the servient tenement

---

[1] Holcroft *v.* Heel, 1 Bos. & P. 403. See Pritchard *v.* Atkinson, 4 N. H. 9; *post,* pl. 8.

[2] Wilson *v.* Wilson, 4 Dev. 154. See Ingraham *v.* Hough, 1 Jones, No. C. 39.

[3] Strickler *v.* Todd, 10 Serg. & R. 63, 69.

[4] Rust *v.* Low, 6 Mass. 90.

shows it was done by leave or favor, or otherwise than under a claim or assertion of right.[1]

Thus, though a way or a watercourse may have been enjoyed for the term of twenty years, or more, it may rebut the presumption of any deed or grant thereof to show that such enjoyment began during a long term for years, or during an estate for life, where the owner of the inheritance, being a reversioner or a remainder-man, would not be bound by such enjoyment which he could not have prevented, it being an essential element of an enjoyment which shall operate as a prescription, that it was had with the acquiescence of him who is seized of the inheritance, and not by his express permission.[2]

And the distinction there is between a length of time which operates as a bar to a claim, and that which is only used by way of evidence, consists in the jury, in the one * case, being concluded by the length of time; in the [*70] other, being left to draw their inference one way or the other according to circumstances. And it is said: " So in the case of prescription, if it be time out of mind, a jury is bound to conclude the right from that prescription, if there could be a legal commencement of the right."[3] Statutes of limitation do not extend to incorporeal hereditaments, with few exceptions, but prescription has been made to conform to the statute by analogy. And by statute in Massachusetts, easements cannot be gained by adverse user and enjoyment for a less period than twenty years.[4]

8. Any seeming discrepancy between the ancient doctrine of *prescription* and the modern notion of a *presumed grant*

[1] Campbell *v.* Wilson, 2 East, 294; Livett *v.* Wilson, 2 Bing. 115; Yard *v.* Ford, 2 Wms. Saund. 175 *a.*

[2] Wood *v.* Veal, 5 Barnew. & Ald. 454; Doe *v.* Reed, Ibid. 232; per *Holroyd,* J., Daniel *v.* North, 11 East, 372; Yard *v.* Ford, 2 Wms. Saund. 175 *d,* note; Coalter *v.* Hunter, 4 Rand. 58; Nichols *v.* Aylor, 7 Leigh, 546, 565; Biddle *v.* Ash, 2 Ashm. 211, 221; Smith *v.* Miller, 11 Gray, 148.

[3] Mayor of Hull *v.* Horner, Cowp. 102; Oswald *v.* Legh, 1 T. R. 270.

[4] Tracy *v.* Atherton, 36 Verm. 510, 514; Edson *v.* Munsell, 10 Allen, 566; Gen. Stat. C. 91, § 22.

where the deed has been lost, as to the conclusiveness of the evidence thereby resulting in favor of a title to incorporeal hereditaments, may be reconciled, if we bear in mind that, to constitute such a user or enjoyment as raises such presumption of a grant, requires, in addition to the requisite length of time, that it should have certain qualities and characteristics, such as being adverse, continuous, uninterrupted, and by the acquiescence of the owner of the inheritance out of or over which the easement is claimed. And if we assume that these have been established by sufficient proof, it would, doubtless, in such a case, and after such a user and enjoyment, be held to create as conclusive a presumption in favor of him who makes the claim, as if it had been established by prescription in its ancient sense.

It may, therefore, be stated as a general proposition of law, that if there has been an uninterrupted user and enjoyment of an easement, a stream of water for instance, in a particular way, for more than twenty-one, or twenty, or such other period of years as answers to the local period of limitation, it affords conclusive presumption of right in the party who shall have enjoyed it, provided such use and enjoyment be not by authority of law, or by or under some agreement between the owner of the inheritance and the party who shall have enjoyed it.[1] And this would extend to the case of a dam, one end of which rests upon the land of another, and has been maintained there the requisite period of time, or the inserting and maintaining a flume or bulk-head in another's dam and thereby drawing water from his pond.[2]

[*71]   *" In a plain case, where there is no evidence to repel the presumption arising from twenty years un-

[1] Strickler v. Todd, 10 Serg. & R. 63; Olney v. Fenner, 2 R. I. 211; Pillsbury v. Moore, 44 Me. 154; Belknap v. Trimble, 3 Paige, 577; Townshend v. M'Donald, 2 Kern. 381; Hazard v. Robinson, 3 Mason, 272; Wilson v. Wilson, 4 Dev. 154; Gayetty v. Bethune, 14 Mass. 51, 53; Mayor of Hull v. Horner, Cowp. 102; Parker v. Foote, 19 Wend. 309, 315; Corning v. Gould, 16 Wend. 531; Hall v. M'Leod, 2 Metc. Ky. 98; Wallace v. Fletcher, 10 Fost. 434; Winnipiseogee Co. v. Young, 40 N. H. 420. See Tracy v. Atherton, 36 Verm. 512.
[2] Burnham v. Kempton, 44 N. H. 88.

interrupted adverse user of an incorporeal right, the judge
may very properly instruct the jury that it is their duty to
find in favor of the party who has had the enjoyment. But
still it is a question for the jury." [1]

And this, it is believed, is in accordance with the language
of Wilde, J., in Coolidge v. Learned: " It has long been
settled, that the undisturbed enjoyment of an incorporeal
right affecting the lands of another for twenty years, the possession being adverse and unrebutted, imposes on the jury
the duty to presume a grant, and in all cases juries are so
instructed by the court. Not, however, because either the
court or jury believe the presumed grant to have been actually made, but because public policy and convenience require that long-continued possession should not be disturbed." [2]

So the English judges, in Knight v. Halsey, speak of the
modern theory that the length of enjoyment is to be taken
as evidence of a lost deed of grant of what is thus enjoyed,
and call it " a novel invention of the judges for the furtherance of justice and the sake of peace, where there has been
a long exercise of an adverse right." [3]

The language of the court of New York, when commenting upon rights gained by enjoyment, may probably be taken
as a brief and accurate statement of the law as now understood upon this point. " The modern doctrine of presuming
a right by grant, or otherwise, to easements and incorporeal
hereditaments, after twenty years of uninterrupted adverse enjoyment, exerts a much wider *influence in [*72]
quieting possession than the old doctrine of title by
prescription which depended upon immemorial usage. The
period of twenty years has been adopted by the courts in
analogy to the statute limiting an entry into lands; but as
the statute does not apply to incorporeal rights, the adverse

[1] Parker v. Foote, 19 Wend. 309.
[2] Coolidge v. Learned, 8 Pick. 504.
[3] Knight v. Halsey, 3 Bos. & P. 172, 206; 3 Dane, Abr. 55.

use is not regarded a legal bar, but only a ground for presuming a right by grant or in some other form." [1]

The question in all these cases is, whether the presumption of a right to the enjoyment of the easement is one of law or of fact. Poland, C. J., in Tracy v. Atherton,[2] examines the point with much learning and discrimination. He cites the language of Aldis, J., in Townsend v. Downer,[3] who seems to regard it as depending upon the purposes for which the evidence of long enjoyment is offered. If it is to raise the presumption of a grant, without regard to the fact whether such a grant was really made or not, it may, with the strictest propriety, be said that the law presumes a grant, and it would be the duty of the court to direct a verdict. But where long possession with other circumstances are admitted as *evidence* that a grant was *in fact* made, the law permits the jury to weigh the evidence, and upon such *presumptive* — not positive — proof to find the fact.

" Where the subject-matter," adds Aldis, J., " is not included in the statute, such as easements " . . . . " the possession is not *primâ facie* adverse. In such cases, courts presume grants in analogy to the statute of limitations. Sometimes these presumptions are held to be conclusive, at others, open to be rebutted. The line between conclusive and disputable presumptions is not well defined." The conclusion of Poland, C. J., is, that " rights to easements acquired by long possession ought to stand on the same ground as rights by possession in lands. The real principle underlying the right is the same, precisely, on which the statute of limitations stands." And while any presumption arising from long enjoyment may be rebutted in various ways, he concludes, " that, in substance, the presumption arising from such long-continued possession, unrebutted, is a presumption of law, and that it is conclusive evidence, or sufficient

---

[1] Parker v. Foote, 19 Wend. 309 ; Curtis v. Keesler, 14 Barb. 511. See also Cooper v. Smith, 9 Serg. & R. 26 ; Hall v. M'Leod, 2 Metc. Ky. 98.

[2] Tracy v. Atherton, 36 Verm. 503.

[3] 32 Verm. 183.

evidence to warrant the court in holding that it confers a right on the possessor to the extent of his use." But the question, after all, seems to be one rather of form than substance, and mainly affecting the manner of instructing a jury, upon the trial of an issue depending upon a long enjoyment of the thing claimed as an easement.

And with the limitations and explanations above stated, this rule of law may now be considered as well settled, although Mr. Dane asks: " Whence comes this modern doctrine of presuming? Not from any statutes, nor from the books of the common law," and declares that it " is of modern date." [1] But it must now be considered as established law.

9. It may be further remarked, that, where a way is claimed by prescription, the character and extent of it is fixed and determined by the user under which it is gained. " The extent of a usage of a way is evidence only of a right commensurable with the use." And it was accordingly held, that,.where the proof by usage was of a carriage-way, it did not necessarily establish a right of way for cattle, though it might be competent evidence to go to a jury, in connection with other evidence, in establishing the extent of the right claimed. [2]

Where, therefore, one acquired a right of way, by user, to a wood-lot, to take off the wood, it was held that he could not use it for other purposes after the wood had been taken off. [3]

So, if one acquire a right to corrupt the water of a stream by one use, or to a limited extent, it will not avail him if he corrupts it in a different manner or to a greater extent. [4]

[1] 3 Dane, Abr. 55. It is stated by Bell, J., in Wallace v. Fletcher, 10 Foster, 446, that the Court of Chancery was the first to adopt this doctrine of presuming the existence and loss of a deed in 1707; but that it was not till 1761 that the courts of common law adopted it.

[2] Ballard v. Dyson, 1 Taunt. 279; Allan v. Gomme, 11 Adolph. & E. 759; Güter, Bracton, 99.

[3] Atwater v. Bodfish, 11 Gray, 152.

[4] Holman v. Boiling Spring Co., 1 M'Carter, 346.

Where a water-way had been used to bring goods to a tavern-yard for the use of the tavern, it did not authorize the use of the way for other occupants of the land and other purposes than the occupancy of the tavern.[1]

10. But if a way is created by express grant, user is not evidence to restrict the usual import of the terms [*73] of the *grant. But if the grant is lost, usage alone indicates the extent of the way. All prescriptions are *stricti juris;* a way for carriages includes a horse-way, but not a drift-way for cattle. The use of a way for pigs does not imply a right of way to drive oxen.[2]

And where the way claimed was a *general* right by prescription, it was necessary to show a user of it for all purposes, time out of mind. But if it is shown that the defendant, and those under whom he claims, have used the way whenever they have required it, it is such evidence of a general right to use it for all purposes, that a jury might infer from it such right.[3]

11. If now we consider in what cases prescriptions may be gained, and by what means, it will be found, in the first place, that prescriptions can only be for things which are the subjects of grant. And though sometimes the term is loosely applied to titles to corporeal hereditaments, when used with technical accuracy it is predicated of incorporeal hereditaments alone.[4]

12. To constitute a title, therefore, by prescription, there

[1] Bower v. Hill, 2 Bing. N. C. 339.

[2] Ballard v. Dyson, 1 Taunt. 279, 288. See Co. Entr. 5, 6, for form of pleading a prescriptive right of way.

[3] Cowling v. Higginson, 4 Mees. & W. 245. See Allan v. Gomme, 11 Adolph. & E. 759 ; Dare v. Heathcote, 36 Eng. L. & Eq. 564. Smith v. Miller, 11 Gray, 148.

[4] 1 Lomax, Dig. 614 ; Potter v. North, 1 Ventr. 383, 387 ; Strickler v. Todd, 10 Serg. & R. 69 ; Carlyon v. Lovering, 1 Hurlst. & N. 784 ; Rochdale Canal Co. v. Radcliffe, 18 Q. B. 287, 314 ; Davis v. Brigham, 29 Me. 391 ; Cortelyou v. Van Brundt, 2 Johns. 357 ; Gayetty v. Bethune, 14 Mass. 53 ; Thomas v. Marshfield, 13 Pick. 240 ; M'Cready v. Thomson, Dudley, 131 ; Golding v. Williams, Dudley, 92 ; Pearsall v. Post, 20 Wend. 111, 129 ; Ferris v. Brown, 3 Barb. 105 ; 2 Sharsw. Blackst. 264, note. Hill v. Lord, 48 Maine, 96 ; Luttrel's case, 4 Co. 87.

must be a thing claimed which may be granted, and a person to whom a grant may be made, and who may be a party to such grant. And in this consists one great distinction between a proper *prescription* and a *custom*, the latter being applicable to rights by way of easement which the public or the inhabitants of a particular locality may acquire by *long enjoyment, without having been incorporated [*74] or capable of collectively becoming grantees in any deed of conveyance.[1]

13. Prescriptions and customs both relate to incorporeal hereditaments, and the main difference between them is, that prescriptions are always personal, and belong to some person, using the term in its broad sense as including corporations, while customs are always local, and predicated of something to be enjoyed by individuals living in certain districts. And accordingly it is said: " Another difference was taken and agreed between a prescription, which always is alleged in the person, and a custom, which always ought to be alleged in the land; for every prescription ought to have, by common intendment, a lawful beginning; but otherwise it is of a custom, for that ought to be reasonable, but need not be intended to have a lawful beginning."[2] By this it would seem that " lawful beginning " must imply a beginning by means of an original grant, there being in the case of a prescription some one capable of taking the grant, whereas in case of custom there are no such grantees capable of taking, from the very fact that it belongs to such and to such only as, for the time being, belong to a particular locality, not as successors of persons gone before, but as dwellers there, irrespective of the circumstances under which they became such. Another thing may be repeated for the purpose of explanation. Prescriptions are often more extensive in their operation upon the rights of the owners of estates out of

---

[1] Lockwood *v.* Wood, 6 Q. B. 50, 64 ; Smith *v.* Gatewood, Cro. Jac. 152 ; Grimstead *v.* Marlowe, 4 T. R. 717 ; Curtis *v.* Keesler, 14 Barb. 511 ; Perley *v.* Langley, 7 N. H. 233. See *post*, chap. 3, sect. 10.

[2] Lockwood *v.* Wood, 6 Q. B. 50, 66 ; Litt., § 170 ; Co. Litt. 113 *b*.

which they are enjoyed, than customs, since in the case of prescriptions it is supposed the parties in interest settled the terms and extent of the grant made by the one to the other, whereas in the case of customs no such contract or [*75] agreement could have been *made, and the law supplies the only limit, and requires that it should be reasonable. Thus the difference which has been spoken of between a prescription for a profit, and a claim of *profit à prendre* under a custom. The court hold such a custom unreasonable, for if one of the dwellers in a particular vill or neighborhood may carry off turf, soil, or other parts of the land of another, others may do the same without limit or stint, and the effect may be that it may all be carried away or destroyed.[1]

" That which is a matter of interest, as the taking a profit from the soil, must from its existence have some person in whom it is, and a *flux body*, which has no entirety or permanence, cannot take that interest which, by the supposition, is immemorial and permanent, because, from its nature, it cannot prescribe for anything." [2]

14. And it may be added, though already implied if not expressly stated, that, in order to establish a prescriptive right, it must be claimed under and through some one who had a right to grant or create the easement claimed. Thus, where a company were authorized by act of Parliament to construct and operate a canal for public use, and the defendant erected a steam-engine upon its banks, and drew water therefrom for operating the same, and to an action for doing this he pleaded a prescriptive right, by long enjoyment, the court held that such right could not be main-

---

[1] Jones v Robin, 10 Q B 620, Rogers v. Brenton, Ibid 26, 60 ; Gateward's case, 6 Rep. 59 , Day v. Savadge, Hob. 85 ; Co. Litt. 110, *b*, 113 ; Bell v. Wardell, Willes, 202 ; Cortelyou v Van Brundt, 2 Johns 357 , Donnell v Clark, 19 Me 174, 2 Blackst Comm 263, 264 ; *ante*, sect. 1, pl. 6   Nudd v Hobbs, 17 N H 527.

[2] Rogers v Brenton, 10 Q. B. 26, 60 ; Day v. Savadge, Hob 86 ; Gateward's case, 6 Rep 59.

tained, for it implied an original grant thereof by the company to him, and they had no right to make any such grant, or to use the water for any purpose except for that of a canal.[1]

15. Thus, in the case of Lockwood *v.* Wood, the court *say: "A custom which has existed from time im- [*76] memorial, without interruption, within a certain place, and which is certain and reasonable in itself, obtains the force of a law, and is, in effect, the common law within that place to which it extends, though contrary to the general law of the realm." "A custom that every inhabitant of such a town shall have a way over such land, either to church or market," is said to be good, because "they are an easement, and no profit." And it was held, in the same case, that "the inhabitants of E.," not being incorporated, could not prescribe for an easement *in alieno solo,* nor claim it by a modern grant. The court, by way of illustration, cite the case of a *custom* for all fishermen within a certain precinct to dry their nets upon the land of another, as being a good one, though a *grant* of such an easement to fishermen within the district, *eo nomine,* would be held void.[2]

And, in accordance with the doctrine above stated, the language of the court, in the case last cited, is: "In case of a *custom,* it is unnecessary to look out for its origin. But in case of a prescription, which founds itself upon the presumption of a grant that has been lost by process of time, no prescription can have had a legal origin where no grant could have been made to support it."[3]

As will be seen more fully hereafter, inhabitants of localities like towns when incorporated may prescribe for easements in the same way as individuals. But a few cases are cited below to show the extent to which inhabitants of particular localities may claim easements by custom, though not incorporated.

[1] Rochdale Canal Co. *v.* Radcliffe, 18 Q. B. 287.
[2] Lockwood *v.* Wood, 6 Q. B. 50, 65.   [3] See *post,* chap. 3, sect. 10.

16. The test seems to be the reasonableness or unreasonableness of the claim, having reference to the character and condition of those who are to enjoy the right claimed, and to the fact which forms a leading and discriminating distinction between customs and prescriptions, that while the [*77] latter *may be released or extinguished by the act of those who are entitled to the right, the former cannot be, since the right attaches to whoever, for the time being, happens to live or dwell in a certain locality ; nor can one or more of these bind those who may afterwards take their places, by any act of release which they may see fit to execute.[1]

And in respect to what is reasonable, courts do not extend the rights and privileges which are valid by custom to the public at large, but restrict them to such as live or dwell in particular neighborhoods. Thus, in Fitch v. Rawling, it was held that, though a custom for all the inhabitants of a parish to enter upon a certain close and play at cricket was good, it could not be claimed as a good custom for all the people of England to do this. So it would be bad if the claim was in favor of all persons happening to be in the parish at the time of their engaging in such play.[2]

17. So, though there may be a dedication of many rights which the public may enjoy, a right like that to use a landing-place upon the shore of navigable waters for depositing articles such as wood and the like cannot be claimed *for the public*, nor for all the inhabitants of a state, by prescription or custom. The court, in Pearsall v. Post, say : " If subsequent English cases have allowed customary and prescriptive rights to invade and exclusively enjoy the soil of another, to permanent inhabitants of a certain town, they have never extended, but uniformly denied it to the inhabitants of the kingdom generally. . . . . None of the English cases, that I

---

[1] Grimstead v. Marlowe, 4 T. R. 717; Mellor v. Spateman, 1 Wms. Saund. 341, note 3.

[2] Fitch v Rawling, 2 H. Blackst. 393.

find, have ever allowed a custom permanently to enjoy the soil of another to the inhabitants of the whole nation. On the contrary, they hold that the English law denies such right." [1]   " The law is well settled, that a customary accommodation in the lands of another, to be good, *must be confined to the inhabitants of a local dis- [*78] trict, and cannot be extended to the whole community or people of the state." [2]   It was accordingly held, that the public could not gain a right to deposit manure, wood, and the like, on a public landing-place on the bank of navigable waters; and that no one could claim such a right except in favor of particular farms, so that whoever claims it by long usage must prescribe in a *que estate*.[3]

18. Not only must the custom be reasonable in its subject-matter, but in the mode of its enjoyment, in order to be a lawful one. Thus it was held that a custom would not be sustained by law, for all the inhabitants of a certain town or county to walk or ride over a certain close at such times of year as the owner had corn growing or standing thereon, because it would tend to destroy the profits thereof altogether.[4]

But a custom for all the inhabitants of C, to go upon a certain close for the purpose of horseracing, on a certain day in the year, was held to be a good one.[5]

So a custom for the inhabitants of a place, or the owners of a particular estate, to pass over the soil of another wherever their convenience requires, and where least prejudicial to the owner, would be an unreasonable one, being too indefinite and uncertain.[6]

And where one claimed a right to extend his bay-window beyond the line of his house and over a part of the street by

---

[1] Pearsall *v.* Post, 20 Wend. 111, 128 ; Manning *v.* Wasdale, 5 Adolph. & E. 758.

[2] Post *v.* Pearsall, 22 Wend. 425, 432, per *Walworth*, Ch.

[3] Ibid. 434 ; State *v.* Wilson, 42 Me. 9 ; Gardiner *v.* Tisdale, 2 Wisc. 153.

[4] Bell *v.* Wardwell, Willes, 202.

[5] Mounsey *v.* Ismay, 25 Law Rep. 370.

[6] Jones *v.* Percival, 5 Pick. 485.

the custom of the city in which he lived, the court held that if such householder had no freehold in the soil of the street, the custom was an unreasonable one and not to be sustained.[1]

So a custom, in order to be good, must be in favor of a class of persons who are susceptible of being identified and ascertained; for where a right by custom was claimed in favor of the poor and indigent householders of a certain village to take rotten wood, as well as boughs of trees, in a certain close, it was held to be bad on two grounds; — 1st, because it was wholly undefined who came under such a description, and could avail themselves of it; and, 2d, because it is a claim to take the profits of land, which can only be prescribed for in a *que estate*.[2]

[*79]   Among the instances of customary easements, as *distinguished from those by prescription, which have been recognized as valid, are a right of way to a church,[3] to dance upon a close for recreation,[4] to dry or mend fishermen's nets upon a close,[5] a right of way to a market, and a right to be quit of toll, a right to turn one's plough upon another's land, a right of a gateway or of a watercourse,[6] a right to take water from a spring or well in another's land for culinary and domestic purposes,[7] a right to a public landing-place to land upon and pass over, but not to occupy for storage of articles.[8]

19. Whatever may be claimed by custom may also be

---

[1] Codman v. Evans, 5 Allen, 310.

[2] Selby v. Robinson, 2 T. R. 758.

[3] Smith v. Gatewood, Cro. Jac. 152.

[4] Abbot v. Weekly, 1 Lev. 176; Bland v. Lipscombe, 4 Ellis & B. 714, note; *ante*, sect. 1, pl. 6.

[5] Baker v. Brereman, Cro. Car. 418.

[6] Pain v. Patrick, 3 Mod. 289, 294; Perley v. Langley, 7 N. H. 233; Commonwealth v. Newbury, 2 Pick. 59, per *Putnam*, J.; 17 Viner, Abr. 256, *Prescription*, A, note.

[7] Race v. Ward, 4 Ellis & B. 702. Lord Campbell cites Year B. 15 Edw. IV., fol. 29, pl. 7; Weekly v. Wildman, 1 Ld. Raym. 405; Emans v. Turnbull, 2 Johns. 313.

[8] Coolidge v. Learned, 8 Pick. 511; Pearsall v. Post, 20 Wend. 111, 128.

claimed by prescription.[1]   But the extent of the claim which may be made by the latter is much broader than that by the former, and this is commonly illustrated by the general proposition that the one extends to *profits à prendre*, the other does not.[2]

Among the prescriptions, but similar in many respects to rights by custom coming under the class of *profits à prendre*, are rights in the inhabitants of a town, if incorporated, to take sand or soil, stone, grass, or turves on another's land, such as sand, for instance, that is washed up by the sea ;[3] or to pass over land to angle and fish.[4]   Or to take sea-weed from another's land,[5] or to pile wood or lumber for purposes of sale or shipment.[6]

* But, in the language of Maule, J., " A claim to [*80] enter upon another man's land, and dig a hole there, can hardly be called a *profit à prendre*." [7]

20. In order to claim a right of *profit à prendre*, by the inhabitants of a town, it must be done by them in their corporate capacity, and must be prescribed for in a *que estate*.[8]   But to gain this right requires more than the individual acts of the inhabitants.   It must be done as a corporate act.   It was, accordingly, held that the taking of sea-weed, or landing upon a beach by individual inhabitants of a town, was no evidence of a prescriptive right to do this

[1] Perley *v.* Langley, 7 N. H. 233 ; Cortelyou *v.* Van Brundt, 2 Johns. 357 ; Pearsall *v.* Post, 20 Wend. 111, 129.

[2] Hardy *v.* Hollyday, cited in 4 T. R. 718, 719 ; 1 Wms. Saund. 341, note 3 ; Gateward's case, 6 Rep. 59 ; Waters *v.* Lilley, 4 Pick. 145 ; Post *v.* Pearsall, 22 Wend. 425.

[3] Perley *v.* Langley, 7 N. H. 233 ; Blewett *v.* Tregonning, 3 Adolph. & E. 554.

[4] Waters *v.* Lilley, 4 Pick. 145.

[5] Hill *v.* Lord, 48 Maine, 100 ; Nudd *v.* Hobbs, 17 N. H. 527.

[6] Littlefield *v.* Maxwell, 31 Maine, 134.

[7] Peter *v.* Daniel, 5 C. B. 568.

[8] Grimstead *v.* Marlowe, 4 T. R. 718, per *Kenyon*, C. J. ; Abbot *v.* Weekly, 1 Lev. 176 ; Hardy *v.* Hollyday, cited in 4 T. R. 719 ; Perley *v.* Langley, 7 N. H. 233 ; Hill *v.* Lord, 48 Maine, 98 ; Foxhall *v.* Venables, Cro. Eliz. 180 ; Fowler *v.* Dale, Ib. 362 ; Weekly *v.* Wildman, 1 Ld. Raym. 405 ; Whittier *v.* Stockman, 2 Bulst. 87.

in their corporate capacity.[1] Nor would it be claimed by custom, being a *profit à prendre*.[2]

In respect to the distinction between easements, properly so called, and a *profit à prendre*, when claimed by individuals, it is said by Walworth, Ch., that " such easements are either personal and confined to an individual for life merely, or are claimed in reference to an estate or interest of the claimant in other lands as the dominant tenement ; for a *profit à prendre* in the land of another, when not granted in favor of some dominant tenement, cannot properly be said to be an easement, but an interest or estate in the land itself." [3]

But an easement like that of taking water from a spring or well on another's land is not a *profit à prendre*, though an interest in land and an incorporeal hereditament, and would be the subject of grant or prescription, and might be prescribed for by reason of occupying an ancient messuage, though the prescription must always be laid in him who has the inheritance.[4] But one cannot prescribe [*81] *except in his own person for an easement proper, in gross, since such a right cannot be created by grant so as to be assignable or inheritable.[5]

21. And if one prescribes in a *que estate*, he can claim nothing under his prescription but such things as are incident, appendant, and appurtenant to lands.[6]

---

[1] Sale *v.* Pratt, 19 Pick. 191 ; Green *v.* Chelsea, 24 Pick. 71 ; Nudd *v.* Hobbs, 17 N. H. 524.

[2] Hill *v.* Lord, Sup.

[3] Post *v.* Pearsall, 22 Wend. 425, 432 ; *ante,* sect. 1, pl. 7, 12.   See Ferris *v.* Brown, 3 Barb. 105.

[4] Manning *v.* Wardale, 5 Adolph. & E. 758 ; Tyler *v.* Bennett, Ibid. 377.   See Hill *v.* Lord. Sup. as to taking water being a *profit à prendre.*   Perley *v.* Langley, 7 N. H. 233 ; Co. Litt. 121 *a* ; 2 Sharsw. Blackst. 264, note ; Pain *v.* Patrick, 3 Mod. 289, 294 ; Smith *v.* Kinard, 2 Hill, So. C. 642 ; Baker *v.* Brereman, Cro. Car. 419.

[5] Ackroyd *v.* Smith, 10 C. B. 164, 187.   But see White *v.* Crawford, 10 Mass. 183, as to ways in gross, and *ante,* pp. *8, *10 ; Bailey *v.* Stephens, 12 C. B., N. S., § 110.

[6] Donnell *v.* Clark, 19 Me. 174 ; Ackroyd *v.* Smith, 10 C. B. 164, 188.   Sargent *v.* Gutterson, 13 N. H. 467 ; Muskett *v.* Hill, 5 Bing. N. C. 694.

In Wickham *v.* Hawker, it was held that the liberty of
fowling, hawking, and fishing, where one takes fish to his
own use, are *profits à prendre,* and by a grant to one and
his heirs of either of those rights, it may be exercised by him
or his servants. Whereas, a personal license to hunt and
the like could only be exercised by the party himself to
whom it was given.[1]

22. Whether one can set up a claim to a right in another's land, both by prescription and by custom, or must rely
upon one as being inconsistent with a claim by the other,
was a question which Denman, C. J. declined to answer, in
Blewett *v.* Tregonning.[2]   But in Kent *v.* Waite,[3] the court
use this language : " It has been urged that the evidence
proved a custom, and not a prescriptive right ; but we think
it proved both a prescriptive title in the plaintiff and a right
by custom in others, and their rights are not inconsistent.
Different persons may have a right of way over the same
place by different titles, one by grant, another by prescription, and a third by custom, and each must plead his own
title ; and if he proves it, it is sufficient, although he may
also prove a title in another, provided the titles are distinct
and not inconsistent."

*Bearing in mind that it is now settled beyond a [*82]
doubt that the inhabitants of a town, in their corporate capacity, are capable of taking an easement or other incorporeal hereditament, and that they may become seized of
a right by grant, prescription, or reservation,[4] the following
language of the court, in Perley *v.* Langley,[5] presents, perhaps, as good a summary of the law, as it bears upon the

---

[1] Wickham *v.* Hawker, 7 Mees. & W. 63 ; *ante,* pp. *7, *28. Davies' case, 3
Mad. 246 ; Wolfe *v.* Frost, 4 Sandf. ch. 93.

[2] Blewett *v.* Tregonning, 3 Adolph. & E. 554.

[3] Kent *v.* Waite, 10 Pick. 138.

[4] Commonwealth *v.* Low, 3 Pick. 408 ; Valentine *v.* Barton, 22 Pick. 75 ;
Green *v.* Chelsea, 24 Pick. 71 ; Rose *v.* Bunn, 21 N. Y. 275 ; Smith *v.* Kinard,
2 Hill, So. C. 642 ; Hardy *v.* Hollyday, cited in 4 T. R. 718, 719 ; Avery *v.*
Steward, 1 Cush. 496.

[5] Perley *v.* Langley, 7 N. H. 235.

distinction between public rights claimed by custom and like rights claimed by prescription, and such as are claimed by individuals, as can be readily found. " If these rights are common to any manor, district, hundred, parish, or county, as a local right, they are holden as a *custom*. If the same rights are limited to an individual and his descendants, to a body politic and its successors, or are attached to a particular estate, and are only exercised by those who have the ownership of such estate, they are holden as a *prescription*, which prescription is either personal in its character or is a prescription in a *que estate*."

But individuals cannot gain a prescriptive right of way by passing over an open passage-way across a private estate where the user is not in connection with some estate of their own.[1]

23. Like a custom, a prescription to be good must be a reasonable one. Thus, where one owning a brick-kiln undertook to justify carrying away from another's land a quantity of clay, under a prescriptive right to dig and carry away therefrom clay indefinitely as to quantity, it was held to be bad, as it was virtually prescribing for a right to carry away the entire close.[2] So is a prescription to cut all the wood and timber on a lot of land void, because of its being unreasonable.[3] So where one owning a mine, undertook to claim a prescriptive right to excavate coal, though by so doing he undermined and injured an ancient dwelling-house, it was held that it could not be sustained, because it was not to be presumed, in the absence of positive evidence of a grant, that the tenant of such a house would ever have *come into such an agreement, it being unreasonable [*83] from its being destructive in its effect.[4] So a right

---

[1] Crossman v. Vignaud, 14 Louis, 173; In State v. McDaniel, 8 Jones, L. 284.

[2] Clayton v. Corby, 5 Q. B. 415, 422; Wilson v. Willes, 7 East, 121.

[3] Bailey v. Stephens, 12 C. B., N. S., 108. See Hoskins v. Robins, 2 Wms. Saund. 323.

[4] Hilton v. Granville, 5 Q. B. 701, 730. See Rowbotham v. Wilson, 6 Ellis & B. 593; s. c., 8 H. of L. Cas., 348; Humphries v. Brogden, 12 Q. B. 739. See

cannot be claimed by prescription to pass over another's estate in several different directions, to suit the convenience of him who claims the right of way.[1]

As nothing but incorporeal hereditaments can be claimed by prescription, it was held that a man could not prescribe for a right to erect a building on another man's land for the purpose of fishing in the adjacent waters, nor for a right to use a saw-mill on another's land. Such rights are not the subjects of prescription, in the sense in which the term is properly applied, and an exclusive right to possession of land cannot be established by prescription.[2]

But a right to convey water across the land of another to one's mill is an incorporeal hereditament, for an injury to which trespass *qu. cl.* would not lie.[3]

One might prescribe for the privilege of taking coals for use in another's land, but he could not prescribe for a vein of coal itself lying in another's land.[4]

And it is no answer to a claim of way by prescription, that the claimant has another way to the premises.[5]

It may be remarked, in passing, that, in setting forth a claim of an easement by prescription, the same particularity should be observed as if the person claimed by express grant.[6]

A tenant at will or for years may prescribe for a right *of way, but it must be done in the name of his [*84] landlord, the tenant of the fee.[7]

24. In considering user and enjoyment as evidence of the

also Blackett *v.* Bradley, 1 B. & Smith, 954 ; where it is said that though the reasoning in Hilton *v.* Granville had been impugned, the case itself has not been overruled, and that case itself was also decided upon it as an authority.

[1] Jones *v.* Percival, 5 Pick. 485 ; Brice *v.* Randall, 7 Gill & J. 349 ; Holmes *v.* Seeley, 19 Wend. 507.

[2] Cortelyou *v.* Van Brundt, 2 Johns, 357 ; Ferris *v.* Brown, 3 Barb. 105 ; Donnell *v.* Clark, 19 Me. 174 ; 2 Sharsw. Blackst. 263, 264, note.

[3] Baer *v.* Martin, 8 Blackf. 317.

[4] Wilkinson *v.* Proud, 11 Mees. & W. 33.   Caldwell *v.* Copeland, 37 Penn. 431.

[5] Staple *v.* Heydon, 6 Mod. 1 ; Com. Dig. *Chimin.*

[6] Wright *v.* Rattray, 1 East, 377, per *Dodderidge;* Sloman *v.* West, Palm. 387 ; *post,* chap. 6, sect. 2, pl. 16.

[7] Smith *v.* Kinard, 2 Hill, So. C. 642.

possession of a prescriptive right, it will be proper to inquire what the nature and character of such use must be, in order to constitute such evidence, before attempting to apply the same to the different classes of easements.

In the first place, the possession or enjoyment of what is claimed must be long continued as well as peaceable, — *" longus usus, nec per vim, nec clam, nec precario."* [1]

What shall be taken to be a sufficiently *long period* of use or enjoyment to create a prescription or presumptive grant, in the modern use of the term, is understood to correspond with the local period of limitation for quieting titles to land.[2] In England it is twenty years.[3] So it is in South Carolina,[4] New Jersey,[5] North Carolina,[6] Alabama,[7] Kentucky,[8] Maine,[9] Massachusetts,[10] and New York.[11] In New Hampshire, Rhode Island, Delaware, Virginia, Mississippi, Missouri, Indiana, Illinois, Wisconsin, and Florida the rule would be the same, if, as is doubtless the case, the period of prescription and limitation as to lands is the same.[12]

In Vermont it is fifteen years.[13] So in Connecticut.[14]
[*85]   *In Texas it is two years.[15] So in Louisiana,[16] Arkansas, and Iowa.[17]

[1] Bract, fol. 222 *b* ; Co. Litt. 114 *a* ; Thomas *v.* Marshfield, 13 Pick. 240.
[2] 1 Greenl. Ev., § 17, note ; Sherwood *v.* Burr, 4 Day, 244 ; Polly *v.* McCall, 37 Ala. 29.
[3] Wright *v.* Howard, 1 Sim. & S. 190, 203.
[4] Cuthbert *v.* Lawton, 3 M'Cord, 194.
[5] Campbell *v.* Smith, 3 Halst. 140.
[6] Felton *v.* Simpson, 11 Ired. 84 ; Griffin *v.* Foster, 8 Jones L. 339.
[7] Stein *v.* Burden, 24 Ala. 130. It is now ten years, Wright *v.* Moore, 38 Ala. 596.
[8] Manier *v.* Myers, 4 B. Monr. 514.
[9] Rev. Stat. c. 147, § 14 ; Pierre *v.* Fernald, 26 Me. 436.
[10] Sargent *v.* Ballard, 9 Pick. 251 ; Gen. St. c. 91, § 33.
[11] Parker *v.* Foote, 19 Wend. 309 ; Miller *v.* Garlock, 8 Barb. 153.
[12] Angell, Limit., 4th ed., Appendix of Statutes. Gentleman *v.* Soule, 32 Ill. 278 ; Evans *v.* Dana, 7 R. I. 311.
[13] Rogers *v.* Page, Brayt. 169 ; Tracy *v.* Atherton, 36 Verm. 515.
[14] Sherwood *v.* Burr, 4 Day, 244.
[15] Haas *v.* Choussard, 17 Texas, 588.
[16] Delahoussaye *v.* Judice, 13 La. Ann. 587.
[17] Angell, Limit., 4th ed., Appendix of Statutes.

In Pennsylvania it is twenty-one years.[1] So in Ohio.[2] In Georgia and Tennessee the period is seven years.[3] In Michigan it is twenty-five years,[3] and in California five.[3]

The earliest case in Massachusetts in which the doctrine of twenty years' enjoyment was allowed as evidence of a grant of an easement was Hill v. Crosby.[4]

The doctrine upon the subject maintained by the Supreme Court of the United States is thus stated : " In general, it is the policy of courts of law to limit the presumption of grants to periods analogous to those of limitations, in cases where the statute does not apply." [5]

By the law of France, possession and enjoyment of continuous and apparent easements for the period of thirty years create a prescriptive title to the same.[6]

25. But no time of enjoyment less than the term of prescription can give one a right of easement in the land of another, or raise any presumption in favor of such a right. In one case, cited below, the enjoyment and acquiescence had been for nineteen years ; in another, between fifteen and twenty years.[7]

There must, moreover, be what answers in law to an *actual enjoyment, in order to create a prescrip-   [*86] tion. It is laid down as an invariable maxim by writers upon the civil law, *Tantum præscriptum, quantum possessum.* Prescription acquires for the possessor precisely what he has possessed, but nothing beyond that. *Prescriptiones tantum habent de potentia quantum habent de actu.*

---

[1] Okeson v. Patterson, 29 Penn. St. 22.

[2] Angell, Limit., 4th ed., Appendix of Statutes.

[3] Ibid.

[4] Hill v. Crosby, 2 Pick. 467.

[5] Ricard v. Williams, 7 Wheat. 110.

[6] 2 Fournel, Traité des Servitudes, 338, § 221 ; Code Nap., Art. 690.

[7] Gayetty v. Bethune, 14 Mass. 49, 55 ; Campbell v. Smith, 3 Halst. 140 ; Prescott v. Phillips, cited 6 East, 213 ; King v. Tiffany, 9 Conn. 162 ; Gilman v. Tilton, 5 N. H. 231 ; Dyer v. Depui, 5 Whart. 586 ; Haight v. Price, 21 N. Y. 241 ; Thurston v. Hancock, 12 Mass. 220 ; Green v. Chelsea, 24 Pick. 71 ; Lawton v. Rivers, 2 M'Cord, 445 ; Jeter v. Mann, 2 Hill, So. C. 641 ; Stuyvesant v. Woodruff, 1 N. J. 133 ; Griffin v. Foster, 8 Jones, L. 339.

The possession, therefore, of a part only of a divisible thing is not the possession of the whole.[1]

26. In the next place, the use and enjoyment of what is claimed must have been *adverse, under a claim of right, exclusive, continuous, uninterrupted*, and with the knowledge and acquiescence of the owner of the estate in, over, or out of which the easement prescribed for is claimed, and while such owner was able, in law, to assert and enforce his rights, and to resist such adverse claim, if not well founded. And it must, moreover, be of something which one party could have granted to the other. Out of the numerous cases that might be cited to sustain the above proposition, in part or as a whole, a few have been selected as a matter of convenient reference.[2]

27. In analyzing the essential requisites to the gaining of a right by prescription, by *adverse* is meant that it was not a matter of permission asked by the one party and granted by the other, for an adverse right of easement cannot grow out of a mere permissive enjoyment.[3] The real point of distinction is between a tolerated or permissive user, and one which is adverse or as of right. The former will not mature into a title by prescription.[4] Thus a tenant cannot prescribe for

[1] 3 Toullier, Droit Civil Français, 485 ; *post*, sect. 39.

[2] Colvin v. Burnet, 17 Wend. 564; Luce v. Carley, 24 Wend. 451; Sargent v. Ballard, 9 Pick. 251, 255; Gayetty v. Bethune, 14 Mass. 49, 55; Parker v. Foote, 19 Wend. 309, 313; Hart v. Vose, Ibid. 365; Stokes v. Appomatox Co., 3 Leigh, 318; Golding v. Williams, Dudley, 92; Arnold v. Stevens, 24 Pick. 106; Yard v. Ford, 2 Wms. Saund. 175 *d*, note; 3 Dane, Abr. 251, 252; Watkins v. Peck, 13 N. H. 360; Thomas v. Marshfield, 13 Pick. 240; Tickle v. Brown, 4 Adolph. & E. 369 ; Bradbury v. Grinsell, cited 2 Wms. Saund. 175 *d*; Olney v. Gardner, 4 Mees. & W. 496; Miller v. Garlock, 8 Barb. 153; Mebane v. Patrick, 1 Jones, No. C. 23; Ingraham v. Hough, Ibid. 39; Esling v. Williams, 10 Penn. St. 126; Gentleman v. Soule, 32 Ill. 279; Tracy v. Atherton, 36 Verm. 514; Harper v. Parish, &c., 7 Allen, 478; Edson v. Munsell, 10 Allen, 560, 568; Evans v. Dana, 7 R. I. 311.

[3] Bachelder v. Wakefield, 8 Cush. 243; Howard v. O'Neill, 2 Allen, 210; Medford v. Pratt, 4 Pick. 222; Kilburn v. Adams, 7 Metc. 33; Gayetty v. Bethune, 14 Mass. 50; Tickle v. Brown, 4 Adolph. & E. 369; Hall v. M'Leod, 2 Metc. Ky. 98; Ingraham v. Hough, 1 Jones, No. C. 39.

[4] Polly v. M'Call, 37 Ala. 20; s. c., Select Cases, Ala. 255; Pierce v. Cloud, 42 Penn. 113.

an easement against his landlord,[1] and so long as a way is used under a license, it cannot be claimed by prescription.[2] Where A, by permission of B, dug a drain from B's land through A's to draw off water standing on B's land, and this was used for more than twenty years in that state, and a third party purchased B's land while the drain was in existence, it was held that the owner of B's land gained no right of easement to have the same drained thereby, by means of such use.[3]

*It is an important circumstance, in determining [*87] whether the user of the right claimed is adverse or not, that it is contrary to the interest of the owner of the land.[4]

If, therefore, it appears that the enjoyment has been by permission asked, or for a rent paid, or other equivalent acts done by the one exercising the privilege, showing that it was not done adversely or under a claim of right, it effectually rebuts the presumption of a grant. Thus an offer, within the twenty years, by the claimant of the easement, to purchase the right of the owner of the land, was held to be an act of this character.[5] And the language of the court of New York upon the point is very significant and strong: "It is well known that a single lisp of acknowledgment by a defendant that he claims no title, fastens a character upon his possession which makes it unavailable for ages." [6]

But asking permission to use an easement once actually acquired, does not affect the right. It would only bear upon the question whether the prior use had been adverse or permissive in a trial of that issue.[7]

"There must be an adverse possession or assertion of

1 Phillips *v.* Phillips, 48 Penn. 184.
2 Crounse *v.* Wemple, 29 N. Y. 542.
3 Smith *v.* Miller, 11 Gray, 145.
4 Arnold *v.* Stevens, 24 Pick. 106.
5 Watkins *v.* Peck, 13 N. H. 360.
6 Colvin *v.* Burnet, 17 Wend. 564.   See Betts *v.* Davenport, 13 Conn. 286.
7 Perrin *v.* Garfield, 37 Verm. 310.

right, so as to expose the party to an action, unless he had a
grant ; for it is the fact of his being thus exposed to an action,
and the neglect of the opposite party to bring suit, that is
seized upon as the ground for presuming a grant in favor of
long possession and enjoyment, upon the idea that this adverse state of things would not have been submitted to if
there had not been a grant." [1]

Thus in Doe v. Wilkinson, which, though not a case of
easement, illustrates the principle above stated, the defendant had been in possession of a parcel of land which he enclosed over thirty years previous to 1822. In 1808 the plaintiff purchased it of the true owner, and in 1816 called on
the defendant to pay him sixpence as rent, and the
[*88] *defendant paid it three times. In an action to recover the land in 1822, the court held this payment
of rent conclusive evidence that the occupation by the tenant
was a permissive one, and that he was the plaintiff's tenant.[2]

So the yielding by the owner of the dominant estate to
the demand of the owner of the servient one, that he
should forbear to exercise the right claimed during the period of alleged enjoyment under which the claim is made,
would rebut the idea that such enjoyment was adverse under
a claim of right. Thus where the owner of a lower mill had
been accustomed, during a state of low water, to place flash-
boards upon his dam, and continued this usage for more than
twenty years, but during these years had complied with the
requirements of the owner of an upper mill to remove them,
at times, and did not claim a right to maintain them to the
injury of the upper mill, it negatived the claim of a prescriptive right to enjoy the use of such flash-boards.[3]

28. But though a right of way cannot be gained by the
parol agreement of him who creates it, yet where, under

[1] Felton v. Simpson, 11 Ired. 84; Mebane v. Patrick, 1 Jones, No. C. 23.

[2] Doe v. Wilkinson, 3 Barnew. & C. 413; Lisle's Lessee v. Harding, cited in
Buller, N. P. 104. See also Church v. Burghardt, 8 Pick. 327.

[3] Sumner v. Tileston, 7 Pick. 198.

such agreement, the owner of the dominant estate used
the way thus created for twenty years, and the same was
acquiesced in by the owner of the servient estate, it was
held to be such an exercise of the way, under a claim
of right, as to gain thereby a prescriptive right to the
same.[1]

And it is no objection to gaining an easement by prescription, that the same was originally granted or bargained for
by parol. That the use began by permission does not affect
the prescriptive right, if it has been used and exercised for
the requisite period, under a claim of right on the part
of the owner of the dominant tenement. Land *itself [*89]
may be gained in that way, as well as an easement in
it.[2]

In Monmouth Canal Co. v. Harford, Lord Lyndhurst says :
" The simple issue is, whether there has been a continued
enjoyment of the way for twenty years, and any evidence
negativing this is admissible. Every time that the occupiers
asked for leave, they admitted that the former license had
expired, and that the continuance of the enjoyment was
broken." [3]

And in Golding v. Williams the language of the court is :
" The use must be adverse, and such as would show that no
one could dispute the exercise of it." [4]

29. An enjoyment of a thing may be continued long
enough in respect to time, and yet under such circumstances as to rebut the idea of its being an adverse, though
not permissive, user. Thus, where a party owned land adjoining a beach which he depastured, but, there being no
fence between his land and the beach, his cattle were accustomed to pass on to the beach, and thence over the adjoining beaches, which were unfenced, it was held not to be such

---

[1] Ashley v. Ashley, 4 Gray, 197.

[2] Arbuckle v. Ward, 29 Vt. 43, 52. See Sumner v. Stevens, 6 Metc. 337.

[3] Monmouth Canal Co. v. Harford, 1 Crompt. M. & R. 631. See Church v.
Burghardt, 8 Pick. 327.

[4] Golding v. Williams, Dudley, 92.

an adverse enjoyment of a right to run upon these beaches
as to gain a prescriptive right thereby, since it was in no
way injurious to the rights of the owners of the beaches, nor
likely to produce resistance or opposition.[1]

So no one will acquire a title by prescription, by pasturing
his cattle on an open common, training-field, or highway ;
for, these being kept open for public use, no one by using
them can raise any presumption of a particular grant in his
favor.[2]

In accordance with this idea, that the enjoyment of
[*90] a *thing by one cannot be held to be adverse to another who is in no way injured thereby, especially if
he is not cognizant of such enjoyment; where one raised
water upon his land which percolated into the land of an
adjoining proprietor, but did no harm to the same, nor was
the fact known to the land-owner until he had occasion to
build upon it, when, upon beginning to excavate the same,
he found that the water beneath the surface interfered with
his occupying his land, it was held that, though this raising
of the water had been long continued, no prescriptive right
to continue it had thereby been acquired, since prescription
does not begin till the act by which it is claimed has begun
to work some injury to the right of the other party, of which
he might be cognizant.[3]

So where one, having diverted the waters of a stream by a
ditch dug within his own land, but occasioned no damage
thereby to his neighbor's land, so long as he kept the ditch
clear, afterwards suffered it to become filled up and clogged, whereby the lands of his neighbor were damaged, it
was held that the prescription to maintain such diversion
must date from the time it began to cause injury, and not
from the time of digging the ditch.[4] And where one under-

[1] Donnell v. Clark, 19 Me. 174, 183 ; Thomas v. Marshfield, 13 Pick. 240.

[2] Thomas v. Marshfield, 13 Pick. 240; First Parish in Gloucester v. Beach,
2 Pick. 60, note.

[3] Cooper v. Barber, 3 Taunt. 99 ; ante, pl. 4. See also Cooper v. Smith, 9
Serg. & R. 33.

[4] Polly v. M'Call, 37 Ala. 30.

took to prescribe for the right to throw cinders, &c., into a stream, which injured a mill below, it was held that it must date from the time that such injury began.[1]

And the cases last cited are so nearly identical in principle with the two cited below,[2] that it is unnecessary to repeat the facts at length.

30. It is not, however, necessary to show that the act which forms the basis of the prescription did any actual damage to the party against whom it is claimed, provided it was an invasion of his right.[3]

31. And if there has been the use of an easement for twenty years unexplained, it will be presumed to be under a claim of right, and adverse, and be sufficient to establish a title by prescription, and to authorize the presumption of a grant, unless contradicted or explained.[4]

An instance of the application of this doctrine was that of White v. Chapin, very recently decided, wherein Foster, J. gave an elaborate opinion. One ancient ditch connected with another still more ancient, by which the water accumulating upon a considerable tract of land flowed from the first into the second ditch, and thence into a natural stream. The two estates through which these ditches ran, came into the same owner's possession. After a while he sold the lower

---

[1] Murgatroyd v Robinson, 7 Ellis & B 391

[2] Roundtree v Brantley, 34 Ala. 544, Crosby v Bessey, 49 Me. 539. See also Flight v Thomas, 10 Ad & El. 590, *post.* p. *100, 10 Law M. & R 182.

[3] Bolivar Mg Co. v. Neponset Mg. Co, 16 Pick 241, 247; Bliss v Rice, 17 Pick. 23, Hobson v Todd, 4 T R 71, Atkins v Bordman, 2 Metc. 457, Parker v. Foote, 19 Wend. 309, 314, Hastings v Livermore, 7 Gray, 194; *post*, chap 6, sect. 2, pl. 1.

[4] Miller v Garlock, 8 Barb 153; Chalk v M'Ahly, 11 Rich 153, Williams v Nelson, 23 Pick 141, 147, Yard v. Ford, 2 Wms. Saund 172; Blake v Everett, 1 Allen, 248; Ricard v. Williams, 7 Wheat. 59, 109, Hammond v. Zehner, 21 N. Y 118, Bolivar Mg Co. v. Neponset Mg. Co, 16 Pick 241; Colvin v. Burnet, 17 Wend. 564, Olney v Fennet, 2 R I 211, Pue v. Pue, 4 Md Ch. Dec. 386, Esling v Williams, 10 Penn St 126, Steffy v. Carpenter, 37 Penn. St 41, Worrall v Rhoades, 2 Whart 427, Garrett v Jackson, 20 Penn. St 331, Ingraham v. Hough, 1 Jones, No. C. 39; Polly v M'Call, 37 Ala. 30; Perrin v. Garfield, 37 Verm 310, Hammond v. Zehner, 23 Barb. 473.

parcel to the defendant's grantor; and then sold the upper
to the plaintiff's grantor.   The estates thus remained for
more than twenty years, when the owner of the lower parcel
stopped the ditch.   The upper owner claimed a prescriptive
right to maintain the same, and this right was sustained by
the court.[1]

It may, however, be remarked, in passing, that the plaintiff, it would seem, might have asserted the same right under
an implied grant, when his grantor severed the two heritages
through which these drains had been constructed, and were
openly in use when he conveyed them to separate and distinct owners, agreeably to the doctrine of Pyer v. Carter,
hereinbefore commented on at length.[2]

Accordingly the court, in Garrett v. Jackson, say:
[*91]   " Where *one uses an easement whenever he sees fit,
without asking leave, and without objection, it is adverse, and an uninterrupted adverse enjoyment for twenty-
one years is a title which cannot be afterwards disputed.
. . . . The owner of the land has the burden of proving
that the use of the easement was under some license, indulgence, or special contract inconsistent with a claim of right
by the other party.[3]

But to bring a case within the principle above stated, it is
apprehended that it must clearly be such a use as would be
the invasion of another's property in a manner indicating a
claim of right on the part of one party, and a yielding to
such right by the other.   Thus, in Miller v. Garlock, the
right used was that of a private way, and in Chalk v. M'Alily,
it was that of setting back water upon another's land by a
permanent dam.   But where one had exercised the right to
pass over an open piece of ground around a public academy,
to his own house, whenever he pleased, and this was done by

---

[1] White v. Chapin.   Allen not yet reported.

[2] 1 H. & Norm. 916 ; ante, *44 ; Copie's case, ante, p. *49 ; Dunklee v. Wilton
R. R., 4 Foster, 489 ; post, p. *530 ; Dodd v. Burchell, 1 H. & Colt. 121 ; Elliot v.
Rhett, 5 Rich. 405.

[3] Garrett v. Jackson, 20 Penn. St. 331 ; Pierce v. Cloud, 42 Penn. 102, 113, 114.

the proprietors of the academy and other people generally, whenever they had occasion, it was held to be a permissive and not an adverse use as to the owners of the land. Nor did it make any difference, that the owner of the house crossed the land in one uniform track, provided the same be not wrought by him into a way for his distinct and separate use.[1]

And it has accordingly been held, that, under the statute of 2 & 3 William IV. c. 71, § 5, it would be no allegation of a prescriptive right of way, to aver in a plea, simply, that the same had been enjoyed for twenty years. In order to avail as such, it must be alleged to have been done " as of right." [2]

And the mere enjoyment of what is in the nature of an easement in favor of one parcel in or over another parcel of *land, for the requisite period of time, will [*92] not, under the statute of 2 & 3 William IV., gain a prescriptive right, if, during any portion of that time, both tenements have been in the occupation of the same person.[3]

Upon the same principle, where one owns land adjoining a highway, the soil of which belongs to another, and occupies it by laying wood, logs, or other materials upon it, in front of his land, he would not, by such use, acquire an easement against the owner of the soil of the highway. It would be considered permissive on the part of the public, and not adverse to the owner of the soil, and one reason would be, that he had not the right of possession during the time.[4]

32. It is upon the ground above stated, that the use is neither an injury to the owner of the land, nor evidence of any assertion of a right adverse to him, that the courts of South Carolina have repeatedly held that no one gains an easement of way or of hunting on another's land, which is wild and unenclosed, by travelling across or hunting over it,

[1] Kilburn v. Adams, 7 Metc. 33 ; see ante, pl. 31, note.
[2] Holford v. Hankinson, 5 Q. B. 584; Olney v. Gardiner, 4 Mees. & W. 496. See Mebane v. Patrick, 1 Jones, No. C. 23.
[3] Harbridge v. Warwick, 3 Exch. 552.
[4] Parker v. Framingham, 8 Metc. 260.

such use by the public being regarded as a permissive one, from the condition of the country, and the general understanding of the people who enjoy it, unless evidence is offered to give a different character to such use.[1]

It does not depend upon the land being unenclosed, but upon the intention with which the act of passing over it is done, as indicated by the nature of the use. If one were notoriously to use a way across the unenclosed or forest land of another from a highway to his own premises, not casually, as in hunting or simply travelling across it, but for [*93] purposes *of occupying or cultivating his own land, under some notorious assertion of right, he may thereby acquire an easement of way over such unenclosed or forest land.[2]

The rule, as stated in one case, is, that the way, in order to be gained by such use, must be a definite one, " with an *a quo* and an *ad quem*." [3]

33. And in Maine, the courts, in applying the doctrine of adverse use to cases where mill-owners have exercised the statute right to flow the lands of others, have held that, inasmuch as no claim of damages can be prosecuted until some injury has been sustained by the land-owner, no easement of right to flow can be acquired by the mill-owner in such cases by merely continuing the act of flowing for twenty years. It must be such as to cause damage to the land-owner, in order to raise a presumption of grant from twenty years' enjoyment; otherwise the law will presume it to have

[1] Rowland v. Wolfe, 1 Bailey, 56; Lawton v. Rivers, 2 M'Cord, 445; Turnbull v. Rivers, 3 M'Cord, 131; M'Kee v. Garrett, 1 Bailey, 341; Nash v. Peden, 1 Speers, 17; Sims v. Davis, Cheves, 1; Hogg v. Gill, 1 M'Mull, 329; Golding v. Williams, Dudley, 92; Prince v. Wilbourn, 1 Rich. 58; Watt v. Trapp, 2 Rich. 136; Gibson v. Durham, 3 Rich. 85; Hale v. M'Leod, 2 Metc. Ky. 98. See also Mebane v. Patrick, 1 Jones, No. C. 23.

[2] Worrall v. Rhoades, 2 Whart. 427; Smith v. Kinard, 2 Hill, So. C. 642; Jeter v. Mann, Ibid. 641; Reimer v. Stuber, 20 Penn. St. 458; Watt v. Trapp, 2 Rich. 136; Nash v. Peden, 1 Speers, 17; Gibson v. Durham, 3 Rich, 85; Hall v. M'Leod, 2 Metc. Ky. 98.

[3] Golding v. Williams, Dudley, 92.

been done by authority of the statute, and subject to the payment of damages in the mode prescribed by statute.[1]

34. But such is not held to be the law in Massachusetts. The enjoyment of the right to flow another's land for twenty years, if unexplained, will raise a presumption of grant, although no actual damage could be shown to be occasioned thereby. " It may be deemed adverse, if in any degree it tend to impose any servitude or burden on the estate of another." [2]

35. And in New York it was held, that a continued user of a right upon another's land, injuriously affecting the same, for twenty years, such as flowing it, creates a *presumption of a grant, and if the owner of the land [*94] would rebut it, he must show it to have been done by license or permission.[3]

So where one abutted his mill-dam upon another's land, without claiming any right to the soil, and continued to use and enjoy the same for twenty years, it was held that he thereby had acquired an easement to maintain his dam and flowing.[4] And where a mill-owner used and maintained a dam and pond of water to supply his mill, situate about a mile below this dam, and continued so to use it the requisite length of time to gain a prescription, it was held that he thereby acquired a right to the use of such dam and pond of water for his mill, and that this passed as appurtenant to the mill upon a sale thereof, although the dam and pond were upon another person's land.[5]

36. One may acquire a negative easement in another's land by adverse judgment for the term of twenty years, as

---

[1] Tinkham v. Arnold, 3 Me. 120 ; Nelson v. Butterfield, 21 Me. 220 ; Underwood, v. No. Wayne Scythe Co., 41 Me. 291 ; Gleason v. Tuttle, 46 Me. 288 ; Seidensparger v. Spear, 17 Me. 123 ; post, chap. 3, sect. 5, pl. 9.

[2] Williams v. Nelson, 23 Pick. 141.

[3] Hammond v. Zehner, 21 N. Y. 118.

[4] Trask v. Ford, 39 Me. 437.

[5] Perrin v. Garfield, 37 Verm. 304. See Brace v. Yale, 10 Allen, 441 ; post, p. *272.

well as an affirmative one. Thus in case of a mill upon a
stream, from which an ancient ditch had formerly caused the
waters of such stream to flow in a direction so as not to
reach the mill, the owner stopped the ditch, and thereby
the water of the stream flowed uninterruptedly to his mill.
This he enjoyed for twenty years, when, the owner of the
ditch having attempted to open it, it was held that the mill-
owner had thereby acquired the right to have the same kept
closed.[1]

37. It is no objection to the acquiring of an easement by
adverse enjoyment, that, to a certain and defined extent, it
is an excess of user beyond what has been granted by deed.
Thus, where one to whom a foot-way had been granted used
it as a carriage-way also for the space of twenty years, it was
held that he had gained a carriage-way by prescription.

But where an easement has been created by grant or
reservation, no use of it will be held to be adverse which can
be construed to be consistent with the terms of the grant or
reservation, and, consequently, the extent of the easement will
be limited by the terms of such grant or reservation.[2]
[*95]   *38. In other words, the law never presumes a
grant nor raises a prescription from a use, where
there has been an express grant to which the use substantially conforms.[3]

39. An easement, moreover, cannot be prescribed for,
unless the party claiming it has actually used and enjoyed
it, as well as claimed it as of right. The prescription grows
out of the user and intent, and not the claim or intent without the user, however strongly expressed. Thus it was held
not to be competent for one to establish a right of way over
another's land, by showing that, while standing on his own
land, he declared to a third person that he had a right of

[1] Drewett v. Sheard, 7 Carr. & P. 465.
[2] Atkins v. Bordman, 20 Pick. 291 ; s. c., 2 Metc. 457 ; Gayetty v. Bethune,
14 Mass. 49 ; Wheatley v. Chrisman, 24 Penn. St. 298.
[3] Atkins v. Bordman, 2 Metc. 457, 465.

way over the land in question, but did not point it out or do anything upon the last-mentioned close.[1]

40. As an instance of what enjoyment would be held to be adverse, and under a claim of right, although partaking somewhat of the character of permissive use, B. and H. owned adjacent lots running back from the street, on which they occupied houses which were separated by an open passage-way, along and near the middle of which the dividing line of their land ran. This passage-way they both had made use of for over twenty years, and at one time there was a gate at the street which opened into the same. A street having been opened from the first-mentioned street along the other side of H.'s house, whereby he could reach his back land, and having no occasion to use this passage-way any longer, he built upon it, and insisted that B. had no other right to use it than by way of indulgence and permission. But the court held that, so far as either had used the other's land for a way, it was to be presumed to be adverse, and, having been continued more than twenty years, an easement was thereby gained. The court refer to the circumstances and situation of the premises in respect to the way, as tending to confirm this view; and held that, *after [*96] such use, the burden of proof would be upon the party resisting the claim, to show that the use had been permissive.[2]

41. But it is otherwise where the subject-matter of enjoyment is owned in common, and is in its nature indivisible, like a water-power, though its parts are divided by the line of ownership of the land. Thus, where the owners of land upon the opposite sides of a stream have a water-power between them, through which the dividing line of their lands runs, and one of them occupies the whole power, he does not thereby gain any prescriptive right to such exclusive use, so long as the opposite proprietor neither uses nor seeks to

1 Ware v. Brookhouse, 7 Gray, 454; ante, sect. 25.
2 Barnes v. Haynes, 13 Gray, 188.

use, nor makes any provision nor has any occasion for the use of any part of the stream to which he is entitled. Such use by the one owner is not deemed to be adverse to the right of the other owner, for in using his own part of the privilege he is obliged to use the whole as one entire thing.[1]

42. The case of Wheatley v. Chrisman presents an instance where a right was gained by a constructive adverse enjoyment of what had been granted to one by the party against whom he claimed it. The defendant had granted to the plaintiff a right to carry water across the defendant's land for the purpose of irrigating the land of the plaintiff. This he had enjoyed for more than twenty years, and during that time he had enjoyed the privilege of watering his cattle at the ditch within his own land. The defendant, after this, having fouled the water, it was held that the plaintiff might have an action for the injury thus done to him by depriving him of the benefit of the water in a state suitable for his cattle to drink, although the watering of them upon his own land had not been done adversely to the defendant.[2] Another case of constructive, adverse possession arose out of the situation of a party-wall standing upon an arch, one leg of which rested on A.'s and the other on B.'s land, and it was held, after twenty years, that A. had a right to have the wall thus supported on B.'s land.[3]

43. Another requisite of a prescription is, that the enjoyment of the right claimed thereby should be *ex-*
[*97] *clusive,* *which the court, in Davis v. Brigham, say must mean, " that the enjoyment of the easement, as claimed, whether it be a limited or more general enjoyment, should exclude others from a participation of it." [4]

So it said that the use of a way, if continued uninterruptedly, under a claim of right, and exercised in favor of a

[1] Pratt v. Lamson, 2 Allen, 275; Stillman v. White Rock Co., 3 W. & Min. 341, 343.

[2] Wheatley v. Chrisman, 24 Penn. St. 304.

[3] Dowling v. Hennings, 20 Md. 184.

[4] Davis v. Brigham, 29 Me. 391, 403.

proprietor, *sui juris*, may ripen into a right by an enjoyment for the requisite length of time.[1]

44. It would seem that it is not necessary that the one who claims the easement should be the only one who can or may enjoy that or a similar right over the same land, but that his right should not depend for its enjoyment upon a similar right in others, and that he may exercise it under some claim existing in his favor, independent of all others. This is illustrated by the case of Kilburn *v.* Adams, where Shaw, C. J. says : " The rule, we think, is, that where a tract of land attached to a public building, such as a meeting-house, town-house, school-house, and the like, and occupied with such house, is designedly left open and unencumbered for convenience and ornament, the passage of persons over it, in common with those for whose use it is appropriated, is in general to be regarded as permissive, or under an implied license, and not adverse. And though an adjacent proprietor may make such use of the open land more frequently than another, yet the same rule will apply, unless there be some decisive act indicating a separate and exclusive use, under the claim of right. A regularly formed and wrought way across the ground, paved, macadamized, or gravelled, and fitted for use as a way from his own estate to the highway, indicating a line distinct from any use to be made of it by the proprietors, would, in our view, be evidence of such *exclusive* use and claim of right. So would any plain, unequivocal act, indicating a peculiar and *exclusive* claim, open and ostensible, and distinguish- [*98] able from that of others." [2]

In accordance with the views above expressed, the court, in Nash *v.* Peden say : " But I must not be understood as meaning that, where a clear right of private way is established, it is to be defeated because other persons than the plaintiff have

---

[1] Pierce *v.* Selleck, 18 Conn. 321.

[2] Kilburn *v.* Adams, 7 Metc. 33. See Smith *v.* Higbee, 12 Vt. 113 ; Curtis *v.* Angier, 4 Gray, 547.

used the road, such use being in no wise inconsistent with the right. . . . . Nor do I suppose the proposition can be maintained, that a private right of way must be exclusive. I can see no reason why two or even more may not acquire a right in the same way, and by the same adverse use by which one may acquire it." [1]

It is accordingly said, that "no one can prescribe for a privilege which is common to every one." [2]

And upon this principle it is assumed, in Hamilton v. White, that one by passing over a public highway for twenty years does not thereby acquire a private right of way over the land occupied by the highway.[3]

45. So where the plaintiff claimed a right to divert the waters of one stream into another by an artificial channel cut through intermediate meadows, upon the ground that he had enjoyed it for the requisite period of time, it was held to be no answer to this claim, that the owners of the intermediate meadow had a right, at certain seasons of the year, to divert the waters running in such ditch into the original stream, the question of such right to divert the water from one stream to the other being between other parties than the owners of the meadows.[4]

46. And different prescriptions may exist in favor [*99] of *different persons in respect to the same land.

That is, one may have a prescriptive right of use for one purpose, and another may have a like right, but for another purpose. Thus one may have a right to flow A. B.'s land for the purpose of floating logs, while another may acquire it to flow the same land for the purpose of working mills.[5]

And this seems to be in accordance with the doctrine of

---

[1] Nash v. Peden, 1 Speers, 22.

[2] Thomas v. Marshfield, 13 Pick. 240 ; First Parish in Gloucester v. Beach, 2 Pick. 60, note.

[3] Hamilton v. White, 1 Seld. 9.

[4] Bolivar Mg. Co. v. Neponset Mg. Co., 16 Pick. 241.

[5] Davis v. Brigham, 29 Me. 391.

Kent *v.* Waite, that different parties may have rights of way over the same land, one claiming it as appurtenant to his estate, and others by custom by reason of living in a certain locality.[1]

Nor would it make any difference in acquiring the right, as in the cases of Bolivar Manufacturing Co. *v.* Neponset Manufacturing Co., and Davis *v.* Brigham, that, as between the two who exercised the right which laid the foundation for the prescription, one had such a paramount right that the exercise of it operated as a suspension of the exercise of the right of the other.[2]

So where, a town having made a road across a navigable stream, a mill-owner erected his mill and applied the road as a dam for the same, whereby land of a third party was flowed, and this had been continued for more than twenty years, it was held that he had thereby acquired a prescriptive right to flow the land. Although he may have been liable to indictment, by so doing, in a public prosecution for a nuisance to the highway.[3]

47. The case of Curtis *v.* Angier illustrates the doctrine that one may gain an easement by adverse, exclusive enjoyment, though others are, at the same time, using it for other purposes than those intended by him. In that case the proprietors of a canal changed the public travel from an *existing highway on to the tow-path of their canal. [*100] The owner of a farm, through which the canal passed, had used this tow-path for access to and the accommodation of his farm for over twenty years, when the canal and tow-path were discontinued. It was held that, if the way had not, by such user, become a public highway by dedication, it had become a private one by adverse use and enjoyment by the owner of the farm, which he had a right to assert over and along the course of the tow-path.[4]

---

[1] Kent *v.* Waite, 10 Pick. 138.

[2] Davis *v.* Brigham, 29 Me. 391; Bolivar Mg. Co. *v.* Neponset Mg. Co., 16 Pick. 241.

[3] Boiden *v.* Vincent, 24 Pick. 301.   [4] Curtis *v.* Angier, 4 Gray, 547.

48. Another requisite in a valid prescription is, that the use and enjoyment by virtue of which it is claimed should have been *continuous* for the requisite period of time.[1] This involves two inquiries : — first, What may be regarded as continuous acts of enjoyment ? and, second, how far the acts of one person may be united with those of another to constitute a continuity for the requisite period of enjoyment.

49. It may be stated, generally, that the time from which the period is to be reckoned in computing the duration of a continuous enjoyment, is when the injury or invasion of right begins, and not the time when the party causing it began that which finally creates the injury.   Thus, where one claimed a prescriptive right to flow another's land by a mill-dam, it was held that the period of prescription began when the dam was so far completed as permanently to raise the water and set it back upon the land flowed, and did not include the time during which it was in the progress of construction.[2]

50. What shall constitute a requisite continuity of enjoyment to gain thereby a prescriptive right to an easement depends, of course, upon the character and nature of the right claimed.   To exercise a right of way, for instance, *consists in passing over the land of another [*101] more or less frequently, and at greater or less intervals of time, according to the nature of the use to which its enjoyment may be applied; whereas a right to use a drain or a watercourse through another's land, or to flow the same for the purposes of operating a mill, or for other hydraulic uses, implies a constant and continued enjoyment of the right.

The terms of the definition are *continuous* and *uninter-*

---

[1] Pollard v. Barnes, 2 Cush. 191 ; Monmouth Canal Co. v. Harford, 1 Crompt. M. & R. 614 ; Co. Litt. 113 b.

[2] Branch v. Doane, 17 Conn. 402 ; s. c., 18 Conn. 233 ; Hurlbut v. Leonard, Brayt. 201 ; *ante,* p. *90. Crosby v. Bessey, 49 Maine, 543 ; Polly v. M'Call, 37 Ala. 20. See 2 Wood's Civ. L. 127, 128 ; *post,* c. 6, § 2, 10, Law Mag. & R. 182.

rupted, which implies that the enjoyment shall neither have been interrupted by the act of the owner of the land in, over, or across which the right is exercised, nor by a voluntary abandonment of the same by the other party. As it is ordinarily impossible to show an actual enjoyment of what is claimed as an easement, every day, for twenty years, or in fact to maintain such an uninterrupted enjoyment, each case, it would seem, may present a matter for the jury, to inquire whether the suspension of the enjoyment, if any, was voluntary, or by some act of interruption on the part of the land-owner, or was the result of accident or causes which the party claiming the right could not control, and not with any intent to abandon a right to the same.[1]

Coke, quoting Bracton, says: " Continuam dico ita quod non sit legitime interrupta." [2] Whatever breaks the continuity of the possession and enjoyment of an easement, whether by a cessation to enjoy it, or by any act of the owner of the servient tenement, destroys altogether the *effect of the previous user, and this is an *interrup-* [*102] tion* within the meaning of the (Massachusetts) statutes.[3]

In the case of Pollard *v.* Barnes, the claim was of a right to pile boards upon another's land. It had been enjoyed from 1822 to 1846, except from the years 1829 to 1834, during which no such use was made of the land. And it was held to be a voluntary interruption which destroyed the continued enjoyment of the right for twenty years.[4]

---

[1] Pollard *v.* Barnes, 2 Cush. 191 ; 2 Washb. Real Prop. 46.

[2] Co. Litt. 113 *b.* The entire passage from Bracton is as follows: " Nunc autem dicendum qualiter transferunter sine titulo, et traditione per usucaptionem, s. per longam, continuam, et pacificam possessionem, ex diuturno tempore et sine traditione : sed quam longa esse debeat, non definitur a jure, sed ex justitiariorum discretione. Continuam dico, ita quod non sit interrupta ; interrupi enim poterit multis modis, sine violentia adhibita, per denuntiationem et impetratio-nem diligentem, et diligentem prosequutionem, et per talem interruptionem nunquam acquiret possidens, ex tempore, liberum tenementum. Pacificam dico, quia si contentiosa fuerit, idem erit quod prius," &c. — Bract., fol. 51, 52.

[3] Pollard *v.* Barnes, 2 Cush. 191.

[4] Ibid. 191 – 199.

In Watt v. Trapp, the party claiming a right of way passed over the land in 1819, and then again in 1824 and 1825, and continued passing to 1843. But it was held not to be a continuous use except from 1824.[1]

In Dana v. Valentine, the easement claimed was the right to carry on an offensive trade in the claimant's buildings, which had stood more than twenty years, and in which he had carried on the business for eighteen years uninterruptedly; and it was held that the mere suspension of the business for two years, where there had been no interference with the enjoyment of the right, was not an interruption which should affect the right, unless done with an intent to abandon the business and not resume it. The intention, in such a case, becomes a material inquiry.[2]

A ready illustration would present itself to the mind where, from analogy to the above cases, there would seem to be no want of continuity, although the easement was but rarely used. Suppose a man had been accustomed to go across another's land to a meadow, once a year, for the purpose of cutting and bringing away the grass growing thereon, and had continued this for twenty years or more under a claim of right, it would be sufficient, it is believed, to acquire thereby an easement of way for that purpose. [*103] *Nor would this right be affected by the long intervals between the times of the user.[3]

In Wood v. Kelly, the easement claimed was a right to flow land, but the flowing had been suspended during the time in which the owner of the dam was repairing it. It was held not to be such an interruption to the continuity of the user and enjoyment as to affect the right. So it would be if the stream were at times too low, by reason of a drought, to operate his mill.[4]

---

[1] Watt v. Trapp, 2 Rich. 136.

[2] Dana v. Valentine, 5 Metc. 8, 13.

[3] Carr v. Foster, 3 Q. B. 581.

[4] Wood v. Kelly, 30 Me. 47; Gerenger v. Summers, 2 Ired. 229. See Winnipiseogee Co. v. Young, 40 N. H. 420.

Where a party maintained a dam, and raised the water of his pond to the height of his dam, whenever the water was high enough in the stream, and continued this more than twenty years under a claim of right, it was held that the height of his dam fixed the extent of his easement or right of flowing, although, at times, the water of the pond was below the top of the dam.[1]

In Cuthbert v. Lawton, the court, in speaking of a right of way which was claimed by user, say : "If it had only begun to accrue, the obstruction of one year in twenty would prevent its legal consummation; but after twenty years of uninterrupted use, it could only be defeated by an adverse and continued obstruction, for," &c.[2]

It seems to be an unquestioned proposition, that a mere succession of acts of trespass will not give the trespasser such possession as to gain for him a prescriptive right.[3]

51. And the language of the court in Olney v. Gardiner, given by way of illustration, presents the proposition in a clear light: "For instance, if the occupier had used the road openly for a year or two, and then uniformly asked permission on each occasion, or only used it secretly and by stealth for some years, and then resumed the enjoyment of it, no one would pretend that a grant could have been presumed, because the intervals of enjoyment united might amount to twenty years. A similar reason applies to intervals of unity of possession, during which there is no one who could complain of the user of the road."[4]

Whether there has been an interruption to the enjoyment *of what is claimed as an easement, is a [*104] question for the jury. To bring it within the meaning of the statute of 2 & 3 William IV. c. 71, it must be an interruption caused by an obstruction of some other person, and not a mere cesser to use the right. Where actual en-

---

[1] Winnipiseogee Co. v. Young, 40 N. H. 436 ; post, p. *105.

[2] Cuthbert v. Lawton, 3 M'Cord, 195.

[3] Cooper v. Smith, 9 Serg. & R. 34.

[4] Olney v. Gardiner, 4 Mees. & W. 500.

joyment is shown before and after the period of intermission, it may be inferred from that evidence that the right continued during the whole time. How many times the right has been exercised is not the material question, if the jury are satisfied that the claimant of the right exercised it as often as he chose. There must be some overt act indicating that the right is disputed.[1]

52. Questions often arise, especially in respect to easements in the use of water, in consequence of changes made in the mode and extent of user and enjoyment. And the rule seems to be this: while the law does not require the use to be, in all respects, identical and the same, both in manner and extent, in order to gain an easement; any material change in these respects, while the right is being gained by prescription, may defeat the same. If it shall have been actually gained, a mere failure to use it to the extent to which the right has been acquired will not affect such right.

Thus, where one had enjoyed the use of a drain from his land over that of another for more than twenty years, but during the twenty years it had been materially changed in its size, direction, and termination, it was held that no right had thereby been gained. In order to acquire an easement in such drain, there must have been an enjoyment of it twenty years after such change had been made.[2]

[*105]   *So where one flowed the land of another, by a dam of a certain height, for ten years, and then increased its height, and thereby flowed additional land for ten years more, it was held that he had thereby only acquired an easement to flow the parcel which was flowed by the original dam.[3]

---

[1] Carr v. Foster, 3 Q. B. 581. See Lane v. Carpenter, 6 Exch. 825; Winship v. Hudspeth, 10 Exch. 5. The following cases bear upon the same subject of the continuity of enjoyment requisite to acquire an easement, and are cited for the purpose of convenient reference. Esling v. Williams, 10 Penn. St. 126; Ingraham v. Hough, 1 Jones, No. C. 39; Battishill v. Reed, 18 C. B. 696.

[2] Cotton v. Pocasset Mg. Co., 13 Metc. 429; Stein v. Burden, 24 Ala. 130.

[3] Baldwin v. Calkins, 10 Wend. 167; Morris v. Commander, 3 Ired. 510; Whittier v. Cocheco Mg. Co., 9 N. H. 454; Gerenger v. Summers, 2 Ired. 229; Wright v. Moore, 38 Ala. 598.

53. But where the locality of the dam by which the flowing is caused is not material, the prescriptive right to flow may be acquired, if continued the requisite length of time, though the place of the dam, or that of using the water, be changed, provided it be used for the same purpose during the requisite time.[1]

Nor is it necessary that the water should have been used in the same precise manner during the twenty years, or applied to propel the same machinery. All that the law requires is, that the mode or manner of using the water should not have been materially varied to the prejudice of others.[2]

54. But it is not always easy, in case of flowing lands by means of artificial dams, to fix a precise limit to what has been enjoyed for the requisite period of time to establish a prescriptive right. The state of the water in most streams is constantly varying, and the condition of the dam, as to its capacity to pen it back, is often affected by the state of repair in which it may be. As a general rule, the height of the dam fixes and limits the extent of the right to flow. By height of a dam, as thus used, is meant its height when completed and finished, with its rolling dam, waste-ways, &c., in good repair and condition, without regard to the height of other parts of the structure, which have no operative effect in causing the water to flow back. When, *therefore, one has acquired a prescriptive right to [*106] maintain a dam which, in its usual operation, would raise the water to a given height, and has used it at his pleasure at that height, without the claim of any other person to have it drawn or kept down, he has a right to retain it at the same height, although, from the former leaky condition of the same, the construction of the machinery, or

---

[1] Davis v. Brigham, 29 Me. 391 ; Stackpole v. Curtis, 32 Me. 383, 385 ; Whittier v. Cocheco Mg. Co., 9 N. H. 454, 458.

[2] Belknap v. Trimble, 3 Paige, 577 ; Bullen v. Runnels, 2 N. H. 255; Whittier v. Cocheco Mg. Co., 9 N. H. 454.

10

lavish use of the water, the water in the pond is not, in fact, constantly or usually kept at that height ; and he would not be liable for rendering his dam tight, or using the water in a different mode, though he thereby constantly flows more land than he had hitherto usually done.[1]

The proposition that the extent of the right to flow is determined by the height of the dam, is limited by the courts of New Hampshire, so that, though the owner of the dam may maintain it at the height to which it has been kept by twenty years user, the easement of flowing by it is fixed not by the height of the dam but by the limits and extent of the user of the water itself. " The same proof of user which establishes the right, is equally conclusive in establishing the limitations of that right." [2]

In New York, the court recognizes the doctrine of Cowell v. Thayer as law, and applied it to the case of using flash-boards upon a dam for the purpose of retaining the water in seasons when it was low. Having acquired a right to do this, the owner of the dam was at liberty to raise his dam to the height of the flash-boards by a permanent structure, provided he did not flow it any higher, or for a longer time in the year, than he had done by the flash-boards.[3] And in another case the mill-owner was held liable for keeping up the water a longer time in the year than he had done by his flash-boards, although he had not erected his dam any higher than his flash-boards had been kept, nor any higher than he had a right to raise it. And he would be liable, also, if by such a dam he flowed more land than the dam with its flash-boards had done, when in good and suitable repair.

And if the owner of the dam, or his predecessors, have in fact enjoyed and exercised the right of keeping up his dam

---

[1] Cowell v. Thayer, 5 Metc. 253, 258 ; Alder v. Savill, 5 Taunt. 454 ; Vickerie v. Buswell, 13 Me. 289 ; Ray v. Fletcher, 12 Cush. 200 ; Lacy v. Arnett, 33 Penn. St. 169 ; Bliss v. Rin, 17 Pick. 33. Marcly v. Shultz, 29 N. Y. 354.

[2] Burnham v. Kempton, 44 N. H. 90. See also Smith v. Ross, 17 Wisc. 227 ; ante p. *103.

[3] Hynds v. Shultz, 39 Barb. 600 ; Marcly v. Shultz, 29 N. Y. 352.

and flowing the land of another, for a period of twenty years, without paying damages therefor, or any claim or assertion of a right to damages for such flowing, it is in itself evidence of a prescriptive right to continue such flowing.[1]

55. Though no mere temporary suspension of flowing to any particular height by reason of failing to keep up a head of water in an artificial pond, by the lavish use of the same, or by a want of repair of the dam, would prevent the owner from exercising the right to flow to its original height, which he may have acquired by prescription, by restoring the dam to its original condition, it would seem that, in acquiring the right by use and enjoyment, reference is had to the actual extent to which the flowing has been exercised during the twenty years, rather than to the form or height of the dam. Thus, where A had flowed B's land for more than twenty years to a certain height, during all which time his dam was leaky, and at the end of that period he repaired and tightened the same without increasing its height, *whereby he set back the water upon B's land to a [*107] greater extent than had been done during the twenty years, it was held that he was responsible in damages for this excess in flowing B's land.[2]

56. Nor may the nature of the use be changed from that by which the prescription may be gained. The flow of the water, if it be a watercourse which is the subject of the prescription, must remain substantially the same, both as to quantity and rapidity of the current, as it had been during the period in which the easement was acquired. Thus, if a man shall have acquired a right to turn water through an artificial trench across another's land for purposes of irrigation, and to enter and clear the same, he would not have a right to convert the same trench into the tail-race of a mill, and to widen and deepen it for that purpose. So he may

---

[1] Williams v. Nelson, 23 Pick. 141 ; Perrin v. Garfield, 37 Verm. 310; Brace v. Yale, 10 Allen, 443.

[2] Mertz v. Dorney. 25 Penn. St. 519.

not change the use of the trench by increasing the quantity flowing through the same.[1]

✗ 57. And in considering further how far a change in the mode of using an easement, while in the process of acquiring it by use and enjoyment, will defeat the necessary continuity, it may be stated in general terms, that, while a way, for instance, must be used in the same course and direction without change or variation, — not in one place to-day and in another to-morrow, — every immaterial change in this respect ought not to be construed into a destruction of its identity. In determining this, regard ought to be had to the situation of the country and habits of the people in respect to public ways, in a new country, for instance. And something of the sort might be allowed in a private way without destroying a prescriptive right; such as changing a road between two points for the purpose of straightening it for the convenience of the parties, the way being kept open and used all the time.[2] But a prescriptive right of way, whether public or private, cannot be gained to pass over land generally, it must be confined to a specific line of travel.[3]

[*108]   *58. As prescriptions are often partly personal and partly incidental to the possession of an estate, it sometimes becomes a question whether the death of a party, or his ceasing to own or occupy the estate with which the easement is connected, operates as such a break in the continuity of enjoyment as to defeat the prescription. In other words, what is the effect upon an inchoate prescription for an easement of the death of either of the parties, or the ceasing by one to own or to occupy the dominant or servient estate? And, first, if such death or ceasing to own or occupy is on the part of the one exercising the acts of easement. Where a user and enjoyment of an easement has

[1] Darlington v. Painter, 7 Penn. St. 473 ; ante, p. 53.

[2] Lawton v. Rivers, 2 M'Cord, 445.

[3] Gentleman v. Soule, 32 Ill. 278 ; 3 Kent, p. *419. See Gage v. Pitts, 8 Allen, 527.

been begun by an ancestor for the benefit of an estate which, upon his death, descends to his heirs, and the use is continued by the heir so long that the two periods united will be equal to twenty years' adverse enjoyment, the prescription will be complete. The same would be true in case of vendor and vendee, or any person claiming as privy in estate with a previous occupant, provided the enjoyment were continuous though no mention is made in the deed of the easement.[1] But if there is an actual break or interruption in the occupancy or user, a new occupation or user would be the commencement of a new period of prescription. Nor can the time of one adverse enjoyment be united with that of a second, who does not claim under the first by privity of estate.[2]

59. Thus, where successive persons had flowed another's land for a period exceeding twenty years, it was held that, in order to gain a prescriptive right to do this, the flowing must have been continued for twenty years by the same person, or some one under whom he claims title. And if it be done by a succession of persons, each of whom has acted independently of any right acquired from his predecessor, no one of them will thereby have acquired an easement or prescription in his favor. So if one of *successive [*109] owners, who have enjoyed the right claimed for twenty years, had done so by permission of the owner of the servient estate, it would prevent the twenty years' enjoyment creating a prescriptive right.[3]

60. So where the owner of the dominant estate used a way for two years, and then, after some years' interval, sold his

[1] Leonard v. Leonard, 7 Allen, 277 ; Kent v. Waite, 10 Pick. 138 ; Hill v. Crosby, 2 Pick. 466 ; Sargent v. Ballard, 9 Pick. 251 ; Williams v. Nelson, 23 Pick. 142.

[2] Sargent v. Ballard, 9 Pick. 251 ; Melvin v. Whiting, 13 Pick. 184 ; 3 Kent, Comm. 444, 445 ; M'Farlin v. Essex Co., 10 Cush. 304 ; Inst. 2, 6, 8 ; Okeson v. Patterson, 29 Penn. St. 22. Tracy v. Atherton, 36 Verm. 503.

[3] Benson v. Soule, 32 Me. 39 ; Winship v. Hudspeth, 10 Exch. 5 ; Perrin v. Garfield, 37 Verm. 309.

estate to one who used it for eighteen years, it was held not
to give a prescriptive right by what the law considers an
uninterrupted and continuous use.[1]

61. So if the owner of the dominant estate were to become
the occupant of the servient estate, by a lease from the
owner thereof, during the twenty years of his using and
enjoying the easement claimed, it would so break the continuous adverse enjoyment as to defeat a prescription therefor.[2]

In one case the owner of land upon one side of a stream
leased it for thirty-four years to the owner or tenant of the
land upon the opposite side. The lessee then went on and
erected a dam above the plaintiff's land, and thereby raised a
head of water, and by a canal dug therefrom to works erected
upon the side opposite the plaintiff's land, and thereby
diverting the water from the bed of the stream, created a
large manufacturing establishment thereon. About the time
of the expiration of the lease, the lessor conveyed his land
to the plaintiff, who, after a few years, sought to enjoin the
defendant from diverting the water of the stream from its
former channel and the plaintiff's land. It was held that
this enjoyment of the diversion being under a lease, where
the owner of the land could not interfere, was not, in law,
adverse, and gave the lessee no right to continue it after
such lease had expired. Nor was the land-owner estopped
by standing by and seeing the defendant incur heavy charges
in constructing his works, inasmuch as he had no right to
interfere by way of assent or dissent with the erection of the
works. And the injunction was granted, though the effect
of restoring the stream to its original watercourse and the
plaintiff's land, was to destroy the defendant's works.[3]

62. So where there were two adjacent estates, and the
owner of the one had charge of the other, as agent of the

---

[1] Kilburn v. Adams, 7 Metc. 33.

[2] Clay v. Thackrah, 9 Carr. & P. 47; Olney v. Gardiner, 4 Mees. & W. 496;
Holland v. Long, 7 Gray, 486.

[3] Corning v. Troy Iron, &c. Co., 39 Barb. 311; s. c., 22 How. Pr. Cas. 217.

owner, which was occupied by a succession of tenants for short periods of time, amounting to twenty years, it was held that no easement was gained by the owner of the second estate, by user of a way over the other, while such second estate was in possession of these successive tenants; — 1st, because, having charge of both, it could not be treated as adverse ; and 2d, because, these successive tenants not being in privity with each other, there could be no continued adverse enjoyment as against the servient estate.[1]

63. One owning land upon one side of a highway occupied a parcel, for piling lumber, upon the opposite side of the way, for the space of two years, by an arrangement with the owner by which he was to purchase the same, and in the mean time was tenant at will of the parcel. At the *end of the two years he sold his land to a third [*110] party, who continued to occupy that on the opposite side of the road for the next eighteen years. It was held that here had not been an adverse possession for twenty years, since, during the first two, the occupancy was not adverse ; and, besides, the possession of a tenant at will was not assignable, so that the purchaser could avail himself of the benefit of it.[2]

64. On the other hand, if the owner of the servient estate die during the period of twenty years' enjoyment by the dominant estate, leaving only minor heirs, it is held by some courts to be an interruption to the prescription, so long as such minority remains. But it would not so far defeat it but that, if the user were continued long enough after the minor heirs became of age to make the period before the ancestor's death and that after the minority of the heirs had ceased together equal to twenty years, it would make a good prescription.[3]

[1] Holland v. Long, 7 Gray, 486.
[2] Plumer v. Brown, 8 Metc. 578.
[3] Melvin v. Whiting, 13 Pick. 184, 188 ; Watkins v. Peck, 13 N. H. 360 ; Lamb v. Crosland, 4 Rich. 536. See Arbuckle v. Wood, 29 Vt. 43, where the exception of minority of the heirs is not alluded to by the court, and post, pl. 73.

65. As a general proposition, as will hereafter appear, an easement cannot be acquired by prescription against a re-versioner of the servient estate, by use and enjoyment during the occupation thereof by a tenant; yet if the use be begun adversely to the owner of the servient estate, and he part with his possession thereof to a tenant, such possession by the tenant will not operate as an interruption to the acquisition of a prescriptive right to such easement, if the enjoyment thereof is continued.[1]

And it may be added, that, unless the acts of prescription operate against all persons having estates in the premises, the party exercising them gains thereby no prescriptive rights against the tenant or any one. Thus, where one has used a right of way adversely to a tenant for years [*111] or for *life, for more than twenty years, inasmuch as it did not affect the right of the reversioner, it did not operate to create any prescriptive right against the tenant.[2]

By a recent English statute one tenant for years may gain an easement of light against another tenant for years, after an adverse enjoyment of twenty years, though both tenants hold by simultaneous leases from the same landlord.[3]

66. In the next place, to gain a prescriptive right to the use and enjoyment of any easement by a long continuance of the same, it must have been done with the knowledge and acquiescence of him who was seized of an estate of inheritance as owner of the servient estate.[4]

The maintaining of a mill-dam is such an act of notoriety, that the law will presume a knowledge of it on the part of the land-owner living near it.[5]

---

[1] Cross v. Lewis, 2 Barnew. & C. 686. See Pearsall v. Post, 20 Wend. 111; Bright v. Walker, 1 Crompt. M. & R. 211; post, pl. 70. McGregor v. Wait, 10 Gray, 75.

[2] Bright v. Walker, 1 Crompt. M. & R. 211; Tud. Lead. Cas. 118.

[3] 2 & 3 Wm. 4, 671; Frewen v. Philipps, 11 C. B., N. S. 449.

[4] Bradbury v. Grimsel, 2 Saund. 175 d; Daniel v. North, 11 East, 372; Ingraham v. Hough, 1 Jones, No. C. 42; La. Civ. Code, Art. 727; ante, sect. 4, pl. 4.

[5] Perrin v. Garfield, 37 Verm. 311.

67. What shall constitute the evidence of such knowledge and acquiescence depends upon the circumstances of the case. The language of the court in Blake *v.* Everett is this: " There need not be a claim of right to the way in words, or an admission by the owner of the land in words, that he knew of the adverse use and claim of right : twenty years of adverse use, continually and uninterruptedly, with the knowledge and acquiescence of the owner of the land, in the absence of any evidence of permission and license, is sufficient proof of the existence of such easement." [1]

The court, in Beasley *v.* Clarke, which was a case under the statute 2 & 3 William IV. c. 71, § 5, held that, to a plea of a right of way by user, &c., " the plaintiff is at liberty to show the character and description of the user and enjoyment of the way during any part of the time ; as that it was used by stealth or in the absence of the occupier of the close, and without his knowledge ; or that it was merely a precarious enjoyment by leave and license, or any other circumstances which negative that it is an user or enjoyment under a claim of right." [2]

And in Solomon *v.* Vintners' Co., Bramwell, B. says: " It was an enjoyment *clam*, not open, and consequently not as of right." [3]

This doctrine was applied in the case of a drain constructed by the owner of two or more houses which he afterwards conveyed to different purchasers, and the drain remained more than twenty years, but was not known by the owner of either house to exist. It was held that such an enjoyment of the drain did not give the upper estate a right to maintain it through the lower one as a prescriptive easement. [4]

[1] Blake *v.* Everett, 1 Allen, 248 ; Gray *v.* Bond, 2 Brod. & B. 667 ; Smith *v.* Miller, 11 Gray, 148.
[2] Beasley *v.* Clarke, 2 Bing. N. C. 705 ; Tickle *v.* Brown, 4 Adolph. & E. 369.
[3] Solomon *v.* Vintners' Co., 4 Hurlst. & N. 602.
[4] Carbrey *v.* Willis, 7 Allen, 368.

[*112]   *And Putnam, J., in Sargent v. Ballard, quotes
the words of Bracton: " Possessio per longum con-
tinuum et pacificum usum, sine consensu expresso,
per patentiam veri domini, qui scivit et non prohibuit, sed
permisit de consensu tacito," — " It must be with the knowledge and permission of the owner, and not merely of the
tenants." [1]

68. The maxim is, " Ita quod, nec per vim, nec clam, nec
precario." [2]

If, therefore, it should appear that, during the period of
the alleged acquisition of an easement by use and enjoyment, the owner of the servient tenement resisted such
claim, or opposed such use, it would negative the claim.

It was accordingly held that a prescriptive right to divert
water from a stream could not be acquired by an enjoyment
for the requisite period, where it appeared that the party,
against whom it was claimed, during that time remonstrated
against such diversion, and consulted counsel for a prosecution therefor.[3]

Thus where, though one had flowed another's lands for
more than twenty years, it appeared that the latter had complained thereof, and denied his right so to do, it was held
that it rebutted the presumption of its having been enjoyed
under a grant.[4]

So in Powell v. Bagg, the defendant claimed an easement
of an aqueduct across the plaintiff's land, by an enjoyment
for the term of thirty-eight years, which he proved. It was
held that, if the owner of the land, being upon it, forbade
the other party to enter upon the land, and make use of the
aqueduct, it was enough to prevent his acquiring an ease-

---

[1] Sargent v. Ballard, 9 Pick. 251 ; Bract. 52 b. c. 23, § 1.   Edson v. Munsell,
10 Allen, 567.

[2] Bract., fol. 222 ; D. 39, 3, 23 ; Co. Litt. 114 a ; Eaton v. Swansea Water-
works Co., 17 Q. B. 267.   Per *Bramwell*, B., Solomon v. Vintners' Co., 4 Hurlst.
& N. 602.

[3] Stillman v. White Rock Co., 3 W. & Min. 549.   See Bealy v. Shaw, 6 East,
216.

[4] Nichols v. Aylor, 7 Leigh, 546, 565.

ment by such use and enjoyment. Nor was it necessary, in order to defeat such a claim, that the land-owner should show that he resisted the claimant by acts of violence or force to eject him. To have one gain an easement, it not only must be claimed adversely, but it must be acquiesced in by the owner of the land, under a claim of right. And if, before the expiration of twenty years from the time the right was first claimed, the owner of the land, by a verbal *act on the premises in which the easement is [*113] claimed, resists the exercise of the right, or denies its existence, the presumption of grant is rebutted, his acquiescence is disproved, and the essential elements of a title to an easement by adverse use are shown not to exist. In this respect there is a material difference between an actual disseizin of lands, where the disseizor continues in possession, and an easement; for in the latter case the owner of the land remains in possession, and there is no disseizin, and the title to the easement rests chiefly on an acquiescence in an adverse use.[1]

So in the case of Eaton v. Swansea Waterworks Co., above cited, it was held that, to gain an easement, it must have been enjoyed without contention or resistance by the owner of the land: "It seems clear that, if the enjoyment is clandestine, contentious, or by sufferance, it is not of right. Enjoyment of a right must be *nec clam, nec vi, nec precario.*" And it was accordingly held that, where the servant of one claiming an easement to draw water was prosecuted for exercising that right, and the master paid the penalty, without appealing, it was competent evidence to prove that he had not enjoyed it as a matter of right for twenty years.[2]

And in another case, where one had used a way over twenty years, but it appeared that it had always been a subject of contention, it was held that the jury were justified

---

[1] Powell v. Bagg, 8 Gray, 441. See Ingraham v. Hough, 1 Jones, No. C. 39. Tracy v. Atherton, 36 Verm. 514.

[2] Eaton v. Swansea Waterworks Co., 17 Q. B. 267, 269.

in negativing a prescriptive grant. "Nothing but an uninterrupted usage can raise a presumption of a grant." [1]

69. Another essential circumstance in the use and enjoyment of an easement, in order to gain thereby a prescriptive right to the same, is that, while it was thus being gained, the owner of the servient estate was able, in law, to assert and enforce his rights, and to resist such adverse claim, if not well founded.

[*114]   *No presumption of grant, therefore, arises from adverse enjoyment against a *feme covert* or a minor,[2] or an insane person,[3] nor would the admission of a *feme covert* that such grant existed be admitted as evidence against her.[4]

But where a female minor married after the period of adverse enjoyment had begun to run, it was held that such second disability is disregarded in determining the question of a prescriptive right thus acquired.[5]

This involves the effect of the servient estate being in the occupation of a tenant, or the owner thereof being a minor during all or a portion of the alleged period of prescription.

70. In addition to what has already been said, it may be stated, with few if any qualifications, that neither a remainder-man nor a reversioner can be affected by any use or enjoyment of an easement in or over the servient estate, by way of thereby creating a prescriptive right in respect to the same, while his land is in the possession and occupation of a tenant for life or years.[6]

---

[1] Livett v. Wilson, 3 Bing. 115.   Smith v. Miller, 11 Gray, 148.

[2] Watkins v. Peck, 13 N. H. 360; Melvin v. Whiting, 13 Pick. 184; Reimer v. Stuber, 20 Penn. St. 458, 463.   See Mebane v. Patrick, 1 Jones, No. C. 26; [3] Toullier, Droit Civil Français, 418, 419 ; Merlin, Repertoire de Jurisprudence, tit. *Prescription*, Sect. 1, § 7, Art. 2 ; Lalaure, Traité des Servitudes Réelles, 34 ; *ante*, sect. 3, pl. 1.

[3] Edson v. Munsell, 10 Allen, 557.

[4] M'Gregor v. Wait, 10 Gray, 74.

[5] Reimer v. Stuber, 20 Penn. St. 458, 463; Schenley v. Commonwealth, &c., 36 Penn. St. 29.

[6] Bradbury v. Grimsel, 2 Saund. 175 *d* ; Daniel v. North, 11 East, 372; Parker v. Framingham, 8 Metc. 260; Pierre v. Fernald, 26 Me. 436; Blanchard v.

In the case of Daniel *v.* North, there is a doubt expressed as to the effect upon the rights of the reversioner of an enjoyment of an easement for twenty years in an estate while in a tenant's hands, if the reversioner had been cognizant thereof. But the case of Barker *v.* Richardson, as well as the reasoning of the court in Daniel *v.* North, seems to settle the point, that no adverse enjoyment of an easement by a dominant over a servient estate can affect the rights of the reversioner, though enjoyed adversely by the owner of the *former, if the latter were in the possession of [*115] a tenant for life during such adverse enjoyment.

The reason of this is, that a prescription operates only against one who is "capable of making a grant." And a tenant for life cannot make a grant which shall affect the estate, when it shall come into a reversioner's hands.[1]

In Wood *v.* Veal, the premises over which a way was claimed, by adverse use and enjoyment for a long space of time, — longer, in fact, than human memory, — had been during this time in the possession of a tenant for ninety-nine years, which had then recently expired, and it was held that no right was thereby gained against the owner of the inheritance.[2]

But, as already stated, it would seem that if, after such adverse use and enjoyment had begun by the owner of the dominant estate, the owner of the servient estate should part with his possession to a tenant, and the same should continue to be used as before, an easement might be gained by prescription after twenty years' enjoyment.[3]

Bridges, 4 Adolph. & E. 176 ; Barker *v.* Richardson, 4 Barnew. & Ald. 579 ; Bright *v.* Walker, 1 Crompt. M. & R. 211 ; Baxter *v.* Taylor, 4 Barnew. & Ad. 72 ; Reimer *v.* Stuber, 20 Penn. St. 458 ; Schenley *v.* Commonwealth, &c., 36 Penn. St. 29 ; Tud. Lead. Cas. 116 ; Runcorn *v.* Doe, 5 Barnew. & C. 696 ; *ante*, sect. 3, pl. 32.

[1] Barker *v.* Richardson, 4 Barnew. & Ald. 579. See Davies *v.* Stephens, 7 Carr. & P. 570 ; Merlin, Repertoire de Jurisprudence, tit. *Prescription*, Sect. 1, § 7, Art. 2, Ques. 13 ; McGregor *v.* Waite, 10 Gray, 75.

[2] Wood *v.* Veal, 5 Barnew. & Ald. 454.

[3] See Cross *v.* Lewis, 2 Barnew. & C. 686 ; Mebane *v.* Patrick, 1 Jones, No. C. 23.

But, for various reasons, if the owner of the dominant estate becomes himself a tenant of the servient estate, no enjoyment of an easement during such unity of possession could be adverse, or lay the foundation for a prescription.[1]

71. On the other hand, though it is clear that a tenant for life of a dominant estate may acquire an easement in a servient one by adverse enjoyment, it does not seem to be settled whether it would, when acquired, enure in favor of him who has the inheritance by way of reversion.[2]

But though in the above-cited case the court avoid the question, it would seem that, if the tenant held by [*116] lease *from the tenant of the fee of the dominant estate, an easement gained by such a holding by the tenant would enure to the landlord's benefit, in analogy with the doctrine of a class of cases which hold that, if a tenant by disseizin extends his holding over a neighboring parcel of land till a prescriptive title is gained, it will enure to the benefit of his landlord.[3]

72. But in respect to the principal proposition, it may be stated that, if an easement is claimed by an adverse enjoyment, with the knowledge of the owner of the servient estate, it must be while he or those under whom he claims have the absolute ownership thereof. And if it shall have begun while the premises were in the possession of one having a particular estate therein, which may have continued for any part of the time it was enjoyed, so much thereof is to be deducted, and there must have been twenty years of such enjoyment, exclusive of the period for which the tenant of the particular estate thus held possession.[4]

But it is said by Bell, J., in Wallace v. Fletcher,[5] that " the tenant for life or years may grant easements or permit them to be acquired by user, and they will be valid against

---

1 Clay v. Thackrah, 9 Carr. & P. 47.

2 Holland v. Long, 7 Gray, 487.

3 Andrews v. Hailes, 2 Ellis & B. 349, and cases therein cited.

4 Pearsall v. Post, 20 Wend. 111 ; La. Civ. Code, Art. 725.

5 Wallace v. Fletcher, 10 Foster, 453.

himself and those who hold his estate during its continuance, and perhaps not afterwards, where the reversioner had previously neither cause nor right to complain."

But it would seem that, if the servient estate be in the possession of one having a conditional or determinable fee in the same, a servitude may be gained against him, which would be defeated if afterwards the estate of the servient tenant fails.[1]

73. The effect of the death of the owner of the servient estate before an easement shall have been acquired by the requisite period of enjoyment, has been somewhat anticipated. There would ordinarily be no difficulty in fixing the rule to be applied in such cases, if the heir who succeeded to the ancestor were of age, and suffered the use and enjoyment to be continued till it had extended to the period of prescription.

But if the heir were at the time under a disability like that of being a minor, it is held by writers upon the French law, as well as by some of the American courts, that during the period *of his minority the prescription is [*117] suspended. Thus if, after five years' adverse enjoyment against the owner of an estate, he dies, and it comes by descent to a minor heir of the age of five years, it would require a continued enjoyment against this heir of thirty-one years before the easement could be gained by adverse use, the law allowing the owner of the dominant estate to add the period of enjoyment during the ancestor's life to that while the heir is tenant, after his arriving at the age of twenty-one.[2]

The identity of the doctrine above stated with that of the French law will be perceived by the following quotation from Merlin, Repertoire de Jurisprudence : " Au surplus, remarquez que, dans les cas où la prescription temporaire ne court

---

[1] 3 Toullier, Droit Civil Français, 419.
[2] Lamb v. Crossland, 4 Rich. 536 ; Watkins v. Peck, 13 N. H. 360 ; Melvin v. Whiting, 13 Pick. 184.

pas contre les mineurs, la minorité de l'heriter suspend bien la prescription commencée contre le defunt, mais n'empêche pas qu'on ne joigne au temps durant lequel on a possédé contre celui-ci, le temps qui a suivi sa majorité." [1]

The same writer remarks further, that a prescription which does not run against a minor will not, upon the same principle, run against his heir during his minority.[2]

The rule, as stated in the Civil Code of Louisiana, is this: " It is not sufficient to be an owner in order to establish a servitude : one must be master of his own rights, and have the power to alienate. Thus minors, married women, persons interdicted, cannot establish servitudes on their estates, except according to the forms prescribed for the alienation of their property." [3]

[*118]   *73 a. On the other hand, some of the American courts hold that the analogy between the doctrine of a presumed grant from twenty years enjoyment and the statute of limitations is so strong that, inasmuch as there is no exception in favor of infants, insane persons, and women under coverture in the latter, unless the disability exists when the statute begins to run, there should be none in the acquisition of an easement by lapse of time, except under the same circumstances. That the exception in the statutes of limitations is thus qualified is settled in the cases cited below.[4]

Gray J., in Edson v. Munsell, has examined the law in an exhaustive manner, upon the effect of the disability of insanity of the owner of the servient estate when the adverse possession began, and shows clearly that no length of enjoyment can

[1] Merlin, Repertoire de Jurisprudence, tit. *Prescription*, Sect. 1, § 7, Art. 2. Ques. 2.

[2] Ibid.

[3] La. Civ. Code, Art. 727 ; see Code Nap., Art. 2252.

[4] Mebane v. Patrick, 1 Jones, N. C. 23 ; Allis v. Moore, 2 Allen, 306 ; Currier v. Gale, 3 Allen, 328 ; Edson v. Munsell, 10 Allen, 557 ; Dekay v. Darrick, 2 Green, N. J. 294 ; Reimer v. Stuber, 20 Penn. 463 ; M'Farland v. Stone, 17 Verm. 174 ; Tracy v. Atherton, 36 Verm. 517 ; Wallace v. Fletcher, 10 Foster, 454.

give a prescriptive right of easement thereon, however open
and adverse it may be. The easement claimed in that case
was an aqueduct which had been enjoyed forty-three years uninterruptedly. But as the owner of the land was all the
time insane, it was held that no right had thereby been acquired. In two of the other cases cited, the disability was
insanity, which began after the statute had begun to run, and
in another the disability was coverture, assumed after such
commencement of the running of the statute. The reasoning of the court, in Watkins v. Peck, seems to sustain the idea
that no deed can be presumed to have been given, in accordance with the theory of modern prescription, unless the owner
of the land against whom it is claimed has been of ability to
give it or to resist the user of the easement, during the whole
and every part of the twenty years, and that prescription is
not like the statute of limitation, an arbitrary and technical
rule of law. Thus the C. J. in that case says : " We are of
opinion that no grant can be presumed from an adverse use
of an easement in the land of another for the term of twenty
years, where the owner of the land was, at the expiration of
the twenty years and long before, incapable of making a
grant, whether the disability arose from infancy or insanity."
" Perhaps a disability intervening during the lapse of the term
but not extending to the termination of the period of twenty
years, might not be sufficient to rebut the presumption ; but
it would be absurd to *presume* a grant where it was clear that
no such grant could have existed." And in Edson v. Munsell, Gray, J. remarks, that " a grant cannot be presumed
against a person legally incapable of making it." Neither of
these cases go the length of settling the question whether the
occurrence of a disability on the part of the owner of the
servient estate, after prescription has begun to run, and before a title has thereby become established, suspends the
force of the prescription. And the language of Merrick, J.,
in Currier v. Gale, would seem to settle the point, that if such
disability were assumed, like becoming covert, it would not

11

suspend the prescription. After stating that if, after a disseizin and a lapse of time reasonably sufficient to enable the disseizee to take measures for the protection of his rights, a disability occurs, it would not delay or postpone the operation of the statute of limitations, he adds : " The same rule must, for the same reason, prevail in relation to easements or other rights acquired by prescription, or to titles established and confined by open adverse possession." And this language is quoted with approbation by Gray, J., in Edson v. Munsell. But in Lamb v. Crosland, and Melvin v. Whiting, the point was distinctly ruled, that, if the ancestor die before the prescription becomes complete, and the estate descends to a minor heir, the prescription is suspended during his minority.

On the other hand, the courts of Vermont, North Carolina, and New Hampshire hold the same rule as to prescription as they do as to the statute of limitation. If there is no disability when it begins to run, no subsequent disability will arrest or suspend the operation of the prescription. In the case of Tracy v. Atherton,[1] Poland, C. J., in an able and elaborate opinion maintains, that if the adverse enjoyment of a way be begun during the life of the owner of the servient estate, and he die before the term of prescription has expired, and the estate descends to his heir, then a minor, it would not work a suspension of the prescription. And in the case of Mebane v. Patrick, where a like doctrine is maintained, the court say : " Such being the law as to the statute of limitations, it follows it must be so in regard to prescriptions." The disability in that case was insanity.[2] The same doctrine was expressly held in Wallace v. Fletcher,[3] where it was denied that any different doctrine was sustained in Watkins v. Peck, and where, of a disability of minority in an heir, to whom the estate descended from an ancestor after the ad-

---

[1] Tracy v. Atherton, 36 Verm. 503.

[2] Mebane v. Patrick, 1 Jones, N. C. 26.

[3] Wallace v. Fletcher, 10 Foster, 434, 454.

verse enjoyment had commenced, the court say, " Such intervening disabilities should not defeat the presumption of
title resulting from twenty years possession."

Story, J., in Tyler v. Wilkinson,[1] in speaking of the effect
of the presumption which arises from the long enjoyment of a
privilege, says : " Its operation has never yet been denied in
cases where personal disabilities of particular proprietors
might have intervened, such as infancy, coverture, and insanity."

But the court, in Lamb v. Crosland, assume, that when
making this ruling, " he did not bear in mind the distinction
between a right claimed by prescription and a presumption
of right from a non-existing grant." And it is questionable
if the same criticism might not apply to the case of Wallace
v. Fletcher. But there is one remark in the latter case
which has a very important bearing upon the question under
consideration : " It strikes us that the legitimate and natural
tendency of evidence of user may, in many cases, be rather
to prove a deed existing *before* the commencement of the
user, than one executed during the time of the use, or at its
termination."

The court of Pennsylvania seem also to adopt the same
rule as to prescription as they do in respect to the statute of
limitations, in the matter of its running against a minor or
feme covert.[2]

It would not, probably, be possible to reconcile these different rules. And while one class of courts hold that the
doctrine of prescription is merely the statute of limitations
applied to incorporeal hereditaments, and the other that in
order to imply the existence of a grant there must have been
an adverse enjoyment for the term of twenty years, during
the whole of which time there was some one in possession of
the servient estate who could have granted or resisted the
enjoyment, there will be two sets of rules, the one or the

---

[1] Tyler v. Wilkinson, 4 Mason, 402.
[2] Reimer v. Stuber, 20 Penn. 463.

other to be applied according to the local law of the State where the case may arise.

74. The last clause in the definition of what is necessary to create a prescription, — that it must be of something which could have been granted by one party to the other, — has been pretty fully anticipated ; and yet it may be well to refer to one or two authorities bearing upon this proposition, although it is implied from the familiar doctrine, that every prescription is based upon an assumed original grant.

If, for instance, two adjacent proprietors of lands occupy them in a manner which each would have a legal right to do, without obtaining any leave or permission from the other, neither can insist, as a prescriptive right, that the [*119] other shall *continue such mode of occupation, although in its effect it operates a benefit to his own estate. Such benefit, though derived from another's estate, is not an easement in or out of the same in favor of his own. Thus, one built a dam upon his own land, which so regulated and controlled the flow of the water of the stream that it no longer was discharged upon the land of a proprietor below in such quantities as to flood the same, as it had been accustomed to do before the erection of the dam, and the owner of the land, by digging ditches therein, was able to drain it and cultivate it. This he enjoyed for more than twenty years, when the owner of the dam cut it away, and suffered the water to flow as formerly, and the land of the lower proprietor was, consequently, again flooded and damaged. But it was held that he was without a remedy for the injury, since he had acquired no easement to have the water kept back, for he had done nothing adverse to the rights of the upper owner, nor had the latter done anything adverse to him. The benefit derived to the land below was merely incidental to the lawful act of another's erecting the dam upon his own land above. The law would not presume, in such use, that either of these owners had granted anything to the other, since each had whatever he enjoyed, independently of the other.[1]

And it is said in Wheateley v. Baugh, that " no man, by the mere prior enjoyment of the advantages of his own land, can establish a servitude upon the land of another." [2]

And, as stated by Swift, J., in Chalker v. Dickinson, it is always competent to rebut a presumption arising from the enjoyment of what answers to an easement, by proof of such circumstances as show that no grant could have been made.[3] As there can be no grant by a man to himself, nor an adverse use of his own land by one as against himself, it may *be regarded as a mere truism to say that no [*120] length of use of a way, for instance, by a man over one parcel of his land to another, can create an easement of way in favor of the latter parcel. No one can prescribe in his own land.[4]

75. But by the cases cited, as has been more fully explained in another connection, though a way, for instance, thus used for the benefit of one of two parcels of land over another belonging to the same owner, would not pass as appurtenant to such parcel upon a grant of the same, it might pass if the parcel were conveyed " with all ways." [5]

76. The following case has been selected, though somewhat complicated in its facts, as furnishing an illustration of several of the propositions to which the reader's attention has been called. The case is Watkins v. Peck, and was very elaborately and ably considered by Parker, C. J. The facts were briefly these. An aqueduct had been laid from a spring of water to the estate S., from which point an aqueduct was laid in 1796 or 1797 to the Bellows House, and had continued to run there till 1838. In 1812, aqueducts

[1] Felton v. Simpson, 11 Ired. 84.

[2] Wheateley v. Baugh, 25 Penn. St. 528.

[3] Chalker v. Dickinson, 1 Conn. 382.

[4] Atkins v. Bordman, 2 Metc. 457 ; Ritger v. Parker, 8 Cush. 145 ; Cooper v. Barber, 3 Taunt. 99 ; Gayetty v. Bethune, 14 Mass. 49.

[5] Staple v. Heydon, 6 Mod. 3.

were laid from the Bellows House to the estates of Gage and Watkins, by which the surplus water not needed at the Bellows House was conducted to these estates, and used there up to 1838.   Subsequent to 1812, Buffum laid an aqueduct from S. to his own house, and took a portion of the water which flowed from the spring to that point, and which did not flow to the Bellows House.   This he continued to use up to 1838.   In 1812, Cochrane became the owner of the estate S., and held it till his death in 1821, but never interfered with the use of either of the aqueducts.   He left four children, one a minor, to whom his estate passed.   In 1838, Peck purchased S. estate of these children, one [*121] of them still being a minor, and denied the *rights of Buffum and Bellows, and Gage and Watkins, to draw water by the aqueducts then in use.   Whatever rights they had to any of the aqueducts depended upon user and enjoyment, as no deeds had ever been made granting their use.

One objection to the claim of an easement in such aqueducts by an enjoyment thereof was, that, by the death of Cochrane in 1821, leaving one of his heirs a minor, and the estate S. having remained undivided till 1838, no user and enjoyment between these periods could gain an easement in the S. estate.   And the court held that such was the law, and that it made no difference that the other children had been of age during that time, since the easement claimed was of that which was of itself indivisible, and could not be used without being done adversely to the minor, and therefore could not be done at all, at least until partition had been made of the estate among the children, and the land through which the aqueduct passed had been assigned to another than the minor.   No grant could be presumed from adverse enjoyment against such minor, since no grant could be presumed against a person who was incapacitated to make it.   " It would be absurd," say the court, " to presume a grant where it was clear that no such grant could have existed." So far, therefore, as Buffum was concerned, it was held that he had not gained a prescriptive right to use the aqueduct to his estate. But inasmuch as the Bellows estate had enjoyed the aqueduct to that estate for more than twenty years before Cochrane's death, it had acquired the same as an easement. And as to the claims of Gage and Watkins, it was held that, as they took what water they used from the Bellows estate, and the surplus only of what flowed to that, their enjoyment of their aqueducts was not adverse to any one but the owner of that estate, and they were not affected by the minority of the heir of Cochrane ; and having enjoyed the use of their aqueducts for more than twenty years by the acquiescence *of the owner of the Bellows estate, they had ac- [*122] quired a prescriptive right to the same.[1]

But it seems to be settled now, as already stated, that, even if the prescription might be suspended during the minority of an heir, where the ancestor dies after an adverse enjoyment has begun, if enjoyed after such heir comes of age, the two periods of adverse user might be added together to make the requisite period of prescription.[2]

77. The cases above cited, as well as the express language of the courts in several cases, are directly opposed to the doctrine of Story, J., in Tyler v. Wilkinson, where he says : " By our law, upon principles of public convenience, the term of twenty years of exclusive uninterrupted enjoyment has been held a *conclusive* presumption of a grant or right. I say of a grant or right, for I very much doubt whether the principle now acted upon, however in its origin it may have been confined to presumptions of a grant, is now necessarily limited to considerations of this nature. The presumption is applied as a presumption *juris de jure*, wher-

---

[1] Watkins v. Peck, 13 N. H. 360 – 381.

[2] Melvin v. Whiting, 13 Pick. 184 ; Lamb v. Crosland, 4 Rich. 536. See Guernsey v. Rodbridges, Gilb. Eq. Cas. 3 ; La. Civ. Code, Art. 727. See Stat. 2 & 3 Wm. IV. c. 71, § 7, as to exceptions in case of disabilities of owners; *ante*, pl. 73.

ever, by possibility, a right may be acquired in any manner known to the law. Its operation has never yet been denied in cases where personal disabilities of particular proprietors might have intervened, — such as infancy, coverture, and insanity, — and where by the ordinary course of proceeding grants would not be presumed. In these, and like cases, there may be an extinguishment of right by positive [*123] limitations of time, by *estoppels, by statutable compensations and authorities, by election of other beneficial bequests, by conflicting equities, and by other means. The presumption would be just as operative, as to these modes of extinguishment of a common right, as to the mode of extinguishment by grant." [1]

In Lamb v. Crosland, the court insist, as already stated, that Story, J. did not make the proper distinction between a prescription, properly so called, and a presumption of a non-existing grant, the latter of which arises after an enjoyment for twenty years, the former goes beyond legal memory. [2] And Putnam, J., in Sargent v. Ballard, says: " We cannot suppose that the mere use of the easement for twenty years is conclusive of the right, nor do we think that was the meaning of Story, J., in Tyler v. Wilkinson. He could not have intended an enjoyment which had been by favor, and at the will of the owner for twenty years." [3] And in Watkins v. Peck, the Chief Justice says: " It would be absurd to presume a grant where it was clear that no such grant could have existed." [4]

This subject has already been treated of, and was only resumed from its connection with the doctrine of a suspen-

[1] Tyler v. Wilkinson, 4 Mason, 402. See also Mebane v. Patrick, 1 Jones, No. C. 23.

[2] Lamb v. Crosland, 4 Rich. 536.

[3] Sargent v. Ballard, 9 Pick. 251. See also 3 Kent, Comm. 444; Colvin v. Burnet, 17 Wend. 564; Nichols v. Aylor, 7 Leigh, 546; Yard v. Ford, 2 Wms. Saund. 175, note; Mayor of Hull v. Horner, Cowp. 102; Parker v. Foote, 19 Wend. 309, 315; ante, pl. 73.

[4] Watkins v. Peck, 13 N. H. 377.

sion of prescription, under certain circumstances, in case of a personal disability of the owner of a servient estate.

Nor does the distinction seem to be of sufficient practical consequence to occupy much time in its discussion. But it was resumed by the court of New Hampshire, in Wallace v. Fletcher, already referred to,[1] where it is said, " the current of English authorities has gone no further than to hold that long-continued and uninterrupted possession is evidence from which a jury may presume a deed." But the judge (Bell) maintains that, by the American law, such an enjoyment is something more than a presumption. He quotes 2 Greenl. Ev. § 539, and the authorities there cited, as well as sundry others, and concludes, that " this may properly be regarded as a species of prescription established here by a course of judicial decisions, by analogy to the statute of limitations of real actions." But the admission he makes of the exceptions there must be to this as a positive rule of prescription, really seems to leave it very much where the cases of Sargent v. Ballard and Watkins v. Peck had done, that, in order to be conclusive, it must be shown affirmatively to have all the qualities of an adverse enjoyment; 1, for the requisite time ; 2, against the owner of the estate who was in a condition to grant the easement, and who, 3, had knowledge of and did not object to the uses by which the right was acquired.

[1] Wallace v. Fletcher, 10 Foster, 446. See also Hall v. M'Leod, 2 Metc. Ky. 98, that twenty years' enjoyment is only evidence, it raises a presumption but not a prescription.

*1. IT has already been stated, that public corpo- [*125]
rate bodies, like the inhabitants of towns, may acquire
rights in the nature of easements, by continued corporate
acts of enjoyment, amounting to a prescription. The subject is in some respects so far distinct from mere private prescriptions, that it has been reserved for a place by itself,
to be followed by that of rights acquired by dedication,
though, as will appear, these differ in many essential par-
ticulars.

But the effect in the matter of ways, which is given, in
many cases, to a user, in establishing a public way and a
dedication of a way to public use, are so nearly identical,
that they can hardly be treated of separately. A way,
however, which is gained by a corporate body by prescription, properly so called, is limited to the use of those constituting that body. It is strictly a private easement, and
does not come within the category of public ways.

2. In a dissenting opinion, in Commonwealth v. Newbury,
Putnam, J. says: " I am of opinion that the inhabitants of
a town may prescribe for a way, as well as individuals." [1]
He cites a remark, " that the prescription may be that the
usage of the vill D. has been time out of mind that the inhabitants, &c., have had a way over the land of the plaintiff
to the church, &c., and that the inhabitants may prescribe
for an easement." [2]

In Commonwealth v. Low, the court say : " There is no
doubt that the inhabitants of a town, in their corporate
capacity, are capable of taking an easement or other incorporeal hereditament, and that they may become seized of a
right of way by grant, prescription, or reservation. A grant,
also, may be presumed from continued occupation, as well in
favor of a corporation as of an individual. . . . . If a grant of
the way be presumed, it will not support the indictment. It
will operate in favor of the town only, and will give no right

---

[1] Commonwealth v. Newbury, 2 Pick. 51.
[2] 17 Viner, Abr. 256 ; Nudd v. Hobbs, 17 N. H. 525.

[*126] of passage to any but the inhabitants. It *will be technically a private way, and any person other than an inhabitant passing upon it will be a trespasser."[1]

3. So in New York, the court held that the inhabitants of a town might gain a right of easement of pasturage by prescription or grant, and that, consequently, any inhabitant of the town might turn his sheep upon the land without thereby being a trespasser.[2]

4. So it was held that the inhabitants of a town might prescribe for a right to maintain a gate across a highway, when the same was necessary to preserve the grass in the close through which it leads.[3]

5. The language, however, of the courts in many cases would lead one to infer that ways for public use, whether town ways or public highways, might be established by prescription. Thus in Stedman v. Southbridge it is said: "It has been argued as if the question was, whether a town way, under any circumstances, can be proved by prescription or by presumption, arising from use and enjoyment. It is, perhaps, too much to say that such a way, or any other kind of easement cannot be thus proved, but it would be manifestly difficult, because, in general, the facts which would tend to prove the existence of such a way would prove the larger easement of a public highway."[4]

The use of a way by the public for twenty years gives a prescriptive right of a public as well as a similar user does of a private way, and this right, when once established, continues until it is clearly and unmistakably abandoned. A transient or partial non-user will not work an abandonment. It must be total, and of sufficient length of time.[5]

But to establish a public way by prescription, there must

[1] Commonwealth v. Low, 3 Pick. 408; Smith v. Kinard, 2 Hill, So. C. 642; Green v. Chelsea, 24 Pick. 71; Avery v. Stewart, 1 Cush. 496.
[2] Rose v. Bunn, 21 N. Y. 275.
[3] Spear v. Bicknell, 5 Mass. 124.
[4] Stedman v. Southbridge, 17 Pick, 162; post, p. *142.
[5] Lewiston v. Proctor, 27 Ill. 417.

have been a user for twenty years in substantially the same line and direction, and if a line once used is abandoned, and another adopted changing, in fact, the thread of the road, and it remains so for eight or nine years, it is not such a continuous use as to establish a presumptive right.[1]

So in Avery v. Stewart, it is said: " It may be difficult to decide whether the long user of a way by the inhabitants of a town, and by others, would authorize the presumption of its being a public highway or a town-way." [2]

Now, in all these cases, it is apprehended the court intended to speak of a way open for the use of all persons indiscriminately, whether known and called a town or a *public way or road,[3] and not a mere private way, [*127] belonging only to the inhabitants of a town.

The court say, in Commonwealth v. Low: " Ways of various kinds may be proved, not only by prescription, but by a continued and uninterrupted use of them for a period much within the memory of man. And it cannot be doubted that public highways may be shown by evidence of a user, as well as by the record of their laying out." [4]

And parol evidence of the existence and user of an ancient highway is admissible to establish it as such.[5]

So in Folger v. Worth, it is said: " It is now, we think, too late to contend that the existence of a highway cannot be proved by immemorial usage." [6]

6. From what has heretofore been said of the distinction between prescription, — where there is assumed to have been a grant, with a grantor and grantee, — and a custom, — where, from the nature of the case, if there is a grant and a

1 Gentleman v. Soule, 32 Ill. 278.

2 Avery v. Stewart, 1 Cush. 496.

3 Craigie v. Mellen, 6 Mass. 7 ; Commonwealth v. Low, 3 Pick. 408 ; Valentine v. Boston, 22 Pick. 75. See Nash v. Peden, 1 Speers, 17.

4 Commonwealth v. Low, 3 Pick. 412.

5 Green v. Canaan, 29 Conn. 167.

6 Folger v. Worth, 19 Pick. 108. See also Williams v. Cummington, 18 Pick. 312 ; State v. Hunter, 5 Ired. 369 ; State v. Marble, 4 Ired. 318 ; Nash v. Peden, 1 Speers, 17.

grantor, there is no grantee, the persons who were to enjoy under it being incapable of taking in their collective capacity, — there could, obviously, be no prescription, properly speaking, for a right in the public to use a way, for the reason that there is no grantee in the assumed grant. It comes under the category of dedications, and the court, in Valentine v. Boston, remark: " When those decisions [Commonwealth v. Newbury and Commonwealth v. Low] were made, the doctrine of dedication had not been recognized as the law of this State." [1]

In the last case, the plaintiff, and those under whom he claimed, had suffered a small piece of ground in front of his store to be used as a part of the street for a great [*128] length of *time, and it was held that the public had acquired an easement to use the same as a way. And where a man had opened a way across his land, which has been used as a highway for the term of twenty years, it was held that it might be treated as a public way, and one which he could not close. But if the user had been for a shorter period, the land-owner might close it. [2]   " Whether it may have been acquired by grant or dedication, or the presumption of a laying out, and whether it may be viewed as a private way for the town, or as a highway for the public, seem to us to be useless speculations."

This may be true in settling the question of damages then before the court. But, in its bearing upon other cases, it may not be so unimportant to fix whether the right claimed was gained by prescription or dedication, in respect to which such different rules will be found to prevail. To authorize a dedication does not require the existence of a corporation to whom it is made, or in whom the title should vest. It may be valid without any specific grantee *in esse* at the time, to whom the fee could be granted. And in this respect it forms an exception to the general rule of transferring or creating

[1] Valentine v. Boston, 22 Pick. 75.
[2] Estes v. Troy, 5 Maine, 368.   But see State v. M'Daniel, 8 Jones, L. 284.

an interest in lands, as it may be done without a deed, and
without any person competent to accept the grant as grantee.[1] The public is an ever-existing grantee, capable of taking a dedication for public uses.[2]

7. The court also recognize the distinction above referred
to, between a prescription and a dedication, as applicable to
ways for public use, in the case of Larned v. Larned,[3] where
there had been a way which the public had used for forty
years, across certain lots of land between certain termini.
The way across the plaintiff's close had been changed, eight
years previous to the action, by his consent and that of the
defendant, who was the plaintiff's grantor, and of the other
owners of the parcels over which the way passed, the termini
remaining the same. The court held this to be a
*dedication of the new way. They say a way may [*129]
be established by dedication of the owner of the soil,
with the assent of those who are interested in the way.
" And this," they add, " is true, not only of a highway, but
of a town-way, or a private way." By " private way," as
here used, must obviously have been intended that class of
ways known to the law of Massachusetts, which are laid out
by public authority under that name, and are open to the use
of the public, though designed for the accommodation of the
proprietors of particular estates ; for the court say, " Length
of use is not a necessary element, without which a dedication cannot be proved." And there was nothing in the case
which called for an overthrow of all preconceived and well-
settled rules in relation to a grant or prescription being necessary to gain an easement of a private way. Besides, in
Commonwealth v. Newbury,[4] the court say : " We do not see

1 Hunter v. Trustees of Sandy Hill, 6 Hill, 407 ; 3 Kent, Comm. 450 and note ;
Abbott v. Mills, 3 Vt. 521 ; State v. Wilkinson, 2 Vt. 480 ; Cincinnati v. White,
6 Pet. 432 ; Pawlet v. Clark, 9 Cranch, 292, 331 ; Kennedy v. Jones, 11 Ala. 63 ;
Brown v. Manning, 6 Ohio, 298.
2 Warren v. Jacksonville, 15 Ill. 236.
8 Larned v. Larned, 11 Metc. 421. See Lawton v. Tison, 12 Rich. 88.
4 Commonwealth v. Newbury, 2 Pick. 57. See Dawes v. Hawkins, 8 C. B.,

how the principle of dedication to the public can be applied to a private way, for the very evidence which would tend to show a dedication would disprove it as a private way."

A dedication is properly only to the public use; there can be no dedication, properly speaking, to private uses. A private pass-way cannot be created by dedication.[1]

Although the authority cited directly sustains the statement here made, it is apprehended that though there may not be technically a dedication of a way to private uses, there are many cases where, from acts like those of a dedication to a public use, rights are secured to individuals for their private benefit. Thus in laying out streets, alleys, &c., by the owner of land, who sells lots bounding upon them, it does not constitute them public streets until the public shall have, in some way, accepted and adopted them as such, and yet the proprietors of those lands have a right to the use of those streets beyond their being ways or easements by necessity. Thus, in Bissell v. N. Y. Central R. R., one M. opened a new street over his own land, and sold lots upon it. And the court say, " his grantees acquired the right to have the strip remain open for the purpose of a street." " By the sale of the lots, nothing passed to the several grantees but this right and a perpetual easement over this ground of egress to and from their lots." [2]

This must obviously be so, if, as is laid down in Holdane v. Trustees, &c.,[3] a way, in order to become a public highway by dedication, must be a thoroughfare, and, if a *cul de sac*, it could not be.

The language, however, of the court of Massachusetts upon this point is in a hypothetical form: " If a private way can be established between the parties by dedication, it must

___

N. s. 848; Pope v. Devereux, 5 Gray, 409, where the court seem to assume that " private way " in the above case was a private way at common law. See also Lawton v. Tison, 12 Rich. 88.

[1] Hale v. M'Leod, 2 Metc. Ky. 98; *post*, pp. *133, *141.
[2] 26 Barb. 633. See Clements v. W. Troy, 16 Barb. 251. See *post*, p. *138
[3] 23 Barb. 103.

appear to have been done with a full knowledge of the rights of the parties, thus indicating a clear intent by the party owning land to devote his land to such purpose, so as to give to others an irrevocable right to use it." [1]

8. The effect upon the public in the matter of right is so nearly identical, whether the way has become a public one by prescription or dedication, that the line of distinction between the two, as modes of acquiring it, is often overlooked. The case of Jennings v. Tisbury may be cited as recognizing, if it does not fully explain, the distinction. That was the case of a narrow lane in Tisbury through open, unenclosed lands, which had been used as a road by the public more than twenty years, and was determined irrespective of *any statute now in force in Massa-   [*130] chusetts on the subject of dedication.   There was no record in this case of a laying out of the road, and the plaintiff placed his claim that it was a public highway upon a dedication, because the town had not, under a statute authorizing them to give notice, disavowed it as a public way.   But the court treat of it as not being affected by that statute.   " This leaves untouched the case of public ways by prescription, and perhaps it would not be too much to say, that a large proportion of the public ways, whether they be considered public highways or town-ways, stand upon no other title but prescription.   No doubt, in the early settlement of the country, when lands were commonly granted to a company of proprietors, public ways were reserved when .the lands were surveyed and allotted, which have remained open and public ways to the present time, of which there is no record.   That these are in all respects highways, is a point too well established to require authorities.   To establish such a way, where there is no proof of dedication, and where the element of dedication does not subsist, it will be necessary to prove actual public use, general, uninterrupted, continued

---

[1] Atwater v. Bodfish, 11 Gray, 152 ; post, p. *142. For the distinction between a way by dedication and one by license, see post, p. *133.

for a certain length of time.   In general, it must be such as
to warrant a presumption of laying out, dedication, or appropriation by parties having authority so to lay out, or a right
so to appropriate, like that of prescription or non-appearing
grant in case of individuals.   It stands upon the same legal
grounds, a presumption that whatever was necessary to give
the act legal effect and operation was rightly done, though
no other evidence of it can now be produced except the
actual enjoyment of the benefit conferred by it."   And upon
the question of length of enjoyment requisite to raise the
legal presumption of its being a public highway, the judge
says : " It is put upon the ordinary ground of prescription
and presumption of a non-appearing grant or record, which
we now consider as fixed at twenty years.   If such evidence
      of the existence of a highway is proved, the court
[*131] are of *opinion that it will be sufficient, independ-
      ently of any such supposed dedication." [1]

Whether the foregoing opinion is open to criticism or not,
in failing to define what would be a dedication, so far as it
goes to establish the doctrine that there may be a public highway whose existence may be proved by prescription, independent of any evidence of an original dedication, the same is
reaffirmed by the court in the above-cited case of Durgin v.
City of Lowell.

9. The whole doctrine of dedication of easements to the
public use seems to be of comparatively modern date.   Thus
it is stated by Gibson, C. J., in Gowen v. Philadelphia Exchange Co.,[2] that the doctrine of dedication to the public,.
without the intervention of trustees, began in 1732, Rex v.
Hudson,[3] and was next applied in Lade v. Shepherd,[4] in
1735.   It then slept until 1790, in the case of Rugby v.
Merriweather.[5]

---

[1] Jennings v. Tisbury, 5 Gray, 73.   See Williams v. Cummington, 18 Pick.
312 ; Durgin v. City of Lowell, 3 Allen, 398 ; Valentine v. Boston, 22 Pick. 75.
[2] Gowen v. Phila. Exchange Co., 5 Watts & S. 141.
[3] Rex v. Hudson, 2 Strange, 909.
[4] Lade v. Shepherd, 2 Strange, 1004.
[5] Rugby Charity v. Merryweather, 11 East, 375.

In Wisconsin, it is declared to be a part of the common law of that State. So in Tennessee.[1]

In Hinckley *v.* Hastings, the court of Massachusetts doubt if the doctrine of dedication had ever been adopted in this Commonwealth. This was as late as 1824.[2]

But in Hobbs *v.* Lowell, the court, with one dissenting opinion, held that a highway could be established here by dedication. This was in 1837.[3]

The doctrine had gained currency slowly, for in the year before that, the same court, speaking of dedication, say : *" The doctrine of dedication, *if* it be adopted in [*132] this State," &c.[4]

The matter had been fully considered in the case of Cincinnati *v.* White,[5] in the Supreme Court of the United States, and settled in 1832, which was a case of dedication of an open square in a city ; and this had been preceded by the case of Pomeroy *v.* Mills, in 1830, in Vermont.[6]

It may now be assumed to be a settled doctrine, at common law, in this country generally. It can best be stated and illustrated by a reference to some of the cases which have occurred, with the language of the courts in respect to the same.[7]

10. Although the idea of dedication implies an appropriation of property, by the act of the owner, for the use and benefit of others, without any formal and specific contract between them, like the making and receiving of a grant by deed or otherwise, yet to a complete dedication there is assumed to be an acceptance of the offered benefit by those for whom it was intended. In the language of the court, in

---

[1] Gardiner *v.* Tisdale, 2 Wisc. 153 ; Connehan *v.* Ford, 9 Wisc. 240 ; Scott *v.* State, 1 Sneed. 632.

[2] Hinckley, *v.* Hastings, 2 Pick. 162.

[3] Hobbs *v.* Lowell, 19 Pick. 405.

[4] Green *v.* Chelsea, 24 Pick. 71.

[5] Cincinnati *v.* White, 6 Pet. 431.

[6] Pomeroy *v.* Mills, 3 Vt. 279.

[7] Pearsall *v.* Post, 20 Wend. 115, per *Cowen,* J., and cases cited. See *post,* chap. 3, sect. 9, pl. 17.

Green v. Chelsea, " Dedication must originate in the voluntary donation of the owner of the land, and be completed by the acceptance of the public." [1]

Nor can one of two or more tenants in common dedicate the common lands belonging to himself and his cotenants.[2]

11. And in respect to who may dedicate lands to public uses, the rule seems to be the same as in making grants of any kind. Thus the land of a married woman may be dedicated where the acts of herself and husband are such as to indicate an intention to do so. But it can only be done by one having the fee in the land.[3] It cannot be done by a trespasser or a tenant.[4]

12. To constitute a dedication of land to a public [*133] use, *there must first be an intention to do it on the part of the owner. And this must be unequivocally and satisfactorily proved. But it may be manifested by writing, by declaration, or by acts.[5] Dedications have been established in every conceivable way by which the intention of the party could be manifested.[6] Without that, no dedication can take place, and if, for instance, in opening a passageway of a character which might otherwise be deemed a public way, the owner of the land should place a gate at its entrance, by which such passage may be closed, it would be regarded as evidence negativing the intention to make it a public way. Nor would it become so by the gate being suffered to go to decay, or ceasing to be used. It was accordingly held, in Commonwealth v. Newbury,[7] that there must be a manifest intention to accommodate the public through a man's land, before he shall be held, by implication, to have

---

[1] Green v. Chelsea, 24 Pick. 71 ; Child v. Chappell, 5 Seld. 256.

[2] Scott v. State, 1 Sneed. 629.

[3] Schenley v. Commonwealth, &c., 36 Penn. St. 29 ; Ward v. Davis, 3 Sandf. 502.

[4] Gentleman v. Soule, 32 Ill. 279 ; State v. Atherton, 16 N. H. 208.

[5] Gentleman v. Soule, 32 Ill. 280 ; Godfrey v. Alton, 12 Ill. 29 ; Scott v. State 1 Sneed. 633.

[6] Waugh v. Leech, 28 Ill. 492.

[7] Commonwealth v. Newbury, 2 Pick. 51.

given it, so that even when, at the first opening of such way, a post only had been put up, which soon after was knocked down, and remained down for twelve years, and the passage had been uninterrupted all that time, it was determined that the owner might maintain trespass against those who used the way ; and the court cite, as sustaining that doctrine, Roberts v. Karr.[1]

The doctrine that the erection of a post or a gate at the entrance of a passage-way, or similar acts, may negative the intention of the owner to dedicate it, and thereby prevent it becoming a highway, is undoubtedly well sustained, both in England and this country.[2] But the modern authorities, it is believed, instead of holding one a trespasser who should pass over a way in a city apparently open for use, would hold that the very opening of the way would be a license to the public to use it, if it had the ordinary indicia of being intended for public convenience. It would otherwise serve as a trap to innocent passengers.[3]

If the owner of land open a way across it, having the ordinary indicia of an open way for the public, he would be considered as licensing its use so long as he keeps it open, although he may, by posts, gates, or public notice at its entrance, negative the dedication of it as a public way. Nor would one be liable in trespass for travelling over it while in this state. Nor would the city or town be liable to any one passing over it who should sustain damage by reason of its being defective or unsafe for travel. Nor would it make any difference that the way is a *cul de sac*, open at only one end. The measure of the implied license is fixed by the apparent use for which it is proposed and used. The traveller has no

---

[1] Roberts v. Karr, 1 Campb. 262, note. See also Woolr. Ways, 12; Lethbridge v Winter, 1 Campb 263, note

[2] Rugby Charity v Merryweather, 11 East, 376, note, Carpenter v. Gwinn, 35 Barb 395, 406, Proctor v. Lewiston, 25 Ill. 153, 2 Smith, Lead. Cas, 5th Am ed, 203.

[3] Stafford v Coyney, 7 Barnew & C 257, Bowers v. Suffolk Mg Co, 4 Cush. 332, Morse v Stocker, 1 Allen, 154, Commonwealth v. Fisk, 8 Metc. 238; Cleveland v. Cleveland, 12 Wend. 172.

occasion to inquire whether the way is a public or private one, so far as it is a question of license.[1]

The owner of the land would be estopped to deny that it was a highway if opened and used as such, though never accepted by the public.[2]

So where a manufacturing company opened a street on their own premises, and built houses upon each side, and wrought the way as a street, and the houses were occupied by the operatives employed in their works, but it had not been their intention to dedicate it as public way, and they had posted up at the opening of the street, " Private way," it was held to be such only, and the city was not responsible to a person who, in passing through it, sustained injury.[3]

And where the owners of two adjoining estates in a city, left an open space between their houses leading from the street to the rear of their lots, and suffered the public to pass over the same for thirty or more years, but the way had never been laid down upon any plot of the town or city, nor recognized as such by the municipal officers, and there was no evidence of an actual dedication of it having been made, it was held that one of the owners might enclose his part of the land, although the other had erected a building fronting upon this passage-way. Nor could any one, by merely passing over this way, have acquired a prescriptive right to use it as a way.[4]

[*134]   *The acts and declarations of the land-owner, indicating the intent to dedicate his land to the public use, must be unmistakable in their purpose and decisive in their character to have that effect. In one case, a landowner in the village of Newburgh, laid out a strip of land of the ordinary width of a street, from one public street to another, and wrought it, at the expense of several thousand dollars, into the condition of a street fit for public use.

1 Danforth v. Durell, 8 Allen, 244.
2 Greene v. Canaan, 29 Conn. 172.
3 Durgin v. Lowell, 3 Allen, 398.
4 Crossman v. Vignaud, 14 Louis, 176.

When he began to work it, he had gates at each end. He took down one as he progressed, and in the end he removed the other ; and while he was working it, people on foot and some in vehicles passed over it. After it was completed he replaced one of his gates. A citizen of the town insisted upon passing over it, on the ground that it was a dedicated way. The court held it was a question of intention on the owner's part. " The plaintiff must be shown, in the present case, to have declared by words or by actions, or both, his irrevocable intention to make this strip of land, forthwith, not merely a road, or a way of passage, but a public way." The taking down the gates here was accounted for by its being necessary in constructing the way. It was held not to be a dedicated highway.[1]

A similar doctrine was held in Proctor v. Lewiston, where a party fenced out a strip of land which the public used for a way. Whether it was a public way depended upon the intention with which this was done on his part. If once dedicated, it could not be retracted. But his acts and declarations at the time of making the road might be shown to negative such intention.[2]   And the question of dedication is always one of mixed fact and law.[3]

And in Poole v. Huskinson, it was held that the user of a way by the public is, at best, only evidence of intention on the part of the owner of the land to dedicate it, and that *a single act of interruption by the owner is of [*135] much more weight upon the question of intention, than many acts of enjoyment on the part of the public ; the use, without the intention to dedicate it as a public way, not being a dedication.[4]

[1] Carpenter v. Gwynn, 35 Barb. 395, 406.

[2] Proctor v. Lewiston, 25 Ill. 153. See Bowers v. Suffolk Mg. Co., 4 Cush. 332.

[3] Cowles v. Gray, 14 Iowa, 8.

[4] Poole v. Huskinson, 11 Mees. & W. 827 ; Barraclough v. Johnson, 8 Adolph. & E. 99 ; Stafford v. Coyney, 7 Barnew. & C. 257 ; Stacey v. Miller, 14 Mo. 478, no dedication, though used for fifteen years ; Dwinel v. Barnard, 28 Me. 554 ; Skeen v. Lynch, 1 Robins, Va. 186.

But " it is every day's practice to presume a dedication of land to the public use, from an acquiescence of the owner in such use." [1]   And the doctrine is well established, that a dedication of real estate to public use may be made by mere verbal declarations, accompanied with such acts as are necessary for that purpose.[2]

It is upon the ground of want of intention to dedicate it to the public, that no man, ordinarily, loses his right to enclose a strip of land lying between his buildings and the highway, though suffered to remain open to the same for ever so long a period of years.[3]

13. And where a way is opened as a private way, and intended as such, and this can be shown, no length of use by others will make it a public way.[4]

14. There may, moreover, be a dedication of land for special uses.   But it must be for the benefit of the public, and not for a particular portion of it.   A permissive use of a way by certain portions of the community constitutes a license, and not a dedication, and is ordinarily something that may be revoked.

Thus in Stafford v. Coyney, the land-owner suffered the public to use a road through his estate for several years for all purposes except that of carrying coals.   It was held, at best, to be but a partial dedication of the way as a highway to the public.   " The public must take *secundum formam doni ;* if they cannot take according to that, they cannot take at all." [5]

And though the judges in that case expressed doubts whether there could be such a partial dedication, the point was settled in Poole v. Huskinson, where it was held [*136] that *there might be a dedication to the public for a

. [1] Knight v. Heaton, 22 Verm. 483.

   [2] Hall v. M'Leod, 2 Metc. Ky. 104.

   [3] Gowen v. Phila. Exchange Co., 5 Watts & S. 141 ; Tallmadge v. E. River Bank, 26 N. Y. 108.

   [4] Hall v. M'Leod, 2 Metc. Ky. 98.

   [5] Stafford v. Coyney, 7 Barnew. & C. 257.

limited purpose, as for a foot-way, a horse-way, or a drift-way, though there cannot be a dedication to a limited part of the public.[1]

In Barraclough v. Johnson, the owner of the land opened the way for public use, upon an agreement by an iron company and the people of the hamlet to pay him five shillings a year, and to find cinders to repair the way with. It was held to be a revocable license only, and not a dedication, though it had been used by any person wishing to pass over it for nineteen years. Denman, C. J. says in that case: " A dedication must be made with intention to *dedicate*. The mere acting so as to lead persons into the supposition that the way is dedicated does not amount to a dedication, if there be an agreement which explains the transaction."

And in Hemphill v. City of Boston, the court held that it was competent to dedicate a way as a foot-way, without making the city liable to keep it in suitable repair for the passage of carriages.

15. Waiving, for the present, what would be sufficient evidence of a dedication, the purposes for which the use of land may be dedicated are various, and the effect of such a dedication varies according to the nature of the use to which the land is to be applied.[2]

Thus, by the civil law, if a thing was dedicated to sacred and religious uses, it ceased to belong to individuals, and a piece of ground became such by depositing within it a dead human body; and this conforms in some measure with the common law.[3]

*At common law, it has been held that there may [*137] be a dedication to public and pious uses, such as

[1] Poole v. Huskinson, 11 Mees. & W. 827; Barraclough v. Johnson, 8 Adolph. & E. 99; Gowen v. Phila. Exchange Co., 5 Watts & S. 141; Hemphill v. City of Boston, 8 Cush. 195. See Woolr. Ways, 13; The King v. Northampton, 2 Maule & S. 262; State v. Trask, 6 Vt. 355; Danforth v. Durell, 8 Allen, 244.

[2] Rowan v. Portland, 8 B. Monr. 248.

[3] Inst. 2, 1, 7 and 9; Bract., fol. 8; Abbott v. Mills, 3 Vt. 521; Pawlet v. Clark, 9 Cranch, 293, 331.

glebe land or land for the erection of a church, for the use of a non-existing church,[1] or for purposes of burial of the dead.[2]

So there may be a dedication of a spring of water to public use,[3] or land for a public square in a city,[4] or for a street or public highway,[5] or for a public quay or landing-place upon the bank of a river,[6] or for public commons, or for sites for court-houses or other public buildings,[7] and it would seem that " all sorts of easements and rights to enjoyment of land, whether for use or of pleasure, which may be acquired by an individual by grant or prescription, may also be acquired by the public by actual dedication."[8]

16. It is not necessary, in order to effectuate a dedication, that the owner of the land dedicated should part with the fee of the same. Nor is it inconsistent with an effectual dedication, that the owner should continue to make any and all uses of the same which do not interfere with the uses for which it is dedicated.[9] And where one who had dedicated a public way, between which and the land of a third [*138] person there was a ditch, and the latter, in order *to gain access from his land to the way, laid a bridge across the ditch, one end of which rested upon the way, it

[1] Pawlet v. Clark, 9 Cranch, 293.

[2] Beatty v. Kurtz, 2 Pet. 566, 583.

[3] M'Connell v. Lexington, 12 Wheat. 582.

[4] Cincinnati v. White, 6 Pet. 431 ; Commonwealth v. Alburger, 1 Whart. 469 ; 2 Smith, Lead. Cas., 5th Am. ed., 222.

[5] Denning v. Roome, 6 Wend. 651.

[6] New Orleans v. United States, 10 Pet. 662, 712; Gardiner v. Tisdale, 2 Wisc. 153 ; Godfrey v. City of Alton, 12 Ill. 29 ; Bolt v. Stennett, 8 T. R. 606.

[7] Hunter v. Trustees of Sandy Hill, 6 Hill, 407 ; Watertown v. Cowen, 4 Paige, 510 ; Abbott v. Mills, 3 Vt. 521.

[8] Post v. Pearsall, 22 Wend. 480, per *Verplanck* ; Rowan v. Portland, 8 B. Monr. 232.

[9] Abbott v. Mills, 3 Vt. 521 ; Hunter v. Trustees of Sandy Hill, 6 Hill, 407 ; State v. Wilkinson, 2 Vt. 480 ; Hobbs v. Lowell, 19 Pick. 405 ; Post v. Pearsall, 22 Wend. 451 ; Cincinnati v. White, 6 Pet. 431 ; Barclay v. Howell, 6 Pet. 498 ; Gardiner v. Tisdale, 2 Wisc. 153, 194 ; Connehan v. Ford, 9 Wisc. 240 ; Scott v. State, 1 Sneed. 632 ; Commissioners, &c. v. Taylor, 2 Bay, 290 ; Schurmeier v. St. P. & Par. R. R. 10 Min. 104.

was held that the owner of the soil, notwithstanding the dedication, might have trespass against the party who constructed the bridge.[1]

17. The doctrine of prescription is not applicable to the case of dedication, so as to require evidence of a long user in order to establish the right. A valid dedication may be made by a single act, if positive and unequivocal in its nature, and especially where purchases have been made upon the faith which the act was meant to induce. To constitute a public use, it is not necessary that the public at large, that is, all persons without distinction, shall be able or be entitled to share in its advantages, but it is sufficient that its advantages are meant to be shared, and may be shared, by the inhabitants, or a portion of the inhabitants, of a city, town, or village, or other locality. Though the above is the language of the court, Duer, J., in Ward *v.* Davis, and is believed to be, in most respects, sustained by other decided cases, it will be seen that a different doctrine is mentioned in other cases as to a dedication, properly speaking, being limited to certain portions of the public.[2]

18. It has accordingly been held, that the proprietors of town lots adjoining a street which has been dedicated to the public acquire, thereby, rights in the street of a private character distinct from that which the public have, and may have an action for damages for any obstruction in or injury to such street;[3] whereas, if one purchase a village or town lot bounded upon a public street, he acquires thereby no right of a private character, distinct from the use which every one of the public may claim, although the fee of his *land in fact extends to the centre line of the [*139] street, subject only to the public easement.[4]

[1] Lade *v.* Shepherd, 2 Strange, 1004.

[2] Ward *v.* Davis, 3 Sandf. 502.

[3] Indianapolis *v.* Croas, 7 Ind. 9; Haynes *v.* Thomas, Ibid. 38; Tate *v.* Ohio & Miss. R. R. Co., Ibid. 479. But see Mercer *v.* Pittsburg, &c. R. R. Co., 36 Penn. St. 99; *post,* pl. 25; *ante,* p. *129.

[4] Kimball *v.* City of Kenosha, 4 Wisc. 321. See Barclay *v.* Howell, 6 Pet. 498.

19. To constitute a dedication requires, however, no grant
or conveyance by deed or writing on the part of the owner
of the land.   If he shall do such acts *in pais* as amount to a
dedication, the law regards him as estopped *in pais* from denying that the public have a right to enjoy what is dedicated,
or from revoking what he had thus declared by his acts.
And there may be a dedication to the use of a town before
it shall have been actually incorporated, or it may be to the
public, — a body not capable of taking a grant, — the only
limit being, that what is dedicated is suited to the wants of
the community at large.[1]

20. And a dedication, when once made to and accepted
by the public, is in its nature irrevocable.[2]

If one make a dedication of his land to public uses, he will
be at liberty to revoke this at any time before the same has
been accepted, but not afterwards.[3]

21. If, in this connection, it is asked what length of time
is necessary in order to have a dedication become effectual,
it is believed there is no period or term of enjoyment necessary, as in the case of prescription.   Length of enjoyment
may be regarded, when the evidence of a dedication having
been made depends upon a user by the public of the thing
dedicated.   But as all that is requisite to constitute a good
dedication is, that there should be an intention and an act
of dedication on the part of the owner, and an acceptance on
the part of the public, as soon as these concur, the dedi-

---

[1] 2 Smith, Lead. Cas., 5th Am. ed. 209; Cincinnati *v.* White, 6 Pet. 431;
New Orleans *v.* United States, 10 Pet. 662, 712; Cady *v.* Conger, 19 N. Y. 256;
Haynes *v.* Thomas, 7 Ind. 38; Warren *v.* Jacksonville, 15 Ill. 236; Cole *v.*
Sprowl, 35 Me. 161; Skeen *v.* Lynch, 1 Robins. Va. 186; Vick *v.* Vicksburg, 1
How. Miss. 379; Connehan *v.* Ford, 9 Wisc. 240; Commonwealth *v.* Fisk, 8
Metc. 238; Ward *v.* Davis, 3 Sandf. 502; Wright *v.* Tukey, 3 Cush. 294.

[2] State *v.* Trask, 6 Vt. 355; New Orleans *v.* United States, 10 Pet. 662; Commonwealth *v.* Alburger, 1 Whart. 469; Missouri Institute, &c. *v.* How, 27 Mo.
211; Huber *v.* Gazley, 18 Ohio, 18; Rowan *v.* Portland, 8 B. Monr. 232, 247;
Ragan *v.* M'Coy, 29 Mo. 356; Scott *v.* State, 1 Sneed. 632; Dubuque *v.* Malony, 9 Iowa, 455.

[3] Baker *v.* St. Paul, 8 Min. 494.

cation is complete. Ordinarily, there is no other mode of
showing an acceptance by the public of a dedication,
than *by its being made use of by them, and this [*140]
must be sufficiently long to evince such acceptance,
depending, of course, upon the circumstances of each case.
It is not compulsory, at common law, upon the public to
accept the user of a way when offered;[1] but, when accepted,
the dedication is complete.[2] Six or seven years have, in some
cases, been held to be sufficient, and in no case has the time
been measured by that required to create a prescription.

As there may be a qualified or limited dedication, having
regard to the uses and purposes for which the thing dedicated may be applied, so there may be a limited or partial
acceptance of what has been dedicated in a more general
form, and in that case the dedication takes effect only in its
limited or qualified form. But when, and so far as the dedication is accepted, it takes effect, and the owner of the
soil is thenceforward excluded from reasserting his ancient
rights.[3] If, however, the only evidence of the dedication of
a way is its having been used as such by the public, such
user, in order to constitute sufficient evidence of such dedication, must have continued for at least twenty years.[4] And
it seems that it must have been so used as to show that the
public require it for their accommodation, and that the owner intended to dedicate it.[5]

[1] Fisher v. Brown, 2 B. & Smith, 770; Robbins v. Jones, C. B. 26 Law Rep.
291.

[2] Baker v. St. Paul, 8 Min. 494.

[3] Abbott v. Mills, 3 Vt. 521; Denning v. Roome, 6 Wend. 651; Woolard v.
M'Cullough, 1 Ired. 432; State v. Trask, 6 Vt. 355; State v. Marble, 4 Ired. 318;
Shaw v. Crawford, 10 Johns. 236; Post v. Pearsall, 22 Wend. 425; Gowen v.
Phila. Exchange Co., 5 Watts & S. 141; Green v. Chelsea, 24 Pick, 71; Bar-
clay v. Howell, 6 Pet. 498, 513; Cincinnati v. White, 6 Pet. 431; Woodyer v.
Hadden, 5 Taunt. 125; Pritchard v. Atkinson, 4 N. H. 1, 13; State v. Campton,
2 N. H. 513; Child v. Chappell, 5 Seld. 246; Carpenter v. Gwynn, 35 Barb. 395;
Schinley v. Commonwealth, &c., 36 Penn. St. 29; Connehan v. Ford, 9 Wisc.
240; Commonwealth v. Fisk, 8 Metc. 238; Scott v. State, 1 Sneed. 633.

[4] Hoole v. Attorney-General, 22 Ala. 190; Gould v. Glass, 19 Barb. 179;
Smith v. State, 3 N. J. 130; Hutto v. Tindall, 6 Rich. 396.

[5] State v. Nudd, 3 Fost. 327.

In Jarvis v. Dean, four or five years use of a passage-way by the public, with the full assent of the owner of the soil, was held sufficient to constitute it a thoroughfare.[1] While in Rugby Charity v. Merryweather, though, by fifty years' use of a way as a thoroughfare, it was held to have [*141] become a *public highway, which the owner of the soil might not close, it would have been otherwise if he had had a bar across the passage-way, which could be, and occasionally was closed, as this circumstance bore upon the question of intent.[2]

On the other hand, the court, in Woodyer v. Hadden, in speaking of the length of time requisite to effect a dedication, say : " If the act of dedication be unequivocal, it takes place immediately ; for instance, if a man builds a double row of houses opening into an ancient street at each end, making a street, and sells or lets the houses, that is instantly a highway." [3] User for a short time by express and unequivocal treatment of the strip of land as a street, is sufficient.[4]

22. In some States, as will more fully appear, there are statutes which prevent a way becoming a highway by a mere dedication to and user by the public. There are cases where the streets of a village, for instance, are laid out upon a plan of lots, and these are sold in reference to the plan, whereby the purchasers of the lots acquire rights of way along these streets as easements appurtenant to their lots, and yet the streets do not necessarily become dedicated to the public use, though used by the people having occasion to do so. Thus in Child v. Chappell, where a partition of a parcel of

---

[1] Jarvis v. Dean, 3 Bing. 447.

[2] Rugby Charity v. Merryweather, 11 East, 376, note. See Post v. Pearsall, 22 Wend. 425.

[3] Woodyer v. Hadden, 5 Taunt. 125. See also Hobbs v. Lowell, 19 Pick. 405 ; Woolr. Ways, 10 ; Child v. Chappell, 5 Seld. 246 ; Hunter v. Trustees of Sandy Hill, 6 Hill, 407, 414 ; Ward v. Davis, 3 Sandf. 502 ; Rhea v. Forsyth, 37 Penn. St. 503 ; Missouri Institute, &c. v. How, 27 Mo. 211 ; State v. Atherton, 16 N. H. 211.

[4] Bissell v. N. Y. Cent. R. R., 26 Barb. 635.

land into lots was made, with a part left for a mill-yard and a basin and a road, all laid down upon a plan, it was held to bind the parties to permit the parts thus indicated to be used for the purposes designated. " As between the parties, their heirs and assigns," say the court, " it fixes the servitude of a public way upon the land thus laid out as streets." But the Judge (Morse) was of opinion, that such an appropriation would not be a dedication as between the owners and the public. " I take a dedication to the public *of land for a public highway to be something [*142] more than an act of the owner of the land. The dedication is not complete or binding until accepted by a public user, or some other indication of acceptance. . . . . As a rule of wisdom, the acceptance of a dedication of land for public use may be presumed from the beneficial nature of the dedication."[1] The necessity of an acceptance by the public of a dedicated way before it can become a public way, seems to be admitted as almost an elementary principle. The difficulty lies in what shall be such an acceptance. Thus it is stated in Gentleman v. Soule, there must be an intention to dedicate on the part of the owner of the land, and an acceptance on the part of the public, evinced by acts such as taking charge of and repairing the highway by the proper county or town authorities.[2] In New Hampshire, it was held that there must be an acceptance which may be shown by twenty years' user without objection, or by making repairs or setting up guide-boards or other official recognition.[3]

23. In the case of Clements v. West Troy, the proprietors of that village laid out the same by a plan, upon which an alley was laid down, and house-lots were conveyed bounding on this alley. The court say: " As between the original proprietors and those to whom they conveyed, this act of the

---

[1] Child v. Chappell, 5 Seld. 246 ; post, chap. 2, sect. 3, pl. 6. See also Oswego v. Oswego Canal Co., 2 Seld. 257 ; Clements v. West Troy, 16 Barb. 251 ; Commonwealth v. Rush, 14 Penn. St. 186.

[2] 32 Ill. 280 ; ante, p. *126.

[3] State v. Atherton, 16 N. H. 210.

proprietors secured a right of way. But the alley thus designated, and in respect to which the purchasers of the lots
had acquired an indefeasible right of way, did not thereby
become a public highway. The dedication must be accepted.
The highway must be laid out. Until that is done, the alley
would remain the property of the original proprietors, subject to the right of way in those who had taken the deeds of
lots bounded upon the alley." [1]

24. The case of Bowers v. Suffolk Manufacturing Co. serves
further to illustrate how far there may be acts of dedication
of ways as public ways, so that, though not actually dedicated
so as to become a highway, the public may use them so long
as they are kept open, and yet the proprietors of lands over
which they pass, and those to whose estates they are appurtenant, may still have all the rights in respect to the same as
if they were strictly private ways. It was one of the instances
where an easement may become appurtenant to each of many
estates by a process like that of dedication, and be common to them all, without becoming a public easement, and
without detracting from the right of each, to whose
[*143] *tenement the right of easement has become appurtenant, to seek a private remedy for any injury to his
own enjoyment of the same. The facts were these. Certain
proprietors of an extensive tract of land, water-power, &c.,
laid out R. Street over the same from a county road to H.
Street (which they also laid out), and marked R. Street for
a carriage-way and public travel, and the same was used by
any person having occasion to do so, no gate nor barrier having been erected thereon. In 1832, after these acts done,
the proprietors sold to the defendants the lands lying on both
sides of the northerly end of R. Street, and the land over
which that part of the street was laid out, by an indenture
in which it was covenanted that the streets described therein

[1] Clements v. West Troy, 16 Barb. 251. See Child v. Chappell, 5 Seld. 246;
Rhea v. Forsyth, 37 Penn. St. 503; ante, p. *129; Holden v. Trustees, 23 Barb.
103.

should be maintained as roads, " for the common use of the parties hereto, their successors and assigns, each keeping in repair those parts which pass over their respective estates," and referring to a plan on which R. Street was laid down fifty feet wide from the county road to H. Street. In 1844 the proprietors sold the plaintiff a lot bounding on R. Street, with all privileges and appurtenances, on which he built a house and resided therein. Before this, four other house-lots on R. Street had been sold by the proprietors to other persons. In 1845 the proprietors sold at auction all their remaining lands on R. Street and in the neighborhood, reference being made to printed plans and conditions of sale. And on this plan R. Street was laid down fifty feet wide. One of the conditions of sale was as follows : " The streets mentioned in the catalogue, and laid down on the plans, are all to be reserved and kept open for the benefit of the abutters, but they are not all graded. Any street reserved, and not graded, may be altered or discontinued with the consent of all the abutters thereon." There were twenty lots then sold on R. Street, on which buildings were afterwards erected. In 1846 the city laid out R. Street as a public street over a part of the distance from the county road to H. Street, the plaintiff's house being upon the part thus laid out.

In *1847 the defendants dug up R. Street at a point [*144] beyond where it had been located as a highway, towards H. Street, for the purpose of putting in hydraulic works for their use, which rendered R. Street in that place for the time impassable ; and when the work should be completed, it would permanently occupy and obstruct a part of the fifty feet in width. For this obstruction the plaintiff brought his action. The question was, whether the plaintiff, as owner of a tenement on R. Street, had a right of action for this obstruction, at a point remote from his own estate, no special damage having been shown. It was insisted that, the way having become public by dedication, the remedy was by indictment, and that a private action would not lie without

13

showing actual damage to the plaintiff. The court held that, though this was true if such were the fact, the street had not been dedicated as a public highway. If it had simply been opened and used, it might be evidence of an intent to dedicate it. But in the deed of the land over which R. Street was laid out, it was to be maintained for the common use of the parties thereto, each keeping in repair those parts that passed over his respective estate. And, at the auction, the streets were reserved and kept open for the benefit of the abutters, and any street not graded might be discontinued by the consent of the abutters thereon. The use actually made by the public could not alter the intention with which the street was laid out, as thus indicated. But even if it was the intention of the proprietors to dedicate the street, it could only become such by the assent of the city, express or implied, so as to make the city liable for its repair. The landowners, in such case, might not be entitled to maintain trespass against any one who might pass over it while it remained open.[1] But they might shut up the way, and the right of passing over it would thereby be terminated, the opening of the street being a license, and not a grant or dedication.

The court held that the action could be maintained. [*145] "The plaintiff, by a grant from the proprietors *of the land over which R. Street had been laid out by them, did acquire a good title to the right of way claimed, for the disturbance of which the defendants are liable."[2]

25. But where a street has been actually dedicated to the public by the act and intent of the owner of the soil, and by what shows an acceptance by the public, it becomes a public highway, and the owners of the adjacent land, whether the original proprietors or purchasers under them, have no other rights in it than the adjoining owners of any other public highway.[3]

---

[1] *Ante*, p. *133.

[2] Bowers *v.* Suffolk Mg. Co., 4 Cush. 332. See Rowan *v.* Portland, 8 B. Monr. 232.

[3] Mercer *v.* Pittsburg, &c. R. R. Co., 36 Penn. St. 99. See *ante*, pl. 18.

And one who shall obstruct a dedicated highway, would be liable to an indictment, but not to a civil action by any one to recover the land over which it is laid.[1]

26. Citations might easily be multiplied, where streets have become dedicated as public highways, so far, at least, as the owner of the soil is concerned, although the same may never have been opened or wrought. And among them are cases where the owner of city lots has sold them by a plan on which streets have been designated by the proper officers to locate and establish the same, and has bounded the lots sold by such streets. The soil of the streets in such cases is dedicated thereby to the public use.[2] And the same was held in the case of the city of Pittsburg, without the same having actually been designated as highways by an officer qualified to locate the same.[3]

26 a. In some of the Western States there seems to be, sometimes by statute and sometimes by usage, a mode of dedicating streets, public landings, quays, squares, &c., in towns, by the proprietors laying down and describing these by plats upon the plan of the location of the town or village, and in some cases causing this plat to be recorded for general reference. Though, carrying out the notion of dedication at common law, these, in some measure, form a class by themselves. Several of these cases have already been cited. A few others have been collected for illustrating the subject. Thus, in Minnesota, a statute provides for dedicating lands for city purposes by recording a plat of the same duly acknowledged by the owners thereof, and certified by the surveyor. If this has been done it cannot be revoked by the owner. But if

[1] Commissioners v. Taylor, 2 Bay, 291.

[2] Matter of Thirty-second Street, N. Y., 19 Wend. 128; Matter of Twenty-ninth Street, N. Y., 1 Hill, 189; Wyman v. Mayor of New York, 11 Wend. 486; Livingston v. Mayor of New York, 8 Wend. 85; Matter of Thirty-ninth Street, N. Y., 1 Hill, 190; Matter of Seventeenth Street, 1 Wend 262, 270; Vick v. Vicksburg, 1 How. Miss. 379; Rector v. Hartt, 8 Mo. 448. See Underwood v. Stuyvesant, 19 Johns. 181, as to effect of commissioners refusing to open the street. Dubuque v. Malony, 9 Iowa, 455.

[3] Barclay v. Howell, 6 Pet. 498, 504.

streets are laid out by such plan or plans, they must have been accepted on the part of the public in order to be effectual. After they have been accepted they cannot be revoked. And acceptance may be evidenced by their being used by the public. The fee, however, remains in the dedicator.[1]

And although the plat or the record of it is defective, it may become a valid dedication, if the public accept it before it is withdrawn by the owner.[2]

So, in Indiana, the laying down of streets, &c., on a town plat, and recording the same, is a dedication of these to the public.[3]

The dedication of streets, &c., by laying them down upon plats of villages, is recognized as valid in Wisconsin.[4]

The same seems to be the law of Missouri, where all such plats are required to be recorded.[5]

In Iowa, where an owner lays down upon the plat of a town the streets, &c., and has it recorded, the title to such parts as are set apart for public use, or charitable, educational, and religious purposes, passes, thereby, to the public, but nothing outside of the lines upon the plat. So that, where the line of dedication next to the Mississippi river left a strip between that and the bank, it was held not to be a dedication of that strip. But no one but he who has the title can make a valid dedication. Nor does the dedication take effect until the public shall have accepted it.[6]

In Louisiana, a dedication will not be proved by a mere plat, unless the intention to dedicate the land is found on the plat itself, such as a designation of it as a street, a square, and the like.[7]

In Illinois, a dedication may be made by a survey and plat alone, without any declaration either oral or on the plat,

---

[1] Baker v. St. Paul, 8 Minn. 493, 494 ; Schurmeier St. P. & Pac. R. R., 10 Minn. 108.

[2] Ib. 491.   [3] Evansville v. Page, 23 Ind. 527.

[4] Sanborn v. Chicago, &c. R. R., 16 Wisc. 19; Yates v. Judd, 18 Wisc. 118.

[5] Rev. St. c. 148 ; Callaway Co. v. Nolley, 31 Misso. 393.

[6] Cowles v. Gray, 14 Iowa, 1 ; Grant v. Davenport, 18 Iowa, 186.

[7] David v. New Orleans, 16 Louis. An. 404.

where it is evident, from the face of the plat, that it was the intention to set apart certain grounds for public uses, even if the ways shall not have been actually used by the public. And such a plat of a town and street may operate as a dedication of the ways, though not so recorded as to pass the fee to the city corporation.[1]

26 b. But while it is not difficult to lay down intelligible rules as to what shall be an act of dedication, it is far more difficult to define what is to be received as sufficient evidence of an acceptance on the part of the public to consummate and give effect to such dedication. In Connecticut, the court divided upon the point, two of the judges holding that something more than mere user by the public was requisite to constitute the acceptance of a dedicated way.[2]

But in a subsequent case, the court reviewed the law of dedication, and held that, as there are no statutes upon the subject, it is governed by the common law, that if one dedicates his land to the public, he is estopped from recalling the act, and an acceptance by the public may be presumed, if the thing dedicated be of public convenience and necessity, and therefore beneficial to the public. Among the direct evidences of this would be an express acceptance by the town, a reparation of the way, for instance, by its officers, a tacit acquiescence in its public use, recognizing it in maps, boundaries in deeds, or reference to it in advertisements, and especially its public use as a highway without objection, by all who have occasion to use it as such.[3]

By the English common law, any man might dedicate a highway to the public, which thereupon was to be kept in repair by the people of the parish or township. But this was altered by the statute of 5 & 6 Will. IV., requiring sundry preliminary things to be done before such a way can be made a public charge.[4]

---

[1] Waugh v. Leech, 28 Ill. 492; Godfrey v. Alton, 12 Ill. 35; Banks v. Ogden, 2 Wall. U. S. 57.

[2] Green v. Canaan, 29 Conn. 172.

[3] Guthrie v. New Haven, 31 Conn. 321.

[4] Reg. v. Dukinfield, 4 B. & Smith, 172.

The question has come up, several times, in Vermont. In the first of these it was held that mere use of a way by common travel was not enough, it required some act of the town by their officers recognizing the road to be a public highway, to make it such.[1] In the next, a miller had opened a way from his mill to the highway, and it had been used for many years. But the court held, that though a way may be proved to be a highway by its having been recognized as such by a town, by doing labor upon it, or authorizing the surveyor to collect and expend the highway tax upon it, no individual can lay out a way for his benefit, and compel the town to adopt it.[2] But in the next case it was held that the town might adopt a highway for travel, and thereby become liable on account of the same. If the town or selectmen as their agents were to shut up an old road, and have no other avenue for travel except on a road which they had made or caused to be worked, or if they put the same into the rate-bills of the highway surveyors on which the highway tax is to be worked, the town would be liable. But the *consent merely* of the selectmen, that any person should travel on any path, whether a public or private road, is no *act* by which the town is made responsible, nor would the knowledge of the selectmen, that the traveller supposed it to be a public highway, have that effect.[3]

The last of the cases was one where a bridge in a highway had been carried away, and the public had used a ford across the stream, which was wholly outside of the line of location of the original way, for the term of twenty days, and the question was, if the town were liable for the condition of this ford as being a dedicated way. The court say, that to make a public way by dedication, there not only must be a dedication by the owner of the land, but an acceptance by the town. Nor would acts of highway surveyors adopt such a

[1] Bailey *v.* Fairfield, Brayt. 128.

[2] Paige *v.* Weathersfield, 13 Verm. 429.

[3] Blodgett *v.* Royalton, 14 Verm. 294.

road, since that is not within their agency. Nor is it enough
that the town has suffered the way to be travelled. But
Redfield, C. J., in a dissenting opinion, held that the town
would be liable, if they suffered a road to remain open to
public use, and one sustained an injury by reason that the
same was unsafe for such use.[1]

In Michigan, although the governor and judges of the
Territory, in laying out the city of Detroit, had laid down
streets and alleys upon the plat, it was held that before this
dedication could become effectual in respect to any of these
streets, it must have been accepted by the proper authorities
on behalf of the public, and manifested by some act, such as
ordering it to be opened, or doing acts of improving or regulating the same.[2]

In Illinois, where a canal company had erected a bridge
over the canal, in a street of the town, it did not render the
town liable in consequence of its condition, unless the town
had adopted it as a way, or the approaches to it had been
constructed by the town, fitting it for use by the public, and
the like.[3]

In New York, the question has come up in different forms,
and it is difficult to draw from the cases any uniform rule
upon the subject. Thus it is said that a way may be dedicated, and will become a highway, when laid out as such by
the constituted authorities, by an acceptance of the dedication by those authorized to act for the public. But it is not
competent for an individual, by a simple act of dedication,
to impose upon the public the burden and responsibility of
maintaining a highway. Nor will the mere use of the way
by the public make an acceptance, if for a less time than
twenty years. Nor could the public prosecute the one who
had dedicated it, for having shut it up before the same was
accepted.[4]

---

[1] Hyde v. Jamaica, 27 Verm. 443.   See Coggswell v. Lexington, 4 Cush. 307.
[2] Tillman v. People, 12 Mich. 401 ; People v. Jones, 6 Mich. 176.
[3] Joliet v. Verby, 35 Ill. 58.
[4] Trustees, &c. v. Otis, 37 Barb. 50.

In another case the court held that the acceptance must be by some express corporate or official act, or *by user, distinct and unequivocal,* of such street as a public road or highway.[1]

But in Holdane *v.* Trustees, it was held by the other judges, against Strong, J., that a dedicated way may acquire the character and qualities of a highway, if it has been openly used as such, though there had been no formal act of acceptance done by the public authorities, and that it then becomes a way for all persons.[2]

And in one case in Massachusetts, where streets had been laid out in anticipation of the future wants of the town, and a plan of these made which was regarded as a dedication of these by the owners of the land, it was held that appropriating money and labor in working any of these, was an acceptance of such as were thus wrought by the town, and made them " complete highways." [3]

27. But in case of the dedication of a public square for the accommodation of county buildings, for instance, and they are erected upon another locality, or for that of a church, which is erected and afterwards removed [*146] to another *locality, the owners of the soil may resume the possession and occupancy of the land, and the public right therein ceases. It might be otherwise if, under such a dedication, the square had been enclosed and ornamented for public use, and the public had actually enjoyed it for purposes aside from a mere space for the accommodation of the public buildings.[4]

28. In Trustees of Watertown *v.* Cowen, this doctrine seems to be extended to all cases where, to use the language of the court, " the owners of urban property have laid it out into lots, with streets and avenues intersecting the same, and have sold their lots with reference to such plat. It is too

1 Bissell *v.* N. Y. Cent. R. R., 26 Barb. 634.
2 23 Barb. 123.
3 Wright *v.* Tukey, 3 Cush. 295.
4 Commonwealth *v.* Fisk, 8 Metc. 238, 245 ; State *v.* Trask, 6 Vt. 355.

late for them to resume a general and unlimited control over
the property thus dedicated to the public as streets, so as to
deprive their grantees of the benefit they may acquire, by
having such streets kept open. And this principle is equally applicable to the case of similar dedications of lands in a
city or village, to be used as an open square or a public
walk." [1]

29. But although the mode of dedicating land to the public use may be substantially the same, whether it be for a
highway, a public square, or a public common, yet the uses
and purposes intended being different, the character of the
easements acquired in the lands dedicated will vary according to the nature of these uses. Thus, if it be a public way,
every one may pass over it at his will and convenience, in
any usual and suitable mode of travelling. But if it be a
public common or square in a village, the same may be enclosed, improved, and ornamented in any suitable manner
by the authorities of the town or village, at their discretion, for purposes of health, recreation, or business,
*and the public must conform to these in their use [*147]
of the same.[2]

Nor will the law extend an easement, which is claimed by
construction from an alleged dedication by a sale of city lots,
in which reference is made to plans, &c., beyond what may
fairly be supposed and understood to be appurtenant to the
particular lot sold, and to be enjoyed therewith. Thus,
upon the sale of a township, a plan of the lots into which it
was divided was exhibited at the sale, having streets, squares,
&c., thereon, and, among other things, lots designated as sites
of churches. One of these was indicated as the site of a Bap-
tist church, although no such society had then been organized.

[1] Trustees of Watertown v. Cowen, 4 Paige, 510 ; Rives v. Dudley, 3 Jones,
Eq. No. C. 126. See Barclay v. Howell, 6 Pet. 498, 507, as to effect of misapply-
ing lands dedicated for particular purposes.
[2] Langley v. Gallipolis, 2 Ohio St. 107 ; Rowan v. Portland, 8 B. Monr. 232 ;
Wellington Petitioners, 16 Pick. 87 ; Commonwealth v. Rush, 14 Penn. St. 186,
190.

Such a society subsequently took possession of the lot, and erected a church thereon, and proposed to sell the remainder of the lot. The other purchasers of lots objected, and insisted that they had an easement in this lot, not to have it appropriated to other than church purposes. Nothing had been said in the deeds of any of the lots of any easements belonging to the same, and the court held that no such right as was here claimed passed as incident to.the lots at the time of the original purchase.[1]

30. But it is not, after all, the laying down of streets or squares upon the plat of a contemplated city or village, even though the same may be publicly exhibited or declared by the proprietors thereof, that constitutes a dedication of these to the public. There must be a sale of some of these lots, having reference to such streets or squares, and some adoption thereof by the public as such, in order to create a dedication of these to the public use.[2]

[*148]   *31. And in several of the States, a mere user of streets or ways, as such, by the public, does not constitute an acceptance or adoption of them as highways by dedication, unless there shall have been a location of the same, as public ways, by the proper officers of the town, city, or county, authorized by the statutes of the State to make such location. The statutes in these States supersede or control the common law in this respect. Such is understood to be the case in New York, Virginia, and Massachusetts.[3]

The above cases in New York were those of streets or ways laid out by the proprietors of village lots. And in that of Clements v. West Troy, the court say : " It is assumed in all

[1] Chapman v. Gordon, 29 Ga. 250.

[2] Logansport v. Dunn, 8 Ind. 378; Child v. Chappell, 5 Seld. 246; Badeau v. Mead, 14 Barb. 328; People v. Beaubien, 2 Dougl. Mich. 256; Rowan v. Portland, 8 B. Monr. 232; Vick v. Vicksburg, 1 How. Miss. 379; Westfall v. Hunt, 8 Ind. 174; People v. Jones, 6 Mich. 176; Tillman v. People, 12 Mich. 405; Bissell v. N. Y. Cent. R. R., 26 Barb. 634; David v. N. Orleans, 16 Louis, An. 406. See Green v. Canaan, 29 Conn. 171; Elsworth, J., dissenting opinion.

[3] Oswego v. Oswego Canal Co., 2 Seld. 257; Clements v. West Troy, 16 Barb. 251; Commonwealth v. Kelly, 8 Gratt. 632.

these cases that the mere dedication of a street to a public use does not make it a public street, until the dedication is ratified by the public authorities. The same proceedings must be had for opening or laying out such street as if there had been no dedication." [1]

32. In Connecticut, it seems all that is necessary to create a way dedicated to the public a public highway, is evidence that it has been used as such and accepted as such, and this may result from a public use and enjoyment, though such use have not continued for the ordinary period of prescription.[2]

It seems, therefore, to be a mere question of evidence of acceptance, for it was said in Holmes v. Jersey City, that " an individual cannot, by opening a road upon his own land, burden the public with maintaining and repairing it, or constitute it a public highway, within the meaning of the road act. The public were at liberty to accept this dedication in whole or in part, or utterly to disregard it. . . . . *The mere fact of dedication by map and [*149] survey, and the opening the streets as laid out, did not constitute them public highways, until such street was in some way accepted and ratified by public authority." [3]

33. The subject has been, of late, fully considered in Massachusetts, in connection with a statute of that State relating to the same. The case of Hobbs v. Lowell, decided in 1837, was the first in which the doctrine of dedication of a highway was adopted in that State. In 1846 a statute (chap. 204) was passed, declaring that " No way hereafter opened and dedicated to the public use shall become chargeable upon any city or town," unless laid out in a manner prescribed by statute. The general statutes adopt this pro-

[1] Clements v. West Troy, 16 Barb. 251, 253.

[2] Curtiss v. Hoyt, 19 Conn. 154; Noyes v. Ward, 19 Conn. 250, 265. See also, in New Jersey, Holmes v. Jersey City, 1 Beasl. 299; and, in Louisiana, David v. 2d Municipality, 14 La. Ann. 872.

[3] Holmes v. Jersey City, 1 Beasl. 299. See David v. 2d Municipality, 14 La. Ann. 872.

vision, and also declare that a mere grading of a street, in pursuance of an order of the officers of a city or town, shall not be construed a dedication of the same to the public use.[1] The case of Jennings v. Tisbury,[2] before cited, was one where the way had become public by prescription, and in Hayden v. Attleborough,[3] the court held the town liable, they having, without any formal dedication of the way, treated it as such, and assumed to work and repair it as a highway.

But in Bowers v. Suffolk Manufacturing Company,[4] the court were inclined to deny that a way could, after the statute of 1846, become a public one by dedication. And in Morse v. Stocker,[5] the court use this language: " No way or street could be made a public way by merely throwing it open to the public, or permitting the public to use it, without the assent of the public authorities, and its ac-
[*150] ceptance *by them as a street; and this assent and acceptance, after the statute of 1846, could only be given by laying out the street according to the ordinary mode prescribed by law."

And in Gurney v. Ford, where there was a public highway near a mill, and out of this a lateral way led across the stream, around the mill, and back again into the public way, which people were accustomed to use in going to the mill, and when the highway in that place was out of repair, and when they wished to water their horses at the stream, it was held not to have become a highway, the town never having done anything to it as such.[6]

34. But the limitation of the power of dedicating lands to public uses in Massachusetts, under the statute, as well

---

[1] Hobbs v. Lowell, 19 Pick. 405 ; Mass. Gen. Stat., chap. 43, §§ 82, 86.

[2] Jennings v. Tisbury, 5 Gray, 73,

[3] Hayden v. Attleborough, 7 Gray, 338.   See also Wright v. Tukey, 3 Cush. 295.

[4] Bowers v. Suffolk Mg. Co., 4 Cush. 332, 340.

[5] Morse v, Stocker, 1 Allen, 150.   See Durgin v. City of Lowell, 3 Allen, 398,

[6] Gurney v. Ford, 2 Allen, 576.

as in other states, seems to be confined to ways, and is
adopted for the purpose of avoiding the liability to which
towns might otherwise be subjected in case of a want of repair of such ways.   But the law remains, it would seem, as
at common law, in respect to public squares and other subjects of dedication.

35. And it may be added, that, as to ways, it is not competent for the public to make them public without their
being located by proper authority, and thereby to impose
duties and burdens, in respect to the same, upon the land-
owners, by a mere use of them against the intention of such
land-owners to dedicate the same.   Thus, where the public
were accustomed to go over the land of a corporation which
had constructed a private way for the accommodation of the
dwelling-houses of their operatives, and a person travelling
through the same sustained an injury from an alleged want
of repair, it was held that the city was not liable therefor.[1]
So, where the public were in the habit of going across another's land to shorten the distance of the neighboring highway, but in so doing were *trespassers, the [*151]
same being against the wishes of the land-owner, it
was held that the public had not, by these successive tres-
passes, acquired such a right of way over said land, that, if
the owner have occasion to dig a pit in his land, and a person passing over the same were to fall into it, he could have
an action to recover damages occasioned by such injury.[2]

And where the owner of land in a city laid out a street
over it, and sold house-lots thereon, but did not dedicate the
same to the public, nor had the public used it but a part of
the distance, on account of obstructions therein, but had
been permitted for many years to pass over a part of it, and
the officers of the city undertook to order the grade of the
street under the stat. 1853, chap. 135, and to require the owners of the street to cause the same to be made, it was held that

[1] Durgin v. City of Lowell, 3 Allen, 398.
[2] Stone v. Jackson, 16 C. B. 199 ; Commonwealth v. Fisk, 8 Metc. 238.

the act was unconstitutional, inasmuch as the owners had a right to use their land as they saw fit, in a manner not injurious to others; and permitting it to be used by the public did not make it public property, since it was a mere license, revocable at pleasure.[1]

So in Woodyer v. Hadden, the owner of the land opened a *cul de sac* from a public street in a city, upon which he built houses on each side, and the same was closed at one end by a fence between his and the land of an adjoining owner; and this had been opened in this state for twenty-one years, and had had houses upon it for nineteen years, when the latter owner removed this fence so as to open the *cul de sac* into a way across his land. It was held not to be a way dedicated to the public use, because the evidence showed that such was not the intention of the owner when he opened it.[2]

36. Without attempting further to lay down any [*152] general *rules whereby to distinguish between a public use by license, and a dedication of ways, public squares, and the like, the following cases may be referred to as illustrations from which these rules may be drawn in their application to particular cases. Thus it is said : " To lay off a road through one's plantation, and for his own convenience, cannot be construed into a dedication of it to public use. If it has become a public market-road, or even if he had permitted a church or other public buildings to be built at the end of the avenue, it might have admitted of that construction." [3]

37. In Gowen v. Philadelphia Exchange Co., Gibson, C. J., while commenting upon the difference between a dedication and a license, and whether the one construction or the other should be ascribed to the fact of leaving an open space

---

[1] Morse v. Stocker, 1 Allen, 150 ; Mass. Gen. Stat., chap. 43, § 85.

[2] Woodyer v. Hadden, 5 Taunt. 125. See Woolr. Ways, 11. People v. Jackson, 7 Mich. 432 ; Tillman v. People, 12 Mich. 400 ; Holdane v. Trustees, 23 Barb. 103. But see Wiggens v. Tallmadge, 11 Barb. 457.

[3] Witter v. Harvey, 1 M'Cord, 67.

before one's premises which is accessible to the public, refers to cases where it has been held that, by opening a street which is closed at one end, the owner indicates decisively that it is not intended to be a thoroughfare. And he adds: "There are a thousand circumstances connected with a man's calling which imply a license to enter his premises, subject to his regulation and control. The publican, the miller, the broker, the banker, the wharfinger, the artisan, or any professional man whatever, licenses the public to enter his place of business, in order to attract custom. But when the business is discontinued, the license is at an end. It is a license which is dependent on the use of property to which it is annexed, and which cannot, without permission of the owner, be annexed to anything else." And it was accordingly held, that a piece of land left open for the accommodation of the owner was not thereby dedicated to the public.[1]

On the other hand, where the owner of a narrow strip of land, lying between the highway and the enclosed land of a *third party, suffered this strip to lie unen-   [*153] closed, it was held to be so far a dedication of it to the public, that an action would not lie for passing over it against a stranger, as otherwise it would serve as a trap to the traveller.[2]

38. In the case of New Orleans v. United States, the dedication was of a quay along the bank of the river, on which goods were landed from vessels. It was held that, not only was the quay dedicated to the use of the city, but that it carried with it, and embraced within such dedication, the gradual increment by alluvion formed by the river. It was also held that, where public land had been dedicated by the government to a public use, it was withdrawn from commerce; and so long as it continued to be thus used, it could not become the property of an individual.[3]

---

[1] Gowen v. Philadelphia Exchange Co., 5 Watts & S. 143.

[2] Cleveland v. Cleveland, 12 Wend. 172.

[3] New Orleans v. United States, 10 Pet. 662, 712; Rector v. Hartt, 8 Mo. 457; Commonwealth v. Alburger, 1 Whart. 469, 485.

But the public have no highway along the margin of the navigable rivers and lakes in New York, unless the same shall have been acquired by express grant or prescription.[1]

39. In State v. Trask, a deed had been made by a grantor to individuals who were empowered to convey the premises to the county, to be used as a yard or green for the State and county buildings. It was held that this deed was evidence of an intent to dedicate the land to public use, and it did not require a second deed to the county to effectuate this; that if such second deed had been made, and the county had, by deed, relinquished the land, it would not have defeated the dedication, — a dedication to the public being in its nature irrevocable. "All that seems necessary," say the court, "is that the owner shall clearly manifest an intention to dedicate the land to public use, and that the public should, relying upon that manifestation, have entered into the use and occupation of it, in such manner as renders it unjust and injurious to reclaim it. . . . . . It is not only necessary that there be some act of dedication on the part of the owner, but there must also be something equivalent to an acceptance on the part of the public. . . . . . Towns [*154] *and cities may be projected, streets, public squares, and roads may be laid out; but if no town or city is built, there is no effectual dedication." It was held further, that there might be a partial acceptance of what had been dedicated, and beyond such partial acceptance the dedication would be defeated.[2]

40. In the case of Abbott v. Mills, the dedication was of a public square left in a village, around which the inhabitants had built their houses; and it was held a sufficient dedication, that the proprietors of the town had exhibited such a square upon the plan of the town, and had suffered persons to go on and incur expense in erecting their houses,

[1] Ledyard v. Ten Eyck, 36 Barb. 127.

[2] State v. Trask, 6 Vt. 355, 364, 367 ; Commonwealth v. Fisk, 8 Metc. 238, 243, 244. See Noyes v. Ward, 19 Conn. 250 ; Oswald v. Grenet, 22 Texas, 94 ; Cincinnati v. White, 6 Pet. 431.

although they had not marked off the same by monuments upon the ground, and they were accordingly prohibited from making use of the land for purposes inconsistent with its use as a public square.[1]

And it was held, in the above cases from the Vermont reports, that " the enjoyment of a public highway, square, common, or other common privilege or immunity, for a period short of fifteen years (the period of limitation), may afford conclusive evidence of a right so to do." [2]

41. The subject of dedication of lands to public uses is fully considered in Hunter *v.* Trustees of Sandy Hill, by the court of New York, in which several of the cases above cited are referred to. " Lands," say the court, " may be dedicated for pious and charitable uses, as well as for public ways, commons, and other easements in the nature of ways, so as to conclude the owner who makes the dedication. . . . . A dedication may be made without writing, by act *in pais,* *as well as by deed. It is not at all neces- [*155] sary that the owner should part with the title which he has, for dedication has respect to the possession, and not the permanent estate. Its effect is not to deprive a party of his land, but to estop him, while the dedication continues in force, from asserting that right of exclusive possession and enjoyment which the owner of property ordinarily has. Where, as in the case of a highway, the public acquire but a mere right of passage, the owner, who makes the dedication, retains a right to use the land in any way compatible with the full enjoyment of the public easement." [3]

But if he or any other person put obstructions in such way as renders the travelling over it unsafe, he who placed them

---

[1] Abbott *v.* Mills, 3 Vt. 521 ; State *v.* Catlin, 3 Vt. 530 ; Pomeroy *v.* Mills, 3 Vt. 279 ; State *v.* Wilkinson, 2 Vt. 480 ; Cincinnati *v.* White, 6 Pet. 431 ; Cady *v.* Conger, 19 N. Y. 256 ; Doe *v.* President, &c. of Attica, 7 Ind. 641 ; Commonwealth *v.* Rush. 14 Penn. St. 186.

[2] Abbott *v.* Mills, 3 Vt. 521 ; State *v.* Catlin, 3 Vt. 530.

[3] Hunter *v.* Trustees of Sandy Hill, 6 Hill, 411 ; Tallmadge *v.* E. River Bank, 26 N. Y. 108 ; Dubuque *v.* Malony, 9 Iowa, 455, 456.

14

there would be liable in damages to any one who should receive an injury while passing over it with proper care.[1]

But if there be an erection or excavation existing in the way, when it is dedicated, the owner is not liable for accidents thereby occasioned. The public accept the way subject to the inconvenience or risk arising from the existing state of things.[2]

42. Though the doctrine of the case above, of Trustees of Watertown v. Cowen,[3] may be considered as settling the respective rights of the owner of the soil of such a street or square, and of those who may have built houses or purchased lots bounding upon the same, it does not seem to cover the question how far the public can be made responsible for the safe condition of such streets, when used by others for the general purposes of a way or thoroughfare.

In one case in England, Bayley, J. held that there might be a dedication of a way to the public by the land-owner, and yet the public not be liable for the repair of the same; and that to make a parish liable for repairs of a way, there must have been some act of acquiescence or adoption of it as a public way on their part.[4]

Whatever may be the rule of law applicable to the [*156] cases *above supposed, it seems to be now settled that the proper authority to take charge of what has thus been actually dedicated is the local corporate body within which the same is situate, having charge of similar interests, and this from the incapacity of an indefinite entity like " the public " to manage or take care of the same.[5]

A question of this kind came up in respect to a public square in Philadelphia, which Penn had dedicated to the

[1] Corby v. Hill, 4 C. B. N. s. 556.
[2] Fisher v. Prowse, 2 B. & Smith, 770; Robins v. Jones, C. B. 26 Law Rep. 291.
[3] Trustees of Watertown v. Cowen, 4 Paige, 510.
[4] The King v. St. Benedict, 4 Barnew. & Ald. 449. See Hobbs v. Lowell, 19 Pick. 405.
[5] 2 Smith, Lead. Cas., 5th Am. ed. 222.

city. It was held that, after such a dedication, the owner of the soil could not grant away an exclusive right to any part of it. Nor could any length of occupation destroy·the right of the public, in the absence of positive statute, short of a strict prescription. " Public rights cannot be destroyed by long-continued encroachments; at least, the party who claims the exercise of any right inconsistent with the free enjoyment of a public easement or privilege must put himself on the ground of prescription, unless he has a grant or some valid authority from the government. . . . . When property is dedicated or transferred to public use, the use is indefinite, and may vary according to circumstances. The public being unable themselves to manage or attend to it, the care and employment of it must devolve upon some local authority or body corporate as its guardian, who are in the first place to determine what use of it, from time to time, is best calculated for the public interest, subject, as charitable uses are, to the control of the laws and the courts, in case of any abuse or misapplication of the trust. The corporation has not the right to these squares, so as to be able to sell them, or employ them in any way variant from the object for which they were designed." [1]

43. It was held that, where a township had been laid out by a plan showing streets, landing-place, &c., and the lots *were sold, it constituted a dedication of [*157] these to the public. Yet where an individual enclosed a part of the land thus dedicated, and held exclusive possession of the same for twenty years, he gained a valid prescriptive title to the same. [2]

So where an owner had dedicated a lot of land to a town, in a manner recognized by the law of Missouri, and afterwards sold the same to one who enjoyed it long enough to

[1] Commonwealth v. Alburger, 1 Whart. 469, 485. See Commonwealth v. Rush. 14 Penn. St. 186 ; Trustees of Watertown v. Cowen, 4 Paige, 510 ; Dubuque v. Malony, 9 Iowa, 460.

[2] Alves v. Town of Henderson, 16 B. Monr. 131, 172 ; Rowan v. Portland, 8 B. Monr. 232 ; Knight v. Heaton, 22 Verm. 480.

gain a prescriptive right, under ordinary circumstances, it was held that the town was thereby barred of any rights gained by dedication.[1]

So where the public forebore to use what was dedicated as a way, for the term of twenty-five years, and in the mean time the grantees of the land continued to occupy it exclusively, it was held that the public had lost their right in the premises.[2]

[1] Callaway Co. v. Nolley, 31 Misso. 393.

[2] Baldwin v. Buffalo, 29 Barb. 396; Commissioners, &c. v. Taylor, 2 Bay, 292.

*CHAPTER II. [*158]

EASEMENTS AND SERVITUDES OF WAY.

SECT. 1. Ways defined, and how they affect the Right of Freehold.
SECT. 2. Of Ways of Necessity.
SECT. 3. Of Ways created by Grant.
SECT. 4. How Ways may be used.
SECT. 5. Rights of the Owners of the Land and of the Way, in the Land.

SECTION I.

WAYS DEFINED, AND HOW THEY AFFECT THE RIGHT OF FREEHOLD.

1. Rights of servitude do not affect general rights of property.
2. Rights of land-owners in the soil of highways.
3. Of ways, and their several classes.
4. Divisions of ways in the civil law.
5. Ways when in gross and when appendant, &c.

1. PASSING from the modes in which easements may be acquired, to the rules which apply to the several classes into which they are divided in reference to the subject-matters to which they relate, it may be remarked, that the existence of a servitude upon an estate does not affect the general rights of property in the same. All these remain, subject only to the enjoyment of the existing easement. Thus it is no objection to the owner of the fee maintaining a writ of entry against one, that he has an easement of a right of way over the demanded premises. The rights are independent, and each owner may have an appropriate action to vindicate or establish his right, — the one to protect his seizin, the other to prevent the disturbance of his

[*159] *easement without having any right to recover the land itself in a real action.[1] And yet it has been held, in Pennsylvania, that the existence and exercise of a private way over granted premises, is an eviction, *pro tanto*, so far as to be the ground of an action upon the covenant of *warranty* in a deed.[2]

2. Highways, for instance, are regarded as easements. The public acquire, by their location, a right of way, with the powers and privileges incident to that right, such as digging the soil, using the timber and other materials found within the limits of the road, in a reasonable manner, for the purpose of making and repairing the road and its bridges. The former proprietor of the soil still retains his exclusive right in all the mines, quarries, springs of water, timber, and earth, for every purpose not incompatible with the public right of way. The person in whom is the fee of the road may maintain trespass, or ejectment, or waste, in respect to the same. And upon the discontinuance or abandonment of the right of way, the entire and exclusive property and right of enjoyment revest in the proprietor of the soil.[3]

And this doctrine extends to railroads as well as highways.[4] But the language of Story, J. on this subject, is as follows: " Where a highway is made over another man's land, the soil still remains in the owner subject to the easement. If there are trees on it they are his. If it be neces-

---

[1] Morgan *v.* Moore, 3 Gray, 319; Hancock *v.* Wentworth, 5 Metc. 446; Jerman *v.* Mathews, 2 Bail. 271; Atkins *v.* Bordman, 2 Metc. 457; Winslow *v.* King, 14 Gray, 321; Miller *v.* Miller, 4 Pick. 244; Perley *v.* Chandler, 6 Mass. 454; Pomeroy *v.* Mills, 3 Vt. 279; Matter of Seventeenth Street, 1 Wend. 262; Viner, Abr., *Chimin Private*, B.; Underwood *v.* Carney, 1 Cush. 292; O'Linda *v.* Lothrop, 21 Pick. 292; Green *v.* Chelsea, 24 Pick. 71; Lade *v.* Shepherd, 2 Strange, 1004; Jackson *v.* Hathaway, 15 Johns. 447; Westbrook *v.* North, 2 Me. 179; Maxwell *v.* M'Atee, 9 B. Monr. 20.

[2] Wilson *v.* Cockran, 46 Penn. 233.

[3] Jackson *v.* Hathaway, 15 Johns. 447; Westbrook *v.* North, 2 Me. 179; Robbins *v.* Borman, 1 Pick. 122; Adams *v.* Emerson, 6 Pick. 57; Harback *v.* Boston, 10 Cush. 295; Harris *v.* Elliott, 10 Peters, 55; Hollenbeck *v.* Rowley, 8 Allen, 473; Lyman *v.* Arnold, 5 Mason, 198.

[4] Blake *v.* Rich, 34 N. H. 282; Quimby *v.* Verm. Cent. R. R., 23 Verm. 387.

sary to cut them and remove them in order to make the highway, still the property in the trees so cut down is unchanged."[1] If the adjacent owner of lands enclose a portion of the highway by a fence, and keep the same so enclosed for forty years, under a claim of right, he thereby acquires a right to maintain his occupation as against the public.[2]

And the owner of the soil may maintain an action of ejectment against any one who shall erect a permanent structure upon the soil of a highway or public landing-place, to the exclusion of the public and the owner.[3]

The proprietors of West Boston Bridge, however, acquired the fee of the land conveyed to them, though created a corporation for the construction and maintenance of a public bridge.[4]

* 3. One of the most common class of easements [*160] or servitudes known to the law is that of *Ways*, or the right of one man to pass over the land of another in some particular line. " A way, *ex vi termini*, imports a right of passing in a particular line."[5]

And it seems that A could not claim a way from one part of B's land to another part, over B's land, though he may claim such way from one part of his own land, over B's, to another part of his own.[6]

These ways are of various kinds, though classed into four by Mr. Woolrych, in his treatise upon the subject, to wit: *Foot-ways ; Foot-ways and Horse-ways; Foot, Horse, and Carriage-ways; and Drift-ways.*[7]

[1] Lyman v. Arnold, 5 Mason, 198. This is regulated by statute in Massachusetts. Such trees are forfeited if not removed by the owner in a prescribed time. Gen. St. c. 43, § 13.

[2] Cutter v. Cambridge, 6 Allen, 20. See Fox v. Hart, 11 Ohio, 414; Knight v. Heaton, 22 Verm. 480.

[3] Gardiner v. Tisdale, 2 Wisc. 153; Goodtitle v. Alker, 1 Burr. 133; Blake v. Rich, 34 N. H. 284; Barclay v. Howell, 6 Peters, 498.

[4] Harlow v. Rogers, 12 Cush. 291.

[5] Jones v. Percival, 5 Pick. 485; Jennison v. Walker, 11 Gray, 426.

[6] Staple v. Heydon, 6 Mod. 3.

[7] Co. Litt. 56 a; Woolr. Ways, 1.

A grant of " *a* way " over one's premises will be understood to be a general way for all purposes.[1] A " carriage-way " always includes a " foot-way." [2] So it does a " horse-way," but not a " drift-way." [3] A " drift-way " is a common way for driving cattle, and was held to intend a way for the passage of teams.[4] A right to " lead " manure is a right to carry it in a cart, since " leading " implies " drawing in a carriage." And a way " on foot, or for horses, oxen, cattle, and sheep," does not give one a right to carry manure in a wheelbarrow, although he who wheels it travels on foot.[5] A " way of necessity " extends only to a single track or way.[6] And where one grants a right of way across his land, he may shut the termini of the same by gates, which the grantee must open and close when using the same, unless an open way is expressly granted.[7]

4. The division of ways, by the civil law, was into [*161] *Iter, * Actus,* and *Via; — Iter* being a way on foot or horseback, over another man's land, to one's own ; *Actus*, a right of walking, riding, driving cattle or a cart, over another man's land, though sometimes it did not include the right of driving a cart or wagon. *Via*, sometimes called *Aditus*, answered to a highway, including the right of walking, riding, driving cattle, carts, and the like. One having an *iter* had not an *actus*, but he who had an *actus* had also an *iter ;* and a *via* included an *iter* and an *actus*.[8]

5. A way is an incorporeal hereditament, and consists in the right of passing over another's ground. It may arise

---

[1] Warner *v.* Green, Com. 114.

[2] Davies *v.* Stephens, 7 Carr. & P. 570.

[3] Ballard *v.* Dyson, 1 Taunt. 279, per *Heath*, J.

[4] Smith *v.* Ladd, 41 Maine, 320.

[5] Brunton *v.* Hall, 1 Q. B. 792.

[6] M'Donald *v.* Lindall, 3 Rawle, 492.

[7] Maxwell *v.* M'Atee, 9 B. Monr. 20; Bean *v.* Coleman, 44 N. H. 539, 544; Bakeman *v.* Talbot, 31 N. Y. 366; *post*, pp. *186, *195.

[8] Ayl. Pand. 307 ; Inst. 2, 3. For the different classes of ways known to the French law, their width, and how they may be used, see 1 Fournel, Traité du Voisinage, 233, § 88.

either from grant, necessity, or prescription, and is either *in gross* or *appendant* to land. By prescription, a grant is implied, as, if all the owners and occupiers of such a farm have immemorially used to cross another's ground, such usage supposes an original grant of the right. A right of way may be *in gross*, that is, attached to the person using it, or appurtenant to land, but a way is never presumed to be in gross when it can fairly be construed to be appurtenant to land.[1]

But the grant of a way across a man's land conveys no right to the soil, rocks, or other things within the bounds of the way.[2]

Ways are said to be appendant or appurtenant when they are incident to an estate, one terminus being on the land of the party claiming. They must inhere in the land, concern the premises, and be essentially necessary to their enjoyment. They are of the nature of covenants running with the land, and like them must respect the thing granted or demised, and must concern the land or estate conveyed. A way appendant cannot be turned into one in gross, because it is inseparably united to the land to which it is incident.

So a way in gross *cannot be granted over to an- [*162] other, because of its being attached to the person.[3]

Nor can one have a private way over and along a public highway.[4]

In the foregoing definition of a way, borrowed from the language of the court of Pennsylvania, the usual classification of modes is retained, by which ways may be created, though it is hardly necessary to repeat, that, when analyzed, they resolve themselves into simple grants, the difference consisting in the character of the proof, and not in the mode

---

[1] Case of Private Road, 1 Ashm. 417; Garrison *v.* Rudd, 19 Ill. 558; Derrickson *v.* Springer, 5 Harringt. 21.

[2] Smith *v.* Rome, 19 Giv. 91; Jamaica Pond *v.* Chandler, 9 Allen, 164. See Lyman *v.* Arnold, 5 Mason 198.

[3] Garrison *v.* Rudd, 19 Ill. 558, 565.

[4] State *v.* Jefcoat, 11 Rich. 529.

itself. For the sake of convenience, however, ways of necessity will be treated of as a class by themselves, and will be considered before the nature, character, and extent of enjoyment of different kind of ways shall be illustrated or explained.

SECTION II.

OF WAYS OF NECESSITY.

1. Ways of necessity only exist over lands of grantors.
2. In what cases ways of necessity exist.
3. Same rule, if grantor reserves "a way of necessity."
4. Such ways exist only so long as the necessity continues.
5. Effect of owning adjoining land with a private right of way.
6. Executor may by grant create a way of necessity over his own land.
7. A tenant in common cannot create a way over common land.
8. Rights of way over parcels of land not dependent on priority of grant.
9. Whether a way passes, dependent on state of the premises.
10. Who is to designate the course of a way of necessity.

1. A WAY of necessity can only be created over one of two parcels of land of which the grantor was the owner when the same was conveyed or reserved ; and it arises in [*163] favor of *such parcel when the same is wholly surrounded by what had been the grantor's other land, or partly by this and partly by that of a stranger.[1] This arises from the effect of the grant or reservation of the land itself, and it is so far appurtenant to it as to pass with the land to another, provided he have no other way of access to the same.[2]

[1] N. Y. Life Ins. & Tr. Co. v. Milnor, 1 Barb. Ch. 353, 366 ; Collins v. Prentice, 15 Conn. 39 ; 1 Wms. Saund. 323, note; Brice v. Randall, 7 Gill & J. 349 ; Marshall v. Trumbull, 28 Conn. 183; Kimball v. Cocheco R. R., 7 Fost. 449. See Trask v. Patterson, 29 Me. 499 ; Tracy v. Atherton, 35 Verm. 52.

[2] Clarke v. Rugge, 2 Rolle, Abr. 60 ; Woolr. Ways, 21 ; Jorden v. Atwood, Owen, 121 ; Howton v. Frearson, 8 T. R. 50 ; Lawton v. Rivers, 2 M'Cord, 445 ; Nichols v. Luce, 24 Pick. 102; Proctor v. Hodgson, 10 Exch, 824 ; White v. Leeson, 5 Hurlst. & N. 53; Wissler v. Hershey, 23 Penn. St. 333.

2. It would be simply absurd under the common law to pretend that A could, by any form of grant, create a servitude upon the land of a stranger in favor of land which he should convey to his grantee.[1] But both by the civil codes of France and Louisiana, one whose lands cannot be reached from a highway, except by passing over the lands of another person, may pass in the shortest feasible distance over such third person's land, paying him an indemnity therefor.[2] And as to the question, what constitutes a necessity sufficient to raise an implied grant of a right of way, some courts have been inclined to hold that it need not be absolute and irresistible, and that a mere inconvenience may be so great as to raise such an implication.[3] But the same court held, in another case, that where the land conveyed was surrounded on all sides but one by water, and there was no access to it by land except over the grantor's land, it was not such a necessity as to raise an implied grant of a right of way over this land, and that mere convenience was not the test.[4] And the law seems to be now settled beyond controversy, that, in the language of the court in M'Donald v. Lindall : " The right of way from necessity over the land of another is always of *strict necessity*, and this necessity must [*164] not be created by the party claiming the right of way.

It never exists where a man can get to his property through his own land. That the way through his own land is too steep or too narrow, does not alter the case. It is only where there is no way through his own land that the right of way over land of another can exist. That a person claiming a way of necessity has already one way, is a good plea, and bars the plaintiff." [5] A way of necessity, *ex vi termini*, im-

---

[1] 2 Rolle, Abr. 60, pl. 18 ; 1 Wms. Saund. 323 b, note ; Bullard v. Harrison, 4 Maule & S. 387 ; Woolr. Ways, 21 ; Tracy v. Atherton, 35 Verm. 52.

[2] Martin v. Patin, 16 Louis. 57 ; Code Nap. §§ 682 – 685.

[3] Lawton v. Rivers, 2 M'Cord, 445 ; Morris v. Edgington, 3 Taunt. 230. But see Screven v. Gregorie, 8 Rich. 158, convenience not sufficient.

[4] Turnbull v. Rivers, 3 M'Cord, 131. See also Cooper v. Maupin, 6 Mo. 624 ; Anderson v. Buchanan, 8 Ind. 132.

M'Donald v. Lindall, 3 Rawle, 492 ; Com. Dig. *Chimin*, D. 4 ; Staple v.

ports a right of passage through the lands of another as being indispensable.[1] Nor can one claim a way by necessity because of its superior convenience over another way which he has.[2]

Or, as stated by another class of cases, a right of way exists only where the person claiming it has no other means of passing from his estate into the public street or road.[3]

The same rule applies where the grantor conveys land surrounding a parcel retained by him; he has a way of necessity over the granted land to the parcel retained.[4]

3. Nor would the rights of a grantor be any more extensive or different, though by the terms of his deed he reserved to himself " a way of necessity."[5]

4. And so limited is the right of way of necessity in respect to its duration, that, though it remains appurtenant to the land in favor of which it is raised so long [*165] as *the owner thereof has no other mode of access, yet the moment the owner of such a way acquires, by purchase of other land or otherwise, a way of access from a highway over his own land to the land to which the way belongs, the way of necessity is at an end; or in other words, a way of necessity ceases as soon as the necessity ceases. The necessity limits the duration of the grant, and this applies as well to a subsequent owner of the estate to which such way attaches, as to the first grantee in whose

Heydon, 6 Mod. 1; Seabrook v. King, 1 Nott & M'C. 140; Kimball v. Cocheco R. R., 7 Fost. 448; Leonard v. Leonard, 2 Allen, 543; Trask v. Patterson, 29 Me. 499; Ogden v. Grove, 38 Penn. St. 487; Hall v. M'Leod, 2 Metc. Ky. 98.

[1] Hyde v. Jamaica, 27 Verm. 460.

[2] Dodd v. Burchell, 1 H. & Colt. 122; Pheysey v. Vicary, 16 M. & W. 496, per *Alderson*.

[3] Gayetty v. Bethune, 14 Mass. 49; Grant v. Chase, 17 Mass. 443; Smyles v. Hastings, 22 N. Y. 217; Collins v. Prentice, 15 Conn. 39; Hyde v. Jamaica, 27 Vt. 443.

[4] Clark v. Cogge, Cro. Jac. 170; Brigham v. Smith, 4 Gray, 297; Seymour v. Lewis, 13 N. J. 444; White v. Bass, 7 H. & Norm. 732.

[5] Viall v. Carpenter, 14 Gray, 126.

favor it was originally raised.   It is not enough that it continues to be a way of convenience, if it ceases to be indispensable as a means of access to the land.[1]

5. It would not be enough, however, that one having such
way of necessity should acquire a parcel of land adjoining
that to which such way belongs, to which there is access by
a prescriptive right of way, since the owner of such a way
could only use it as a means of access to the particular
parcel to which it is appurtenant.[2]

6. A right of way will be raised between the parties to
the transfer of one of two or more estates or parts of
estates, where the part granted or retained can be reached
only over the other part ; and this not only applies to cases
of levies of executions upon parts of an estate, but has been
held to extend so far, that, if one as an executor sells land
to which there is no means of access except over his own
land, the purchaser may pass over the executor's land to
that which he has purchased. So if an executor, in the
execution of his trust to sell lands of his testator, sell a
front lot to one, and then a rear lot to another, the
*latter may, if necessary, pass over the front lot to [*166]
reach that in the rear of it.[3] So if a creditor levy
his execution upon his debtor's land in such a mode that it
is necessary to pass over the part levied upon, in order to
reach the other parts of the estate, a right of way over the
same at once attaches to the other parts.[4] But not if there

[1] Pierce v. Selleck, 18 Conn. 321; Holmes v. Seely, 19 Wend. 507; Collins
v. Prentice, 15 Conn. 39; Morris v. Edgington, 3 Taunt. 23; Lawton v. Rivers,
2 M'Cord, 445; Viall v. Carpenter, 14 Gray, 126; Holmes v. Goring, 2 Bing.
76, 83; New York Life Ins. & Tr. Co. v. Milnor, 1 Barb. Ch. 353; Nichols v.
Luce, 24 Pick. 102; Staple v. Heydon, 6 Mod. 1; White v. Leeson, 5 Hurlst.
& N. 53; Seeley v. Bishop, 19 Conn. 128; Gayetty v. Bethune, 14 Mass. 49
Woolr. Ways, 72.
[2] New York Life Ins. & Tr. Co. v. Milnor, 1 Barb. Ch. 353.
[3] Collins v. Prentice, 15 Conn. 39; Howton v. Frearson, 8 T. R. 50; Woolr.
Ways, 20.
[4] Russell v. Jackson, 2 Pick. 574; Pernam v. Wead, 2 Mass. 203; Taylor v.
Townsend, 8 Mass. 411.

is a way left from the highway to the back land which might
be rendered feasible at no disproportionate cost.[1]

7. But this would not give one tenant in common a right
to create an easement of way over the common estate to land
sold by him belonging to himself alone.[2]

8. In determining whether, as between two or more
parcels, a right of way exists in favor of one over the
other, as a way of necessity, it does not depend upon the
order or priority of the conveyances. Thus, suppose lots A,
B, and C lying in the above order, A lying in front, and B
being accessible only over A, and C only over A and B,
all of which originally belonged to the same owner, and it
cannot be shown whether the one or the other was granted
first. It would make no difference in the result, for if it
was C, a right of way was thereby created in its favor over
A and B, and would pass therewith, so long as it remained
one of necessity. If it was B, then, by the principle heretofore stated, a right of way was thereby reserved to the
grantor from A over B to C, and would pass as appurtenant
to those lots so long as the necessity continued, so that the
same rights in favor of one over the other of said parcels
exist, irrespective of the priority or order of the conveyance
of the parcels.[3]

[*167]   *9. And whether a way passes as one of necessity,
with the parcel of land to which it may have belonged, depends upon the condition of the estate at the time
of the conveyance. Thus, where there were two parcels of
land, upon one of which there had once been a barn to
which there was a way of necessity over the other parcel,
and the owner of the estate suffered the barn to go wholly
to decay, it was held that the right of way over the other

<hr />

[1] Allen v. Kincaid, 11 Me. 155.

[2] Collins v. Prentice, 15 Conn. 39; Gayetty v. Bethune, 14 Mass. 49; Marshall v. Trumbull, 28 Conn. 183; Brice v. Randall, 7 Gill & J. 349; 1 Wms.
Saund. 323, note.

[3] Pinnington v. Galland, 9 Exch. 1; White v. Bass, 7 H. & Norm. 732.

parcel of land thereby became extinct, and ceased to be appurtenant to it.[1]

10. In respect to who shall designate the way which is to be used by the grantee, where it is claimed as a way of necessity, it would seem that, if a way had been in use for the benefit of such parcel before its conveyance, it would be understood that the same would be to be continued if reasonably convenient.[2] But if it is to be designated anew, it seems that the right of selecting the place over which it shall be used lies with the owner of the land over which it is to pass, provided, upon request, he shall designate it in a reasonable manner, and he may so do it as to be least inconvenient to himself.[3] But if the owner of the land fail to designate such a way when requested, the party who has the right to use it may select a suitable route for the same, having regard to the interest and convenience of the owner of the land over which it passes. And when he has once selected the way, he may not change it at will, but must be confined to the way thus selected.[4] And in this respect it seems the law differs between ways claimed by necessity and *those claimed by grant, where there is [*168] no designation made of the particular part of the tenement in which it is to be exercised. In the latter case, the selection is left to the owner of the dominant tenement, but he must not make such a selection as would unnecessarily occasion detriment to the servient tenement. And the same rule would apply to aqueducts.[5]

[1] Gayetty v. Bethune, 14 Mass. 49 ; M'Donald v. Lindall, 3 Rawle, 492.

[2] Pinnington v. Galland, 9 Exch. 1.

[3] Capers v. Wilson, 3 M'Cord, 170; Russell v. Jackson, 2 Pick. 574; Holmes v. Seely, 19 Wend. 507; 2 Rolle, Abr. 60, pl. 17; Smiles v. Hastings, 24 Barb. 44; Pearson v. Spencer, 1 B. & Smith, 584.

[4] Nichols v. Luce, 24 Pick. 102; Morris v. Edgington, 3 Taunt. 23; Holmes v. Seely, 19 Wend. 507.
There are rules in the French law as to which of several adjoining estates, one having a right of way, by necessity, from a highway to a parcel of land surrounded by the lands of others, shall pass over. It is not a matter of mere election on his part. 2 Fournel, Traité du Voisinage, 301.

[5] 3 Burge, Col. & F. Law, 441.

Where the grantor of land, who had reserved a right of way over it within certain limits, opened it in a direction not authorized by the reservation, and he was enjoined from using it, it was held he might make a new designation of the way.[1]

SECTION III.

OF WAYS CREATED BY GRANT.

1. Ways may be created by express or constructive grant.
2. How far grants of ways affected by ways in use.
3. O'Linda v. Lothrop. Grantor estopped to deny a way.
4. Effect on private rights of discontinuing a highway.
5. Smyles v. Hastings. Right of way created by plans of premises.
6. Child v. Chappell. Easements passing on partition of estates.
7. Effect of bounding land by a contemplated street.
8. When bounding by a street conveys a right of way in it.
9. How far bounding by a street implies any width thereof.
10. Osborn v. Wise. How far parol may explain what is granted.
11. Emerson v. Wiley. Constructive grant of a general way.
12. Hartshorn v. South Reading. General grant limited by nature of use.
13. White v. Leeson. Case of way not passing, though on a plan.
14. Morris v. Edgington. Two ways used by grantor, which passes.
15. Kirkham v. Sharp. Grantor of way limited to same use as grantee.
16. Salisbury v. Andrews. State of premises defines way granted.
17. Lewis v. Carstairs. Way for one purpose may not be extended.
18. How far a way passes with the several parts of an estate.
19. Grant of a right of maintaining a bridge, held to be of a right of way

1. IN considering the subject of ways created by grant, it chiefly remains, after having treated already of what [*169] will pass *by implication, with the principal thing granted, to state and apply the rules which courts have adopted for limiting and defining the nature, use, and extent of such ways as pass by grants of lands with which they are to be enjoyed. These may be defined by the express terms of the deed by which they are created, or they may be ascertained by construction, having reference to the state and condition of the principal estate granted.

[1] Hart v. Conner, 25 Conn. 331.

2. As a general proposition, a grant of an estate with "ways heretofore used," or "ways in use," or the like, would pass all existing ways in actual use at the time, whether the same are used by the grantor over other parts of his own estate, and so are not properly appurtenant to such granted parcel, or are appurtenant to the same, by having been in use over the land of another.[1] But a mere reference in the deed to an intended way, without an express grant, will not pass such way.[2] And where a right of way is granted, but its locality and duration are not defined, it may become fixed by use and acts of acquiescence of the parties. And where there are two ways which will answer the description in the grant, the grantor's declaration may be admitted as evidence as to which was intended.[3] And when once fixed by user, it may not be changed except by a sufficiently long acquiescence therein by the parties in interest.[4] And this applies to an aqueduct as well as a way.[5] And if the deed granting the way defines its course, &c., it is not to be controlled by parol testimony as to what the parties intended, or to contradict the terms of the grant.[6]

But where both parties claimed under one remote grantor and grantee, and the question was as to the width of the way, reference was had to the deed of the original grantor, who created it.[7]

3. Among the numerous illustrations which are to be found in decided cases, of ways passing either by being referred to in deeds and taking effect by way of estoppel, or by

[1] Plant v. James, 5 Barnew. & Ad. 791; Harding v. Wilson, 2 Barnew. & C. 96; Staple v. Heydon, 6 Mod. 1.

[2] Harding v. Wilson, 2 Barnew. & C. 96; Roberts v. Karr, 1 Taunt. 495.

[3] French v. Hayes, 43 N. H. 32; Osborn v. Wise, 7 C. & P. 761.

[4] Bannon v. Angier, 2 Allen, 128; Wynkoop v. Burger, 12 Johns. 222; French v. Hayes, 43 N. H. 32; Osborn v. Wise, 7 C. & P. 761; Jennison v. Walker, 11 Gray, 426; Jones v. Percival, 5 Pick. 487.

[5] Jennison v. Walker, 11 Gray, 426.

[6] Shepherd v. Watson, 1 Watts, 35; Ballard v. Dyson, 1 Taunt. 279, 288.

[7] Brown v. Stone, 10 Gray, 65.

having been laid down upon plans used by the parties, or by having been actually in use when the grant of the principal estate was made, are the following.

[*170]   *In O'Linda v. Lothrop, the grantor, owning a parcel of land, sold the north part of it, and bounded the part sold on the south by an intended street where none existed, and sold the south part, bounding it north by a street. Nothing, however, was said in the deed of a right of way over the street. But it was held that the grantor was estopped to deny that it was a street or way to the extent of the land so referred to. It was an implied covenant on his part that there was such a street.[1]

But in the case above stated, had there been an existing way a part of the length of the line of the granted premises, but not the whole of it, it would be considered as limiting the grant to the existing way, and not as extending the covenant as to the way to the whole length of line of the premises.[2]

4. So where one sells land bounding it upon the highway, and the same is discontinued by act of law, although the same reverts to the owner of the fee of the soil, the grantor as such, in such a case, would have no right to deprive his grantee of the right to use the discontinued road for the purposes of a way.[3]

5. In order to a partition of a common estate, a plan was prepared of the premises, and of the several parcels into which it was to be divided, and in the deeds of partition reference was made to the plan. Upon this plan a street or road was laid down, upon which one of the lots was bounded, and to which there was no other mode of access from a public highway, except over the lands of third persons. It was held that the right of way as thus laid down became appurte-

---

[1] O'Linda v. Lothrop, 21 Pick. 292; Tufts v. Charlestown, 4 Gray, 537; Parker v. Smith, 17 Mass. 413; Howe v. Alger, 4 Allen, 206.

[2] Parker v. Smith, 17 Mass. 413; Parker v. Framingham, 8 Metc. 260.

[3] Parker v. Framingham, 8 Metc. 260.

nant to the lot thus bounded, and passed with it as a proper appurtenance.[1]

*6. The case of Child v. Chappell, already cited, [*171] may serve to illustrate more than one of the forego-ing propositions. In that case, three tenants in common of one hundred acres of land, adjoining falls in a river, made partition of it by deed, by a plan annexed to it, showing a mill-yard, mill-races, water, and alleys, which were to be en-joyed for their common use forever. Five years after, by another partition deed, reciting the former one, they laid out new lots upon a part of the " mill-yard," altered some of the lines, and made a new division of these lots. It was mutu-ally covenanted that a basin should be made on the annexed plat upon a part of the mill-yard, which was to be common property of the parties, their heirs and assigns. The road was to be forever kept open as a common way to the mills, to the basin, and to the warehouses adjoining the same. The plaintiff purchased one of these lots, and the defendant another, from the original grantees in the partition deed. It was held that the undivided parts of the estate became a servient tenement to the several parcels divided and sold, and the easement and privilege of the way, the basin, &c., became permanently annexed to the lots. The act of laying out these basins and ways, and selling one of the lots to the defendant with express reference to the deed containing the plan and covenants, " was *quoad* the purchaser and the land purchased a dedication of it to the use for which it was con-structed." Morse, J. considers the point of its being a dedication. " As between the original owner of the land and the several grantees of parcels thereof, these rights are fixed; but until the public has in some way become a party to the transaction, the whole arrangement is subject to be rescinded by the joint act of the original owner, and all of those who own and have the right to represent the land sold.

---

[1] Smyles v. Hastings, 22 N. Y. 217, 224; s. c., 24 Barb. 44. See Van Meter v. Hankinson, 6 Whart. 307.

. . . . In other words, there might be impressed upon this mass of private property, by private contract, rights in the strictest sense of the word analogous to the ordinary public rights of highway, and yet these rights confined to [*172] the owners and *representatives of the land forming the subject of the compact, and liable to be ended and rescinded by the mutual consent of all who have an interest in the subject. . . . . But until they did mutually agree to the contrary, the mill-yard remained a common way, common to those who had interests in the mill-seat lots fronting upon it, constituting to each lot an easement appurtenant to it, not by prescription, but by what a prescription implies, a grant." [1]

7. But where land was bounded upon a contemplated street laid down upon a plat of village or city lots, and the commissioners, who had jurisdiction of the matter, prevented its being opened, it was held that the purchaser of the lot would have no right of way over it, if he has another convenient way of access to his lot. [2]

8. In Roberts v. Karr, the grantor conveyed a parcel of land adjoining a new way *over his own land*, on which houses had been erected, and described the parcel by lines measured by feet and inches, "abutting on the road or street." It was held to carry with it a right of access to this road or street at every point along this front. Nor was the grantor permitted to show, by parol, that the line intended was along the street a part of the distance, and then along a narrow space of land between the granted parcel and the road, which still belonged to the grantor, although that corresponded with the admeasurement and lengths of the lines mentioned in the deed. The grantor would not be admitted to deny that the land on which the parcel abuts is the road. [3]

---

[1] Child v. Chappell, 5 Seld. 246, 256, 260 ; *ante*, chap. 1, sect. 5, pl. 22.

[2] Underwood v. Stuyvesant, 19 Johns. 181 ; Bellinger v. Burial Ground, &c., 10 Penn. 135.

[3] Roberts v. Karr, 1 Taunt. 495.

In the case above cited, the way in respect to which an implication of appurtenancy was raised, it will be remembered, was over and upon the land of the grantor himself. But it seems not to be entirely clear how far the *law would raise a covenant that the use of such a [*173] way existed in favor of the granted premises, and might be enjoyed with them, by merely bounding the same upon it, where it lies over the land of another person.

The question came up in Howe v. Alger,[1] where the court held, that bounding land in a deed upon a street neither conveyed any right of way in the street, nor was it a covenant that there was such a street, if the grantor had no interest in the soil of the same. If he owned the soil of the street, and bounded land by it, describing it as a street, he would be estopped to deny that it was one, or that his grantee had a right to use it.

In Maryland, the court holds that if one grants land in a city, and bounds it by streets designated as such in the conveyance, or on a map made by the city, or by the owner of the property, such sale implies, necessarily, a covenant that the purchaser shall have the use of such streets. The grantor would be estopped to deny that there was such a street as he describes in his deed.[2]

9. In Walker v. Worcester, the owner of a large tract of land laid out streets upon it for the purpose of selling house-lots bounding upon the same, and caused a plan of it to be made. One of these streets was called " Park," and was laid out sixty feet wide. He then sold the whole land together, and his grantee made a fence around it, enclosing it, and ploughed and cultivated it. He then sold a house-lot, a part of this estate, bounding it on one side by an existing street, and " westerly on Park Street, one hundred and fifty feet." The owner of the general parcel graded

---

[1] 4 Allen, 206 ; Matter of Mercer Street, 4 Cow. 542.
[2] White v. Flannigain, 1 Md. 540, 542   Moale v. Mayor, &c. of Baltimore, 5 Md. 321.

this street anew and reduced it to forty feet in width, and sold the other part of the estate, including twenty feet formerly within Park Street, to the defendants. In an action for preventing the purchaser of the house-lot passing over the whole original width of Park Street, the court held that, in order to constitute a street, it must be open and appropriated, and adopted by the public or the owner for purposes of travel, so that a person passing over it, while it was open, would not be liable for a trespass. Though once open, if closed before any house-lots were sold, the deed amounted to an implied covenant and grant, if the grantor owned it, that the grantee should have the right to a convenient street or passage-way. But there was nothing to designate or limit the dimensions of the way thus granted by implication. The law would imply a way necessary and convenient to accommodate the grantee in the use of the land granted, to the extent granted of one hundred and fifty feet.[1]

10. In Osborn v. Wise, there was a grant of a [*174] house, with *a passage-way ten feet wide on the east side of the premises, with a reference to a plan which showed a passage-way on that side, but of only five feet in width in parts of it, and it did not, moreover, all pass over the grantor's land. The grantee claimed a way running in another direction wide enough for a carriage-way, and offered evidence to show that the grantor declared the road was what the owner of the estate claimed it to be. The court refused the evidence, but held that evidence was competent to show the state of the property at the time when the grant was made, and that, if the way granted was of no use, the grantee had a way of necessity over the grantor's land to the nearest public highway then existing. But the acts of the parties, before or after the grant, would not be evidence of what was granted.

---

[1] Walker v. Worcester, 6 Gray, 548. See Harding v. Wilson, 2 Barnew. & C. 96.

The deed was to be construed by the state of the premises when the grant was made. Nor does the grant that carries with it a right of way of necessity necessarily imply a carriage-way, even though the thing granted be a house. But the grant of tillage-land implies a carriage-way, because such a way is necessary in order to carry off the crops, unless, by the custom of the vicinage, the crops are carried off by men instead of teams. But if there had been two ways on the east side of the premises answering to the description in the deed, parol evidence would have been competent to show which of these was intended.[1]

11. The proprietors of a town voted that certain land should remain unfenced, among other things, " to accommodate the neighbors that live bordering on said lands, for their more convenient coming at and improving their own lands and buildings, and to the use of the old parish and neighborhood forever," &c. The parish granted a parcel of land, " bounded all round by the land given by the town, to the first parish, &c., with all the privileges *there- [*175] to belonging." It was held that this conveyed to the grantee the right to cross this open land in all directions, and amounted to a covenant that the same should not be enclosed without consent of the owners abutting upon it.[2]

12. In Hartshorn v. South Reading, the subject of an easement in the same public land as in Emerson v. Wiley came under the consideration of the court. The plaintiff's land fronted upon the common land, which by vote of the town was to lie unfenced " for the use of the old parish, for highways, a training-field, and burying-place, and the more common coming at the pond with flax and creatures, and also to accommodate the neighbors that live bordering on said lands, for their more convenient coming at and improving their own lands and buildings." The town enclosed a part of this common, and the plaintiff

---

1 Osborn v. Wise, 7 Carr. & P. 761.
2 Emerson v. Wiley, 10 Pick. 310.

brought his action because he was thereby deprived of a right of way over it, and over every part of it in all directions, which he claimed was appurtenant to his land under this vote. The court held, in the first place, if the injury complained of was of the same nature with that which all persons having occasion to use the same would sustain, except in degree, the only remedy was by indictment, and not by an action for an injury to a private easement. In the second place, the uses to which this land was devoted by the original action of the town were distinct and separate, some necessarily of a public character, to be controlled by the public authorities. These are to be used by individuals and the public so as to be consistent with each other. The public could not use the common directly in front of the plaintiff's land for a burying-ground, so as to prevent access to the same by him; and, on the other hand, if a burying-ground were allotted upon a part of it, the [*176] plaintiff would have no right to travel over or among the *graves and monuments, or drive his cattle over these. The extent of his right as owner of the land which belonged to him was that of passage over so much of the common as was reasonably sufficient for coming to his lands and buildings, and for access to the pond. And as the evidence did not show that the enclosure complained of obstructed these, it was held that the action of the plaintiff could not be sustained.[1]

13. In White v. Leeson, a devisee of lands was authorized by private act of Parliament to lay out the same for building-lots, and to make ways, streets, &c., " for the general improvement of the estate, and the accommodation of the tenants and occupiers thereof." He laid out the lands and made certain streets, one of which led to the sea. He then granted several of the lots to the defendant, without mentioning any right of way, and granted other lots to

---

[1] Hartshorn v. South Reading, 3 Allen, 502. See Brainard v. Connecticut River R. R. Co., 7 Cush. 506 ; Harvard College v. Stearns, 15 Gray.

others, with rights of way in express terms. This street to
the sea was a mere private way, and does not seem to have
been necessary to the occupation of the defendant's lots.
But he seems to have claimed the right to use it, because
it was laid out for the general improvement and accommodation of the tenants of the parcels into which the estate
was divided. But the court held that, being a mere private
way, the defendant had no right to make use of it beyond
what had been expressly granted to him. The judge, Watson, B. says: "The argument for the defendant would go
to show that, if a square of large houses was set out with an
enclosure, all the tenants must have a right to walk in it,
though they lived in cottages at a distance."

It will be observed that no question of dedication or necessity was raised, but merely of the construction to be given
to the deed of the defendant, taken in connection with the
condition of the property, and the omission to grant a
*right to use this private way was conclusive that it [*177]
did not pass with the parcels granted.[1]

This subject is thus treated of by Chancellor Cottenham,
in Squire *v.* Campbell: " I will suppose it [plaintiff's affida-
vit] to state that a plan was shown by some person authorized to act for the lessors, and that the plan showed a space
such as has hitherto existed." (This was of an open square
in which defendant proposed to erect a statue.) " This
will raise the question, whether, in the absence of all fraud,
mistake, or misapprehension, the mere exhibition of the plan
of property, part of which the lessee takes, gives such lessee
a right to say that all the other parts of the property exhibited upon such plan shall continue during his lease in the
same state in which it was exhibited upon the plan; or, if it
was not at that time in such state, shall be made to assume
such state, and to have the assistance of this court to enforce
such right, the lease granted to each lessee being wholly
silent as to any provision for that purpose. . . . . This

[1] White *v.* Leeson, 5 Hurlst. & N. 53.

proposition would evidently lead to most absurd consequences. A man who is about to sell a corner of an estate
may exhibit a plan of the whole estate, in order to show the
relative position of that part which he is about to sell; but
is he, on that account, to have his hands forever tied up from
the enjoyment and use of all other parts of the estate, and is
he to preserve it in exactly its present state?"[1]

14. The case of Morris v. Edgington, though somewhat
complicated in its facts, may serve to show the principles of
construction which courts apply in determining the nature
and extent of a way, where one is granted but not defined.
The defendant owned an estate consisting of a coffee-room,
a passage east of this, which led from the street into a close
yard, in which carriers deposited goods, entering through
this passage. East of the passage was a tap-room,
[*178] *and over the passage was another room. There
was a door from the passage-way into the tap-room,
so that persons could go directly from the street through the
passage-way to the tap-room by this door. There was also a
door from the street into the coffee-room, and then from the
coffee-room into the passage, so that one could reach the tap-
room by passing from the street through the coffee-room and
across the passage to the door of the tap-room, although the
gate between the street and the passage-way was closed.
The defendant let to the plaintiff the coffee-room and tap-
room, " and all ways to the demised premises belonging and
appertaining," reserving the yard and the passage-way to the
yard. Soon after letting the premises, the defendant closed
the gate to the passage-way after seven o'clock in the even-
ing, in order to make the goods deposited in the yard safe
and secure, and the plaintiff brought his action for this
obstruction of his way to the tap-room through this passage-
way from the street. The defendant insisted that the way
through the passage was not one of necessity, since the
tenant had another way through the coffee-room, and that

[2] Squire v. Campbell, 1 Mylne & C. 459, 478.

it did not pass as appurtenant, because, so long as the entire
estate was in the defendant's hands, there could properly be
no such thing as a way appurtenant to one part over another.
But the court held that, though neither of the ways was in
itself a way of necessity, since there was another way of
access, and though, technically, neither of them was appurtenant to the leased premises, yet as there were but two ways,
and one of them must have been intended to pass by the
lease, that through the passage was to be taken as the way
intended, by reason of its being so much more convenient
for the accommodation and use of the leased premises.[1]

15. The facts in Kirkham v. Sharp are still more complicated, but the case is referred to as illustrating the manner
in which the general owner of land may so grant a
right *of way over it as to restrict himself to a like [*179]
use of the way, although there is nothing in his deed,
in express terms, limiting his use or enjoyment of the same.
The defendant's grantor owned two house-lots forming one
estate, fronting west on Fourth Street, and extending back
one hundred feet. In the rear of these lots he had a stable
and yard, separated from the house-lots by a wall, to which
he had a way by an alley from Market Street, which ran in
a direction at right angles with Fourth Street. On the
north of these house-lots he had a house in the occupation of
A. B. He conveyed to the plaintiff's grantor one of these
house-lots bounding him on the west by Fourth Street, and
also " the full and free privilege and authority of ingress,
egress, and regress by, through, and upon a four-feet-six-
inches alley, extending in and about forty-five feet from
Fourth Street, to be forever left open between the lot hereby
granted and the house now occupied by A. B.," &c. It will
be perceived that the way was over the soil of the defendant's grantor, and that, in passing from the end of the forty-
five feet to the stable and yard in rear of his lot, he would
pass only over his own land. The defendant, wishing to

[1] Morris v. Edgington, 3 Taunt. 24; *ante*, chap. 1, sect. 3, pl. 14.

pass from Market Street through his stable estate, and thence
to Fourth Street, extended the alley above described over
his own land, and, by breaking down the wall, into the stable
yard, used the same as a passage way; for doing which
the plaintiff brought his action. The court sustained it, on
the ground that, by the terms of the deed, the alley was
limited to forty-five feet in depth, and the grantor had
thereby restricted himself from extending and enlarging its
use. "The ungranted residue of a right of way," say the
court, " may be annexed to a particular messuage or close,
either by express stipulation or necessary implication, according to the occasion of the grant. An instance of this might
be found in the disposal of houses surrounding a court originally destined to be a common avenue to them, in which it
                would be sufficiently obvious, from the disposition of
[*180] the property, that the right *of way had been appended
                to the houses, and not the owner of them. By the act
of laying out the ground as a court, it would be allotted to
the houses intended to adjoin it, so as to pass with them as
an appurtenance, and the right of the owner would be cor-
respondingly qualified by the nature of the use to which it
was dedicated. Sales of houses would successively abridge
it, till it was, ultimately, extinguished along with his property in the last of them, when the purchasers might, by common consent, bar the entrance against his person, notwithstanding his legal title, just as they might bar it against a
stranger. During his ownership of but a part of the property, he would be entitled to no privilege that he had not
originally annexed to it, nor could his right to use the court,
as a thoroughfare to a messuage or close adjoining him on the
farther side, be greater than that of his grantees."
In applying this doctrine, the court held that, as the way
here was only over a part of the entire length of the lots,
and over this the plaintiff had full and free ingress and
regress, there was an implied restriction upon the owner of
the other parcel to be accommodated by it, that a similar

use to that which his grantee could make it, should only be
made of it by him, and therefore the grantor could not, in
addition to that, use the way for the accommodation of other
and more remote lands.[1]

16. In the case of Salisbury v. Andrews, the question was,
whether a right of access to, and to use, a sidewalk, passed
with the principal estate granted. The house was situate
upon Central Court, so called. The description of the parcel on which it stood was by feet and inches from point to
point at the four corners, " together with the land in front
of said house under the stone steps, with a right to pass and
repass on foot, and with horses and carriages, to said
house *and land, through said Central Court, at all [*181]
times." The grantee was to be at half the expense
in keeping the sidewalk in front of the house in good repair.
The injury complained of by the owner of this house was,
the narrowing of the court and passage-way. In commenting
upon the effect to be given, in a deed, to the state and condition of the premises thereby conveyed, in construing its
meaning, the court say that it is the natural presumption,
" when a man erects a house on his own land, and makes a
sidewalk in front of it, paved with brick, and thereby fitted
for the passage of persons and wheelbarrows, and especially if
he opens doors and gates upon such passage, forming convenient means of access to different parts of the house and
grounds, and adapts the construction of the house and
grounds to such means of access, it is intended that such
passage shall remain for the use and benefit of all those who
hold, use, or purchase the house, and that they are intended
to be annexed to the house as permanent easements. . . . .
Still, it is competent for the one to sell, and the other to purchase, the house without the easements. . . . . But where
the language is not clear and explicit, where it is open to
doubt, and the question is, what was the intent of the parties,

---

[1] Kirkham v. Sharp, 1 Whart. 323. See Howell v. King, 1 Mod. 190; Lawton v. Ward, 1 Ld. Raym. 75; Jamison v. M'Credy, 5 Watts & S. 129, 140.

the presumption arising from such original adaptation and annexation of the easements to the house is of considerable importance." The court refer to the language of the deed in reference to the "court" and the "sidewalk," and the condition of the premises, for the purpose of ascertaining what the parties intended, and conclude that a way of some kind was intended; that here being a paved way, with a side-walk, it must be the one intended. "A right to pass and repass, if over vacant and unoccupied land where no way actually exists or is used, would be the grant of a conven-ient way, the direction and width of which would be deter-mined by various circumstances. But similar words being used in regard to a place over which a way is already fixed by buildings or permanent enclosures, would be con-[*182] strued *to be a grant of a way thus located, fixed, and defined." And such was held to be the proper construction to be given to this deed, and that the plaintiff acquired thereby a right of way over the sidewalk of the width at which it was at the time of making the deed.[1]

17. The case of Lewis v. Carstairs was somewhat similar in its facts to that of Kirkham v. Sharp, and the same doc-trine is there sustained by the court, limiting the use of a way created for the accommodation of certain lots to these lots, and excluding its use for other purposes. The facts were briefly these. Plaintiff's grantor owned an estate at the intersection of two streets, E. and C. The defendant owned an adjacent estate on C. Street. Plaintiff's grantor conveyed to him a part of his estate, bounding him on E. Street, and agreed to open an alley from E. Street along the side of the lot sold to the plaintiff, and along the rear of his remaining lot fronting on C. Street, "bounded on an alley of the width, &c., intended to be left open by the grantor, together with the free use and privilege of the said alley as a passage, in common with the grantor and his heirs, and those to whom he may grant the same privilege." Afterwards the

[1] Salisbury v. Andrews, 19 Pick. 250, 253.

plaintiff's grantor conveyed his estate on C. Street to the defendant, who undertook to use said alley to pass from E.
Street, along the rear of the parcel last conveyed to him, to
the rear of the adjoining parcel.   And the court held he had
no right thus to extend the use of the alley to other lands
than those to which the original parties who created it made
it appendant.[1]

18. The above case has been referred to thus specially,
partly to illustrate the application of the doctrine of Kirkham v. Sharp, and partly to suggest a limitation to the proposition elsewhere made, that, where an easement becomes
appurtenant to an estate, it remains appurtenant to
*every part of it into which it may be divided, which, [*183]
though generally true, is often limited by the nature
of the easement, and the condition of the estate to which it
is attached.

The distinction seems to depend upon whether the easement — a way, for instance — is indefinite in its limitation,
or, from the nature of the use to be made of it, is restricted
and defined. " If," says Jervis, C. J., " I grant a way to a
cottage which consists of one room, I know the extent of the
liberty I grant, and my grant would not justify the grantee
in claiming to use the way to gain access to a town he might
build at the extremity of it." [2]

So it was held that a way to a dwelling-house, wash-house,
and stable does not justify the use of it for access to a field.
A way to a cottage ceases, if the cottage be changed into a
tan-yard.   But if the grant be of a cottage, with all ways to
the same, the right of way is not lost by altering the cottage.
If the grant be of a way from a highway to the grantee's
dwelling-house, he may not open it to his field, and drive
his cattle over the grantor's land along such way to his
field.   And if the way be to a particular corner of a field,

[1] Lewis v. Carstairs, 6 Whart. 193.

[2] Metropolitan Cemetery Co. v. Eden, 16 C. B. 42. See Allan v. Gomme,
11 Adolph. & E. 759 ; ante, chap. 1, sect. 3, pl. 38.

the grantee may not use it to enter his field at any other point.[1]

And this may be further illustrated by a case put by Denman, C. J., in giving an opinion in Allan v. Gomme, of the grant of a small parcel of land, part of a large field devoted to the culture of crops, for the purpose of a yard to the house of the grantee, if a way were reserved across the same to the field ; the grantor could not sell this field into house-lots, and thereby turn this way into one for the accommodation of a town or village.[2]

19. The following case is stated here, because it is treated of as coming under the category of ways, though not [*184] easily *assigned to any of the classes already mentioned. There was a grant of a "river landing, so far as the same shall be necessary for erecting, maintaining, and supporting an intended bridge." The court held it to be a grant of a servitude or easement in land for a defined purpose. "It is a right of way of a specified kind, and nothing more. . . . . The grant being of an easement, the occupation under it must be regarded as the exercise of the right granted. Long enjoyment of an easement will establish a right to an easement, but not to the land itself." [3]

SECTION IV.

HOW WAYS MAY BE USED.

1. Case of way, "across," "over and along," &c., "to get hay," &c., how to be used.
2. Cases of special ways and for special purposes, rule of construction.
3. Grantee of way held strictly to the terms of his grant.
4. How far a "carriage-way" is a "drift-way."
5. When one not in possession may use a way appurtenant, &c.
6. How far a way for agricultural purposes a general one.
7. Atkins v. Bordman. Rights of way defined and explained.

---

[1] Henning v. Burnet, 8 Exch. 187.

[2] See *ante*, chap. 1, sect. 3, pl. 38.

[3] Schuylkill Nav. Co. v. Stoever, 2 Grant, Cas. 462.

8. Bounding by an intended way only implies a suitable one.

9. A right to pass over twenty feet is only so far as it is necessary.

10. Right of way carries all that is necessary to enjoy it.

11. Metropolitan Cemetery Co. v. Eden. Right to pass from any part of a way to land.

12. Allan v. Gomme. Restricting ways to the special objects of the grant.

13. Henning v. Burnet. Specific ways not to be changed in their use.

14. Dand v. Kingscote. Adopting improved modes of using ways.

1. THIS leads to a consideration of the extent and uses to which ways of a particular description may be applied, and how far this is limited and controlled by the nature and condition of the estates for whose benefit the same is created.

A grant of a way *across* a parcel of land does not give a right to enter upon the parcel on one side, and, after going *partly across, to come out upon the same [*185] side. And where one under such a grant drew timber from his own land on to the servient parcel and turned it round, which he could not do on his own land, it was held that he was not justified under his right of way.[1] So where one had a way " in, through, over, and along " a certain strip of land from A to B, it was held that he had not thereby a right to a way across the strip of land.[2] Where the grant was of a convenient way to get hay, &c., over the grantor's land, it was limited to one line ; and though at first an indefinite one, when it had been once designated, it could not be changed at the election of the grantee.[3] But what is a reasonable use of a way, where the purposes are not defined, is a question for the jury.[4]

Where a right of way has been created, but no time or hour in the day is fixed in which it may be used, the French law seems to be this : if it is to be exercised over an unenclosed place, it may be used at any hour, whether by night or by day ; but if the place is designed to be closed for the security of the owner or that of the public, it may be used at any convenient hour, but he who is to enjoy it cannot in-

[1] Comstock v. Van Deusen, 5 Pick. 163.

[2] Senhouse v. Christian, 1 T. R. 560, 569 ; Woolr. Ways, 33.

[3] Jones v. Percival, 5 Pick. 485.

[4] Hawkins v. Carbines, 3 Hurlst. & N., Am. ed. 914.

16

sist that it should be kept open all hours of the night. But if the right of passing in the night in such a case is granted, the owner of the land cannot prevent its being enjoyed at any hour; and if, on the other hand, the owner of the dominant estate chooses to exercise the right, he must have a key by which to unlock the gate of the enclosure, and must not leave it open after having passed through it.[1]

2. A grant of way on foot, and for horses, oxen, cattle, and sheep does not authorize one to carry manure over the way in a wheelbarrow.[2] A way to Green Acre is a [*186] way for *any purposes for which that field could be used. But, as will be shown, if it was to a particular open space described in the grant, and that was afterwards occupied by a building, the right of way is defeated, since it could only be used for the purposes for which it was granted, and that could no longer be done.[3] If granted or acquired over Black Acre to Green Acre, and the grantee of the way, having passed over Black Acre, pass over and beyond Green Acre, he will be a trespasser, because the right of way did not justify such a use of it. But it is suggested that if, after having reached Green Acre, the owner thereof had proceeded thence over his own land or a public way to a mill, it might be otherwise.[4] And it is held, moreover, that if, in the case supposed, the owner of the way was passing over Black Acre with an intent to pass beyond Green Acre, he would be liable in trespass, the character of the act, whether justified or otherwise, depending upon the intention with which he entered upon Black Acre; and this is for the jury to determine.[5]

3. The proposition in regard to confining the use of a

---

[1] 3 Toullier, Droit Civil Français, 497, 498.

[2] Brunton v. Hall, 1 Q. B. 792.

[3] Henning v. Burnet, 8 Exch. 187 ; Allan v. Gomme, 11 Adolph. & E. 759.

[4] Howell v. King, 1 Mod. 190 ; Davenport v. Lamson, 21 Pick. 72 ; Lawton v. Ward, 1 Ld. Raym. 75 ; Woolr. Ways, 34 ; Shroder v. Brenneman, 23 Penn. St. 348 ; 1 Rolle, Abr. 391, pl. 50.

[5] French v. Marstin, 4 Fost. 440, 451.

way strictly to the purposes for which it was granted, is
thus stated in the case of French v. Marstin, above cited:
" The grantee of a way is limited to use his way for the
purposes and in the manner specified in his grant.   He
cannot go out of his way, nor use it to go to any other place
than that described, nor to that place for any other purpose
than that specified, if the use in this respect is restricted." [1]
So where there was a grant of a right of way and a free open
road from a highway to a mill privilege, it was held that the
grantee had not thereby any right to pile lumber upon the
way so granted.[2]

4. Although it was held, as elsewhere stated, that a prescriptive way for a carriage did not include a drift-way,
Chambre, J. was inclined to hold that a carriage-
way was *prima facie* and strong presumptive evi- [*187]
dence of the grant of a drift-way.   The grantee in
such cases might send back his horses without his carriage,
or he might draw his carriage by oxen as well as horses, and
in either case he might send back his horses or oxen loose,
in order to drive them to pasture.[3]

5. In one instance, at least, it has been held that a man
may exercise a right of way appurtenant to an estate,
although he is not in possession of the same; and that is,
where the owner of a tenement to which there is a way
appurtenant lets the same to a tenant, he may use the way
to view waste, demand rent, and remove obstructions from
the premises.[4]

6. It has been questioned how far the grant of a way for
agricultural purposes is a general right of way.   It seems,
however, to be one of a limited and qualified character.   It
was held not to include the right to transport coals over such

---

[1] French v. Marstin, 4 Fost. 440, 449. See Regina v. Pratt, 4 Ellis & B. 860;
Knight v. Woore, 3 Bing. N. C. 3.   Bakeman v. Talbot, 31 N. Y. 366; Colchester v. Roberts, 4 M. & W. 774.

[2] Kaler v. Beaman, 49 Maine, 208.

[3] Ballard v. Dyson, 1 Taunt. 279, 288.

[4] Proud v. Hollis, 1 Barnew. & C. 8; Woolr. Ways, 35.

a way,[1] nor to transport lime from a quarry.[2] So a right to draw water from a river will not sustain a plea of a right to draw goods and water,[3] and a right to cart timber will not sustain a plea of a general right of way on foot, and with horses, carts, wagons, and other carriages.[4]

7. The whole subject of the rights of way and their limitations was most elaborately and ably examined by Shaw, C. J., in the case of Atkins v. Bordman, so frequently cited in the course of this work. In that case there was a grant of a parcel of land, which was described as having a gate and passage-way about five feet wide on one side, and a right of way was reserved " through and upon the said gate or passage-way, for carrying and recarrying wood or any other thing through the same, and over the yard or ground [*188] *of said messuage hereby granted, into and from the housing and land of me (the grantor), for the use and accommodation thereof." It was held to intend a convenient passage-way, but not of a definite width. An easement of way, as observed by the Chief Justice, consists in the right to use the surface of the soil for the purpose of passing and repassing, and the incidental right of properly fitting the surface for that use. But the owner of the soil has all the rights and benefits of ownership consistent with such easement. All which the person having the easement can lawfully claim is the use of the surface for passing and repassing, with a right to enter upon and prepare it for that use, by levelling, gravelling, ploughing, and paving, according to the nature of the way granted or reserved; that is, for a foot-way, a horse-way, or a way for all teams and carriages.

If the way is not bounded or limited, or there be no one in existence, the grant of a way would be, in point of width

1 Cowling v. Higginson, 4 Mees. & W. 245.
2 Jackson v. Stacey, Holt, N. P. 455.
3 Knight v. Woore, 3 Bing. N. C. 3.
4 Higham v. Rabett, 5 Bing. N. C. 622.

and height, such as is reasonably necessary and convenient
for the purposes for which it is granted. If a foot-way, it
shall be high and wide enough for persons to pass with such
things as foot-passengers usually carry. If for teams and
carriages, it shall be sufficient to admit carriages of the
largest size, or loads of hay and other vehicles usually moved
by teams. So that, what is reasonable is partly law and
partly fact ; the facts are found by the jury, and then the
court declare whether it is convenient or not. When no
dimensions of a way are defined, but the purposes of it are
expressed, the dimensions will be held to be sufficient for the
accomplishment of that object. Where the way reserved
was for a house, it excluded the idea of such a use as might
be required for a store, such as bales, boxes, and the like.
And when "wood or any other thing" is mentioned in
connection with a house, it implies fire-wood, and not timber
for sale ; or things usually used in dwelling-houses, such as
vegetables, provisions, furniture, and the like.   And
the reservation of a way " for carrying and *re-carry- [*189]
ing wood or any other thing . . . . into and from
the housing and land of, &c., for the use and accommodation
thereof," was held to be a convenient foot-way to and from
the grantor's dwelling-house, of suitable height and dimensions to carry in and out furniture, provisions, and neces-
saries for family use, and to use for that purpose wheelbarrows, hand-sleds, and such small articles as are commonly
used for that purpose in passing to and from the street to
the dwelling-house in the rear, through a foot-passage in a
closely-built and thickly-settled town.[1]
    The easement reserved was " a right of passage " over the
agricultural lands which were set off on partition made.
Nothing passes as incident to such a grant but what is requisite to its fair enjoyment. That must be the reasonable and
usual enjoyment and user of such a privilege. The land-
owner may nevertheless appropriate his land to such pur-

[1] Atkins v. Bordman, 2 Metc. 457.

pose as he pleases, consistent with the right of the grantee of the passage to and fro.[1]

The general principles applicable to questions of this kind are here so fully stated and enforced, that little more is necessary than to refer to particular cases for purposes of illustration. Thus, in the case above stated, it was held that the owner of the land across which the way was reserved might erect a building over it, provided he left a convenient passage-way beneath it of a suitable height, and sufficiently lighted to be conveniently used.[2]

8. So, where one let a parcel of land, bounding it upon an intended way of thirty feet, and afterwards occupied a part of it so as to reduce it to twenty-seven feet in width, it was held that the recital did not amount to a covenant as to the way or as to its width; that under it the lessee was entitled to a way of a suitable width, and if one of twenty-seven feet answered that description, it was all he could insist upon under his lease, inasmuch as, it not being an existing way at the time of the grant, no inference as to its actual width was to be derived from what then was apparent.[3]

9. So, where there was a grant of a parcel of land, " with a right of passing and repassing over the space of twenty feet, between the west wall of the store and east line of the granted premises," it was held not to describe the [*190] limits of *the way granted, but that it was a grant of a convenient way within those limits, adapted to the convenient use and enjoyment of the land granted, for any useful and proper purpose for which the land might be used, considering its relative position. And what is a suitable and convenient way must depend upon circumstances. It could not, therefore, necessarily follow that the grantor would be liable for obstructing some part of this space, and it would

---

[1] Bakeman v. Talbot, 31 N. Y. 371.

[2] Atkins v. Bordman, 2 Metc. 466, 468.

[3] Harding v. Wilson, 2 Barnew. & C. 96. See Walker v. City of Worcester, 6 Gray, 548.

be for the jury to say whether the owner of the easement was thereby impeded in the use of a convenient way.[1]

But where the grant was of a right " in and over and through a forty feet street," it was held to give a way unobstructed over any and every part of it, as a strip of land dedicated to the purposes of a street in the neighborhood of the locality of the premises.[2]

10. The grant of a right of way carries with it all rights to the use of the soil which are properly incident to the free exercise and enjoyment of the right granted or reserved. Thus, a right of way to a warehouse would authorize the tenant of such warehouse to place on the ground goods brought to the warehouse, and to keep them a reasonable and convenient time to put them in store, and to place and keep goods on the ground a reasonable length of time, which are to be carried from the warehouse. And what would be such reasonable and convenient time would be a question of fact depending upon many circumstances. What would be an unreasonable length of time to leave goods upon a sidewalk, or in a street which was much frequented, would not be so on rear ground, where they would encumber no one having an equal right of way. In applying these general principles, it was held that, where a warehouse was granted with a right of passage which had been used for carrying goods to and from the same, " in as full and ample a manner as they now are or heretofore have been used and enjoyed," these were not words of restriction nor limitation of the use to such as had been made of it, and none other. If, for instance, the way used had been over the natural surface of the earth, the grantee might improve it by macadamizing, paving, or planking it, being limited to the use of *the same right, in a manner more convenient and [*191] beneficial to himself, without injury to those having the common right, but he might not use it for another and

---

[1] Johnson v. Kinnicutt, 2 Cush. 153.
[2] Tudor Ice Co. v. Cunningham, 8 Allen, 141.

distinct purpose. If the tenant in such case were to lay a railway track in such passage-way, for the purpose of moving his goods thereon, it would be a question for the jury whether the same interrupted other abutters in their use of the surface as a passage-way, or caused any actual damage to the owner of the soil, or was or was not a use of the soil for a distinct purpose beyond that of a right of way. But if what the tenant did was only an improvement of the surface, to fit it the better for the passage of persons, teams, and carriages, and the transportation of merchandise not injurious to the other abutters, nor to the owner of the soil, it would not be a new and distinct use of the soil. It was within the right of way reserved to the abutters, and not adverse to the right of the owner, and no action therefor would lie.[1]

11. In Metropolitan Cemetery Company *v.* Eden the question was to determine the extent of the way granted, where the grant was of a parcel of land, referring to a plan, on one side of which was a way or road, " together with full and free liberty, license, &c., to the grantees and all persons coming to or going from the same land, or any part thereof, to use and enjoy," &c., " the roads or ways leading to and from the same land, as the same ways were described in the said map or plan." On the plan there was a hedge by the side of the parcel of land next to the way, in which were two gates. The purchaser cut down that hedge and laid a heavy wall in its place, with gates in different places from those indicated on the plan, and formerly standing in the hedge. A purchaser of the land upon the opposite side of the way, the fee of which still remained in the original grantor, altered the way by digging it down in front of these new gates. And

[*192] the question was, whether the first purchaser *was not restricted to the gates as they were originally placed, and whether he had a right to complain of the obstruction to gates placed at different points

[1] Appleton *v.* Fullerton, 1 Gray, 186, 194; Brown *v.* Stone, 10 Gray, 65; Lyman *v.* Arnold, 5 Mason, 198.

from these.   But the court held that the right of access to
the lot over the way indicated upon the plan was indefinite,
and might be used anywhere ; that making this wall did not
deprive him of the right to use any other way of access,
whenever he chose to open such a way, and that the rule
was altogether different where the way is indefinite from
what it is if defined.   In the latter case, it cannot be exceeded or used in any other place or mode than that expressed in the deed.[1]

And this will probably serve for a clew to reconcile what
may sometimes seem an inconsistency in referring, as courts
often do, to the state and condition of the premises or plans
thereof, in determining what rights and easements pass therewith ; as in this case, though there was a defined way laid
down upon the plan, it was to be used by persons coming
from or going to " any part " of the granted premises, and
did not specify the gates on the plan as the mode of access
to the premises.

12. To illustrate, further, the principles of construction
which courts adopt in ascertaining the limits of grants of
ways, the case of Allan *v.* Gomme, which was elaborately
considered, is referred to, not only for the principal point
raised and settled in it, but for sundry collateral points
which received the attention of the court and were applied
in settling the main question.   The grant in that case was
of " a right of way and passage over said close, &c., to the
stable and loft over the same, and the space and opening
under the said loft, and then used as a wood-house."   The
grantee of this way, after this, converted this loft and
space under it used as a wood-house into a cottage,
and undertook to use the way for the purposes of the
cottage.   The question was, whether this grant of
way was to the *place occupied by the loft and space   [*193]
for any purposes to which they might be appropriated, or was limited to the use of it as a wood-house, or what

[1] Metropolitan Cemetery Co. *v.* Eden, 16 C. B. 42.

was its limit. The court held that it was not limited to
purposes of a wood-house alone, and that a reference to the
wood-house was to indicate the terminus of the way ; nor was
it a way for all purposes, for if so, a grant of a way to go
across a man's yard might be turned into a way for a village
to be built at the end of it. They held it was to be taken
as intending a way to an open space of ground generally,
which was to be in the same predicament in which it was at
the time of making the deed, but to be used for any purposes the grantee chose, provided it continued in the same
open state, and not to be used for buildings to be erected
thereon. One case, put for illustration by Denman, C. J.,
was that of a way to a field of many acres, then in corn or
pasture, reserved over a small parcel granted for a man's
yard ; and if the grantor were to build a village on his field,
it would not be claimed that the reservation of such a way
could be extended to such a use.[1]

13. In the case of Henning v. Burnet, the extent to which
the doctrine of Allan v. Gomme might lead, from the terms
there employed, was somewhat modified, though its general
doctrine, that reference is to be had to the existing state of
things at the time the grant is made in construing its terms
and meaning in respect to the nature and extent of the easements that pass with it, is not impugned.

In that case the owner of a dwelling-house, coach-house,
and stable had a field which belonged and was used with
the same, constituting together one estate. There was a
private carriage-way from a turnpike to his dwelling-house
and coach-house, and also to the field, by a gate from the car-
riage-road opening into the field at a particular point
[*194] *at the end of the carriage-way. He conveyed the
above premises, " with free liberty of ingress with
cattle," &c., in, over, and upon the carriage road, &c., to
the dwelling-house, coach-house, and stables. The purchaser of the estate tore down the carriage-house and stables,

---

[1] Allan v. Gomme, 11 Adolph. & E. 759.

and built a wall across the private way, and opened a gate from the carriage-way to another corner of the field. It was held that he had no right to use this new entrance into the field. In fact, there was no way, in terms, granted in respect to the field, and the only way which had been used to reach it was from the end of the carriage-way, which only authorized the grantee to go through the old gate, and was the only way that passed by the grant.[1]

14. In Dand v. Kingscote, a grant of land was made, reserving the mines within it, with sufficient " way leave " and " stay leave," with liberty of sinking and digging pits. It was held that by this reservation the grantor had no right to use this way for the purpose of drawing coal from under an adjacent lot of land, and in so doing he was a trespasser, and that the limit of the easement reserved, and the mode of using it, were what was reasonably convenient, according to the mode in general use when the right was to be exercised. If, therefore, in the progress of improvement, better or more feasible ways are devised and applied to use than those known and used at the time when the grant was first made, the mine-owner, under a reservation in this general form, might adopt the improved way ; as, for instance, he might substitute a railway for a wagon-way, by which to transport the coal from the pit across the granted premises, although the construction of such new way would subject the land-owner to the inconvenience of having it laid down in the place of the former one. Under this reservation, the grantor, moreover, might fix such machinery upon the premises as would be necessary to drain the mines, and *draw [*195] the coal from the same, and, in that case, he was held justified in erecting thereon a steam-engine and an engine-house, and constructing a pond upon the premises to supply water for working the engine.[2]

1 Henning v. Burnet, 8 Exch. 187.
2 Dand v. Kingscote, 6 Mees. & W. 174.

SECTION V.

OF THE RIGHTS OF THE LAND-OWNER AND WAY-OWNER IN LAND.

1. Land-owner may do anything not injurious to owner of the way.
2. Land-owner has same rights as to private as to public ways.
3. Owner of way may, and ordinarily must, repair it.
4. Limitations and exceptions as to general duty to repair.
5. Williams v. Safford. Of going *extra viam*, if way is impassable.
6. What way-owner may do with or upon the soil.
7. Egress, regress, fishing, and fowling give no right to things growing.
8. Right of way to carry coals, what is embraced in it.
9. How far one way may be exchanged for another.

1. The respective rights of the owners of the soil and of the easement to do acts upon the soil over or adjoining which the easement of way exists, were considered in Underwood *v.* Carney, where it was held that, if one grant a way across his land, he has no right to make any such use of the land adjoining it as produces any serious inconvenience to the owner of the easement. He may make a reasonable use of it, having reference to the public and general use which others make of their lands which are similarly situated. And in addition to what is said of the right to maintain fences across a way by the land-owner (ante p. *160), it seems to be now settled that if the land-owner is not restrained by the terms of the grant of a right of way across his lands for agricultural purposes, he may maintain fences across such way, if provided with suitable bars or gates for the convenience of the owner of the way. He is not obliged to leave it as an open way, nor to provide swing gates, if a reasonably convenient mode of passage is furnished.[1] Thus, in the case of a grant of a right of way over a place or court in Boston, the owner of the soil of the court erected stores upon the adjacent land, and laid sidewalks in front of the

---

[1] Bakeman *v.* Talbot, 31 N. Y. 366; Bean *v.* Coleman, 44 N. H. 539; Maxwell *v.* M'Atee, 9 B. Mon. 20; Cowling *v.* Higginson, 4 M. & W. 245. See State *v.* Pettis, 7 Rich. 390.

same, and opened passages into the cellars under the stores, and swung window-shutters over the line of the way, and it was held to be a lawful use of the adjacent land, being a customary one.[1] So the owner of land *ad- [*196] joining a way may dig cellars by the side of it, if in towns or cities, and may lay building materials thereon, if he takes care not improperly to obstruct the same, and removes the materials within a reasonable time.[2]

2. So the owner of the soil of a way, whether public or private, may make any and all uses to which the land can be applied, and all profits which can be derived from it consistently with the enjoyment of the easement. He may, as before stated, maintain ejectment to recover the land, and if the way is discontinued, he holds it again free from encumbrance. He may sink a drain or a watercourse below the surface, if he do it so as not to deprive the public of their easement.[3] He may have an action of tort against one who erects his house fronting upon the line of the street, and extending his bay window over the land of the highway though it be so high above the vehicles passing along the same as not to affect the travel injuriously. The act in the case cited, being of the character of a permanent occupation, rests upon a different ground from that of O'Linda v. Lathrop,[4] or Underwood v. Carney,[5] which was a temporary use connected with the purposes of the way.[6] So the owner of the land occupied by a highway, may have trespass for entering upon the same and digging into the side of it to widen the travelled part of it, though such act by a highway surveyor would be a lawful one.[7]

[1] Underwood v. Carney, 1 Cush. 292.
[2] O'Linda v. Lothrop, 21 Pick. 292.
[3] Perley v. Chandler, 6 Mass. 454 ; Green v. Chelsea, 24 Pick. 71 ; Pomeroy v. Mills, 3 Vt. 279 ; Lade v. Shepherd, 2 Strange, 1004 ; Adams v. Emerson, 6 Pick. 57 ; Atkins v. Bordman, 2 Metc. 457.
[4] 21 Pick. 292.
[5] 1 Cush. 292.
[6] Codman v. Evans, 5 Allen, 308.
[7] Hollenbeck v. Rowley, 8 Allen, 476.

3. The owner of a private way may enter upon the same and repair it, or put it into a condition to be used, and, ordinarily, it is incumbent upon the owner of the way to keep it in repair.[1] The owner of the way, for this purpose, has a right to do what is necessary upon the soil to make it safe and convenient for use, such as removing rocks to make the way, &c. The rocks, however, would belong to the owner of the soil, except so far as they were needed in making or repairing the way,[2] and this doctrine was extended to constructing and using a canal under a grant of an easement of a canal across another's land.[3] Nor would he have a right to go outside of the limits of such way, if defined and designated, in passing from one point to another, although the way were impassable by being overflowed or out of repair.[4] But a different rule prevails in respect to public ways.[5] Though, even then, he could only justify removing enough of the fences of the adjoining close to enable him to pass around the obstruction, doing no unnecessary injury.[6]

[*197]   *4. The exceptions to these rules are few, and grow out of the peculiar circumstances of particular cases. Thus the grantor of a way over his land may be bound by covenant to keep the same in repair, or the owner . of the soil may be bound by prescription to support and

---

[1] Gerrard v. Cooke, 2 Bos. & P. N. R. 109; Osborn v. Wise, 7 Carr. & P. 761; D. 8, 1, 10; 1 Fournel, Traité du Voisinage, 258; Wynkoop v. Burger, 12 Johns. 222; Doane v. Badger, 12 Mass. 65, 70; Atkins v. Bordman, 2 Metc. 457.

[2] Smith v. Rome, 19 Geo. 92; Brown v. Stone, 10 Gray, 65; Appleton v. Fullerton, 1 Gray, 186; Maxwell v. M'Atee, 9 B. Mon. 20; Bean v. Coleman, 44 N. H. 539.

[3] Lyman v. Arnold, 5 Mason, 198.

[4] Taylor v. Whitehead, 2 Doug. 745; Bullard v. Harrison, 4 Maule & S. 387; Miller v. Bristol, 12 Pick. 550; Holmes v. Seely, 19 Wend. 507; Capers v. M'Kee, 1 Strobh. 168; Williams v. Safford, 7 Barb. 309; Bakeman v. Talbot, 31 N. Y. 372.

[5] Taylor v. Whitehead, 2 Doug. 745; Campbell v. Race, 7 Cush. 408; Bullard v. Harrison, 4 Maule & S. 387; Holmes v. Seely, 19 Wend. 507; 3 Dane, Abr. 258; State v. Northumberland, 44 N. H. 631.

[6] Williams v. Safford, 7 Barb. 309.

maintain the way.[1] If the public locate a way across an existing watercourse, the public must maintain a bridge across the same, and may not stop the watercourse. But if the owner of the soil constructs a watercourse under the highway already existing, he must keep the bridge over the same in repair, or be liable to indictment.[2] And if one has a right of way across the land of another, which is not limited and defined, and the owner of the land obstruct the same, the owner of the way may pass over the adjacent lands of such land-owner, doing no unnecessary damage thereby.[3] And if the way is claimed and enjoyed as one of necessity, and the way previously in use shall be obstructed without the fault of the owner of it, by flood, for instance, it is stated by some authorities that he may, if necessary, pass over other lands of the owner of the soil of such way, doing no unnecessary damage thereby.[4]

Mr. Tudor, upon the strength of a case cited by counsel in Henn's case,[5] says : " If a way becomes impassable through want of repairs which ought to have been done by the owner of the land, the owner of the dominant tenement may, it seems, justify his trespass by deviating from the ordinary track." [6]

The case from Sir William Jones was this. It was trespass *qu. cl.* The defendant pleaded a right of way by a " common footpath through the close." The plaintiff replied, that the defendant went out of the path. The *de- [*198] fendant rejoined, that the footpath was founderous, &c., " in default of the plaintiff, who ought to amend it," and therefore he passed along as near the path as he could. " And this was resolved a good plea and justification."

---

[1] Doane *v.* Badger, 12 Mass. 65, 70 ; Taylor *v.* Whitehead, 2 Doug. 745.

[2] Perley *v.* Chandler, 6 Mass. 454.

[3] Leonard *v.* Leonard, 2 Allen, 543 ; Farnum *v.* Platt, 8 Pick. 339.

[4] Holmes *v.* Seely, 19 Wend. 507 ; Woolr. Ways, 51. See Taylor *v.* White head, 2 Doug. 749 ; Capers *v.* M'Kee, 1 Strobh. 168.

[5] Henn's case, W. Jones, 296.

[6] Tud. Lead. Cas. 127.

Whether calling it a " common footpath " took this out of the category of private ways, is not stated.

5. Several of the questions involved in the foregoing propositions were considered in Williams v. Safford. It was there held, that the owner of a private way had no right to go upon other land than the way itself, although the owner of the land shall have put obstructions in the way. The law gives the owner of the way no remedy but by abating the nuisance, or an action for damages. The grantee of a private way is himself bound to keep it in repair. He alone has the right of using it. He alone can prosecute for an obstruction of it. " In Taylor v. Whitehead," says Willard, J., " Buller, J. observes that, if the way pleaded in that case had been a way of necessity, the question whether in case it became founderous the owner might go *extra viam* would have required consideration. This dictum has given rise to the intimation, in Woolrych on Ways,[1] and of Nelson, C. J., in Holmes v. Seely, that ' there is a distinction between a private way by grant and one of necessity, resting upon the ground that the one is the grant of a specific track over the close, while the other is a general right of way over it ; the one an express specific grant, the other a more general, implied one.' It is believed, however, that there is no such distinction between them. A private way of necessity is nothing else but a way by grant. Such way does not give the owner a right to go at random over the entire close. He has a right merely to a convenient way, due regard being had to the convenience of both parties. But after the way has been once assigned, or selected, it rests on the same footing as any other way by grant, and [*199] both *parties are bound by it; the grantor not to obstruct it, and the grantee to be confined to it. . . . . It makes no difference whether the road was obstructed by the plaintiff or a stranger, or by the act of God. In neither case can the defendant justify a trespass *extra viam*. . . . .

[1] Woolr. Ways, 51.

The same doctrine applies with respect to a private road by prescription, that governs in the case of grants." [1]

6. The grant of a parcel of land bounded upon a passage-way gives the grantee a right of way over the same, but not a right to take and carry away the materials thereof. But he would have a right to use the sand, gravel, stone, &c., within the passage-way for grading, fitting, and repairing it. [2]

And where one owning the soil of a way, upon which his own house stood, granted to the owner of another house which abutted thereon, a right to pass over the same as a foot or carriage way for twenty yards from H. Street, it was held that such grantee might make the way dry and safe for use in a manner most convenient to himself, provided he did not thereby cause inconvenience to his grantor. And it was accordingly held, that he might, for that purpose, lay a flag-stone at his door within the passage-way. [3]

7. But a grant of a right of ingress and regress over land, and of fishing and fowling thereon, gives no right to take wood, grass, or any other thing properly appertaining to the ownership of the soil. [4]

8. The grant of a way to carry coals gives such grantee a right to lay down such tracks in the grantor's land, between the termini of the way, as are usually adopted for that purpose, provided the same are necessary to enable the grantee to carry out the purposes of the grant. [5]

*So where there was a grant of land reserving the [*200] mines, with a right of necessary and convenient ways for the purpose, " and particularly of laying, making, and granting wagon-ways in and over the said premises, or any part thereof." It was held that this was limited to such ways as were necessary to get at and remove the mineral. Nor would the grantee of the land have any cause of action

[1] Williams v. Safford, 7 Barb. 309. See also Boyce v. Brown, 7 Barb. 80.
[2] Phillips v. Bowers, 7 Gray, 21.
[3] Gerrard v. Cooke, 2 Bos. & P. N. R. 109.
[4] Emans v. Turnbull, 2 Johns. 313.
[5] Senhouse v. Christian, 1 T. R. 560.

17

by reason of constructing such a way upon the land, though intended to be used for other purposes. But if the road actually made be not of the description mentioned in the deed, the owner of the soil would have a right of action therefor.[1]

9. Questions have occasionally arisen in respect to substituting one way for another, and how far, where this has been done, it is binding upon the parties. The head-note of the case of Pope v. Devereux is in these words: "Evidence of an executed oral agreement between the owners of the dominant and servient tenements, to discontinue an old way and substitute a different one, is competent evidence of a surrender of the old way."[2]   And in the case of Smith v. Lee, the language of the judge, though it may be considered as somewhat *obiter*, is: "When a right of way in a certain locality exists, it may be changed by the verbal agreement of the parties in interest, and when the change is actually made, and a new way is thus adopted by them, it fixes and determines their respective rights."[3]

It was held by the same court, that, where one undertook to change a way, which had been acquired by prescription, over his land, a part of which land he had sold to B., for the purpose of relieving the part so conveyed from the encumbrance of the way, but by mistake he made the new way, for a part of the distance, over B.'s land, so purchased by him, and the same was used fifteen years; whether this shall be an effectual substitution by which the parties shall be bound, depended upon whether it was known and acquiesced in by B. If it was, he would be bound by it. If he did not know it, no use, short of twenty years, would make it valid and binding upon the owner of the land.[4]

The case of Crounse v. Wemple involved the question of

---

[1] Durham & Sunderland R. R. Co. v. Walker, 2 Q. B. 940, 966; Bowes v. Ravensworth, 15 C. B. 512.

[2] Pope v. Devereux, 5 Gray, 409.

[3] Smith v. Lee, 14 Gray, 473.

[4] Gage v. Pitts, 8 Allen, 531.

a substitution of one way for another, though the vague manner in which the opinion is given can aid but little in settling the principle upon which other like cases are to be determined. In that case the way in question was one from a highway to a mill, passing through a swamp. The owner of the way used a new way a part of the distance, so as to avoid the swamp, and it was held that he did not thereby lose his prescriptive right over the other parts of the way. Nor would it affect his right that the way had, by reason of a new way being opened, ceased to be of as much importance to him as it once had been. A part of the charge of the judge to the jury who tried the case, and which seems to have been approved by the Court of Appeals, was, " that it was competent for the owner of the right of way and of the land over which it runs, to alter its location, and when it is changed it was for the jury to say whether such change was intended to be a permanent one or merely temporary, and if the new way has been used by the party owning the easement, and the owner of the land forbids the use of the new road, if the right to use it exists by license, the owner of the way may go back to the old road. But if such change was the result of an agreement to make a permanent change, then the right to change back did not attach, in the event of the owner of the land closing the new way." In other words, it would seem, though not so directly ruled, that in the latter case the original way is lost by abandonment, though the new way has not been enjoyed long enough to give a prescriptive right to the same, if this case is to stand as law.[1]

If it was intended to say that one who has a definite way over another's land can exchange that with the owner of the land for another definite way across his land, by a mere parol agreement, followed by an enjoyment of the new way for less than twenty years, and thereby lose his title to the first and gain a legal title to the second, as of an

---

[1] Crounse v. Wemple, 29 N. Y. 540.

[*201]   *incorporeal hereditament, it seems to be doing
         violence to the notion, that such an independent
easement can only be created and acquired by deed of grant,
as well as to modern English authorities. If I cannot acquire a right of way as appurtenant to my land over my
neighbor's land without a deed, where the consideration
which I pay him therefor is a sum of money, or an article
of merchandise, would it be otherwise if I paid for it by giving up to him an interest in land like another easement, even
in his own land ?   Could A acquire a right of way as an appurtenant to Black Acre, over another's land without a deed,
by giving in exchange by parol a right to maintain a trench
across other lands of the same man ?

Several of the authorities upon the subject are collected
by Woolrych, and, although cases have occurred where the
stoppage of one way and the opening of another have been
held to be a *license* to use such new way, it was, after all, a
revocable license, and the party was thereupon remitted to
his original right of way.   Among the cases cited was that of
Reignolds v. Edwards,[1] and of Horne v. Widlake.[2]

The case of Lovell v. Smith expressly holds that a parol
agreement to substitute a new way for an old prescriptive
way, though followed by a discontinuance of the use of the
old way, would not amount to an abandonment of it.[3]

Nor is the doctrine sustained by cases like that of Larned
v. Larned,[4] where a way gained by *dedication* has been given
up in favor of another way *dedicated* in its stead, since a
dedication neither requires a formal grant nor a long-continued enjoyment to give it effect.

In the case of Reignolds v. Edwards, the owner of the
land over which the defendant had a right of way fenced it
         up, but opened another, which the defendant used
[*202]   for *several years, when the owner of the land shut

---

[1] Woolr. Ways, 22, 51 ; Reignolds v. Edwards, Willes, 282.
[2] Horne v. Widlake, Yelv. 141.
[3] Lovell v. Smith, 3 C. B. N. s. 120.
[4] Larned v. Larned, 11 Metc. 421 ; 2 Washb. Real Prop. 57.

up the new way, and the defendant, having occasion to use it, broke down the fence and passed over the new way. But the court say : " This new way was only a way by sufferance, and either party might determine it at his pleasure ; and the plaintiff, in this case, has determined his will by fastening the gate, and so the defendant ought to have had recourse to his old way."

The case of Hamilton v. White, though in many respects like some of those cited above, does not seem to be very satisfactory, as settling the question, either way. But it does not hold that there can be a valid and effectual substitution of one way for another by parol, whereby the first is extinguished and the second becomes a permanent easement in the servient tenement, though followed by use for less than twenty years.

In that case, one had a right of way by prescription from a highway to his land, over the plaintiff's land. By agreement between the parties, this was changed, the first one closed and another opened, and was used for ten or twelve years. This way lay across a ditch or stream, over which was a bridge. The plaintiff took up this bridge, leaving the way otherwise open as usual, and the defendant, having occasion to use it, passed along the way to the stream, and, finding the bridge gone, threw in earth, over which he passed, though forbidden by the owner, and the owner of the land brought trespass.

The court, Ruggles, C. J., referring to Reignolds v. Edwards, says : " But the difference between that case and the present is, that the new way in the present case remained open. The bridge across the ditch had been removed, but the way was not fenced up, and the defendants in passing it were not compelled to break down or remove any wall, fence, or enclosure." He also cites Horne v. Widlake, above cited, and dwells upon the fact that the plaintiff, instead of objecting to the use of the new way, and offering   ·
*the use of the old in its stead, objected to the de- [*203]

fendant's using either, and denied his right to any way, when in fact the defendant had a right of way over the land. He adds: "If it be admitted that the right to the new track, not being created by grant, nor acquired by user of twenty years, was held at the will of the plaintiff, he ought not to be permitted to put an end to that will, without opening the old route or consenting that the defendants might use it. . . . . If he chose to put an end to the defendants' right of passing by the new way, he should have opened the way to which the defendants had a lawful title. By denying the defendants' right of way altogether, the plaintiff showed his intention of putting the controversy between himself and the defendants, on the ground that the defendants had no right at all; and on that point the cause was tried."[1]

The case, therefore, obviously turns upon the peculiar circumstances under which the way was used, and does not, in terms or by implication, affirm that the owner of the way had become entitled to the new one, by the way of substitution or exchange, as a permanent easement.

It is more like the case where the owner of the land over which another has a right of way should put an obstruction in it at some point, and the owner of the way, having occasion to pass over it, should avoid such obstruction by going upon the adjacent land of the servient tenement, which some authorities, as has been before stated, maintain he might do.

And though not directly in point, the language of Patteson, J., in Payne v. Shedden, in applying the doctrine of the statute of 2 & 3 Wm. IV. c. 71, has a bearing upon the question examined above. "So if, instead of the direct path from A to B, another track over the plaintiff's land from A to C, and thence to B, had been substituted [*204] by parol *agreement of the parties for an indefinite time, yet the user of this substituted line may be considered as substantially an exercise of the old right, and evidence of the continued enjoyment of it." This was pre-

[1] Hamilton v. White, 1 Seld. 9. See s. c., 4 Barb. 60.

faced by the remark, that "the agreement to suspend the enjoyment of the right does not extinguish, nor is it inconsistent with the right." [1]

And in Carr v. Foster, in speaking of the above case, he says : " I thought there, that if I have a right over another's land, and he for a time gives me a consideration for ceasing to exercise it, I enjoy the right while receiving the compensation." [2]

[1] Payne v. Shedden, 1 Mood. & R. 382.
[2] Carr v. Foster, 3 Q. B. 581.

*CHAPTER III.

OF EASEMENTS AND SERVITUDES OF WATER.

SECTION I.

OF PROPERTY IN STREAMS AND WATERCOURSES.

1. ANOTHER class of the prædial servitudes, known to the civil law as *rural* or *rustic*, in distinction from those called *urban*, relate to " the conducting and using of water." It embraces a variety of forms, bearing different specific names. And, besides these, there were *urban* servitudes connected with the conducting of water, such as that of *eaves' drip*, called *Stillicidium*, and that of a sewer of an adjacent owner's estate.[1]

It is proposed to treat of both these classes under one head, under the name of easements and servitudes, and to apply to them the rules of the common law.

2. It will be borne in mind, that, as by a servitude or easement is meant a right which is granted for the advantage of one piece of land in or over another, it always presupposes two parcels, and these belonging to different proprietors, one of which is burdened with the servitude called the servient, and one for the advantage of which the servitude is conferred, called the dominant estate.[2]

3. As water, from its nature, is ordinarily passing from a higher to a lower level, till it reaches the point where it is lost by absorption, evaporation, or discharge into the ocean ; and inasmuch as its use may not only be available when wholly enjoyed upon the estate of a land-owner, but its benefit may often be derived, more or less immediately, from its being managed or controlled by such land-owner, in its passage through the estate of another, — it becomes important to define what a land-owner's rights and duties are in respect to water found within his premises. This becomes *the more important, in order to discrimi- [*207]

[1] Kauff. Mackeldey, 342 – 345 ; Wood, Inst. Civ. Law, 91 - 93; 1 Brown, Civ. Law, 182.

[2] Kauff. Mackeldey, 335 ; 1 Brown, Civ. Law, 182.

nate between what rights one may claim as naturally incident to the ownership of his estate, and those to which he is entitled, or is subject, in respect to such ownership, in its connection with other estates, and constituting, in respect to his own, a servitude or easement.

4. As forming the subject of property, in connection with the realty, water may be viewed in two lights; — one, as constituting one of the elements of which an estate is composed, and giving, by its qualities and susceptibilities of use, a value to such estate; the other, as being valuable alone for its use, to be enjoyed in connection with the occupation of the soil.

In the latter sense, it constitutes an incorporeal hereditament, to which the term *easement* is applied. But in neither light is it the water itself of which property is predicated. And it is of its use alone as an element, and the right to enjoy it in connection with some portion of the soil, that it is proposed to treat in the present chapter.[1]

5. In considering, then, what are the rights of a land-owner in respect to the use of water which naturally belongs to his freehold, in order to see what will make his a dominant or servient estate in respect to acquiring new rights or losing those originally belonging to it, resulting from the use of the water by himself or others, it will be necessary to treat the subject under different heads. And it is proposed, for purposes of general classification, to consider, — 1st. The rights of the land-owner as such, or as the owner of works to be operated by the same, to running streams or watercourses generally; 2d. The rights and [*208] *duties of persons interested in surface or natural drainage; 3d. Their rights in respect to underground or percolating waters.

---

[1] Gould v. Boston Duck Co., 13 Gray, 443; Cary v. Daniels, 8 Metc. 466, 480; Campbell v. Smith, 3 Halst. 140, 145; Gardner v. Trustees of Village of Newburgh, 2 Johns. Ch. 162; Hendrick v. Cook, 4 Ga. 241, 255; Plumleigh v. Dawson, 1 Gilm. 544; Woolr. Waters, 117; Stein v. Burden, 29 Ala. 127; s. c., 24 Ala. 130; Burden v. Stein, 27 Ala. 104; Crittenton v. Alger, 11 Metc. 281; 5 Duranton, Cours de Droit Français, 200; Davis v. Getchell, 50 Maine, 604.

6. The term *Watercourse*, in this classification, is intended to include all running streams of water, though writers often describe these by different distinctive terms, such as *Rivers,* *Brooks*, and the like.

Woolrych, borrowing from Callis, defines a *river*, "A running stream, pent in on either side with walls and banks, and it bears that name as well where the waters flow and reflow, as where they have their current one way."[1]

Callis defines a *sewer*, "A fresh-water trench, compassed in on both sides with a bank, and is a small current, or little river."

"A *gutter* is of less size, and of a narrower passage and current, than a sewer is." "A *sewer* is a common public stream, — a *gutter*, a straight private running water."

"A *ditch* is a kind of current of waters in *infimo gradu*." But the law only recognizes ditches as such, "which have a kind of current, and which in some sort partake with rivers."[2]

The term "watercourse," when used in a grant, may mean the channel through which water flows, or the stream that flows through it, and whether it be the one or the other depends upon the context. If used in the first sense, it is a corporeal hereditament; if in the second, it is an incorporeal one.[3] And it was held that a grant of "a river as it winds and turns, including the same," passed no land, recognizing the doctrine, as stated by Coke, that, "if a man grant *aquam suam*, the soil shall not pass, but the piscary within the water passeth therewith."[4]

A stream may acquire the name of a river, in the channel *of which, at some seasons of extreme [*209] drought, no water flows.[5]

[1] Woolr. Waters, 31 ; Callis, Sewers, 54.
[2] Callis, Sewers, 57, 58, 59.
[3] Doe v. Williams, 11 Q. B. 688, 700 ; Woolr. Waters, 117.
[4] Jackson v. Halstead, 5 Cow. 219 ; Co. Litt. 4 b.
[5] Reynolds v. M'Arthur, 2 Pet. 417, 438 ; Ashley v. Wolcott, 11 Cush. 195 ; Bangor v. Lansil, 51 Maine, 525.

And, as a general proposition, wherever there is a steady, uniform current of water, it constitutes a river, though this does not include a lake through which there is a current from its head to its outlet.[1] And where a river is divided by an island or intervening parcel of land, each branch becomes a watercourse with all its incidents, and this though the island be formed in the stream, and there would be a *filum aquæ* to each of the streams or watercourses.[2]

To maintain the right to a *watercourse* or *brook*, it must be made to appear that the water usually flows in a certain direction, and by a regular channel with banks or sides; mere surface drainage at certain seasons of the year, when the water is high, is not a stream or brook.[3]

Among the definitions of a watercourse which may be found in the books, the following by Bigelow, J., in Luther *v.* Winnisimmet Company, is perhaps the most accurate and compendious: "A stream of water usually flowing in a definite channel, having a bed, sides, or banks, and usually discharging itself into some other stream or body of water. To constitute a watercourse, the size of the stream is not important; it might be very small, and the flow of the water need not be constant. But it must be something more than a mere surface drainage over the entire face of a tract of land, occasioned by unusual freshets or other extraordinary causes."[4] It was accordingly held, in another case, that "the accustomed, though not continuous, flowage of waters" (in this case from springs) "is a stream in the eye of the law, and its channel is no more to be obstructed than if it was the channel of a stream that never failed."[5] So where water rose from a spring and ran off several rods in a de-

---

[1] State *v.* Gilmanton, 14 N. H. 467, 476; s. c. 9 N. H. 461.

[2] Luttrel's Case, 4 Co. 88; Trustees. &c. *v.* Dickinson, 9 Cush. 549.

[3] Ashley *v.* Wolcott, 11 Cush. 192; Bangor *v.* Lansil, sup.

[4] Luther *v.* Winnisimmet Co., 9 Cush. 171, 174; Ashley *v.* Wolcott, 11 Cush. 192; Ward *v.* Metcalfe, Clayt., ed. 1651, 96; Shields *v.* Arndt, 3 Green, Ch. 234; Kauffman *v.* Griesemer, 26 Penn. St. 407; Earle *v.* Hart, 1 Beasl. 280, 283.

[5] Kauffman *v.* Griesemer, 26 Penn. St. 407.

fined stream with a current, and then came to marshy land, where it spread itself over the ground, but still continued to flow sluggishly in a defined bed or depression, but not with a sufficiently strong current to destroy the grass or break the sod, till it reached another owner's land, who had a watering-place for his cattle which was supplied by this water, it was held to be a watercourse of which the owner of the higher land had no right to stop the current and flow.[1] Nor is it essential to a watercourse, that the banks should be absolutely unchangeable, the flow constant, nor the water entirely unmixed with earth, nor moving with any fixed velocity.[2] It need not be shown to flow continually, it may be dry at times, but it must have a well-defined and substantial existence.[3] It is immaterial how small it may be, if it be well defined, nor, so far as *the rights of prop- [*210] erty of the land-owner in a stream of water are concerned, is it material whether it flows above or below the surface, provided it be an ascertained current of flowing water.   And whatever may be its source, as soon as water becomes a part of a natural stream, it belongs to him in whom is the property of the stream itself.[4]

7. But the watercourses above described do not include water flowing in the hollows or ravines in land, which is the mere surface water from rains or melting snows, and is discharged through these from a higher to a lower level, but which at other times are destitute of water.   And although, when hereafter treating of servitudes which one parcel of land may have in another in respect to surface water, the circumstance of there being outlets for the same will be seen to be an important consideration, it is not the right of

[1] Gillett v. Johnson, 30 Conn. 180.

[2] Basset v. Company, 43 N. H. 578.

[3] Ashley v. Wolcott, 11 Cush. 195.

[4] Dudden v. Guardians of Poor, &c., 1 Hurlst. & N. 627 ; Rawstron v. Taylor, 11 Exch. 369 ; Broadbent v. Ramsbotham, 11 Exch. 602 ; Wheatly v. Baugh, 25 Penn. St. 528 ; Arnold v. Foote, 12 Wend. 330 ; Dickinson v. Grand Junction Canal Co., 7 Exch. 282, 301 ; Wood v. Waud, 3 Exch. 748, 779 ; Eddy v Simpson, 3 Cal. 249.

property in such waters, or in their use, that is at present the subject of examination. Where a spring rises out of the ground within one's estate, in such a manner as to flow from its outlet or head in a defined current to the land of another proprietor, he thereby acquires a right of property in the use of its water, of which no one has a right to deprive him. But where the water rose from subterranean sources into a well which occasionally overflowed, and diffused itself upon the surface, and was conducted off in an artificial channel which was often dry, it was held not to come within the category of running water, the benefit of which a lower proprietor could claim as such. The same rule applies to water which collects in low or swampy places upon land, but has never formed for itself a defined channel by which it reaches an existing watercourse, although if left to itself it would by force of gravity eventually find [*211] its way *into and help supply a stream which is running through another's land. The owner of the land in which water thus situated is found, may do what he will with the same, though he thereby prevents its reaching the land of another, as it has been accustomed thus indirectly to do.[1]

In one case, where the land adjoining a highway was swampy, and received the water which flowed from the highway, and the owner filled it up so as to prevent the water any longer flowing from the highway on to it, it was held that he might lawfully do it.[2] And in another case, the court held that the owner of land over which the surface water from another tract was accustomed to flow, might protect his land by raising it, though he thereby prevented the flow of the water from the adjacent tract.[3]

[1] Broadbent v. Ramsbotham, 11 Exch. 602 ; Rawstron v. Taylor, 11 Exch. 369, 382 – 384 ; Wadsworth, v. Tillotson, 15 Conn. 366, 373. In Ashley v. Wolcott, 11 Cush. 192, the court waive the question of the right to stop the flow of the surface water on one's land.

[2] Bangor v. Lansil, 51 Maine, 525.

[3] Parks v. Newburyport, 10 Gray, 28 ; post, pp. *225, *355 – *359, *362.

And yet, if the doctrine elsewhere laid down is a sound and tenable one, it would seem that, though for purposes of occupying a lot by building upon it, or by raising it up for purposes of cultivation, the owner may prevent the surface water of an upper lot from flowing on to it, he may not stop it by a dike or bank along the upper line of his land, leaving it as it was before in other respects.[1]

Where there is no watercourse by grant or prescription, and no stipulation between conterminous proprietors of land concerning the mode in which their respective parcels shall be occupied and improved, no right to regulate or control the surface drainage water can be asserted by the owner of one lot over that of his neighbor. The owner of land may occupy it in such manner or for such purpose as he sees fit, either by changing the surface, or the erection of buildings or other structures thereon, and this right is not restricted or modified by the fact that his own land is so situated, in reference to that of adjoining owners, that an alteration in the mode of its improvement or occupation, in any portion of it, will cause water which may accumulate thereon by rains and snows falling on its surface or flowing on to it over the surface of adjacent lots, either to stand in unusual quantities on other adjacent lands, or pass into and over the same in greater quantities or in other directions than they are accustomed to flow. Nor is it at all material whether a party obstructs or changes the direction and flow of surface water by preventing it from coming within the limits of his land, or by erecting barriers or changing the level of the soil so as to turn it off in a new course after it has come within his boundaries.[2]

A similar question to that discussed above, arose in a case where the owner of land adjoining a highway filled it up, and, at one point where there had been a gorge through

[1] See *post*, § 6, and cases cited.
[2] Gannon *v* Horgadon, 10 Allen, 106 ; Luther *v* Winnisimmet Ferry, 9 Cush

174

which the water from the street escaped on to his land, he built a dwelling-house stopping the flow of the water entirely, and it was held that he had a right so to do, although it obliged the town to construct a drain to take off this water. The town may make its roads so that the water therefrom may flow on to the adjacent lands, and the land-owner can only protect himself by erecting proper structures on his land to guard against it.[1]

The same principle, under a somewhat different form, was involved in the decision of Dickinson v. Worcester, where the court held that " a conterminous proprietor may change the situation or surface of his land, by raising or filling it to a higher grade by the construction of dikes, the erection of structures, or by the improvements which cause water to accumulate from natural causes on the adjacent land, and prevent its passing off from the surface." " Nor can a party gain a right to the flow of surface water over his neighbor's land, by collecting it in drains or culverts or artificial channels, unless he maintains them for a length of time sufficient to acquire a right of easement by adverse user. He cannot by his own act merely, without the assent or acquiescence of the adjoining owner, change their relative rights or duties, and convert a flow of surface water into a stream with all the legal incidents of a natural watercourse." The force of this latter remark resulted from the fact that the plaintiff had maintained a ditch for some time, into and through which the surface water and underdraining from his land had flowed, which the defendant had stopped upon his own land below. Had this been a permanent stream of water, the rights of the parties would have been entirely different, and defendant would have been liable for thus stopping the flow of the water.[2]

The recent case of Earle v. De Hart, in New Jersey, involves several of the questions discussed in the last few

[1] Flagg v. Worcester, 13 Gray, 601; Wheeler v. Worcester, 10 Allen, 603.

[2] Dickinson v. Worcester, 7 Allen, 19. See Bangor v. Lansil, 51 Maine, 526.

pages, and presents a state of facts combining somewhat of the law of surface water and that arising from springs, in respect to constituting watercourses, and being governed by the general rules relating to them. The land in that case lay in the city of Elizabeth. The plaintiff's land was so situated that at certain seasons of the year the water collected upon the surface in such quantities as to discharge itself through a certain duct or channel, uniformly in one place, across the defendant's land, into an existing gutter which led to a river. The defendant stopped this duct or channel on his land, and the plaintiff prayed to have such obstruction abated. It was denied that such a channel as this, in which water only occasionally discharged itself, was a watercourse, within the eye of the law. But the Chancellor says : " If there is a quantity of water collecting at different seasons of the year on the complainant's land, to such an extent as requires an outlet to some common reservoir, and if such is always the case in times of heavy rain and melting of snow, and if, as far back as the memory of man runs, that flow of water produced a natural channel through the defendant's land, where such accumulated surplus water had always been accustomed to run, the right of the complainant to have the water discharged in the same channel, for the relief of her land, is so clear, that a court of equity would not refuse to protect her right," &c. " But I *think the facts admitted in the answer [*212] show that this is an ancient stream or watercourse, and that it is a natural watercourse in the etymological use of the term. . . . . It may be natural, as where it is made by the natural flow of the water, caused by the general superficies of the surrounding land, from which the water is collected into one channel, or it may be artificial, as in case of a ditch or other artificial means used to divert the water from its natural channel, or to carry it from lands from which it will not flow in consequence of the natural formation of the surrounding land. It is an ancient watercourse,

18

if the channel through which it naturally runs has existed from time immemorial. Whether it is entitled to be called an ancient watercourse, and as such, legal rights can be acquired and lost in it, does not depend upon the quantity of water it discharges. . . . . If the face of the country is such as necessarily collects in one body so large a quantity of water, after heavy rains, and the melting of large bodies of snow, as to require an outlet to some common reservoir, and if such water is regularly discharged through a well-defined channel, which the force of the water has made for itself, and which is the accustomed channel through which it flows, and has flowed from time immemorial, such channel is an ancient natural watercourse. . . . . This water having run in the same course for more than twenty years, and the complainant and those under whom she holds having enjoyed it as a right during that period, in its present channel, no one has a right to dam up the channel, or to divert the course of the water, to the injury of the complainant's land." [1]

8. In considering, then, the nature and extent of property in running water, and its use belonging to a land-owner who, as such, derives a benefit from its enjoyment, it may be repeated, that a *stream* is a part of the freehold. [*213] Every *land-owner has a property in the stream which flows through his land, while he has no property in the water itself of which it is composed, save for the gratification of his natural or ordinary wants.[2] And Lord Campbell, when speaking of a claim set up by the inhabitants of a place, of a right, by custom, to take water from a spring in the land of another, for domestic purposes, says : " The water which they claim a right to take is not the produce of the plaintiff's close, it is not his property, it is not the subject of property. . . . . It is not disputed

---

[1] Earle v. De Hart, 1 Beasl. 280.

[2] Stein v. Burden, 29 Ala. 127 ; s. c., 24 Ala. 130 ; Burden v. Stein, 27 Ala. 104 ; Cary v. Daniels, 5 Metc. 236 ; Crittenton v. Alger, 11 Metc. 281 ; Hart v. Evans, 8 Penn. St. 22.

that this would be so, with respect to the water of a river, or any open, running stream. We think it equally true as to the water of a spring when it first issues from the ground. . . . . While it remains in the field where it issues forth, in the absence of any servitude or custom giving a right to others, the owner of the field, and he only, has a right to appropriate it, for no one else can do so without committing a trespass upon the field. But when it has left his field, he has no more power over it or interest in it than any other stranger." [1]

9. But still, water, though an element, is not " a movable, wandering thing, and must of necessity continue common by the law of nations," as represented by Blackstone.[2] Nor is " flowing water " so far " originally *publici juris*," that, though, " so soon as it is appropriated by an individual, his right is coextensive with the beneficial use to which he appropriates it, subject to that right, all the rest of the water remains *publici juris* "; — as stated by Bailey, J., in Williams *v.* Morland ;[3] if by that form of expression is meant *that any one can appropriate it to his use [*214] or convenience, except as he is the owner or occupant of land in connection with which it is to be enjoyed.

There are, on the other hand, in many of the cases, especially the earlier ones, forms of expression adopted in respect to the rights of land-owners in the waters of streams flowing through their premises, which are as much too limited as those above quoted are too broad. The formula in which the law as to running water has, from an early date, been stated, is *Aqua curret et debet currere ut currere solebat.* And the language of the Vice-Chancellor in Wright *v.* Howard [4] is : " Without the consent of the other proprie-

[1] Race *v.* Ward, 30 Eng. L. & Eq. 187, 192 ; s. c., 4 Ellis & B. 702, 709 ; Pratt *v.* Lamson, 2 Allen, 275 ; 1 Fournel, Traité du Voisinage, 319.

[2] 2 Blackst. Comm. 14 – 18.

[3] Williams *v.* Morland, 2 Barnew. & C. 910, 913. See also Liggins *v.* Inge, 7 Bing. 682, 692, per *Tindal,* C. J. *Contra,* Mason *v.* Hill, 5 Barnew. & Ad. 1.

[4] Wright *v.* Howard, 1 Sim. & S. 190, 203 ; 3 Kent, Comm. 439 ; and lan-

tors, who may be affected by his operations, no proprietor can either diminish the quantity of water which would otherwise descend to the proprietors below, or throw the water back upon the proprietors above."

10. Now the rights of a riparian proprietor of land, over which there is a flowing stream of water, are to use it for any and all lawful purposes, while it is passing, in its natural current, over his land.[1] But the specific water that may be thus passing is not his property except through its use ; nor has he a right to detain it otherwise, since the rights of all riparian proprietors upon any stream, in respect to the waters thereof, are, in the eye of the law, equal and the same. The obligation of any one of these to suffer it to flow to the proprietor below is equally stringent and imperative as his right was to have it flow to him from the proprietor above.

These rights of riparian proprietors, though coming [*215] under * the head of what are called " Natural Easements," are not, in fact, the result of any supposed grant, evidenced by long acquiescence on the part of a superior proprietor, of the flow of the water from his land to the land below. The right of enjoying this flow, without disturbance or interruption by any other proprietor, is one *jure naturæ,* and is an incident of property in the land, not an appurtenance to it, like the right he has to enjoy the soil itself, in its natural state, unaffected by the tortious acts of a neighboring land-owner.[2] It is an inseparable incident to

guage almost as strong and unqualified is used by *Denio,* J., in Bellinger *v.* N. Y. Central R. R., 23 N. Y. 47, though the facts of the case carry an explanation of the limitation with which it must have been intended to be used.

[1] *Shaw,* C. J., thus defines a "riparian proprietor " : " By this designation I understand an owner of land bounded generally upon a stream of water, and as such having a qualified property in the soil to the thread of the stream, with the privileges annexed thereto by law." Bardwell *v.* Ames, 22 Pick. 333, 355.

[2] Dickinson *v.* Grand Junction Canal Co., 7 Exch. 282, 299 ; Rawstron *v.* Taylor, 11 Exch. 369, 382 ; Sury *v.* Pigot, Poph. 166 ; Wood *v.* Waud, 3 Exch. 748, 775 ; Embrey *v.* Owen, 6 Exch. 353 ; Tyler *v.* Wilkinson, 4 Mason, 397 ; Evans *v.* Merriweather, 3 Scamm. 492 ; Gardner *v.* Trustees of Village of Newburgh, 2

the ownership of land, made by an inflexible rule of law an absolute and fixed right, and can only be lost by grant or twenty years' adverse possession.[1]   And the proprietor may begin to exercise his rights as to the water whenever he pleases.   His right does not depend upon the exercise of it.[2] Shaw, C. J., in Johnson v. Jordan, thus states in a summary form, the right of a land proprietor to a natural watercourse flowing through the same: "Every person through whose land a natural watercourse runs has a right, *publici juris*, to the benefit of it, as it passes through his land, to all the useful purposes to which it may be applied; and no proprietor of land on the same watercourse, either above or below, has a right, unreasonably, to divert it from flowing into his premises, or obstruct it in passing from them, or to corrupt or destroy it.   It is inseparably annexed to the soil, and passes with it, not as an easement, nor as an appurtenance, but as parcel.   Use does not create it, and disuse cannot destroy or suspend it.   *Unity of possession [*216] and title in such land with the lands above it or below it does not extinguish it or suspend it."[3]

11. In determining, therefore, what these rights of the respective riparian proprietors upon a stream are, two things are to be taken into consideration; — first, that, to derive a value from this incident to his property, requires that the

Johns. Ch. 162; Campbell v. Smith, 3 Halst. 140; Pugh v. Wheeler, 2 Dev. & B. 50; Elliot v. Fitchburg R. R. Co., 10 Cush. 191; Wright v. Howard, 1 Sim. & S. 190, 203; Sampson v. Hoddinott, 1 C. B. N. S. 590; Parker v. Foote, 19 Wend. 309; Johnson v. Jordan, 2 Metc. 234; Canham v. Fisk, 2 Crompt. & J. 126; Rowbotham v. Wilson, 8 Ellis & B. 123, per *Bramwell*, B.; Williams v. Morland, 2 Barnew. & C. 910; Mason v. Hill, 2 Barnew. & Ad. 1; Shreve v. Voorhees, 2 Green, Ch. 25; Tourtellot v. Phelps, 4 Gray, 370; Cary v. Daniels, 8 Metc. 466; Davis v. Fuller, 12 Vt. 178; Hendricks v. Johnson, 6 Port. 472; Wadsworth v. Tillotson, 15 Conn. 366; Plumleigh v. Dawson, 1 Gilm. 544; M'Coy v. Danley, 20 Penn. St. 85; Blanchard v. Baker, 8 Me. 253; Webb v. Portland Mg. Co., 3 Sumn. 189; Stockoe v. Singers, 8 Ellis & B. 31.

[1] Corning v. Troy, &c. Factory, 39 Barb. 311.

[2] Crossley v. Lightowler, L. R. 3 Eq. 296.

[3] Johnson v. Jordan, 2 Metc. 234, 239; Holsman v. Boiling Spring Co. 1 M'Carter, 335.

proprietor should apply the water to *use* in some form ; and, second, that whatever is true of his own right is true of every other proprietor above and below him.   And from these a rule has been deduced, which is as near uniform as the nature of the case admits, and that is, that each proprietor may make any reasonable use of the water upon his premises, provided he do not thereby essentially or materially diminish the quantity or corrupt the quality of water in the stream, so as to deprive other proprietors of a fair and reasonable participation in the benefits thereof.   The uses to which water may be applied are so various, and the circumstances of the several cases where this is to be done are so diverse, that no more definite rule than this can be laid down.   And whether, in any given case, a use shall have been reasonable or otherwise, must, as will be seen hereafter, ordinarily be referred, as a question of fact, to a jury.[1]

The case of Holsman *v.* Boiling Spring Co., may be cited as illustrating the general propositions above stated.   The plaintiff had a valuable estate and pleasure grounds upon a small stream, upon which the defendant had a bleachery above the plaintiff's works.   The chemicals used in the bleachery and thrown into the stream, corrupted the water, and rendered it unfit for the uses to which it had been applied by the plaintiff.   In settling the respective rights of the parties upon the plaintiff's application for an injunction to the fouling of the water by the defendant, the court held that every riparian proprietor had a right to the natural flow of the water of a stream, as well in quality as quantity. The right of a riparian proprietor to the use and enjoyment of a stream of water in its natural state, is as sacred as the right of soil itself.   If a mill has acquired a prescriptive right to foul the water in one mode or to a certain extent, it will not justify fouling it in another mode or to a greater extent.   This does not depend upon what a riparian proprietor

[1] Davis *v.* Getchell, 50 Maine, 604.

may have expended upon his estate, but applies to riparian estates universally.[1]

The following extended quotation from the opinion of Story, J., in the case of Tyler *v.* Wilkinson, presents views of the law upon this subject which have met the approbation of American courts, and been liberally cited and commended by the English courts, especially by the very able judges of the present Court of Exchequer. " *Prima facie,* every proprietor upon each bank of a river is entitled to the land covered with water in front of his bank, to the middle thread of the stream. In virtue of this ownership, he has a right to the use of the water flowing over it, in its natural current, without diminution or obstruction. But, strictly * speaking, he has no property in the water [*217] itself, but the simple use of it while it passes along.

The consequence of this principle is, that no proprietor has a right to use the water to the prejudice of another. It is wholly immaterial whether the party be a proprietor above or below in the course of the river, the right being common to all the proprietors on the river, no one has a right to diminish the quantity which will, according to the natural current, flow to a proprietor below, or to throw it back upon a proprietor above. This is the necessary result from the perfect equality of right among all the proprietors of that which is common to all. The natural stream, existing by the bounty of Providence for the benefit of the land through which it flows, is an incident annexed, by operation of law, to the land itself. When I speak of this common right, I do not mean to be understood as holding the doctrine that there can be no diminution whatsoever, and no obstruction or impediment whatever, by the riparian proprietor, in the use of the water as it flows, for that would be to deny any valuable use of it. There may be, and there must be allowed, of that which is common to all, a reasonable use. The true test of

[1] Holsman *v.* Boiling Spring Co., 1 M'Carter, 335 ; Crossley *v.* Lightowler, L. R. 3 Eq. 297.

the principle and extent of use is, whether it is to the injury of the other proprietors or not. . . . . The maxim is applied, *Sic utere tuo ut alienum non lædas*." [1]

And Shaw, C. J., in Bardwell *v.* Ames, in speaking of the rights of a riparian owner upon one side of a river, [*218] like the *Connecticut, says: " Such owner, like every other owner of land over which there is a stream of water, has a right to appropriate to himself, and apply to any useful and beneficial purpose, the force to be derived from the natural flow of the water as it passes over his land, subject only to this limitation, that he does not thereby injuriously affect the common and equal rights of other proprietors of lands above or below his own on the stream." [2]

This is further illustrated by Parke, B., in the case of Embrey *v.* Owen, above cited, where he says: " The right to have the stream flow in its natural state, without diminution or alteration, is an incident to the property in the land through which it passes; but flowing water is *publici juris*, not in the sense of *bonum vacans*, to which the first occupant may acquire an exclusive right, but that it is public and common in this sense only, that all may reasonably use it who have a right of access to it; that none can have any property in the water itself, except in the particular portion which he may choose to abstract from the stream and take into his possession, and that during the time of his possession only. But each proprietor of the adjacent land has the

---

[1] Tyler *v.* Wilkinson, 4 Mason, 397; 3 Kent, Comm. 439; Gardner *v.* Trustees of Village of Newburgh, 2 Johns. Ch. 162; Soc. for establishing Manufactures *v.* Morris Canal & Banking Co., Saxt. Ch. 157, 188; Merritt *v.* Parker, Coxe, 460; Shreve *v.* Voorhees, 2 Green, Ch. 25; Cary *v.* Daniels, 8 Metc. 466; Haas *v.* Choussard, 17 Texas, 588; Hendrick *v.* Cook, 4 Ga. 241, 255; Dilling *v.* Murray, 6 Ind. 324; Embrey *v.* Owen, 6 Exch. 333; Dickinson *v.* Grand Junction Canal Co., 7 Exch. 300; Wood *v.* Waud, 3 Exch. 748, 775; Evans *v.* Merriweather, 3 Scamm. 492; Tourtellot *v.* Phelps, 4 Gray, 370; Gould *v.* Boston Duck Co., 13 Gray, 442; Twiss *v.* Baldwin, 9 Conn. 291; Platt *v.* Johnson, 15 Johns. 213; Howell *v.* M'Coy, 3 Rawle, 256; Blanchard *v.* Baker, 8 Me. 253; Davis *v.* Getchell, 50 Maine, 604; Hayes *v.* Waldron, 44 N. H. 584.

[2] Bardwell *v.* Ames, 22 Pick. 354; Davis *v.* Getchell, 50 Maine, 604.

right to the usufruct of the stream which flows through it."[1]

Shaw, C. J. has also defined the rights of the several riparian proprietors upon a stream, in respect to the use of the water thereof, in Cummings *v.* Barrett, in these words: "The upper proprietor has a right to make any use of the stream, which is beneficial to his estate and himself, which is reasonable, and does not either wholly take away the right of the lower proprietor, or does not practically, and in a perceptible and substantial degree, diminish and impair an equal and common right of the lower proprietor." And whether it has this effect, he says, is often a *ques- [*219] tion of fact depending upon the peculiar circumstances of the case.[2]

The owner of land may apply the water that flows in a stream over it to domestic, agricultural, or manufacturing purposes, provided he uses it in a reasonable manner, and so as to work no material, actual injury to others, or to the infringement of the rights of others. And this extends to the depositing in such stream waste matter and foreign substances which are the results of processes of manufactures, provided it be a reasonable use of the same, which is a question of fact to be determined by a jury. And what is reasonable, must depend upon a variety of conditions, such as the size and character of the stream and the uses to which it can be applied.[3]

12. It follows, as a corollary from the doctrine of the above cases, that, in the language of Parke, B., in Embrey *v.* Owen, cited above, "it is only for an unreasonable and unauthorized

---

[1] Mason *v.* Hill, 5 Barnew. & Ad. 1; Pugh *v.* Wheeler, 2 Dev. & B. 50; Howell *v.* M'Coy, 3 Rawle, 256; Thomas *v.* Brackney, 17 Barb. 654; Wright *v.* Howard, 1 Sim. & S. 190, 203.

[2] Cummings *v.* Barrett, 10 Cush. 186; Elliot *v.* Fitchburg R. R. Co., 10 Cush. 191; Thomas *v.* Brackney, 17 Barb. 654; Parker *v.* Hotchkiss, 25 Conn. 321; Gould *v.* Boston Duck Co., 13 Gray, 442; Hendrick *v.* Cook, 4 Ga. 241; Selden *v.* Del. & Hud. Canal, 29 N. Y. 642.

[3] Hayes *v.* Waldron, 44 N. H. 584; Housee *v.* Hammond, 39 Barb. 95; 95 *post*, *282.

use of this common benefit that an action will lie," though,
it may be added, for such a use an action will lie, though no
actual damage may thereby have accrued to the proprietor
whose right has been invaded.[1]

13. Though the courts, both of England and this country,
seem to be so well agreed in the general principles applicable
to the rights of water, the uses to which it may be put are
so various, that it is often difficult to apply any general rule
to the practical operations of the several riparian proprietors.
One may wish to use the stream for mill purposes, another
for the irrigation of his land, and a third for household
purposes, or supplying the necessary drink for his cattle.
The use to which one may wish to apply it will leave the
waters of the stream pure and healthy, while the business of
another, if suffered to be carried on, renders it foul or deleterious to health. It is this diversity of uses and interests
which, in its practical workings, has led to many of the multiplied questions which, especially of late, have engaged the
attention of the courts. Ever since the 32 Edw. III., the
uniform rule of law has been, that an action will lie for an
actual diversion of the water of a stream.[2] Yet the cases
are numerous where a diversion of water, under certain circumstances, has been held lawful, one of which is given
here, for purposes of illustration.

[*220]   *In the case of Wadsworth v. Tillotson, which was
an action for an alleged diversion of water which
ought to flow to the plaintiff's land, there was a spring in
the defendant's land which naturally overflowed and discharged its waters by a defined channel, running through the
plaintiff's land adjoining that of the defendant. The defendant laid an aqueduct from this spring to his house for supply-

[1] Embrey v. Owen, 6 Exch. 353, 369; Johns v. Stevens, 3 Vt. 308; Thomas
v. Brackney, 17 Barb. 654; Ripka v. Sergeant, 7 Watts & S. 9. Compare the
above with the unguarded language of the court in Bellinger v. N. Y. Central R.
R., 23 N. Y. 47.

[2] Year B., Book of Assize, 32 Edw. III. pl. 2; 2 Rolle, Abr. 140; Com. Dig.
Action upon the Case for a Nuisance, A.

ing it with water, and for watering his cattle ; and in order to keep it pure and prevent its freezing, he suffered portions of it, more than he wanted for the above uses, to escape, and either applied it in irrigating his lands, or suffered it to run to waste, so that the plaintiff lost the benefit of a part of the natural flow of the stream through his land. It was held that the defendant had a right to divert what was reasonably necessary for supplying his family use, and that he might use the water in a reasonable manner, and so as not to destroy or render useless, or materially diminish or affect the application of the same by the proprietors upon the stream below. And it was further held, that the rule that water ought to flow as it is wont, without diminution or alteration, and cannot be diverted in whole or in part, but must be returned, after it is used, to its ordinary channel, is not to be understood literally, so as to prevent a small, unessential, or insensible diminution, variation, or loss of the water incident to the beneficial use of it. And the question was submitted to the jury, whether the mode in which the diversion was made in this case was or was not a reasonable one, with a direction that, if it was, the defendant was not liable therefor, though the plaintiff thereby suffered some loss.[1]

But it should be remembered, that a riparian proprietor may, by long exercise of the right, acquire a right to stop the flow of water from his premises to those below him, and wholly deprive the owner thereof of the same.[2]

*But nothing short of twenty years' continued di- [*221] version authorizes a presumption of grant or license to create it.[3]

14. Though the interest in the water of a stream has thus far been treated of as a subject of separate and individual property, there is often a joint interest in it which involves

---

[1] Wadsworth v. Tillotson, 15 Conn. 369. See Perkins v. Dow, 1 Root, 535 ; Chatfield v. Wilson, 31 Vt. 358; Gillett v. Johnson, 30 Conn. 183.

[2] Ennor v. Barwell, 2 Giff. 410, 420.

[3] Haight v. Price, 21 N. Y. 241.

rules as to the respective rights of two or more joint owners, of a somewhat peculiar character. Thus, if one proprietor owns land upon one side of a stream, in which the tide does not ebb and flow, and another owns upon the opposite side, the dividing line of their lands is the thread or centre line of the stream between the banks, irrespective of the circumstance that a larger or smaller quantity or current of water flows upon one side or the other of that line.[1]

But each proprietor does not thereby become the owner of any distinct portion of the waters flowing in the stream, regarding them, in their capacity for use, as heretofore explained. Viewed in that light, the property in the stream is one and indivisible, and each riparian proprietor is bound to use it accordingly as an entire stream in its natural channel; or, in other words, he cannot sever the stream, for a severance of it would destroy the rights of both. One proprietor cannot, however, so appropriate or use the stream as materially to injure others jointly interested in it. Each having a right to only one half of the water, he may use the same, but must use it as it is accustomed to flow down the channel.[2]

If the owner of one side of a stream to the thread thereof, divert the water from the stream, the owner of the other part of it may restrain him from so doing, as he has a right to the natural flow of the stream over his part of the bed of it.[3]

Accordingly, where a riparian owner on one side of a stream erected a dam wholly within his own land, and by means thereof created and used a water-power on his own land for more than twenty years, it was held that he [*222] was *only exercising his own right, and not adversely to the rights of the owner of the other side; and that it did not derogate from his right to enjoy the use of his

[1] Pratt v. Lamson, 2 Allen, 275, 284; Trustees, &c. v. Dickinson, 9 Cush. 544, 552; Schurmeier v. St. P. & Par. R. R., 10 Min. 102.

[2] Canal Trustees v. Haven, 11 Ill. 554; Vandenburgh v. Van Bergen, 13 Johns. 212; Plumleigh v. Dawson, 1 Gilm. 544, 551; Ersk. Inst., fol. ed. 358; Pratt v. Lamson, 2 Allen, 275, 287.

[3] Corning v. Troy Iron, &c. Co., 22 How. Prac. Cas. 219; s. c., 39 Barb. 311.

undivided share of the stream whenever he should see fit to apply the same, unless the first occupant shall have done that which positively excluded the other owner from enjoying the same.[1]

15. Attempts have, at times, been made to lay down something like arbitrary rules by which to determine, in cases where, from drought or other cause, there fails to be water enough in a stream to supply the wants of several successive owners upon its banks, to which of them a prior right to the water is to be accorded. Thus, for instance, suppose the case of a stream the water of which is applied by one to domestic uses, by another to irrigate his land, and by a third to operate a mill ; may either claim a precedence in right to the same, or is the water to be equally shared by them all, or is it to depend upon the order in which their estates stand upon the stream ?

The question arose in Evans v. Merriweather, where the court of Illinois undertook to prescribe rules applicable to cases like the one supposed. The stream, in that case, was a small and natural one. The plaintiff and defendant both had mills upon its banks, which were operated by steam, for generating which the waters of the stream, in connection with those of certain large wells, were used, and, ordinarily, were sufficient. But a drought having prevented such supply, the defendant, who owned the upper mill upon the stream, placed a dam in it, by which the water flowing therein was turned into his well, and the plaintiff's mill was wholly deprived of the same. As both were mill-owners, the determination of the question raised between them would not seem to call for a solution of the question above proposed. But the court proceed to discuss it, under the inquiry whether the entire consumption of a stream by *an upper proprie- [*223] tor can, in any case, be a reasonable one ?

" To answer this question satisfactorily," say the court,

---

[1] Pratt v. Lamson, 2 Allen, 275, 289 ; Corning v. Troy, &c. Co., 39 Barb. 311.

"it is proper to consider the wants of man in regard to the
element of water. These wants are either natural or artificial. Natural are such as are absolutely necessary to be
supplied, in order to his existence; artificial, such only as,
by supplying them, his comfort and prosperity are increased.
To quench thirst, and for household purposes, it is absolutely
indispensable. In civilized life, water for cattle is also necessary. These wants must be supplied, or both man and beast
will perish." The court then go on to state, that, for manufacturing purposes, or those of irrigation, the use of water is
not essential to man's existence in this climate, whatever it
might be in hot and arid climates, and add: "From these
premises would result this conclusion, that an individual,
owning a spring upon his own land, from which water flows
in a current through his neighbor's land, would have a right
to use the whole of it, if necessary, to satisfy his natural
wants. He may consume all the water for his domestic purposes, including water for his stock. If he desires to use it
for irrigation or manufactures, and there be a lower proprietor to whom its use is essential to supply his natural wants,
or for his stock, he must use the water so as to leave enough
for such lower proprietor. Where the stream is small, and
does not supply water more than sufficient to answer the
natural wants of the different proprietors living on it, none
of the proprietors can use the water for either irrigation or
manufactures. . . . . Each proprietor, in his turn, may, if
necessary, consume all the water for these purposes," that
is, for the supply of these natural wants. The case goes on
to affirm, that if, beyond the supply of these, any surplus is
left, all have a right to participate in its benefits, and no rule
can be laid down as to how much each may use, without in-
fringing the rights of others. The question in such
[*224] cases must be referred to a jury, to say whether *a
party has, under all the circumstances, used more
than his just proportion of the water. And, tried by the
tests which had thus been premised, the court had no dif-

ficulty in holding the diversion complained of to be unwarranted.[1]

The opinion thus advanced by the court of Illinois, and which seems to be favored more or less directly by the other cases cited, may be considered as deriving weight from what will appear in the following pages ; namely, that, while numerous questions have arisen as to the liability of land-owners for the manner in which they have applied the water of running streams for irrigation and mill purposes, no case is recollected where one has been held to have violated the rights of any other proprietor by any use made by him upon his own premises for purely domestic purposes, or watering of his cattle. And further, that the rule is a universal one, that no man has a right so to use or apply water flowing through his land as to foul the same or render it corrupt or unhealthy, and unfit to be used by the land-owner on the stream below him, for domestic purposes, or watering his cattle.

The following are some of the cases illustrating the application of the foregoing doctrines. The plaintiff owned a paper mill, which derived its water, among other sources, from what fell upon a hillside, and found its way into a cavern through which it flowed in a current, and found its way into the stream on which the plaintiff's mill was situate, and so to the plaintiff's mill. The defendant began works upon the top of the hill, using water which was thereby fouled and corrupted, and was suffered to find its way through fissures into the cavern where it mingled with the water flowing through it, and thereby fouled the water that came to the plaintiff's mill, and rendered it unfit for his use. It was held that he was liable in an action for

---

[1] Evans v. Merriweather, 3 Scamm. 492. See Ingraham v. Hutchinson, 2 Conn. 584; Arnold v. Foot, 12 Wend. 340; Pugh v. Wheeler, 2 Dev. & B. 50, 54; Omelvany v. Jaggers, 2 Hill, So. C. 634; Blanchard v. Baker, 8 Me. 253; Elliot v. Fitchburg R. R. Co., 10 Cush. 191; Stein v. Burden, 29 Ala. 127; s. c., 24 Ala. 130; Smith v. Adams, 6 Paige, 435; Brown v. Best, 1 Wils. 174; Johns v. Stevens, 3 Vt. 308, 316; Chatfield v. Wilson, 31 Vt. 358; Pardessus, Traité des Servitudes, § 114; 1 Fournel, Traité du Voisinage, 347.

thus fouling the water, although it passed a considerable part of its way through the earth and underground.[1]

16. It may be stated, though it might seem to result necessarily from what has already been said, that the owner of land through which a stream of water flows has, as incident to such ownership, a right to have the water flow from his land, without obstruction, upon that of the next adjoining proprietor below, and for creating any such obstruction he may have his action, as for the diversion which prevented its flowing to and upon his land.[2]

The owner of a swamp or wet land may drain the same into a stream in his own land, without being liable therefor, though it increase the quantity of water in the stream to the injury of the owner below. But he may not thus throw the water upon land below him by an artificial trench.[3]

If the public, in making or repairing a highway, stop the water that naturally flows into it, so as to throw it back on to the adjoining owner's land, the surveyor who does it, would be held liable in damages.[4] And such would be the law as to railroads. But if it is necessary, in making a railroad, to stop the flow of water, and thereby to flood the adjacent land, it would be considered that a right to do this was incident to and embraced in the easement acquired by the location.[5]

In a case before the Lords of the Privy Council, the court use this language: " Every riparian proprietor has a right to what may be called the *ordinary* use of water flowing past his land, for instance, to the reasonable use of the water for his domestic purposes and for his cattle, and this without re-

---

[1] Hodgkinson v. Ennor, 4 B. & Smith, 229 ; *post*, p. *364.

[2] Johns v. Stevens, 3 Vt. 308, 316 ; Pugh v. Wheeler, 2 Dev. & B. 50, 53 ; Overton v. Sawyer, 1 Jones, No. C. 308 ; Tillotson v. Smith, 32 N. H. 90 ; Martin v. Jett, 12 La. 501 ; Martin v. Riddle, 27 Penn. St. 415, note ; Kauffman v. Griesemer, 26 Penn. St. 407, 413.

[3] Miller v. Laubach, 47 Penn. 154.

[4] Rowe v. Addison, 34 N. H. 313 ; Haynes v. Burlington, 38 Verm. 361.

[5] Johnson v. Atlantic, &c. R. R., 35 N. H. 572 ; Proprietors, &c. v. Nashua, &c. R. R., 10 Cush. 388.

gard to the effect which such use may have, in case of deficiency, upon proprietors lower down the stream.   He has a right to use it for any purpose, or what may be deemed the extraordinary use of it, provided that he does not, thereby, interfere with the rights of other proprietors, either above or below him.   Subject to this condition, he may dam up the stream for the purpose of a mill, or divert the water for the purpose of irrigation.   But he has no right to interrupt the regular flow of the stream, if he thereby interferes with the lawful use of the water by other proprietors, and inflicts on them a sensible injury." [1]

The Court of Alabama cover the point that has sometimes been made whether, if there is not water enough in the stream to supply the wants of both upper and lower owner, the upper one can use it all, or is bound to share it with the lower owner.   " Each riparian proprietor has the right to use the water which flows from or through his lands for all ordinary purposes and for the gratification of natural wants, even though in such use he consumes the entire stream ; this right extends to the use of the water *ad lavandum et potandum,* both by himself and all living things in his legitimate employment."   " Such proprietor has also the right to the extraordinary or artificial use of the stream of water composing it, provided that, by such use, the water is not forced back upon the lands of the proprietor above, is not unreasonably and injuriously precipitated on the lands of the proprietor below, and after its use is restored without material diminution, and before it leaves the land of the person diverting it to its accustomed channel." [2]

So, if the effect of erecting a bridge for a highway across a stream, in a reasonable and proper manner, be to damage a mill upon the same stream, the remedy of the mill-owner is not by an action against the town for damages, but by resort to the same mode for relief which is provided for the recov-

---

[1] Miner *v.* Gilmore, 12 Moore, P. C. 156 ; 1 Lepage Desgodets, 16.
[2] Stein *v.* Burden, 29 Ala. 132.

ery of damages in cases where private property is taken for public uses, and the same rule applies to a railroad if, in erecting such bridge, it acts within the scope of the powers given it by its charter.[1]

But if a town, by failing to provide a proper culvert, or keep it in repair to carry off the water of a watercourse, thereby flows back water on to land above, it would be liable in an action for damages.[2]

[*225]   *And this principle, it may be remarked, though more fully illustrated hereafter, applies to surface water as well as to that flowing in a proper watercourse.[3]

17. But if, from natural causes, the channel by which the water flows from one's land becomes clogged or obstructed, it is incumbent upon him to cause the same to be cleared, if he would avail himself of it to relieve his land.[4] He has, however, no right to deepen the bed by removing natural obstructions in the land of another, nor obstructions long existing therein, though originally artificial. And if the owner of the land remove these, he will not be liable to the owner above, though he replace them by artificial obstructions, provided the latter do not set back the stream any higher than the natural obstructions had previously done.[5]

18. It may be added, that it is the natural right of a riparian proprietor, not only that the water of the stream should come to him uncorrupted, but unchanged in its natural temperature by the proprietors above, through or by whose lands it shall have flowed.[6] And this applies, also,

[1] Sprague v. Worcester, 13 Gray, 193; Perry v. Worcester, 6 Gray, 546; Mellen v. Western R. R., 4 Gray, 302; Hazen v. Essex Co., 12 Cush. 475; Wheeler v. Worcester, 10 Allen, 603.

[2] Haynes v. Burlington, 38 Verm. 362.

[3] Martin v. Riddle, 26 Penn. St. 407, note; Laumier v. Francis, 23 Mo. 181; Bellows v. Sackett, 15 Barb. 96; ante, p. *211.

[4] Brisbane v. O'Neall, 3 Strobh. 348; Prescott v. Williams, 5 Metc. 429; Prescott v. White, 21 Pick. 341.

[5] Brown v. Bush, 45 Penn. 64 – 66.

[6] 2 Rolle, Abr. 141; Cary v. Daniels, 8 Metc. 466, 476; Alfred's case, 9 Rep. 59; Mason v. Hill, 5 Barnew. & Ad. 1; Magor v. Chadwick, 11 Adolph. & E. 571; Wood v. Waud, 3 Exch. 748, 777; Howell v. M'Coy, 3 Rawle, 256; Davis v. Getchell, 50 Maine, 604.

to cases where the riparian proprietor owns only upon one side of the stream.   Thus where the owner of mills upon a stream, who was accustomed to foul the water by dye-stuffs, &c., thrown into it, sold the land upon one side of the stream below his mills without any reserve, it was held that the purchaser, as riparian proprietor, had a right to the flow of the water over his half of the bed of the stream, pure and uncorrupted, and that the vendor had no longer any right to foul it.[1]

19. Though, with the foregoing idea of property in the use of water in connection with the ownership of real estate, it may seem hardly consistent to treat that as an easement which is naturally incident to the rightful enjoyment of one's own land, yet it is common to speak of the right of one riparian owner upon a stream to have the water thereof flow from the land of an owner above in an uncorrupted state upon and along his own land, and thence to discharge it into and upon the land of the owner below in an unobstructed manner, as a *natural easement* and *servitude*.   And the land of such owner is regarded in such case, in respect to the flow of such water, both a dominant and servient estate, in respect to those above and below it upon the same stream. It is, at least, so much like an easement or servitude, that it may not be considered as doing any violence to the terms, although a natural *incident to the property [*226] in such lands, and not the result of grant, either direct or by implication, under the name of *prescription*.[2]

Thus the right of having water flow unobstructed from one's land is considered by the court " as a claim of right to a natural easement," though sometimes it is called " a secondary easement " in another's land.[3]

---

[1] Crossley v. Lightowler, L. R. 3 Eq. 297.

[2] See Johnson v. Jordan, 2 Metc. 234; Soule v. Russell, 13 Metc. 436 ; *ante*, chap. 1, sect. 1, pl. 19, 20.

[3] Cary v. Daniels, 5 Metc. 236 ; Prescott v. Williams, 5 Metc. 429 ; Crittenton v. Alger, 11 Metc. 281 ; Ashley v. Ashley, 6 Cush. 70; *ante*, chap. 1, sect. 2, pl. 11.

The law is, where two parcels of land lie adjoining each other, belonging to different persons, and one parcel lies lower than the other, that the lower one owes a *servitude* to the upper, to receive the water that *naturally* runs from it, provided the industry of man has not been used to create the *servitude*.[1]

And the court, in Kauffman *v.* Griesemer, use the following language, in speaking of this as a natural easement or servitude : " Because water is descendible by nature, the owner of a *dominant* or superior heritage has an *easement* in the *servient* or inferior tenement, for the discharge of all waters which by nature rise in or flow or fall upon the superior. . . . . This obligation applies only to waters which flow naturally without the art of man. Those which come from springs, or from rain falling directly on the heritage, or even by the natural dispositions of the place, are the only ones to which this expression of the law can be applied. . . . . Hence the owner of a mill has an easement in the land below for the free passage of the water from the mill [*227] in the natural channel of the stream," &c. * " This easement," referring to that which the superior has in the inferior as the servient tenement, " is called a servitude in the Roman law." [2]

20. From the familiar fact above referred to, that water is descendible by nature, there are few uses which can be made of it by any one upon his own premises that do not more or less sensibly affect either the quantity or quality of the water received from an upper tenement and discharged upon a lower one, or the uniformity or rate of impetus with which it is allowed to flow through one's land or be discharged upon that of another. It results, almost as a matter of

---

[1] Martin *v.* Jett, 12 La. 501; Orleans Navigation Co. *v.* Mayor of New Orleans, 2 Martin, 214, 233; Delahoussaye *v.* Judice, 13 La. Ann. 587; *ante*, p. 15; 1 Fournel, Traité du Voisinage, 337, 339; Code Nap., Art. 640; 5 Duranton, Cours de Droit Français, liv. 2, tit. 4, § 1, pp. 152 – 166; Pardessus, Traité des Servitudes, §§ 82, 83, pp. 113 – 118, ed. 1829; Miller *v.* Laubach, 47 Penn. 154.

[2] Kauffman *v.* Griesemer, 26 Penn. St. 407, 413. See *ante*, p. *211.

course, that easements, in the proper sense of the term, in numerous forms, may be acquired in reference to such use, just to the extent to which such use may vary the state and condition in which the water would have been, if it had been suffered to flow in a strictly natural manner.

It becomes necessary, therefore, in pursuing the subject, to point out how far the various modes in which flowing water is ordinarily applied to use are in conformity with the natural rights which are incident to the ownership of the land, and how far such use, though not in conformity with such natural right, may have become lawful by grant or prescription as a servitude or easement. And it may be stated, as a general proposition, that, from the earliest history of the common law, it has been deemed an actionable tort for one man to obstruct the natural flow of water in a stream running through another's land, if thereby another is deprived of the use of it, or his land is submerged by such obstruction, or his mill is hindered in its operation.[1]

And the owner of the land through which it flows, has no right to fill up a watercourse, or divert the water from the land below, nor to flow it back upon the land above.[2]

21. In considering the law as to the uses to which water may be applied, it becomes necessary to treat of these under different heads. And for that purpose, it is proposed, first, to consider the subject of irrigation, next, the application of *water to the operation of mills, as gov- [*228] erned by the rules of the common law, and then to inquire into the character and extent of the rights which may be acquired in respect to water flowing in artificial channels, together with some of the rights of water for the operation of mills, created by statute.

1 2 Rolle, Abr. 140; Com. Dig., *Action on the Case for a Nuisance*, A.
2 Bangor *v.* Lansil, 51 Maine, 526.

SECTION II.

OF RIGHTS OF IRRIGATION.

1. BY irrigation, as here used, is meant, unless otherwise expressed, the application of the waters of a running stream by a riparian proprietor in the cultivation of his land by artificial means, and not the overflowing of its natural banks by periodical or extraordinary freshets or swellings of the stream beyond the customary quantity flowing therein. This, of course, implies a greater or less degree of diversion of water from the stream, and the difficulty to which it gives rise, of determining the respective rights of successive riparian proprietors upon a stream, is, that while a right to divert water for such purposes, to some extent, and under certain circumstances, is incident to the ownership of the soil, if it is carried to a greater extent, or exercised [*229] under *different circumstances, it becomes a wrong, for which the one causing it is responsible in damages, unless it can be justified by evidence of grant or assent on the part of him whose property is thereby injuriously affected.

The point to be determined in these cases is, where the right ends, and the wrong begins, in the scale of admeasure-

ment of such diversion ; for if a riparian proprietor transcends the right, he is subject to an action by other riparian
proprietors whose rights are thereby affected, although no
actual damage can be shown to have been thereby occasioned.
The reason of this rule, which is now established by a multi-
tude of cases, is, that for every wrong the law professes to
provide a remedy, and if a party whose right in respect to
his land has been invaded were obliged to show an actual
damage sustained before he could vindicate his right by an
action at law, the repetition of the act might often be continued till a prescriptive right were gained by such adverse
user in favor of one whose original act was confessedly a
wrong.

Bearing in mind that it is not for every diversion of water
that an action will lie, but only for such as violates the right
of some other person, as explained in Elliot v. Fitchburg R.
R. Co., cited below, the following cases have been selected
from a much larger number, to show that such action may
be sustained, though no actual damages can be shown to
have been occasioned by such diversion, since the law will
imply a damage in such cases, and establish the right of
the party assumed to be injured by a solemn judgment of
court.[1]

*2. Therefore, to limit a land-owner to the mere [*230]
benefit of having a stream flow through his land, without any right to divert the same or any part of it, would be

. [1] Hastings v. Livermore, 7 Gray, 194 ; Elliot v. Fitchburg R. R. Co., 10
Cush. 191 ; Bolivar Mg. Co. v. Neponset Mg. Co., 16 Pick. 241 ; Grant v. Lyman, 4 Metc. 470 ; Atkins v. Bordman, 2 Metc. 457 ; Newhall v. Ireson, 8
Cush. 595 ; Dane v. Valentine, 5 Metc. 8 ; Butman v. Hussey, 12 Me. 407 ;
Whipple v. Cumberland Mg. Co., 2 Story, 661 ; Webb v. Portland Mg. Co., 3
Sumn. 189 ; Parker v. Foote, 19 Wend. 309, 313 ; Hendrick v. Cook, 4 Ga. 241,
260 ; Plumleigh v. Dawson, 1 Gilm. 544, 552 ; Stein v. Burden, 24 Ala. 130,
148 ; Welton v. Martin, 7 Mo. 307 ; Hulme v. Shreve, 3 Green, Ch. 116 ; Parker v. Griswold, 17 Conn. 288 ; Chatfield v. Wilson, 27 Vt. 670 ; Sampson v.
Hoddinott, 1 C. B. N. s. 590 ; Wood v. Waud, 3 Exch. 748, 772 ; post, chap. 6,
sect. 2, pl. 1. Roundtree v. Brantley, 34 Ala. 553 ; Munroe v. Stickney, 48
Maine, 462 ; Graver v. Sholl, 42 Penn. 67 ; Delaware Canal v. Torrey, 33 Penn.
143.

defeating, in a great measure, the purposes for which Providence had supplied these sources of comfort and convenience
to man, and the means of fertilizing the soil, and giving a
profitable employment for industry and art ; it is accordingly
held, that if, in any question of diversion the jury should
find, it was only of such water as the complaining party
could not have used for any beneficial purpose, or that it
was made in a reasonable manner, and for a proper purpose,
an action for the same would not lie.   But as every diversion
is, *prima facie*, a violation of the right of the riparian proprietor below to have the benefit of the stream, *ut currere
solebat*, an action will lie therefor, unless the party causing
it can ground his defence upon such a use of it as is above
supposed.[1]

3. The right to divert water, in applying it to use above
spoken of, will of course be understood as one that is
naturally incident to property in the land, and if any one
should lose this, or should acquire other and more extensive
rights in this respect, it could only be by having become
subject to a *servitude*, or by having acquired an *easement*
under some grant, actual or implied.

4. It may be further remarked, that, in determin-
[*231] ing what *is a reasonable use of water by diversion,
reference is to be had to the injury sustained thereby
by one as well as the benefit obtained by the other.   Thus it
might be of great advantage to the owner of a dry and
porous parcel of land upon a stream, to spread the waters
thereof over its surface at frequent intervals.   But if, in so
doing, the water which operated an existing mill below

[1] Elliot v. Fitchburg R. R. Co., 10 Cush. 191, 195 ; Howell v. M'Coy, 3
Rawle, 256, 269 ; Shreve v. Voorhees, 2 Green, Ch. 25, 34 ; Williams v. Morland, 2 Barnew. & C. 910, 916 ; Thompson v. Crocker, 9 Pick. 59 ; Cooper v.
Hall, 5 Ohio, 320 ; Parker v. Griswold, 17 Conn. 288, 299 ; Embrey v. Owen,
6 Exch. 353 ; Sampson v. Hoddinott, 1 C. B. N. S. 590 ; Webb v. Portland Mg.
Co., 3 Sumn. 189, 198 ; Wright v. Howard, 1 Sim. & S. 190, 203 ; Tyler v. Wilkinson, 4 Mason, 397, 400 ; Wadsworth v. Tillotson, 15 Conn. 366, 373 ; Pugh
v. Wheeler, 5 Dev. & B. 50, 59 ; Van Hoesen v. Coventry, 10 Barb. 518 ; 3
Kent, Comm. 438 ; Davis v. Winslow, 51 Maine, 290.

should be absorbed and wasted, it would, obviously, be an unreasonable use of what ought to be, within proper limits, for the benefit of both.

And in respect to the general principles applicable to cases of diversion of water, there is no difference between the rights of the riparian proprietor, whose land extends only to the centre of the stream, and of him who owns upon both sides of it. Thus, in the case of Parker v. Griswold,[1] the plaintiff owned land upon one side only of the stream, and the action was for diverting the water thereof by an artificial trench, and not returning the same into the stream until after it had passed the plaintiff's land. The action was sustained, although the plaintiff had never appropriated the water of the stream to use, and no damages were shown to have resulted to him from such diversion. So, in the case of Tyler v. Wilkinson,[2] the language of Story, J. upon this point is: " *Prima facie*, every proprietor upon each bank of a river is entitled to the land covered with water in front of his bank to the middle thread of the stream. In virtue of this ownership he has a right to the use of the water flowing over it, in its natural current, without diminution or obstruction. . . . . The consequence of this principle is, that no proprietor has a right to use the water to the prejudice of another. . . . . In their character as riparian proprietors, they have, annexed to their lands, the general flow of the river, so far as it has not been already *acquired by some [*232] prior and legally operative appropriation."

5. The application of the foregoing principles to the subject of irrigation may be best illustrated by a reference to a few leading cases involving an inquiry into the mode and extent to and in which this may be done.

In the case of Weston v. Alden,[3] the controversy was between two owners of meadows upon the same stream. The

---

[1] Parker v. Griswold, 17 Conn. 288.

[2] Tyler v. Wilkinson, 4 Mason, 397, 403. See 5 Duranton, Cours de Droit Français, 205.

[3] Weston v. Alden, 8 Mass. 136.

defendant, by sluices cut in the bank of the stream, diverted the water thereof on to his meadow, whereby some part of it was absorbed and wasted, but returned all the remainder into the stream before reaching the plaintiff's meadow below. The court held, that " a man owning a close on an ancient brook may lawfully use the water thereof for the purpose of husbandry, as watering his cattle, or irrigating the close, and he may do this, either by dipping water from the brook and pouring it upon his land, or by making small sluices for the same purpose. And if the owner of a close below is damaged thereby, it is *damnum absque injuria*."

In Blanchard *v.* Baker,[1] Weston, J., in referring to the rights of a riparian proprietor, connected with the remark, that " he may make a reasonable use of the water itself for domestic purposes, for watering cattle, or even for irrigation, provided that it is not unreasonably detained, or essentially diminished," adds, that, " although by the case of Weston *v.* Alden the right of irrigation might seem to be general and unlimited, yet subsequent cases have restrained it consistently with the enjoyment of the common bounty of nature by other proprietors, through whose land a stream had been accustomed to flow. And the qualification of the right by these later decisions is in accordance with the common law."

The case of Perkins *v.* Dow [2] is earlier than either [*233] of the *above, and was one between the owner of an ancient mill and a riparian proprietor above, for diverting the water for purposes of irrigation. The court held that he had a right to diminish the quantity of water in the stream as against the mill owner below, by spreading it upon the land to manure and enrich it, provided he did it prudently, and did not deprive the mill-owner of the surplus.

The case of Colburn *v.* Richards [3] differs from that of

[1] Blanchard *v.* Baker, 8 Me. 253, 266.
[2] Perkins *v.* Dow, 1 Root, 535.
[3] Colburn *v.* Richards, 13 Mass. 420.

Weston *v.* Alden by the fact that the land-owner stopped the stream altogether by a dam, in order to raise a head of water whereby to irrigate his land, until it rose and ran over the dam, and thereby an ancient mill of the plaintiff was injuriously affected ; and it was held to be an unlawful act on the part of the land-owner.

So in Anthony *v.* Lapham,[1] in which the controversy was between two owners of meadows upon a stream, the upper one stopped the water by a dam, so that a large portion of it was diverted on to his land, where much of it was absorbed or evaporated, and the same was not returned into the stream. The court recognize the general right of diverting water for purposes of irrigation, and, in giving judgment in favor of the lower owner, lay stress upon the circumstance that the upper one had stopped the water by a dam, and remark, in regard to irrigation, " he must use it in this latter way so as to do the least possible injury to his neighbor, who has the same right."

6. The discussion can hardly be complete without referring to two or three recent English cases where the subject of irrigation is considered, and in which the courts take occasion to speak of several of the American cases, already cited, with approbation, and to intimate that the American law upon the subject is much less stringent than that of England ; which, perhaps, may be accounted for by the size and *quantity of water of many of the mill- [*234] streams in this country compared with those of England.

In Embrey *v.* Owen,[2] the plaintiff was a mill-owner upon a stream upon which the defendant owned meadows situate above this mill, which he had been in the habit of irrigating at irregular intervals, but only when the stream was full, and when no actual damage was thereby done to the plain-

[1] Anthony *v.* Lapham, 5 Pick. 175.
[2] Embrey *v.* Owen, 6 Exch. 353.   See Mason *v.* Hill, 3 Barnew. & Ad. 304 ; Crooker *v.* Bragg, 10 Wend. 260.

tiff's mill. And it was held, that by so doing he violated no rights of the plaintiff, but simply exercised such as belonged to himself. Parke, B., in giving judgment, examines the respective rights of the parties as to diverting water for purposes of irrigation, and intimates that it would not be allowed, as in the United States, to cut sluices for the purpose in the banks of the stream, but states that each case must depend upon its own circumstances. It is, in his judgment, a question of degree, and it is impossible to draw precise limits between what is a reasonable and what a wrongful use. And the only general rule to be drawn from the case seems to be, that while each riparian proprietor has a right to the usufruct of the stream flowing through or along his land, this right is subject to similar rights on the part of the proprietors on each side of the stream, within reasonable limits of enjoyment, while an action will lie only for an unreasonable and unauthorized exercise of the right.

The other case referred to is that of Sampson v. Hoddinott,[1] where the question was between two owners of meadows. The defendant had stopped the water of a stream running through the meadows of the parties, for the purpose of irrigating the upper meadow. The effect was that the water, instead of reaching the lower meadow in the early part of the day, did not reach there till so late in the afternoon that the owner of the meadow could not usefully apply it in irrigating it as he wished to do.

[*235] *The court treat the right of irrigation as one belonging to a riparian proprietor as an incident to his estate, which he is at liberty to use or not, but does not lose it by neglecting to use it, although a proprietor below him may have exercised the like right upon his own land, and although the lower proprietor may be somewhat injured in the enjoyment of his right by the upper one beginning to ex-

---

[1] Sampson v. Hoddinott, 1 C. B. n. s. 590; Crossley v. Lightowler, L. R. 3 Eq. 296.

ercise that belonging to himself. No user by a riparian proprietor affects the natural rights of other proprietors above or below him, unless it be of a nature to affect the use they have made, or the power to use such rights, and thereby to raise a presumption of a grant, and so as to render the tenement above or below a servient one. Merely using the stream for irrigation, in the exercise of a natural right, however long continued, would not have the effect to make the upper or lower tenement a servient one, or, in any way, affect the natural right of the owner as to the use of the water. If the use be of more than the natural right, the owner of the other tenement may have an action, whether he has begun to use it on his own land or not, for it is an invasion of his right, and he may defend it by a suit, though he may not be able to show actual damages. The owner of an upper tenement might divest himself, by grant, of his right to use the water for irrigation. But a mere non-user of the right would raise no presumption of such a grant. But the court held that the mode of using the defendant's right in this case, by penning up the entire water for a part of the day, and thereby, during that time, wholly depriving the plaintiff of the natural flow of the stream, was an unreasonable one, for which he was liable in the present action.

7. In the latter position the court assume the same ground as that upon which the case of Colburn v. Richards, above cited, seems to have been decided. And the suggestion, that an upper proprietor may lose his right to irrigate his lands by grant, is in accordance with the doctrine of *the case of Cook v. Hull,[1] where it was held that [*236] the owner of a mill may, by long exclusive enjoyment of the entire waters of a stream, the same being necessary for the working of the mill, exclude the riparian proprietor above from diverting any part thereof for purposes of irrigation, if by such diversion he is injuriously affected in the operation of the mill. In that case the mill had enjoyed the

---

[1] Cook v. Hull, 3 Pick. 269.   See also Colburn v. Richards, 13 Mass. 420.

water adversely for forty years, but, under the modern rule as to prescription, twenty years would undoubtedly be equally effectual.

8. The court of Pennsylvania considered this subject in the case of Miller v. Miller,[1] where the defendant had conveyed to the plaintiff a parcel of land situate upon a stream, and subsequently diverted portions of the water for the purpose of irrigating his other lands lying upon the same stream. As no reference is made to any mill, it is to be presumed that the question was simply between two land-holders, where one claimed damages for being deprived of the natural flow of the stream running through his land. In speaking of the rights of such proprietors, the court say : " The law requires of the party that he should use the stream in a reasonable manner, and one of the conditions of the use is, that he do not destroy, or render useless, or materially lessen or affect the application of the water by those situated above or below him on the stream. . . . .

" The reasonableness of the detention of the water by the upper proprietor, must depend on the circumstances of each case, and is to be judged of by the jury." And they illustrate the remark, by supposing the case of a large stream, where the diversion for purposes of irrigation might hardly be perceptible in its effects upon the volume of the stream ; and another, of a very small stream, where such diversion might absorb, substantially, the whole of the stream ; [*237] in *regard to which different rules would be applied in determining the reasonableness of the use. The only practical test which they suggest is, that an action would be for a diversion, " whenever so much of the volume of water is obstructed as to be plainly perceptible in its practical uses below."

9. This reference to the size and state of a stream, in determining the respective rights of riparian proprietors along its course, to apply its waters for purposes of irrigation, is

---

[1] Miller v. Miller, 9 Penn. St. 74.

adopted by the court of New York, also, in the case of Arnold v. Foot,[1] above cited.

The action in that case was for diverting and wasting the waters of a spring, which had previously flowed from the defendant's land through that of the plaintiff's. The court say : " The defendant had a right to use so much of the water as was necessary for his family and his cattle, but had no right to use it for irrigating his meadow, if thereby he deprives the plaintiff of the reasonable use of the water in its natural channel," and cite the language of Nelson, J., in Crooker v. Bragg.[2] When speaking of the right to running water, he says: " We cannot take from one party a right for the sake of the convenience of another."

So, where the owner of land, in which was a spring of water with a watercourse from it into the land of an adjacent owner, stopped the flow and used it for irrigation on his land in a proper manner, but thereby wholly deprived the adjacent land-owner of the same, it was held that he had no right thus to do. While he had a right to apply it in a reasonable manner and in a reasonable quantity for irrigation, he was not at liberty to deprive the adjacent owner of what he needed for his cattle.[3]

10. But the point is so fully considered, and so clearly stated and illustrated, by Shaw, C. J., in Elliot v. Fitchburg R. R. Co., that little need be added to the doctrine there laid down. The stream, in that case, was a small one, and was fed, in part, by a spring.

The defendants, under a grant from the owner of the land, had erected a dam just below the spring, whereby they raised a reservoir, from which, by means of pipes, they drew water to supply their engines used upon their railroad.

The plaintiff owned land through which the original stream flowed ; the land of another proprietor intervening between

[1] Arnold v. Foot, 12 Wend. 330. See ante, chap. 3. sect. 1, pl. 15.

[2] Crooker v. Bragg, 10 Wend. 264.

[3] Gillett v. Johnson, 30 Conn. 180.

the lot in which was the dam and the plaintiff's land. The
     action was for this diversion by means of the
[*238] *pipes laid from the reservoir, in which the plain-
          tiff claimed to recover, though he failed to show
any actual damages occasioned thereby. But the court
held that he could not recover unless he could show some
actual appreciable damage, because, to a certain extent, a
right to divert the water for use was incident to the land on
which the dam was, and if they had not transcended this, the
defendants had violated no right of the plaintiff.

"This appears," says the Chief Justice, "to have been a
small stream of water, but it must, we think, be considered
that the same rules of law apply to it, and regulate the rights
of riparian proprietors through and along whose lands it
passes, as are held to apply to other watercourses, subject to
the consideration that what would be a reasonable and
proper use of a considerable stream, ordinarily carrying a
large volume of water, for irrigation, or other similar uses,
would be an unreasonable and injurious use of a small
stream just sufficient to furnish water for domestic uses, for
farm-yards, and watering-places for cattle. . . . .

"The right of flowing water is now well settled to be a
right incident to the property in the land. It is a right
publici juris, of such a character that, while it is common
and equal to all through whose land it runs, and no one can
obstruct or divert it, yet, as one of the beneficial gifts of
Providence, each proprietor has a right to a just and reasonable use of it as it passes through his land, and so long as it
is not wholly obstructed or diverted, or no larger appropriation of the water running through it is made than a just and
reasonable use of it, it cannot be said to be wrongful or injurious to a proprietor lower down. What is a just and
reasonable use may often be a difficult question, depending
on various circumstances.

"To take a quantity of water from a large running stream
for agricultural or manufacturing purposes would cause no

sensible or practicable diminution of the benefit to the prejudice of a lower proprietor, whereas, taking the same
quantity *from a small running brook, passing [*239]
through many farms, would be of great and manifest injury to those below who need it for domestic supply,
or watering cattle, and therefore it would be an unreasonable use of the water, and an action would lie in the
latter case, and not in the former. It is, therefore, to a
considerable extent a question of degree. Still the rule is
the same, that each proprietor has a right to a reasonable use
of it for his own benefit, for domestic use and for manufacturing and agricultural purposes. . . . . It has sometimes
been made a question, whether a riparian proprietor can
divert water from a running stream for purposes of irrigation. But this, we think, is an abstract question, which
cannot be answered either in the affirmative or negative, as
a rule applicable to all cases. That a portion of the water
of a stream may be used for the purposes of irrigating land
we think is well established as one of the rights of the proprietors of the soil along or through which it passes. Yet a
proprietor cannot, under color of that right, or for the
actual purpose of irrigating his own land, wholly abstract
or divert the watercourse, or take such unreasonable quantity of water, or make such unreasonable use of it, as to
deprive other proprietors of the substantial benefit which
they might derive from it, if not diverted or used unreasonably. . . . . The right to the use of flowing water is
publici juris, and common to all the riparian proprietors ;
it is not an absolute and exclusive right to all the water
flowing past their land, so that any obstruction would give a
cause of action, but it is a right to the flow and enjoyment
of the water, subject to a similar right in all the proprietors,
to the reasonable enjoyment of the same gift of Providence.
It is only, therefore, for an *obstruction* and *deprivation* of
this common benefit, or for an unreasonable and unauthorized use of it, that an action will lie. But for such depriva-

20

tion or unwarrantable use an action will lie, though there be
no actual, present damage."

11. Two things, however, should be kept in mind
[*240] in *considering this subject : — 1. That any *diversion* of water, properly so called, except for domestic
use or purposes of irrigation, is a violation of the natural
rights of property in the riparian proprietors below ; and, 2.
As seems to be more than indicated by the cases already
cited, a riparian proprietor may not stop the flow of the
entire stream by a dam, and pen the same back for the
purposes even of irrigation, if thereby he substantially deprives other proprietors upon the stream of the natural flow
thereof. " Whether or not," in the language of Harris, J.,
in Van Hoesen *v.* Coventry, " a *diversion* of water is reasonable, is a question not so much as mentioned by any writer
or judge. The very proposition assumes the right of the
proprietor above to use the water for his own purposes, to the
exclusion of the proprietor below, a proposition inconsistent
with the doctrine universally admitted, as we have seen, that
all the proprietors have the same rights." [1]

12. As the uses above spoken of are not, properly, those
of servitude or easement between dominant and servient
estates, nor is it easy to define them, except as they are
something gained to one estate or lost to the other beyond
what naturally belongs to it of right ; it may be well to
repeat, that the right of a riparian proprietor, *jure naturæ*,
to divert water from a stream, when reduced to a simple
proposition, seems to be this. He may not do it for any
purpose except domestic uses, and that of irrigating his
land ; and whether, and to what extent, he may do the
latter depends, in each particular case, upon whether it is
reasonable, having regard to the condition and circumstances
of other proprietors upon the stream, and this is to be
determined, in all cases of doubt, by a jury. But in no case
may he do this so as to destroy, or render useless, or materi-

---

[1] Van Hoesen *v.* Coventry, 10 Barb. 518, 522.

ally diminish or affect the application of the water by the other proprietors.[1]

*13. It follows, from what has gone before, that if [*241] by any means a proprietor of land upon a stream shall have acquired rights to the enjoyment of the water, beyond those naturally belonging to the same, as above limited and explained, it must have been done at the expense of the right of some other proprietor, by grant or otherwise, in relation to whose estate his own becomes a dominant to the other as a servient one. In other words, his own thereby gains an easement while the other is subjected to a servitude.

How easements may be acquired by grant or an adverse user, which is regarded as evidence of a grant, was considered in a former part of this work.[2] But as this, so far as it is necessary, can better be illustrated when treating of the rights of mill-owners in connection with those of irrigation, than by regarding them separately, whatever is necessary to be added upon the subject of irrigation will be placed under the rights of mill-owners, in order to avoid unnecessary repetition.

14. It is hardly necessary to premise, after what has been said, that one may acquire an easement to divert water, whether for irrigation or other purposes, by grant or adverse user, as against other riparian proprietors below, whether it be to the injury of the land-owner, as such, or of an existing mill upon the stream. But he may not without a grant begin to divert the water of a stream for any purpose, so as materially to injure an existing mill, though it may not have stood for twenty years.[3]

[1] 3 Kent, Comm. 440; approved and commended in Embrey v. Owen, 6 Exch. 353; Wood v. Waud, 3 Exch. 748; Sampson v. Hoddinott, 1 C. B. N. s. 590; Webb v. Portland Mg. Co., 3 Sumn. 189, 199; Platt v. Root, 15 Johns. 218; Wadsworth v. Tillotson, 15 Conn. 366, 375; Twiss v. Baldwin, 9 Conn. 291, 308; Miller v. Miller, 9 Penn. St. 74; Hetrick v. Deachler, 6 Penn. St. 32; Pugh v. Wheeler, 5 Dev. & B. 50, 55, 59.

[2] Ante, chap. 1, sect. 4.

[3] Ward v. Robins, 15 Mees. & W. 237; Arnold v. Foot, 12 Wend. 330, 333;

[*242]   *15. It may be further added, that whatever would constitute a nuisance or injury to an incorporeal right of another, in respect to the use or enjoyment of running water as an element, may, as a general proposition, grow into a right of adverse enjoyment, by grant, or such use as is evidence of a grant, and thereby become an easement which one land-owner may have in that of another. And among the familiar illustrations which have before been mentioned, are those of watering cattle, or taking water for culinary or domestic purposes, at a spring or watercourse in another's land, as easements belonging to an ancient messuage in possession of him who claims to exercise such right.[1]

SECTION III.

OF THE USE OF WATER FOR MILLS.

Frankum v. Falmouth, 6 Carr. & P. 529 ; Mason v. Hill, 5 Barnew. & Ad. 1 ; Cox v. Matthews, 1 Ventr. 237 ; Buddington v. Bradley, 10 Conn. 213, 219.

[1] Manning v. Wasdale, 5 Adolph. & E. 758.

1. ONE of the most common instances of acquiring a right by adverse enjoyment, is that of obstructing the waters of a stream, and often of thereby setting back water upon the land of another, by means of a dam erected upon the owner's land, for the purpose of raising a head of water for the operation of mills or hydraulic works. If this is continued uninterruptedly and adversely for the term of twenty years, the mill-owner acquires thereby an easement, or right to obstruct such stream, or to flow such land, to the extent to which it shall have been enjoyed.[1]

[1] Townsend v. M'Donald, 14 Barb. 460, 467 ; Hart v. Vose, 19 Wend. 365 ; Colvin v. Burnet, 17 Wend. 564, 567 ; Wright v. Howard, 1 Sim. & S. 190, 203 ; Hurlburt v. Leonard, Brayt. 201 ; Middleton v. Gregorie, 2 Rich. 631.

A right to pond water upon another's land is an incorporeal hereditament. It is a freehold interest, and can only pass by deed, if regarded as a permanent right. But if it be a mere license, it is revocable. But equity, in some of the States, will enforce an executed license, though by parol, if granted upon a consideration, or upon the faith of which money has been expended, if the licensee would be without adequate compensation if the license were revoked.[1]

But a mill-dam cannot, lawfully, be maintained so as to interfere with or essentially lessen the use of a naturally navigable stream for purposes of a highway, unless the dam itself creates the navigable quality of the stream.[2]

[*244]   *From the importance of hydraulic works of art, for the comfort and convenience of man, and from the ordinary necessity there is of raising a head of water by means of a dam, in order to create the power requisite to operate the same, a right to do this by any riparian proprietor is deemed to be incident to the property in the land, *jure naturæ*, in the same sense as that of applying water to purposes of irrigation. And inasmuch as to cause this obstruction necessarily hinders the flow of a stream, to a greater or less interference with the enjoyment of the same by other mill or land owners, the same rule of reasonableness in its application is applied in the case of mills as in that of irrigation. And although the exercise of this right, so long as it is confined within the limits of the estate of the mill-owner, can hardly be called a proper easement, or the obligation to suffer it to be done be called a servitude, yet the rights which every mill-owner has to receive the flow of water from a superior riparian proprietor, and to discharge the same upon the land of a lower one, are spoken of by courts and writers as "natural servitudes and easements," although not, even in theory, held by virtue of any grant from these proprietors.[3]

---

[1] Bridges *v.* Purcell, 1 Dev. & Bat. 497; Snowden *v.* Wilas, 19 Ind. 13. *Ante*, pp. 23, 24, and cases cited.

[2] Hall *v.* Lacy, 3 Grant's Cas. 264.

[3] Kauffman *v.* Griesemer, 26 Penn. St. 407; Prescott *v.* Williams, 5 Metc.

2. It becomes necessary, in the first place, to inquire who may avail himself, as a riparian proprietor, of the right to obstruct the flow of the waters of a stream by a dam across the same, under the character of a mill-owner. Although a " mill site," or " seat," or " privilege," — for all these terms are in use, — may not require any definite amount or capacity of power to entitle the owner thereof to exercise the right of penning back the waters of a stream, it does imply the capacity of thereby creating sufficient power by the fall of the water, within the owner's premises, to be susceptible of being applied to some useful purpose of art. One *privilege may be adequate to carry a single mill, [*245] another may put in motion the spindles of a whole village.

3. There have been various definitions of a *mill site, seat,* or *privilege,* which it may be well to refer to in this connection.

Thus, in Russell *v.* Scott, the court say that a " mill-seat," or a " watercourse suitable for the erection of mills," which is " but another expression for mill seat or seats," implies land upon which a mill may be erected, for " it is an absurdity in terms to say that a stream is suitable for the erection of mills upon which no mill can be erected." [1]

In M'Calmont *v.* Whitaker, Gibson, C. J. says : " The water-power to which a riparian owner is entitled consists of the fall in the stream when in its natural state, as it passes through his land, or along the boundaries of it. Or, in other words, it consists of the difference of level between the surface where the stream first touches his land and the surface where it leaves it." [2]

429 ; Gould *v.* Boston Duck Co., 13 Gray, 442 ; Cary *v.* Daniels, 8 Metc. 466 ; 480 ; Brace *v.* Yale, 10 Allen, 441 ; Brown *v.* Bush, 45 Penn. 66.

[1] Russell *v.* Scott, 9 Cow. 281 ; Crosby *v.* Bradbury, 20 Me. 61. See Stackpole *v.* Curtis, 32 Me. 383; Jackson *v.* Vermilyea, 6 Cow. 677 ; Moore *v.* Fletcher, 16 Me. 63.

[2] M'Calmont *v.* Whitaker, 3 Rawle, 84, 90. Brown *v.* Bush, 45 Penn. 66.

This definition is adopted in terms by the court of Illinois, in Plumleigh v. Dawson.[1]

And Huston, J., in the above cited case, in applying the rule in question, says: " To the lower line of M'Calmont, he (Whitaker) could dam back the water, and no further. . . . . The rule must be, that a man has a right to dam back the water to his own upper line, as the water was, and as the bottom of the creek was, in a state of nature, when he built his dam."

Questions often arise as to the mode of measuring and ascertaining these, especially where one dam has been substituted for another, and the comparative extent of the flowing by one or the other is sought to be measured and ascertained. In one case, it was attempted to measure the natural fall in a stream by a process of instrumental levelling. But the court held that this was less satisfactory than, and must yield to, " actual visible facts," such as a fixed object in the stream, before the dam in question was erected, being out of water but covered afterwards, the rise and fall of the water on the posts and abutments of a bridge above, or drowning out a permanent object upon the bank of the stream, because instrumental measurements are liable to accidents and mistakes. The court instructed the jury that " water will find its level with more certainty than science can do the same work. The instrumental levelling does show that the plaintiff has more fall upon his land than he has elevation at his dam ; but if that does not tell the height of the water set back as clearly as shown by the water itself, then the fact demonstrated upon the ground must govern. We do not undervalue scientific measurements, but the history of all engineering in Pennsylvania has shown that, wherever science has disregarded and set aside the testimony of local experience and observation, it has blundered, and has had to do its work over again." " And then nature has her own secrets which she has not revealed even to science. Who can calculate for

---

[1] Plumleigh v. Dawson, 1 Gilm. 544.

what the watermen call ' piling ' of water, or for the effect of removing a given obstruction a few rods further down stream, whereby the velocity of the current at a particular point is changed, or for atmospheric resistance to water ? " [1]

In Van Hoesen v. Coventry,[2] Harris, J. says : " The general doctrine relating to watercourses is, that every proprietor is entitled to the use of the flow of the water in its *natural course, and to the momentum of its fall [*246] on his own land." While in Davis v. Fuller [3] the Judge (Collamer) limits it by saying : " No man can be said to have a mill-privilege which cannot be used without injury to others."

Chancellor Bland, in Binney's case,[4] undertakes to define a " natural mill-site," by means of a diagram in the form of a right-angled triangle, having for its hypothenuse the line of the slope or descent in the stream, and the other sides formed by a horizontal line extending from the highest point in the stream till it meets a perpendicular erected at the lowest point in the slope of the stream. The points from which the horizontal line is drawn, and from which the perpendicular is erected, must neither of them transcend the limits of the owner's land, if it is intended thereby to define the extent to which a property in the mill-site can be claimed. The mill-power, as here represented, is assumed to be created by conducting the water along the horizontal line to the point of its intersection with the perpendicular, and causing it to propel machinery by falling therefrom to the lowest point in the stream, the horizontal line representing the " head-race," the perpendicular one the " tail-race," which would, of course, be equal to the fall from the upper to the lower points in the stream.[5] It is immaterial what may be the length of the head-

1 Brown v. Bush, 45 Penn. 61.
2 Van Hoesen v. Coventry, 10 Barb. 518, 520.
3 Davis v. Fuller, 12 Vt. 178.
4 Binney's case, 2 Bland, Ch. 99, 114.
5 " Head and Fall," as applied to an occupied mill-privilege, is " the distance of the surface of the water above the dam to the bottom of the race-way,

race, or what that of the tail-race may be, provided it is high enough to have the momentum of fall sufficient to propel the machinery of the mill.   A mill-site, as thus described, is in its nature an entire thing, incapable of division.

In Crittenden v. Field, the grant of a *mill-privilege* was described as commencing at a certain rock and running to a certain dam, and was held to be a right to flow to the [*247] rock, *and limited the privilege from the dam below to the rock above, but not to flow above the rock.[1]

But by "mill-privilege" it would seem that something more was meant than the quantum of power applicable to driving machinery, or the limits and bounds within which this is to be applied.   It embraces, also, the right which the law gives the owner, to erect a mill thereon, and to hold up or let out the water at the will of the occupant, for the purpose of operating the same in a reasonable and beneficial manner.[2]

In Bardwell v. Ames, Shaw, C. J., speaking of what had been granted in that case, says : " We think it was the whole of the water-power and mill-privilege created and established by the artificial works then created for the purpose of appropriating and applying the current of the stream for mill purposes, consisting of the wing dam, the side dam, the guard gates, the pond, reservoir, or general passage above the mills, and the stone flume " ; showing how broad a signification may be given to the term *water-power* and *mill-privilege*, when used as terms of description in a grant.[3]

4.   In whatever terms a mill site or privilege may be described, it is obvious that two or more of these cannot be occupied upon the same stream, within any reasonable distance from each other, without the operation of the one in some

where the water strikes after it has passed the wheels on which it operates." Per *Shaw*, C. J., in Bardwell v. Ames, 22 Pick. 333, 362.

[1] Crittenden v. Field, 8 Gray, 621.

[2] Gould v. Boston Duck Co., 13 Gray, 442, 453 ; Pettee v. Hawes, 13 Pick. 326 ; Brace v. Yale, 10 Allen, 447.

[3] Bardwell v. Ames, 22 Pick. 333, 355.

measure injuriously affecting that of the other. And it often becomes a question of difficulty to determine whether such injury is the foundation or not for an action at law. The mills may be of unequal magnitude and capacity, the one may require a less volume of water to propel it than the other, or one may require the water of the stream to be retained till accumulated in sufficient quantity to carry the works in the same, and the other be thereby delayed while it is so accumulating, and, being incapacitated to use it all *as it shall then be discharged by the upper mill, [*248] the lower one will lose the benefit of the natural flow of the stream. And even if no such inequality in the works exist, there must necessarily be a delay and obstruction, by the upper mill, of the water flowing to supply the lower one. And, on the other hand, the head raised to work the lower one may set back so as to check or diminish the rapidity with which the water is discharged from the tail-race of the upper one.

Questions of this kind have been numerous, and, though it is not intended to examine them in detail, it is desirable to collect enough of them to draw some general rules which may be of practical application in like or analogous cases.

5. The reader whose attention has not already been called to the fact, will be surprised to find how recent, in point of time, have been the cases which are now regarded as the leading ones upon this subject, in England as well as in this country. Few cases, for instance, have been more frequently cited than that of Bealey v. Shaw, which has become a leading authority, and was decided in 1805, and is cited here, somewhat at length, in order to trace the course of the decisions of the several questions which were raised in its discussion. In that case the mill of the defendant, which was an ancient one, was operated by means of a dam and a sluice, which conducted the water from the stream, and after having been used at his mill, the same was discharged into the stream below the site of the plaintiff's mill. The plaintiff's mill had been in operation but eight years, and was worked

by the water of the stream which was not turned into the sluice of the defendant's mill, when the defendant built a new dam, enlarged his sluice and the work at his mill, and took the whole water of the stream, thereby depriving the plaintiff of all means of operating his mill. And for this diversion the action was brought. It was contended that the defendant, by having appropriated the stream to the purposes of a mill, might, as against a recent mill, apply as [*249] much water as he had occasion to use *without being responsible for so doing. But this position was overruled by the court. They held that twenty years' exclusive enjoyment of the water in any particular manner affords conclusive presumption of right in the party so enjoying it, derived from grant or act of Parliament; in which, however, as will be seen hereafter, the language of the court should have been considerably qualified. But that, if this principle were applied, it would not extend to any more water than had been used at the defendant's works at the time of the erection of the plaintiff's mill. And Grose, J. said: "The plaintiff had a right to all the water coming over that *weir* (dam) which had not been carried off by such sluice." And the rule stated by Le Blanc, J., in which he substantially agreed with Lawrence, J., is: "That after the *erection of works*, and the appropriation by the owner of the land of a certain quantity of the water flowing over it, if a proprietor of other land afterwards takes what remains of the water before unappropriated, the first-mentioned owner, however he might, before such second appropriation have taken to himself so much more, cannot do so afterwards."[1]

6. One of the principal points in this case, as it will be perceived, was how far a prior occupation of a mill-site gives the owner and occupant thereof an exclusive right to the control of the waters of the stream, and how far this

---

[1] Bealey v. Shaw, 6 East, 208. See also Cary v. Daniels, 8 Metc. 466, 477 Baldwin v. Caskins, 10 Wend. 167; Canham v. Fisk, 2 Crompt. & J. 126.

depends upon the mill, by which such occupation is had, being an ancient one.   Much discussion has been had upon the subject, nor have the decisions in all cases been the same.

In Platt v. Root,[1] the first occupant of a mill-privilege claimed that he had, thereby, acquired a right to the stream above and below so far that no second occupant could use *or detain the water thereof to the least [*250] injury of his mill.   But this claim, it will be perceived, is not like that in Bealey v. Shaw, of having appropriated the whole waters of the stream by the erection of a mill ; but that, to the extent to which it had actually been appropriated, no one had a right to interfere with the undisturbed enjoyment thereof.   But such a right, as incident to a prior occupancy, was denied by the court.   They adopt the language of Thompson, J., in Palmer v. Mulligan,[2] that " the elements being for general and public use, and the benefit of them appropriated to individuals by occupancy, this occupancy must be regulated and guarded with a view to the individual right of all who have an interest in their enjoyment, and the maxim, *Sic utere tuo ut alienum non lædas*, must be taken and construed with an eye to the natural rights of all.   Although some conflict may be produced in the use and enjoyments of such rights, it cannot be considered, in judgment of law, an infringement of the right.   If it become less useful to one in consequence of the enjoyment by another, it is by accident, and because it is dependent on the exercise of the equal rights of others. . . . . The erection of dams on all rivers is injurious, in some degree, to those who have mills on the same stream below, in withholding water.   Yet this had never been supposed to afford a ground of action. . . . . Each one had an equal right to build his mill, and the enjoyment of it ought not

1 Platt v. Root, 15 Johns. 213. See Panton v. Holland, 17 Johns. 92.

2 Palmer v. Mulligan, 3 Caines, 307. See Davis v. Winslow, 51 Maine, 290.

to be restrained because of some trifling inconvenience to the other." And they mention among these, "insensible evaporation, and decrease of the water by dams, and the occasional increase or decrease of the velocity of the current, and the quantum below." And the language of Livingston, J., in the case of Palmer v. Mulligan, is: "It becomes impossible to attempt to define any case which may occur of this kind. Each must depend on its own circumstances."

[*251]   *It may be stated, as an unqualified proposition, that no priority of occupation or use of water by a mill-owner upon a stream within the limits of his own estate affects the right of a riparian proprietor above to erect and operate a mill, in a suitable and reasonable manner, upon his own land.[1]

This remark applies to cases where, like that of Gould v. Boston Duck Company, there had been no prescriptive rights acquired. But a mill may so use the water of a stream as to give it prescriptive rights against other riparian owners, as where the lower of two mills had exercised the exclusive right to control the water retained by a reservoir dam above the upper mill, it acquired a prescriptive right to do so, as against the upper mill, as was the case in Brace v. Yale.[2]

7. But the rules applicable to the question, what is a suitable and reasonable manner of erecting and operating one mill in reference to the rights acquired by priority of occupation by an existing one, can best be limited and illustrated by particular cases. That of Tyler v. Wilkinson[3] has been recognized as a leading one both in England and this country. Speaking of the rights of a lower mill-owner upon a stream, Story, J., says: "As owners of the lower dam, and the mills therewith connected, they have no rights beyond

---

[1] Thurber v. Martin, 2 Gray, 394; Martin v. Bigelow, 2 Aik. 184; Gould v. Boston Duck Co., 13 Gray, 442, 453. But see Wood v. Waud, 3 Exch. 748, 773.

[2] 10 Allen, 441.

[3] Tyler v. Wilkinson, 4 Mason, 397, 403.

those of any other persons who might have appropriated that portion of the stream to the use of their mills. That is, their rights are to be measured by the extent of their actual appropriation and use of the water, for a period which the law deems a conclusive presumption in favor of rights of this nature. . . . . They are riparian proprietors, and as such are entitled to the natural flow of the river without diminution to their injury. . . . . In their character as mill-owners, they have no title to the flow of the stream beyond the water actually and legally appropriated to the mills. But in their character as riparian proprietors, they have, annexed to the lands, the general flow of the river, so far as it has not been already acquired by some prior or legally operative appropriation."

As a general proposition, every riparian proprietor has a natural and equal right to the use of the water in the stream adjacent to his land, without diminution or alteration. The right to use implies a right to exercise a degree of control over it, and even, to some extent, to diminish its quantity. He may apply it to the purposes of manufacture or the arts, but may not, in so doing, corrupt it. He may use it for hydraulic purposes, but may not unreasonably retard its natural flow, nor injuriously accelerate its motion, by discharging it from his works in an unreasonable manner, nor suddenly, nor in excessive quantities, nor divert it from its accustomed channel without returning it to the same before it passes from his own premises to those of another. But he could not be held responsible for any injurious consequences which might result to others, if he use the water in a reasonable manner, and the quantity used is limited by and does not exceed what is reasonably and necessarily required for the operation and propulsion of works of such character and magnitude as are adapted and appropriated to the size and capacity of the stream and the quantity of water flowing therein.[1]

[1] Davis v. Getchell, 50 Maine, 604; Springfield v. Harris, 4 Allen, 494. See Corning v. Troy, &c. Iron Co., 39 Barb. 311.

8. In Hatch v. Dwight[1] the court state the law to be :
"The owner of a mill-site, who first occupies it by
[*252]   erecting *a dam and mill, will have a right to water
sufficient to work his wheels, if his privilege will
afford it, notwithstanding he may, by his occupation, render
useless the privilege of any one above or below him upon
the same stream ; so if a site once occupied had been abandoned by the owner."

This broad doctrine, of the effect of a mere priority of
occupation, has been somewhat criticised by other courts,
and among them by that of Maine, in Butman v. Hussey,[2]
where, while it is affirmed that a riparian proprietor has a
right to avail himself of the momentum of the water, and
may for this purpose raise a head of water on his own land,
if he do not thereby impair the rights of other proprietors,
it is questioned whether the owner of a mill-privilege, which
had never been occupied, could have an action for an injury
to the same by the erection of a dam below ; and the judge,
Weston, after comparing the doctrine of Hatch v. Dwight
with that of Tyler v. Wilkinson, as to the effect of priority
of occupation, concludes that the weight of authority is with
the latter, and that an exclusive right to a mill-privilege is
not sustained by occupancy alone, for a period less than
twenty years.

Whether or not the doctrine of Hatch v. Dwight may
have been somewhat affected in the extent to which it was
applied by the peculiar laws of Massachusetts upon the
subject of mills, which will hereafter be explained, the subject was deliberately examined by the court in Thurber v.
Martin,[3] wherein it was held that priority of occupation
secures to the first occupant the exclusive right to the use of
the water to the extent of his occupation. But priority of
use at any particular point upon a stream, however long

---

[1] Hatch v. Dwight, 17 Mass. 289, 296.

[2] Butman v. Hussey, 12 Me. 407. See also King v. Tiffany, 9 Conn. 162,
168 ; Omelvany v. Jaggers, 2 Hill, So. C. 634.

[3] Thurber v. Martin, 2 Gray, 394.

continued, can never deprive the owner of the lands bounded
on the same stream, at any point above the mill-pond
of *the first occupant, of the right to have and enjoy [*253]
a similar use of the water as it passes by his land.
In that case, the lower mill had been in operation sixty years,
yet the upper riparian proprietor was held to have a right to
erect and operate a mill upon his own land. But in doing
so he must use the water in a reasonable and proper manner,
in propelling and operating a mill, suited and adapted in its
magnitude to the size and capacity of the stream, and the
quantity of water flowing therein. Nor could he detain the
water an unreasonable length of time, nor discharge it in
such excessive quantity that it would run to waste. He
must use the water in such a way and manner, that every
riparian proprietor, at points further down the stream, will
have the use and enjoyment of it, substantially, according to
its natural flow, subject, however, to such disturbance and
interruption as are necessary and unavoidable in and by
the reasonable and proper use of it, for the operating of a
mill of suitable magnitude, adapted and appropriate to the
size and capacity of the stream, and quantity of water flowing therein. And if any proprietor on the stream claims
any special right to the use of the water, more beneficial to
himself or burdensome to the riparian proprietors below
than what may be called the natural or general right to the
reasonable use of the stream, he must establish it by grant
or prescription. The doctrines of this case were reaffirmed
in that of Chandler v. Howland,[1] and may be considered as
the well-settled common law of Massachusetts, although, as
already stated, this has been essentially modified in some
respects by the statutes of that State.

The question as to the extent and effect of appropriating
the waters of a stream for mill or other purposes has been
discussed in California, where by statute those working

[1] Chandler v. Howland, 7 Gray, 348. See also Cary v. Daniels, 8 Metc. 478;
Smith v. Agawam Canal Co., 2 Allen, 355.

mines are authorized to divert and use the water of [*254] streams *for the purpose of carrying on their mining operations.   In Ortman *v.* Dixon,[1] the defendant had a saw-mill upon a watercourse.   The plaintiff had a ditch by which he took the water of the stream to his mine-works from above the defendant's mill, when the defendant was not using it for his mill.   After this the plaintiff constructed a second ditch above the former one, whereby the chief part of the water of the stream was diverted from defendant's mill.   The court, in passing upon the two rights, concede the prior right of water to the mill, and, in determining how much the ditch-owner might divert, say : " The measure of the right as to extent follows the nature of the appropriation, or the uses for which it is taken.   The intent to take and appropriate, and the outward act, go together. . . . . If, for instance, a man takes up water to irrigate his meadow at certain seasons, the act of appropriation, the means used to carry out the purpose, and the use made of the water, would qualify his right of appropriation to a taking for a specific purpose, and limit the quantity to that purpose, or to so much as is necessary for it.   So if A erects a mill on a running stream, this shows an appropriation of the water for the mill ; but if he suffer a portion of the water, or the body of it, after running the mill, to go on down its accustomed course, we do not see why persons below may not as well appropriate this residuum as he could appropriate the first use.   The truth is, he only appropriates so much as he needs for the given purpose. . . . . He [the defendant] was entitled to all, whenever all was necessary for the mill ; but whenever the mill did not need or could not use it for its operations, the defendant [plaintiff?] could use it for his purposes. . . . . It is enough to hold that this appropriation, according to the finding of facts, was not an appropriation of all this water as the property of the defendant, but only an appropriation of so much as was necessary for the mill, and

1 Ortman *v.* Dixon, 13 Cal. 33.

that *the defendant, after the claim to this residuum [*255] had attached by the plaintiff's appropriation, could not enlarge his right at the expense of the plaintiff's rights already vested.''

The doctrine of the case is believed to be in harmony with that already enunciated by the prior cases above cited. But it has been stated more at large perhaps than otherwise necessary, because of the peculiarity of the local laws of that State, whereby the common law, as to the rights of riparian proprietors to the natural flow of the stream through their lands, is essentially modified in favor of those carrying on mining operations.

Another case illustrative of the application of the law of California, was this. The plaintiff erected a dam on a stream, by which he turned the water from its original bed, for a considerable distance, for the purpose of working the bed of the stream for minerals, between the points where the stream was diverted, and where it again entered the original bed. While things were in this state, the defendant went several miles above the point of this diversion, and, by a ditch, turned the water of the stream, and applied it at works for mining purposes. After that, the plaintiff being desirous of applying the water of the stream for mining purposes and for irrigation, at a point considerably lower down than that at which the water had been returned by the plaintiff into the original stream, brought an action against the defendant on the ground that he had made a prior appropriation of it. But it was held that he had no right to the water, as against the defendant, by reason of his appropriation first made by his dam, since that was done merely to divert the water from the bed of the stream so as to work the bed altogether above the point where he now proposed to use it.[1]

9. A leading case from the English reports, involving some of the questions above suggested, is that of Mason v.

[1] M'Kinny v. Smith, 21 Cal. 374.

Hill,[1] decided in the King's Bench in 1833. The defendant's mill, in that case, was erected in 1818, that of the
plaintiff in 1823. The owner of the land on which the latter
mill was erected had applied the waters of the stream for
more than twenty years before 1818 for watering his cattle
and irrigating this land. In 1818 the defendant diverted
from the stream a part of the water of a spring which had
previously flowed into it. And when, in 1823, the plaintiff
erected his mill, he applied to the same the water of the
stream that flowed over the defendant's dam, and that part
of the water of the spring which the defendant had not diverted, and also that of another spring that flowed into and
fed the stream. Soon after this the defendant changed the
site of his dam so as to divert, at all times, the water from the
plaintiff's mill. The court considered the question of prior
occupancy, and say: " The position that the first occupant of
running water for a beneficial purpose has a good title to it,
is perfectly true in this sense, that neither the owner of the
land below can pen back the water nor the owner of the land
above divert it to his prejudice. . . . . And the
[*256] owner of the land that applies *the stream that runs
through it to the use of a mill newly erected, or
other purposes, if the stream is diverted or obstructed, may
recover for the consequential injury to the mill. . . . . But
it is a very different question whether he can take away from
the owner of the land below one of its natural advantages,
which is capable of being applied to profitable purposes, and
generally increases the fertility of the soil, even when unap-
plied, and deprive him of it altogether by anticipating him
in its application to a useful purpose. . . . . It appears to
us that there is no authority in our law, nor, so far as we
know, in the Roman law, that the first occupant, though he
may be the proprietor of the land above, has any right, by
diverting the stream, to deprive the owner of the land below
of the special benefit and advantage of the natural flow of the

---

[1] Mason v. Hill, 5 Barnew. & Ad. 1.

water therein," unless the same has been gained by prescription or grant.

The court, accordingly, held the defendant liable for continuing to divert the water of the spring, although he had begun to do so before the plaintiff had erected his mill, and they applied the same rule to the stream generally.

10. Regarded in its reference to a diversion of water, the law of the case of Mason v. Hill would probably be adopted as the law of this country, as it is in England. But the rules which are to govern, in the mode of exercising their respective rights to the use of water by the several proprietors upon the same stream, are yet to be considered. Before doing this, however, reference may be had to another somewhat leading case, in which the rights growing out of prior occupancy of water are treated of. Ruffin, C. J., in Pugh v. Wheeler,[1] uses this language: " The defendants say, that such one of the owners as may first apply water to any particular purpose, gains thereby and immediately the exclusive right to that use of the water. That *is [*257] true, in the sense that any other proprietor above or below cannot do any act whereby that particular enjoyment would be impaired, without answering for the damages which are occasioned by the loss of the particular enjoyment. Whereas, before the particular application of the water to that purpose, the damages would not have included that possible application of the water, but been confined to the uses then subsisting. But to render the proposition, even thus far true, the use supposed must be a legitimate one, that is, it must not interfere with any previously existing right in another proprietor; for usurpation does not justify itself. If one builds a mill upon a stream, and the person above divert the water, the owner of the mill may recover for the injury to the mill, although, before he built, he could

_____
[1] Pugh v. Wheeler, 2 Dev. & B. 50, 55 ; Gould v. Boston Duck Co., 13 Gray, 442, 450; Kelly v. Natoma Water Co., 6 Cal. 105 ; Shreve v. Voorhees, 2 Green, Ch. 25.

only recover for the natural use of the water as needed for his family and irrigation. . . . .

" There is, therefore, no prior or posterior in the use, for the land of each enjoyed it alike from the origin of the stream, and the priority of a particular new application or artificial use of the water does not therefore create the right to that use, but the existence or non-existence of that application, at a particular time, measures the damages incurred by the wrongful act of another in derogation of the general right to the use of the water as it passes to, through, or from the land of the party complaining. The right is not founded in user, but is inherent in the ownership of the soil ; and when a title by use is set up against another proprietor, there must be an enjoyment for such length of time as will be evidence of a grant, and thus constitute a title under the proprietor of the land."

The court also, in another case in New York, Merritt v. Brinkerhoff,[1] declared the law to be, that the prior occupancy of a mill-privilege by one upon a stream gave him no exclusive right to the undisturbed use of the water.

[*258]   *It will be unnecessary to dwell any longer upon the cases in which the doctrine applicable to questions of precedence of right, arising from priority of occupation of water-power, is discussed, except as it may be to illustrate the practical operation of the doctrine. But the reader, by referring to other cases cited below, will find it therein more or less prominently sustained.[2]

11. From the consideration that, so far as a property in a

---

[1] Merritt v. Brinkerhoff, 17 Johns. 306.

[2] Heath v. Williams, 25 Me. 209, 216 ; Ingraham v. Hutchinson, 2 Conn. 584, 591 ; Sherwood v. Burr, 4 Day, 244 ; Sumner v. Tileston, 7 Pick. 198, 203 ; Gould v. Boston Duck Co., 13 Gray, 442, 453 ; Cox v. Matthews, 1 Ventr. 237 ; Rutland v. Bowler, Palm. 290 ; Frankum v. Falmouth, 6 Carr. & P. 529 ; Buddington v. Bradley, 10 Conn. 213, 219 ; Tucker v. Jewett, 11 Conn. 311, 323 ; Twiss v. Baldwin, 9 Conn. 291, 306 ; Blanchard v. Baker, 8 Me. 253, 269 ; Shreve v. Voorhees, 2 Green, Ch. 25 ; Thomas v. Brackney, 17 Barb. 654 ; Davis v. Fuller, 12 Vt. 178 ; Hoy v. Sterrett, 2 Watts, 327 ; Hartzall v. Sill, 12 Penn. St. 248.

mill site or privilege is concerned, it is limited by the extent of ownership of the land within which the fall of the water is contained, and as the dividing line between the upper and lower riparian proprietor may so divide the fall in the stream that but one part can be advantageously appropriated, it may sometimes happen that the effect of a prior appropriation of water-power in such case by one may interfere with another riparian proprietor enjoying what he originally had an equal right to avail himself of. And this will be found to have a more extensive application in those States, where, by statute, one may go beyond the limits of his own land in appropriating a water-power by a dam erected wholly or in part upon his own land, and thus it may seem to form somewhat of an exception to the general rule, as the same has been stated above.[1]

12. Two things are to be considered in ascertaining the manner and extent of the use to which the water of a stream may be applied in operating mills thereon.
One *is its effect upon the land of other riparian [*259] proprietors, the other is its effect upon other existing mills, and a third is sometimes presented in cases where a change is necessary, or has been made in the mode of operating, or in the character of the mill.

13. It seems to be settled that a mill-owner has a right, by means of his dam, to swell or set back the water of the stream, in its natural state, to the line of the adjoining riparian proprietor, and to maintain his dam at that height, although at times of freshets the water of his pond shall set back on to the land of such proprietor. If it were not so, it would not be possible to apply the whole power of a mill-privilege arising from the descent of the water within the land of the mill-owner.[2] But by freshets is meant, not the swells of water in the stream which ordinarily occur periodi-

---

[1] M'Coy v. Danley, 20 Penn. St. 85; Burwell v. Hobson, 12 Gratt. 322; Hendrick v. Cook, 4 Ga. 241, 257, 265 ; Cary v. Daniels, 8 Metc. 466, 477.

[2] Monongahela Navigation Co. v. Coon, 6 Penn. St. 379, 383. See Domat, B. 1, Tit. 12, § 5, Art. 4 ; Smith v. Agawam Canal Co., 2 Allen, 355.

cally at certain seasons of the year, by which the same is raised above the ordinary state of the stream at other seasons, but extraordinary rises in the stream; and the language of the court, in a later case than the one last cited, is: "A flood is a different thing. When it does come, it is a visitation of Providence, and the destruction it brings with it must be borne by those on whom it happens to fall." And they hold that a man may not erect his dam so high as to set back water beyond his neighbor's line, in "its natural and ordinary swellings in some seasons of the year."[1]

And in Rex v. Trafford,[2] it is maintained that no man may change or obstruct the flow of the water of a stream for his own benefit, to the injury of another, whether it be in the ordinary state of water while flowing in a bounded channel at all seasons, or the "extraordinary course [*260] which *its superabundance has been accustomed to take at particular seasons."

If a mill-owner flow back water so as to obstruct the natural drainage of land lying near, but not bordering upon the stream, he may be liable, unless the obstruction arose from a reasonable use of his own land or privilege, and what is a reasonable use is a mixed question of law and fact.[3]

14. A question has been raised and discussed, in view of the general principle above stated, whether any riparian proprietor may have an action for damages against a mill-owner for setting back the water of a stream beyond the line of such proprietor, without showing some actual appreciable damage thereby done to his land. The questions have chiefly arisen where, though the water was not flowed back above the banks of the stream upon the adjacent land, the water of the current was deepened, and more water remained therein than otherwise would have been found there at a similar state of water in the stream.

---

[1] M'Coy v. Danley, 20 Penn. St. 85, 89. See also, Burwell v. Hobson, 12 Gratt. 322. See Strout v. Millbridge Co., 45 Me. 76.

[2] Rex v. Trafford, 1 Barnew. & Ad. 874.

[3] Bassett v. Company, 43 N. H. 578.

In Garrett *v.* M'Kie,[1] the majority of the court of South Carolina held, that, in such a case, in order to recover, the riparian proprietor must show some appreciable damage as resulting from setting back the water into the channel upon his land. But a similar question having arisen in Georgia, the court of that State disapproved of the doctrine of Garrett *v.* M'Kie, and, after referring to several English and American cases, maintain the broad doctrine that to flow back water upon a man's land against his consent, whether already submerged or not, is an injury, and that, in the eye of the law, every injury imports a damage, for which nominal damages at least are recoverable by a suit at law, though he cannot prove an actual perceptible damage, and this would extend as well to the owner of half as to the owner of the whole bed of the stream.[2] At a later period, however, the court of the former State take occasion to re-affirm the doctrine of Garrett *v.* M'Kie to this extent, " that backing within the channel, from which no appreciable damage results, is not of itself a legal injury which will sustain an action. The proposition which thus we approve,
* results, we conceive, from the reasonable use of [*261] water, which every one through whose land it flows is authorized to enjoy, considered in connection with the necessities of machinery, upon sluggish streams, and in a flat country." [3]

But in Ripka *v.* Sergeant, Gibson, C. J. says : " The penning back of water in the channel of a stream is an injury to the freehold, though the banks be not overflowed." [4]

Where the dam of one mill set back water into the tail-race of another, it was held to be a ground of action, whether the tail-race was upon the upper mill-owner's land or that of

---

[1] Garrett *v.* M'Kie, 1 Rich. 444.

[2] Hendrick *v.* Cook, 4 Ga. 241, 257, 265.

[3] Chalk *v.* M'Alily, 11 Rich. 153, 161. See also Omelvany *v.* Jaggers, 2 Hill, So. C. 634.

[4] Ripka *v.* Sergeant, 7 Watts & S. 913.

another by the consent of the owner, and though no actual damage could be shown to have arisen.[1]

15. The broad and general language in which courts have spoken of what would or would not be the ground of an action for theoretic injuries, without actual damage, occasioned to the land of one man in a proper and reasonable operation of the mill of another, has tended to leave this still an open question, and, like many other questions as to the use of water, it will remain so until courts will define, somewhat more accurately than some of them have hitherto done, the qualifying limits they intend to apply to the particular cases when making use of general propositions.

Thus it is said by Wright, J., in Waring v. Martin: " Every owner of land over which a watercourse flows has a right to use the water, but he must use it without inflicting any *substantial* injury to another, or he is liable," which seems to negative the idea of a mere theoretic injury.[2]

And in the cases cited below, it was held that one mill-owner upon a stream, in order to have an action against another mill-owner for an alleged injury done to the operation of his mill, must show that the injury was a practical and perceptible one. It would not be enough that it was a mere theoretical one.[3]

16. The above cases, it will be perceived, were between one mill-owner and another, and do not necessarily [*262] involve *a determination of the question between a mill-owner and a riparian land-owner above him. And the language of Hemphill, J., in Haas v. Choussard, may be adopted as correct, that, " Whether an action for throwing back water will lie for merely nominal damages, where there has been no actual injury, is not free from doubt, though supported by American authorities." [4]

---

[1] Graver v. Scholl, 42 Penn. 67.

[2] Warring v. Martin, Wright, 381.

[3] Thompson v. Crocker, 9 Pick. 59 ; Cooper v. Hall, 5 Ohio, 320 ; Shreve v. Voorhees, 2 Green, Ch. 25 ; *contra*, Ripka v. Sergeant, 7 Watts & S. 9.

[4] Haas v. Choussard, 17 Texas, 590.

But in Stout *v.* M'Adams, the court of Illinois held that no one had a right to create an obstruction upon his own land, so as to set back water upon the land of another above, although created for the purpose of operating a mill; nor did it make any difference, in this respect, whether there was a mill standing upon the upper proprietor's land or not.[1]

But where a riparian owner built a dam across a stream, to create a fish-pond thereby upon his own land, but interfered with the flow of the stream in no other way, it was held to be a reasonable use of the water, and a mill-owner below had no cause of complaint on account of it, either at common law or under the statute as to mills in Massachusetts.[2]

17. It seems, however, to be well settled, that a mill-owner may not enlarge the quantity of water flowing in a stream from his mill through the land of a lower proprietor, by turning a new stream, which never was accustomed to flow into the same, into his pond, to increase the capacity of his power or privilege. " The wrong consists," say the court, in Tillotson *v.* Smith, " in turning any water upon the land which does not naturally flow in that place. . . . . It can make no difference, if the water, wrongfully turned upon a man's land against his will, flows in the channel of an ancient stream, or in a course where no water flowed before, if similar damage results." Nor would it be any justification in the party who should thus turn the waters of a *stream into the new channel, that the owner of the   [*263] land below was thereby actually benefited. No one has a right to compel another to have his property improved in any particular manner.[3]

18. But this does not extend to preventing a proprietor upon a stream digging ditches, or doing other acts in the proper cultivation of his land, though the effect of it is to

[1] Stout *v.* M'Adams, 2 Scamm. 67.

[2] Wood *v.* Edes, 2 Allen, 578.

[3] Tillotson *v.* Smith, 32 N. H. 90, 95 ; Merritt *v.* Parker, Coxe, 460 ; Pardessus, Traité des Servitudes, §§ 58, 88.

increase the quantity of water in the stream in ordinary times.[1]

19. Before proceeding to the subject of the use of water, as between mill-owners upon the same stream, it may be remarked, that it seems now to be well settled, that, if one occupies a mill-privilege upon a stream, but does not appropriate and apply the whole power or water of the stream to actual use, he leaves the unappropriated part open for occupation by any riparian proprietor, in the same manner as if no mill had been erected;[2] however, the opinion of the majority of the court in King v. Tiffany,[3] and expressions in the decision of Davis v. Fuller,[4] and Heath v. Williams,[5] might seem to conflict with this position.

The extent of the right to flow in such cases will be the height to which a dam of the same height as that which has been sustained for twenty years would flow, although some part of that time, by leaking and want of repair, the dam has not kept up the water to its original height. The owner of the dam may repair it, and thereby keep up the water uniformly.[6]

[*264]   *20. It should be remembered, then, that the owner of every mill-privilege may, by the common law, hold two relations to other owners of mills or lands upon the same stream, namely, that of riparian proprietor of land and that of a mill-owner. And, as it seems, he may, in the first capacity, maintain an action at common law for acts done by other mill-owners, for which he could not recover in a suit as mill-owner. Thus, as riparian proprietor, he has a

---

[1] Williams v. Gale, 3 Harr. & J. 231 ; Kauffman v. Greisemer, 26 Penn. St. 407 ; Martin v. Jett, 12 La. 501 ; Lattimore v. Davis, 14 La. 161 ; post, p. *354.

[2] Mason v. Hill, 5 Barnew. & Ad. 1 ; Cary v. Daniels, 8 Metc. 466, 478 ; Brown v. Best, 1 Wils. 174 ; Saunders v. Newman, 1 Barnew. & Ald. 262 ; Dagget, J. dissenting.

[3] King v. Tiffany, 9 Conn. 162.

[4] Davis v. Fuller, 12 Vt. 178.

[5] Heath v. Williams, 25 Me. 216.

[6] Jackson v. Harrington, 2 Allen, 243 ; Cowell v. Thayer, 5 Metc. 253 ; Ray v. Fletcher, 12 Cush. 200.

right to the uninterrupted natural flow of a stream, so far, at least, as necessary for domestic purposes, for drinking, washing, watering cattle, and the like, and, in some cases, for those of irrigation.[1]

21. As the owner of a mill-privilege, he has the right to occupy the same, within the limits of his own land, by stopping this flow by means of dams. And this right is as much an element of property as any other quality of the land of which it is an accident. In respect to any question of prior appropriation, that must have regard to the quantum of water, and not the quantum of the fall, since the latter could only be augmented by subtracting from the fall belonging to the proprietor above, by swelling back the stream upon him, or by appropriating a part of the fall of the adjoining proprietor below, by deepening the channel within his boundary, and thereby carrying out the bottom on a level to some point, in the inclined plane of the natural descent, lower than his own line; neither of which he has a right to do. But as the fall in his own land is all his own, he loses no part of what is left within that, by appropriating a portion only of the entire fall at first.[2]

22. And it may be repeated, as a general proposition, that, neither as a mill-owner nor as a riparian proprietor, has any one a right to do any act in his own premises, *which shall cause the water of a stream to flow back [*265] upon either the land or the mill of a proprietor above.
And it was even held in Davis v. Fuller, that if, by reason of a mill-dam, ice accumulates in the pond, and water is thereby caused to be flowed back upon an existing mill to its material injury, the owner thereby becomes liable in damages. But this seems to be overruled and a more reasonable doctrine maintained in Smith v. Agawam Canal Co., where it

1 Evans v. Merriweather, 3 Scamm. 492; Johns v. Stevens, 3 Vt. 308, 316; Tyler v. Wilkinson, 4 Mason, 395, 403.
2 M'Calmont v. Whitaker, 3 Rawle, 84, 90; Gould v. Boston Duck Co., 13 Gray, 442, 453.

was held that, if the lower dam, in the ordinary stages of the water, do not throw back water upon the wheels of an upper mill, the owner will not be responsible, though this is done by the accumulation of ice when the stream breaks up, and though the upper be an ancient mill.[1]

23. Corresponding to this, the prior occupant of a mill-privilege, who owns the land upon both sides of the stream, has a right to an unobstructed flow of the same below his mill for the purpose of *venting*, as it is called by the court, the waters of his pond according to the natural descent and course of the water. Nor can a subsequent occupant of a mill-site below, back the water so as to deprive the first proprietor of this natural descent and flow. But, in order to set up this priority of right, he must own both sides of the stream, or maintain his dam by the consent of the owners of the side not belonging to him.[2]

24. It is competent for the owner of a mill-privilege, as such owner, or as riparian proprietor, to change or deepen the channel of a stream within his own premises, or the mode of applying it to use, as often as he will, provided he return the water on to the land of the next proprie- [*266] *tor at its accustomed point, and do nothing that materially affects the enjoyment of the water by the adjacent proprietors, according to their legal rights.[3]

25. Where two or more owners of mill-privileges upon the same stream shall have occupied the same, as above contemplated, with hydraulic works of art, they have each a right to make use of the same in a reasonable manner, having reference to a like right in the other, but subject to the rights of the riparian proprietors upon the same

---

[1] Cowles v. Kidder, 4 Fost. 364; Tyler v. Wilkinson, 4 Mason, 395, 400; Gilman v. Tilton, 5 N. H. 231; Davis v. Fuller, 12 Vt. 178; Blanchard v. Baker, 8 Me. 253, 266; Pugh v. Wheeler, 2 Dev. & B. 50; Hill v. Ward, 2 Gilm. 285; Cary v. Daniels, 8 Metc. 466, 477; Smith v. Agawam Canal Co., 2 Allen, 355.

[2] Delaney v. Boston, 2 Harringt. 489; Bliss v. Rice, 17 Pick. 23.

[3] Norton v. Valentine, 14 Vt. 239; Ford v. Whitlock, 27 Vt. 265; Stein v. Burden, 29 Ala. 127.

stream, and, as will be more fully shown, if a question arises in any given case what would be such a reasonable use, it is to be referred to the decision of a jury. A large proportion of the cases, where conflicting rights are set up by such mill-owners to the use of water, will be found to have been determined by the application of this broad rule of what is a reasonable use in view of the circumstances of each particular case.[1] What a reasonable use of water may be, in any given case, depends upon the subject-matter of the use, the occasion and manner of its application, its object, extent, necessity and duration, and the established usage of the country, the size of the stream, the fall of water, its volume and velocity and prospective rise and fall, all of which are important elements to be taken into account in determining the question.[2]

26. The mode and extent to which one mill-owner may use and apply the waters of a stream, as between him and another mill-owner, is not what would be reasonable for his particular business, but what is reasonable, having reference to the rights of the other proprietors on the stream, without by such use materially diminishing it in quantity, or corrupting it in its quality. If one requires more than this, he cannot claim it as a natural right. The necessity of one man's business is not to be made the standard of another man's rights.[3]

27. All the cases seem to concur in this, that no mill-

[1] Cary v. Daniels, 8 Metc. 466; Evans v. Merriweather, 3 Scamm. 492; Beissell v. Scholl, 4 Dall. 211; Chandler v. Howland, 7 Gray, 348; Johns v. Stevens, 3 Vt. 308, 316; Hendricks v. Johnson, 6 Port. 472; Gould v. Boston Duck Co., 13 Gray, 442, 450; Pugh v. Wheeler, 2 Dev. & B. 50; Snow v. Parsons, 28 Vt. 459; Parker v. Hotchkiss, 25 Conn. 330; Davis v. Getchell, 50 Maine, 604; Springfield v. Harris, 4 Allen, 494.

[2] Davis v. Winslow, 51 Maine, 297. In Shears v. Wood, 7 J. B. Moore, 345, plaintiff was allowed to recover upon a count that the water did not run to the plaintiff's mills as they were accustomed to have it, though not described as ancient mills.

[3] Wheatley v. Chrisman, 24 Penn. St. 298, 302; Brace v. Yale, 10 Allen. 447; s. c., 4 Allen, 393.

owner has a right to *divert* the waters of a stream,
[*267] and *thereby deprive a lower proprietor of the benefit thereof.[1] And, in one case, this was applied to
its utmost extent, although the diversion was made for the
purpose of enabling the mill-owner to repair his works.[2]
But this does not impugn the right of reasonably detaining
the water by such proprietor by shutting down the gates of
his mill.

28. But precisely to what extent the owner above may use
the water for manufacturing purposes, if he do not divert it
from its accustomed channel, does not seem to be very well
defined. In other words, how far the owner above shall be
allowed to use the water of the stream for mechanical and
manufacturing purposes, where such use may produce injury
to the owner below, does not seem to be very well settled by
any of the adjudged cases in England or this country. Each
case depends upon its own circumstances. "The question
of the reasonable use of the water by the mill-owner above,
depending as it must upon the size of the stream, as well as
the business to which it is subservient, and on the ever varying circumstances of each particular case, must be determined by the jury and not by the court."[3]

29. Questions of this kind have often arisen, where the
owner of the upper mill, upon its first being put in operation, has shut down the gate and wholly stopped the water
till the pond could fill; or has been obliged to shut down his
gate and detain the water to raise his pond to a sufficient
height to drive his works, and the lower mill has suffered by
reason of such detention. Such were the cases of Hartzall

---

[1] Thomas *v.* Brackney, 17 Barb. 654; Snow *v.* Parsons, 28 Vt. 459; Newhall
v. Ireson, 8 Cush. 595; Sackrider *v.* Beers, 19 Johns. 241; Butman *v.* Hussey,
12 Me. 407; Judd *v.* Wells, 12 Metc. 504.

[2] Van Hoesen *v.* Coventry, 10 Barb. 518, 520.

[3] Thomas *v.* Brackney, 17 Barb. 654, 656; Parker *v.* Hotchkiss, 25 Conn. 321;
Patten *v.* Marden, 14 Wisc. 473; Hayes *v.* Waldron, 44 N. H. 584; Davis *v.*
Winslow, 51 Maine, 295.

v. Sill,[1] and Hoy *v.* Sterrett,[2] Hetrich *v.* Deachler,[3] and *Wheeler *v.* Ahl,[4] all of which were decided by [*268] the courts of Pennsylvania, and in all of which the idea of precedence of right, arising from priority of occupation, is discarded. In the case of Hoy *v.* Sterrett, the plaintiff's mill had been in operation more than thirty years, when the defendant erected one on the stream above him. In working his mill, the defendant often detained the water in his pond for two days and a night at a time, for which the plaintiff brought his action. But the court submitted the question to the jury, under the instruction that, " if they believed the water was no longer detained than was necessary for the proper enjoyment of it, as it passed through the defendant's land, for the use of his mill, it was a damage to which the plaintiff must submit."

The doctrine of this case was reaffirmed in Wheeler *v.* Ahl, where the owner of an upper mill enlarged his works, although to carry them he had to shut down his gate at night, and not run his works till the next morning, whereby the water from his mill did not reach the lower mill till eight or nine o'clock in the day, and during the remainder of the day more water was poured into the stream from the upper works than could be used to advantage by the lower mill.

In Hetrick *v.* Deachler, the plaintiff's works were an ancient grist-mill, the defendant's a modern saw-mill, on the same stream. In operating his mill, the defendant sometimes detained the water from three to five days or more, and, besides using the water for driving his mill, applied it in irrigating his land. Besides this, he, at times, let out so much water from his own as to flow the plaintiff's mill. The court were urged to rule that such a detention must

1 Hartzall *v.* Sill, 12 Penn. St. 248.
2 Hoy *v.* Sterrett, 2 Watts, 327.
3 Hetrich *v.* Deachler, 6 Penn. St. 32.   See also Mabie *v.* Matteson, 17 Wis. 1 ; Springfield *v.* Harris, 4 Allen, 496.
4 Wheeler *v.* Ahl, 29 Penn. St. 98.

necessarily be actionable, as being a violation of the plaintiff's rights. But they declined so to do, and submitted the question to the jury, whether it was a reasonable [*269] *detention of the water or not. " If he detained it no longer than was necessary for his proper enjoyment of it, the plaintiff cannot recover," unless, as the court added in their instructions, the defendant detained the water vexatiously or wantonly. And the whole court, in commenting upon and approving those instructions, refer, as a test of what may be done, to " the reasonableness of the detention, depending as it must on the nature and size of the stream, as well as the business to which it is subservient, and on the ever-varying circumstances of each particular case."

But in a case in Indiana, the oldest of three mills, and highest upon the stream, was the defendant's oil-mill; the lowest and next in age was the plaintiff's. After the latter had been in operation fourteen years, the defendant erected a saw-mill between the two, in which he used a different kind of wheel from those in use in the other mills, and which required a great deal more water to work it. The stream did not furnish a constant supply of water to run the mills, and they had to be operated by " gathering heads." In consequence of this erection and mode of operating the defendant's saw-mill, the plaintiff was not able to work his mill more than half as much as before. The court held this detention of water by the defendant unreasonable, and ordered it to be abated, the wheel being unsuited to the stream.[1]

A leading case upon this subject is that of Merritt v. Brinkerhoff,[2] where the plaintiff had a flour-mill situate below the defendant's rolling and slitting mill. The stream was a small one, and, the defendant's dam being twenty-four

---

[1] Dilling v. Murray, 6 Ind. 324.

[2] Merritt v. Brinkerhoff, 17 Johns. 306, 322. See also Heath v. Williams, 25 Me. 209; Twiss v. Baldwin, 9 Conn. 291; Beissell v. Scholl, 4 Dall. 211; Runnels v. Bullen, 2 N. H. 532; Hendricks v. Cook, 4 Ga. 241; Blanchard v. Baker, 8 Me. 253, 270.

feet in height, he stopped the entire waters of the stream, more than an hour at a time, while he was heating his iron, *and then let it out in such quantities as to [*270] run over the plaintiff's dam and be wasted, and the plaintiff's mill was stopped from half an hour to two hours daily. The rule laid down by the court, as governing such a case, was, that the upper mill might apply the water to the best advantage, but not so as to render the lower mills on the stream useless or unproductive. The law will so limit this common right to use the water of the stream, that the owners of the lower mills shall enjoy a fair participation of it, although the upper mills may thereby sustain a partial loss of business and profit. The upper mill must not use the water in an unreasonable manner so as to be materially injurious and destructive to the mills below. The jury found for the plaintiff, and the court sustained the finding.

In Pitts v. Lancaster Mills [1] the defendants erected a mill above the plaintiff's ancient mill, and, while filling their pond, in order to start their own mill, stopped the water and deprived the plaintiff of the use of it. But it was held to be *damnum absque injuria*, since the right to do this, in a reasonable manner, was incident to the property in the mill-privilege of the defendant.

It is, accordingly, held as a general proposition, that the owner of land over which a watercourse flows, is entitled to a reasonable use of the water for a mill, provided his dam is of a magnitude suited to the size of the stream and quantity of water usually flowing therein. Nor will he be liable to the owner of mills below for any injury arising to them from such use, having reference to the general custom and usage of the country in cases of dams upon similar streams.[2] He may not render a mill below useless, but must so use the water as to give such lower mill a fair participation in the same.[3]

---

[1] Pitts v. Lancaster Mills, 13 Metc. 156.

[2] Springfield v. Harris, 4 Allen, 494 ; Davis v. Getchell, 50 Maine, 604 ; Mabie v. Matteson, 17 Wis. 1 ; Davis v. Winslow, 51 Maine, 291 – 293.

[3] Patten v. Marden, 14 Wisc. 473.

30. The subject was also considered by the court in the case of Barrett *v.* Parsons,[1] and in Thurber *v.* Martin,[2] where the rules to be observed in the management of mills upon a stream are stated substantially to be, that those who are lowest upon the stream must take the water subject to the previous rights of those above them, to use and employ it for their mills and works, and to do all that is necessary and usual for the purpose of building dams, forming mill-ponds, and erecting gates, and such other structures and apparatus as may be convenient and proper. But the owners of the upper mills are bound to use and employ the water in a reasonable and proper manner, conformably to the [*271] usages *and wants of the community, and not inconsistent with a like reasonable and proper use of it by others on the same stream below.

So in Gould *v.* Boston Duck Co.,[3] the court states, summarily, the respective rights of two or more owners of mill-powers upon a stream. They are not rights to the natural flow of the stream, in the manner in which it originally run, or, as if no mill were erected upon it, or to be worked by it. A right to erect a dam and change the natural mode of the flow of the current is incident to the right of applying it to the working of mills, and this right is common to every riparian proprietor. Each must, therefore, exercise his own reasonable right with a just regard to a like reasonable use by all the others. In respect to the time and mode of holding up and letting down the water by mills, so far as it is reasonably incidental to the use of the stream for mill purposes, it is the right of the proprietor, and constitutes, in part, the mill-privilege which the law gives him. As priority of occupation, in this respect, gives no priority of right to the use of the stream, beyond the actual extent of such occupancy, where an upper mill, though recent, in the rea-

---

1 Barrett *v.* Parsons, 10 Cush. 367, 371.

2 Thurber *v.* Martin, 2 Gray, 394.

3 Gould *v.* Boston Duck Co., 13 Gray, 442, 453. See also Cary *v.* Daniels, 8 Metc. 466; Chandler *v.* Howland, 7 Gray, 348.

sonable and proper use of it, interrupts, in some measure, the operation of the lower mill, though an ancient one, the owner of the latter is without remedy, even though it were done in a low state of water in the stream, occasioned by drought, and the upper mill-owner, in order to work his mill, is obliged to stop the natural flow of the water while his pond is being filled.

The case cited seems to furnish a proper limitation to the language of the courts in some of the cases, which assumes that a mill-owner has, as incident to the same, the same right, against another mill-owner, to the natural flow of the stream as exists between successive riparian propri- etors in *respect to their respective lands, indepen-   [*272] dent of any application of the water for purposes of art.   And among the cases where this appears to have been assumed by the court as the law, are Davis v. Fuller,[1] and King v. Tiffany.[2]

30 a. Mill-owners often construct dams at considerable distances above their works, for the purpose of creating res- ervoirs of water to be drawn for use when the condition of the stream may require it.   This often gives rise to ques- tions of some difficulty where there are other mill-owners upon the same stream, especially if their mills are situate be- tween the reservoir dam and the mill of the owner of such dam.   It was held that such a dam and pond came within the principle of the Massachusetts mill acts, as to flowing the lands of third persons.[3]

So the above cited case of Gould v. Boston Duck Co., was one where the injury complained of arose from the mainten- ance and management of a reservoir dam by the defend- ants which was situated above the plaintiff's works.   Simi- lar questions came up in the case of Brace v. Yale, the facts of which were substantially these.   The plaintiff owned an

---

1 See ante, pl. 22 ; Davis v. Fuller, 12 Vt. 178.

2 King v. Tiffany, 9 Conn. 162.

3 Wolcott Co. v. Upham, 5 Pick. 292.

ancient mill, and a reservoir had been maintained by him for the benefit of this mill, about a hundred rods above it, for over forty years. The plaintiff ordinarily opened the gate of this reservoir in the morning, and, if no obstacle intervened, the water reached his mill in about twenty minutes. Another owner, the defendant, erected a mill between the plaintiff's mill and reservoir, and raised a dam which stopped this water, often detaining it two hours and a half to fill this new pond. When the gate of the reservoir was closed no water flowed in the stream below, as it was a small one, and when the gates of the middle dam were closed no water flowed to plaintiff's mill until the new pond was filled. Much water was wasted to the plaintiff, by the operations of the defendant's mill, because the same was not wanted for the plaintiff's mill. But the defendant used no more than was advantageous for working his mill. Some days, the plaintiff's mill was, in this way, interrupted half the time. The court held that the plaintiff, by this long user, management, and enjoyment of the water in the reservoir, in stopping the flow of the stream except when the same was let out by gates, and only in such quantities as he needed from time to time for operating his mill, acquired a right which was adverse to the original rights of the riparian proprietor's to the natural flow of the stream, and which he might claim by prescription. The mere erection, however, of a dam across the stream for raising a head of water to work a mill, and the cutting of sluices and waterways for conducting the water to and from such mill, would not be deemed adverse to the other riparian proprietor, although it might, in some measure, change the natural flow of the water in the stream, or cause a temporary obstruction therein, because this is not inconsistent with the rights of such proprietors. Nor would the erection of a reservoir dam and the stopping of the water thereby, until it had filled, be adverse to the rights of such proprietors, if the water was then suffered to resume its accustomed flow, because the obstructions thereby occasioned, would be slight and temporary, and not inconsistent with the rights of proprietors below. But by this long adverse enjoyment by the plaintiff, the riparian proprietors below the reservoir dam lost the right to the natural flow of the stream, as well as the right to control the quantity of water or time of its passage, except in subordination to the plaintiff's acquired rights, and in a way not to interfere with the accustomed working of his mill and machinery. He could not, therefore, lawfully hold back the water flowing from the reservoir for the purpose of filling and refilling his pond, nor let it down in such quantities that the plaintiff could not appropriate it to the operation of his mill, and thereby cause the water to run to waste. The circumstance which chiefly distinguishes this from the case of Gould v. Boston Duck Co., is the prescriptive rights which had been acquired by user in the present case, in favor of the reservoir.[1]

In one case the owner of a stream and its banks erected a dam and grist-mill thereon, and sold the mill and privilege to J. S. He then erected another dam above this, across the stream, with a design to erect a mill at one end of the same. He then sold to the plaintiff one half of this dam, with a privilege to erect and carry on tan works on the bank, but subject to a preferred use of the water for the intended mill upon this dam. He then sold his property in this dam and privilege to J. D.; J. D. then purchased the lower dam and grist-mill of J. S., through whom they came to the defendant. No mill was erected by any of these owners on the end of the upper dam opposite to the plaintiff's tan works; and in times of low water the defendant drew water from the upper dam by a gate therein which had the effect to interrupt the use of the plaintiff's tan works. It was held that the defendant, as owner of the prior mill, might, if the upper dam stopped the water and prevented its reaching his mill,

[1] Brace v. Yale, 10 Allen, 441. See Pitts v. Lancaster Mills, 13 Metc. 156 ; Perrin v. Garfield, 37 Verm. 204 ; ante, p. *94.

draw the water from the upper pond, if necessary, for work-ing his mill, and that his owning the upper dam with the plaintiff made no difference in respect to his rights as owner of the lower mill.[1]

31. From the nature of property in the use of water, it may often happen that there may be a community of in-terest and ownership in a mill-privilege, although the own-ership of the land may be separate, as where two adjacent riparian proprietors, each owning to the thread of the stream, have a water-power in the water of such stream by reason of its descent along the channel between where it enters upon and where it leaves their premises. The privi-lege becomes operative and valuable by the two joining in occupying it by a dam across the stream; in which case they become tenants in common of the water-power, al-though each must apply it upon his own individual land. In such case, if either uses the water in an unreasonable manner, to the injury of the other, he would be liable therefor, since neither can wantonly waste the water to the prejudice of the other. Each owner, in such case, would be bound to keep his part of the dam in repair, so long as he uses the water of the pond, and if either ceases to use it, the other may keep the dam in suitable repair.[2]

Though a water-power, that is, a force or power caused by its flow and fall in a stream, is a thing incapable of partition by metes and bounds like land, it may, nevertheless, be the subject of joint ownership, wherein any one proprietor may become entitled to any given proportion of the whole power or flow of the water.[3] And whenever two persons draw

[1] Miner v. Gilmore, 12 Moore, P. C. 131.

[2] Runnels v. Bullen, 2 N. H. 532, 538; Carver v. Miller, 4 Mass. 559; Con-verse v. Ferre, 11 Mass. 325; Gwinneth v. Thompson, 9 Pick. 31; 2 Dane, Abr. 721; Loring v. Bacon, 4 Mass. 575; Doane v. Badger, 12 Mass. 65; Campbell v. Mesier, 4 Johns. Ch. 334; Mumford v. Brown, 6 Cow. 475; Binney's case, 2 Bland, Ch. 99, 114; Bliss v. Rice, 17 Pick. 23, 36. See Pratt v. Lamson, 2 Al-len, 275, 286.

[3] Monroe v. Gates, 48 Maine, 467.

water for their mills from the same dam, and neither has any peculiar or precedent right by grant or prescription, each may continue to use the water, whatever the effect may be upon the other.[1]

It has accordingly been settled, that, if either mill-owner upon such common mill-dam have occasion to repair his mill standing upon his own land, or the flume or works thereof, he may do so, and if he exercises reasonable care and diligence in prosecuting the work, he will not be *responsible to the other owner of the privilege, [*273] though by accident he sustains damage while such repairs are being made. Nor would the rule be different even if the privilege had been so far divided, as it might be, between them, that each had the exclusive use of the entire power every alternate six months.[2]

When a partition has been made of a water-power, by assigning to each of two or more joint owners a right to occupy it exclusively for a certain period, or it has been enjoyed in that way till a partition may be presumed, the one who for the time being has a right to such use may divert the waters of the pond for irrigation upon his own land, but not to continue such diversion while another of the cotenants has a right to occupy the mill.[3]

The partition above spoken of must have been by mutual arrangement and grant between the several owners in common. At common law, there was no process for dividing incorporeal hereditaments like a joint water-power by what answers to metes and bounds. But, by statute in Massachusetts, partition may now be made by a process in equity.[4]

Where there were a grist-mill and saw-mill occupying a mill-privilege upon one dam belonging to the same person, and the only mills upon the privilege, and he granted one by

---

[1] Brown v. Bowen, 30 N. Y. 538.

[2] Boynton v. Rees, 9 Pick. 528 ; Bliss v. Rice, 17 Pick. 23, 38.

[3] Bliss v. Rice, 17 Pick. 23.

[4] Miller v. Miller, 13 Pick. 237 ; Adam v. Briggs Iron Co., 7 Cush. 361 ; De Witt v. Harvey, 4 Gray, 496, 499 ; Gen. Stat. c. 136, § 77.

the name of the saw-mill, for instance, it passed the proportion or share of the water in the river belonging to such mill, which was such proportion of the whole right in the brook as the water used to drive the mill conveyed bore to that used by the other mill. But had there been several mills upon the stream of different kinds, all drawing from the same level, and there was only sufficient water to supply the power necessary to drive each mill, a grant of one of these mills would carry only the mill and the water actually necessary to drive it.[1]

32. The rights of the respective mill-owners upon a stream, in respect to the diversion thereof, are the same whether the stream be a public or private river. In neither case may the owner of an upper mill divert the water of the stream, and discharge the same into the current [*274] again *below the mill of a lower owner.[2] Nor may a lower mill flow back upon an upper one, though erected upon a stream which is a highway, and, for maintaining his dam across it, he may be liable to indictment for a nuisance. If liable for the nuisance, it is to the public only, and his rights as a mill-owner may not be infringed by another mill-owner upon the stream.[3] And it was held to make no difference, in respect to acquiring a right, by prescription, to flow the land of another, that the mill by which it was done stood upon an embankment or dam formed by a highway across a navigable stream.[4]

33. There are some cases where a lower mill may acquire the benefit of expenditures laid out by the upper mill-owner, without being liable to contribute therefor. Thus if the upper owner increase the capacity of the stream for mill purposes, by enlarging the extent of his pond, or the reservoirs which supply his mill, the lower one has a right to avail himself of the benefit of this, as something incident to the owner-

---

[1] Crittenden v. Field, 8 Gray, 621.
[2] Sackrider v. Beers, 10 Johns. 241.
[3] Stiles v. Hooker, 7 Cow. 266.
[4] Borden v. Vincent, 24 Pick. 301.

ship and situation of his mill. Nor would he be liable to any land-owner above the upper mill, whose land was damaged by such increased flowing.[1] Nor could the upper mill-owner, after having increased the quantity of water in the stream by such additional flowing, erect works between the upper and lower mills, upon his own land, and thereby divert water from the stream, though it did not exceed the quantity which he had thus added to the natural flow of the stream.[2]

34. In addition to what has been said upon the subject of diverting water from a stream in its connection with the rights of mill-owners, it may be stated, that it mat-- ters not how or *for what purposes such diversion [*275] is made, nor whether it be of the waters of the principal stream, or a remote or inconsiderable branch and feeder thereof, provided such feeder be itself a running natural stream, even though it flow underground, if in a well-defined channel. Thus where one dug a large well upon his own premises, into which the waters of a running stream, which supplied in part a mill below, were withdrawn therefrom by penetrating through the earth into the well, and were then pumped into another channel and not returned to the original stream, and it was known when he dug the well that such would be the effect, he was held liable to the mill-owner for such diversion. But the reader will keep in mind the distinction there is between such a case as this, and those cases to be hereafter noticed, where waters percolating through the earth into streams have been prevented from reaching them by excavations made by riparian proprietors on their own lands, though to the injury of mills upon the streams.[3]

---

[1] Tourtellot v. Phelps, 4 Gray, 370, 376.

[2] Eddy v. Simpson, 3 Cal. 249. But see Whittier v. Cocheco Mg. Co., 9 N. H. 454; post, pl. 46, 53.

[3] Dickinson v. Grand Junct. Canal Co., 7 Exch. 282, 301 ; post, p. *370 ; Broadbent v. Ramsbotham, 11 Exch. 602; Wheatley v. Baugh, 25 Penn. St. 528; Arnold v. Foot, 12 Wend. 330 ; Dudden v. Guardians of Poor, &c., 1 Hurlst. & N. 627; Rawstron v. Taylor, 11 Exch. 369; Evans v. Merriweather, 8 Scamm. 492.

Whether and how far a mill-owner, who draws his water from a natural pond,

35. Keeping in mind what rights are incident to the ownership and use of mills, from the nature of such property, the reader will be prepared to understand what are meant by easements and servitudes as applicable to mills and mill-privileges. And it may be stated, in general terms, that if any land or mill owner shall claim a right to a different or exclusive use of a stream, or to use its waters in a manner more injurious to other owners upon the same stream than those which have been above enumerated, he can only maintain it by establishing a claim of easement in favor of his own as a dominant estate, over and upon that of [*276] the other *owner in reference to which it is to be exercised as the servient estate; and this right of easement the dominant estate must have acquired at some time from the servient one, by grant, or its equivalent, prescription.[1]

No proprietor of land on the same stream has a right, at common law, to divert the water or change the use of it to the injury of any other proprietor, unless such right has been acquired by grant or prescription.

Where the mill-owner has, in fact, exercised the right of raising or diverting the water by keeping up his dam and flowing the land of another for a period of twenty years, without objection or claim of damages, it is evidence of a right so to use the water as acquired by prescription or grant. But it is equally well settled by the authorities, that if any riparian proprietor has, by means of a dam, made a special use of the water by penning it up, and throwing it back upon a proprietor above, or holding it back from the proprietor below, or by diverting it, and has so used the

may take the ice that forms thereon, or prevent others from doing it, for use or sale, was left unsettled in the case of Cummings v. Barrett, 10 Cush. 189.

[1] Wright v. Howard, 1 Sim. & S. 190; Arnold v. Foot, 12 Wend. 330, 333; Brown v. Best, 1 Wils. 174; Murgatroyd v. Robinson, 7 Ellis & B. 391; Johns v. Stevens, 3 Vt. 308, 316; King v. Tiffany, 9 Conn. 162, 169; Cary v. Daniels, 8 Metc. 466, 479; Shreve v. Voorhees, 2 Green, Ch. 25; Cowell v. Thayer, 5 Metc. 253.

water without resistance or opposition from other proprietors for the term of twenty years, he thereby establishes a right so to continue to use it by way of prescription or presumed grant.[1]

36. In briefly considering what rights to water-power, in connection with mills, may have been granted or acquired by use, rather by the way of illustration than with a view of anything like a general discussion of how easements may be acquired, which has been considered in a former part of this work, it may be stated, that questions have sometimes been made, whether that which is granted is a right to use *such a measure or quantity of power for a specific [*277] purpose, and none other, or, by naming the purpose for which it is conveyed, it is made a measure of the quantity that is granted, but with liberty to use it for such purposes as the grantee sees fit.

As a general thing, where there is a grant of sufficient water-power to carry a grist-mill or a cotton-factory of such dimensions, and the like, it is construed by courts to be the quantity and not the purposes of the power granted that is meant. And yet it is competent to restrict the grant, as is often done, to the use of the power for some specific purpose or kind of business, in which case any different use would be against right.

These questions may arise either in cases of grants, or reservations, and, it will be observed, the cases are not those where land, with a stream of flowing water, is granted, or reserved, but a right to draw water or use a water-power independent of the ownership of the bed of the stream.

Thus where there was a grant of sufficient water-power to carry a grist-mill and a cotton-factory with not more than five thousand spindles, it was held to be a mere measure or

[1] Cowell v. Thayer, 5 Metc. 253; Bolivar Mg. Co. v. Neponset Mg. Co., 16 Pick. 246; Williams v. Nelson, 23 Pick. 141; Buddington v. Bradley, 10 Conn. 213; Baldwin v. Calkins, 10 Wend. 167.

description of the quantity granted, and not the use to which it must be applied.[1]

In the case of Tourtellot v. Phelps, the grant was of "a privilege to draw water sufficient to carry a water-wheel, well constructed, with twelve feet head and fall, for two common blacksmith's bellows," and was held to be a measure of power. But in Ashley v. Pease, a fulling-mill [*278] and other *mills were standing upon the grantor's land, and his grant was of a piece of land, with a fulling-mill standing thereon, with a right to draw so much water as may be necessary to carry and supply the fulling-mill "which now stands or may hereafter stand on the same spot," with a provision that when there was not a sufficiency of water, &c., the grantee was to draw, &c., "for the use of the said fulling-mill or mills, twelve hours in the twenty-four," &c. It was held to be a limited grant of water to be applied to the use of a fulling-mill alone.

And yet courts always incline to construe such grants as limiting or measuring the quantity of power, rather than defining and restricting the uses to which it may be applied. Thus the grant of land, with the privilege of water to turn the fulling-mill mentioned in the deed, when the same is not wanted for carding wool, reserving water for carding-machines and fulling-mill, was held to be a measure of power, and not a restriction as to the purposes for which the water should be used, and had reference to the mills then in existence, and the use then being made of the water when the deed was made.[2]

---

[1] Bigelow v. Battle, 15 Mass. 313; Tourtellot v. Phelps, 4 Gray, 370; Ashley v. Pease, 18 Pick. 268; Hurd v. Curtis, 7 Metc. 94, 111; Whittier v. Cocheco Mg. Co., 9 N. H. 454; Cromwell v. Selden, 3 Comst. 253; Bardwell v. Ames, 22 Pick. 354; Atkins v. Bordman, 2 Metc. 470; Rogers v. Bancroft, 20 Vt. 250; Adams v. Warner, 23 Vt. 395, 410; Rood v. Johnson, 26 Vt. 64, 72. This is very clearly and satisfactorily illustrated and explained in an able opinion by *Merrick*, J., in Pratt v. Lamson, 2 Allen, 275, 283; Wakely v. Davidson, 26 N. Y. 387; Dewey v. Williams, 40 N. H. 227; Blanchard v. Baker, 8 Maine, 253; Johnson v. Rand, 6 N. H. 22; Kaler v. Beaman, 49 Maine, 208; Deshon v. Porter, 38 Maine, 289; De Witt v. Harvey, 4 Gray, 489.

[2] Wakely v. Davidson, 26 N. Y. 387, 394; Borst v. Empie, 1 Seld. 33; Olmstead v. Loomis, 6 Barb. 152, 159; Fisk v. Wilber, 7 Barb. 395, 402.

The case of Shed *v.* Leslie[1] was similar in principle to that of Ashley *v.* Pease, with the additional circumstance that the habendum in the deed was, " so long as he (the grantee) or they shall carry on clothiers' business, in or near said place," &c. The grant was held to be restricted both in the quantity and purposes of the power granted.

The case of Garland *v.* Hodsdon[2] may also be referred to as an instance of a limited power and use reserved, where there had been a grant of land upon a stream, with part of a dam across the same, with the right and privilege in the dam and stream to take water sufficient for one fulling-mill. The deed " reserved for the use of the grist-mill, or such other grist-mill as may be erected at the place where the grantor's mill then stood, the right at all times to take water sufficient for two run of stones." It prohibited the grantee from taking the water " when the same shall be wanted for the grist-mill," &c. It was held to be a grant of so much power as would carry one fulling-mill, and which the grantee might use as he pleased. But the reservation was a limited one, to be applied only for the use specified, namely, a grist-mill.

So where there was a grant of a parcel of land and " a water-privilege for tanning purposes in all its various branches, which privilege is to come out of the grist-mill dam " which belonged to the grantor, it was held to be limited and restricted to the uses designated in the grant.[3]

Where there was an indenture between several parties, carving out to each interests in a joint water-power, giving to one the right to draw so many feet, and another so *many feet, and so on, with a provision that, if it [*279] should be insufficient at any time to supply so much water, each was to share in the above proportions in what there was ; it was held not to be a grant of a specific power,

1 Shed *v.* Leslie, 22 Vt. 498.
2 Garland *v.* Hodsdon, 46 Me. 511.
3 Deshon *v.* Porter, 38 Maine, 289.

but a grant of a certain proportion of the entire power, measured by the respective quantities mentioned.[1]

.37. If the owner of land on one side of a stream grant.to the owner upon the opposite side a right to extend a dam across the river upon his bank, it is *primâ facie* a grant thereby of the sole ownership of the water-power thereby created, unless the deed contain restrictions in that respect. And, in the absence of any such deed, a user by one of the owners of the entire water-power for the requisite length of time gives him a prescriptive right to enjoy the same. Nor does the fact that he has during this time used it for the purposes of carrying a saw-mill raise any presumption that his right is limited to such a use.[2]

So if one of two owners of a water-power, having separate mills upon opposite sides of the stream, exercise the right of the first use of the water at his mill, when there is not sufficient for both, for the term of twenty years, he will thereby acquire a precedence in favor of his own mill, which will make it, as to the other mill, the dominant, and the latter the servient estate.[3]

So where the owner of land upon one side of a stream maintained a dam across it, resting it upon the land of another upon the opposite side, and enjoyed and maintained the same for twenty years, it was held to be no evidence that he owned the entire water-power or control of the water at that point. The maintenance of a dam in a particular mode, or the user of the water in a particular way for twenty years, is evidence of a grant of a right to build and maintain just such a dam and to make just such a use as have thus been continued for that time. The use limits and defines the extent of the rights. If, therefore, there be a surplus of water in such a case, the owner of the land upon the bank on which the dam rests, might draw it and use it for carrying

---

[1] Bardwell v. Ames, 22 Pick. 354.

[2] Bliss v. Rice, 17 Pick. 23.

[3] Rogers v. Bancroft, 20 Vt. 250.

a mill upon his own premises if he do not interfere with the enjoyment of the right already acquired by the owner of the dam.[1]

38. In determining what would constitute an easement in another's land, in respect to the use of water, which may be acquired by grant or adverse use, it may be stated, generally, in accordance with what has before been said, that whatever would constitute a nuisance or injury by one to the enjoyment or use of running water by another, may grow into a right on the part of him who shall cause such nuisance or injury, if done in the occupation of his own premises as a dominant estate in a particular manner, for twenty years, *or the period of prescription fixed by the [*280] laws of the State in which the premises are situated.

Nor is it necessary that the use should be exercised in precisely the same form during the whole of this period, provided it be adverse, exclusive, and under a claim of right, and it be acquiesced in by the other party. If it is substantially the same mode and extent of use, it will be sufficient.[2]

And in applying this doctrine to the case of two mills, where the dam of the lower one, which had been in operation eighty years, was raised so as to flow back upon one that had been in operation forty years, the court of Connecticut held that the upper mill, having enjoyed the use of the water in a particular manner for fifteen years, the period of prescription in that State, had acquired a right to such enjoyment, with which a lower mill, though more ancient, might not interfere. Although Gould, J., in a dissenting opinion, insisted that such enjoyment could not have been adverse unless the other owners upon the stream had had occasion to exercise their rights, and had forborne so to do,

---

[1] Burnham v. Kempton, 44 N. H. 90.

[2] Belknap v. Trimble, 3 Paige, 577, 605; 3 Kent, Comm. 442; Bealey v. Shaw, 6 East, 208; Pugh v. Wheeler, 2 Dev. & B. 50, Ingraham v. Hutchinson, 2 Conn. 584; Esling v. Williams; 10 Penn. St. 126; Watkins v. Peck, 13 N. H. 360; Johns v. Stevens, 3 Vt. 308, 315; Lapham v. Curtis, 5 Vt. 371, 380; Shreve v. Voorhees, 2 Green, Ch. 25; Sherwood v. Burr, 4 Day, 244.

and had acquiesced in the exercise of the right by the other party.[1]

39. But a right on the part of a mill-owner, acquired by prescription, to flow back water, and control the stream for the use of his mill, gives him no right to prevent a riparian proprietor above from cultivating and making improvements upon his land, or using the waters of the stream for that purpose, unless he thereby sensibly affects the rights of such mill-owner in the use of the water, and works an injury to his mill.[2]

[*281]   *40. Nor does a mill-owner acquire any prescriptive rights in respect to the user and enjoyment of water by another mill, if the user by the first, though long continued, was no invasion of the rights incident to the second.[3]

41. But a proprietor upon a stream may, by adverse user and enjoyment, acquire a right to divert the water of a stream to the injury of mill-owners and riparian proprietors below.[4] And it is even stated in one case, that " an absolute right to a watercourse may be acquired by an uninterrupted possession, use, and occupation, claiming right thereto adverse to all others." [5]

42. So one may acquire a right by prescription to flow the land of another by means of a dam or obstruction in the stream upon his own land.[6] And, because a right to create a permanent obstruction in a stream and watercourse may be acquired by user, it was held that one who had a right to a watercourse for purposes of navigation, might maintain an

---

[1] Ingraham v. Hutchinson, 2 Conn. 584, 592, 594.

[2] Shreve v. Voorhees, 2 Green, Ch. 25. See Bardwell v. Ames, 22 Pick. 354, 356.

[3] Parker v. Hotchkiss, 25 Conn. 321, 330.

[4] Arnold v. Foot, 12 Wend. 330; Wright v. Howard, 1 Sim. & S. 190; Mason v. Hill, 5 Barnew. & Ad. 1; Newton v. Valentine, 14 Vt. 239; Bealey v. Shaw, 6 East, 208; Campbell v. Smith, 3 Halst. 140; Middleton v. Gregorie, 2 Rich. 630.

[5] Rogers v. Page, Brayt. 169; s. c., Ibid. 201.

[6] Hurlbut v. Leonard, Brayt. 201.

action for creating an obstruction therein, although he had
suffered it to become clogged by the deposit of mud in it,
and to remain so for sixteen years.[1]

So one may acquire a prescriptive right to foul and corrupt
the waters of a stream, while carrying on a business upon its
banks which has that effect, as is the case with that of tan-
yards, working of ores or minerals, and various kinds of
manufactures, and chemical works.[2]

*So where the owner of an upper mill had enjoyed [*282]
the privilege of throwing cinders and scoriæ, created
in his business, into the stream, which floated down the
same and filled it up so as to hinder the operation of a lower
mill, and had done this adversely to the lower mill for more
than twenty years, reckoned from the time when it began to
be injured thereby, it was held that a right to continue the
same was thereby acquired in favor of such upper mill.[3]

The same rule substantially holds in cases where there is
necessarily a greater or less deposit of foreign substances in
a stream, when using its waters for purposes of art, such as
saw-dust from a saw-mill, bark from a tan-yard, soap from a
manufactory, and the like. So far as this is reasonable, it
may be done with impunity, though it occasions some loss or
inconvenience to the owners of the mills or lands below. If
it essentially impairs the use of the water below, it would be
deemed to be unreasonable and unlawful. This may, moreover, depend upon the size and nature of the stream ; for
what would be a serious injury upon one, might be of immaterial consequence upon another.[4] The question in each
case is, whether the acts complained of were done in the
reasonable use of the stream, and in determining this, the
jury should consider the necessity or importance of the right

[1] Bower v. Hill, 1 Bing. N. C. 549. See also Hendrick v. Cook, 4 Ga. 241, 261.
[2] Moore v. Webb, 1 C. B. N. S. 673 ; Wright v. Williams, 1 Mees. & W. 77 ;
Carlyon v. Lovering, 1 Hurlst. & N. 784 ; Wood v. Sutcliffe, 8 Eng. L. & Eq. 217.
[3] Murgatroyd v. Robinson, 8 Ellis & B. 391 ; Ingraham v. Hutchinson, 2 Conn.
591 ; per *Gould*, J. See Carlyon v. Lovering, 1 Hurlst. & N. 784.
[4] Snow v. Parsons, 28 Vt. 459.

claimed so to discharge the waste, as well as the extent of the injury likely to be caused to the other party.[1] But a right thus to foul or encumber a stream may be acquired to any extent by an adverse user for the requisite period of time.[2]

One has no right to use the water of a stream so as to fill it or clog it with foreign or noxious matter which would materially interfere with the use of the water below. In this case the upper works were a tan-yard, from which bark, hair, and filth were thrown into the stream and carried to the plaintiff's mill below.[3]

43. Corresponding to the right which may be gained by adverse user, to increase the head of water at one's mill by raising the pond thereof so as to flow the land of another, is that of increasing the fall by deepening the bed of the stream below the mill and beyond the line of the mill-owner's land. If, by doing this, and so placing his wheel as to make use of such increased fall, he shall have enjoyed the benefit thereof the requisite period of time, he may acquire a right [*283] to continue it as a servitude on *the lower estate, and an easement, in respect to which his is the dominant estate.[4]

44. Partly from the necessity there is, in order to make use of a mill-privilege, that the water used in operating a mill should flow freely from the same, and partly from its ordinarily being incident to the ownership of an easement that the same should be kept in a condition to be used by the owner of the estate to which it belongs, it follows that a mill-owner, whenever it is necessary to clear out the tail-race or channel by which the water is discharged from his mill, may do so, though, in order to accomplish it, he is obliged to go upon the land of another,

[1] Veasie v. Dwinell, 50 Maine, 490.
[2] Jones v. Crow, 32 Penn. St. 398, 406; ante, p. *219; Hayes v. Waldron, 44 N. H. 585.
[3] Houser v. Hammond, 39 Barb. 89; post, p. *400.
[4] Townsend v. M'Donald, 14 Barb. 460.

doing no more injury to such proprietor's land than is necessary.[1]

45. So if there be an embankment in another's land, by
means of which the water is retained in a mill-pond, and
the same break away or require repairs, by reason of the
lawful use of the waters of the pond, the mill-owner may
go upon the land where such embankment stands and repair it.

But if he had broken the same by raising his head of
water higher than he had a right to do, he could not justify
going upon such land to repair the embankment.[2]

46. When a right to use or apply water, in any particular manner, or to a certain extent, has been acquired, either
as incident to the land, or by grant or prescription, it will
not be lost or impaired by the mere change in the mode
of using it, provided such change do not materially affect
the rights of other persons. Otherwise there could be no
improvements made in the application of machinery
*or the useful arts. The question in such cases is, [*284]
whether the alteration is of the substance or the
mere quality of the thing.[3] One of the cases illustrating this
point is Hale v. Oldroyd,[4] where one for agricultural purposes had acquired by long usage a right to receive the flow
of certain surplus water of a stream into a pond in his land,
and having filled that, dug three small ones. The proprietor above stopped the flow of the water to these, but it was
held that the owner of the pond had not thereby lost his
right to have the flow of the water.

This question has been raised, more frequently than upon
other grounds, upon changes made in substituting wheels

---

[1] Prescott v. Williams, 5 Metc. 429; Prescott v. White, 21 Pick. 341; Brisbane v. O'Neall, 3 Strobh. 348; Doane v. Badger, 12 Mass. 65; Kauffman v.
Greisemer, 26 Penn. St. 407; Darlington v. Painter, 7 Penn. St. 473; Peter
v. Daniel, 5 C. B. 568, 578, 579; 11 Toullier, Droit Civil Français, 449.

[2] Fessenden v. Morrison, 19 N. H. 226.

[3] Luttrell's case, 4 Rep. 86; Allan v. Gomme, 11 Adolph. & E. 759.

[4] Hale v. Oldroyd, 14 Mees. & W. 789.

of a different size or construction, or in the nature of the business carried on in the works upon the stream.

Thus in Luttrell's case,[1] where one prescribed for a grist-mill *or* fulling-mill, he might sustain it, by proving either; and a change of a mill from a grist-mill to a fulling-mill did not impair the rights belonging to the same, if no prejudice thereby arose to other owners, by diverting or obstructing the water.

In Saunders *v.* Newman,[2] the plaintiff's mill was an ancient one, for operating which he had substituted a large for a small wheel, but placed the same upon the original level of the former one, and it actually took less water to carry it than the former one. The defendant, an owner of a mill below the plaintiff's, altered his works so that by their operation he interfered with the operation of the plaintiff's mill, and claimed a right to do so, inasmuch as the plaintiff had not acquired a right to maintain his present wheel. [*285] But *the court held that the plaintiff had not, by this change, lost the right to have the water flow from his mill as formerly, and might apply it in such manner as he pleased, provided it did not prejudice the rights already acquired by the lower mill. " The defendant, therefore," says Holroyd, J., " had no right to use the water, in this case, after the erection of the plaintiff's mill, in a different manner than it had been accustomed to be used before, for, at all events, by that act the plaintiff appropriated to himself the water flowing in that particular way."

It has accordingly been held, that, where one had acquired a right to draw water for a mill standing upon an ancient dam, he might cease to use the water at that place, and draw it by gates to operate a mill upon another site below, provided he did not increase the quantity so drawn. " It is

---

[1] Luttrell's case, 4 Rep. 86; Johnson *v.* Rand, 6 N. H. 22; Bullen *v.* Runnels, 2 N. H. 255; Blanchard *v.* Baker, 8 Me. 253; Allan *v.* Gomme, 11 Adolph. & E. 759.

[2] Saunders *v.* Newman, 1 Barnew. & Ald. 257, 262; Buddington *v.* Bradley, 10 Conn. 213, 219; Merritt *v.* Parker, Coxe, 460, 463.

immaterial," say the court, " to the plaintiff at what spot the
defendants apply the water to a wheel, or what machinery
that wheel turns, so long as they do not exceed their rights
in the quantity they use." [1]

In the above action, the defendants drew their water
through a gate at one end of a dam, on the other end of
which the plaintiff had a mill. They used the water some
three miles below this dam. But they had, by artificial
reservoirs, increased the quantity in the stream above this
dam at their own expense, and in dry times drew so much
of this extra quantity of water that the plaintiff lost the benefit of it at his mill, though he had the usual and natural supply ordinarily running in the stream at such times. For
this he brought his action, and it was held that the defendants had a right to use this additional supply of water as they
did, for the benefit of their mills.[2]

In King v. Tiffany,[3] which has already been referred to,
the plaintiffs erected their mill in 1802 ; the defendants *theirs, below the plaintiffs', in 1818, and raised [*286]
their head of water so high, that when, in 1832, less
than fifteen years (the period of prescriptive right in Connecticut) after the erection of the defendants' dam, the plaintiffs put a new wheel into their mill, and placed the same
lower than the former one, it was obstructed by the backwater of the defendants' pond. The majority of the court
held that the plaintiffs had a right thus to change their
wheel, theirs being a prior mill, and that the acts of the defendants in keeping up their pond to the obstruction thereof
was against right.

The opinion of Dagget, J. in favor of the defendants, under
such circumstances, seems to be more in accordance with the
modern notions of courts upon the law of the case.

So a mill-owner may adopt improved machinery in his

[1] Whittier v. Cocheco Mg. Co., 9 N. H. 454.
[2] But see ante, pl. 33. See Rogers v. Bruce, 17 Pick. 184; post, pl. 53.
[3] King v. Tiffany, 9 Conn. 162.

mill, which takes less water to carry it than that in use before, although the effect of this may be to keep a higher state of water in his pond.   So he may change, at his pleasure, the point at which the power is applied, as, for instance, he may draw the water on to his wheel from the top instead of the bottom of the flume.[1]

But this right to change the machinery in a mill, even by adopting that of an improved character, may be limited by its effect upon other mills ; as where the defendant erected a saw-mill upon a stream just above the plaintiff's, and introduced into it machinery which required so little water to carry it, that what was discharged from his wheel was insufficient to carry the mill of the plaintiff to advantage, it was held that it was an injury to the plaintiff for which he might sustain an action.[2]

And where the introduction of new machinery into one mill is a nuisance to another, it is no justification that the mill in which it is used is an ancient one.   In respect to the use of such machinery it is a new mill.[3]

[*287]   *Nor is it a defence to the owner of an upper mill for obstructing the natural flow of the stream, to the injury of a mill below, that the owner of the lower mill had changed his works so as to require more than his accustomed supply of water, or had changed the mode of applying the water.[4]

47. The owner of a watercourse, as has heretofore been stated, may change the course of a stream through his own land, provided he does not thereby diminish the beneficial use of the water to the adjacent proprietors.   So he may change the same back to its original channel, unless other proprietors, having a right to the use of the water, have been led by such original change to expend money in order to en-

[1] Cowell v. Thayer, 5 Metc. 253.

[2] Wentworth v. Poor, 38 Me. 243.

[3] Simpson v. Seavey, 8 Me. 138.

[4] Buddington v. Bradley, 10 Conn. 213; Johnson v. Lewis, 13 Conn. 303; Cox v. Matthews, 1 Ventr. 237 ; Merritt v. Parker, Coxe, 458.

joy the benefit of the same, in its new channel, and would be injured by such second change. By suffering them to expend money upon their premises, in reference to the new channel, as if it were to be a permanent one, he dedicates it to their use, in its then state and condition.[1]

So if a new channel has been found for the current of a stream, and the riparian proprietors have enjoyed it in that condition for twenty years, they thereby gain a right to its use, nor can the land-owner change it again, against their consent.[2]

The grantee of a mill would have no right to have the course of the stream from the same over another's land changed into a new place. But it would be otherwise if the water by natural means changed its course and found a new channel.[3]

48. If one, having gained a right to foul the water of a stream by carrying on a trade upon its banks by which a *certain quantity of fouling matter is dis- [*288] charged into it, increase his works, and thereby increase the quantity of such matter discharged, he will be responsible to the proprietors below for such increase. And Cresswell, J. remarked, "If a man goes on increasing the use every year, he has not, actually, used the stream for the whole period in the manner he claims," which remark was applicable to the English statute of prescription.[4]

49. In order to treat this subject with anything like completeness, the mode of using and managing water-power for operating mills should be noticed, in order that a line may be drawn between what would be a legitimate use and what

[1] Ford v. Whitlock, 27 Vt. 265; Norton v. Valentine, 14 Vt. 239; Woodbury v. Short, 17 Vt. 387; Devonshire v. Eglin, 7 Eng. L. & Eq. 39; s. c., 14 Beav. 530; Townsend v. M'Donald, 14 Barb. 460.

[2] Dalaney v. Boston, 2 Harringt. 489.

[3] Miller v. Bristol, 12 Pick. 550.

[4] Moore v. Webb, 1 C. B. N. S. 673; Holsman v. Boiling Spring Co., 1 M'Carter, 345.

ought to be resisted by other proprietors, if they would prevent a mill-owner acquiring rights as against them, by prescription, as well as to ascertain what might be done in de-
fending against such adverse user.

What a mill-owner may or ought to do in the management of his dam and mill, and keeping the same in repair,
often varies with the variant circumstances of the different
cases.

Thus, if there were no other mill upon the stream, and he
were to suffer his dam to go to decay, and the water of his
pond to escape by its breaking away, it might afford no cause
of action to other proprietors upon the stream, who, if they
had had mills standing thereon, to be thereby damaged or
endangered, might have an action for such negligence, or
want of care. A mill-owner, in other words, is bound to use
reasonable care and diligence in keeping his dam and works
safe and in proper repair, and is responsible if, by want of
such care and diligence, a mill-owner below is injured. But
if a mill-dam gives way, or other damage to a lower mill result from inevitable accident to the upper mill, the owner of
the mill causing the damage is not responsible therefor. In
Delaware there is a statute requiring notice to be given
by an upper mill-owner, to those below him upon
[*289] *the stream, of any extraordinary discharge of water,
whether by accident or intentionally on the part of
the upper owner.[1]

50. A question somewhat analogous to that of damages
occasioned by an extraordinary flood in a stream by the
breaking away of an upper dam, is that of damages occasioned to an upper mill, in times of freshets or high floods
in the stream, by the water being prevented by a lower dam
from subsiding as it otherwise would have done. The question supposes such lower dam so constructed as not to occasion any backwater upon the upper mill in any ordinary

[1] Lapham v. Curtis, 5 Vt. 371, 381 ; M'Ilvaine v. Marshall, 3 Harringt. 1 ;
Ross v. Horsey, 3 Ibid. 60 ; Soule v. Russell, 13 Metc. 436.

state of the stream. Some of the cases seem to hold that the lower mill-owner would be responsible to the upper one for such injury. Other cases would only hold him responsible for an injury caused by flowing back the water in its usual state, or in such freshets as usually and periodically occur, and which the mill-owner ought to have regarded in erecting his dam.

In Pugh v. Wheeler,[1] the language of the court was: "One has the right at no time to prevent the water flowing from the land of the proprietor above as it has usually done, more than the proprietor above has the right to divert the stream so as to prevent it from flowing to him below." And they held the party responsible for such temporary obstruction, the difference between a permanent and occasional obstruction being only in the amount of damages. And in the case of Thompson v. Crocker,[2] the court appear to recognize the right of an upper mill-owner to maintain an action for having his mill obstructed "during freshes," where the damage "was caused when the water was unusually high," if his mill had sustained any actual perceptible damage in consequence of the erection of the defendant's dam.

*The court do not in either of the above cases seem [*290] to have considered the distinction which some of the cases make between freshes ordinarily or periodically occurring and those extraordinary floods which sometimes occur in streams, which no foresight can anticipate or guard against, consistently with the reasonable use of the several privileges upon a stream.

Thus in China v. Southwick, one was authorized to erect a dam, but not so high as to flow or injure a certain bridge. After the erection of the dam, by reason of extraordinary rains and high winds, the water flowed back and injured the bridge, which it would not have done had it not been for the dam. The court held that the owner of the dam was not

---

[1] Pugh v. Wheeler, 2 Dev. & B. 50, 53.
[2] Thompson v. Crocker, 9 Pick. 59.

responsible, the true doctrine being, "*causa propinqua non remota spectatur.*"[1]

In Smith *v.* Agawam Canal Co., just cited, the defendants erected a dam below the plaintiff's ancient mill, which only occasioned damage to the plaintiff's works at certain times, when, upon the breaking up of the ice in the stream, it was stopped by the defendant's dam, and, by being piled up, stopped the flow of the water, and set it back upon the plaintiff's works. It was held to be a consequence too remote to be charged upon defendants' dam. The general principle stated is: "Riparian proprietors may erect and maintain dams on their own lands across streams, to raise a head of water for the working of mills, without being liable for consequences which are casual, remote, and uncertain."[2]

51. A peculiar case may be noticed in this connection, in which a party, injured by the act of another, was held to be remediless, because it was incident to a lawful act on the part of the latter. In Pixley *v.* Clark, the defendant [*291] had *purchased of the plaintiff a strip of land along a stream, upon which he erected a mill and dam, and raised a head of water. Upon this strip of land, and adjacent to the plaintiff's land, he erected an embankment for the purpose of thereby raising the water in his pond. The effect of this was found to be, that the water, when thus raised, percolated through the natural banks of the stream, and reached the plaintiff's land and injured it. But inasmuch as the defendant's embankment was properly constructed, and he had a right to erect it on his own land, and thereby to raise a head of water for the use of his mill, the adjacent land-owner was without remedy for the indirect and consequential damages thereby resulting to him.[3]

52. Though the remedy which one has whose right of easement is invaded, as well as what one may do to guard

---

[1] China *v.* Southwick, 12 Me. 238; Smith *v.* Agawam Canal Co., 2 Allen, 355.

[2] Smith *v.* Agawam Canal Co., 2 Allen, 355.

[3] Pixley *v.* Clark, 32 Barb. 268.

against encroachments which, if continued, may grow into easements, are treated of in another part of this work, it may be proper to refer, in this connection, to one or two cases more especially applicable to mills.

Ordinarily, if one wrongfully flows back water upon the mill of another by an obstruction placed by him in the stream within his own land, or prevents the flow of water to such mill, the owner thereof may enter upon the land of the party causing this obstruction, and remove it.[1] But there is often a difficulty in knowing when this may be applied, for there are cases where, from the peculiar nature of the ownership, if a mill-owner is injured by the acts of another, he must resort to an action at law, or process in equity for redress. In one case it was held that, where the upper proprietor turned a second stream into the one naturally flowing through his land, and thereby threw more water than naturally flowed in such stream into the *current in another's land below, the latter had a [*292] right to stop such extra flow, before reaching his land, and, if necessary in order to do it, might stop the stream altogether, without subjecting himself to an action in favor of the one who caused the diversion.[2]

But where of two mill-owners upon opposite ends of a dam, and drawing water from the same pond, one had a right to the exclusive use of the water when insufficient to carry both mills, and the other, in violation of this precedence of right, continued to draw water when insufficient to supply both mills, it was held that the former mill-owner had no right to create a permanent obstruction to the flow of the water to the other mill in order to turn the same towards his own.[3] It is, however, the duty of the one hav-

[1] Hodges v. Raymond, 9 Mass. 316; Baten's case, 9 Rep. 54 b; Colburn v. Richards, 13 Mass. 420; Langford v. Owsley, 2 Bibb. 215; Dyer v. Depui, 5 Whart. 584; Heath v. Williams, 25 Me. 295; Bemis v. Clark, 11 Pick. 452.

[2] Per Kinsey, C. J., Merritt v. Parker, Coxe, 460; Tillotson v. Smith, 32 N. H. 90, 95; Pardessus, Traité des Servitudes, § 88.

[3] Curtis v. Jackson, 13 Mass. 507.

ing the subordinate right, to take notice and not to draw the water when there is a deficiency in quantity for both. But if he continues to draw in such a state of water, the other party may enter upon his premises and stop the passage of the water to his mill, subject, however, to the duty of removing such obstruction as soon as there is again sufficient for both mills.[1]

53. A case of a qualified right to stop another in the use of the water of a stream, not very analogous, it is true, to those above stated, was where a mill-owner had acquired, by use, a right to maintain a dam and flume on another's land, and thereby controlling the waters of a pond which served as a reservoir for his mill below. The owner of the land, having erected a mill on his own land, raised the dam to a much greater height, and much increased the head of water, and proceeded to draw from the same, discharging it into its accustomed channel running to the lower mill. It was held that the lower mill-owner had no right to obstruct [*293] *him in drawing the water in the pond as low as the surface of the former pond.[2]

It need only be added, that, as the law aims to provide an adequate remedy for every legal injury, there is often an election of remedies for a person suffering by the wrongful inteference with his rights as a mill or riparian owner.

SECTION IV.

OF RIGHTS IN ARTIFICIAL WATERCOURSES.

1. Two classes of artificial watercourses defined.
2. Distinction between natural and artificial watercourses.
3. Case of Arkwright v. Gell. Owner may stop the latter.
4. The owner of artificial watercourse may not foul the water.
5. Case of Wood v. Waud. One cannot claim the water on another's land.

---

[1] Sumner v. Foster, 7 Pick. 32.

[2] Rogers v. Bruce, 17 Pick. 184. See Whittier v. Cocheco Mg. Co., 9 N. H. 454; ante, pl. 46.

1. THE watercourses thus far spoken of have been such as exist by nature, and it has been of the use and *appropriation of the water flowing in these, in con- [*294] nection with the riparian ownership of the land through which they flow, that it has been attempted to systematize and embody the rules by which they are governed.

It is proposed, in the next place, to consider watercourses which are artificial in their original construction, and to point out wherein the law as to easements and servitudes, connected therewith, differs from that of those connected with natural streams of water, as they relate to irrigation, the operation of mills, or otherwise.

These may naturally be divided into two classes; first, where the supply of the watercourse is itself created by art; and second, where new and artificial channels are made to serve, in whole or in part, the purposes of natural conduits of water flowing upon or issuing from the earth.

2. The first great distinction between natural and artificial watercourses is, that while the use of the one is incident to the ownership of the land itself in which it exists, that of

the other may exist merely as an easement in such land, belonging to another than the owner of the land. And the distinction between the two classes of artificial watercourses may be generally stated to be, that if the supply of water be artificially created, as well as the course in which it is made to flow, no property like that of a perpetual easement can be acquired in the water by the use thereof, especially if the original purposes of its creation were temporary in their nature, while, if the artificial course be a substitute for a natural one, in conducting the flow of a permanent stream of water, an easement in the case of such water may be acquired by the owner of the land through which it passes, by an enjoyment thereof for a requisite period of time.

This proposition, as well as what is meant by creating an artificial supply for a watercourse, and by creating it for purposes temporary in their nature, can best be illustrated by a few recent English cases, which it will be necessary to state at considerable length.

[*295]   *3. The first of these is Arkwright v. Gell,[1] decided in the Court of Exchequer in 1839. In that case it appeared that, as early as 1705, the proprietors of certain mines then in operation made arrangements with certain persons to drain these mines of water, by a " sough," as it was called, which had its outlet in the land of a third person. The water from the mines flowed through this land into a natural stream, upon which, in 1772, the plaintiff erected a manufactory, and enjoyed the use and benefit of the stream thus enlarged till 1825, when the defendants, being also owners of other mines connected with those drained by the first sough, made an arrangement with the latter owners, but for the benefit of the defendants, to construct a new *sough* which should enter the mines at a lower level, and drain them. The effect of this was that the water

---

[1] Arkwright v. Gell, 5 Mees. & W. 203 ; Wood v. Waud, 3 Exch. 748, 778; Greatrex v. Hayward, 8 Exch. 291 ; Norton v. Valentine, 14 Vt. 239 ; North Eastern Railway Co. v. Elliott, Johns. & H. 154.

from the mines no longer flowed into the first *sough*, and the plaintiff lost so much of what had been thereby supplied for operating his mill.   At his request a barrier was placed in the second sough, which prevented this diversion of this water till 1836, when, in order to test his right to claim it as appurtenant to his mill, the present action for such diversion was brought.

The court did not sustain the action, and held, among other reasons, that what the plaintiff had been thus enjoying was not a natural watercourse, but a supply created by another person under whom the plaintiff did not claim, and who had created it for his own benefit to enable him to work his mines ; that, though the plaintiff had enjoyed the flow of the water for such a length of time, it was in no sense a user adverse to the owner of the mine, to whom it must have been indifferent what use was made of the water after it had been discharged from the *sough;* *that [*296] the plaintiff thereby acquired no right to insist upon the water being kept up to a certain height in the mine, but that the mine-owner, if it was convenient, in working it, to drain from a lower level, had a right so to do.

It will be remarked, as an important circumstance in this case, that the one who dug the second sough and caused the diversion was interested in the mines thereby to be drained.   Had it been otherwise, had he been a stranger, or merely the owner of the land lying between the outlet of the first sough and the place where the water entered into the natural stream, he would have had no right to divert the current issuing from the mine, so as to deprive the plaintiff of the use of the water flowing in the same, after having enjoyed it so long.   Park, B., in illustrating the doctrine intended to be laid down by the court, supposes the case of a current of water made by pumping it from a mine by a steam-engine.   Though it should be continued for twenty years, it could give no land-owner who had thereby derived a benefit from the flow of 'this water over his land a right to maintain an action against the miner for the loss of this, if he should see fit to stop pumping. Another illustration was that of a land-owner having the benefit of the water flowing from his neighbor's eaves for more than twenty years, the owner of the house might, nevertheless, take down the house and stop this flow at any time. "The nature of the case," says the judge, "distinctly shows that no right is acquired as against the owner of the property from which the course of water takes its origin, though, as between the first and subsequent appropriator of the watercourse itself, such a right may be acquired."

4. It should be remarked also, that while, in cases like that last cited, the owner of the land over which the water flows would have no right to divert the water, since to him it is, as to the riparian proprietors below, as a natural stream, it would not be competent for the mine-owner, [*297] though he *might stop it, to foul or corrupt the same to the injury of the proprietors upon the stream. To that extent, if suffered to flow, it had the incidents of a natural stream, even as against the one who had created it.[1]

5. The case of Wood v. Waud, above cited, presented still other features as to the rights of land-proprietors upon a stream created by artificial draining of mines. The plaintiff and defendant each had mills upon a small natural stream. A part of the supply of water for these was derived from two different mines, from one of which a stream had flowed for sixty years, by means of an artificial outlet dug by the owner of the mine for the purpose of draining his mine. From the other mine a stream of water flowed which was caused by pumping. These streams flowed through separate soughs into the natural stream. One of these passed underground through the defendant's land, before reaching the plaintiff's land, and then through that into the stream. The other did

---

[1] Wood v. Waud, 3 Exch. 748; Magor v. Chadwick, 11 Adolph. & E. 571; See Wardle v. Brocklehurst, 1 E. & Ellis. 1059.

not pass through the plaintiff's land at all before reaching and discharging itself into the stream.

The action of the plaintiff was for diverting, or improperly interfering, by the defendant, with the enjoyment by the plaintiff of the water flowing from these soughs. Whatever he did in this respect was done by him upon his own land, before they had entered and united with the waters of the natural stream, and before the water of the sough that run through the plaintiff's land had reached the latter.

The court held, that, if the mine-owner had seen fit to stop the supply of water, or divert it, so that the water from the mines should no longer reach the works of the mill-owners, he would not have been liable therefor, adopting the doctrine of Arkwright *v.* Gell. As between the plaintiff and defendant, no prescription had been set up or relied on, on either side ; neither had any right to complain of any use which * the other should make of the water in his [*298] own land, before it reached that of the other, provided he did not foul it, or turn it into the stream heated, so as to injure the party below. " Each," in the language of the court, " may take and use what passes through his land, and the proprietor below has no right to any part of that water until it has reached his own land. He has no right to compel the owners above to permit the water to flow through their land for his benefit, and consequently he has no right of action if they refuse to do so. . . . . If they polluted the water so as to be injurious to the tenant below, the case would be different." But as soon as the water from either of these soughs had become united with that of the natural stream in its natural watercourse, it partook of the character and incidents of a natural stream. Pollock, C. B., in giving the opinion of the court in the above case, gives, as an illustration of the doctrine which he sustains, the case of a drain made through a man's land for agricultural purposes, which had continued for twenty years, whereby the water from his own land was discharged upon that of another. This would not give a right in the latter to insist upon its continuance, and thereby to preclude the land-owner from altering the level of his drain for the greater improvement of his land. " The state of the circumstances in such cases shows that one party never intended to give, nor the other to enjoy, the use of the stream as a matter of *right*."

The above case makes this important distinction between the right of a lower riparian proprietor to water flowing in a natural stream, and to that created and flowing in an artificial one, for a temporary purpose, that in the former case an action will lie for its diversion by an upper proprietor, although done in his own land, whereas in the latter case no action will lie for the diversion of the water, unless the same shall have reached and become a part of a natural stream.

Such diversion, however, as appears by other cases, [*299] should be made not *wantonly or maliciously, but in the prosecution of some legitimate business.

6. The case supposed by Pollock, C. B., in the above case, of an agricultural drain, arose in that of Greatrex *v.* Hayward, in 1853, and is fully considered, and the doctrine by him stated is fully sustained. It was further held, that no length of enjoyment of what was designed by another for a temporary use, like the discharge of water from a drain designed for such a use, could gain for the recipient a prescriptive right to claim it. In that case the lands of the plaintiff and defendant adjoined each other. As early as 1796 the defendant dug a drain in his land, through which the water, as it collected therein, was discharged into a ditch of the plaintiff that ran along near the defendant's land, and through which it flowed into a large pit in the plaintiff's land, where it was used for watering his cattle and other like purposes. In 1851 the defendant changed the mode of draining his land, whereby the water from the same escaped at a lower level, and the plaintiff lost the benefit of its accustomed flow. And for this he brought this action. The court held that the action would not lie, upon the grounds, among

others, upon which the cases above cited were determined. Alderson, B. says: " In one sense, perhaps, it may be said, that the plaintiff has enjoyed the use of this water as of right, because the defendant has not in any way impeded such use. But it is not such a user as of right as will serve his present purpose, for there has been no adverse user." Parke, B.: " The right of a party to an artificial watercourse, as against the party creating it, must depend upon the character of the watercourse and the circumstances under which it was created. This watercourse is clearly of a temporary nature only, and is dependent upon the mode which the defendant may adopt in draining his land." [1]

7. The case of Magor v. Chadwick, decided in the Queen's * Bench, in 1840, ought to be noticed in [*300] this connection, because of certain expressions made use of by Denman, C. J., in giving the opinion of the court, which have not met the approbation of other eminent judges ; and the doctrine of the case may, at least, be said to have been modified, if not overruled by later cases. The water in that case flowed from a drain originally dug by the owner of a mine for the purpose of draining the same. But the mine had not been wrought for thirty years. The adit of the underground watercourse was in land which did not belong to the plaintiff. The plaintiff, a brewer, cleared out this adit, and applied the water to the use of his brewery, although, in the state in which it was discharged while the mine was in operation, it would have been unfit for such a use ; and he had enjoyed it in this state for more than twenty years. The defendant owned a mine, other than that for which the drain was originally dug, and, in order to drain it, made use of this original passage-way, though not claiming any right to do so, under any grant or title from the original mine-owner, but doing it, first, under a right by usage in the mining regions where the premises were situate, and second, on the ground that the same rules did not apply

---

[1] Greatrex v. Hayward, 8 Exch. 291.

to such artificial outlets of water as to natural watercourses. The use of the channel as a drain for the mine fouled the water, so that the plaintiffs could not use it.   Patteson, J. instructed the jury, "That, in the absence of custom, artificial watercourses are not distinguished in law from such as are natural, that the same rules apply to them, and that twenty years' enjoyment might therefore warrant the jury in finding in favor of the right."   And the Chief Justice, in stating the opinion of the court, says: "The imputed misdirection is, that the law of watercourses is the same, whether natural or artificial.   We think this was no misdirection, but clearly right."[1]

[*301]   *8. As applicable to the case under consideration, where the defendant did not justify under any claim of title to, or ownership of, either the mine drained by the watercourse, ·or the land in which it had its adit, the ruling was doubtless correct.   But the broad terms in which it was announced, it is believed, are not sustained by later and better-considered cases.   The court, in Wood v. Waud, above cited, take this distinction, and, moreover, the distinction there is between diverting water and fouling it, which do not stand upon the same ground in law, and add : "The general proposition, that under all circumstances the right to watercourses arising from enjoyment is the same, whether they be· natural or artificial, cannot possibly be sustained."

The reader will observe, that it is not assumed that prescriptive rights may not be acquired in artificial watercourses, under some circumstances, but it is properly denied that the law, in respect to acquiring these, is the same in all respects as it is as to similar rights in the water of natural streams.   And Crowder, J., in Sampson v. Hoddinott, commenting upon the case of Magor v. Chadwick, says: "That case has been considered not altogether satisfactory, and it is inconsistent with Arkwright v. Gell."   And Cresswell, J., in the same case, in referring to the distinction

---

[1] Magor v. Chadwick, 11 Adolph. & E. 571.

there is, in point of law, between an artificial drain and a natural stream, says: "All authorities, from the Digest downwards, show that there is."[1]

9. The question, how far an easement can be acquired in an artificial watercourse by one not owning the land through which it is constructed, was raised in Beeston v. Weate, in the Queen's Bench in 1856. In that case the defendant owned a piece of land between that of the plaintiff and a natural stream which ran along by the side of the defendant's land. From this stream there was an artificial channel cut through the defendant's land to the land of the *plaintiff, and by putting sods in the stream the [*302] water thereof would flow into this channel, and, when not used by the defendant for irrigating his intermediate land, would reach that of the plaintiff, where it was made use of by him for watering his cattle and the like. The owners of the plaintiff's land had been accustomed to place this dam of sods in the stream whenever they desired the water, and had thereby enjoyed the use of it, except at the times when the defendant saw fit to apply it in irrigating his land, which was a right prior to that of the plaintiff. In this state of things, the defendant removed the dam of sods altogether from the stream, and thereby wholly deprived the plaintiff of the water. In the hearing of the case, the defendant insisted that the artificial trench being in his own land, for his own use, the plaintiff could not acquire an easement therein by user, to draw water therefrom for the use of his land. Lord Campbell, C. J., however, while approving the cases of Arkwright v. Gell, Wood v. Waud, &c., said: "We do not consider that the cases lay down any such rule as that enjoyment and acts, which, without the existence of the easement, would be tortious and actionable, may not be evidence of the right to the use of water, although it flows in an artificial cut. . . . . In the cases referred to, regard was had to the water being obtained artificially by the owner

---

[1] Sampson v. Hoddinott, 1 C. B. n. s. 590.

of the servient tenement, rather than to the water running through an artificial cut. . . . . If it were not that the occupier of the servient tenement has himself used the water flowing through the artificial cut for irrigation, no plausible objection could be made to the easement which the plaintiff claims, and we do not see that the use of the water on the servient tenement takes away from the effect of the use of it for the dominant tenement, regard being had to the positive acts done by the occupier of the dominant tenement for the purpose of enjoying the easement." The court, moreover, held, that the evidence showed that the artificial cut was not originally made for a temporary purpose, [*303] *excluding the case from the principle of some of those above cited. And it was held, that the plaintiff was entitled to recover for this interruption of his right to enjoy the water.[1]

In illustrating some of the positions taken in the above case, the Chief Justice puts the case of water for a mill turned by a *weir* across a stream in a *leat* through the land of another to a mill, and after being used there returned into the natural stream again, where the mill-owner has been accustomed to go upon the land of the intermediate land-owner and clear the *leat* whenever there was occasion therefor, or repair the banks thereof, long enough to acquire, so far as time was concerned, a prescriptive right. " We conceive," says he, " that the right to do so might be established, and that an obstruction to the flow of water through the mill *leat* would be actionable."

10. It was accordingly held, in Baer v. Martin, that a right in one man to convey water through the land of another, by a race to the mill of the former, was an incorporeal hereditament, and, if the same were obstructed, an action of trespass *quare clausum* as to a corporeal hereditament would not lie.[2]

---

[1] Beeston v. Weate, 5 Ellis & B. 986. See Watkins v. Peck, 13 N. H. 360, 3 70, sustaining a similar doctrine.

[2] Baer v. Martin, 8 Blackf. 317.

11. Rights like those indicated by Lord Campbell, in respect to entering upon the land through which an artificial watercourse conducts water to or from a mill, and clearing or repairing the same, may be acquired by user by the mill-owner of such watercourse, although he may never have had occasion before to do such acts, as has been decided in several of the American courts. One of these is Prescott v. White, where there was an artificial race-way from an ancient mill through another's land, whereby the water of such mill was discharged into the natural stream below. It was held that the mill-owner might enter upon such land and clear the channel if necessary, though he had never * done so before, doing only what was customary in [*304] like cases, on the broad ground that, having an easement of discharge of water through another's land, he had, as incident thereto, the means of keeping the same in repair and fit for use. In doing this, however, he must exercise all reasonable care to do no unnecessary injury to the land-owner; and where stones had fallen from the wall of the race-way, he was bound to replace them upon the wall, and if the earth had fallen from the banks into the watercourse, he was bound to replace it again upon the bank for the owner to use if he saw fit; and, if not fit for use, the mill-owner must remove the materials in a reasonable time, in a manner least prejudicial to the land-owner. And if the mill-owner's land adjoined such watercourse on one side of it, he must make use of that for the deposit of such material taken therefrom which is not useful for the land-owner. These rules are applicable to cases where the mode of clearing or repairing such watercourse has not been fixed by grant or prescriptive use.[1]

A similar doctrine is declared in several cases, as being applicable to the case of entering upon and clearing a natu-

---

[1] Prescott v. White, 21 Pick. 341. See also Darlington v. Painter, 7 Penn. St. 473; Brisbane v. O'Neall, 3 Strobh. 348; Kauffman v. Griesemer, 26 Penn. St. 407, 413.

ral watercourse flowing from a mill through another's land. The court in one case call it "a natural easement in the land below," and consider it as belonging to a mill, "independently of any right acquired by compact or by prescription."[1]

How far it is strictly proper to speak of that as an "easement" which is neither acquired by compact nor prescription, but belongs intrinsically to the estate with which it is used, is referred to in another part of this work,[2] and [*305 is *again alluded to here chiefly for illustrating the extent of the doctrine how far an easement may be acquired in watercourses that are strictly artificial.

12. By following out the illustrations adopted by the English courts in treating of rights which may be acquired, by enjoyment, in watercourses artificially created for temporary purposes, considerable has been said which properly belongs to the second division of the subject, which relates to easements which may be acquired in or by artificial watercourses supplied from natural sources and designed for permanent use. And here, again, when treating of these, the reader will find cases cited which might seem more properly applicable to the rights which mill-owners or others may acquire and enjoy in natural streams. But the reason for this will be perceived in the analogy which the courts apply in similar cases between natural and artificial watercourses.

Thus it may be stated, in general terms, that one may acquire an easement to discharge water upon the land of another, pure or foul, as the user may have been, by an artificial channel or pipe, or by having the water from the eaves of his house fall upon his neighbor's land.[3]

The Chancellor, in the case of Earl v. De Hart, above

---

[1] Prescott v. Williams, 5 Metc. 429; Kauffman v. Griesemer, 26 Penn. St. 413; Cary v. Daniels, 5 Metc. 236; Crittenton v. Alger, 11 Metc. 281.

[2] Ante, chap. 3, sect. 1, pl. 10.

[3] 2 Washb. Real Prop. 68; Wright v. Williams, 1 Mees. & W. 77, 78; Ashley v. Ashley, 6 Cush. 70; Carlyon v. Lovering, 1 Hurlst. & N. 784, 798; Earl v. De Hart, 1 Beasley, 280, 285.

cited, in relation to a channel by which water had been discharged from the plaintiff's land, uses this language : " It makes no difference whether it is a natural watercourse or an artificial ditch. If it is a mere ditch, and the complainant's land has enjoyed the use of it for more than twenty years, and as an adverse right, then it is an easement which the owner of the complainant's land has in that of the defendant's ; it is a privilege, without a profit, and is as much the subject of protection as a natural watercourse." [1]

*13. In the case of Watkins v. Peck, the water- [*306] course under consideration was from a natural spring, and in treating of the rights which had been gained by several therein, the court lay down the broad doctrine that the adverse use of the water of an artificial aqueduct for twenty years gains thereby a right to the enjoyment thereof, in the same manner and to the same extent as would have been the case if the water had flowed in a natural channel.[2]

So in Pennsylvania, where it seems an executed license is not revocable, A gave B permission to erect a dam on A's land, by which to turn the water of a stream upon B's land, through a channel, for the purpose of irrigating B's meadow ; and B for twenty years had watered his cattle at the artificial watercourse, when A began a business upon his own land by which he fouled the waters running therein, so that the cattle could not drink it. It was held, that by this user and enjoyment B had acquired an easement to have his cattle supplied with pure water by such watercourse. It was held, in the same case, that one having a watercourse in his own land may conduct the water thereof wherever he pleases upon his land, if he do not materially diminish the quantity to which others below him are entitled. And if, while so managing the water, another were to interfere with the water flowing therein, to the injury of such land-owner, he

---

[1] Earl v. De Hart, 1 Beasley, 280, 285.

[2] Watkins v. Peck, 13 N. H. 360, 370. See Elliott v. Rhett, 5 Rich. 405.

would be liable for such interference in the same manner as if the watercourse had been a natural one.[1]

In California, in order to encourage mining, if one digs a ditch for that purpose, for conducting water to a mine, he acquires the exclusive right to control the waters flowing therein, without being liable to have the same obstructed or diverted by other ditches ; and under this rule it was [*307] *held that a miner might avail himself of a dry ravine for the purposes of an artificial ditch, with all the rights he would have if excavated by art.[2]

14. It should, however, be stated, that, as understood in England and most of the States, a parol license to construct a watercourse in one's land is revocable, and no title is thereby gained either to the land or to any right to maintain the watercourse. An enjoyment under such a license would neither be by grant nor adverse user.[3]

15. Under a statute passed in 1840, giving the Supreme Court jurisdiction in " all actions respecting easements on real estate," the courts of Massachusetts have had occasion several times to consider cases of what, as above explained, have been called " natural easements" in watercourses, in which it became necessary also to treat indirectly of the law of easements in artificial watercourses. In one of these the question raised was, whether the right which a mill-owner has to have the water flow freely from his mill through the land of a lower proprietor in the natural stream, was an *easement*. It was held under the statute that it was. The court make a distinction between the right to have water flow over one's own land and over the land of another, in these words: " The right which a party has to the use of

---

[1] Wheatley v. Chrisman, 24 Penn. St. 298, 303, 304. See Ford v. Whitlock, 27 Vt. 265.

[2] Hoffman v. Stowe, 7 Cal. 46.

[3] Hewlins v. Shippam, 5 Barnew. & C. 221 ; Fentiman v. Smith, 4 East, 107 ; Cocher v. Cowper, 1 Crompt. M. & R. 418 ; 1 Washb. Real Prop. 399 ; Mumford v. Whitney, 15 Wend. 380 ; Cook v. Stearns, 11 Mass. 533 ; Sampson v. Burnside, 13 N. H. 264.

water flowing over his own land is undoubtedly identified with the realty, and is a *real* or *corporeal hereditament*, and *not an easement.* But the right of a party to have the water of a stream or watercourse flow to or from his lands or mill, over the land of another, is an incorporeal hereditament, and an easement or a prædial service, as defined by the civil law. And it is immaterial whether the watercourse be *natural or artificial*, or whether the right is derived *ex jure *naturæ* or by grant or prescription. It [*308] seems, however, that the right to receive the flow of water and transmit it over the land of another, although a natural easement, not beginning by grant or assent of parties, may be claimed by prescription." [1]

This language, cited from the case last named, was adopted in Crittenton *v.* Alger ; [2] and the doctrine was reaffirmed in Ashley *v.* Ashley,[3] that " the right which the plaintiff claims, to have the water from his land run by the ancient watercourse over the defendant's land, is an easement."

This right in a mill-owner to discharge water upon another's land is, in one sense, something so different from that which one land-owner, as such, may claim to have the water flowing through his own land discharged upon that of the next proprietor below, that it may well be called an easement, so far as it respects the upper estate, and a servitude in respect to the lower one, since it changes materially the manner and extent of using the waters of the stream, in stopping them altogether, or discharging them in unusual quantities, instead of suffering them to flow in their accustomed current along the channel. But it is, after all, an easement of a most peculiar character. No unity of possession of the upper and lower estates, though dominant and servient, destroys it as an easement, as in ordinary cases. But it survives to the mill-owner the mo-

---

[1] Cary *v.* Daniels, 5 Metc. 236, 238.
[2] Crittenton *v.* Alger, 11 Metc. 284.
[3] Ashley *v.* Ashley, 6 Cush. 70.

ment the two estates are again owned in severalty, whether
there is any express grant ·or reservation made of the stream
or not.[1]

16. How far a right thus to discharge water from a mill
by an artificial channel may be said to be, in all re-
[*309] spects, *like that by a natural one, it may not be important to inquire, as it is well settled that such a
right would pass with the mill, by implication, in a grant
thereof.[2]

And yet, to prevent misapprehension in the use of terms,
it would seem that when the court, in the cases above cited,
say, " It is immaterial whether the watercourse be natural
or artificial, or whether the right is derived *ex jure naturæ*
or by grant or prescription," when applied to the right of
one land-owner to have the water flow to or from his land,
from or to that of another, their language must have related
to cases like those then under consideration.

Blackstone says : " A prescription cannot be for a thing
which cannot be raised by grant, for the law allows prescription only in supply of the loss of a grant, and therefore presupposes a grant to have existed." [3]   But it is difficult to
conceive that water ever began to flow from a higher to a
lower level along the surface of the earth, by permission or
grant of the lower proprietor.   While it is easy to understand that a right to change and control the mode in which
it should flow, by acts of one owner upon his land, like stopping it, and then suffering it to flow again to the injury of
another, might have originally been the result of compact
between them.

And in Sury *v.* Pigot, Whitlock, J. says : " In our case

[1] Saunders *v.* Newman, 1 Barnew. & Ald. 258 ; Sury *v.* Pigot, Poph. 166 ;
Tyler *v.* Wilkinson, 4 Mason, 395 ; Hazard *v.* Robinson, 3 Mason, 272 ; Brown
v. Best, 1 Wils. 174 ; Wood *v.* Waud, 3 Exch. 748, 776.   And Tucker *v.* Jewett, 11 Conn. 311, 322, where the point is examined at length.

[2] New Ipswich W. L. Co. *v.* Batchelder, 3 N. H. 190 ; 2 Washb. Real Prop.
37 ; Johnson *v.* Jordan, 2 Metc. 234, 240.

[3] 2 Blackst. Com. 265.

the watercourse doth not begin by consent of parties, nor by prescription, but *ex jure naturæ*, and therefore shall not be extinguished by unity of possession. So it was early laid down, that if one have a mill, and sue for a diversion of the water therefrom, if it be upon his own land and upon a natural stream, he need not allege it to have been an ancient mill. But if he claims the water by prescription, he must allege his mill to be an ancient one, in order to recover." [1]

*So Story, J., in Hazard v. Robinson, says: " He [*310] took the distinction that, where a thing hath its being by prescription, unity will extinguish it, but where the thing hath its being *ex jure naturæ*, it shall not be extinguished." [2]

17. While it can hardly be proper to speak of water rights belonging to mills *ex jure naturæ*, or of the right to the natural flow of a stream as one of prescription, it was undoubtedly correct to consider these embraced, under the statute, in the category of " easements on real estate," and that watercourses, though originally artificial, when once created by grant or prescription and applied to purposes of art, or as a means of enjoying the use of water, have most if not all the incidents and rights of natural watercourses attached to them.

This is illustrated by the case of Townsend v. M'Donald. There three owners of land, through which ran a natural watercourse, made division thereof in reference to enjoying the power of the water, by erecting a dam across the same, above their land, for raising a pond of water, and from this artificial channels were cut, through the three parts into which the land was divided, to the river below, for working mills standing upon these several parcels. It was held that, in the mode and extent of using these artificial streams through their respective lands, the owners

---

[1] Palins v. Heblethwait, Skinn. 65 ; Luttrell's case, 4 Rep. 86.
[2] Hazard v. Robinson, 3 Mason, 272, 277.

of the several parcels were to be governed by the same rules as they would have been had each been a natural stream.[1]

The case of Hurd v. Curtis may be referred to in the same connection, though perhaps less positive in the statement of the doctrine above proposed than might have been desirable. In that case a single mill-privilege, sufficient for six paper-mill powers and one fulling-mill power, belonging in common, was divided by indenture, whereby the [*311] owner * of the fulling-mill power was " to use the water at all times without preference," all the rights mentioned being considered " first rights." This " fulling-mill right " was not, in terms, annexed to any particular mill or mill-site, and it was accordingly held that it might be applied at any convenient site, provided no increased burden was imposed for race-ways or otherwise upon the other proprietors of the common supply of the several mills. The one to whom it was assigned had already applied it to operate a mill upon his own land by means of an artificial canal across the same in which the water flowed to his mill.

After this, he conveyed the intermediate land through which this canal passed, but made no reservation of any right to maintain this channel and flow of water. But the court incline to the opinion that, here being a mill in operation, carried by water flowing in this open channel, would raise a reservation, by implication, of a right to maintain it, and that the owner of the land could no more obstruct it than if it had been a natural watercourse.[2]

And a similar doctrine was more definitely declared in Frey v. Witman, where the owner of land on both sides of a natural stream erected a dam thereon, and excavated an artificial canal from the same along the bank of the stream, to a mill below the dam, whereby the water of the stream

---

[1] Townsend v. M'Donald, 14 Barb. 460; Buddington v. Bradley, 10 Conn. 213.

[2] Hurd v. Curtis, 7 Metc. 94.

was turned from its original channel, and flowed in this artificial one.   He then sold the intermediate land to another,
and, among other things, subsequently stopped certain leaks
in the dam, by which a part of the water in the pond had
escaped and flowed down the original channel.   It was held
that the purchaser of the land had no remedy for continuing
this diversion, since he must have known, when he took his
deed, that the grantor did not intend to destroy his mill, and
that it could only be carried on by continuing to divert the natural stream into this artificial *one, and   [*312]
that the stopping of the leaks was but a part of the
reserved right to maintain the diversion.[1]

An instance of the rights of a proprietor of a natural
stream to the flow of the water therein attaching to an artificial one, was this.   The plaintiff was lessee of a mill which
stood some distance from the bank of the stream upon
the lessor's land, and was carried by water taken from the
stream in A's land above the mill by a trench, and through
the land of the plaintiff's lessor who had, by an agreement
with A, cut this trench for the purposes of this mill.   The defendant, at a point above A's land, diverted the water of the
stream to the plaintiff's injury.   And it was held, that as to
this trench and the water flowing in it, the plaintiff had the
rights of a riparian proprietor.   And one of the Barons held,
generally, that a riparian owner may grant the flow of water
in a stream to one who is not a riparian proprietor, to be
used on the premises of the latter, which a higher proprietor
may not disturb by diverting it.[2]

18. Without intending to resume the discussion, how far
the granting of one of several tenements creates an easement
or servitude in either, by implication, it may be proper to
refer in this connection to a few more cases which go to illustrate the extent to which an artificial watercourse, when once
created and attached to another, as a principal estate, be-

[1] Frey v. Witman, 7 Penn. St. 440.
[2] Nuttall v. Branwell, L. R. 2 Exch. 1.

comes like unto, or identical with, a natural one, in respect to the rules by which its ownership is governed. Thus in Pheysey *v.* Vickary, Parke, B., in speaking of what easements would or would not be extinguished by unity of seizin and possession of the dominant and servient estates, says : " If it is necessary to the safety of a house that water should flow down a drain, the right of a watercourse through it is reserved, by implication, in every grant of a house."[1]

But the terms in which the artificial watercourse is created are to be regarded in determining the extent and mode of its use. Thus in Lee *v.* Stevenson, the plaintiff leased certain premises to the defendant, and therein reserved the right to lay a covered drain through these premises in order to drain his other estate to a certain point. The defendant, after it had been constructed, opened a drain from the leased premises into this drain. But as the drain was, by its terms, to be for the use of the plaintiff's other premises, the court held there was no implied right granted of making use of it for the defendant's convenience. Although, had the right which the plaintiff reserved to himself been general, to drain his premises across those of the defendant, it would not have given him such exclusive right, but the same might have been used by the defendant.[2]

[*313]   *19. Upon the principle that an artificial watercourse may acquire the incidents and qualities of a natural one, it was early held that, if the owner of an estate in fee, upon which there was a dwelling-house and spring of water, were to lay aqueduct pipes from the spring to the house, for supplying the latter with water, and should sell the house without the land, or the land without the house, the right of the aqueduct would in the one case pass, and in the other be reserved, by the grant, as an easement incident to the house as the dominant estate.[3]

---

[1] Pheysey *v.* Vickary, 16 Mees. & W. 484.

[2] Lee *v.* Stevenson, 1 Ellis, B. & E. 512.

[3] Nicholas *v.* Chamberlain, Cro. Jac. 121 ; Pyer *v.* Carter, 1 Hurlst. & N. 916 ; Sury *v.* Pigot, Poph. 166 ; Lampman *v.* Milks, 21 N. Y. 505 ; Seymour *v.* Lewis, 13 N. J. 443.

But in one respect they are not identical, for, if the two estates were to become again united in one owner, and he were to cut off the aqueduct from the house, and were to sell the same in that state, it would not carry the right to the aqueduct, being an easement, and not a natural or necessary right.[1]

20. A land proprietor may restrict himself by grant or covenant from changing the course of a stream through his land;[2] and after suffering the water to flow through his land in a new channel for twenty years, he cannot change it to the injury of mill-owners below, or of riparian proprietors above, who have enjoyed the benefit of its flowing in such artificial watercourse.[3]

The case of Hall v. Swift is one where a corresponding right to receive the water upon his land by a new and artificial channel was held to be properly exercised by a landowner, so that a proprietor above him might not interfere therewith. The stream in that case was a small one, and, after leaving the defendant's land, its natural course was *into a narrow lane, which separated the defend- [*314] ant's and plaintiff's lands ; after running a short distance along this lane, it turned into the plaintiff's land. The plaintiff changed its place of entering his land, so that it run directly across this lane from where it left the defendant's land. After this it ceased to flow at all for many years, but began again, and had flowed in this new channel for nineteen years, when the defendant obstructed it. In an action for such obstruction, it was held that the plaintiff's right to have the water flow in this artificial channel was the same as if it had been the natural one, and that he had lost no right to insist upon the then present flow of the water by reason of its having been suspended.[4]

[1] Sury v. Pigot, Poph. 172; s. c., Palm. 446, citing Lady Browne's case ; Robins v. Barnes, Hob. 131.

[2] Northum v. Hurley, 1 Ellis & B. 665 ; Townsend v. M'Donald, 14 Barb. 460.

[3] Belknap v. Trimble, 3 Paige, 577, 605; Delaney v. Boston, 2 Harringt. 489, 491.

[4] Hall v. Swift, 6 Scott, 167 ; s. c., 4 Bing. N. C. 381.

21. In the absence of an express grant, defining the extent and mode of application to use of an artificial watercourse, reference must be had to such use as has actually existed for the requisite period of time to acquire a prescriptive right to the same, and it hardly need be added, that the owner thereof cannot change or increase the extent of such enjoyment as against the riparian proprietors. So that if, for instance, there be a surplus of water in the stream beyond what the owner of such artificial watercourse has acquired a right to appropriate by having applied the same to use, it belongs to the riparian proprietor, and the owner of the trench or watercourse may not appropriate the same by enlarging his trench or making use of an increased quantity of water at his works.[1]

22. Though a land-owner may not divert, or unreasonably obstruct, the water of a stream flowing through his land, so as to deprive the proprietor below of the use of the same through and along its accustomed channel, he may change its direction by artificial channels through his own land at his pleasure, provided he do not thereby diminish the [*315] *beneficial use of the same to other proprietors.

Nor would a lower mill-owner have any better right to disturb the owner of an upper mill, which was placed within the owner's land upon an artificial channel, than if placed upon a natural one. The rights of the mill-owner incident to his ownership as riparian proprietor would be the same in the one case as in the other.[1] But if the landowner, having changed the direction of a natural stream through his land, were to suffer others, who are entitled to a right to the use of the water, to go on and expend money in reference to such use, under a belief that the new channel was to be a permanent one, and this were known to the land-owner, he could not afterwards change the course of

[1] Tyler v. Wilkinson, 4 Mason, 395, 405, 407.
[2] Webster v. Fleming, 2 Humph. 518.

the stream so as to injure the party who expended his money.[1]

23. In these and like cases, where one, who owns a watercourse in which another is interested, or by the use of which another is affected, does or suffers acts to be done affecting the rights of other proprietors, whereby a state of things is created which he cannot change without materially injuring another who has been led to act by what he himself had done or permitted, the courts often apply the doctrine of estoppel, and equity, and sometimes law, will interpose to prevent his causing such change to be made. The reader will take, in this connection, as a general principle of law, that if one gives another a parol license to flow his land by a dam to be built upon the licensee's land,[2] or to build a dam upon the licenser's land and the like, such license is revocable.[3] But in an early case in equity, where A had been at great expense to divert a watercourse which put B to expense and operated as a nuisance as to him, for which *he [*316] brought his action at law, the court granted an injunction against prosecuting the suit, because, while A was engaged in causing this diversion, B stood by, and, so far from objecting, encouraged him to proceed.[4]

24. A case is also stated in Middleton v. Gregorie, by Butler, J., where it would seem that a mill-owner may not always abandon, at his pleasure, a right to stop and divert the flow of a stream by a mill-dam which he has acquired by prescription or grant, if by doing so he will work an injury to a riparian proprietor below him, against whom he shall have acquired this right. He supposes the case of a riparian

---

[1] Ford v. Whitlock, 27 Vt. 265 ; Norton v. Volentine, 14 Vt. 239 ; Woodbury v. Short, 17 Vt. 387 ; Townsend v. M'Donald, 14 Barb. 460 ; Devonshire v. Eglin, 7 Eng. L. & Eq. 39 ; s. c., 14 Beav. 530.

[2] Otis v. Hall, 3 Johns. 450. Contra, McKellip v. M'Ilhenny, 4 Watts, 317 ; Lacy v. Arnett, 33 Penn. St. 169.

[3] 1 Washb. Real Prop. 399. Contra, Rerick v. Kern, 14 S. & R. 267 ; Houston v. Saffee, N. H. Rep. 15 Law Reg. 380.

[4] 2 Eq. Cas. Abr. 522 ; ante, chap. 1, sect. 3, pl. 43 ; Campbell v. M'Coy, 31 Penn. St. 263, adopts the doctrine of the 2 Eq. Cas. Abr. 522 ; post, sect. 25.

proprietor upon a stream, who should yield to a stoppage
and diversion of the water thereof for twenty years, by a
dam erected by another upon his own land above such riparian proprietor, and the latter should, in consequence, appropriate his land to a dry culture, such as corn or cotton,
which, before such diversion, could not have been cultivated
thereon. " Would the defendant " (the owner of the dam),
asks the judge, " have a right to cut his dam and destroy the
growing crop? "   " For all legal purposes," he answers,
" the plaintiff might, under such circumstances, have regarded his land as though the water had never flowed
through it.   Indeed, I think he would have as much right
to enjoy his property in security, as if he had cultivated dry
land above ; and it is very clear that, where one has land
lying adjacent to a stream, and a proprietor below dams the
water back upon him, the former has a right of action to
abate the nuisance." [1]

25. There is one other case which it may be proper to
notice, although it can hardly be regarded as settling many
principles applicable in those States where the same rules
of law as to executed licenses do not prevail as in Pennsylvania, or the rules of equity are not equally liberal
[*317] in *modifying the common law in determining the
rights of suitors.   The case is Le Fevre v. Le Fevre.
The owner of a parcel of land sold a part of it to the owner
of a tanyard, together with a right to draw water by pipes
laid in the earth along a designated line through the vendor's land, from a stream in his land to the vendee's tan-
yard.   After these pipes had been laid and used for a considerable time, it was orally agreed between the parties that
they should be taken up and laid in another place than the
line indicated by the deed, and it was accordingly done by
the vendee at his expense.   After lying in this situation, and
being used for six or seven years in connection with the business of the tanyard, the owner of the latter sold the same

[1] Middleton v. Gregorie, 2 Rich. 631, 638.

with the water right which he had purchased to the present plaintiff. Soon after this the original vendor cut off the pipes within his own land, and stopped the flow of water therein to the tanyard, and for this the plaintiff brought the present action. The court held, that as the pipe was laid in a manner indicated by the owner of the land, at the expense of the owner of the tanyard, a court of equity would treat the latter as owning the right to maintain it there, first, by having incurred expense in laying it down under an agreement with the land-owner that he should have such right, and second, by his being in possession; that the court would require the land-owner to execute this agreement on his part, and would have granted an injunction to prevent the land-owner from prosecuting a suit at law for laying down the pipe, and that courts of law would not suffer him, under these circumstances, to take the law into his own hands by cutting or destroying the aqueduct. To the suggestion that the laying down of the pipe was done by a parol license only, which was revocable, the court held that, after having been executed and expense thereby incurred by the licensee, it could not be revoked so as to make the licensee a wrong-doer. And they held it was competent to show by parol that * another spot was substituted for that de- [*318] scribed in the deed, as the same had been carried into effect, and the original contract could not, therefore, be insisted upon without working a fraud upon one of the parties.

The court cited the case above mentioned from 2 Equity Cases Abridged, and that of Short v. Taylor, said to have been decided by Lord Somers, where Taylor in building a house laid his foundation partly upon Short's land, he standing by and encouraging him; and upon bringing an action therefor, the Chancellor granted an injunction against his proceeding with it. Silent acquiescence would seem from this to have been regarded in the light of an express license, but even that, by the ordinary rules of the common law, might be revoked, though held otherwise in Pennsylvania.[1]

26. Somewhat akin to the case of the change of a natural current by substituting an artificial channel therefor, is that of a change in such current by an extraordinary natural cause, like that of a freshet, for instance. In one case a stream had flowed first through the defendant's and then through the plaintiff's land, until 1830. In that year the course of the current was so changed by the effect of a freshet, that from that time it ran wholly within the land of the defendant, avoiding that of the plaintiff. In 1840, the defendant changed the then course of the stream back to its original line, so as again to run across the plaintiff's land, for doing which the present action was brought.

The court, in giving an opinion, waive the question how far the defendant might have restored the current back to its original course before any act of acquiescence on his part. But they held that, after so long an acquiescence, he was not at liberty to do it. They refer to Hale's De Jure Maris[2] for the doctrine, " that if a river leaves its course, [*319] * and sensibly makes its channel entirely in the lands of A, the whole river belongs to A. *Aqua cedit solo.*" And they likened the case under consideration to that of a quantity of earth suddenly carried away by a flood, or the like, from one man's estate, and lodged upon that of another. If the former suffers it to remain until " it cements and coalesces with the soil, the property is changed, and there is no right to reclaim the soil." [3]

In the last-cited case the court held that, if a river not navigable change its course so as to cut off a point of land, leaving it an island in the stream, it would belong to the

[1] Le Fevre *v.* Le Fevre, 4 Serg. & R. 241 ; *ante,* sect. 23 ; Short *v.* Taylor, 2 Eq. Cas. Abr. 522.   See *ante,* p. *19.

[2] Hargrave's Tracts, pp. 5, 6.

[3] Woodbury *v.* Short, 17 Vt. 387.   See 2 Washb. Real Prop. 453, note ; Trustees, &c. *v.* Dickenson, 9 Cush. 454 ; 1 Fournel, Traité, &c. 157, § 38 ; Code Nap., Art. 559.

original owner. If the bed of the stream gradually fill up
by deposit, and the stream take a new channel, the new land
so formed belongs to the original proprietors of the stream
respectively, to its original thread. If land forms above
such island within the stream, not by accretions to such
island, and becomes an island in the stream, it would belong
to the riparian proprietors according as it was divided by the
filum aquæ, which is the medium line between the banks or
natural water-lines on the shores, at the time the new land
was formed, irrespective of the relative depth of the water in
the different parts of the stream.[1] Soil gained by the gradual and imperceptible accretion upon land bounding upon a
river or the sea, becomes the property of the land-owner, and
this extends to sea-weed accumulating thereon.[2]

*SECTION V.   [*320]

SPECIAL LAWS AS TO MILLS.

    1. Grounds upon which these statutes are based.
    2. How far the acts of Massachusetts constitutional.
    3. The constitutionality of the Virginia system.
    4. How far private property may be taken for private use.
    5. Mill Acts of Massachusetts.

[1] See Pratt *v.* Lamson, 2 Allen, 275 ; Carson *v.* Blazer, 2 Bin. 485.
    The rules laid down in the Digest upon the subjects above treated of are in
these words : " Quod si vis fluminis partem aliquam ex tuo prædio detraxerit,
et meo prædio attulerit, palam est eam tuam permanere. Plane si longiore
tempore fundo meo hæserit, arboresque quas secum traxerit, in meum fundum
radices egerint, ex eo tempore videtur meo fundo adquisita esse." D. 41, 1, 7, 2.
See also Inst. 2, 1, 21.
    " Insula quæ in mari nascitur (quod raro accidit) occupantis sit ; nullius
enim esse creditur. In flumine nata (quod frequenter accidit) si quidem mediam
partem fluminis tenet, communis est eorum qui ab utraque parte fluminis prope
ripam prædia possident, pro modo latitudinis cujusque prædii, quæ latitudo
prope ripam sit. Quod si alteri parti proximior sit, eorum est tantum qui ab
ea parte prope ripam prædia possident." D. 41, 1, 7, 3. See also Inst. 2,
1, 22.
    [2] Emans *v.* Turnbull, 2 John. 313 ; Hargrave's Tracts, p. 28 ; Ford *v.* Lacy,
7 H. & Nomr. 156.

6. Apply only to injuries to land by mill-dams.
7. Extend to injuries below as well as above mills.
8. Do not extend to stoppage of water by an upper mill.
9. Laws of Maine apply only where actual damage done.
10. Of fixing by the jury of the height the mill-owner may flow.
11. Parol release of damages by flowing.
12. The law authorizes construction of reservoirs.
13. Extends only to cases where mill-owner owns both banks.
14. Only extends to an occupied privilege of the owner.
15. Does not extend to tide-mills.
16. What is considered an occupation of a privilege.
17. The first occupant has the prior right to a privilege.
18. Application of this doctrine. Case of Cary v. Daniels.
19. What constitutes a prior occupation.
20. An occupation requires both intent and act done.
21. Action lies for flowing above the prescribed height.
22. Unless height of flowing is fixed by grant.
23. Statute only protects actually existing mills.
24. Effect of decay and abandonment of mill and dam.
25. What would be such abandonment.
26. Statute right to flow lands operates a license.
27. Statute confers no estate in the lands flowed.
28. Power to flow subject to public right of passage.
29. Statute extends to flowing to the injury of drains.
30. Statute protects mills from being flowed.
31. Of remedy for flowing before actual damage done.
32. How far flowing adverse before actual damage done.
33. All mill acts of the States local in their effect.
34. How far the United States affected by State mill acts.
35. Mill Acts of Maine.
36. Mill Acts of Wisconsin.
37. Law of flowing in Rhode Island.
38. Virginia system of mill acts.
39. Laws as to mills in Missouri.
40. Of priority of rights under the Virginia system.
41. Laws as to mills of Arkansas and Kentucky.
42. Laws of Mississippi as to mills.
43. Laws of North Carolina as to mills.
44. Laws of Indiana, Illinois, and Florida.
45. All these laws strictly construed.
46. Statutes of Alabama and Maryland abrogated or repealed.

[*321]   *1. THE stringency with which the common law limited the rights of riparian proprietors upon streams of
water to such uses as it might be applied to, within and upon
the land of each proprietor, and the importance of mills to
the comfort of a community, must necessarily have been at-

tended with great inconvenience to new settlers in a country, like the colonists of America, where, from the nature of
the case, nothing like prescriptive rights could have been
acquired for many years after their settlement. In a colony,
moreover, where the loss of a few acres of land bore but a
slight proportion to the value and importance of grist and
saw mills, it could hardly have been otherwise than that
some policy should be adopted better suited to meet the
condition of such a people than the rules of the common
law, which had their origin and application in a country so
different in its physical as well as its social capacities and
wants.   It is, accordingly, historically true, that, from an
early period in Massachusetts, the common law as to the
rights and liabilities of mill-owners has been essentially
modified by statute. Partly by these statutes, and partly by
the construction of courts in applying existing laws to the
growing exigencies which they were designed to meet, a
system of Mill Laws, as they are called, quite complete in
itself, has grown up in Massachusetts, and forms substantially also the law of Maine and of Wisconsin upon the same
subject.   Other and distinct systems in respect to taking
and appropriating lands for mill purposes have been adopted
in other States. So that to treat of this subject with any considerable degree of completeness requires that an outline, at
least, of those systems should be presented to the reader.

In one sense, so far as the mode and extent of making
use of the land of one proprietor by another for his own
benefit as a mill-owner is concerned, when tried by the
rules of the common law, it is a system of easements and
servitudes. But they are servitudes and easements
*created by law instead of being acquired by grant [*322]
or prescription. This remark applies with more propriety to a system like that of Massachusetts, where the mill-
owner is only authorized to occupy, by flowing the same, the
land of another for the purpose of operating a mill, which,
as well as the dam belonging to the same, are erected on

his own land; but the law does not confer upon him any estate in or title to the land thus occupied. Whereas, under what may be called the Virginia system, the mill-owner acquires a title to so much land as shall be taken under process of law for the purposes of a mill, including, it may be, the land upon which a portion of the dam is placed, as well as such parts thereof as may be flowed thereby.

2. This authority by a general law, under which one man is empowered to take and occupy the land of another for his own profit and advantage, has been questioned on constitutional grounds. The question has been, incidentally, discussed in various forms by the courts of Massachusetts, in which it has, sometimes, been treated as a mere statute remedy for a wrong, assuming that the act of occupancy was a common-law wrong. But in whatever form it is viewed, it is not to be disguised, that the statute does authorize one man not only to recover damages in a particular manner for the act of flowing his land by another, but it authorizes the latter to continue and maintain the nuisance against the will of the owner, in the same manner as if he were the true owner of an easement in the estate. And every pretence upon which this can be deemed to come within the principles of the Constitution must fail unless it can fairly be brought within the broad doctrine that private property may be taken for the public good, upon a compensation being had therefor. A recurrence to a few of the cases where the matter has been discussed may be sufficient for the present. In Boston and Roxbury Mill-Dam Cor-
[*323] poration v. Newman, the court held the act *creating the company, and authorizing them to flow the land of others, so far a public enterprise as to be within the intent of the Constitution, and they held, further, that not only must the land-owner submit to having his land flowed for the purpose of creating a head of water for the plaintiffs' mill, but that he might not fill it up, and thereby diminish the size and capacity of their pond, although he retained the fee,

and the company only had the easement of a right to flow.
But the court, at the same time, admit that the mill-owner
is under no corresponding obligation to grind for any one
against his will.   In that case, the several laws upon the
subject are referred to by Putnam, J., in giving the opinion
of the court, and the constitutional grounds on which they
may be considered to rest are examined.[1]

The first of these statutes was passed in 1713, expressly reciting that " the building of mills is serviceable for the public
good and benefit to the town," and that, in " raising a suitable head of water for that service, it hath so happened that
some small quantity of lands or meadows have thereby been
flowed."   And in order to prevent a multiplication of suits
for such an injury, the statute authorizes a continuance on
the part of the mill-owner to flow the land, and provides for
a mode of assessing damages for the same by a jury, upon
complaint of the land-owner, to be annually paid.   This recital clearly indicated the ground upon which the statute was
based, namely, an act on the part of one party designed to
promote a manifest public benefit, in effecting which an un-
intentional infringement of the legal rights of another had
been occasioned.   And while it provided compensation for
the private injury, it authorized the act to be continued as
something required by the public good.[2]   And when the
statute of 1795 was passed, extending the right to flow *any*
lands of another for the purpose of raising a suita-
*ble head of water for working a mill, the language [*324]
of Parker, C. J., in Stowell *v.* Flagg, was undoubtedly justified, that " he could not help thinking it was in-
cautiously copied from the Colonial and Provincial Acts,
which were passed when the use of mills, from the scarcity
of them, bore a much greater value, compared to the land
used for the purposes of agriculture, than at present." [3]

---

1 Boston and Roxbury Mill-Dam Corporation *v.* Newman, 12 Pick. 467.
2 Col. Laws, 404.
3 Stowell *v.* Flagg, 11 Mass. 364.

The statute, in the case last cited, is regarded as one of remedy alone. Other views of it are presented in other cases, as, for instance, in Bates *v.* Weymouth Iron Co.,[1] by Shaw, C. J., and in Williams *v.* Nelson,[2] by the same judge.

The case of Hazen *v.* Essex Company [3] was one where the general law authorizing mill-owners to flow the lands of others was extended by a special act to the flowing back water upon an existing mill to its destruction, by means of a dam across the Merrimack River, for the creation of an extensive mill-power; and the act was held to be constitutional, as coming within the power of the legislature to pass acts required by the public good. The language, however, of the court in Maine is to a certain extent undoubtedly warranted by the whole history of the "Mill Acts" of that State, as well as of Massachusetts, which, in the sequel, will be found to have practically carried the doctrine to the length, that any one wishing to create a mill-power for his own use and emolument, may appropriate the mowing, or tillage, or woodland of another to such extent as he pleases, and exercise a perpetual easement over the same, which in effect destroys all valuable property therein of the owner of such land, upon paying such sum in damages as a jury shall estimate. "The Mill Act," says Rice, J., "as it has existed in this State, pushes the power of eminent domain [*325] *to the very verge of constitutional inhibition. If it were a new question, it might well be doubted whether it would not be deemed to be in conflict with that provision of the Constitution, — private property shall not be taken for public uses without just compensation, nor unless the public exigencies require."[4]

---

[1] Bates *v.* Weymouth Iron Co., 8 Cush. 548, 553. See also Murdock *v.* Stickney, Ibid. 113.

[2] Williams *v.* Nelson, 23 Pick. 141.

[3] Hazen *v.* Essex Company, 12 Cush. 475.

[4] Jordan *v.* Woodward, 40 Me. 317, 323. See 2 Am. Jurist. 25-39. *Shaw*, C. J., in Murdock *v.* Stickney, *supra*, expressly denies that the statute rests upon the right of eminent domain, or that it is in any proper sense a taking of the property of the owner of the land.

The most sensible ground upon which these statutes are to be placed seems, after all, to be furnished in Talbot *v.* Hudson, in which the court hold that it is as competent for the legislature to authorize a body of land-owners to abate the dam of a mill-owner, if the public good requires it, and thereby relieve their lands from being flowed, as it is to authorize a mill-owner to flow them. The principle applicable and governing in all these cases is, that private interests must yield to public exigencies, and that private property, in such cases, may be appropriated, if compensation therefor is provided.

The opinion of the court was given by Bigelow, C. J., and the following extracts will present the grounds on which these statutes rest in as satisfactory a light as could well be desired. In this case, the legislature had passed an act authorizing the removal of a mill-dam in consequence of the alleged extent of the injury thereby occasioned to the lands of riparian proprietors upon the stream above it. The constitutionality of the act was denied, but sustained by the court.

" If land is taken for a fort, a canal, or a highway, it would clearly fall within the first class (public use). If it was transferred from one person to another, or to several persons, solely for their peculiar benefit and advantage, it would as clearly come within the second class (private use). But there are intermediate cases where public and
* private interests are blended together, in which it [*326]
becomes more difficult to decide within which of the
two classes they may be properly said to fall. There is no fixed rule or standard by which such cases can be tried and determined. Each must necessarily depend upon its own peculiar circumstances. . . . . In a broad and comprehensive view, such as has been heretofore taken of the construction of this clause of the Declaration of Rights, everything which tends to enlarge the resources, increase the industrial energies, and promote the productive power of any consider-

able number of the inhabitants of a section of the State, or which leads to the growth of towns and the creation of new resources for the employment of private capital and labor, indirectly contributes to the general welfare, and the prosperity of the whole community. It is on this principle that many of the statutes of the Commonwealth, by which private property has been heretofore taken and appropriated to a supposed public use, are founded. . . . . One of the earliest and most familiar instances of the exercise of such a power under the Constitution is to be found in the statute for the erection and regulation of mills. . . . . And it is because they thus lead, incidentally, to the promotion of one of the great public industrial pursuits of the Commonwealth that they have been heretofore sanctioned by this court, as well as by the legislature, as being a legitimate exercise of the right of eminent domain justifying the taking and appropriating of private property." [1]

Whatever, therefore, might have been thought of statutes like these in their application to particular cases, if the question were now raised for the first time, their validity may be assumed to rest upon premises at once well founded and intelligible.[2]

3. The Virginia system seems to be open to more [*327] obvious *objections upon constitutional grounds than that of Massachusetts, though the same broad construction which authorizes the appropriation of the use of the property of one man for the benefit of another would seem to reach the taking and appropriating of the property itself. The statutes of Virginia, and of the States which have followed her in their policy, provide, in general terms, that one owning land upon one side only of a stream may, by process of law, acquire a title to sufficient land upon the

---

[1] Talbot v. Hudson, 24 Law Rep. 228. See also Commonwealth v. Essex Co., 13 Gray, 239, 251 ; Chase v. Sutton Mg. Co., 4 Cush. 152, 169.

[2] Newcomb v. Smith, 1 Chand. 71 ; Pratt v. Brown, 3 Wis. 603 ; Fisher v. Horicon, &c. Co., 10 Wis. 351.

opposite side on which to erect his dam and create a water-power. The courts of Alabama in 1859 pronounced a statute of this character unconstitutional, although it had stood upon the statute-book of that Territory and State since 1812, though, had this power been limited to grist-mills, which by § 1112 of the Code of that State are declared to be public mills if they grind for toll, the statute might have been deemed to come within the provisions of the Constitution.[1]

So that the question in all these cases turns upon the point whether the use for which the statute authorizes the taking by one man, or a body of men, of the property of another is a public one or otherwise. This question has been raised in respect to other involuntary easements in the lands of individuals, such as the laying out private ways over the land of one man for the benefit of the estate of another, which is provided for in the statutes of several of the States. And in some of them, the power to do this has been denied, as being against the provisions of their Constitutions. Such has been the case in New York, Tennessee, and Alabama.[2]

4. If the act authorizing the taking of such property can be brought within the proper exercise of the right of eminent domain, it ceases to be one of questionable validity. *But it adds nothing to the validity of an act, if it [*328] transcends this limit, that it makes provision for a full compensation to the owner on the part of him who shall have attempted to appropriate the property of another to his own personal benefit.[3]

The doctrine of the court of New York, in Heyward v. Mayor of New York, is believed to be the sound one, that the right to take private property for public uses is an inherent attribute of sovereignty, which exists in every independent State. But no man can have his property taken from

---

[1] Moore v. Wright, 34 Ala. 311, 333.

[2] Taylor v. Porter, 4 Hill, 140; Clock v. White, 2 Swan, 540; Sadler v. Langham, 34 Ala. 311.

[3] Varick v. Smith, 5 Paige, 137, 159; Matter of Albany Street, 11 Wend. 149; Bowman v. Middleton, 1 Bay, 252; 2 Kent, Comm. 276; Ibid. 340.

26

him without his consent, and given to another, by mere legis-lation.[1] " We know of no case in which a legislative act to transfer the property of A to B, without his consent, has ever been held a constitutional exercise of legislative power in any State in the Union.   Per Story, J.[2]

And where the right of eminent domain has been once exercised by taking one's land for purposes of a street or high-way, and a railroad company are then authorized by act of legislature to lay their way over the land so taken, it is such an injury to the owner of the fee of the soil, as to entitle him to new damages by the creation of this new easement over his land.[3]

But it was held otherwise in case of locating a horse rail-road over a public highway in Connecticut.[4]

It should be remarked, in passing, that, so far as these laws operate to create what answers to a servitude upon one estate in favor of another, the rights and obligations of the owners of the dominant and servient tenements are governed by the *lex loci rei sitæ*.[5]

5. With this brief glance at the principles upon which the acts of legislation of the several States with which they have seen fit to override the rules of the common law in this re-spect are to be sustained, it becomes proper, in the next place, to give an outline of these, although it would obvi-ously be unsuited to a work like the present to enter with any great minuteness upon the practical detail of the modes in which these systems have been carried out in their opera-tion.

But it should be borne in mind that, in all cases where the party is entitled to his damages upon complaint under the " Mill Acts," his common-law remedy is taken away.[6]

[1] Heyward *v.* Mayor of N. Y., 3 Seld. 314.
[2] Wilkinson *v.* Leland, 2 Peters, 627, 658.
[3] Imlay *v.* Union B. R. R., 26 Con. 249 ; People *v.* Law, 22 How. P. C. 109 ; Wetmore *v.* Law, ib. 130.
[4] Elliot *v.* Fair Haven R. R. 32 Con. 579.
[5] 3 Burge, For. &.Col. L., 448.
[6] Veasie *v.* Dwinel, 50 Maine, 485 ; Fiske *v.* Framingham Co., 12 Pick. 69.

Beginning with that of Massachusetts, which has been in operation in most respects in Maine, both before and since *her separation from the former State, and has, [*329] to a considerable extent, been adopted in Wisconsin, its general provisions may be stated in a summary form. It is made lawful for any one to erect a dam upon his own land, across a stream not navigable, for the purpose of raising a head of water for operating a mill, and to maintain the same, provided he do not thereby injure any mill lawfully existing upon the same stream above or below such dam, nor any mill-site upon the same on which a mill or mill-dam has been lawfully erected, unless the right to maintain the same shall have been lost or defeated by abandonment or otherwise. Nor can he erect such dam to the injury of a mill-site which has already been occupied, provided the owner thereof shall within a reasonable time after commencing such occupation complete a mill and put the same in operation, for the working of which the water of such stream shall be applied. But in Wisconsin, the term " navigable," as applied to a stream, does not imply that it is affected by the tides, but is capable of being navigated for purposes of a highway, and declared to be such by statute, as Rock River, for instance.[1]

And to avoid all question of constructive authority, the statute denies to any one a right to place any part of his mill or dam upon the land of another, except by his grant or permission.[2]

The same statute provides for an assessment of damages in favor of any one whose lands shall be flowed or damaged by the erection and maintenance of such dam and mill, and authorizes the jury which shall be impanelled to assess the same, to fix the height to which the dam and flowing may be maintained, and during what parts of the year the owner of

---

[1] Cobb v. Smith, 16 Wisc. 661. See *post*, p. *397 ; Ward v. Hustis, 17 Wis. 416.

[2] Gen. Stat. c. 149.

the mill may flow the lands of the complainant. Various provisions are made for carrying out the purposes of the statute, such as giving the land-owner a lien upon the mill and dam for the enforcement of his damages, and for increasing the amount in certain cases, while the common-law remedy for such injury is taken away, and a right of tender is given to the mill-owner. And to save a multiplici-[*330] ty of *complaints, two or more land-owners, though not jointly interested in the parcels flowed, may join in one complaint, if damaged by the same mill-dam.

While these provisions, so adverse in many respects to the notions of the common law, have furnished a guide to the courts in determining the respective rights of the mill and the land-owner, it has been necessary to resort to many of the principles of the common law in applying the letter of the statute to particular cases, so that a system has been built up here which combines them both to no inconsiderable extent, as will appear by referring to the cases which have been decided by the courts from time to time.

6. The statute in the first place only covers injuries to land occasioned by means of a mill-dam and flowing the same, and does not extend to injuries to other property than land, nor to damages occasioned by any other means than raising water by a dam for mill purposes.[1] So that if the flowing of one's lands occasions offensive smells, and thereby diminishes the value of other lands in the neighborhood of those flowed, the remedy is not under the statute, but by an action at the common law, since the statute does not authorize what would be a private nuisance, beyond the mere act of flowing of land.[2]

7. But where land is flowed by means of a mill-dam, it matters not whether it be situate above or below the dam; it is equally within the statute in either situation.[3]

---

[1] Palmer Co. v. Ferrill, 17 Pick. 58 ; Thompson v. Moore, 2 Allen, 350.

[2] Eames v. N. E. Worsted Co., 11 Metc. 570 ; Murdock v. Stickney, 8 Cush. 116 ; Rooke v. Perkins, 14 Wis. 82.

[3] Gile v. Steven, 13 Gray, 146 ; Shaw v. Wells, 5 Cush. 537 ; Gen. Stat. c. 149, § 4.

8. Under the provision restricting a mill-owner from doing anything under the mill acts injurious to an existing mill, it was held in Maine, under Rev. Stat. c. 126, § 2, that where one erected a mill above an existing one, and adopted such machinery therein that the water applied *in carrying the same was not sufficient in [*331] quantity to carry the works in the prior mill, the owner's remedy, if any, for being deprived of his accustomed flow of water, was by an action on the case, and not under the statute for regulating mills.[1]

9. In one respect, there is an important practical diversity between the statutes of Maine and Massachusetts on this subject. In Maine no complaint lies until the flowing occasioned by the dam shall have caused some actual damage to the land-owner, and, as the common-law remedy is superseded by the statute in such cases, such land-owner is without remedy until actually damaged. This, as will hereafter appear, has an important bearing upon the question, when the party flowing begins to acquire a prescriptive right to maintain it by an adverse enjoyment of the same. In Massachusetts, on the contrary, it is no answer to the complaint of the land-owner for the assessment of damages for flowing the same, that no actual damage has yet been sustained.[2]

If, therefore, under the Massachusetts law, a mill-owner claims a right by prescription to flow the land of another, who seeks to recover damages under the provisions of the statute, he ought to avail himself of such right by denying that of the land-owner to have a warrant issue for the assessment of damages.[3]

10. And where a jury, in fixing the height to which the mill-owner might flow, established the height of the dam by

---

[1] Wentworth v. Poor, 38 Me. 243.

[2] Hathorn v. Stinson, 10 Me. 224; s. c., 12 Me. 183, 188; Nelson v. Butterfield, 21 Me. 220; Seidensparger v. Spear, 17 Me. 123; Wood v. Kelley, 30 Me. 47; Gen. Stat. c. 149, § 8; Williams v. Nelson, 23 Pick. 141; ante, chap. 1, sect. 4, pl. 33; post, pl. 31.

[3] Wilmarth v. Knight, 7 Gray, 294.

certain marks, it was held that he might flow as high as a dam, maintained at the prescribed height, would flow.[1]

But where the mill-owner had a right to raise the [*332] water *two inches above a certain bolt, it was held that his dam must be so built as not to flow the water above that point.[2]

11. Though it is a familiar doctrine, that an easement in another's land can only be acquired by grant, while a parol license to occupy another's land is in most of the states revocable at pleasure, under the construction given to these mill acts, which authorize a mill-owner to occupy the land of another by flowing the same, if the latter release his damages therefor, though by parol, it will bar him of all claim or right to maintain any complaint for such injury. It was accordingly held that where, as an inducement to the owner of a mill-privilege to go on and occupy the same by a mill, a land-owner, whose land would thereby be flowed, orally agreed not to claim damages therefor, if such mill were erected, it was a bar to any claim in his favor for such damages, not in the light of a grant of a right to occupy lands, but of a parol release of a claim to recover a certain amount of money.[3]

But such agreement would not run with the estate so as to bar the claim of the grantee of the land-owner for any flowing done by the mill-owner after such grant.[4]

12. It is, however, proposed to consider this statute only so far as it bears upon the right to enjoy what answers to an easement thereby created in another's land, and not to enter into any detail of the forms of proceeding or the mode of enforcing compensation for the injuries thereby occasioned.

It not only authorizes one who owns land upon both sides

[1] Wilmarth v. Knight, 7 Gray, 294.

[2] Winkley v. Salisbury Mg. Co., 14 Gray, 443.

[3] Smith v. Goulding, 6 Cush. 154; Seymour v. Carter, 2 Metc. 520; Clement v. Durgin, 5 Me. 9; Short v. Woodward, 13 Gray, 86.

[4] Fitch v. Seymour, 9 Metc. 462.

of the stream on which to erect a mill and dam to do so, and
thereby raise a head of water in immediate connection with
such mill, but to do this by way of a reservoir at any distance above his mill, upon the same stream, and
there *pen up the water for the use of his mill, as [*333]
he shall have occasion to draw the same.[1]

13. But the courts restrict these statutes within a pretty
narrow construction of their terms, and hold that this right
of erecting dams for reservoirs must be upon the same
stream upon which the mill is situate.   And therefore that,
where one owning land on two streams built his mill upon
one, and erected a dam for a reservoir upon the other, and
conducted the water of his reservoir by an artificial channel to the pond of his mill, and by the erection of his dam
flowed land of another, he was not justified in so doing by
the statute relating to mills, but was liable as at common
law.[2]

So where a mill-owner having a reservoir dam above his
mill upon the main stream let out the water thereof into the
plaintiff's meadow by an artificial channel, different from
that through which it naturally flowed, and thereby flooded
the meadow, he was held liable in an action of the case, and
not protected by the mill laws, in making such use of the
water to the plaintiff's injury.[3]

14. It will, moreover, be seen that, so far from its conferring a general right upon a mill-owner to flow the lands of
others, there are several prerequisites to be established before this right can be exercised.   And first, the person claiming it must have a water-privilege on which he has erected
a mill and mill-dam.   Thus, where the owner of one half
the stream erected a dam across the same for a mill, and
abutted and built one end of the dam upon the land of the
opposite owner, without his consent, and the latter after-

---

[1] Wolcott Mg. Co. v. Upham, 5 Pick. 292; Fiske v. Framingham Mg. Co.,
12 Pick. 68; Shaw v. Wells, 5 Cush. 537; Nelson v. Butterfield, 21 Me. 220.

[2] Bates v. Weymouth Iron Co., 8 Cush. 548.

[3] Fiske v. Framingham Mg. Co., 12 Pick. 68.

wards built a dam on his own land below, which in that
place extended across the stream, and flowed out the upper dam, it was held that the upper mill-owner had
[*334] *no right to maintain his dam against the consent
· of the other party, and that the latter was justified
in erecting his dam, and submerging that of the upper owner, or he might have taken down the dam, so far as it stood
on his land.[1]

So if there has been an ancient mill upon a mill-privilege,
one may not erect a mill and dam below it and submerge it,
although no mill may at the time be standing thereon, provided the owner of such upper privilege has not abandoned
it as a mill-privilege.[2]

And if one erects a mill-dam on his own land, which flows
back water upon an existing mill, the owner of the latter
may enter upon the premises of the former, and abate so
much thereof as may be necessary to remove the impediment thereby occasioned.[3]

So where one erected his mill on the stream and his dam
for working it, and another owner upon the same stream
then erected his upon his own land above it, the first could
not, by afterwards raising his dam, increase the flowing so
as injuriously to affect the working of the upper mill.[4]

15. It may be remarked, in passing, that the statute does
not extend to mills worked by tide-power, or what are called
tide-mills.[5]

16. The limitations above mentioned are easily and well
defined, in questions between new and actually existing
mills, and especially what are called ancient mills. But a
class of cases has arisen, which are not entirely free from

[1] Jewell v. Gardiner, 12 Mass. 311.

[2] French v. Braintree Mg. Co., 23 Pick. 216 ; Hatch v. Dwight, 17 Mass. 289.

[3] Jewell v. Gardiner, 12 Mass. 311 ; Hodges v. Raymond, 9 Mass. 314 ; post,
chap. 6, sect. 4, pl. 1.

[4] Sumner v. Tileston, 7 Pick. 198, 203 ; Cary v. Daniels, 8 Metc. 466 ; Veasie v. Dwinel, 50 Maine, 486.

[5] Murdock v. Stickney, 8 Cush. 113.

difficulty, when applying to them the rules of the statute. And these are, where the owner of a mill-privilege may, for instance, have taken steps towards occupying it; but before he shall have had an existing mill thereon, another owner on * the same stream below him, by the exer- [*335] cise of greater despatch, or the completion of a cheaper and more easily erected structure, has actually put a mill in operation in advance of the first. One may, for example, be an extensive cotton manufactory, the other a shingle-mill. The question in such cases has been, which of the two shall have the prior right to the privilege, and may the lower mill-owner flow the land of the upper proprietor to the sacrifice of his rights as a mill-owner? Under the law as it stood before the revision of the statutes in 1836, it had been held that, if the upper proprietor had actually built or was building a mill on his privilege, the lower proprietor could not erect a new dam or raise an old one to its injury, for the principle seems to be the same, so as to destroy the upper mill-privilege, under the protection and authority of the mill acts.[1]

By an alteration in phraseology introduced into the revised statutes, nothing but an existing mill could prevent one from erecting a dam and mill, and flowing the land of another above him; and in one case it was held that he might do this, although the upper land-owner had begun to erect a dam and mill upon his own premises before the lower owner had begun the erection of his works.[2]

But, by the present form of the statute, no one can erect a mill-dam whereby to flow the land of another to the injury of a mill-privilege already occupied, provided the owner thereof completes such occupation by putting a mill in operation upon the same, within a reasonable time after commencing such occupation.[3]

17. In the application of this doctrine to practical uses, reference has to be still had to some of the familiar prin

---

[1] Bigelow v. Newhall, 10 Pick. 348.
[2] Baird v. Wells, 22 Pick. 312.
[3] Veasie v. Dwinel, 50 Maine, 485.

ciples of the common law. Before any mills are erected, the right of each proprietor is the same, and that is a right to appropriate the power of the stream by the actual erection of a mill. The necessary consequence is, that, when [*336] *one proprietor under the common right has in fact appropriated the power, the proprietor below is so far restricted in his right to do the same that he cannot erect a mill on his own land, and flow back water to the destruction of the mill already erected by authority of law.[1]

18. But perhaps the best exposition of the nature and effect of this statute, considered in connection with the common-law rights of riparian proprietors upon a stream, may be found in the opinion of Shaw, C. J., in Cary v. Daniels. If, for instance, the descent of the water of a stream through the lands of several successive owners is such as only to supply power for a single mill-privilege, the proprietor who first erects his dam for the purpose of availing himself of this mill power, may claim it as against the proprietors, whether above or below him, upon the stream, and his prior occupancy gives him a prior title to the use of the water for that purpose. Though such an occupancy deprives the upper proprietor of the right to do the same on his own land which he otherwise would have had, it is *damnum absque injuria*. The proprietor below could not, after such erection, raise a dam upon his own land so as thereby to obstruct the wheels of the prior occupant above. Up to the time of this occupation, these rights were equal and the same. But when the first occupant had made an appropriation of the use, to that extent he acquired a priority with which the others had no right to interfere.

But this applies only to the extent to which he shall actually have appropriated and occupied the stream. All the surplus power may be occupied and appropriated by another riparian proprietor for mill purposes, in the same manner as

---

[1] Gould v. Boston Duck Co., 13 Gray, 442, 450; Hazen v. Essex Co., 12 Cush. 475; Kelly v. Natoma Water Co., 6 Cal. 105.

the first had a right to occupy the part he did.   Nor can the
first proprietor, afterwards, raise his dam to the injury of the
second occupier.

*As to such surplus, the second occupier becomes [*337]
the first, with all the rights to the same of a first
occupant.

The upper occupant, though second in point of time, may
place his mill so low that the pond of the lower mill shall
flow upon its wheel, if he pleases.   But he cannot, in that
case, complain of the lower mill for setting back water upon
his works.

So if the occupant leave a surplus of power unappropriated at first, he may occupy it at any subsequent time, by
raising his dam or otherwise, if no one shall, in the mean
time, have occupied it.[1]

19. While the effect to be given to a prior occupation of
a mill-privilege may be considered as settled, there may obviously arise, at times, nice questions as to precedence of
right between the owners of two mill-privileges upon the
same stream, where only one can be practically used, and
each has undertaken to gain this right by prior occupancy.
Thus cases have occurred where two parties have simulta-
neously, or nearly so, begun to do acts in view of occupying
a privilege upon their respective lands.   In one case, one
proprietor began in the morning to cut brush growing upon
the spot on which he was about to erect a dam, and to drive
stakes at different points on each side of the stream, to indicate the position and height of the intended dam, and an
upper owner began at noon to dig stones upon the bank of
the stream, and to place them in the bed of the stream, as a
part of the foundation of his dam.   Both parties proceeded
with all reasonable despatch to complete their respective
dams, and the same were in fact only a few rods apart.   In
an action by the upper owner against the lower one for flowing his land and destroying his occupied mill-privilege, the

[1] Cary v. Daniels, 8 Metc. 466, 477.

question was made, which of the two had the better right by prior occupancy. A case substantially like this was argued before the Supreme Judicial Court in Worcester, [*338] October, *1833, and the opinion of the court, given by Shaw, C. J., though never reported, was to the effect that the one who first commenced work, *upon the soil,* either by cutting trees, or digging stones or earth, for the purpose of actually building a dam, may be deemed to have first begun his dam. But if the acts of cutting brush, setting stakes, &c., were for the purpose of ascertaining whether there existed a fall of water, &c., or whether the situation was a favorable one for the erection of a mill, and the like, it would not be a beginning. These acts were stated as serving to point out the line of demarcation where the acts of building began. That the stakes were driven might, or might not, be evidence. *Was it a part of the operation of building?* If it was, it would be a beginning. If not, but to show his intention, it would not have that effect.[1]

20. It may further be remarked, that no preference which may be acquired by an actual appropriation of a water-power can be gained by an intention to appropriate it, however strongly expressed. Nor will the doing of an act which would, if so intended, be a part of the act of appropriation of a power, such as digging a trench in which to conduct water, operate as an appropriation of the same, unless done with an intention to have that effect.[2] But if one begins a dam in order to appropriate a water-privilege, it will give him a prior right to the same in preference to one who subsequently commences a dam, though he completes it before the first is finished.[3]

If the appropriation be an actual one, and to some useful purpose, it secures the right so far that it may not be infringed by a subsequent appropriation by others.[4] But the

---

[1] Bemis *v.* Upham. See Kimball *v.* Gearhart, 12 Cal. 27.

[2] Maeris *v.* Bicknell, 7 Cal. 261.

[3] Kelly *v.* Natoma Water Co., 6 Cal. 105.

[4] M'Kinney *v.* Smith, 21 Cal. 381.

limit of the claim which is secured by an appropriation, is
the extent to which it is actually made.   If there is any surplus, it is open for others to avail themselves of it.¹

21. Among the restrictions imposed by the statute upon
the right of a mill-owner to flow the lands of a riparian proprietor, is that which has already been mentioned, by which
it is in the power of a jury to prescribe how high, and during
what portion of the year, the flowing may be sustained. And
if in violation of this limitation the mill-owner shall
flow to *a higher point, or during a greater portion [*339]
of the year than that prescribed by such verdict, he
will, as to such excess, be subject to the common-law rights
and remedies of such land-owner for the injury thereby oc-
casioned.²

22. But if one acquires a right to flow the land of another
during certain portions of the year, or to a definite height
by grant, and transcends this right, he will for such excess
be subject to the provisions of the mill act for the recovery
of the damages thereby occasioned.³ But it is left doubtful
whether a party who has taken a conveyance defining his
right to flow as to its extent, or has agreed in a legal form as
to the height to which he shall flow as a substitute for a
legal process, can, afterwards, increase the flowing, and claim
for it the protection or benefit of the mill acts of Massachu-
setts.⁴

23. Another important restriction in the right of flowing
lands is, that the statute extends its protection only to such
as are owners of existing mills, and exercise the right for the
use and operation of such mills. The consequence is, that
if one has a dam, but no existing mill, or if, having had such
mill, he abandons it, but retains his dam, and lands of third

¹ M'Kinney v. Smith, 21 Cal. 381 ; Ortman v. Dixon, 13 Cal. 33.
² Hill v. Sayles, 12 Metc. 142; s. c., 4 Cush. 549; Johnson v. Kittredge, 17
Mass. 76, 80 ; Winkley v. Salisbury Mg. Co., 14 Gray, 443; Gile v. Stevens, 13
Gray, 146.
³ Tourtellot v. Phelps, 4 Gray, 370 ; Judd v. Wells, 12 Metc. 504.
⁴ Burnham v. Story, 3 Allen, 379.

persons are thereby damaged, the owner of such dam is liable to actions at common law in favor of those whose lands are injured.[1]

24. But though he would lose the benefit of the statute by abandoning his mill, yet if his mill or his dam be destroyed by flood or fire, or become dilapidated by age or natural decay, the proprietor will have a reasonable time in which to rebuild or repair the same, depending, as to what that shall be, upon the circumstances of each particular case.[2]

If the mill-owner cease to use and occupy his land for mill purposes beyond a reasonable time, or if he do acts of abandonment, like removing his dam or mill, accompanied by evidence of an express intent, like a declaration [*340] to that *effect, to abandon the right of flowing another's land, it would extinguish his right to do so under the statute, and, for any subsequent flowing, he would be subjected to the liabilities of the common law.

How far this would be the effect, if such abandonment were made by a tenant for life or years of a mill, so as to bind the rights of a reversioner or remainder-man, or how far an infant would be bound by such acts, after he should have arrived at age, may be considered as questions not necessarily involved in the above decision, which is understood to apply only to cases of owners in fee, who are competent to bind the estate. And it may be assumed to be a rule of law that such abandonment can only be made by such as have a disposing power over the estate.

25. In applying the doctrine of abandonment to what would be regarded as sufficient evidence of its having been made, it would be deemed *prima facie* evidence of this, if there had been a discontinuance of the use for twenty years, though even that may be controlled by proof of the existence

---

[1] Baird v. Hunter, 12 Pick. 556; Slack v. Lyon, 9 Pick. 62; Fitch v. Stevens, 4 Metc. 426; Sampson v. Bradford, 6 Cush. 303; Farrington v. Blish, 14 Me. 423; Hodges v. Hodges, 5 Metc. 205.

[2] French v. Braintree Mg. Co., 23 Pick. 220; Cowell v. Thayer, 5 Metc. 253.

of causes, during that time, which have prevented the owner of the privilege from exercising the act of flowing.[1]

So the effect to be ascribed to a cesser to use a right to flow another's land, when once acquired, accompanied by a declaration of intent, may depend upon the circumstance whether the party causing it shall have acquired the right to do so without payment of damages therefor, or whether he is subject to damages for continuing the same. In the one case, the removal of his mill, and a declaration by the mill-owner that the privilege would not be occupied again, would not be deemed a legal abandonment by which his right to resume it at his pleasure was lost, whereas, in the other, it would be an abandonment, and the respective rights of the land-owner and of the owner of the privilege *would be restored as they stood before such right [*341] had been acquired.[2]

26. The law authorizing the mill-owner to flow another's land by making compensation therefor, so far regards this right like a mere license, and not an estate in another's land, that where a jury had assessed a sum in gross, to be paid by such mill-owner for the right to flow the land of the complainant for all future time, and the mill-owner, at once, ceased to flow it, and, by a written declaration, abandoned all right to continue to flow the same, it was held that he thereby exonerated himself from liability to pay the damages assessed for such future flowing.[3]

27. Nor, though the cases speak of this right as one of perpetual easement, is it, in fact, either an easement in all respects, or an estate in another's land, for, in the first place, the land-owner, if he can do so, may prevent the mill-owner from setting back the water of his pond upon the land of the former by erecting dikes or embankments to guard the

[1] French v. Braintree Mg. Co., 23 Pick. 220; Hunt v. Whitney, 4 Metc. 603; post, chap. 5, sect. 6.

[2] Williams v. Nelson, 23 Pick. 141, 147; French v. Braintree Mg. Co., supra; post, chap. 5, sect. 6.

[3] Hunt v. Whitney, 4 Metc. 603.

same;[1] or he may occupy the water upon his land by making a boom thereof, in which to hold his logs, or may erect piers therein, although he thereby diminishes the capacity of the pond to contain a body of water.[2] And such flowing is never regarded a disseizin of the owner of the land, nor an interference with his right to convey the same.[3] Nor does an oral agreement of the land-owner with the mill-owner, not to claim damages, though binding upon him, run with the land, so as to constitute an encumbrance thereon, or prevent a grantee of such land-owner from claiming [*342] damages occasioned by a subsequent flowing of *the land.[4] And it may be remarked, that the claim on the one side and the liability on the other in respect to damages is so far a personal one, that the one is liable only for the time he shall have owned the mill, and the claim of the other begins and ends with his ownership of the estate.[5]

28. Another limitation of the right of a mill-owner, in the exercise of his power to flow under the statute, is, that he holds it subject to the public right to use navigable streams for purposes of highways,[6] and he may not flow so as to injure an existing highway.[7]

29. Although the injuries thus far spoken of, as being occasioned by flowing under the provisions of the mill acts, have been chiefly those done to the surface or the productions of land, it was held that where, by raising a pond of water, it set it back through an existing underground drain into a cellar, the remedy of the person injured thereby was

[1] Williams v. Nelson, 23 Pick. 141; Murdock v. Stickney, 8 Cush. 116; Bates v. Weymouth Iron Co., 8 Cush. 548.

[2] Jordan v. Woodward, 40 Me. 317.

[3] Charles v. Monson & Brimfield Mg. Co., 17 Pick. 70.

[4] Fitch v. Seymour, 9 Metc. 462.

[5] Holmes v. Drew, 7 Pick. 141; Charles v. Monson & Brimfield Mg. Co., supra.

[6] Knox v. Chaloner, 42 Me. 150; Veasie v. Dwinel, 50 Maine, 479, 490; Davis v. Winslow, 51 Maine, 294; Gerrish v. Brown, Ib. 256.

[7] Commonwealth v. Stevens, 10 Pick. 247; Andover v. Sutton, 12 Metc. 182; Commonwealth v. Fisher, 6 Metc. 433; Treat v. Lord, 42 Me. 522, 561.

under the provisions of this act. And where such flowing obstructed a drain which the owner had, without right, entered upon the land of the mill-owner, the latter was not responsible either under the statute or by the common law, to owners of cellars whose drains discharged into the first-mentioned drain, although by obstructing that the cellars were injured.[1]

30. While a mill-owner may flow the land of another under the statute, he is, in turn, protected from having his own mill injured by another mill-owner flowing back water upon the same, if the upper mill be the more ancient one.[2]

31. In one important respect, the construction given by *the courts of Maine to the Mill Acts of that [*343] State differs from that of the courts of Massachusetts to similar acts in the latter State. Thus, while in Massachusetts the act of flowing another's land is in itself a tort which gives him a right to maintain a complaint therefor, and, if continued for twenty years under a claim of right, acquiesced in by the land-owner, will create a prescriptive right to continue it, though no actual appreciable damage shall have, thereby, been occasioned to the land-owner;[3] in Maine, no right to maintain a complaint exists until some such damage has thereby been occasioned. Nor will any prescriptive right be gained until twenty years' enjoyment thereof by user, after the flowing shall have begun to cause damage to the land-owner. And inasmuch as the process by complaint has superseded that at common law, the owner of land is without remedy for the same being flowed, until he can show that he has thereby sustained actual damage.[4]

---

[1] Cotton v. Pocasset Mg. Co., 13 Metc. 429.

[2] French v. Braintree Mg. Co., 23 Pick. 216, 220.

[3] Williams v. Nelson, 23 Pick. 141, 145; Ray v. Fletcher, 12 Cush. 200, 206.

[4] Tinkham v. Arnold, 3 Me. 120; Hathorn v. Stinson, 10 Me. 224; s. c., 12 Me. 183; Seidensparger v. Spear, 17 Me. 123; Nelson v. Butterfield, 21 Me. 220; Wood v. Kelley, 30 Me. 47; Wentworth v. Sandford Mg. Co., 33 Me. 547; Burleigh v. Lumbert, 34 Me. 322; Underwood v. N. Wayne Co., 41 Me. 291; *ante*, chap. 1, sect. 4, pl. 33; chap. 3, sect. 5, pl. 9.

Nor would the flowing of itself be presumptive evidence of damage done; actual damage must be shown.[1]

32. So that if one were to claim a prescriptive right to flow land of another, by twenty years' enjoyment, the claim might be met by evidence that he had voluntarily suspended such flowing for one or more years, whereby the damage to the same was during that time suspended, unless the suspension were accompanied by acts indicating an intention to continue it, such, for instance, as being engaged, during the time, in repairing the dam or the like.[2]

33. These mill acts, and all others of a like character made by the several States in derogation of the com-
[*344] mon *law, are necessarily local in their operation, since no one State can authorize its citizens to violate the common-law rights of citizens of other States beyond the limits of its own territory. Thus where a citizen of New Hampshire erected a dam upon his own land, which set back the water upon the land of another within the State of Maine, as the erection of the mill and dam were not authorized by the law of Maine, and the land-owner was without remedy under the statute process of that court, it was held that he might maintain an action for the injury thereby sustained at common law.[3]

34. In United States v. Ames, Woodbury, J. was inclined to hold that the statute of Massachusetts as to mills did not extend to lands belonging to the United States, though lying within the limits of Massachusetts, and such besides as the United States held as purchasers, and not by the exercise of eminent domain, but over which the State had ceded the jurisdiction. In that case the owner of a mill and dam flowed lands belonging to the United States, but never otherwise appropriated to use. The mill and dam stood within the territory over which the State retained its original juris-

---

[1] Gleason v. Tuttle, 46 Me. 288; Underwood v. N. Wayne Co., supra.

[2] Gleason v. Tuttle, 46 Me. 288.

[3] Wooster v. Great Falls Mg. Co., 39 Me. 246; Worster v. Winnipiseogee Lake Co., 5 Fost. 525; Farnum v. Blackstone Canal Corp., 1 Sumn. 46.

diction. The point was not settled by the judge, though the right thus to flow, he says, " seems to me to be with difficulty vindicated." To other minds it might seem otherwise. The proposition, it will be perceived, is not that the mill-owner may interfere with any mill or works of the United States, but simply that he may, under a general law of the Commonwealth, flow a parcel of land which the United States holds within the Commonwealth under a deed of purchase. It involves the question whether the United States holding lands within a State, by purchase, are exempt from the lawful easements and servitudes to which such lands were subject, in respect to the adjacent *estates before and when they purchased the [*345] same. Suppose it had been a right of way, or an ancient channel by which water flowed to a mill on the adjacent estate, and neither of these interfered with the full enjoyment of the land, so far as it was needed for any practical use by the United States. Could it make any difference that the jurisdiction over the territory had been ceded by the state? That could be done without changing the property or incidents of ownership in the estates within the ceded portions of the state.

Thus, suppose A's grantor, by his mill and dam, had flowed the land of B's grantor, for fifteen years, by paying annual damages therefor, and had been protected in so doing by the statute. If the state should then cede simply the jurisdiction to the United States over a portion of its territory, which should include the estates of A and B, would the latter at once be thereby clothed with common-law power and rights, and have a right of action upon the case for such flowing, against A, or have a right to abate his dam as a nuisance? In the case reported, the statutes upon the subject of mills were in full force when the United States purchased the land, and unless as purchaser they acquired altogether better rights than their vendor had to bestow, it is not easy to see how they could, without some special appro-

priation of the land or water-power to use, exercise other or
different rights in this respect from other land-holders. The
price they paid must have been predicated upon the servitudes and inconveniences under which the vendor had held
the land, as well as the advantages or intrinsic value it may
have had. And it is not easy to see, upon equitable grounds,
how, the moment the property shall have passed hands, the
adjacent owners should be deprived of the incidental advantages which till then belonged to their lands, while the
land thus purchased should be relieved from its disadvan-
tages.[1]

[*346]   *The reasoning of the court of California seems to
be quite as sound, and far more consonant with the
sense of justice of a common mind, when considering the
right in the United States to take gold or control its disposition within the territory incorporated into the State of California. " Nor do we admit that the United States, holding
as they do, with reference to the public property in the minerals, only the position of a private proprietor, with the exemption from state taxation, having no municipal sovereignty or right of eminent domain within the limits of the
state, could, in derogation of the rights of the local sovereign to govern the relations of the citizens of the state, and
to prescribe the rules of property and its mode of disposition
and tenure, enter upon, or authorize an entry upon, private
property, for the purpose of extracting such minerals im-
bedded in the soil, which could only be done by lessening or
destroying the value of the inheritance.

" The United States, like any other proprietor, can only
exercise their rights to the mineral on private property, in
subordination to such rules and regulations as the local
sovereign may prescribe. Until such rules and regulations
are established, the landed proprietor may successfully resist
in the courts of the state all attempts at invasion of his
property, whether by the direct action of the United States,

[1] 1 Woodb. & M. 76.

or by virtue of any pretended license under their authority." [1]

35. The statute of Maine has one provision distinct from
any that is found in that of Massachusetts, authorizing a
mill-owner to divert water from a stream for the purpose of
creating an operative power for his mill, by means of a canal
which shall not exceed one mile in length. Commissioners,
moreover, instead of a jury, are appointed, in the first place,
to appraise the damages, and fix the height to which the
mill-owner may flow back the water.[2]

*36. The statute of Wisconsin is so nearly in sub- [*347]
stance like that of Massachusetts, that it is only necessary to cite it.[3]

37. In Rhode Island, a party aggrieved by the flowing of
his lands, or their being otherwise injured by the mill-dam
of another, whether the same are situate above or below
such dam, may sue for the same in an action at common
law. If he prevails in such suit, his damages are to be assessed as in Massachusetts, and, upon paying the same, the
mill-owner may continue to flow or damage the plaintiff's
land. There is also a provision requiring a mill-owner not
to detain the natural flow of any stream more than twelve
hours, at any one time, except on Sunday, if requested
by a mill-owner below him to suffer the natural flow of the
stream.[4]

38. Under what may be called the Virginia system of
mill acts, an essentially different principle is involved from
that in Massachusetts, in this, that while, by the latter, the
mill-owner acquires, at most, only an involuntary easement
in another's land, by the law of Virginia he acquires a title
to the land occupied. And instead of requiring, as in Massachusetts, that the mill-owner should have so far an entire

[1] Boggs v. Merced Mining Co., 14 Cal. 279, 235. See Hendricks v. Johnson,
6 Port. 472.

[2] Me. Rev. Stat. 1857, c. 92.

[3] Wisc. Rev. Stat. 1858, c. 56.

[4] R. I. Rev. Stat. 1857, c. 88, p. 215. See Mowry v. Sheldon, 2 R. I. 369.

mill-privilege that his dam and mill shall be erected on his own land, it authorizes one owning land upon one side only of a stream to appropriate land lying upon the opposite side, upon which to construct his dam and mill, by a process of law called a *condemning* of the land.

The general provisions of the act are, that any one owning land upon one side of a stream, extending to the thread thereof, or to the opposite bank, but not the bank itself, whereby he could build a dam for occupying a mill-site on his own land, may apply to the court for a writ of *ad quod damnum*, directed to the sheriff, under which a jury is summoned, who are authorized to locate one acre of [*348] land for *the purpose, and appraise the same at its true value. The jury may also examine what lands above or below will probably be thereby overflowed, and the damage which will thereby be occasioned, and whether the health of the neighborhood will be thereby injuriously affected. This may be done with a view of building a mill, machine, engine, and dam.

Similar provisions exist, in most respects, where the mill-owner owns the land in fee on both sides of the stream, but the erection of a dam thereon would cause damage to the owners of land above.

But if, by the erection of such dam and flowing, a head of water for the same, the mansion-house, offices, curtilage, or garden, or orchard of another will be overflowed, or the health of the neighborhood be injuriously affected thereby, the court may not give permission to erect the same. Upon an adjudication by the court in favor of the erection of such mill, and the payment by the applicant of the assessed value of the acres so appropriated, and the damages assessed by the jury, he becomes seized in fee simple of the land appropriated, and is authorized to erect a dam, mill, machine, or engine, provided he begins them within one year, and completes them within three.

It will be perceived that the proceedings as to condemning

the land and assessing the damages are all preliminary to the erection of the dam and mill, whereas in Massachusetts, until the mill-owner shall have erected his dam and mill, he cannot avail himself of the protection of the statute.

Provision is further made for a second writ *ad quod damnum*, in case the mill-owner shall have occasion to increase the extent of the flowing for his mill.

It was a remark of Carr, J., in view of these statutes, that " no man undertakes to build a mill with us until he has obtained leave of the court of the county in which the mill is situate." [1]

*The mills contemplated by these statutes are [*349] " water grist-mills, or other machine or engine useful to the public." [2]   But no power is thereby given to the court to condemn land for a tail-race to a mill.[3]

In applying this law, the court never grants leave to erect a second mill which will destroy a privilege which they have already authorized another to occupy.[4]

39. There is in Missouri a statute in most respects like that of Virginia, extending to cases where the applicant for leave to establish a mill owns the land upon both sides of the stream, and will thereby cause damage to the lands of others, and to those where he owns only upon one side of the stream. And there is a provision for a penalty of double damages to be paid by any one who shall have erected a mill upon a stream whereby the property of others is injured, without having first obtained permission of the court to erect the same, in the manner prescribed, or the court may enjoin or abate the same as a nuisance.[5]

40. While the statutes of Alabama, which were similar to those of Virginia and Missouri, were considered as in force,

[1] Nichols *v.* Aylor, 7 Leigh, 546, 562.
[2] Tate's Dig. Laws of Va., 1841, p. 692 ; Hunter *v.* Matthews, 1 Robins. Va. 468.
[3] Coalter *v.* Hunter, 4 Rand. 58.
[4] Humes *v.* Shugart, 10 Leigh, 332.
[5] Mo. Rev. Stat. 1855, c. 112.

the court held that, in case of a competing of two or more applicants for leave to erect mills, the first applicant acquired an inchoate right to preference.[1] And in a case in Missouri, where S. and M. owned distinct mill-sites upon the same stream, at the distance of a mile and a half from each other ; but from the nature of the stream, if both were occupied, the lower one would flow out the upper one, so that a preference must be given to one or the other, and each made application to the court for leave to occupy his site ; the jury found that, if the upper one were occupied, it would damage the land of the lower one to a small extent, while the [*350] lower one if *occupied would not damage the land of any one, but simply deepen the current of the stream so as to destroy the upper site for mill purposes, and the court granted the leave to the lower site and denied it to the upper one.[2]

41. The statute of Arkansas is substantially the same as that of Missouri.[3] And the same may be said of that of Kentucky in its general effect. But, among some of its provisions, the jury are limited to one acre which shall be needed for the dam, but may condemn land for a canal an hundred feet in width above or below the site of the mill ; but, like the statutes of Virginia and the other States cited, they are restricted from overflowing any house, garden, or orchard, and from injuring any existing mill. Nor may a mill be authorized to draw the water away from any existing mill, or to injure the vested rights of any one in any water-works upon the same watercourse. The effect of being condemned, upon the title of the land to which it is applied, is the same as under the Virginia statute.[4]

An applicant under this statute must own the land, in fee-simple, upon one or both sides of the stream.[5] And the courts are very exact in their requirements of such applicant

[1] Hendricks v. Johnson, 6 Port. 472.   [2] Hook v. Smith, 6 Mo. 225.

[3] Dig. Ark. Stat. c. 114.

[4] 2 Ky. Rev. Stat., Stant. ed. 1860, c. 67.

[5] Smith v. Connely, 1 Monr. 58.

to state clearly in his petition the grounds upon which he rests his claim for the condemnation of another's land.[1]

42. The statute of Mississippi is like that of Virginia and Missouri in all important respects.[2]

43. The statutes of North Carolina partake somewhat of both those of Virginia and Massachusetts. Thus one may, upon a writ of *ad quod damnum*, take land of another for the purpose of erecting a dam. And if by the erection of a dam the land of another is flowed and damaged, *the land-owner may have his annual damages as- [*351] sessed by a jury under a complaint, instead of maintaining an action at common law for a recovery of the same.[3]

Nor can one whose land is flowed, maintain an action at common law for the injury thereby occasioned, until relief shall have been sought by a petition for annual damages.[4]

But he may recover under the statute for damages to his land, by being prevented by the dam of a mill-owner from draining the same, although the waters of the pond do not actually set back upon his land.[5]

44. In most respects, the laws of Indiana and Illinois upon this subject are like those of Missouri, giving the mill-owner a right, upon a writ of *ad quod damnum*, to have land condemned in his favor, upon which to erect a dam, or to assess the damages to be occasioned to the lands of others by erecting a dam upon his own land.[6] And those of Florida are so nearly identical with the statutes of Virginia that it is unnecessary to repeat them.[7]

45. These proceedings under a writ of *ad quod damnum*, in which respect all the States adopting the Virginia system have the same general form, being in derogation of the com-

---

1 M'Afee *v.* Kennedy, 1 Litt. 92.
2 Miss. Stat., Howard & Hutchinson's ed., 1840, c. 13.
3 No. Car. Rev. Code, 1854, c. 71.
4 King *v.* Shufford, 10 Ired. 100.
5 Johnston *v.* Roane, 3 Jones, Law, 523.
6 1 Ind: Rev. Stat. 1852, c. 48 ; Ill. Stat., ed. 1858, p. 768.
7 Thomp. Dig. Flor. Laws, p. 401.

mon-law rights of the parties injured by the loss of, or damage to, his land, must be strictly pursued, or the injured party is remitted to his remedy at common law.[1]

And though, where such proceedings have been regularly conducted, a judgment in the writ of *ad quod damnum* would be conclusive upon the subject of the damages therein provided for, it has been held, in Indiana, that such assessment will not affect the remedy of an injured party [*352] *for an injury which was not foreseen or estimated by the jury.[2]

And so important is it that one should have obtained authority from the court for erecting a mill and dam, in order to avail himself of the protection of the law in respect to the same, that where one had, without preliminary proceedings, begun to erect a dam and mill, and another obtained leave of court upon a writ of *ad quod damnum*, and proceeded to erect a dam and mill below the first, it was held that, though subsequent in time, he was thereby prior in right, and might go on and flow out the works of the upper owner.[3]

But in Kentucky, where a mill had stood thirty-three years, the unobstructed use of it during that time was held to raise a legal presumption that it was, originally, legally established.[4]

46. To complete what is intended to be said of these local statutes, it may be repeated, that the statutes of Alabama, which were substantially like those of Virginia, were declared unconstitutional by the courts of that State, so far as they relate to taking the lands of one man for the use of another.[5] And a statute in Maryland, which had existed for many years, authorizing any person desirous of establishing

---

[1] Hendricks *v.* Johnson, 6 Port. 472 ; Shackleford *v.* Coffey, 4 J. J. Marsh. 40; Wolf *v.* Coffey, Ibid. 41. See Garrett *v.* Bailey, 4 Harringt. 197.

[2] Kepley *v.* Taylor, 1 Blackf. 492; Smith *v.* Olmstead, 5 Blackf. 37; Bell *v.* Elliott, 5 Blackf. 113.

[3] Hendricks *v.* Johnson, *supra.*

[4] M'Dougle *v.* Clark, 7 B. Monr. 448.

[5] Sadler *v.* Langham, 34 Ala. 311.

a *forging* mill, to apply for a writ of *ad quod damnum*, and under it to have an hundred acres of land condemned to him for that purpose, was repealed in 1822.[1]

*SECTION VI.   [*353]

OF RIGHTS IN RAIN AND SURFACE WATER.

1. Rain and surface water flowing from a higher to a lower field.
2. Case of Martin *v.* Riddle.   As to the law in such case.
3. Easement and servitude of water between upper and lower fields.
4. Case of Kauffman *v.* Griesemer, illustrating this doctrine.
5. Law of Louisiana on the same subject.
6. How far the rule in such cases applies in cities.
7. How far upper owner may deprive lower of surface water.
8. Case of Broadbent *v.* Ramsbotham.   On same subject.
9. Case of Rawstron *v.* Taylor.   Right to drain upper field.
10. Rule as to right to divert, if spring become a stream.
11. Case of Luther *v.* Winnisimmet Company.   As to rights in surface water.

1. Before proceeding to consider the law as to water percolating through the earth, beneath its surface, it is necessary to refer to a few principles which seem now to be pretty well settled as to the respective rights of adjacent land-owners, in respect to waters which fall in rain, or are in any way found upon the surface, but not embraced under the head of streams or watercourses, nor constituting permanent bodies of water, like ponds, lakes, and the like.   It may be stated as a general principle, that, where the situation of two adjoining fields is such that the water falling or collected by melting snows, and the like, upon one, naturally descends upon the other, it must be suffered by the lower one to be discharged upon his land if desired by the owner of the upper field.   But the latter cannot, by artificial trenches or otherwise, cause the natural mode of its being discharged to be changed to the injury of the lower field, as by conducting

---

[1] Binney's case, 2 Bland, Ch. 99, 116.

it by new channels in unusual quantities on to particular parts of the lower field.[1]

This question has arisen in several different forms, [*354] and *the law upon the subject can be best illustrated by referring to some of the decided cases.

2. In Martin *v.* Riddle, there were adjacent parcels of land belonging to the plaintiff and defendant, that of the defendant being upon a lower level than that of the plaintiff. The water that fell upon the plaintiff's land in rain, as well as that arising from certain springs in the same, found their way along a natural channel from the plaintiff's on to the defendant's land. A proprietor upon the slope of the acclivity above the plaintiff's land opened certain other springs in his land by excavating the earth, the water from which found its way into the plaintiff's land, and thence through this natural channel to the defendant's land, increasing the quantity usually flowing therein, and injuring the defendant's land. In order to prevent this, the defendant constructed an embankment across this natural channel, and thereby prevented the water from flowing from the plaintiff's land, and for this he brought his action. It was held, that, while the owners of land are entitled to the benefit of waters naturally running to the same, they are bound to bear the inconvenience thereof, if any, and that living springs are to be suffered to flow in their natural channel, and may not be stopped by one proprietor to the injury of another. In general, the same rule applies to rain-water as to living springs, in respect to its draining from lands upon which it

---

[1] *Ante,* chap. 3, sect. 1, pl. 7 ; Pardessus, Traité des Servitudes, 130; 3 Toullier, Droit Civil Français, 374, ed. 1824. There is a statute in Massachusetts which authorizes the owner of a swamp or meadow, under certain limitations, to construct a drain or ditch from his own across the land of an adjacent owner for the purpose of draining the same. But this extends only to the draining one's land through another's to a pond or stream capable of receiving the water, without causing injury to his neighbor's land. It does not authorize his conducting the water from his own land on to that of his neighbor to its injury. He would be liable to an action for so doing. Gen. Stat. c. 148 ; Sherman *v.* Tobey, 3 Allen, 7.

falls, a lower field being subject to the flow of such water from the higher one. Nor may the owner of the lower one construct embankments which will prevent this. On the other hand, the owner of the upper field may not construct drains or excavations so as to form new channels on to the lower field, nor can he collect the water of several channels and discharge it on to the lower field so as to increase the *wash* upon the same. He may, however, make whatever drains in his own land are required by good husbandry, either open or covered, and may discharge these into the natural channel or channels, even though by so doing he *increases the quantity flowing therein. And [*355] if there is any difficulty in ascertaining what the natural channel is, that will be taken to be such in which the water has been accustomed to flow for the period requisite to acquire a prescriptive right. But if the owner of the upper field throw an unnatural quantity of water upon the lower one, he may not stop it altogether, if, in so doing, he throws back the water upon the land of an intermediate proprietor, as, in the present case, the increase was occasioned by the act of a more remote proprietor. And the court held the defendant in the action liable for creating the obstruction complained of.[1]

3. The owner of the upper field, in such a case, has a natural easement, as it is called, to have the water that falls upon his own land flow off the same upon the field below, which is charged with a corresponding servitude, in the nature of dominant and servient tenements.[2] It may be dif-

---

[1] Martin v. Riddle, 26 Penn. St. 415, in note; 3 Toullier, Droit Civil Français, 356 ; Miller v. Laubach, 47 Penn. 155.

[2] Laumier v. Francis, 23 Mo. 181 ; Bellows v. Sackett, 15 Barb. 96, 102 ; Code Nap., Art. 640; Ersk. Inst. 352, fol. ed. ; Orleans Navigation Co. v. Mayor, &c., 2 Mart. 214, 232; Adams v. Harrison, 4 La. Ann. 165; Lattimore v. Davis, 14 La. 161 ; Hays v. Hays, 19 La. 351 ; Kauffman v. Griesemer, 26 Penn. St. 407, 413.

The same rule applies to all matters which, from the relative situation of two estates, are naturally cast from the one upon the other, such as rocks, slides of earth, and the like, falling from a higher upon a lower parcel. The

ficult to reconcile what is here said with some of the positions to be found in an earlier part of this work (p. *211 *et
seq.*), especially the language of the court of Massachusetts,
that "the obstruction of surface water or an alteration in the
flow of it affords no cause of action in behalf of a person
who may suffer loss or detriment therefrom, against one who
does no act inconsistent with the due exercise of dominion
over his own soil."[1] But the doctrine as above stated is
in accordance with recent opinions of some of the American
Courts. Thus in Beard *v.* Murphy,[2] the defendant stopped
the surface flow from the plaintiff's land on to his by a barrier of boards and clay upon the defendant's land. The
court say "the plaintiff claimed, that, if the surface water
naturally falling on his land would run off upon the defendant's land, the defendant had no right to put up any obstruction to prevent its continuing to do so." "This the court
granted and charged to be law." But inasmuch as what
the defendant did was to prevent filthy water flowing from
plaintiff's house into his well, it was held that he was justified in stopping the same, although he, at the same time,
stopped some of the natural flow of proper surface water.
On the other hand, the owner of an upper parcel cannot drain
the water that stands thereon by artificial channels on to a
lower one belonging to another without his consent. This
was the point in Miller *v.* Lauback. The owner may drain
his land by ditches within his land, for agricultural purposes,
but one owner has no right to insist that another shall suffer
the water in his land to percolate and come into that of the
former though it would be for his benefit.[3]

lower tenement in such case is obliged to receive what is thus cast upon it,
though the owner thereof may protect it, if possible, by works of art, to guard
against injuries thereby occasioned. 3 Toullier, Droit Civil Français, 356.

The owner of the upper tenement may by prescription acquire a right to
roll the stones from his land upon that of his neighbor. But, without gaining
such a right, he may not cause those upon his land to roll on to that of his
neighbor. 2 Fournel, Traité du Voisinage, 177.

[1] Gannon *v.* Hargadon, 10 Allen, 110.

[2] Beard *v.* Murphy, 37 Verm. 104. See also Miller *v.* Lauback, 47 Penn. 155.

[3] Buffum *v.* Harris, 5 R. I. 253.

And the prevailing doctrine, applicable to cases like these, seems to be this, if, for purposes of improving and cultivating his land, a land-owner raises or fills it, so that the water which falls in rain or snow upon an adjacent owner's land, and which formerly flowed on to the first-mentioned parcel, is prevented from so doing, to the injury of the adjacent parcel, the owner of the latter is without remedy, since the other party has done no more than he had a right to do. It was accordingly held in Bentz v. Armstrong, that where several owners of house lots on which houses had been erected, divided them into separate estates, each parcel was to take care of the surface water which gathers upon it, without its flowing from the one on to the other.[1] And in a recent case in New York, the court say, " I know of no principle which will prevent the owner of land from filling up the wet and marshy places on his own soil for its amelioration and his own advantage, because his neighbor's land is so situated as to be incommoded by it. Such a doctrine would militate against the well-settled rule, that the owner of land has full dominion over the whole space above and below the surface." [2]

4. This matter is further treated of in Kauffman v. Griesemer, above cited, in which case there was a spring of water upon the plaintiff's land, which, as well as the rain that fell upon his field which sloped towards the defendant's land, *found its way to a point near the land of the [*356] defendant, but was prevented from flowing upon it,
by a small natural elevation or rise in the land, except in times of freshets. The plaintiff dug a channel through this elevated portion of his land into the defendant's land, whereby the water from the land of the plaintiff flowed on to that of the defendant. To prevent this, the latter created an effectual obstruction, whereby the discharge of the water from

[1] Bentz v. Armstrong, 8 W. & Serg. 40.
[2] Goodale v. Tuttle, 29 N. Y. 467. See also Frasier v. Brown, 12 Ohio St. 300. See post, p. *357.

the plaintiff's land was prevented, except in times of freshet. The court held, in accordance with the doctrine of Martin *v.* Riddle, above cited, that, though a man may drain his own land by discharging the water in the channels through which it naturally flows, and may clear the impediments in a stream within his own land, though the effect should be to increase the quantity of water flowing through these channels upon the land of a neighboring proprietor, he has no right to dig an artificial ditch or drain whereby to conduct the water from his own land upon that of another in any but its natural course. And, consequently, that in the present case the defendant was justified in creating the obstruction he did to the flow of the water in this ditch. And not only so, but so far as the defendant's land was upon a higher level than a part of the plaintiff's, he had a right to have the water flow from his land upon that of the plaintiff. The language of the court upon the subject is : " Because water is descendible by nature, the owner of a dominant or superior heritage has an easement in the servient or inferior tenement for the discharge of all waters which by nature rise in or flow or fall upon the superior." The limit or extent to which this remark reaches is indicated by the language of the court, who add : " This obligation " (to receive the water flowing from the superior heritage) " applies only to waters which flow naturally without the art of man ; those which come from springs, or from rain falling directly on the heritage, or even by the natural dispositions of the place, are the only [*357] ones to which this expression of the law can be *ap-plied. . . . . This easement is called a *servitude* in the Roman law." [1]

5. The courts of Louisiana agree with that of Pennsylvania in limiting this servitude in the lower heritage to the water that *naturally* runs from the superior one, and only

---

[1] Kauffman *v.* Griesemer, 26 Penn. St. 407, 413 ; 5 Duranton, Cours de Droit Français, 167 ; *ante,* pp. *15, *226 ; Pardessus, Traité des Servitudes, § 86, pp. 119 – 122 ; Ibid., § 92, pp. 130, 133.

where the industry of man has not been employed to create the servitude. And while the lower heritage may raise no obstruction to the flow of the water to this extent, the superior one may· do nothing to render the servitude more burdensome, though this does not prohibit fitting the same for agricultural uses by clearing it, or constructing proper ditches and canals for that purpose.[1]

The lower owner, however, is not obliged to open ditches on his own land to draw off the water from his neighbor's land.[2] Nor to suffer the upper owner to cut ditches in his land, and thereby drain the upper lot into a canal in the lower one.[3]

6. But it would seem that this doctrine of a lower estate owing servitude to a superior one, to receive the water that falls upon the latter, and would naturally flow therefrom to the former, does not apply to house-lots in towns and cities, where the same have been occupied by the erection of houses thereon. In such cases each proprietor must, if the same can be done, so grade his lot as not to throw the water which collects upon the same upon the adjacent lot. This question arose in the city of Pittsburg, in the case of Bentz v. Armstrong, where two proprietors of a lot made partition thereof into two, each taking one of these. There was a spring of water upon one of them, which, together with the rain, as it fell, naturally flowed from it upon the other lot, and the owner of the latter, in order to prevent this, raised an embankment upon his land, which caused this water to set back into the cellar upon the lot in which it originated.

*The court held that he had a right so to do, and   [*358] that it was the duty of the owner of the upper lot to

---

[1] Martin v. Jett, 12 La. 504 ; Orleans Navigation Co. v. Mayor, &c., 3 Mart. 214, 233 ; Delahoussaye v. Judice, 13 La. Ann. 587 ; La. Civ. Code, Art. 656 ; Code Nap., Art. 640 ; 5 Duranton, Cours de Droit Français, 167 ; Pardessus, Traité des Servitudes, §§ 85, 86 ; Lattimore v. Davis, 14 La. 161 ; Hebert v. Hudson, 13 La. 54. See also Earle v. De Hart, 1 Beasl. 280 ; ante, chap. 3, sect. 1, pl. 7.

[2] Goodale v. Tuttle, Sup.

[3] Minor v. Wright, 16 Louis. An. 151.

drain the same into the common sewer, if there was one, or in some other way, if possible, to relieve the adjacent house-lot.[1]

But in a case in New Jersey, where the land lay in Elizabeth City, and the waters that were accustomed to collect upon its surface from rains, &c., were accustomed to flow over the defendant's land by an ancient watercourse, it was held that, though within a city, he had no right to stop such watercourse. "To have this water discharged upon the complainant's land is as great an injury to her building lot as it is to the defendant's lot to have it discharged there. There can be no such difference in the application of the law as to building lots as will impose a burden upon one which properly and of right belongs to another."[2]

In that case it was held to make no difference in the rights of the parties that the complainant might at small expense turn the water so as not to flow on to the defendant's land. She was not bound to do it.

7. In considering the subject of surface water, thus far, reference has been chiefly had to the right of the superior land-owner to claim, in the nature of a servitude in the land below, the right to have such water discharged thereon, as an easement belonging to the upper tenement. But the subject admits of another view, and that is, how far the owner of the upper tenement may use and apply such water upon his premises, and deprive the lower tenement of any benefit which might otherwise result to the same by such water finding its way over or through the earth to such lower tenement, provided it be not in the form of a proper watercourse. Thus there are often more or less extensive tracts of land in which water rises or collects in a stagnant state, forming swamps or *swails*, and which occasionally con-
[*359] *tribute to the supply of running streams upon the land of others by overflowing or soaking through

---

[1] Bentz v. Armstrong, 8 Watts & S. 40.
[2] Earle v. De Hart, 1 Beasl. 280.

the intermediate soil. And attempts have been made by those interested in such streams to prevent the owner of the land on which such waters have collected from interrupting their transit into the stream.

But water, whether it has fallen as rain or has come from the overflow of a pond or a swamp, which sinks into the topsoil and struggles through it, following no defined channel, is deemed, by law, absolutely to belong to the owner of the land upon which it is found, for the purpose of enabling him to cultivate his land by controlling or draining it off in the mode most convenient to him.

But the right of the owner of such land over the water therein, is not affected by any right in the owner of an adjoining river, pond, or tank which it may chance, for the time, to feed, though that time has been ever so long protracted. It is, in the eye of the law, as well as of common sense, the moisture and a part of the soil with which it intermingles, to be there used by the owner of the soil if to his advantage, or to be got rid of if he pleases, if it is to his detriment.[1]

8. One of these cases was Broadbent v. Ramsbotham. The plaintiff owned a mill, which had been operated for fifty years by the waters of a natural stream which flowed along the foot of a range of hills, upon the side of one of which was the farm of the defendant. On this farm there were *boggy* places in which water collected from the want of proper drainage. And on another part of this slope was a swamp occasioned by a small ridge of land which prevented the surface water from flowing into the valley, and in this water was generally to be found.

There were two or more wells upon the premises, which were supplied from these marshy and swampy places, and by subterranean waters, and occasionally overflowed, and the water thereof ran into the stream, but not in a defined channel. The defendant constructed several drains in his land,

[1] Buffum v. Harris, 5 R. I. 253 ; *ante*, p. *211.

and partly filled up the swamp and some of the wells, the effect
of which was to prevent the water that fell upon these slopes
of the hills, or were collected in these swampy places, or
in these wells from underground sources, from penetrating
into or flowing over the land and reaching the stream as it
had formerly done.   And for this diversion the plaintiff
brought his action.

The court held that the plaintiff's rights were limited to
"the flow of water in the stream itself, and to the water
flowing in some defined, natural channel, either subterranean or on the surface, communicating directly with the
brook itself.   No doubt all the water falling from heaven,
and shed upon the surface of a hill, at the foot of which a
brook runs, must by the natural force of gravity find its
way to the bottom, and so into the brook; but this
[*360] does not *prevent the owner of the land on which
this water falls from dealing with it as he may
please, and appropriating it" before it arrives at some natural channel already formed.   They held that the owner of
the soil had a right to drain the shallow pond at his pleasure.   The same was true of the boggy or swampy place in
which the water formerly stood, nor did it make any difference that there must have been subterranean courses con-
necting these with the stream, since they were not traceable,
nor did the fact that one of the wells sometimes overflowed
affect the defendant's right to control or divert the water in
it.   And as to the other well, which occasionally overflowed,
and the water, when it did, spread itself upon the surface,
and did not form any natural channel until it reached the
valley, it was held that the defendant had a right to appropriate and divert the same at any time before they had
reached the valley and formed themselves into a natural
channel.[1]

In one case the owner of a parcel of land in which was
a spring which had a defined outlet or fountain, sold the

[1] Broadbent v. Ramsbotham, 11 Exch. 602.

spring and the right to draw water from it to its full extent of supply. He afterwards laid drains through his land to drain the top surface of the soil and render it susceptible of cultivation. And it was held that he had a right so to do, though, possibly, by so doing he might divert some portion of water that would otherwise have percolated through the earth to the spring, and increased its supply. But he would have no right to do this on purpose to prevent the water from supplying the spring, nor would he have a right to construct his drain so carelessly or negligently as to draw the water off from the spring or lessen the quantity of water therein. The owner, in granting the spring, would be presumed to retain the right of surface drainage for agricultural purposes, unless plainly negatived by the terms and operation of the grant.[1]

But where there were springs upon the upper parcel, which rose upon the surface into ponds or pools, with a constant supply, and found their way into the lower parcel, but the space where they rose upon the surface was so near the boundary of the lower parcel that the water could not form for itself a defined channel or channels, it was held that the owner of the upper parcel had no right to pump up and divert the waters of these ponds or pools, and thereby deprive the lower parcel of the use and benefit thereof, although no defined watercourse or channel had been formed from the one into the other.[2]

9. The court, in Broadbent v. Ramsbotham, refer to the case of Rawstron v. Taylor, as confirming the views sustained by them. In that case, plaintiff owned and occupied mills and a reservoir, fed by streams flowing to the same, and his claim for damages was for the diversion of water which had formerly gone to supply these, by acts done by *the defendant upon his own land. The [*361] facts are very numerous and difficult of explanation without a plan. But the opinion of the court will be suffi-

[1] Buffum v. Harris, 5 R. I. 243.
[2] Ennor v. Barwell, 2 Giff. 410, 426.

ciently explicit to show the rule of law in cases such as are above supposed. As to one of the alleged diversions, the court say : " This is the case of common surface water rising out of springy or boggy ground, and flowing in no definite channel, although contributing to the supply of the plaintiff's mill. This water having no defined course, its supply being merely casual, the defendant is entitled to get rid of it in any way he pleases." So as to the other case of diversion they say : " This water has no defined course, and the supply is not constant; therefore the plaintiff is not entitled to it, and the defendant is entitled to get rid of this also, for the purpose of cultivating his land, in any way he pleases."

There was one other source of supply which the defendant had diverted, which consisted of an artificial channel, but which was controlled by a deed between the parties, which can throw no light upon the general question under consideration, and is therefore omitted, except to say that, not being a natural watercourse, the plaintiff would have no right of action against the defendant for diverting the water flowing therein, independent of the grant under which the plaintiff claimed. Platt, B., in giving his opinion upon the first two cases of diversion, says, " As this was merely surface water, and the defendant had a right to drain his land, and the plaintiff could not insist upon the defendant maintaining his fields as a mere water-table," the defendant was entitled to judgment. And Martin, B. adds : " He is at liberty to get rid of the surface water in any manner that may appear most convenient to him ; and I think no one has a right to interfere with him, and that the object he may have had in so doing is quite immaterial." It may be stated, though it seems not to have been made a point in the case, that the plaintiff's mill was an ancient one, and had enjoyed the benefit of the water from the swamps [*362] and *the surface of the defendant's land, which was the subject of the suit, from an ancient period.[1]

[1] Broadbent v. Ramsbotham, 11 Exch. 369. See Stetson v. Howland, 2 Allen, 591.

10. The rule is briefly stated in Dickinson v. Canal Co.: "Where the springs come to the surface, and form streams and rivers, the established rules apply, that each riparian owner is entitled, not to the property in the flowing water, but the usufruct of its stream, for all reasonable purposes, to drink, to water his cattle, or to turn his mills, according to the nature and situation of the stream." [1]

11. A question of this kind arose in Luther v. Winnisimmet Company, where the rule of law was stated to be as follows: "If there was a watercourse or stream of water running through the land conveyed, the right to the continued flow thereof would pass to the plaintiff under his deed as parcel of his grant. But if there were no such watercourse or stream of water, the plaintiff could not claim a right of drainage or flow of water from off his land on to or through the defendant's land, merely because the plaintiff's land was higher than the defendant's, and sloped towards it, so that the water which fell in rain upon it would naturally run over the surface in that direction." The court go on to define what is meant by a watercourse, the stopping of which would be a cause of action, namely, "A watercourse is a stream of water usually flowing in a definite channel, having a bed and sides or banks, and usually discharging itself into some other stream or body of water. To constitute a watercourse, the size of the stream was not important; it might be very small, and the flow of the water need not be constant; but it must be something more than the mere surface drainage over the entire face of a tract of land, occasioned by unusual freshets or other extraordinary causes," and it is a question for a jury whether, in any given case, a watercourse exists or not.[2]

[1] Dickinson v. Grand Junction Canal Co., 7 Exch. 301.

[2] Luther v. Winnisimmet Co., 9 Cush. 171; Ashley v. Wolcott, 11 Cush. 192; as to what is a channel, see Dudden v. Guardians of Poor, &c., 1 Hurlst. &. N. 627 ; Rawstron v. Taylor, 11 Exch. 369 ; Shields v. Arndt, 3 Green, Ch. 234, 246; Goodale v. Tuttle, 29 N. Y. 466, 467; Beard v. Murphy, 37 Verm. 104 ; Bangor v. Lansil, 51 Maine, 525 ; Park v. Newburyport, 10 Gray, 28.

[*363]   *SECTION VII.

OF RIGHTS IN SUBTERRANEAN WATERS.

1. Subject a recent one in courts.
2. No action lies for diverting underground springs.
3. Otherwise, if water runs in a defined channel.
4. Rule of the Civil Law in such cases.
5. Case of Acton v. Blundell. Diverting underground waters.
6. No one may damage another by underground water.
7. Case of Chasemore v. Richards. Right to underground water.
8. Distinction between underground channels being known or not.
9. One may not divert a stream by digging wells on its banks.
10. Law as to waters collecting in mines.
11. American cases. As to diverting underground supplies of water.
12. Case of Roath v. Driscol. No prior right by prior use of such water.
13. Different rule as to prescriptive right gained in such waters.
14. Ellis v. Duncan. Case of diverting sources of a spring.
15. Wheatley v. Baugh. Same subject.
16. One may not divert such sources except in his own land.
17. Of fouling underground sources of a well.
18. How far one may prescribe for underground waters.

1. WHILE the rights and liabilities of adjacent land-owners in respect to streams of water flowing upon the surface have come under the frequent cognizance of courts for a period as long almost as courts have been known, the law regulating the use and enjoyment of springs and currents of water existing underground has been but little discussed until a comparatively recent day.

We are authorized by Pollock, C. B.[1] to say, that the distinction was made for the first time between underground waters and those which flow on the surface, in the case of Acton v. Blundell,[2] which was decided as recently as 1843, though it is believed that there may be found earlier [*364] causes, both in England and this country, where *the doctrine therein maintained was enunciated as law. Since the decision of that case, the question has come up in various forms in both countries, and the same general course

---

[1] 7 Exch. 300.   [2] Acton v. Blundell, 12 Mees. & W. 324.

of ruling in respect to it has been pursued by the several courts.

2. It may be stated as a general principle of nearly universal application, that, while one proprietor of land may not stop or divert the waters of a stream flowing in a surface channel through it, so as to deprive a land-owner whose estate lies upon the stream below that of the proprietor first mentioned of the use of the same, or essentially impair or diminish the use thereof; if, without an intention to injure an adjacent owner, and while making use of his own land to any suitable and lawful purpose, he cuts off, diverts, or destroys the use of an underground spring or current of water which has no known and defined course, but has been accustomed to penetrate and flow into the land of his neighbor, he is not thereby liable to any action for the diversion or stoppage of such water.

Thus it is said, " no land-owner has an absolute and unqualified right to the unaltered natural drainage or percolation to or from his neighbor's land.   In general, it would be impossible to avoid disturbing the natural percolation or drainage without a practical abandonment of all improvement or beneficial enjoyment of his land." [1]   " We are of opinion that the law of the land can recognize no such claims (claims in respect to subsurface waters without any distinct and definite channel), and that, subject only to the possible exception of a case of unmixed malice, *cujus est solum ejus est usque ad cœlum et ad inferos*, applies to its full extent."   " In the absence of express contract, and of positive, authorized legislation as between proprietors of adjoining lands, the law recognizes no correlative rights in respect to underground waters percolating or filtrating through the earth, and this, mainly, from considerations of policy." [2]   In the case, from the opinion of the court in which these extracts are made, the defendant dug " a hole "

1 Bassett *v.* Company, 43 N. H. 573.
2 Frasier *v.* Brown, 12 Ohio, St. 304, 311.

iñ his land, which cut off and stopped the sources and supply
of a spring which had previously risen in and supplied the
plaintiff's land with water. "We are not to be understood
as intimating that an owner may maliciously or negligently
divert, even an unknown subterranean stream, to the damage of a lower proprietor. But, in the enjoyment of his
land, he may cut drains or mine a quarry, though, in so
doing, he interfere with the flowage of water in hidden,
unknown, underground channels."[1] In this case the defendant opened a mine in his own land, 300 feet from the
plaintiff's spring, which had never been dug, and cut off the
supply of water, and it was held to be no legal wrong. On
the other hand, no one can claim a right to have underground percolating waters drained from his land into or
through that of another, or compel the owner of the latter
to abstain from doing that on his land which will prevent the water from draining from the parcel first mentioned.[2]

But he may not foul or poison the water which percolates
through his land, so as to come to that of another in a state
to be deleterious to the health of man or beast.[3]

3. This, it will be understood, does not include well-
defined streams of water which are found in some parts of
the country, which in their course sometimes appear upon
the surface, and then become subterranean for a longer or
shorter distance. Nor, for the present, does it intend to
touch upon the point how far one can acquire an easement
in subterranean waters.

The cases in which the question has been considered may
be stated, generally, to have been those of springs of water
flowing naturally from the earth above ground, wells where
the water is obtained by artificial excavation, and waters

---

[1] Haldeman v. Bruckhardt, 45 Penn. 521.

[2] Goodale v. Tuttle, 29 N. Y. 466.

[3] Hodgkinson v. Ennor, 4 B. & Smith, 229; ante, p. *224; 12 Am. L. Reg. 240,
by Redfield.

accumulating in mines, while working them, by percolation and draining through the adjacent formation.

4. The civil law upon the subject is thus stated in the Digest [1] : " Denique Marcellus scribit cum eo qui in suo fodiens, vicini fontem avertit, nihil posse agi, nec de dolo *actionen. Et sane non debet habere, si non [*365] animo vicino nocendi, sed suum agrum meliorem faciendi id fecit." The English of which, as given by Maule, J., is, " If a man digs a well in his own field, and thereby drains his neighbor's, he may do so unless he does it maliciously." [2]

5. This doctrine of Marcellus is approved by Tindal, C. J., in Acton v. Blundell, who says, in regard to the questions in that case, that no case bearing directly was cited on either side.

The case was this. The plaintiff, Acton, owned a mill which was operated by water flowing from a well dug in his own premises by a former owner of both the mill and the land in which the well was dug. About four years before commencing the present action the plaintiff had enlarged the well for the purpose of supplying more water for his mill. The defendant subsequently opened and sunk a coal-mine in his own land, at the distance of three quarters of a mile from the plaintiff's well, the effect of which was to cut off the underground veins and currents of water which supplied the plaintiff's well, and to prevent his operating his mill. To an action for this injury, the judge at Nisi Prius held, that if the defendant, in properly working a mine in his own premises, caused a diversion of the water from the

[1] D. 39, 3, 1, 12.

[2] Acton v. Blundell, 12 Mees. & W. 336 ; While Bartlett, J., in Bassett v. Company, 43 N. H. 579, expresses a doubt as to our decisions having tended in the direction of Acton v. Blundell, the English court, Crompton J., in New River Co. v. Johnson, 2 E. & Ellis, 445, says it is a decision of great authority, and that the case of Dickinson v. G. Junction Co., 7 Exch. 282, not only did not and could not overrule it, but was itself virtually overruled by the judgment of the House of Lords in Chasemore v. Richards, 7 H. L. Cas. 349, in which Acton v. Blundell is approved and acted upon.

plaintiff's well and mill, he would not be liable therefor. A point was made by the plaintiff's counsel, that, if the well had enjoyed the water, though underground, for twenty years, the defendant would have no right to divert it. But in the present case the well had been dug in 1821, and the defendant began his mine in 1837.

The court held, that "there was a marked and substantial difference" between the law as to the right to enjoy an underground spring of water and that by which a watercourse flowing on the surface is governed; "they are not governed by the same rule of law."

[*366]   *Among the considerations upon which this difference is based is, that the one being notorious, whoever buys or grants it, knows what passes, while the other is secret and unknown at the time of purchase and sale, and may be in its nature constantly shifting. Nor can it ordinarily be ascertained what part of the supply comes from one's own land, and what from that of another. Nor can there be any implied mutual consent or agreement as to what shall be the future course of the current of the water from its having previously flowed in a known channel.

Another suggestion made by the court was, that, in the case of running surface water, the land-owner could only appropriate the use of the water while flowing; whereas, if by excavating a well, the land-owner can appropriate the water which supplies it underground, it would be creating a property in the water itself, and would, moreover, prevent an adjacent land-owner from enjoying the water that is in his own premises, after having incurred expenses in excavating for it within his own land, though ignorant of any injury it might occasion to the owner of the prior well. Besides, the benefit to the one may be altogether disproportioned to the damage to the other, if the rule of prior occupancy were applied, as in the one case a well might be designed for the use of a cottage only, or a drinking-place for cattle, while, in order to preserve it, the owner of an extensive and valuable mine might be prevented from working it, to his own and 'the public injury. And lastly, there can be no definite limits within which the restriction, if applied, could be held to operate.[1] The court, moreover, were inclined to hold, that the right to interfere with underground springs as supplies for the wells upon the lands of adjacent proprietors was incident to the general right of property which every man has in and over his own land, whereby whatever is in a man's *land beneath the surface is his, whether rock [*367] or porous earth, whether in part soil and part water, or wholly soil, which he may dig into and apply to such uses as he pleases; and if in doing so, without intent to injure his neighbor, he cuts off or drains away the underground springs which had supplied his well, it would be, as to him, *damnum absque injuria*.

The same doctrine applies to injuries occasioned by depriving the owner of land of the water percolating underground through that in which public works are being constructed, by which the flow is stopped. Such land-owner has no remedy by action for the loss.[2]

What rule the court would apply had the well been an ancient one, in the sense in which that term is ordinarily used in respect to prescriptive rights, the judge raises a query which is not answered by the case.[3]

6. The court in the above case refer to the case of Cooper *v.* Barber, which they say was the nearest to a case of underground currents of water which had till that time been decided. The case is not a very satisfactory one, but is referred to from being thus alluded to by the court. In that case, the owner of one parcel of land diverted water from a natural stream by an artificial channel for the purpose of

---

[1.] The Artesian well at the Abattoir de Grenelle, in Paris, is said to draw a part of its supply from a distance of forty miles underground. 5 Hurlst. & N. 986.

[2] New River Co. *v.* Johnson, 2 E. & Ellis, 446.

[3] Acton *v.* Blundell, 12 Mees. & W. 324; Radcliff's Exrs. *v.* Mayor, &c., 4 Comst. 195.

irrigating his own land. The water from this artificial channel percolated through the plaintiff's land lying near it, which was of a light porous structure. But this did not show itself, nor do any damage to the latter owner, until, wishing to erect a dwelling-house thereon, he dug a cellar, and found that the water from this channel of the defendant penetrated into it, doing damage to the owner. It was sought to justify the right thus to manage the water by the defendant, because he had enjoyed the same for a space of time long enough to give him a prescriptive right. But the court held that the owner of the first-mentioned parcel and channel could not acquire a prescriptive right as against the other land-owner, to keep up the water on his own land to the injury of the other, so long as the injurious effect to the land of the latter could not be known to him.[1]

[*368]   *The court, in Humphries v. Brogden,[2] allude to the case of Acton v. Blundell, and point out a marked distinction between the right which one has to have his land supported by subjacent or adjacent lands, and the right to running water. And Maule, J. again refers to it with approbation in Smith v. Kenrick,[3] and Wightman, J., with Lord Chelmsford, in the House of Lords, more fully express their approval of the doctrines of that case, in Chasemore v. Richards.

7. The case of Chasemore v. Richards is an interesting one from the importance of the questions decided, and from the circumstance, as stated by Lord Wensleydale, that the House of Lords thereby decided for the first time the question as to underground water.

The case was first heard and decided in 1857, in the Exchequer Chamber,[4] and afterwards, upon error, in the House of Lords, in 1859,[5] and in both in favor of the defendant,

---

[1] Cooper v. Barber, 3 Taunt. 99.

[2] Humphries v. Brogden, 12 Q. B. 739, 753.

[3] Smith v. Kenrick, 7 C. B. 515, 552.

[4] Chasemore v. Richards, 2 Hurlst. & N. 168.

[5] Ibid., 5 Hurlst. & N. 982; 7 H. of L. Cas. 349.

though in one, Coleridge, J. was inclined in favor of the plaintiff, and in the other, Lord Wensleydale hesitated to go as far as the Judges and House of Lords in sustaining the doctrine contended for in behalf of the defendant.   The facts, as stated in the opinion of the Judges, were substantially these.   The plaintiff had an ancient mill, operated by the waters of the river Wandle.   This he had enjoyed for over sixty years.   The river was supplied, in part, by the water falling upon a pretty large territory, above the mill, including the town of C.   This water sank into the earth, and found its way, percolating at different depths through the earth, to the river, but in no defined course or current. The Board of Health of C. sunk a well in their land, about a quarter of a mile from the river, for procuring water for their use, and pumped it up therefrom, in great quantities, *for a supply of the town, and diverted so much   [*369] of the underground water which would otherwise have found its way to the river as sensibly to affect the working of the plaintiff's mill.   The action was for this diversion.

In respect to the right set up by the plaintiff, the judges say : " It is impossible to reconcile such a right with the natural and ordinary rights of land-owners, or fix any reasonable limits to the exercise of such a right. . . . . . Such a right as that claimed by the plaintiff is so indefinite and unlimited, that, unsupported as it is by any weight of authority, we do not think that it can be well founded, or that the present action is maintainable."

Thus, one whose well is drained by constructing public works near it, whereby the percolating waters which supply it are cut off, can have no action for the injury.[1]

Lord Chelmsford, after speaking of water flowing in defined channels, remarks : " But these principles, applicable to streams, whether above or under ground, did not seem to be applicable to water merely percolating through the ground, which had no certain course or defined limits whatever.

_____
[1] New River Co. v. Johnson, 2 E. & Ellis, 435.

The right to water so percolating was of too uncertain a description. When did it commence? If the owner of the land could not intercept it in its course through his land, could he catch it in rain-water tubs, and prevent its reaching the ground at all?"

Lord Cranworth remarked: "The argument founded on the use to which the defendant applied this water did not affect his mind at all, because he thought there was no difference in the case whether one owner sunk a well to supply a thousand other owners, or each of these sunk a well to supply himself."

8. It is not, however, the circumstance of a stream being under or above the surface which determines the right of the land-owner to interfere with the waters which are found within his premises, but "its being or not being ascertained and defined as a stream." If there is a natural spring, the water from which flows in a natural channel, it cannot be lawfully diverted by any one, to the injury of the riparian proprietors. If the channel or course underground [*370] is known, *it cannot be interfered with. It is otherwise when nothing is known as to the sources of supply. In that case, as no right can be acquired against the owner of the land under which the spring exists, he may do as he pleases with it, and if, in mining or draining his land, he taps a spring, he cannot be made responsible.[1]

So in Dickinson v. Grand Junction Canal Co., the same judge says: " If the course of a subterranean stream were well known, as is the case with many which sink underground, pursue for a short space a subterranean course, and then emerge again, it never could be contended that the owner of the soil under which the stream flowed could not maintain an action for the diversion of it, if it took place under such circumstances as would have enabled him to recover, if the stream had been wholly above ground."[2]

---

[1] Per *Pollock*, C. B., Dudden v. Guardians of Poor, &c., 1 Hurlst. & N. 627, 630; Frasier v. Brown, 12 Ohio St. 300.

[2] Dickinson v. Grand Junction Canal Co., 7 Exch. 301.

9. On the other hand, if there be a diversion of the waters of a stream by any land-owner, within his own premises, to the injury of a lower proprietor, it matters not that it is done by digging a well into which the water is diverted, unless, perhaps, if the one who digs the well is ignorant, and cannot, by any reasonable degree of care, have ascertained, beforehand, that the digging of the well would have the effect to divert the water, and when the effect is discovered, is unable to repair the mischief.[1]

In addition to the cases above cited may be mentioned that of Hammond v. Hall,[2] decided in 1840, which relates to subterranean water rights, but did not lead to any important ruling, and is only referred to in order to introduce the remark of the reporter, as a reason why he gives the case, that "a question was raised in arguing it, which was said never to have been discussed before, namely, *whether a right or easement could be claimed [*371] with respect to subterranean water."

There was the ancient case of Prickman v. Tripp,[3] for diverting water from plaintiff's well by digging a cistern near it. But it does not appear what was the nature of the supply of water which had been thus diverted, whether by a defined stream or the percolations through the adjacent earth.

10. The questions as to the rights of parties in respect to underground water, in its effect upon the working of mines, have grown out of causing or suffering the waters which have collected by percolation into one mine to flow into another to the injury of the latter. The rule in such cases seems to be, that, while one may not maliciously, or without reason, cause the water which collects by percolation through the earth in his own mine to flow into that of another to the injury of the latter, if he does this in the usual

---

[1] Dickinson v. Grand Junction Canal Co., 7 Exch. 282, 301.

[2] Hammond v. Hall, 10 Sim. 551. See also Broadbent v. Ramsbotham, 11 Exch. 602, 615.

[3] Prickman v. Tripp, Skinn. 389.

and proper mode of working his mine, he is not responsible therefor.   In such case, neither mine owes servitude to the other, and each mine-owner may work his own in the manner most convenient and beneficial to himself, although the natural consequence may be, that some prejudice will accrue to the owner of the adjoining mine, so long as that does not arise from the negligent or malicious conduct of the party. As was remarked by the court in the case cited below: " The water is a sort of common enemy, against which each man must defend himself.   And this is in accordance with the civil law, by which it was considered that land on a lower level owed a natural servitude to land on a higher, in respect of receiving, without claim to compensation, the water naturally flowing down to it." [1]

11. The American law, it is believed, conforms to the English in the matter of underground currents, although
[*372] it is apprehended that it is more liberal in allowing the *diversion of water flowing upon the surface for the purposes of irrigation, than would comport with the doctrine of some of the English cases.

Among the cases where the question of diverting underground streams has arisen, is Greenleaf v. Francis, where the plaintiff, in digging his cellar, struck upon a spring of water which he deepened and converted into a well within the cellar, and had used it for the purposes of his family for about twelve years, when the defendant, having occasion to dig a well in his own land, near the plaintiff's, struck upon the vein of water which supplied the well of the latter, and stopped the supply therein.   The court held that the defendant did no more than he had a right to do, and the plaintiff was without remedy.   Considerable stress is laid by the judge, in giving the opinion, upon the fact that the plaintiff had not enjoyed the supply of water for his well for twenty years, though it is not in terms held that he would thereby have acquired any better rights as against the acts of the

[1] Smith v. Kenrick, 7 C. B. 515, 566 ; D. 39, 3, 1, 22.

defendant. But the court expressly held that the defendant would not in either case have had the right to disturb the plaintiff in the enjoyment of the supply of water for his well, if done from malice.[1]

The above case of Greenleaf v. Francis was decided in 1836, seven years prior to Acton v. Blundell. In 1837 a question somewhat similar arose in New York, before the Chancellor, upon an application for an injunction, which is stated here, in order, among other things, to give the chronological sequence of the questions as they arose. In the case referred to, of Smith v. Adams, the plaintiff had a spring of water in his premises within a few feet of the defendant's land. He had conducted water from this spring by an aqueduct to other parcels of his land, and had used the water thereof in this way for more than twenty years. The defendant then dug in his own land, and struck the * vein of water which supplied the spring near [*373] the line of his land, and laid an aqueduct therefrom to his house, thereby withdrawing a small portion which would otherwise have flowed into the stream.

The Chancellor, in denying the right of the defendant thus to divert the water, assumes that the same rule applies as if the stream had issued upon the defendant's land, treating it of course as if it had become a defined watercourse, though underground. Another circumstance in the case was, that the defendant dug into his own ground with the knowledge and intent that by so doing he could and would .divert the water which would otherwise supply the spring in the plaintiff's land. And because the water, thus diverted, " is a part of the larger stream which naturally issued from the earth upon the spring lot (the plaintiff's) below," the plaintiff, in the opinion of the Chancellor, had a legal right of action against the defendant for such diversion, although,

---

[1] Grreenleaf v. Francis, 18 Pick. 117. See also N. Albany R. R. v. Peterson, 14 Ind. 112.

for reasons stated in his opinion, he did not see fit to grant the injunction prayed for.[1]

The next case in the order of time was Dexter v. Providence Aqueduct Co.,[2] in 1840. The plaintiff in that case was the owner of a meadow in which there was a spring of water which he had applied to purposes of irrigation and watering his cattle for more than twenty years. The defendants dug a large well near the plaintiff's meadow, for the purpose of obtaining water with which to supply the city of Providence, the effect of which was to divert the water from the spring, and to render it dry. The judge, chiefly upon the strength of the case of Balston v. Bensted,[3] which will be hereafter considered, held that the plaintiff was entitled to an injunction restraining the defendants from thus diverting the water. But the case is not [*374] *elaborately considered, and the opinion seems to be rather in the light of an interlocutory judgment than a final opinion upon the matter as a question of law.

12. The case of Roath v. Driscoll,[4] decided in 1850, is a much more fully and ably considered case, in which the court discuss the general doctrine of underground waters as the subject of property. In that case the plaintiff sunk a well or reservoir in his land, into which the water percolated and stood in considerable quantity, but did not rise to the surface. The defendant, without any intent to injure the plaintiff, or cut off the supply of water in this well, dug a like well or reservoir in his own land, near the plaintiff's, and the plaintiff brought his bill to enjoin the continuance of this, on the ground that the water that would otherwise come to his reservoir was diverted to his injury. The plaintiff had applied artificial means, by way of a siphon, to raise the water from his well over a higher level, to another reser-

[1] Smith v. Adams, 6 Paige, 435. See Wheatley v. Baugh, 25 Penn. St. 528.

[2] Dexter v. Prov. Aqueduct Co., 1 Story, 387.

[3] Balston v. Bensted, 1 Campb. 463.

[4] Roath v. Driscoll, 20 Conn. 533.

voir, which he thereby supplied, which was also stopped after the defendant opened his well or reservoir. But this artificial use of the water had not been continued long enough to gain thereby any prescriptive rights.

It was expressly found, that whatever water came to the well of either party percolated through the earth, and not in any defined channel or course. The court waive any question that might have been made to any prescriptive rights under a different state of things ; " for nothing," say they, " is gained by a mere continued preoccupancy of water, *under the surface*. Why should any advantage be gained by preoccupancy ? Each owner has an equal and complete right to the use of his land, and to the water which is in it. Water combined with the earth, or passing through it by percolation, or by filtration, or chemical attraction, has no distinctive character of ownership from the earth itself, not *more than the metallic oxides of which [*375] the earth is composed. Water, whether moving or motionless, *in the earth*, is not, in the eye of the law, distinct from the earth. . . . . Priority of enjoyment does not in like cases abridge the natural rights of adjoining proprietors. . . . . No man is bound to know that his neighbor's well is supplied by water percolating his own soil, and he ought not, therefore, to be held to lose his rights by such continued enjoyment. He cannot know that the first well requires any other than the natural and common use of water under the surface, nor can he know from whence the water comes, nor by what means it appears in one place or the other, nor which of the persons who first or afterwards opens the earth encroaches upon the right of the other. The law has not yet extended beyond open running streams."

The court of Vermont adopted the doctrine of Roath *v.* Driscoll, that undergound water filtering through the earth is to be taken as a part of the soil, and the owner thereof may take measures to prevent the water therein from percolating into the land of an adjacent owner without thereby violating the legal rights of the latter. In which respect the rights of adjacent land-owners, in the matter of underground waters, do not correspond with those which govern the enjoyment of waters flowing upon the surface in defined currents.

The facts in the case to which these doctrines were applied were these. One land-owner, in order to avail himself of water which percolated through another's land into his own, sunk a hole in his own land, and inserted a cask therein to receive the water. But the adjacent owner, in order to prevent the water penetrating to the land of the first-named owner, dug into his own land and placed hard earth therein, which stopped the percolation of the water into the other's land ; and it was held that the latter was without remedy for the injury thereby occasioned.[1]

[*376]   *There was a point made in the case of Chatfield v. Wilson, which is purposely omitted here, in order to consider it more fully hereafter, and that is, how far the owner of land adjacent to that in which there is an existing well or spring can wantonly and maliciously cut off the underground supply of water therefor, which is derived through or from his land, by acts done upon his own premises.

13. Two inferences may fairly be drawn from the language of the court in the case of Roath v. Driscoll, although not directly stated. First, that a different rule from that applicable to water percolating through the earth would be adopted in respect to water flowing in a known, defined current, though underground. And, second, that no mere length of enjoyment of such percolating water, by means of artificial wells or reservoirs, gives the one in whose land they are dug any prior prescriptive right to such enjoyment as against the proprietor of other lands, who, in digging a well or reservoir for his own use, cuts off or diverts the supply of the wells of the former owner.

---

[1] Chatfield v. Wilson, 28 Vt. 49 ; s. c., 31 Vt. 358. See Harwood v. Benton, 32 Vt. 724.

14. In 1855, another case was decided in the Supreme Court of New York,[1] where it was attempted to enjoin the defendant from opening ditches in his own land, and working a quarry of stone thereon, because by so doing he intercepted the waters of an underground source of a spring in the plaintiff's land which supplied a small stream of water flowing partly through the lands of both parties. It will be perceived that this presented a different question from that in the last-cited case, inasmuch as the spring which was affected was a natural one, the head and source of a stream of water flowing upon the surface ; and the purposes of the party occasioning the loss were partly for the cultivation of his farm, and partly the opening and working a quarry, and had no reference to making use of the underground water upon his own premises. The court refused the application, *remarking : " It seems to me that the [*377] rule that a man has the right to the free and absolute use of his property, so long as he does not directly invade that of his neighbor, or consequentially injure his perceptible and clearly defined rights, is applicable to the interruption of the sub-surface supplies of a stream by the owner of the soil, and that the damage resulting from it is not the subject of legal redress." In this, as in most of the later American cases, the case of Acton v. Blundell, before cited, is referred to with approbation. But it was conceded by the counsel on both sides, that the American courts have considerably modified the English law of easements generally.

The doctrine of Acton v. Blundell, above cited, as to cutting off underground streams of water which supply the well of another, is recognized and reaffirmed by Bronson, C. J., in Radcliff's Exrs. v. Mayor, &c.[2]

15. In the same year (1855) the case of Wheatley v.

---

[1] Ellis v. Duncan, 21 Barb. 230.
[2] Radcliff's Exrs. v. Mayor, &c., 4 Comst. 195, 200. See also Bellows v. Sackett, 15 Barb. 96.

Baugh[1] was decided in a full and elaborate opinion by Lewis, C. J. The facts of the case were these. The plaintiff, as lessee, occupied premises having upon them a valuable spring from 1824 to 1853, the water of which was important for the carrying on his business as a tanner. In 1852 defendant began to work a valuable copper-mine on his own premises, five hundred and fifty yards from the spring. And in 1853, in prosecuting his work, he cut off the supply of water from the spring, to the great injury of the plaintiff. The court, in the first place, recognizing the distinction between mere percolating waters and those flowing in a stream, and applying the same rule to such streams, whether above or underneath the surface, add : " To entitle a stream to the consideration of the law, it is certainly necessary that it be a *watercourse*, in the proper sense of the term. [*378] . . . . *A subterranean *stream* which supplies a spring with water cannot be diverted by the proprietor above for the mere purpose of appropriating the water to his own use. . . . . When the filtrations are gathered into sufficient volume to have an appreciable value, and to flow in a clearly defined channel, it is generally possible to see it, and to avoid diverting it without serious detriment to the owner of the land through which it flows. But percolations spread in every direction through the earth, and it is impossible to avoid disturbing them without relinquishing the necessary enjoyment of the land. Accordingly, the law has never gone so far as to recognize in one man a right to convert another's farm to his own use for purposes of a filter. . . . . Neither the civil law nor the common law permits a man to be deprived of a spring or stream of water for the mere gratification of malice. . . . . The owner of land on which a spring issues from the earth has a perfect right to it against all the world, except those through whose land it comes. He has even a right to it, against them, until it

[2] Wheatley v. Baugh, 25 Penn. St. 528. See Whetstone v. Bowser, 29 Penn. St. 59. See Haldeman v. Bruckhardt, 45 Penn. 518, affirming Wheatley v. Baugh.

comes in conflict with the enjoyment of their right of property. Strangers cannot destroy it, even though it be derived from lands which do not belong to the owner of the spring." These extended quotations state so fully and accurately what is believed to furnish the true criterion between the rights of owners of adjoining lands in respect to waters found flowing above or underneath the surface of their respective estates, that it is unnecessary to add to the statements therein contained, except to remark, what will be repeated hereafter, that the court held in that case that the mere length of time for which the owner of the spring had enjoyed it had no effect to give him any prescriptive right to the use of it, as against the defendant. And judgment in the case was in favor of the defendant.

16. The case of Parker *v.* Boston and Maine Railroad,[1] is in affirmance of the position first stated, that if one in *sinking a well upon his own premises causes the [*379] water to flow from a well in another's land into his own, it is, as to the latter, *damnum absque injuria;* and, second, if one, without being such owner, does acts upon the land of another, which he was not authorized by the owner to do, and which cause the diversion or loss of the water which supplies the well upon another's land, he will be liable to the latter in damages. The case was one where a railroad company, in constructing their road across the land of A, adjoining that of B, by their excavation cut off the sources of supply of B's well, which had been derived through A's land, and were held responsible for the damage thereby occasioned.[2]

If now we resume the inquiry above referred to,[3] how far one may *maliciously* do acts within his own land, whereby he cuts off the underground supply of water which the spring or well of his neighbor derives from or through the same, we must recur to the case of Chatfield *v.* Wilson.[4]

---

[1] Parker *v.* Boston & Maine R. R., 3 Cush. 107, 114.
[2] But see New Albany R. R. *v.* Peterson, 14 Ind. 112.
[3] *Ante,* pl. 12.   [4] Chatfield *v.* Wilson, 28 Vt. 49.

The facts in this case, it will be remembered, were, that the defendant placed within his own land, and near the line of the plaintiff's land, dry, hard earth, which prevented his availing himself of the water which had before, percolated into the plaintiff's land, and supplied an artificial reservoir placed therein, from which he had drawn it by pipes for the use of his buildings. The court, in giving their opinion, say : " The case, so far as it is sent up to us, only concerns the right of the defendant to cut off the filtration of the water from his own land to the plaintiff's tub by artificial means, and the consequences, if *wantonly* done." They further say : " The act of the defendant in the obstruction of the water being in itself lawful, could not subject the defendant to damages, unless by reason thereof some right of [*380] the plaintiff has been violated. The *maxim, *sic utere tuo ut alienum non lædas*, applies only to cases where the act complained of violates some legal right of the party ; . . . . and it may be laid down as a position not to be controverted, that an act legal in itself, violating no right, cannot be made actionable on the ground of the motive which induced it." And they refer, by way of analogy, to the case of a man building upon his own land a high fence for the purpose of darkening or obscuring the light from the windows of a neighboring house, which, it has been held, may lawfully be done. They also refer to a remark of the court, in Greenleaf *v.* Francis,[1] " that the rights of the defendant should not be exercised from mere malice," and add : " We think, as applied to a case like the one then at bar, or the one now before us, the position was unsound, and against principle and authority."

The case had come up, upon the ruling of Poland, J., late Chief Justice of that court, wherein he instructed the jury that, " If they found that the acts of the defendant did prevent the usual and natural flow of the water in or under the ground from the defendant's soil to the plaintiff's, and that

[1] Greenleaf *v.* Francis, 18 Pick. 117.

these acts were done by the defendant solely with the purpose of injuring the plaintiff, and depriving him of water, and not with any purpose of usefulness to himself, then he would be liable to the plaintiff for such damages as he thereby sustained."

In determining how far other courts have adopted the one or the other of these two opposite opinions emanating from such respectable sources, it will be necessary to refer to some of the cases already cited, with the passing remark, as to the case of the obstruction of windows above referred to, that it has been held to be the only way in which, at common law, a man could prevent his neighbor from acquiring a prescriptive right to enjoy the light over his land in process of time, resulting from merely having been suffered to *enjoy it, whereas, as will be shown hereafter, [*381] courts do not agree that one can acquire a prescriptive right to an underground supply of water for his spring or well by having enjoyed it for any length of time.

In the next place, the courts clearly and unequivocally recognize the right to have a well or spring upon one's land supplied by underground sources as so far an existing one, which the law will protect, and punish the invasion of, that if a stranger who has no right in the same go upon an adjacent lot from which this supply is derived and cut it off, he will be liable therefor in an action by the owner of such spring or well.[1]

It would therefore seem to constitute a something of which *meum* and *tuum* might be predicated, and in regard to which the maxim *sic utere tuo,* &c., would not be wholly foreign, especially when the party destroying it does it by using his property, not for his own benefit, but solely for the purpose of depriving his neighbor of what he would otherwise have rightfully enjoyed.

So far as authority goes upon the principal point, the

[1] Parker *v.* Boston & Maine R. R., 3 Cush. 107 ; Wheatley *v.* Baugh, 25 Penn. St. 528, 533.

court of Pennsylvania cite with approbation the language of the court of Massachusetts, in Greenleaf v. Francis, which, in the opinion of the court of Vermont above cited, is said to be unsound and against principle and authority, and add, in connection therewith: " Neither the civil nor the common law permits a man to be deprived of a well or spring of water for the mere gratification of malice. . . . . . In this description of property it is therefore peculiarly necessary that each should be mindful of the necessities and rights of the others. The owner of land on which a spring issues from the earth has a perfect right to it against all the world, except those through whose land it comes."

In Roath v. Driscoll,[1] the court, in giving their [*382] opinion in *a like case of diversion of underground water, are careful to say, " It is found that the defendant is acting from honest motives to advance his interest, without any design unnecessarily to injure the plaintiff's " ; and they quote from Greenleaf v. Francis, adopting the language as their own : " In the absence of all right acquired by grant or adverse user for twenty years, the owner of land may dig a well on any part thereof, notwithstanding he thereby diminishes the water in his neighbor's well, unless in so doing he is actuated by a mere malicious intent to deprive his neighbor of water."

The court of Vermont, in a subsequent case to that of Chatfield v. Wilson, in remarking upon that case, say : " The only criticism that we have heard upon that decision was in respect to excluding the wanton and improper motive as an element in the ground of the defendant's liability. In the present case there is no imputation of such motive."[2]

There was not, it is true, any occasion, for the reason stated, to concur or otherwise in that part of the former ruling. But it is at least noticeable that the court purposely avoid expressing any opinion thereon, while they do,

1 Roath v. Driscoll, 20 Conn. 533.
2 Harwood v. Benton, 32 Vt. 737.

upon the main point, refer to it " as a sound exposition and application of the law."

The civil law expressly places the exemption from liability to an action of one who by digging in his own land interrupts the course of the water that supplies his neighbor's fountain, upon the intent with which the act is done : " Et sane non debet habere (sc. de dolo actionem) si non animo vicino nocendi, sed suum agrum meliorem faciendi, id fecit." [1]

The case of Panton v. Holland was one for injuring the foundations of a building placed by the plaintiff upon his own land, near the line of the defendant's, by excavations *made by the defendant in his own land. [*383] The house was a recent one, and the injury was proved ; but the court held the defendant was not liable, unless he had made the excavation in a careless manner. But the court say : " Suppose Holland (the defendant) had declared that he would exercise his right of digging on his own ground, contiguous to the plaintiff's wall, not to benefit himself, but for the sole purpose of injuring the plaintiff, and digs, accordingly, below the plaintiff's foundation, but takes care that there be no ground for the charge of negligence or unskilfulness in the exercise of his right ; considering himself safely intrenched within the protection of the law, he desists from further operations, his object is accomplished, the adjoining foundation is loosened, and the building is materially injured, — is there a question that in such a case the party injured would be entitled to recover damages ? The *gravamen* would, in the case put, arise from the fact that the act was *maliciously* done." [2]

In giving an opinion in the House of Lords, in Chasemore v. Richards, Lord Wensleydale, referring to the civil-law doctrine in relation to cutting off the underground supply of a

[1] D. 39, 3, 1, 12. See 2 J. Voet. ad Pandect. 669 ; 1 Lacroix, La Clef des Lois Romains, 152, tit. *Eau.*

[2] Panton v. Holland, 17 Johns. 92, 98.

well above referred to, says: " Every man, therefore, had a right to the natural advantages of his land; but those advantages were to be obtained subject to the principle *sic utere tuo*, &c., and the civil law and the law of Scotland did the same, forbade an act which was otherwise lawful, if done *animo vicino nocendi*." [1]

17. In Brown *v.* Illius[2] the court were inclined to the position, that if, in the prosecution of a business, like the manufacture of gas, not a nuisance *per se*, one use materials upon his land which penetrate into the earth and corrupt underground sources of supply by percolating to a well upon a neighbor's land, he would not be liable therefor. It [*384] does *not stand upon the ground of corrupting running streams of water flowing to another's land.[3]

18. A point has been alluded to more than once, in considering the cases upon the subject of rights to subterranean water, and which never seems to have been deliberately settled either in England or this country, and that is, how far these rights are within the rules of prescription, or are susceptible of being maintained on the ground of exclusive enjoyment for a length of time sufficient to establish such right in ordinary cases of easements.

Courts, in giving opinions, have occasionally referred to the case of Balston *v.* Bensted,[4] as settling the question, without stopping to examine the soundness of the opinion expressed therein at Nisi Prius. The case was of a spring which the plaintiff had enjoyed within his own land, for more than twenty years, in supplying water for a bathhouse. The defendant having occasion to work a quarry in his land near the plaintiff's, dug a drain therefrom, which was necessary to rid himself of the water accumulating therein, and by so doing drew down the head of water

---

[1] Chasemore *v.* Richards, 5 Hurlst. & N., Am. ed. 990.

[2] Brown *v.* Illius, 25 Conn. 583.

[3] But see Hodgkinson *v.* Ennor, 4 B. & Smith, 229 ; 12 Am. L. Reg. 240 ; Redfield's note.

[4] Balston *v.* Bensted, 1 Campb. 463.

in the plaintiff's spring, so as to deprive him of water for his bath-house. Lord Ellenborough, upon the trial, remarked, "That there could be no doubt but that twenty years' exclusive enjoyment of water in any particular manner affords a conclusive presumption of right in the party so enjoying it." Story, J., in Dexter v. Providence Aqueduct Co.,[1] refers to this case with approbation, as being "directly in point, if indeed the same principle of law had not been fully recognized from very early times"; and cites Sury v. Pigot,[2] where the illustration drawn by the court from the law as to running-water applies to the case of streams upon the surface.

The case from Campbell, if law, is certainly a peculiar *one, and seems to come more nearly within [*385] the case of Smith v. Adams[3] than the ordinary case of water supplying a spring or well by mere percolation, being rather of the nature of a defined though underground stream of water. It is described as "a gush of water from a hole in the plaintiff's close, which used to run from thence on the surface of the ground into the river." And so the Chancellor, in the case above cited, seems to have regarded it when he refers to it in giving his opinion.

The court in Massachusetts discuss, somewhat, the subject of easements acquired by adverse possession, as connected with the enjoyment of underground water for the supply of wells, in the case of Greenleaf v. Francis,[4] but it was not called for by the case, as the well alleged to have been injured had been in existence only twelve or fourteen years.

In the case of Chasemore v. Richards,[5] Creswell, J. comments upon the case from Campbell above cited, remarking that Lord Ellenborough seems to have supposed the right of a riparian owner arises out of some presumption of grant by

---

[1] Dexter v. Providence Aqueduct Co., 1 Story, 387, 393.
[2] Sury v. Pigot, Poph. 166, 169.
[3] Smith v. Adams, 6 Paige, 435.
[4] Greenleaf v. Francis, 18 Pick. 117.
[5] Chasemore v. Richards, 2 Hurlst. & N. 168, 183.

those higher up the stream. " It is, therefore, probable that, in the case then before him, which related to the water springing up in the plaintiff's land, he meant that the enjoyment of it for twenty years raised a presumption of grant, — a presumption not generally made against those who had no knowledge of the existence of that which they are presumed to have granted." He states that no one in the case under consideration had insisted upon the doctrine of presumption being applicable, although it will be recollected that the mill-owners who complained of the loss of water in that case had enjoyed it more than sixty years. He states also that the idea of a presumed grant in favor of riparian proprietors

[*386] of the enjoyment of running water was repudiated *in the case of Dickinson v. Grand Junction Canal Co.,[1] since it is *ex jure naturæ*, and an incident of property, and adds : " It would seem, therefore, that the Court of Exchequer, as constituted when that judgment was given, would not have rested an opinion in favor of the plaintiff, in Balston v. Bensted, on the ground stated by Lord Ellenborough."

The court, in Roath v. Driscoll,[2] state the question, and intimate their opinion upon the subject in the following words : " Have they, by mere prior occupancy, acquired an advantage over the defendant, in the use of this water ? Or, in other words, can one of two adjoining proprietors, by first opening a watering-place, prevent other persons from doing the same on their own lands, though by so doing water is prevented from percolating the land so as to supply the first-made reservoir ? . . . . As to adjoining proprietors, who open the earth for reservoirs of water, this distinction (whether it had been enjoyed a certain number of years or not) is not the rule, for nothing is gained by a mere continued preoccupancy of water *under the surface*. Why should

1 Dickinson v. Grand Junction Canal Co., 7 Exch. 282. See, as to this case, Crompton J., in New River Co. v. Johnson, 2 E. & Ellis, 445.
2 Roath v. Driscoll, 20 Conn. 533.

any advantage be gained by preoccupancy? Each owner
has an equal and complete right to the use of his land and
to the water which *is in it*."

The ruling in this case seems to settle the law in respect
to wells or artificial reservoirs which are fed by percolating
waters, and the case already cited, of Wheatley *v.* Baugh,[1]
with equal directness, and at much greater length, applies
the same rule to cases of open natural springs within one's
land which are affected by excavations made for proper
purposes in the lands of others. "The prior occupancy of
the spring for the uses of a tannery gave no right of servitude over or through the land of the adjacent proprietor.
No man, by mere prior enjoyment of the advantages of his
own land, can establish a servitude upon the land
of * another." Speaking of the effect of the enjoy- [*387]
ment of the spring for the period of twenty-one
years: "This depends upon the question whether the enjoyment of the spring was of such a character as to have
invaded his neighbor's rights, so as to enable the latter to
maintain an action for the injury. . . . . No presumption
can arise against a party, on the ground of long enjoyment
of a privilege by another, until it is shown that the privilege
in some measure interfered with the rights of the party
whose grant is proposed to be presumed, and that he had a
legal right to prevent such enjoyment by proceedings at law.
Presumption is when the conduct of the party out of possession cannot be accounted for without presuming a conveyance.   Silence, or acquiescence, where one is not injured,
and has no cause of complaint, can never deprive him of his
rights, on the ground of presumption of a grant." The court
fully sustain the doctrine, that, if a spring thus situated, depending upon percolations alone, and not a distinct watercourse leading to it, was diverted by the owner of the adjacent
land in the exercise of his proper business, and without negligence or malice on his part, it could make no difference

---

[1] Wheatley *v.* Baugh, 25 Penn. St. 528.

that the owner of the spring had enjoyed the same for any
length of time prior to such disturbance. And, as a rule as to
what would be a legal presumption in such case, the court cite
Hoy v. Sterrett,[1] that " to raise the presumption of a grant,
the enjoyment must have been adverse ; there must be a continued, exclusive enjoyment of the easement, with the knowledge and acquiescence of the owner of the inheritance, for
twenty-one years (that being the period of limitation in Pennsylvania), which would be evidence from which a jury might
presume a right by grant or otherwise to such easement."

These cases seem to cover the whole ground upon which
a prescriptive right to underground water, not flow-
[*388] ing in a *defined stream, could be placed, and to
settle that such a right cannot be maintained ; and
the later English cases substantially affirm the same doctrine.
Wightman, J., in giving the opinion of the judges, in the
House of Lords, in Chasemore v. Richards,[2] speaking of
Balston v. Bensted, says the opinion therein expressed
" amounted only to the *dictum* of an eminent judge, followed
by no decision of the case, ... and is directly at variance with the judgment of the Court of Exchequer, in the
case of Dickinson v. Grand Junction Canal Co." And, in
commenting upon the question, whether the use of the water
by the plaintiff for over twenty years for working his mill
raises any presumption of a grant, says: " But what grant
can be presumed, in the case of percolating waters, depending upon the quantity of rain falling, or the natural moisture
of the soil, and, in the absence of any visible means of
knowing to what extent, if at all, the enjoyment of the
plaintiff's mill would be affected by any water percolating
in and out of the defendant's or other land ? The presumption of a grant only arises where the person against whom it
is to be raised might have prevented the exercise of the
subject of the presumed grant ; but how could he prevent

[1] Hoy v. Sterrett, 2 Watts, 330.
[2] Chasemore v. Richards, 5 Hurlst. & N., Am. ed. 982.

or stop the percolation of water? . . . . The right, if it exists at all in the case of subterranean percolating water, is *jure naturæ*, and not by presumed grant, and the circumstances of the mill being ancient would in that case make no difference." Lord Chelmsford in the case rebuts the doctrine of Balston *v.* Bensted, and Lord Wensleydale, though he differed from the opinion of the judges in some respects, remarked that "he did not think that the principle of prescription could be applied to this case. The true foundation of the right was, that it was an incident to the land *ex jure naturæ*." Though it should be stated that Coleridge, J., in Chasemore *v.* Richards,[1] in a *dissenting opin- [*389] ion, inclines to sustain the plaintiff's right to water percolating through the earth, on the ground of long and uninterrupted enjoyment by means of a mill, which was operated by the means of a river into which such water found its way from the adjacent land.

So Gould, J., in the case of Ingraham *v.* Hutchinson, in commenting upon the case of Balston *v.* Bensted, says: "But I am unable to perceive why the plaintiff's right to recover would not have been the same if his works had been erected less than twenty years, or had not been erected at all. For his natural right to the use of the spring was as absolute, I conceive, as if the water had flowed in a rivulet upon the surface through the defendant's land and his own, in which case the diversion of the water would have been an infraction of his natural right, though the diversion had commenced immediately after his title to the land accrued."[2]

The court of Ohio hold, that the doctrine of prescription or presumption of grant from lapse of time, can have no proper application to the law of percolating waters, the using of one's own property, being lawful in itself, cannot make it adverse to the lawful right of another.[3]

· When, in addition to the foregoing authorities, it is re-

1 Chasemore *v.* Richards, 2 Hurlst. & N. 186.
2 Ingraham *v.* Hutchinson, 2 Conn. 584, 597.
3 Frasier *v.* Brown, 12 Ohio, 311. See Haldeman *v.* Bruckhardt, 45 Penn. 519.

membered that the common-law idea of prescription implies
a grant from an intelligent grantor of something with which
he intends to part, to a grantee who intends to accept it, and
that open adverse enjoyment in such cases is nothing more
nor less than evidence of such a grant, it is difficult to see
how the idea of such a grant having been made can be
raised, when neither party could have known that the one
was deriving anything from the other, and where the first
knowledge that the supposed grantor had of any water being
used by the supposed grantee, which had been derived from
the land of the former, was when, in the exercise of his own
right to dig within his own premises, he struck the vein that
fed and supplied the well of his neighbor. The rule, as laid
down in the Code Napoleon, in respect to acquiring servitudes by length of enjoyment, is: " Servitudes *apparent* and
continual may be acquired by writing, or by a pos-
[*390]   session of *thirty years. . . . .* Continual servitudes
non-apparent, and continuable servitudes, apparent
and non-apparent, cannot be created but by writing." [1]

SECTION VIII.

OF RIGHTS TO EAVES' DRIP.

1. Nature and character of this servitude.
2. How far it may exist in favor of the land-owner.
3. How far it is an easement in favor of a building.
4. Not hitherto recognized by common law in favor of land.
5. Enjoyment of eaves' drip does not authorize use of gutters.
6. It may not be changed to increase the burden.
7. Effect on this servitude if the building is destroyed.
8. Rule of the Code Napoleon as to eaves' drip.
9. Land-owner may not interfere with the right by building.
10. Effect of acts done on the land by consent of owner of the building.
11. How the right of eaves' drip should be exercised.

1. THIS right, which the owner of one estate may acquire

[1] Art. 690, 691. See D. 8, 5, 21 ; 2 Fournel, Traité du Voisinage, 411.

in and upon the estate of an adjacent owner, was a servitude known to the civil law under the name of *stillicidium* or *flumen*, according to the circumstances under which it was enjoyed. It is also a well-known servitude or easement at common law, and, under the name of *droit de gouttière*, or *droit d'égout des toîts*, is treated of at large in the French law. It is in its character sufficiently akin to the servitudes of water, which have already been treated of, to be considered in this connection.[1]

It grows out of the fact, that, for one to construct the roof of his house in such a manner as to discharge the water falling thereon in rain, upon the land of an adjacent proprietor, is a violation of the right of such proprietor, if done without his consent, and this consent must be evidenced by express grant or prescription.

*The mode in which this injury may be occasioned [*391.] may be by extending the roof of such building beyond the line of separation between the two estates, or by so constructing it as to throw the water falling thereon, by its own impulse and direction, across this line, and thereby causing it to be discharged upon the estate of the adjacent land-owner. For an injury of this kind, occasioned in either way, the owner of the land may have an action against the owner of the house. But where it is caused by projecting the roof beyond the imaginary line that separates the two estates, it is moreover violating the familiar principle of law by which *cujus est solum ejus est usque ad cœlum*, since it matters not, so far as a right of action is concerned, whether one breaks another's close by crossing this imaginary line that bounds it, upon, beneath, or above the surface, provided it be done against his consent.[2]

[1] Toullier, Droit Civil, 397 ; 2 Fournel, Traité du Voisinage, 113 ; 1 Le Page Desgodets, 208, 209, 445.

[2] 2 Rolle, Abr. 140, citing 18 Edw. III. 22 *b*; Baten's case, 9 Rep. 53 ; Tucker *v.* Newman, 11 Adolph. & E. 40 ; Fay *v.* Prentice, 1 C. B. 828, 838 ; Thomas *v.* Thomas, 2 Crompt. M. & R. 34 ; Bellows *v.* Sackett, 15 Barb. 96 ; D. 8, 2, 1 ; 2 Fournel, Traité du Voisinage, 113, 114.

In considering a case arising from the flow of water from the eaves of a house upon adjoining land, the court said it presented three questions : 1. Whether the grant of the land extended to the body of the house. If it did, and the owner of the house had openly claimed a right to have his eaves hang over and the drip fall on to the adjacent land for the requisite time, it would be an acquisition of the land. 2. If the grant made the house a monument, the line of the eaves would be the line of the land. 3. If, without claiming the land, the eaves' drip had been enjoyed for the requisite time, it would gain an easement in the land to that extent, unless done by permission of the land-owner.[1]

2. But though one may by prescription or grant acquire a right to project the roof of his house beyond the line that bounds his land, it is only of the servitude *stillicidii vel fluminis recipiendi* that it is now proposed to treat. It may be remarked, however, that there was a servitude the reverse of what is above expressed which might be acquired by the civil law, by which one was not at liberty to turn the water flowing from the eaves of his house upon his own land, when the same had been enjoyed by another for the benefit of his land for the requisite period to establish a prescription.[2]

3. The right of the owner of a building thus to discharge the rain falling upon its roof upon the land of another, it may be repeated, was a servitude by the civil law and an easement at the common law. It was *stillicidium*, [*392] *if the water fell in drops from the eaves, but took the name of *flumen*, if conducted in a stream by a spout or gutter.[3]

4. But the servitude *stillicidii vel fluminis non avertendi*, above mentioned, that is, the right in the land-owner to

---

[1] Carbrey v. Willis, 7 Allen, 370.

[2] 2 Toullier, Droit Civil, 396, 397 ; 2 Fournel, Traité du Voisinage, 114 ; D. 8, 2, 2.

[3] 1 Kauff. Makeldey, § 312 ; Vinnius, Lib. 2, tit. 3, § 4 ; Domat, Lib. 1, tit. 12, § 2, Art. 2 ; 2 Fournel, Traité du Voisinage, 114, and note ; Cherry v. Stein, 11 Md. 1, 25 ; Vincent v. Michell, 7 La. 52 ; Alexander v. Boghel, 4 La. 312.

insist upon having the water from another's eaves discharged upon his land, does not seem to be one that has hitherto been recognized by the common law. So that, if the owner of such building were to remove the same or change its roof, and thereby stop such discharge, the land-owner would be without remedy for any loss thereby sustained.[1]

5. If one acquire the right to have the water from his roof discharged upon another's land in drops from the eaves thereof, it does not give him a right to collect it in a spout or gutter, and have it discharged in a united stream.[2]

6. If one acquires for his house the easement of eaves' drip upon another's land, he cannot do anything to increase the injurious effect thereby occasioned to such land, nor add to the quantity by receiving water from other roofs upon his own; but he may change the form in which it is enjoyed, provided he does not increase such effect. It has accordingly been held that he might raise his house higher, but could not reduce its height, because in the one case the drops from the eaves would be less, and in the other more injurious in their fall. If the owner of the house become the owner of the land, the servitude as such would be extinguished so long as the two were united in one ownership. But upon conveying the house again the servitude would revive.[3]

*7. If the house to which this servitude belongs be [*393] destroyed, the owner does not lose the easement if he rebuilds the house in the same form and size of the former one. He may not alter its proportions or parts so as to render the servitude more burdensome than it had previously been.[4]

And so strict was the civil law in this respect, that it did not admit of covering the roof from which the water flowed

---

[1] Arkwright v. Gell, 5 Mees. & W. 203, 233; Wood v. Waud, 3 Exch. 748, 778.

[2] Reynolds v. Clark, 2 Ld. Raym. 1399.

[3] Thomas v. Thomas, 2 Crompt. M. & R. 34, 40; 2 Toullier, Droit Civil, 398; 2 Fournel, Traité du Voisinage, 115; post, chap. 5, sect. 2, pl. 1.

[4] D. 8, 2, 20, 2; 2 Fournel, Traité du Voisinage, 115.

with a material from which it fell with more force than from that which had constituted the former covering of the roof.[1]

8. The Code Napoleon simply declares that " Every owner ought so to fix his eaves that the rain-water shall run on to his own soil or upon the public way ; he cannot turn it upon the land of his neighbor." [2]

It is accordingly laid down in the French law, that if one build a house near the premises of another, he ought to leave space enough next the wall of his house, upon his own land, to receive the water from its roof as well as from its court and kitchen. And rules are given in some cities fixing what this space shall be in certain cases. And a different rule applies where the water falls directly from the eaves from what it is if it is conducted off in a gutter or spout.[3]

9. Where one has acquired an easement of eaves' drip upon another's land, the latter cannot deprive him of it by erecting upon the spot on which the water falls, any building of different height to prevent the discharge of the water from the gutters or eaves of the dominant building.[4]

[*394]   *10. But if one, having such an easement, give permission to the owner of the land on which the water from his roof falls to build thereon so as to obstruct the discharge of the water, the easement is thereby lost. It is like the common case of the effect given to a license by the owner of the dominant estate to the owner of the servient, to do something upon the latter estate which deprives the former of his easement. It operates to extinguish the easement.[5]

[1] D. 8, 2, 20, 4, 3 Toullier, *supra*, 398.

[2] Code Napoleon, Art. 681.

[3] Pardessus, Traité des Servitudes, 322.

M. Pardessus examines at some length the question of legal presumption of possession and ownership of the strip of land adjoining one's house upon which the water falls from its eaves, where the owner of the adjoining land cultivates it up to the wall of the house for a long period of years. Ibid. 323. See also 2 Fournel, Traité du Voisinage, 422 ; " Tour de l'echelle," &c.

[4] D. 8, 2, 20, 3 & 6 ; 3 Toullier, Droit Civil, 398 ; 2 Fournel, *supra*, 115.

[5] D. 8, 6, 8 ; 2 Fournel, Traité du Voisinage, 117 ; 3 Toullier, Droit Civil, 399 ; *post*, chap. 5, sect. 7, pl. 4.

11. The obligation of the owner of a house, which has by prescription or otherwise the right of eaves' drip, so to manage the same as not to increase the injury thereby occasioned to the adjacent owner, was considered in the case of Bellows v. Sackett, already cited.[1] The defendant's house had stood twenty-five years, the plaintiff's about fifteen, and was within two feet of the defendant's eaves. The water from the defendant's house had been conducted by a gutter to the ground upon his own premises, but he suffered this to become decayed, and the water from that side of the roof all fell between the houses upon one spot about midway between one end of the house and the other, and by percolation found its way into the plaintiff's cellar. The court, in an opinion of no little ambiguity, growing out of the fact that the water fell upon the defendant's own land, say: " Here the defendant had the clear right to erect his house, to cover it with a roof which would prevent the rains falling upon the surface it covered, and to turn the water falling upon such roof upon any portion of his own soil, at any point, and in any quantity he might choose. But for such interruption or diversion to the manifest injury of another, he is clearly responsible. Here, owing to a want of suitable repairs, the water falling upon an area of twenty-five feet by thirteen is collected at a single point, and precipitated *in an unnatural and unusual quantity and [*395] manner so near the plaintiff's premises as necessarily to cause him an injury." The judgment which was for the plaintiff in this case, must, it would seem, rest upon the last two or three lines of the above extract from the opinion of the court.

[1] Bellows v. Sackett, 15 Barb. 96, 102.

SECTION IX.

OF RIGHTS OF PASSAGE IN PUBLIC STREAMS.

1. The public have a right of way in public streams.
2. Of navigable streams at common law.
3. Other than navigable streams may be public.
4. Artificial streams, though navigable, not public.
5. Of the test of what streams are public.
6, 7, 8. Rule in the United States as to what are public streams.
9. Property in public streams, and use of their banks.
10, 11. What streams public in the several States.
12. Of property in the banks and beds of streams.
13. How far the public may use the banks of a stream.
14, 15. How far one may occupy the stream and landings in using it.
16. Right to use banks of stream limited by what is necessary.
17. Of the doctrine of dedication to public use.
18. The public have no right to use the banks of a navigable river.
19. Pearsall v. Post. Case of claim to occupy such bank.
20. When the public may use a private channel for passage.
21. Limit of one's power to dam a public stream.

1. This work would evidently be incomplete without noticing, at least briefly, two other subjects growing out of the existence of watercourses, considered in their broader and more comprehensive sense of streams, both navigable and not navigable; and these are the easement of way which the public has in them, and the rights of fishing, connected with an interest more or less extensive in the banks and waters of such streams.

It may be stated, in general terms, that the public have a right of passage or way, like a public highway, by [*396] ships, * boats, or other craft, upon and along the course of all public rivers or streams.[1]

[1] Hale, De Jure Maris, Hargr. Law Tracts, 8, 9; Woolr. Waters, 33; 13 Co. 33; Bullock v. Wilson, 2 Port. 436; Morgan v. Reading, 3 Smedes & M. 366, 407; People v. St. Louis, 5 Gilm. 351; O'Fallon v. Daggett, 4 Mo. 343; Hooker v. Cummings, 20 Johns. 90; Baker v. Lewis, 33 Penn. St. 301; Brown v. Chadbourne, 31 Me. 9; Commonwealth v. Chapin, 5 Pick. 199; Arnold v. Mundy, 1 Halst. 1; Cox v. State, 3 Blackf. 193; Gavit v. Chambers, 3 Ohio, 495; La Plaisance Bay Harbor Co. v. Monroe, Walk. Ch. 155; Bailey v. Phila.

But every stream is not a public one, nor does the common law agree in this respect with the law of many of the States, nor are the rules adopted in regard to it by some of the States the uniform law of all.

2. As a general proposition, all streams, whether of fresh or salt water, are *prima facie* public so far, if at all, as the tide ebbs and flows in the same, and are classed under the generic term of "navigable streams," and are public highways.[1]

This doctrine is uniformly applied, by the English courts, as laid down by Lord Hale, and especially in respect to islands formed in the stream. In the one case they belong to the crown, in the other to the riparian owner or owners, as the case may be.[2]

And yet every stream is not navigable because the tide ebbs and flows in it. " Nor is it every small creek in which a fishing-skiff or gunning-canoe can be made to float at high-water, which is deemed navigable. But, in order to have this character, it must be navigable to some purpose useful to trade or agriculture. It is not a mere possibility of being used under some circumstances, as at extraordinary high tides, which will give it the character of a navigable stream, but it must be generally and commonly useful to some purpose of trade or agriculture." [3]

3. But public rivers are not necessarily navigable, in the sense that the tide ebbs and flows therein. They may

---

B. & W. R. R. Co., 4 Harringt. 389; Blundell *v.* Catterall, 5 Barnew. & Ald. 268; Schurmeier *v.* St. P. & Pac. R. R., 10 Min. 103. See Peck *v.* Smith, 1 Con. 133; Davis *v.* Winslow, 51 Maine, 264; Gerrish *v.* Brown, Ib. 256.

[1] Hargr. Law Tracts, 6; Woolr. Waters, 31, 32, 33; Commonwealth *v.* Charlestown, 1 Pick. 180; Arundell *v.* M'Culloch, 10 Mass. 70; People *v.* Tibbetts, 19 N. Y. 523; Anon., 1 Mod. 105, per Lord *Hale;* Rex *v.* Smith, Doug. 441; 3 Kent, Comm. 414; Rhodes *v.* Otis, 33 Ala. 593; Ellis *v.* Carey, 30 Ala. 725. *Contra,* Wilson *v.* Forbes, 2 Dev. 30, North Carolina; Veasie *v.* Dwinel, 50 Maine, 484.

[2] Ford *v.* Lacy, 7 H. & Norm. 151.

[3] Rowe *v.* Granite Bridge Corp., 21 Pick. 344, 347, per *Shaw,* C. J.; Burrows *v.* Gallup, 32 Con. 501.

[*397] * become so by act of the legislature, or by immemorial usage.[1]

4. On the other hand, the mere fact that a river may be
navigated by boats or water-craft does not make it a public
stream, if it was made so by deepening or widening a private
stream by the owner of the bed and banks thereof.[2]

And the capacity to be made navigable does not make it a
public river, unless it shall have been made navigable and
declared a public highway by legislative act.[3]

5. The difficulty has been in finding any discriminating
test, which may be applicable alike to all streams, in determining whether their capacity is of a character to make them
public in their use or not. In England, the Thames above
London Bridge was held to be a public river.[4] And the Wey
and Severn, as well as sundry other streams.[5]

6. There seems to be a rule, pretty generally received in
the United States, that all streams are highways which are
capable of floating to market the produce of the mines, forests, or tillage of the country through which they flow.[6]

But if it be above tide-water, the burden of proving it to
be a public river is upon the party making the claim.[7]

7. In New York and Maine, a stream seems to be
[*398] a *public one if it is capable of floating logs thereon

[1] Hargr. Law Tracts, 8, 9; Callis, Sewers, 216; Woolr. Waters, 31, 33;
M'Manus v. Carmichael, 3 Iowa, 1; State v. Gilmanton, 10 N. H. 467; Col-
lins v. Benbury, 5 Ired. 118; Berry v. Carle, 3 Me. 269; Baker v. Lewis, 33 Penn.
St. 301; Morgan v. King, 30 Barb. 9.

All "navigable rivers" in the territory northwest of the Ohio are declared
public highways by act of Congress. 2 Dane, Abr. 691; Tyler v. The People,
8 Mich. 320.

[2] Hargr. Law Tracts, 9; Woolr. Waters, 33; Wadsworth v. Smith, 11 Me.
278. See People v. Platt, 17 Johns. 195; Veasie v. Dwinel, 50 Maine, 479,
486.

[3] Cates v. Wadlington, 1 M'Cord, 580.

[4] Rex v. Smith, Doug. 441.

[5] Hale, De Jure Maris, Hargr. Law Tracts, 9.

[6] Browne v. Scofield, 8 Barb. 239; Stuart v. Clark, 2 Swan, 9; Walker v.
Shephardson, 4 Wisc. 486; Lorman v. Benson, 8 Mich. 18; Morgan v. King,
30 Barb. 9.

[7] Rhodes v. Otis, 33 Ala. 578; Ellis v. Carey, 30 Ala. 725.

to market.   If this were true only for a few days in
the year, however, it would not be sufficient.[1]   But if a
stream will float logs, for several weeks in a year, the distance of a hundred and fifty miles, it would be a navigable
stream for that purpose.   And the doctrine is said to be one
of common law in Maine, that all rivers, capable, in their
nature, of being used for commerce, or the floating of logs,
rafts, boats, or vessels, are highways, and may be used by
the public for these purposes whenever their condition is
such as to admit of such use.[2]

In North Carolina and Pennsylvania the ebb and flow of
the tide is no test of a river being navigable.[3]

Rock and Fox Rivers in Wisconsin are held to be navigable streams.[4]

8. In California, rivers are not regarded navigable unless
sufficient to float a vessel used in transporting freight or passengers, or rafts of timber.   But a mere capacity to float a
log would not be sufficient.[5]

In Alabama the court held that a creek which could only
be used for floating timber for six or seven miles, where there
were no extensive forests to be accommodated by such a use,
and could only be used for floating rafts occasionally, according to the state of the water, could not be deemed to be a
public, navigable stream, although it might be used to advantage by a single individual.   " The public must be interested before it can become a public highway."   And whether
a stream is a public highway or not is a question of law, after
the facts are ascertained.[6]

---

[1] Curtis v. Keesler, 14 Barb. 511 ; Morgan v. King, 18 Barb. 277, 288. See
Munson v. Hungerford, 6 Barb. 265.

[2] Morgan v. King, supra; Brown v. Chadbourne, 31 Me. 9 ; Moor v. Veazie,
32 Me. 343, 357 ; Treat v. Lord, 42 Me. 552, 562; Knox v. Chaloner, 42 Me.
150 ; cites 1 Allen, N. B. 326.

[3] Wilson v. Forbes, 2 Dev. 30 ; Ingraham v. Threadgill, 3 Dev. 59 ; Carson
v. Blazer, 2 Binn. 475 ; Barclay Road v. Ingham, 36 Penn. 201 ; Flanagan v.
Philadelphia, 42 Penn. 229.

[4] Wood v. Hustis, 17 Wisc. 417 ; Cobb v. Smith, 16 Wis. 661 ; Harrington v.
Edwards, 17 Wisc. 586.

[5] American River Water Co. v. Amsden, 6 Cal. 443.

[6] Rhodes v. Otis, 33 Ala. 578.

9. In Alabama, the right of property in navigable streams
is vested in the State, and the citizens have a right
[*399] of *easement in the banks of the same for the purposes of using them for navigation.[1] And this extends to every watercourse in the State suitable for the ordinary purposes of navigation, as well above as below the
tide, and as such they are highways.[2]

In Mississippi, Illinois, Iowa, Minnesota, and Missouri, the
Mississippi River is held to be a public highway.[3]

10. In Pennsylvania, the Ohio,[4] Alleghany,[5] and Susquehanna[6] are held to be public highways. So is the Ohio in
Indiana[7] and in Ohio.[8] And the Hudson, whether above or
below the tide, is a navigable river in New York.[9] So are
the Schuylkill,[10] Youghiogheny and Towanda[11] and Monongahela[12] and Mohawk.[13] And these, though expressly stated
to be such, may be taken rather as representatives than as
exceptions in respect to most of the States wherein there are
considerable streams of water, for, in other cases, the principle is extended to all streams in New York which are actually navigable, whether above or below tide-waters.[14] The
same is the case in Massachusetts.[15] In New Jersey the doctrine is stated, that navigable rivers, ports, bays, and coasts

[1] Mayor, &c. v. Eslava, 9 Port. 577, 604.
[2] Bullock v. Wilson, 2 Port. 436.
[3] Morgan v. Reading, 3 Smedes & M. 366, 407; People v. St. Louis, 5 Gilm.
351; O'Fallon v. Daggett, 4 Mo. 343; Godfrey v. City of Alton, 12 Ill. 29;
M'Manus v. Carmichael, 3 Iowa, 1 Schurmeier v. St. P. & Pac. R. R., 10 Min. 82.
[4] Baker v. Lewis, 33 Penn. St. 301.
[5] Dalrymple v. Mead, 1 Grant's Cas. 197.
[6] Commonwealth v. Fisher, 1 Penn. 462; Carson v. Blazer, 2 Binn. 475.
[7] Porter v. Allen, 8 Ind. 1.
[8] Gavit v. Chambers, 3 Ohio, 495.
[9] Palmer v. Mulligan, 3 Caines, 307; Hooker v. Cummings, 20 Johns. 90.
[10] Flanagan v. Philadelphia, 42 Penn. 230.
[11] Barclay Road v. Ingham, 36 Penn. 200.
[12] Monongahela Bridge v. Kirk, 46 Penn. 120.
[13] People v. Canal Comrs. 33 N. Y. 461.
[14] People v. Platt, 17 Johns. 195, 211; Shaw v. Crawford, 10 Johns. 236; Post
v. Pearsall, 22 Wend. 425.
[15] Commonwealth v. Chapin, 5 Pick. 199; Knight v. Wilder, 2 Cush. 208.

of the sea are common to all citizens for passing over, fishing, or fowling.[1]

The public are held to have a right of way in all navigable streams in Indiana[2] and Ohio.[3]   And the same, though *applied to the river Raisin, was held [*400] to be the law of Michigan.[4]   And all navigable rivers are highways in Delaware.[5]

11. So in Connecticut and New Hampshire, the Connecticut River has been held to be a public highway for all citizens, for the purposes of boating and rafting, it having become so in the latter State by long usage.   And in Maine, all rivers above the flow of tide which have long been used for the passage of boats, rafts, and the like, are public highways, and may be used accordingly.   And this extends to passing upon the ice of these streams when frozen.[6]

In consequence of the superior capacity of the rivers in America for practical navigation over those in England, there is a general tendency to regard the civil rather than the common law, in determining whether a stream is navigable or not.   If the same is large enough to admit of navigation, it partakes of the character of a navigable river, although it is not affected by the flood or ebb of the tide.   Such rivers are regarded as highways which it is unlawful to obstruct.   And in some of the States the principle of the common law is applied, that the riparian owner is bounded by the low-water mark of the stream, instead of extending to its thread, as is the case with streams at common law where there is no tide.   Thus in Pennsylvania, low-water mark is the boundary of riparian proprietorship.[7]   While

---

[1] Arnold v. Munday, 1 Halst. 1.   See O'Fallon v. Daggett, 4 Mo. 343.

[2] Cox v. State, 3 Blackf. 193.

[3] Gavit v. Chambers, 3 Ohio, 495.

[4] La Plaisance Bay Harbor Co. v. Monroe, Walk. Ch. 155; Lorman v. Benson, 8 Mich. 18; Rice v. Ruddiman, 10 Mich. 141.

[5] Bailey v. Philadelphia W. & B. R. R. Co., 4 Harringt. 389.

[6] Scott v. Willson, 3 N. H. 321; Adams v. Pease, 2 Conn. 481; Berry v. Carle, 3 Me. 269; Spring v. Russell, 7 Me. 273; French v. Camp, 18 Me. 433.

[7] Flanagan v. Philadelphia, 42 Penn. 229; M'Keen v. Delaware Division, &c., 49 Penn. 440.

in some of the States bounding on the Mississippi, it is the thread of that river.[1] A like doctrine to that of Pennsylvania is maintained in New York.[2] In Maine, the Penobscot above tide-water is a highway, but not a navigable stream.[3] But it seems that, in one respect, streams navigable by statute or custom here, are not like those which are so by the common law, since in respect to the latter the shore, the space between high and low water, belongs to the sovereign ; here it belongs to the owner of the upland, and may be built upon by him.[4]

The consequence of holding a stream navigable and public is, that any obstruction placed therein may be treated as a nuisance, and is the subject of indictment.[5]

From the character of highways given to streams which are capable of affording navigation in their natural state, no one may lawfully obstruct the passage of boats, &c., by erecting and maintaining a permanent dam across the same, unless he make provision for a convenient passage way through or by his dam, for the public to use.[6] He may make and maintain temporarily a boom to collect and hold the logs, though he may not permanently interfere with others in floating logs upon the same stream.[7]

This extends to throwing into it any waste material, filth, or trash, such as edgings of boards and the like.[8] Nor does

[1] Morgan v. Reading, S. & Marsh, 404 ; Middleton v. Pritchard, 3 Scam. 510.

[2] People v. Canal Comrs. 33 N. Y. 461 ; impugning former decisions upon the same subject, Lawler v. Wells, 13 How. P. C. 454.

[3] Veasie v. Dwinel, 50 Maine, 479.

[4] Flanagan v. Philadelphia, 42 Penn. 229 ; Clement v. Burns, 43 N. H. 609, 617 ; Gough v. Bell, 2 Zabriskie, 441 ; Thurman v. Morrison, 14 B. Mon. 367 ; O'Fallon v. Daggett, 4 Mo. 343.

[5] Rhodes v. Otis, 33 Ala. 578.

[6] Veasie v. Dwinel, 50 Maine, 479, 484 ; s. c., 44 Maine, 167 ; Davis v. Winslow, 51 Maine, 289 ; Brown v. Chadbourne, 31 Maine, 9 ; Knox v. Chaloner, 42 Maine, 150.

[7] Gerrish v. Brown, 51 Maine, 256 ; Davis v. Winslow, sup.

[8] Veasie v. Dwinel, 50 Maine, 490 ; ante, p. *282.

any length of enjoyment give a party a right to prescribe for a *public* nuisance.[1]

So a party obstructed in the use of a stream as a highway, may himself remove it, as was held where one fastened his raft of logs to the bank in such a manner as to prevent another from landing at his own wharf in a boat.[2]

If one is authorized by the legislature to erect a bridge across a navigable stream, and, in so doing, he flows back the water on to another's land, he is liable in damages to the owner, and the act of the legislature merely justifies him as against an indictment for a nuisance to a public highway.[3]

But a state may authorize obstructions to be maintained in navigable streams within it.[4]   And if the natural and necessary effect of a bridge in a highway or railroad is to flow back water on to another's land, it is regarded as one of the incidental damages which are to be estimated and paid for upon the location of the same, and not the ground of an action on the case as for a wrong done.[5]

12. While the doctrine as to a public easement in navigable streams, using the term in its broader sense as above stated, seems to be well settled, the only question being, what streams answer to that description, the respective rights of the owners of the banks, and of those navigating the streams, have been variously stated by different courts and writers, and are not, perhaps, uniform at this day, under the laws of the different States.

As a general proposition, though there are exceptions to

<hr/>

[1] Veasie *v.* Dwinel, 50 Maine, 496. Commonwealth *v.* Upton, 6 Gray, 476 ; People *v.* Cunningham, 1 Denio, 536 ; Davis *v.* Winslow, 51 Maine, 293 ; Gerrish *v.* Brown, Ib. 256.

[2] Harrington *v.* Edwards, 17 Wis. 586.

[3] Eastman *v.* Company, 44 N. H. 143 ; Crittenden *v.* Wilson, 5 Cow. 165 ; Ang. Water C. § 476 ; Thacher *v.* Dartmouth Bridge, 18 Pick. 502 ; Gardner *v.* Newburgh, 2 Johns Ch. 162 ; Hooksett *v.* Amoskeag Co., 44 N. H. 105.

[4] Flanagan *v.* City of Phila., 42 Penn. 231 ; Wilson *v.* Blackbird Creek, &c. 2 Peters, 250 ; U. S. *v.* New Bedford Bridge, 1 W. & Minot, 407 ; Cobb *v.* Smith, 16 Wis. 661.

[5] Sprague *v.* Worcester, 13 Gray, 193 ; *ante*, p. *224.

this in some States in respect to large rivers, like the Mississippi, the owner of land upon the bank of a stream in which the tide does not ebb and flow, is owner of the land under the stream to its centre, or *filum aquæ.* While, if it be one in which the tide does ebb and flow, he only owns to the water's edge at high water.[1]

[*401]   *But the riparian proprietor holds, in the first-mentioned case, subject to the use of the stream as a highway over it, and may do nothing to obstruct such use.[2] And this doctrine applies to the small lakes in the country.[3]

But if lands border upon what are, technically, navigable streams, the tide ebbing and flowing therein, and the public see fit to stop the use of such stream as a highway, such riparian proprietors have no better right for compensation for such appropriation than any other individuals in the community, since they own no part of the bed of the stream.[4]

13. In some of the States the courts have been inclined to hold, that the right on the part of the public to use a stream as a highway, by boats, rafts, and the like, carries with it the right to land upon the bank of such stream as occasion may require, or to secure boats to the trees standing on the bank, and for like uses. Thus in Mississippi, the court, in speaking of the right of the navigator, say, that in case of necessity he may *perhaps* use the bank, or trees growing upon it, to secure his boat upon.[5]

The extent of the right which the public may exercise in the banks of rivers, in connection with the use of the stream

---

[1] 2 Washb. Real Prop. 632, 634 ; Bardwell *v.* Ames, 22 Pick. 354, as to the Connecticut River ; Lorman *v.* Benson, 8 Mich. 18, as to Detroit River. But see, as to the Mississippi, M'Manus *v.* Carmichael, 3 Iowa, 1 ; D. 8, 3, 17. See, as to the ownership of the shores of American lakes and rivers, Clement *v.* Burns, 43 N. H. 616 *et seq.; ante,* p. *399 ; Grant *v.* Davenport, 18 Iowa, 185.

[2] Cox *v.* State, 3 Blackf. 193 ; Gavit *v.* Chambers, 3 Ohio, 495 ; People *v.* St. Louis, 5 Gilm. 351 ; Morgan *v.* King, 30 Barb. 9.

[3] Rice *v.* Ruddiman, 10 Mich. 143.

[4] Bailey *v.* Phila. W. & B. R. R. Co., 4 Harringt. 389.

[5] Morgan *v.* Reading, 3 Smedes & M. 366, 407. See also Lewis *v.* Keeling, 1 Jones (Law), 299. But see Blundell *v.* Catterall, 5 Barnew. & Ald. 268, per *Bayley,* J. ; Inst. 2, 1, 4.

as a highway, within the former Territory of Louisiana, seems to be somewhat peculiar, and to have been borrowed from the Spanish legislation to which it once was subject. The matter is considered in the case of O'Fallon v. Daggett, wherein M'Girk, J. cites the language of the Partidas, subject to which the grants along the Mississippi were made by the Spanish crown, that "rivers, ports, and public roads belong to all men in common, so that strangers coming from foreign countries may make use of them in the same manner *as the inhabitants of the place where they [*402] are, might do; and though the dominion or property of banks of rivers belongs to the owner of the adjoining estate, nevertheless every man may make use of them to fasten his vessel to the trees that grow thereon, or to refit his vessel, or to put his sails or merchandise there. So fishermen may put and expose their fish for sale there, and dry their nets, or make use of the banks for all like purposes which appertain to the art or trade by which they live." The court accordingly recognize these rights, but restrict them, in the case of the navigator, to cases where, in the actual prosecution of a voyage, his vessel needs repairs to enable her to proceed, but leaving the bank, if private property, as soon as practicable. The right must be limited to cases of emergency, and not extended to cases of mere convenience. The navigator cannot obstruct the owner's enjoyment of his land upon the bank beyond the reasonable limits of necessity imposed on him at the time.[1]

14. In Pennsylvania, upon the ground that the Alleghany is a public river for the transit of timber, it was held, that any one wishing to make up a raft to be run upon the stream had a right to make use of an eddy in the stream for that purpose for a reasonable time, to the exclusion of another, if he was the first occupant thereof, while its pools, bars, inlets, and fastening-places are open and free for the

---

[1] O'Fallon v. Daggett, 4 Mo. 343. See 4 Hall, Law Journ. 550; post, sect. 12, pl. 13.

use of every one while using it, consistently with the same right being enjoyed by every one else.[1]

15. So, the Ohio having been declared by that State a public stream or highway for the passage of boats and rafts, it has been held that it carried with it the right to moor boats and other craft at "the well-known landings and wharves on the stream"; and that one who "moors his craft at an accustomed landing must be careful to leave sufficient [*403] room *for the passer-by. . . . . On the other hand, the vessel in motion must, if possible, steer clear of, and avoid, the one moored or at anchor."[2]

It will be perceived that neither of these cases goes the length of the case cited from Missouri, as to landing at any point the boatman might see fit along the bank of a navigable stream. Nor do they state how the places indicated became "well-known" or "accustomed" "landings."

That the public may acquire a right to use such "landings" by dedication on the part of the owner of the soil, and may thereby acquire an easement in an individual owner's land, is now well settled, as has been heretofore shown. It was so held in Godfrey v. City of Alton, in respect to the landing-place at that city upon the banks of the Mississippi.[3]

But the right, for instance, to raft logs in a stream does not involve the right of *booming* them upon private property for safe keeping and storage.[4]

16. In regard to the right to land upon other points upon the banks of a navigable stream than those which have in some way become public landings, the law would seem to confine it to cases of necessity, where, in the proper exercise of the right of passage upon the stream of water, it becomes unavoidable that one should make use of the bank for landing upon, or fastening his craft to, in the prosecution of his passage.

[1] Dalrymple v. Mead, 1 Grant. Cas. 197.
[2] Baker v. Lewis, 33 Penn. St. 301.
[3] Godfrey v. City of Alton, 12 Ill. 29; *ante*, chap. 1, sect. 5.
[4] Lorman v. Benson, 8 Mich. 33; Harrington v. Edwards, 17 Wis. 586.

Thus in Maine it has been held that, if necessary in driving logs upon one of these streams for one to go upon its bank in order to remove a log resting upon or against such bank, he would have a right so to do. But he would not have a right to use such bank for towing logs along the stream.[1]

*17. The doctrine of dedication of property to [*404] public use, so far as it partakes of the nature of a grant, forms an exception to an almost universal rule, that a right by grant or prescription can only be acquired by some person in existence who may be a grantee and grantor in a deed. No case can be found in the English books where a grant has enured to the personal use of *all mankind*. The public cannot, therefore, claim an easement by *prescription*, though corporations and individual inhabitants of towns may.[2]

The doctrine of dedication, moreover, applies generally to rights like those of public streets and highways, open commons or squares, landing-places upon navigable streams, and the like. And though in one case it was held that a spring of water might be reserved for public use in laying out a village or city, it may be regarded rather as a customary right of the residents of a particular locality, than as a public right like that of passing along a highway or navigating a public stream.[3]

18. In the first place, there is no common-law right to make use of the banks of a stream in navigating it.[4] Nor is there a general custom for persons navigating such stream to deposit goods on the banks thereof.[5] And even if such

---

[1] Treat *v.* Lord, 42 Me. 552 ; Ball *v.* Herbert, 3 T. R. 253, 260. See also Lewis *v.* Keeling, 1 Jones (Law), 299 ; Regina *v.* Cluworth, 6 Mod. 163.

[2] Cincinnati *v.* White, 6 Peters, 436 ; Pearsall *v.* Post, 20 Wend. 111 ; Curtis *v.* Keesler, 14 Barb. 511.   See *ante*, chap. 1, sect. 5.

[3] M'Connell *v.* Lexington, 12 Wheat. 582.   See Cincinnati *v.* White, *supra*. See *ante*, chap. 1 sect. 5.

[4] Ball *v.* Herbert, 3 T. R. 253, 260.   See Blundell *v.* Catterall, 5 Barnew. & Ald. 268 ; 3 Kent, Comm. 417, note ; Bickel *v.* Polk, 5 Harringt. 325.

[5] Chambers *v.* Furry, 1 Yeates, 167.

a right is exercised by individuals, upon one or more places upon the bank of such stream, it does not give the public a right to do the same, against the consent of the owner.[1]

It seems that such right of landing upon the es-
[*405] tate of *another may be acquired by the public as an easement, for the purposes of a passage.[2]

19. What may be claimed as a public easement by way of dedication was elaborately considered by the court of New York, in Pearsall v. Post, already referred to. The question in that case was, whether a public landing-place upon the bank of waters navigable at common law, it being in that case the shore of Long Island, could be claimed as a matter of right for all the citizens. It will be observed, the claim is not set up as a right necessary to the prosecution of a continuous passage by water, nor as being part of a highway over which the public passed to reach other localities, to which such way led. The court reviews, at considerable length, the doctrine of the English, Scotch, and American cases, wherein it is clearly maintained that the right of streets, highways, and public passages may be gained to the public by dedication. But they deny that any English case warrants a claim, by dedication, to anything more than the use of a passage-way, or of a public square and the like, or recognizes any existing right in the public, irrespective of living within the limits of some particular corporation, to enjoy the use of the soil of another. They refer to Waters v. Lilley[3] as sustaining these views of the court, and criticise the language of the court in Coolidge v. Learned[4] that the right there claimed, that the *locus in quo* was a public landing-place which every citizen of the Commonwealth had a right to use, " is a prescriptive right, and as such is well pleaded," as being inconsistent with the idea of a prescrip-

---

[1] Bethune v. Turner, 1 Me. 111; Blundell v. Catterall, 5 Barnew. & Ald. 253, 268.

[2] Chambers v. Furry, 1 Yeates, 167; Cooper v. Smith, 9 Serg. & R. 26, 33.

[3] Waters v. Lilley, 4 Pick. 145.

[4] Coolidge v. Learned, 8 Pick. 504.

tion which implies somebody to be grantees, as well as somebody to grant, which that indefinite thing *the public* could not be.

The right claimed in Pearsall *v.* Post was that of landing upon the plaintiff's premises, occupying them as a *place of deposit of articles in transit, which the pub- [*406] lic had been accustomed to do for more than twenty years. The right was denied both in the Supreme Court, and, upon revision, by the Court of Errors of New York, who held that the doctrine of dedication could not be carried beyond using it for purposes like those of public squares, markets, highways, and promenades, excluding the right of individuals to occupy the land of another for private use.[1]

And it may be incidentally remarked, that the mere leaving an open space between one's house and the line of the street or highway, is not a dedication of the same to the public.[2]

20. It was held that if a man were to construct a channel through his own land, whereby the water of a navigable stream is made to flow through the same, he might be compelled to stop the same as being a public nuisance, and if he stopped or obstructed the use of the stream as a highway, the public might use his new channel in the same manner as they had done the original stream. But it would not give them that right, if the obstruction to the use of the stream was caused by another, and not by the owner of the land through which the artificial channel was constructed.[3]

But if the public use such artificial channel for twenty years for purposes of navigation, they acquire a right to the same by the way of dedication.[4]

21. In one respect, a public company, incorporated with authority to erect a dam across a public stream, would not

[1] Pearsall *v.* Post, 20 Wend. 111 ; 22 Wend. 425. See Cortelyou *v.* Van Brundt, 2 Johns. 357.

[2] Biddle *v.* Ash, 2 Ashm. 211, 220.

[3] Dwinel *v.* Barnard, 28 Me. 554, 562 ; Dwinel *v.* Veazie, 44 Me. 167.

[4] Delaney *v.* Boston, 2 Harringt. 489.

have, in respect to such dam, as broad rights as a riparian proprietor who should have erected the same dam for his own purposes. In the latter case, if in the ordinary [*407] state *of the stream, the water raised by the dam did not set back on to the proprietor's land above, the dam-owner would not be responsible if, at times, the swell in the stream overflowed the same ; whereas, if it were done by a dam erected by such company, they would be responsible for the damages thereby occasioned.[1]

SECTION X.

OF RIGHTS IN WATER BY CUSTOM.

1. Custom as distinguished from dedication.
2. Does not extend to taking the profits of land.
3. What may be acquired by custom.
4. One may claim a right by custom, another by prescription.
5. Easement of bathing in another's stream.
6. How such easement or custom may be defeated.

1. WHAT has been said of the distinction there is between a dedication and prescription leads to a consideration of those easements which belong to the inhabitants of certain localities, as distinguished from a dedication, in the proper sense of the term. Such of these easements, however, only as relate to the use and enjoyment of water will now be considered. Where easements of this character belong to such inhabitants, not personally, nor by reason of holding any particular estate to which the same has attached as a particular easement, they are said to exist by *custom*. In technical accuracy, they are not, indeed, easements, but are sufficiently like them to be treated of under that general character.

2. Nothing can be claimed in this right which partakes of the profits or productions of the land in which it is

[1] Monongahela Navigation Co. *v.* Coon, 6 Penn. St. 379.

claimed. Thus one may claim a right by custom to take
water from a stream in another's land for culinary
or *domestic purposes. But he cannot, under such [*408]
custom, claim a right to catch and carry away fish
in the stream.[1]

3. Mr. Woolrych thus states the law upon this subject:
" Inhabitants or particular persons residing in certain vills
may also have a right to water their cattle in rivers at
spots where they have had an immemorial usage so to do,
and there may be other customs and prescriptions to use
water in various ways."[2]

In Race v. Wood, the claim set up, and sustained by the
court, was an immemorial custom in the township of H.
for all the inhabitants for the time being in the said township to have the liberty and privilege to have and take water
from a certain well or spring of water in a certain close, and
to carry the same to their own houses to be used and consumed therein for domestic purposes. The same would have
been the law had it been a running stream of water. And
a claim of a right to take water does not come within the
principle of claiming a right to take sand or gravel, grass,
turves, or any *profit à prendre*.[3]

Lord Campbell, in giving the opinion in Race v. Wood,
cites an early analogous case from the Year Book,[4] in which
such a right is spoken of as a *prescription*, though, as he
remarks, " There is no prescription stated in a *que estate*."
And there are other authorities for holding that " prescription applies only to incorporeal hereditaments ; and whether
the right claimed be considered as strictly a *custom* or *prescription* the principle is the same. The only material dis-

---

[1] Bland v. Lipscombe, 4 Ellis & B. 714, note; Grimstead v. Marlowe, 4
T. R. 717 ; *ante*, chap. 1, sect. 4, pl. 15 - 19.

[2] Woolr. Waters, 3. See more fully as to custom, *ante*, chap. 1, sect. 4.

[3] Race v. Wood, 4 Ellis & B. 702 ; Weekly v. Wildman, 1 Ld. Raym. 407 ;
Manning v. Wasdale, 5 Adolph. & E. 758.

[4] 15 Edw. IV., fol. 29 A, pl. 7.

tinction between them is, that one is local and the other personal in its nature." [1]

[*409]   *4. The purpose of the above citation is rather to show what a custom is like in its nature, than as illustrating or limiting the extent of its application. Nor is there any incompatibility in the same easement being enjoyed by different individuals in different rights, one claiming it by custom, another by reason of holding a particular estate to which it has become attached. [2]

5. Among the easements in water known to the common law, which may be mentioned, is that of bathing in ponds or streams in another's land. Such an easement may be acquired by prescription or exist by custom. But the right does not, as a natural one, belong to the public, even to bathe in the sea, if to do so the persons using it must pass over the land of another. The latter question was very elaborately considered in Blundell v. Catterall, [3] where the language of Bracton, borrowed from Justinian, favoring such a claim as of right, is criticised and restricted as being at variance with the principles of the common law. And if it is a right which may not be exercised by passing over the land of another bordering upon the sea, much less may it be done in streams whose banks and beds are private property. [4]

6. But such an easement or custom would be subject to be discontinued or destroyed by the erection of dwelling-houses in the vicinity of such bathing place, which should render it indecent to bathe there in public. [5]

---

[1] Cortelyou v. Van Brundt, 2 Johns. 357; Pearsall v. Post, 20 Wend. 111, 119.

[2] Kent v. Waite, 10 Pick. 138.

[3] Blundell v. Catterall, 5 Barnew. & Ald. 268; Bract. fo. 8.

[4] Woolr. Waters, 2, 6, 10. See the case of the Westminster boys bathing in the Thames by immemorial custom at Millbank. 2 Campb. 89.

[5] Rex v. Cremden, 2 Campb. 89.

*SECTION XI.   [*410]

OF RIGHTS OF FISHERY.

1. Of rights to fish in the sea and tide-waters.
2. Right of soil carries right to fish in streams not navigable.
3. Easements of right to fish, how gained.
4. Exclusive right of fishery in tide-waters, how gained.
5. To gain it, the enjoyment must be exclusive.
6. No prescription to fish in the sea by a *que estate*.
7. How far one may have a several fishery independent of soil.
8. The owner of several fishery may grant it alone.
9. What rights of fishery the owner of the soil may grant.
10. Three classes of fisheries defined.
11. Easements only in such as are subjects of private property.
12. Fisheries regulated by State statutes.
13. Rights to fish subject to public right of passage.

1 ANOTHER easement, connected of course with the presence of water, is that of a right to take fish. To distinguish between what would be an easement in this respect, and what a man may enjoy at common law, or as the owner of the estate within which the right is exercised, it may be premised that a right to take fish, including shell-fish, in the sea and the arms and bays thereof, and in rivers where the tide ebbs and flows, below high-water mark, is common to all citizens, unless restrained by some act on the part of the government or State having sovereignty over the same, though this does not extend to a right to land fish, when taken or while taking them, upon the soil of a riparian proprietor above high-water mark.[1]

[1] 2 Dane, Abr. 689, 690, 693; Mass. Ordinance, 1641; Col. Laws, c. 63; Warren *v.* Matthews, 1 Salk. 357; s. c., 6 Mod. 73; Carter *v.* Murcot, 4 Burr. 2164; Hargr. Law Tracts, 11; Word *v.* Creswell, Willes, 265; Parker *v.* Cutler Mill-Dam Co., 20 Me. 353, 357; Melvin *v.* Whiting, 7 Pick. 79; Collins *v.* Benbury, 5 Ired. 118; Delaware, &c. R. R. *v.* Stump, 8 Gill & J. 479, 510; Woolr. Waters, 60; Coolidge *v.* Williams, 4 Mass. 140; Lay *v.* King, 5 Day, 72; Bickel *v.* Polk, 5 Harringt. 325; Moulton *v.* Libbey, 37 Me. 485; Weston *v.* Sampson, 8 Cush. 357, 351. The ordinance of 1641 extends the right of fishing to "great ponds" of ten acres or more, in the same manner as in bays, coves, &c. Colony Laws, c. 63.

[*411]   *2. But at common law a right to take fish belongs so essentially to the right of soil in streams where the tide does not ebb and flow, that, if the riparian proprietor owns upon both sides the stream, no one but himself may come within the limits of his land and take fish there. And the same rule applies so far as his land extends, to wit, to the thread of the stream, where he owns upon one side only. Within these limits, by the common law, his right of fishery is sole and exclusive.[1]

3. But not only may this common right in all the citizens be superseded by an exclusive right in individuals to fish within certain limits, but the right of fishery incident to the ownership of the soil of a river may be granted to another by the owner thereof, while retaining the soil and freehold of the premises, either to be enjoyed in common with himself, or to be exclusively enjoyed by such grantee as a separate incorporeal hereditament. And it is but repeating a familiar principle, that such rights may be acquired by prescriptive user and enjoyment to the same extent as by grant. It will be understood, unless otherwise explained, that the rights here spoken of are such as exist at common law, independent of any local laws or usages of the several states in this country.[2]

Thus, in speaking of the owner of the land upon both sides of a stream having a presumptive right of fishing therein, Lord Hale remarks: " But special usage may alter that common presumption, for one man may have the river, and others the soil adjacent, or one man may have the river and soil thereof, and another the free or several fishing in that river." [3]

[1] Case of Banne Fishery, Davies, 152, 155 ; Hargr. Law Tracts, 5 ; Bract. fol. 207 ; Woolr. Waters, 87 ; Chalker v. Dickinson, 1 Conn. 382 ; Waters v. Lilley, 4 Pick. 145 ; Ingram v. Threadgill, 3 Dev. 59 ; Commonwealth v. Chapin, 5 Pick. 199 ; Hooker v. Cummings, 20 Johns. 90 ; M'Farlin v. Essex Co., 10 Cush. 304 ; 2 Fournel, Traité du Voisinage, § 212.
[2] Woolr. Waters, 89 ; per *Yates*, J., Carter v. Murcot, 4 Burr. 2165.
[3] Hargr. Law Tracts, 5.

*4. So, in speaking of the rights of all citizens to [*412]
fish in the sea and creeks and arms thereof, " as a
public common of piscary," he says that they " may not,
without injury to their right, be restrained-of it, unless in
such places, creeks, or navigable rivers, where either the
king or some particular subject hath gained a propriety, exclusive of that common liberty." [1]

He then states how an individual may acquire the right
to fish in a creek or navigable river to the exclusion of the
public : 1st, by the king's grant ; and 2d, by custom or prescription. " And I think it very clear that the subject may,
by custom and usage or prescription, have the true propriety
and interest of many of these several maritime interests.
. . . . A subject may, by prescription, have the interest of
fishing in the arm of the sea, in a creek or port of the sea,
or in a certain precinct or extent, lying within the sea, and
these not only *free* fishing, but *several* fishing."   The meaning of which terms will be more fully explained.[2]

5. But there must be something more than a mere enjoyment by the person claiming such exclusive right of fishing
in order to acquire it; for he has the right originally, in
common with all the citizens, and the exercising of such a
right by one is in no sense adverse to, or exclusive of, that
of another, whenever he shall see fit to exercise it.   Thus in
the case of Carter *v.* Murcot, cited above, Lord Mansfield
says, when speaking of an exclusive right to fish in a navigable river : " If he can show a right by *prescription*, he may
then exercise an exclusive right, though the *presumption* is
against him, unless he can *prove* such a prescriptive right." [3]

This matter is treated of by the court of Connecticut in *Chalker v.* Dickinson, where the plaintiff [*413]
claimed an exclusive right to fish in a part of Con-

---

[1] Hargr. Law Tracts, 11.

[2] Woolr. Waters, 60 ; 2 Dane, Abr. 690 ; Mayor of Orford *v.* Richardson, 4
T. R. 437, 439 ; Carter *v.* Murcot, 4 Burr, 2164 ; Day *v.* Day, 4 Md. 262, 270 ;
Gould *v.* James, 6 Cow. 369, 376.

[3] See Anon, 1 Mod. 104, per *Lord Hale.*

necticut River in which the tide ebbed and flowed. By the
common law no right could be acquired by use, possession,
and occupation, unless it had been from time immemorial,
and this is called a right by prescription. "The general
rule is, that certain rights may be acquired against individuals by fifteen years' uninterrupted possession and use, un-
answered and unexplained. . . . . But the case under consideration is of a very different description. The fishery in
Connecticut River, below high-water mark, is common to all
the citizens. The use and possession of the plaintiffs was
lawful, and the mere lawful exercise of a common right for
fifteen years, has never been considered as conferring an exclusive right. This case, therefore, does not compare with
the cases where a right is acquired by uninterrupted use and
possession. Further, it does not appear that the plaintiffs
were the *sole* possessors and occupiers of this fishery. . . . .
The public may grant an exclusive right of fishery in a navigable river, and if it may be granted,·it may be prescribed
for. Such a right shall never be presumed, but the contrary. It is, however, capable of being proved." [1]

So in Delaware, &c. Railroad *v.* Stump, the court of Maryland, while they recognize the right of one citizen to an
exclusive fishery in a public, navigable river, acquired by
long enjoyment, insist that it is not the mere enjoyment,
but the enjoyment by such claimant must be to the exclusion of all others, — "long *exclusive* possession and use," to
give the right.[2]

It is necessary that it should appear that all other persons
        have been kept out, by the claimant and his grantors,
[*414] from *fishing in any manner in the waters to which
        he lays claim.[3]

6. But a prescription of a right to fish in the sea gener-

---

[1] Chalker *v.* Dickinson, 1 Conn. 382 – 384; Collins *v.* Benbury, 5 Ired. 118,
124; Gould *v.* James, 6 Cow. 369, 376.

[2] Delaware, &c. R. R. *v.* Stump, 8 Gill & J. 479, 510.

[3] Collins *v.* Benbury, 5 Ired. 118, 124; 2 Sharsw. Blackst. Comm. 40; 3
Kent, Comm. 418.

ally, by reason of owning a certain estate, would be idle, as it is a right which belongs to all citizens, whether owning lands or not.[1]

A right to a several or exclusive fishery in a part of the sea or a navigable river will be regarded as an incorporeal hereditament, unless, as may often be the case, there may be an ownership in the soil over which it is claimed, presumed in favor of the claimant of the fishery.[2]

7. And the court of North Carolina, in citing the case of Somerset v. Foggwell, add : " But the right of several fishery not derived by special grant from the crown, as above, or by prescription, which supposes a grant, cannot exist independently of the right of soil." [3]

The same doctrine is advanced by Blackstone.[4]　But Hargrave[5] controverts the doctrine, and says: " Nor do we understand why a *several* piscary should not exist without the soil as well as a several pasture "; while the point is left unsettled in Seymour v. Courtenay.[6]

And in one of Hargrave's notes it is said : " The truth is, that the authorities on this subject are very numerous, and seem contradictory," [7] the question being whether a several fishery and the soil may be in different persons.

Woolrych, in the page of his work just cited, says : " Indeed, so far from a several fishery being necessarily incident *to the soil, it should seem that in strictness *[415] it must be separated therefrom."

The doctrine maintained by Hargrave and Coke, that it is not necessary that the owner of a several fishery should have a property in the soil, is sustained in Melvin v. Whiting.[8]

---

[1] Ward v. Cresswell, Willes, 265.

[2] Somerset v. Foggwell, 5 Barnew. & C. 875.

[3] Collins v. Benbury, 5 Ired. 118, 126.

[4] 2 Blackst. Comm. 39.

[5] Co. Litt. 122, note, 181.

[6] Seymour v. Courtenay, 5 Burr, 2814.　See Smith v. Kemp, 2 Salk. 637 and note.

[7] Co. Litt. 4 b, note 20.　See Woolr. Waters, 89.

[8] Melvin v. Whiting, 7 Pick. 80, 81 ; s. c., 13 Pick. 184.

But the question is again opened in M'Farlin *v.* Essex Co., by Shaw, C. J., who does not consider it settled in the case of Melvin *v.* Whiting, as he regards the claim set up there by the owner of the several fishery to have been connected with a particular estate upon the bank of the stream.[1]

And in the last-cited case, the point was not taken in the hearing, but the Chief Justice says: " Whether a party can prescribe for a several fishery in the estate of another, without alleging some estate of freehold, is an important question which was not discussed in the present case. As a general rule, a party cannot allege a custom to claim an interest or *profit à prendre* in the estate of another without a prescription in a *que estate.* . . . . And yet we believe it has sometimes been said that a piscary is a freehold in itself, in which there is no occasion to show to what freehold it is appendant."[2]

This discussion, it will be perceived, has taken rather a wide range, and is somewhat in anticipation of the doctrines contained in some of the authorities that follow, where the distinction between the case of a piscary and ordinary prescription of *profit à prendre*, above alluded to, seems to be sustained.

8. The right to take fish within the limits of one's land bounding upon and including a stream not navigable, is considered so far a subject of distinct property or ownership, that it may be granted, and will pass by a general [*416] grant of *the land itself, unless expressly reserved; or, as seems to be settled by the weight of authority, it may be granted as a separate and distinct property from the freehold of the land, or the land may be granted while the grantor reserves the fishery to himself. Whether the grant or reservation shall have one effect or another depends, of course, upon the terms in which it is expressed. Thus it has been held: " If one grants to another *aquam suam*, the piscary in it shall pass by the grant, because it is

---

[1] M'Farlin *v.* Essex Co., 10 Cush. 311.

[2] Ibid. 310, in which he refers to Davies, 155.

included in the word *aqua*. And so by the grant of a piscary the soil shall pass," though Comyn says, " By the grant
of a piscary the soil or water does not pass." [1]

Or, as stated by Coke, in which he is sustained by the
court of New York, " If a man grant *aquam suam*, the soil
shall not pass, but the piscary within the water passeth therewith." [2]

And though the doctrine has been questioned, Lord Coke
maintains that, " If a man be seized of a river, and by deed
do grant *separalem piscariam* in the same, and maketh
livery of seizin *secundum formam chartæ*, the soile doth not
pass, nor the water, for the grantor may take water there,
and if the river become drie, he may take the benefit of the
soile, for there passed to the grantee but a particular right,
and the livery being made *secundum formam chartæ*, cannot
enlarge the grant." [3]

  9. Woolrych, adopting the language of another writer upon
aquatic rights, Mr. Shultes says : " That property in private
rivers may be subjected to every kind of restriction by con-
vention and agreement; a man may grant the soil
for *the purpose of erecting a weir or mill, and re-   [*417]
serve the right to fish or take water. He might
yield his own prerogative of fishing, on the other hand, and
so confer upon his grantee an exclusive or several fishing,
without the ownership of the soil, or he might grant a
license to other persons to fish in common with himself."
And he himself concludes : " The owner of a territorial fishery, so to speak, may either make a grant and thereby exclude himself, or he may permit another to enjoy a co-

[1] Trockmorton *v.* Tracy, Plowd. 154 ; Case of Baune Fishery, Davies, 150 ;
Com. Dig. *Grant,* E. 5.

[2] Co. Litt. 4 b ; Jackson *v.* Halstead, 5 Cow. 219 ; Com. Dig. *Grant,* E. 5 ;
Somerset *v.* Fogwell, 5 Barnew. & C. 875.

[3] Co. Litt. 4 b ; Ibid. 122 ; Hargr. note, 20. See Somerset *v.* Fogwell, 5
Barnew. & C. 875. See Smith *v.* Kemp, per *Holt,* J., Salk. 637 ; Seymour *v.*
Courtenay, 5 Burr. 2816 ; Woolr. Waters, 89 ; Melvin *v.* Whiting, 7 Pick. 81 ;
s. c., 13 Pick. 184.

32

extensive or limited right of fishing in his own water, still reserving his ownership."[1]

In the case of Cortelyou v. Van Brundt, Thompson, J. says: "A right to fish in any water gives no power of the land."[2] He refers to Ipswich v. Browne, where the court say, "If one have a piscary in any water, he has no power over the land without the assent of the tenants of the freehold.[3]

10. But it is not the purpose of this work to treat of the law of fisheries in all its bearings, and it has been rather with a view of ascertaining under what circumstances a right to take fish in another's premises may be the subject of a grant or prescription, and so come within the category of easements, than to discuss the effect of certain forms of grants relating to the same. To do this, a brief reference must be had to the classification of fisheries and the terms by which they are distinguished. But here, again, it would be impossible to reconcile the use of these terms, as applied by different courts and writers, especially those of an earlier day. It is believed that it will be sufficiently accurate to say that there are three classes of fisheries, viz. *several, free,* and *common.* The first is such as a man has in his own land, where the ownership of the soil and freehold is separate and distinct in himself. The second is a right derived by grant from one having a several fishery in connec-
[*418] tion *with his estate in the land, to be enjoyed not separately and alone, but in conjunction with the grantor himself. It is in some measure like a fishery in common, since it may be to be shared with others deriving their titles thereto, by grant originally derived from the landowner. The third is the right which all citizens have to fish in the sea and navigable waters, and is derived by no grant and belongs to no particular estate. It would, more-

---

[1] Woolr. Waters, p. 89.

[2] Cortelyou v. Van Brundt, 2 Johns. 357, 362.

[3] Ipswich v. Browne, Sav. 14.

over, seem, from what has gone before, that though a several fishery was originally based upon the ownership of land, it may be separated therefrom by grant or reservation, and forever after be held and pass independent of the ownership of the land. So a free fishery, though derived from the ownership of the land, may be enjoyed independent of such ownership. Thus Lord Mansfield says: " We agree in the position that, in order to constitute a several fishery, it is requisite that the party claiming it should so far have the right of fishing, independent of all others, as that no person shall have a coextensive right with him in the subject claimed ; for where any person has any such coextensive right, there it is only a *free* fishery." [1]

Lord Coke says : " A man may prescribe to have *separalem piscariam* in such a water, and the owner of the soil shall not fish there. But if he claim to have *communiam piscariæ* or *liberam pischariam*, the owner of the soil shall fish there." [2]

And the court in Melvin *v.* Whiting hold that the views of Lord Coke are law here, and that a free fishery is not a several or exclusive one.[3]

It is moreover said, in a subsequent report of the same case, that a free fishery and a several, exclusive fishery are in some sense inconsistent as titles in a claim of right to exercise the act of fishing in the soil of another, although *there is nothing in the way of the same [*419] person setting up and relying upon both or either at his election. In that case it was held that one might prescribe for a several or exclusive fishery on the soil of another, situate upon the Merrimac River, above tide-water, by showing an adverse, uninterrupted, and exclusive use and enjoyment of the right and privilege claimed, for more than twenty years, and an action on the case was sustained against the owner of the soil for interrupting such fishery.[4]

[1] Seymour *v.* Courtenay, 5 Burr. 2817.   [2] Co. Litt. 122 a.
[3] Melvin *v.* Whiting, 7 Pick. 80, 81.
[4] Melvin *v.* Whiting, 13 Pick. 184. But see M'Farlin *v.* Essex Co., 10 Cush. 304, for comments upon the case.

The doctrine of Coke, above cited, is sustained by the court in Pennsylvania, in Carson *v.* Blazer. A man may prescribe to have *separalem piscariam* in such a water, and the owner of the soil shall not fish there. . . . . The right of piscary must be a right appurtenant to the soil covered with water. It must be a part of the fee-simple of that soil, and must be supposed to have been originally granted out of it by him who had the fee-simple. . . . . In order to have an exclusive fishery in a river, all that was necessary was that the party seized of the river should by his deed grant *separalem piscariam* in it." [1]

Woolrych [2] examines at length the different senses in which courts have used the term " free fishery," and concludes " that to consider the *free fishery* as the same with *common of fishery* will be a reasonable as well as a legal conclusion." But he admits that " there is no modern decision which can warrant us in uniting them." And it will be sufficiently accurate for the purposes of this work to treat a common fishery as one open to all the citizens, as in the sea, though a free fishery, originally derived from a private grant, may be shared in by many persons, who, as to that particular fishery, may be said to have a common fishery.

[*420]　*11. But whether called *several, free,* or *common,* it is only of fisheries which may be the subject of private property that easements can be predicated, and to such only it is intended to refer.

If the right is a part of and incident to the ownership of the soil, it cannot be regarded as an easement in such soil. But if the right in an individual in severalty, or to be shared with others, be to take fish within another's freehold, it is an easement, and may be acquired by grant from the owner thereof, or by such a user as is evidence of such a grant

---

[1] Carson *v.* Blazer, 2 Binn. 475, 489.

[2] Woolr. Waters, 97, 101 ; per *Burrough* and *Dallas,* JJ., in Bennett *v.* Costar, 8 Taunt. 183.

under the name of a prescription, and it may be to the entire exclusion of the owner of the soil from all right to share in the fishery. But it must be shown to have been an actual and exclusive possession of the fishery, adverse to the right of the riparian proprietor, uninterrupted and continued at least twenty years.[1]

And where one has a several fishery, he has a property in the fish, and may maintain trespass for taking them.[2]

12. It will be observed that the rights of fishery thus far discussed have been such as are recognized by the common law. But these are in many cases modified by local statutes. Thus in several of the States many rivers, in respect to their fisheries, are regarded as navigable streams, and the fisheries therein are common, though there be no ebb or flow of tide therein. Such is the case with the Susquehanna in Pennsylvania,[3] and the other large rivers in the State,[4] and the owners of the banks have not an exclusive right to fish in the stream opposite to the same.

The same doctrine prevails in North Carolina as to rivers declared navigable by act of the legislature. But in those *parts of the same rivers which are above the [*421] point of their being actually navigable, as well as in streams not navigable, the doctrine of the common law as to fisheries prevails.[5]

So also is the law in South Carolina in respect to rivers actually navigable, though not declared so by statute.[6]

So in Massachusetts and Maine, the legislature has the power to regulate the fisheries, and, in numerous cases, has exerted the power within streams which by the common law would be private property.[7]

---

[1] Melvin v. Whiting, 13 Pick. 184; M'Farlin v. Essex Co., 10 Cush. 304; Woolr. Waters, 105.

[2] Collins v. Benbury, 5 Ired. 118; Smith v. Kemp, 2 Salk. 637; Holford v. Bailey, 13 Q. B., Am. ed., 426 and n.

[3] Carson v. Blazer, 2 Binn. 475.   [4] 2 Sharsw. Blackst. Comm. 40, note.

[5] Collins v. Benbury, 5 Ired. 118; Ingram v. Threadgill, 3 Dev. 59.

[6] Cates v. Wadlington, 1 M'Cord, 580; 3 Kent Comm. 418.

[7] Peables v. Hannaford, 18 Me. 106; Parker v. Cutler Mill-Dam Co., 20 Me.

13. But in those States where the common law prevails, the right of several fishery in the lands of proprietors bordering upon streams of water in which the tide does not ebb or flow, is not affected by the circumstance that the stream is a public one by being of sufficient capacity to float vessels, boats, rafts, and the like. But the right to fish upon one's own land, or in a several fishery, in such cases, must be enjoyed, if at all, in subordination to the public use of the river for passage. The public right of passage is prior and paramount.[1]

[*422]   *SECTION XII.

OF SERVITUDES OF WATER BY THE CIVIL LAW, ETC.

1. Affirmative and negative servitudes of water.
2. Servitudes of water by the Civil Law.
3. What servitudes of water real and what personal.
4. Rights of drain and of drawing water affirmative servitudes.
5. Servitudes did not depend on being necessary.
6. Why no servitudes in the Civil Law as to mills.
7. Rivers and their banks highways by the Civil Law.
8. Law of Scotland as to servitudes of water.
9. Code Napoleon as to servitudes of water.
10. Servitudes under Code of Louisiana.
11. Owner of servitude has the right and duty to repair.
12. Code of Louisiana as to use of river banks.
13. Provisions of the Partidas as to use of river banks.
14. General agreement as to servitudes between common and civil law.
15. Peck v. Bailey. Judgment of Hawaii.

1. ALTHOUGH these, as well as other servitudes known to the civil law, have already been spoken of to a greater or less extent, it seemed to be desirable to refer to them collectively in a brief and summary manner, that the analogy

353; Commonwealth v. Chapin, 5 Pick. 199, 203; Vinton v. Welsh, 9 Pick. 87; 2 Dane, Abr. 695; Moulton v. Libbey, 37 Me. 472, 494.
[1] Hooker v. Cummings, 20 Johns. 90, 99; Adams v. Pease, 2 Conn. 481; 3 Kent, Comm. 418; Jackson v. Keeling, 1 Jones (Law), 299; Moulton v. Libbey, 37 Me. 472, 493.

which exists in this respect between the civil law and the modern systems now in use may be more readily perceived. And among these may be mentioned the Scotch and the French systems, as well as the laws of Louisiana, and so much of the Spanish Partidas as still prevail in Louisiana, for which the English reader is indebted to Messieurs Lislet and Carleton, whose translation of these was published in 1820.

The number and variety of servitudes known to the civil law seem to have been almost unlimited, and in numerous cases where one estate had a servitude in or upon another, the latter might have had a counter servitude in or upon the former. As, for instance, the servitude of *stillicidium* or *flumen*, heretofore described, consisted in the right that the owner of a house had to discharge the water that fell in rain upon its roof upon the land of an adjacent *proprietor. But the land-owner might have ac- [*423] quired, as an easement in favor of his land, and the owner of the house should not thus discharge the water from his roof, *jus stillicidii vel fluminis non recipiendi.* Or he might gain as an easement the right to insist that the water from the roof should be discharged upon his land, or into his cistern, *jus stillicidii vel fluminis non avertendi.*[1]

2. Among the servitudes relating to the use or management of water known to the civil law was that of *cloacæ mittendæ*, which was urban in its character, and consisted in the right of maintaining and using a sewer through the house or over the ground of an adjacent owner. A servitude answering to this among those known as rural, was that of *aquæ ducendæ*, or right of leading or conducting water through another's land by a pipe or rivulet for the use of the premises of the owner of such servitude. It might apply whether the stream of water was conducted above or below the surface of the earth. It might, moreover, extend

---

[1] *Ante*, sect. 8; 3 Toullier, Droit Civil Français, 397; 2 Fournel, Traité du Voisinage, 114; D. 8, 2, 2; Inst. 2, 3, 1.

through the whole year, or be limited to certain seasons. Nor might the owner of the servitude change the place of direction of the course of the water when once fixed. Where the supply of water was sufficient, others might share in it with the first owner of the servitude. But a second grant could not be made of a right to draw water which should derogate from the right first granted. Under the servitude *aquæ hauriendæ*, one might draw water for his own use from a spring or well or brook, in another's land, which implied a right of way to and from the place of supply as a means of access to the same. By another servitude, the owner of one estate might drive his cattle to water, over the neighboring estate, to a spring or other source of supply within the same.

There was another servitude *aquæ ducendæ*, whereby [*424] one might lead *or conduct off from his land the water thereon through the estate of another.[1]

3. If the person having a right to draw water within another's premises had no land in the neighborhood in connection with the ownership whereof he exercised such right, it was considered a personal one, which died with the person. But all these servitudes took the character of *real* services, where they were possessed in virtue of the occupancy of some other estate for the use and advantage whereof the same were enjoyed. The limit and extent of these several easements were defined by the grant or pre-scription under which they were claimed, and the owner thereof might not exceed this limit. If, for instance, one having a right to water a certain number of cattle under-took to supply a larger number, the owner of the servient estate might hinder the owner of the servitude from using it beyond the prescribed number.[2]

4. A servitude of drawing water to, or of drain or gutter

---

[1] Ayliffe, Pandects, 307, 308 ; Kauff. Mackeldey, §§ 309, 312, 315 ; 1 Domat, Lib. 1, Tit. 12, § 1, Art. 7 ; § 2, Art. 1, 2, 3 ; § 3, Art. 1, 3, 4, 5, 6 ; D. 8, 1, 7 ; Ibid. 43, 20, 1, 3 ; Wood's Inst. Civ. Law, 90 – 93 ; Vinnius, Lib. 2, Tit. 3, § 7 ; Ibid. Tit. 3, §§ 4, 5. See Lalaure des Servitudes, 30.

[2] Ayliffe, Pandects, 308.

from, one's premises, through those of another, was an affirmative one.[1]

5. These servitudes did not depend for their existence upon any supposed necessity of enjoyment, and when once acquired they continued, though the owner of the dominant estate might, for instance, have water enough upon his own premises without drawing any from those of his neighbor.[2]

6. One might naturally be surprised to see so little, or rather nothing, said of the use of water for mills in the Roman law. And the same may be said of hydraulic *works generally, but this is explained by the fact [*425] stated by M. Fournel, that water-mills were not in use among the Romans until after Justinian, their mills before that time having been moved by animal power.[3]

7. By the civil law, not only were navigable rivers highways, but the traveller upon the same might use the banks thereof as a tow-path, provided such use did not interfere with trees growing thereon belonging to the land-owner, or other obstacles lawfully upon the bank.[4]

8. By the law of Scotland, on some of the foregoing subjects, as stated by Erskine, in his Institutes of the Law of Scotland, the servitude of aqueduct is the right that one has of carrying water in conduits or canals along the surface of the servient tenement, for the use of one's own property, and such servitude may be acquired by immemorial possession. Much like to this is the servitude of a dam-head, by which one acquires a right of gathering water on his neighbor's grounds, and of building banks or dikes for containing that water. These servitudes are generally constituted for the use of water-mills or engines, and the owner of the dominant tenement, as he has the benefit of the servitude, is obliged to

---

1 Ibid. 310 ; Wood, Inst. Civ. Law, 92.

2 1 Domat. Lib. 1, Tit. 12, § 1, Art. 17.

3 " Les lois romains ne contienent aucune disposition sur les moulines à eau et à vent, parceque cette construction étoit inconnue aux Romains à l'époque de la rédaction du corps de droit civil." 2 Fournel, Traité du Voisinage, 222.

4 2 Domat, Lib. 1, Tit. 8, § 2, Art. 9.

preserve the aqueducts and dam-heads in such condition
that the adjacent grounds may suffer no prejudice by the
breaking out of the water. *Aquahaustus* is a right of the
land-holder to water his cattle at the river, brook, well,
or pond that runs through or stands upon his neighbor's
grounds.[1]

9. By the Code Napoleon, low lands are subjected to those
more elevated, to receive the waters naturally running from
them without the hand of man contributing thereto. The
owner of the low land cannot erect a bank to pre-
[*426] vent this. *The owner of the high land can do
nothing to aggravate the servitude of the low land.
He who has a spring on his land may use it according to his
pleasure, saving the right which the owner of the low land
may have acquired by title or by prescription. He whose
property abuts upon a running water may cut a way for it
for the irrigation of his property. He through whose estate
such water runs may even make use of it for the space it so
runs, but as the charge of restoring it, where it leaves the
property, to its ordinary course.[2]

10. The Civil Code of Louisiana recognizes the servitudes
of drawing water from the well of another, of conducting
water, or aqueduct, and of watering cattle, substantially like
those of the civil law, and includes those of aqueduct and
drain as among *continuous*, and that of drawing water among
the *discontinuous*, servitudes.[3]

11. And the principle of the common law is here declared
by the terms of the code, that he to whom a servitude is due
has a right to make all the works necessary to use and preserve the same. Such works are at his expense, and not at
the expense of the owner of the estate which owes the servitude, unless the title by which it is established shows the

---

[1] Fol. ed. B. 2, § 13, p. 358.

[2] Cod Nap., Barrett's ed., Arts. 640, 641, 643, 644 ; 1 Le Page Desgodets, 211.

[3] La Civ. Cod., Arts. 716, 717, 719, 720, 721, 723 ; Polden v. Bastard, 4 B. &
Smith, 258, 264.

contrary.   And he may enter upon the servient estate so far as it is necessary to accomplish this purpose.[1]

12. In respect to the use of navigable rivers and their banks, they are declared public so far, that every one may bring his vessel to land there, may make the same fast to trees planted there, to unload his vessels, to deposit his goods, or dry his nets, and the like.   At the same time, the property in the soil of the banks is declared to be in such as possess the adjacent lands.   A bank of a river is de- *fined to be " that which contains the water in its [*427] utmost height." [2]

13. The banks of public rivers are declared public by the civil law.[3]   And by the provisions of the Partidas, recognized within the former Territory of Louisiana, this right is declared to be that " every man may make use of them to fasten his vessel to trees that grow there, or to refit his vessel, or to put his sails or merchandise there.   So fishermen may put and expose their fish for sale there, and dry their nets, or make use of the banks for all other like purposes which appertain to the art or trade by which they live." [4]   In this respect the rule of the common law differs from the civil law, as has been before shown ; [5] and the courts of Missouri have been disposed to limit the language of the Partidas to cases of reasonable necessity.[6]

To pursue the subject of servitudes of water into detail, either under the civil or the French laws, would be opening many topics which either have not yet been adjudicated at common law, or upon which the rule of the common law would be found variant from that of one or both these codes, and would lead to a wider discussion than the plan or the utility of this work would warrant.   But whoever may wish to pursue the inquiry will readily find the works cited below,

[1] La. Civ. Code, Arts. 768, 769, 770.

[2] Ibid., Art. 446 ; D. 43,12, 3, 1.

[3] D. 43, 12, 3.

[4] Partid. 3, Tit. 28, Law 6.   [5] *Ante*, sect. 9, pl. 18.

[6] *Ante*, sect. 9, pl. 13 ; O'Fallon *v.* Daggett, 4 Mo. 343.

which are among the treatises which will throw light upon the subject of these servitudes.[1]

14. The following extracts, however, from a writer of acknowledged authority, will serve to show, after what has been said of easements at common law, how intimate the relations are between that and the civil law in their [*428] *bearing upon this subject. " *Servitus*, a service, is a right by which one thing is subject to another thing or person, contrary to common right. . . . . Here one is the ruling estate, the other subject to the rule, either to suffer something from the other, or not to do a thing without the leave of the owner of the ruling estate. . . . . A man's estate cannot owe service to himself." [2]

15. A very recent case has been decided by the Supreme Court of the Hawaiian Islands, in Equity, by the Hon. Ch. J. Allen, Chancellor, which is interesting, not only from the importance of the questions it involved, and the great ability evinced by the Chancellor in their discussion, but the facility with which the principles of the common law in which the Chancellor, born and educated in Massachusetts, was trained, may be adapted and applied to a country whose physical condition differs essentially from that in which the common law originated. In these islands, the agricultural productions on which the people chiefly subsist, can only be raised by the artificial application of water, by way of irrigation. This, as it seems, is not done by mere sluices cut in the natural banks of a stream, by which the water flushes over on to the adjacent lands, but by lateral artificial trenches by which the water is taken from its natural bed and diffused over large tracts on which it is absorbed, so that the lower proprietor is materially affected by the manner and to the extent in which the upper owner makes use of the water. As this use is not what would ordinarily be regarded as a

[1] 5 Duranton, Cours du Droit Français, 144–231 ; Pardessus, Traité des Servitudes, 96–174 ; Merlin, Répertoire de Jurisprudence, Tit. *Cours d'Eau.*
[2] Wood's Inst. Civ. Law, 90.

natural incident to the land bordering upon a watercourse,
it becomes a matter of easement or servitude if continued
long enough, and under proper circumstances to create a
prescriptive right. Such, in brief, was the case referred to,
and the questions involved were: 1st. If the upper owner
had diverted more water than he had a prescriptive right to
do, to the injury of the lower owner's mill and crop which
he was cultivating? 2d. Whether, as he had acquired a
prescriptive right to divert the water for the production of
a certain crop (kalo) upon certain lands, he had a right to
use it upon other lands in growing a crop of cane? 3d.
Whether, as in the use of the water upon the kalo land, a
portion of it reached the plaintiff's land, whereby it was
benefited, and this had been continued from time immemorial, the defendant had a right to cease using it upon his
kalo land and to use it on his cane land, and thereby deprive the plaintiff of the enjoyment of the water from the
kalo land? And 4th. What rule should be applied as to
the extent of enjoyment of the parties, if at any time there
should be deficiency of water by reason of an extraordinary
drought? Upon these points the Chancellor held that the
rights of the parties as to the extent to which either could
apply the waters of the streams running through their lands,
must be measured by the prescriptive rights of user acquired
by each; that the right attached to the estates owned by
them, and had reference to the quantity to be used and not
the particular mode in which it should be applied, and that
it was indifferent whether it was used in growing kalo or
cane; that inasmuch as the use of the water upon his kalo
land was artificial and for his own benefit, the owner was
not bound to continue it, although its discontinuance worked
an injury to the adjacent owner; and that the use of the
water of the stream was so far the common property of both,
that if, from extraordinary causes, there was a deficit in the
quantity necessary to supply the wants of both, the loss
should be borne pro rata, by the estates of the parties in

interest. All these points are fully considered in the light of authorities drawn from English and American decisions and elementary treatises. And the case itself and its decision furnish palpable and gratifying evidence of the change which has come over the social and political condition of a people who, within the memory of living witnesses, have emerged from barbarism and idolatry, and are now enjoying the gladsome light of jurisprudence in its dispensation by a learned and able judiciary and an educated bar.[1]

[1] Peck v. Bailey, Pacific Com. Advertis., Feb. 9, 1867.

OF EASEMENTS AND SERVITUDES OTHER THAN OF
WAY AND WATER.

SECTION I.

EASEMENT OF LATERAL SUPPORT OF LAND.

1. AMONG the rights which adjacent proprietors of lands
may have to enjoy the benefit of their contiguity, is that of

[*430] *having one parcel laterally supported by the other.

It is a right incident to the ownership of the respective lands, rather than an easement which one has in the other. It does not result from the idea of an adverse enjoyment, nor is it derived from any grant, as something superadded to the dominion which the owner of the fee has as such, over the soil of the particular close that is supposed to be benefited by it. So far as it partakes of the character of an easement it is that of a natural easement, like the right of a riparian proprietor to the flow of a natural stream along its accustomed water-course.[1] A writer in the London Law Magazine and Review, in treating of this subject, thus states the law : " But the right being a right to support from land in its natural state to land in its natural state, on the one hand, it includes only the right to such support as is furnished by the permanent conditions of land, not by its accidental circumstances, and, on the other hand, if the support required is increased, either by increasing the weight of the supported land, or by diminishing its self-supporting power, no right exists to have this additional support supplied by the neighboring land, and no subsidence resulting from this cause gives a right of action." [2] But where the owner of one parcel undertakes to claim, as a right, this lateral support of an adjacent parcel to sustain an additional burden thereon, as a dwelling-house, an artificial embankment, and the like, it becomes a servitude so far as the adjacent parcel is concerned, and an easement in favor of the parcel sharing the benefit of such support.[3]

[1] M'Guire v. Grant, 1 Dutch. 356, 368; Humphries v. Brogden, 12 Q. B. 739; Lasala v. Holbrook, 4 Paige, 169; Farrand v. Marshall 19 Barb. 380; Hunt v. Peake, Johns. Ch. (Eng.) 705; No. East. R. W. Co. v. Elliot, 1 Johns. & H. 145; Foley v. Wyeth, 2 Allen, 131; Rowbotham v. Wilson, 8 Ellis & B. 123, 152; Solomon v. Vintners' Co., 4 Hurlst. & N. 585; Bonomi v. Backhouse, Ellis, B. & E. 622, 642, 644; Caledonian R. W. Co. v. Sprot, 2 Macq. H. of L. Cas. 449; Napier v. Bulwinkle, 5 Rich. 311, 323.
[2] 20 Law Mag. & R. 82.
[3] Humphries v. Brogden, 12 Q. B. 739, 748, 750; Thurston v. Hancock, 12 Mass. 226; Bonomi v. Backhouse, Ellis, B. & E. 622, 646; Hunt v. Peake,

From the circumstance that there may be in mining regions an upper and a lower freehold, questions of the right of support of the superior by an inferior stratum of earth or mineral often arise, and, as a general proposition, the same distinction in this respect prevails between the superior tenement in its natural condition, and when burdened by buildings and other structures, as there is in the case of lateral support.[1]

*2. And although it is proposed to confine these [*431] inquiries, principally to the common law, it seems proper to refer briefly to the provisions of the civil law upon the subject, and the systems which have been borrowed from it. The rule as laid down in the Digest [2] required, " that, if a man dig a sepulchre or a ditch, he shall have (between it and his neighbor's land) a space equal to its depth ; if he dig a well, he shall have the space of a fathom." [3]

By a law of Solon, no one could dig a ditch upon his own land without allowing as much space between the ditch and his neighbor's land as the same was deep. No wall could be placed nearer to a neighbor's land than the distance of one foot. A house must be two feet distant. Trees might not be planted nearer the outer line of one's land than nine feet, and olives ten. The laws of the XII. Tables in Rome were borrowed from those of Solon.[4]

The subject is, in a measure, regulated by the Code Napoleon and that of Louisiana,[5] and the principles applicable in cases of making excavations, or erecting structures upon lands adjoining those of other proprietors, are further explained by Pardessus.[6]

3. The test of this right of lateral support is the limit

Johns. Ch. (Eng.) 705, 712 ; Partridge v. Scott, 3 Mees. & W. 220 ; Rogers v. Taylor, 2 Hurlst. & N. 828 ; Hide v. Thornborough, 2 Carr. & K. 250.

[1] *Post*, sect. 4, pl. 3 – 5.   [2] D. 10, 1, 13.

[3] 9 C. B. 412.

[4] Barrett's Introd. Code Nap. cxi, cxxxv.

[5] La. Civ. Code, Arts. 674, 688 – 691.

[6] Traité des Servitudes, §§ 199 – 201.

which one is bound to observe in excavating his own soil in the direction of his neighbor's close, for, aside from the injury that may be done by removing thereby the support which his neighbor may lawfully claim to derive from his land, there is no limit as to the extent to which such excavation may be carried. The rule to be observed, where the rights of the parties relate to the soil in its natural state, is generally stated to be, that neither shall excavate his own soil so as to cause that of his neighbor to be loosened and fall into such excavation. This rule, as stated by Rolle in his Abridgment, is often cited as a sound one, and embraces the distinction which the law makes between land in a natural state and the same land burdened with buildings or other structures. " If A be seized in fee of land next adjoining the land of B, and A erect a new house on the confines of his land, next adjoining the land of B, and if B afterwards digs his land so near the foundation of A's house, but no part of the land of A, that thereby the foun-

[*432]   *dation of the house and the house itself fall into the pit, yet no action lies by A against B, because it was A's own fault that he built his house so near to B's land, for he by his act cannot hinder B from making the best use of his own land that he can. . . . . But *semble*, that a man who has land next adjoining my land cannot dig his land so near mine that thereby my land shall go into his pit ; and therefore if the action had been brought for that, it would lie." [1]

If any diversity of opinion is found among the judges in the modern cases, it is believed, it is only as to how far one is bound to exercise more care in digging in his own land, in respect to its injury upon that of his neighbor who has recently erected a house thereon, than if there were no such structure there.

4. The case of Thurston *v.* Hancock is a leading one

---

[1] Wilde *v.* Minsterley, 2 Rolle, Abr., *Trespass*, I. pl. 1 ; Beard *v.* Murphy, 37 Verm. 101.

upon this subject, and often referred to, wherein the facts were as follow. The plaintiff in 1802 purchased a lot of land upon a hill, and in 1804 built a house thereon, within two feet of the line of his land. In 1811 the defendant purchased the adjoining lot, and began to dig down the hill, and had dug up to within five or six feet of the plaintiff's land, when the earth gave way, and exposed the foundations of the plaintiff's house, and he had to take it down. For this he brought his action, the digging having been done with full knowledge, on the part of the defendant, that he was thereby endangering the property of the plaintiff. But the court held that he was without remedy for the injury to the house. A man, in digging upon his own land, is to have regard to the position of his neighbor's land, and the probable consequences to his neighbor. If he digs too near his line, and if he disturbs the natural state of the soil, he shall answer in damages. But he is answerable only for the natural and necessary consequences of his act, and not *for the value of a house put upon or near the [*433] line by his neighbor. For in so placing the house the neighbor was in fault, and ought to have taken better care of his interest. . . . . He (the plaintiff) built at his peril, for it was not possible for him, merely by building upon his own ground, to deprive the other party of such use of his as he should deem most advantageous. There was no right acquired by his ten years' occupation to keep his neighbor at a convenient distance from him. . . . . It is, in fact, *damnum absque injuria*. . . . . For the loss of or injury to the soil merely, his action may be maintained. The defendants should have anticipated the consequences of digging so near the line, and they are answerable for the direct consequential damage to the plaintiff, although not for the adventitious damage arising from his putting his house in a dangerous position." [1]

Although, in Farrand *v.* Marshall, Harris, J. expressed a

[1] Thurston *v.* Hancock, 12 Mass. 226.

decided impression that, upon the facts of the case of Thurston v. Hancock, the same was incorrectly decided, yet he sustains the general view of the law as there stated, that while, as an incident to property, every owner of land has a right to a lateral support thereof by the adjacent soil of another, he has no right to claim such support for an increased burden upon his land.[1]

5. The case of Farrand v. Marshall was one where one owner, for the purpose of procuring clay for the manufacture of brick, dug for the same in his own soil so deep and so near to the line of the adjacent owner as to cause the soil of the latter to fall into the excavation. It was again argued and decided upon an appeal, in which Wright, J. gave the opinion confirming that given by Harris, J., above stated. He admitted that it might be too late to question the soundness of Thurston v. Hancock, and repeated [*434] the *position in several forms, that one may dig on his own land, but not so near that of his neighbor as to cause the land of the latter to fall into his pit.[2]

6. So far as the rights of adjacent owners to the support of each other's soil in its natural state is concerned, the rule above stated has been recognized as law in the following cases, in some of which the doctrine was applied to cases of excavations made by companies in constructing railroads and other public works.[3]

7. The case of Lasala v. Holbrook involved also the ques-

---

[1] Farrand v. Marshall, 19 Barb. 380, 385, 386. See also Richardson v. Vt. Cent. R. R. Co., 25 Vt. 465.

[2] Farrand v. Marshall, 21 Barb. 409, 415.

[3] Lasala v. Holbrook, 4 Paige, 169; Radcliff v. Mayor, &c., 4 Comst. 195; Hunt v. Peake, Johns. Ch. (Eng.) 705; Charless v. Rankin, 22 Mo. 566; M'Guire v. Grant, 1 Dutch. 356, 363, 368; Com. Dig., *Action on Case for a Nuisance*, A; Slingsby v. Barnard, 1 Rolle, 430; Panton v. Holland, 17 Johns. 92; Wyatt v. Harrison, 3 Barnew. & Ad. 871; Humphries v. Brogden, 12 Q. B. 739, 744; Barnes v. Ward, 9 C. B. 392, 412; Bonomi v. Backhouse, Ellis, B. & E. 622, 642, 657; Hay v. Cohoes Co., 2 Comst. 159; Richardson v. Vt. Cent. R. R. Co., 25 Vt. 465; No. Eastern R. W. Co. v. Elliot, 1 Johns. & H. 145; Foley v. Wyeth, 2 Allen, 131; Rowbotham v. Wilson, 8 Ellis & B. 123, 142; 2 Dane, Abr. 717; Howland v. Vincent, 10 Metc. 371, 373.

tion how far the existence of a house upon one man's land prevents the adjacent owner from digging in his land adjoining that upon which the house is standing. In that case the complainants owned a church which had stood on their land for thirty-eight years. The line of the defendant's land was six feet distant from the church. He commenced excavating for the purpose of erecting a building covering his lot. The effect was to crack the walls of the church, by the settling of the land, and the application was for an injunction to such excavation. The Chancellor states the law as follows : " I have a natural right to the use of my land, in the situation in which it was placed by nature, surrounded and protected by the soil of the adjacent lots. And the owners of those lots will not be permitted to destroy my land, by removing this natural support and barrier. . . . . My neighbor has the * right to dig a pit upon his own land, if necessary [*435] to its convenient or beneficial use, when it can be done without injury to my land in its natural state. I cannot, therefore, deprive him of this right by erecting a building on my lot, the weight of which will cause my land to fall into the pit which he may dig, in the proper and legitimate exercise of his previous right to improve his own lot." [1] He cites Thurston v. Hancock, with approbation of the doctrine there maintained, and also the case of Panton v. Holland, stated hereafter. " From the recent English decisions it appears that the party who is about to endanger the building of his neighbor, by a reasonable improvement on his own land, is bound to give the owner of the adjacent lot proper notice of the intended improvement, and to use ordinary skill in conducting the same, and that it is the duty of the latter to shore or prop up his own building, so as to render it secure in the mean time." [2] He then goes

[1] See also Beard v. Murphy, 37 Verm. 102.

[2] Peyton v. Mayor, &c., 9 Barnew. & C. 725 ; Massey v. Goyder, 4 Carr. & P. 161.

on to state that there is a class of cases where the owner of a building is protected from the consequences of excavations or alteration of the adjoining premises. " These are ancient buildings, or those which have been erected upon ancient foundations, and which by prescription are entitled to the special privilege of being exempted from the consequences of the spirit of reform operating upon the owners of the adjacent lots, and also those which have been granted in their present situation by the owners of such adjacent lots, or by those under whom they have derived their title."[1] The Chancellor held that the owners of the church had acquired no prescriptive right, and as they did not hold directly or indirectly from the grantor of the respondent, an injunction was refused.

But the law, as stated by the Chancellor, seems to [*436] be * well settled by that and other cases, namely, that the owner of a building standing near the land of another has no right to hold the same protected from any excavation in the adjacent land, which would not injuriously affect the soil on which it stands, if not burdened with such building,[2] unless the owner of both parcels had conveyed the parcel and the dwelling-house; for in that case the right of having it supported passed with the same for the benefit of whoever may be the owner thereof, and the owner of the adjacent parcel took it charged with the duty or servitude of supporting the house, as well as the natural soil on which it stands.[3] Or, unless the house shall have

---

[1] *Ante*, p. 50; Dodd *v.* Holme, 1 Adolph. & E. 493; per *Littledale*, J., *post*, sect. 4, pl. 7; Hide *v.* Thornborough, 2 Carr. & K. 250.

[2] M'Guire *v.* Grant, 1 Dutch. 356, 362; Gayford *v.* Nichols, 9 Exch. 702, 708; Richardson *v.* Vt. Cent. R. R. Co., 25 Vt. 465; Hunt *v.* Peake, Johns. Ch. (Eng.) 705, 710; No. East. R. W. Co. *v.* Elliot, 1 Johns. & H. 145, 153; Smith *v.* Kenrick, 7 C. B. 515, 565.

[3] Cox *v.* Matthews, 1 Ventr. 237; Palmer *v.* Fleshees, 1 Sid. 167; s. c., under name of Palmer *v.* Fletcher, 1 Lev. 122; M'Guire *v.* Grant, 1 Dutch. 356, 365; Richards *v.* Rose, 9 Exch. 218; Humphries *v.* Brogden, 12 Q. B. 739, 746; Caledonian R. W. Co. *v.* Sprot, 2 Macq. H. of L. Cas. 449; Harris *v.* Ryding, 5 Mees. & W. 71; No. East R. W. Co. *v.* Elliot, 1 Johns. & H. 145, 153; Solomon *v.* Vintners' Co., 4 Hurlst. & N. 585, 597; United States *v.* Appleton, 1 Sumn. 492, 500; Eno *v.* Del Vecchio, 4 Duer, 53.

stood so long as to have acquired a prescriptive right to such support as an easement, in either of which latter cases, if the owner of the adjacent parcel dig the same to the injury of such house he will be held responsible.[1]

8. While the doctrines above stated are sustained by Panton v. Holland, another important principle is there established, that, although one may dig in his own land for all lawful purposes, and by so doing may injure a dwelling-house recently erected by another upon the adjacent parcel of land, yet he has no right to do this carelessly, nor with an intent * to injure the occupant of the neigh-   [*437] boring tenement. In that case the defendant, in erecting a house in New York, dug the foundations deeper than those of a house standing upon the adjacent parcel, whereby the walls of the house were injured. The court, Woodworth, J., says: " On reviewing the cases, I am of opinion that no man is answerable in damages for the reasonable exercise of a right, when it is accompanied by a cautious regard for the rights of others, when there is no just ground for the charge of negligence or unskilfulness, and when the act is not done maliciously." The court cite Thurston v. Hancock, with approbation. " The result of my opinion is, that the plaintiff has not shown a right to recover damages in this case, unless it be on the ground of negligence in not taking all reasonable care to prevent the injury. That is a question of fact." [2]

[1] Lasala v. Holbrook, supra; Hide v. Thornborough, 2 Carr. & K. 250; Stansell v. Jollard, 1 Selw. N. P. 457, cited by Parke, B.; Humphries v. Brogden, 12 Q. B. 739, 749; Bonomi v. Backhouse, Ellis, B. & E. 622, 646, 660; Partridge v. Scott, 3 Mees. & W. 220; M'Guire v. Grant, 1 Dutch. 356, 364; Eno v. Del Vecchio, 4 Duer, 53, 64; Brown v. Windsor, 1 Crompt. & J. 27.

[2] Panton v. Holland, 17 Johns. 92; Foley v. Wyeth, 2 Allen, 131; Trower v. Chadwick, 3 Bing. N. C. 334; Bradbee v. Christ's Hospital, 4 Mann. & G. 714, 758; Dodd v. Holme, 1 Adolph. & E. 493; Radcliff v. Mayor, &c., 4 Comst. 195, 203; Richart v. Scott, 7 Watts, 460; M'Guire v. Grant, 1 Dutch. 356, 361; Thurston v. Hancock, 12 Mass. 220; Shrieve v. Stokes, 8 B. Monr. 453; Massey v. Goyder, 4 Carr. & P. 161; Hay v. Cohoes Co., 2 Comst. 159; Richardson v. Vt. Cent. R. R. Co., 25 Vt. 465; Charless v. Rankin, 22 Mo. 566; Hart v. Baldwin, 1 N. Y. Leg. Obs. 139. See also Humes v. Mayor, &c. 1 Humph. 407.

9. This doctrine is fully sustained in the English courts, both as to excavations upon the surface and in working mines. If a stranger digs away the support of one's soil or his house, and the same is thereby injured, he is liable in damages. So is the adjacent land-owner, if he do it wrongfully, carelessly, and negligently.[1]

10. In Radcliff v. Mayor, &c., Bronson, C. J. is not disposed to limit the power of any man over his own premises by rules even as narrow as those above stated. "He may dig in his own land, though the house which his neighbor has previously erected at the extremity of his land be thereby undermined and fall into the pit." He criticises [*438] the *language used in Lasala v. Holbrook, as carrying the doctrine of a natural right to hold one's land free from interference by the adjacent owner's removing its natural support too far, especially in a city. "I think the law has superseded the necessity of negotiation by giving every man such a title to his own land that he may use it for all the purposes to which such lands are usually applied, without being answerable for the consequences, provided he exercises proper care and skill to prevent any unnecessary injury to the adjacent land-owner."[2]

11. One of the cases relied on in the above case was that of Wyatt v. Harrison, where the court, in speaking of a party's right to dig on his own land, say: "But if I have laid an additional weight upon my land, it does not follow that he is to be deprived of the right of digging in his own ground because mine will then become incapable of supporting the artificial weight which I have laid upon it."[3]

12. Whoever erects a house upon his own premises must, in order to complain of an injury by excavation in the ad-

---

[1] Jeffries v. Williams, 5 Exch. 792; Bibby v. Carter, 4 Hurlst. & N. 153.

[2] Radcliff v. Mayor, &c., 4 Comst. 195, 201, 203. But see Farrand v. Marshall, 21 Barb. 409, negativing the doctrine that one may dig in his own land so as to cause the soil of his neighbor to fall, and declaring the above doctrine of Bronson, J., an obiter dictum. See 2 Washb. Real Prop. 75, note.

[3] Wyatt v. Harrison, 3 Barnew. & Ad. 871.

jacent soil affecting such structure, not only build of proper materials and in a proper manner, but he cannot otherwise acquire a prescriptive right to have the foundations of his house undisturbed by excavations made with ordinary care and diligence in the adjacent premises. " If the first builder, in the construction of his wall, use materials unfit for the purpose, or the materials, though suitable, are so unskilfully built in the wall that it cannot be preserved and supported by ordinary care and diligence, with the use of the ordinary and usual means resorted to in practice for that purpose, when the second builder comes to dig out the foundation for his house, but notwithstanding the use of such care, *diligence, and means by the latter to prevent it, the [*439] walls give way, and with it a part or the whole of the first building falls, occasioning small or great loss to the owner thereof, it must be regarded as *damnum sine injuria,* for which the second builder is in no wise responsible." It was contended that, as the house had stood over twenty-one years, the adjacent owner had no right to disturb it by excavations in his premises, although the house were improperly or insufficiently built. But the court repudiate the doctrine in express terms : " Such a principle, when carried out, may go to exclude the owner of a lot in a situation similar to that of the defendant from building on it altogether, which would be inconsistent with principles of sound policy, as well as of law and natural justice." [1]

So, though one by excavating within his own premises cause an injury to his neighbor's premises, he would not be responsible therefor, if he had no just cause for supposing such a consequence would follow, and it resulted from some unforeseen cause.[2]

13. In determining whether a party had been guilty of carelessness in excavating his own land, reference may be

[1] Richart *v.* Scott, 7 Watts, 460 - 464. See *Littledale,* J., in Dodd *v.* Holme, 1 Adolph. & E. 493 ; Hunt *v.* Peake, Johns. Ch. (Eng.) 705, 711.

[2] Shrieve *v.* Stokes, 8 B. Monr. 453 ; Chadwick *v.* Trower, 6 Bing. N. C. 1.

had to what is usually done by other builders in similar cases, since the law does not impose upon any owner the exercise of extraordinary means of precaution, unless such care was obviously needed from the situation of the property.[1]

14. The recent case of Hunt v. Peake sustains the doctrine which the Vice-Chancellor regarded as a controverted one, that, if one enjoys the support of a dwelling-house upon land adjoining that of another for twenty years, the latter may not withdraw that support by excavations made [*440] in his *land.[2] And in a still more recent case, it was settled, that, "if a land-owner conveys one of two closes to another, he cannot afterwards do anything to derogate from his grant; and if the conveyance is made for the express purpose of having buildings erected on the land so granted, a contract is implied on the part of the grantor to do nothing to prevent the land from being used for the purpose for which, to the knowledge of the grantor, the conveyance is made." This is said of the right which one may acquire thereby to the support of buildings which he may erect upon his own land against the adjacent land of another.[3]

15. A question involving several of the matters above considered was raised in a late case in Massachusetts, Foley v. Wyeth, where, after assuming the law to be well settled, that, "if the owner of land makes an excavation in it, so near to the adjoining land of another proprietor that the soil of the latter breaks away and falls into the pit, he is responsible for all the damage thereby occasioned," the court dis-

---

[1] Shrieve v. Stokes, 8 B. Monr. 453, 457. See Charless v. Rankin, 22 Mo. 566, 574.

[2] Hunt v. Peake, Johns. Ch. (Eng.) 705 ; Partridge v. Scott, 3 Mees. & W. 220 ; Rogers v. Taylor, 2 Hurlst. & N. 828, 833 ; Smith v. Kenrick, 7 C. B. 565 ; Stansell v. Jollard, 1 Selw. N. P. 457 ; Humphries v. Brogden, 12 Q. B. 736, 750 ; Rowbotham v. Wilson, 8 Ellis & B. 140, per *Bramwell*, B.

[3] No. East. R. W. Co. v. Elliot, 1 Johns. & H. 145, 153 ; Caledonian R. W. Co. v. Sprot, 2 Macq. H. of L. Cas. 449 ; Rowbotham v. Wilson, 8 H. of L. Cas. 348.

cuss the point, how far the owner of land adjoining that on which a house has been recently erected would be liable for an injury to the same by digging within his own premises, if he was not chargeable with a want of due care and skill or positive negligence in so doing. And the conclusion to which they arrive is, that, in the absence of any proof of carelessness, negligence, or unskilfulness in the execution of the work, so far as the house was concerned, a jury had no right to regard, as an element of damage, the fact that such digging caused the foundation of the plaintiff's house to crack and settle, although he were entitled to re- cover for *causing the natural soil of the plaintiff [*441] to fall into the excavation made by the defendant.

And in this they coincide with the rule which was practically applied in Thurston v. Hancock.

In the case of Foley v. Wyeth, the defendant had not only caused the soil upon the plaintiff's premises to fall into the place excavated, and also the soil under a way that led to the plaintiff's premises, but had also caused the foundation of his house standing thereon to crack and settle. But as there was no evidence of this having been done carelessly, it was held that he could recover for the first, but not for the last injury alleged. As to the first, the court say : " This does not depend upon negligence or unskilfulness, but upon the violation of a right of property which has been invaded and disturbed." [1]   And similar language is used by the court of Vermont, in Richardson v. Vermont Central Rail- road Co.[2]

Nor is it enough to hold the defendant liable for an in- jury to adjacent land arising from his digging in his own, that what he did *contributed* to the injury, the plaintiff must show that he did not, himself, contribute to the injury com- plained of.[3]

[1] Foley v. Wyeth, 2 Allen, 131.
[2] Richardson v. Vt. Cent. R. R. Co., 25 Vt. 465, 471.
[3] Smith v. Hardesty, 31 Mo. 412.

But, say the court, in Foley *v.* Wyeth, " this unqualified rule is limited to injuries caused to the land itself, and does not afford relief for damages by the same means to artificial structures. For an injury to buildings which is unavoidably incident to the depression or slide of the soil upon which they stand, caused by the excavation of a pit on adjoining land, an action can only be maintained when a want of due care and skill, or positive negligence has contributed to produce it."

It will be perceived that the court here consider an estate in land with buildings thereon, if recently erected, as made up of two parts or elements, so far as the claim of the owner thereof for damages by removal of its lateral support is concerned. In respect to the land, they hold it to be an invariable rule of property, that a removal of its lateral support by excavation in the adjacent parcel is a violation of the [*442] right *of property, and is actionable, independent of the consideration whether it was done with or without negligence or unskilfulness. Whereas, whether the injury to the house shall be actionable depends upon its being done with a want of due care or skill, or not.

Regarding the first part of this proposition as *res adjudicata,* although it is said by Harris, J., in Farrand *v.* Marshall, that the rule, as stated by Rolle, had never been formally adopted as a rule of law, except by the *obiter dicta* of some of the judges, it only remains to ascertain by what rule the second part of the above proposition is to be applied. What is the measure of the care and diligence necessary to be observed in respect to such house, in excavating the soil of the adjoining lot ?

It seems to be conceded, in all the cases, that no man has a right to claim any aid or support in respect to his house, if a modern one, from the land of the adjacent owner. So far as the right of support of his land by that of his neighbor is a servitude, or in the nature of a servitude, upon the latter, he has no right to add to or increase it by putting any new burden upon his land. In other words, no man can claim for his land and house together any greater amount of support from his neighbor's land than he had originally a right to claim for merely his land alone, while unburdened by a house.[1]

But as the case supposes that the house may be injured by the digging in the adjacent soil, and its owner may be without remedy therefor, though such digging may have removed the necessary natural support of his soil, under one state of facts, and for a similar injury he may have a remedy under a different state of facts, and that this difference consists in the degree of care with which it is done, it becomes important to ascertain what rule or test *is to be ap- [*443] plied in measuring the degree of care which is to be exercised by the one causing the excavation in his own land.

It is obvious that the court mean to apply a different test than the mere fact of removing the natural support, for that was done in Foley v. Wyeth, and it was held that, in order to recover for the house, the owner must show, positively, want of due care or skill, or actual negligence. Besides they say: " To make a justifiable use of his own, he (the one causing the excavation) must have a proper respect to the appropriation which has already been made by the owners of the surrounding territory, and, therefore, when one undertakes to make an excavation on his land, he must consider how it will be likely, in view of the existing and actual occupation of others, to affect the soil of his neighbor." And this was said in answer to the ground taken, that if the injury complained of was in any degree caused by, or would not have occurred but for the additional weight of buildings erected on their land by persons other than the plaintiff, he could not recover in the action, and was a kind of corollary to the proposition, that " he who, in the execution of an enterprise for his

[1] Charless v. Rankin, 22 Mo. 566, 571 ; Partridge v. Scott, 3 Mees. & W. 220 ; Farrand v. Marshall, 19 Barb. 380, 387.

own benefit, changes the natural condition of the parcel of territory to which he has title, and thereby takes away the lateral support to which the owner of the adjoining estate is entitled, cannot exonerate himself from responsibility by showing that the particular injury complained of would not have occurred if other persons had never made alterations in or improvements upon their respective closes."

The way to reconcile these views and suggestions, and still to retain the distinction between an injury to the natural soil and an injury to the same soil burdened by a house or other structure thereon, seems to require some such rule as this; not only must the owner of the land, when caus-[*444] ing an excavation thereon to be made, so *conduct it as not to disturb the soil of the adjacent lot in its natural state, but if there be a dwelling-house thereon, he must use such care in the *mode* of excavating, to the *extent* above stated, as not to injure the house, provided this can be done without subjecting himself to extraordinary expense in guarding against such injury. He might, for instance, if there were no house standing upon the land, dig and remove portions of the lateral support for a considerable distance without substituting any such safeguard as a wall, and no injurious consequences would follow. Whereas if there were a house standing thereon, in order safely to carry the excavation to the same extent, bordering upon the land of his neighbor, he must expose only small portions of the soil at a time, as was done in Lasala v. Holbrook, where the defendant, as fast as he dug away his soil near the land of the plaintiff, supplied a support by the cellar-wall on which he was to rest his own house.

Still, even in this respect, he would only have to use reasonable care and diligence. Thus he would not have to prop up his neighbor's house, if the owner was cognizant of the excavation being made, in order to prevent its falling.[1]

[1] Peyton v. Mayor, &c., 9 Barnew. & C. 725; Charless v. Rankin, 22 Mo. 566, 574.

In forming a judgment of what would be a safe and proper mode of conducting his work of excavation, he may have a reasonable regard to the judgment of other practical, judicious, and skilful men.[1]

But a possible damage to another, in the cautious and prudent exercise of a lawful right, is not to be regarded, and if a loss is the consequence, it is *damnum absque injuria*. And the owner of the house would have no right to recover damages, unless it be upon the ground of *negligence in not taking all reasonable care to pre- [*445] vent the injury.[2]

16. Another circumstance to be regarded in measuring the degree of care which one must exercise in such cases, is the means and opportunity he had to know, or have reasonable ground to believe, that he was endangering his neighbor's property by his acts. This matter is somewhat considered in Shrieve *v.* Stokes,[3] above cited. The court there assume that it was the defendant's duty in digging, even upon his own ground, and for his own lawful purposes, to proceed with reasonable care and a due regard to the safety of the neighboring house. But they say : " We are of opinion that upon the question of reasonable care, in digging the defendant's cellar near the plaintiff's house, it was admissible to prove what was usually done by builders in digging cellars under similar circumstances. . . . . In order to impose upon the defendant the duty of using any extraordinary means for the protection of the plaintiff's house, it must have been apparent, upon common observation, that the digging of his cellar would probably cause the house to fall." There was in that case an alley of two or three feet in width between the cellar and the house, and the court say : " Unless the

---

[1] Charless *v.* Rankin, *supra.*

[2] Panton *v.* Holland, 17 Johns. 92, 100, 101.

[3] Shrieve *v.* Stokes, 8 B. Monr. 453, 459. See also Richardson *v.* Vt. Cent. R. R. Co., 25 Vt. 465, 471 ; Chadwick *v.* Trower, 6 Bing. N. c. 1 ; Dodd *v.* Holme, 1 Adolph. & E. 493 ; Walters *v.* Pfeil, Mood. & M. 362 ; *post*, sect. 3, pl. 7.

nature of the intervening earth was such as to render it
highly probable that it would give way, upon the cellar being
dug out, and thus cause the plaintiff's house to fall, there
could be no obligation on the defendant to take any precaution, except that he should not disturb or break down the
alley. . . . . Unless the plaintiff was entitled to have his
house supported not only by the alley, but by the compact
earth on the defendant's lot adjoining the alley, the mere
removal of that earth was not a breach of duty in
[*446] the *defendant. And in that case he could not be
said to have caused the loss to the plaintiff, nor be
held liable for it, unless he knew, or had good reason to
believe, that the removal of the earth up to his own line
would occasion the loss before the necessary support should
be supplied by building up his cellar wall, or unless the loss
could be fairly attributed to his want of ordinary skill or
care in loosening or removing the earth from his own lot." [1]

It may be stated, in this connection, that the question of
the right of the owner of the house to recover damages does
not depend upon the state of repair of the house. It was held
that such owner might recover in an action, although it
appeared that the house, if let alone, would not have stood
six months.[1]

Further illustrations of the doctrine of the right of easement and servitude of lateral support for land will be found
when the subject of subjacent support of land is considered,
in a subsequent part of this work, as the analogy between
the two renders it unnecessary to repeat in respect to one
what, upon several points, may be said of the other.[2]

The case, however, of Dodd v. Holme may be properly
referred to at some greater length, as it bears upon several
of the points already referred to. In this case the plaintiff
had an ancient house standing on his own land near that of
the defendant. The latter, in order to build a house on his
land, dug a cellar which came within about four feet of the

---

[1] Dodd v. Holme, 1 Adolph. & E. 493.   [2] Post, sect. 4, pl. 4, et seq.

plaintiff's house. The house began to give way, when the defendant attempted to shore it up. The weather was unusually wet, and partly from this cause, and partly from a want of shores, the house fell. The question submitted to the jury was, " Whether the fall was occasioned by the defendant's negligence ? " The jury found for the plaintiff, and the court sustained the verdict. But in doing this, a part of the judges regard the fact of the house having been *an ancient one as an important cir- [*447] cumstance, taken in connection with the fact of negligence found by the jury. Taunton, J. said : " If the building had fallen down merely in consequence of its infirm condition, that would not have been a damage by the act of the defendant." And Williams, J. : " If it was true that the premises could have stood only six months, the plaintiff still had a cause of action against those who accelerated its fall ; the state of the house might render more care necessary on the part of the defendants not to hasten its dissolution." But it will be perceived that throughout the case, the plaintiff's house being ancient, that and the land are treated of as an entire thing, each part having an equal right to protection, no distinction being made, as in Thurston v. Hancock, and Foley v. Wyeth, between the damage to the land and that to the house.[1]

In this connection reference may also be made to Walters v. Pfeil,[2] where the court held, that though if there be two houses adjoining each other, and it is necessary to take down one, the owner of the other ought to shore it up, if necessary to its security, yet, though he omit to do this, he would not be without remedy if the other party so irregularly and improperly took down his house as thereby to cause the other house to fall ; or, in the words of the judge (Tenterden), if " the house of the defendant was pulled down in a wasteful, negligent, and improvident manner, so as to occasion

[1] See also Hide v. Thornborough, 2 Carr. & K. 250.
[2] Walters v. Pfeil, Mood. & M. 362.

34

greater risk to the plaintiff's than in the ordinary course of doing the work they would have incurred."

17. Questions somewhat related to those above alluded to, incidentally arose in the case of Chadwick v. Trower, which was an action for so carelessly taking down the defendant's vault, that the plaintiff's wine-vault and wine were injured. After discussing the form of the declaration, and what was averred therein in respect to the de-[*448] fendant's * obligation to do certain things in respect to the plaintiff's vault that adjoined his, the judge, Parke, B., says : " The question is, whether the law imposes upon the defendant an obligation to take such care in pulling down his vaults and walls as that the adjoining vault shall not be injured. Supposing that to be so, where the party is cognizant of the existence of the vault, we are all of opinion that no such obligation can arise where there is no averment that the defendant had notice of its existence ; for one degree of care would be required where no vault exists, but the soil is left in its natural and solid state ; another, where there is a vault; and another, and still greater degree of care would be required where the adjoining vault is of a weak and fragile construction." [1]

18. And there is great force in the remark of Wardlaw, J., in Napier v. Bulwinkle, as to the gaining rights by one, and imposing duties upon another, of two adjoining estates by mere length of time in which a certain state of things has existed. " Where the enjoyment was in its nature hidden, or, although it was apparent, there was no ready means for resisting it within the power of the servient owner, assent was not implied, and the influence of twenty years' time, therefore, not acknowledged." [2]

[1] Chadwick v. Trower, 6 Bing. N. C. 1.
[2] Napier v. Bulwinkle, 5 Rich. 311, 324.

EASEMENT OF SUPPORT OF HOUSES.

1. Right of support of houses on each other gained by grant or prescription.
2. Rules of the civil law upon the subject.
3. Right of mutual support when incident to adjoining houses.
4. Right limited to adjoining houses, where it exists.
5. Of the care to be used in taking down a house adjoining another.
6. Right of support of houses may be gained by prescription.
7. One responsible for want of care in taking down his house.

1. OF a character somewhat analogous to that of the ease-ment which the owner of a house may acquire by grant or prescription, of having it supported by the soil of an adjacent proprietor, and which has been above considered, is that which the owner of a house may acquire of having the same supported by an adjacent house.   As both these are artificial structures, this right can, in no sense, be a natural one, and if, therefore, it exist at all, it can only have been acquired by grant or prescription.[1]

2. As a servitude, it was known to the civil law under the name of *oneris ferendi,* by which the wall or pillar of one house is bound to sustain the weight of the buildings of the neighbor, and the owner of the servient building was bound to keep it in repair, and sufficiently strong for the weight it had to bear, unless it was otherwise expressly stipulated by agreement, or it had otherwise been practised for a sufficient length of time.   And while the wall was being rebuilt, the support of the dominant house was to be provided by the owner thereof.[2]

3. There may be a mutual right of support by two or more houses arising from grant or reservation, where they

---

[1] Solomon v. Vintner's Co., 4 Hurlst. & N. 598.

[2] Ayl. Pand. 309 ; 3 Burge, Col. & F. Law, 402 ; Domat, B. 1, t. 2, § 2, p. 7 ; D. 8, 2, 33. 2 Fournel, Traité du Voisinage, 413, § 248.   The distinction be-tween the above right or servitude and the "Droit d'appui," or a simple right of support, is pointed out in the above work of M. Fournel, § 31.

[*450]   *are erected by one owner, and are so constructed as
          to require such support, and are then conveyed to
different owners, or one is conveyed and the other retained
by the original owner. The right of support, in such cases,
is incident to the property so far as to pass with it, unless
excluded by the terms of the grant. The law in such cases
presumes a grant or reservation of the right of support in
favor of each of the tenements.[1]

4. A question how far an easement of support may arise
in favor of one house against another came up in Solomon v.
Vintners' Co., where there were three houses in a block.
The plaintiff owned the first, the defendant the third, and
the intermediate house standing between them belonged to
a third person. The houses stood upon a hill, and for over
thirty years had been out of perpendicular, the first leaning
towards and upon the second and third. The defendant's
house being out of repair, he pulled it down in order to rebuild it. In consequence of this the intermediate house
leaned more than before, and the plaintiff's house fell. And
for this he brought his action. There had never been a
common ownership of the houses, nor did it appear under
what circumstances they were originally constructed.

The court assumed that the one who took down the defendant's house was negligent in the manner in which the
work was done. The plaintiff insisted that he had, by long
enjoyment, acquired the right to have his house supported
by the adjacent house. But Pollock, C. B., in treating of
this, says: "If the house removed had been the next
adjoining the plaintiff's, we should have felt much em-
barrassed by some cases and *dicta*. In Stansell v. Jollard,[2]
and Hide v. Thornborough,[3] such a right of support is stated

[1] Richards v. Rose, 9 Exch. 218. See Partridge v. Scott, 3 Mees. & W. 220 ;
Webster v. Stevens, 5 Duer, 553; Eno v. Del Vecchio, 4 Duer, 53 ; United
States v. Appleton, 1 Sumn. 492, 500; Partridge v. Gilbert, 15 N. Y. 601 ; 1
Fournel, Traité du Voisinage, § 31.

[2] Stansell v. Jollard, 1 Selw. N. P. 457.

[3] Hide v. Thornborough, 2 Carr & K. 250.

to be *gained if the houses have stood for twenty [*451] years, and in Humphries *v.* Brogden [1] Lord Campbell refers to these cases. It is extremely difficult to see how the circumstance of the houses having stood for twenty years makes any difference, or creates a right where houses are supposed to have been built by different adjoining land-owners, each with its own separate and independent walls, but, upwards of twenty years ago, one of them got out of perpendicular, and leaned upon and was supported in part by the others, so that if the latter were removed, the other would fall. . . . . And it seems contrary to justice and reason, that a man, by building a weak house adjoining to the house of his neighbor, can, if the weak house gets out of the perpendicular, and leans upon the adjoining house, thereby compel his neighbor either to pull down his own house, within twenty years, or to bring some action at law, the precise nature of which is not very clear. Otherwise, it is said, an adverse right should be acquired against him." But as the plaintiff's house did not adjoin that of the defendant, the court held the latter could not be responsible to the former for the injury to his house by the removal of the defendant's house.

Bramwell, B. agrees with the Chief Baron in his conclusions, but avoids the point of how far and when the owner of one house can gain an easement of support against another, as involving questions of very great difficulty and importance, and on which he would rather not pronounce an opinion, without a great deal more consideration than he had been able to give them.[2]

The case of Stansell *v.* Jollard, however, was that of a claim of a right to have an ancient house supported by the adjacent soil, and not of support of one house by another. The same was true of Hide *v.* Thornborough.

*5. In Peyton *v.* Mayor, &c., the action was for [*452]

[1] Humphries *v.* Brogden, 12 Q. B. 739, 749.
[2] Solomon *v.* Vintners' Co., 4 Hurlst. & N. 585 – 603.

pulling down, by the defendant, of his own house without shoring up that of the plaintiff, which leaned upon it,
by reason of which the latter fell. The defendant's house
was old, and required to be taken down. The count in the
plaintiff's writ assumed that the defendant, when he took
down his house, was bound to shore up the plaintiff's house,
and it did not aver that defendant failed to give him notice,
so that the plaintiff could have done it himself; so that
whether such notice was necessary was not a question raised
in the case. It did not appear whether both houses were
built at the same time or at different times. The freehold of
the two was then in different hands. The plaintiff must,
from his situation in this case, have known of the act of taking down the defendant's house. From the want of any
evidence of a grant of a right of support of plaintiff's house
upon defendant's, the court held, under the plaintiff's declaration, he could not recover for the injury to his house.[1]

No obligation or servitude of support of one building by
another arises from their mere juxtaposition, however long
continued. Nor, as it would seem, from the one house, tot-
tering and resting against the other, which stands erect, in
its original position.[2]

6. But, from the cases before cited, it seems to be understood that one may, under some circumstances, acquire the
right of supporting his house against that of his neighbor,
if enjoyed for a sufficient length of time. And this will, at
any rate, be shown to be the case if there be a wall of mutual support between them answering to a party wall.[3]

7. Still one may not, recklessly, and in a wasteful
[*453] and *negligent manner, take down his own house
upon his own land, and thereby cause injury to the
adjacent buildings of another. In taking down his own

---

[1] Peyton v. Mayor, &c., 9 Barnew. & C. 725 ; Partridge v. Gilbert, 15 N. Y.
601, 612.

[2] See Napier v. Bulwinkle, 5 Rich. 311, 324.

[3] Wiltshire v. Sidford, 8 Barnew. & C. 259, note ; Cubitt v. Porter, 8 Barnew.
& C. 257.

house he is bound to exercise reasonable care, and either to give the adjacent owner notice of the proposed alteration in the premises, and an opportunity to protect his premises by proper props and guards, or to provide them himself, unless the structure which he takes down is wholly his own and upon his own land. But if he give the other party notice, and he fails to protect his buildings from injury, the party who takes down the house is not bound to use any extraordinary care in preventing an injury to the premises of the other party.[1]

SECTION III.

EASEMENT OF PARTY WALLS.

1. Servitude of the civil law answering to party walls.
2. What constitutes a party wall.
3. Either party may build upon his part of the wall.
4. Either party may repair or enlarge his part of the wall.
5. Cubitt v. Porter. How far one may rebuild the whole wall.
6. When a wall is deemed a party wall.
7. Degree of care to be used in repairing a party wall.
8. How far one may underpin a party wall.
9. Of the respective rights of the owners to repair party walls.
10. Right to use the wall by one, though the other house be destroyed.
11. Covenant to pay for party wall runs with the land.
12. Common wall erected by tenants for years not a party wall.
13. Sherred v. Cisco. Of recovering expense of rebuilding a party wall.
14. How far destruction of premises destroys the easement.
15. Easement mutual, though property in the wall several.
16. Burlock v. Peck. How far agreements bind successive owners.
17. Neither party may impair the wall on his own land.
18. Rules of civil law as to repair of party walls.
19. French law as to party walls.
20. Law of Pennsylvania as to party walls.

*1. AMONG the urban servitudes of the civil law [*454]

---

[1] Walters v. Pfeil, Mood. & M. 362; Massey v. Goyder, 4 Carr. & P. 161 ; Trower v. Chadwick, 3 Bing. N. C. 334 ; s. c., 6 Bing. N. C. 1, reversing the former judgment; 2 Washb. Real Prop. 77 ; Charless v. Rankin, 22 Mo. 566, 572 ; Eno v. Del Vecchio, 4 Duer, 53, 66 ; s. c., 6 Duer, 17 ; Hart v. Baldwin, 1 N. Y. Leg. Obs. 139 ; 3 Kent, Comm. 437 ; Brown v. Windsor, 1 Crompt. & J. 20 ; Humphries v. Brogden, 12 Q. B. 739, 751 ; Partridge v. Gilbert, 15 N. Y. 601, 612.

was that of a right in one man to fix a beam or piece of timber or stone in his neighbor's wall, *immitendi tigna in parietem vicini.*[1]

2. Corresponding in many respects to this, and the servitude of *oneris ferendi*, already mentioned, is that of party walls at the common law. By *party walls* are understood walls between two estates which are used for the common benefit of both, in supporting, for instance, timbers used in the construction of contiguous buildings standing thereon. But the mere circumstance that a wall stands between two contiguous buildings, and the timbers of the one are supported upon one side of the wall and those of the other upon the other side will not necessarily make them tenants in common of the wall. It may have been built by the parties so as to stand one half upon the land of each. But it does not, thereby, make them tenants or owners thereof in common. Each would still own his half in severalty, though each may make use of it for the purposes of the support of his building erected upon or against it. But if such joint use of such wall were continued for twenty years, each acquires such a right, in common with the other, to enjoy the use and benefit of it, that it becomes thereby properly a party wall, and neither could remove it or render it insufficient to support the building of the other upon it.

So, if one proprietor erect two adjoining houses, with a wall between them for the purpose of supporting both buildings, and the same is necessary for that purpose, and he then conveys one of these dwellings by metes and bounds, by a line running through the centre of this wall, the grant would not only carry what was within the limits described, but pass, as an easement appurtenant to the grant, a right of support of the house by the entire wall, as well [*455] that *not included as that within the limits mentioned in the deed.[2]

[1] Ayl. Pand. 309 ; D. 8, 2, 2.
[2] 2 Washb. Real Prop. 78 ; 3 Kent, Comm. 437 ; Eno v. Del Vecchio, 4 Duer,

Although party walls, *murs mitoyens*, are fully defined, and the law in respect to them stated at much length in the treatises upon the French law,[1] its rules seem to be much less satisfactorily settled by the common law, although the cases under it are multiplying with the growth and increase of our cities. Thus it is said that " what the legal rights and burden of a ' party wall ' are, as even its definition, is as yet scarcely settled definitively. The term is commonly applied to a wall of which, if divided longitudinally, the two parts rest on land belonging to different owners, built solidly, of materials not easily divided, or whose parts cannot be taken down, without danger to the whole structure. In such case, either party may remove the half on his own land, if it does not injure the other half, unless one or the other owner has an easement by grant to have his neighbor keep his half to support his own. Walls, however, built entirely on one man's land may acquire, by grant, the characteristics of *party walls*," the rights of the parties in such cases depending, exclusively, on the character of the grant. Another Judge in the same case defines a party wall in its general, ordinary signification, as " a dividing wall between two houses, to be used equally for all the purposes of an exterior wall by both parties, that is, by the respective owners of both houses." " This use, in its full, unrestricted sense, embraces not only the use of the interior face or side of the wall, but also such use of it as is necessary to form a complete and perfect junction in an ordinary, good mechanical manner between it and the exterior walls of the house." " And the right of the grantee of such unrestricted use would be the same whether the wall stood one half on the land of one owner and one half on the land of the other, or stood wholly upon land of the grantor of the unrestricted

53, and 6 Duer, 17 ; Sherred *v.* Cisco, 4 Sandf. 480 ; Matts *v.* Hawkins, 5 Taunt. 20 ; Cubitt *v.* Porter, 8 Barnew. & C. 257 ; Webster *v.* Stevens, 5 Duer, 553 ; Murly *v.* M'Dermott, 8 Adolph. & E. 138 ; 3 Kent, Comm. 437 ; 1 Fournel, Traité du Voisinage, 110 ; 2 Ibid. 217.

[1] 1 Le Page, Desgodets, 39 – 122.

use." But he adds, that the term " party wall " has never been judicially defined.[1]

In another case, the question grew out of the terms of the grant, but in determining it the court goes somewhat into the nature of the right claimed. The owner of two lots upon a street which faced to the south, upon the eastern one of which was a three-story brick house against whose west wall there was a one-story brick building standing upon the western lot. He conveyed the western lot bounding it on the east by the west line of this three-story building, " the owners on both sides to have mutual use of the present partition wall." A question was made as to the height to which the purchaser might raise his house, and avail himself of the west wall of the three-story house as a party wall. The purchaser claimed a right to insert joists, &c., into the same to its whole extent, as had been done with the one-story building then standing. The court held that as a general principle the use of such a wall was mutual, but that it must be a reasonable use, and such that neither of the parties shall thereby inflict substantial injury upon the other, and that neither had a right to remove it or destroy it, nor appropriate it exclusively to his own use. But that, as in the terms of the grant in this case, " the present partition wall " was the subject-matter conveyed, it excluded the idea of a reservation or grant of the whole wall as being a partition wall, and therefore the owner of the west lot could only use it as a party wall to the height of his original building.[2]

3. In Matts v. Hawkins, where the wall had been built half upon the land of each land-owner, it was held that either party had a right to carry up his half of the wall above that of the half of the other proprietor, if he saw fit.

4. The case of Eno v. Del Vecchio reviews the cases upon the subject of party walls, and states, in addition to what is embraced in the above propositions, that so long as the wall is capable of answering the purposes for which it was erected,

[1] Fettretch v. Leamy, 9 Bosw. 525.   [2] Price v. McConnell, 27 Ill. 255.

the owner of either part may underpin the foundation, sink it deeper and increase its thickness within the limits of his own lot, or its length or height, if he can do so without injury to the building on the adjoining lot. But he cannot interfere with the wall in any manner, unless he can do so without injury to the adjoining building, or without the consent of the owner of such building. He cannot pare off the part of the wall that stands on his own land, so as to render the remainder insufficient or unsafe, or excavate under the part of the wall upon his own premises, to the permanent injury thereof.[1]

The ground on which the rights and liabilities of the owners or occupants of party walls rest, are thus stated by the court of Pennsylvania, in considering the law of that State upon the subject: " When it (the wall) is constructed, the regulation of its enjoyment and repair is as plain as that belonging to any other property in common."[2]

5. In the case of Cubitt v. Porter, Bayley, J. says: " The jury found it was a party wall. They did not, in terms, find that it was common property. . . . . Where a wall is *common property, it may happen either that a [*456] moiety of the land on which it is built may be one man's, and the other moiety another's, or the land may belong to the two persons in undivided moieties." In that case, one of the parties took down the dividing wall, and rebuilt it of a greater height than the former one, and it was held he was not liable in trespass to the owner of the house upon the other side of the wall, the jury having found it was a party wall.

Holroyd, J. says: " The presumption arising from the acts of enjoyment is, that the wall was the property of the plaintiff and defendant as tenants in common, for the law will presume that what was done without opposition for a considerable time was done rightfully, and that these acts

1 See Webster v. Stevens, 5 Duer, 553.
2 Evans v. Jayne, 23 Penn. St. 36.

of enjoyment were lawful. That being the case, there was abundant evidence upon the trial to raise a question to go to the jury, whether the wall was or was not the common wall of both. There having been a joint use of the wall by both, each must have had the right, originally, or have acquired the right, in the course of time, by legal means. The jury have found, in effect, that it was their common property." [1]

6. So, in Wiltshire v. Sidford, the wall in question had been used by the adjacent owners for near a century, and the court say : " Where the quantity of land contributed by each was not known, the reasonable presumption from the common use of the wall was, *prima facie*, that the wall and the land on which it was built were the undivided property of both." [2]

These citations have been made to show the inclination of the courts to regard the long enjoyment of a wall by the adjacent owners as evidence of its being not only a party wall, but one in which there is a common owner-
[*457] ship, * although, for purposes of remedy, and defin-
ing the respective rights of such adjacent owners, it is always open to be shown that each owns the part of the wall that stands upon his own land. [3]

7. In Hart v. Baldwin, the two houses were erected together with a common wall between them, about fifteen years before the injury complained of. The defendant dug a cellar adjoining it, in consequence of which the front wall of the plaintiff was injured by reason of the party wall being insufficient. It was held that the defendant, as purchaser of the estate, was not presumed to know the insufficiency of the wall, and having used all the requisite care in doing his work, which would have been sufficient to guard against in-

---

[1] See 3 Kent, Comm. 438.

[2] Wiltshire v. Sidford, 8 Barnew. & C. 259, note.

[3] See Sherred v. Cisco, 4 Sandf. 480, 490 ; Murly v. M'Dermott, 8 Adolph. & E. 138.

jury if the wall had been a sufficient one, he was not liable for the injury to the adjacent owner's estate.[1]

8. But it was held, in Bradbee *v.* Christ's Hospital, that one owner of a party wall had no right to underpin the same partially or wholly, unless he can do so without injury to the adjacent messuage, whether the interest in the wall were several in the owners, one half in each, or they were tenants in common of the same. The finding in that case by the arbitrator was, however, that there was carelessness, negligence, and unskilfulness in the defendant in underpinning the wall partially, and in not underpinning the whole of the wall, whereby the plaintiff's house sunk and sustained damage.[2]

9. But, as it is obvious there may be occasions where such walls must be repaired or rebuilt, an inquiry arises, how can one of the parties effectually call upon the other *to join in such repair or reconstruction ? In [*458] a case before Kent, Chancellor, the party wall was between two old houses, and the plaintiff, owner of one of them, wished to tear his down, and erect a new one in its place. He gave notice to the other party, and requested him to join in the reconstruction of the wall; but he declined to act, and forbade his pulling down the wall. The plaintiff then tore down his house and the wall, and erected new ones on the sites of the former house and wall, and requested the other owner to contribute his share of the expense of the wall. The case found that it was a party wall in which both parties had an equal interest, and that the wall was in a state of ruin and decay, and that the plaintiff could not rebuild without taking it down. The Chancellor states the French law to be as follows : " A common or party wall, by that law, is where it has been built at common expense, or if

---

[1] Hart *v.* Baldwin, 1 N. Y. Leg. Obs. 139. See Shrieve *v.* Stokes, 8 B. Monr. 453.

[2] Bradbee *v.* Christ's Hospital, 4 Mann. & G. 714, 761 ; Webster *v.* Stevens, 5 Duer, 553, 556. See Pardessus, Traité des Servitudes, 265, ed. 1829 ; Dowling *v.* Hemmings, 20 Md. 179.

built by one party, where the other has acquired a common right to it."

Every wall of separation between two buildings is presumed to be a common or party wall, if the contrary be not shown, and this not only is a rule of positive ordinance, but is a principle of ancient law. If the common wall be in a state of ruin, and requires to be rebuilt, one party can compel the other by action to contribute to the expense of rebuilding it. But the necessity of the reparation must be established by the judgment of men skilled in the business, and made on due previous notice; and if the new wall be made wider or higher, &c., the party building must bear the extra expense. And in this case the Chancellor decreed that the owner of the other estate should contribute his equal share in the expense of reconstructing the wall.[1]

[*459]   *10. The case of Brondage v. Warner was one where the owner of a store granted to another the right of placing the wall for the third story of his house upon the top of the wall of the grantor's store, and of occupying the end of the store as the end of the house to be erected by the grantee. The grantee erected his building accordingly, and enjoyed the use of the wall of the grantor's store. It was held to be the grant of an easement only, but to continue either as long as the wall stood, or in fee. And he was held to have a right to make use of it, although the rest of the grantor's store had been burned down.[2]

11. So where the owner of one city lot granted to the owner of an adjoining lot the use of six inches of his land for the purpose of erecting a party wall, and covenanted for himself, his heirs, and assigns, that whenever he should erect a new building on his lot, he would pay the owner of the other lot, his heirs, or assigns, one half part of the value

---

[1] Campbell v. Mesier, 4 Johns. Ch. 334; 2 Fournel, Traité du Voisinage, 217, 236–242. See Peck v. Day, 1 N. Y. Leg. Obs. 312; 3 Kent, Comm. 438; Cubitt v. Porter, 8 Barnew. & C. 257; Partridge v. Gilbert, 15 N. Y. 601; *post*, sect. 19.

[2] Brondage v. Warner, 2 Hill, 145.

of such portion of the wall as he should use, it was held to
be a grant of an easement, that it was an incorporeal hereditament, and the covenant connected with it bound, and
was a charge upon the land.[1]

12. But where the common or party wall between two
tenements was erected by two tenants for years, it did not
create mutual easements in perpetuity of support by such
wall in favor of the adjacent estates, for the reason that
neither could grant a permanent interest in the land in his
occupation. There would be a right of such easement between the respective tenants who constructed the wall, but
it would not continue beyond this common term. Nor
would the respective reversioners be bound by such arrangement between their tenants.[2]

13. How far one of two adjacent owners of premises is
bound to join in building or repairing a party wall
between *the same was fully considered in the case　[*460]
of Sherred v. Cisco, where the case above cited of
Campbell v. Mesier is referred to. In that case, the plaintiff
had for many years owned a lot of land in New York, having
a warehouse upon it adjoining another warehouse, from
which it was separated by a brick wall, one half of which
rested on her land, and the other upon the land of the other
owner; and the beams of each warehouse rested on this
common or party wall. The owner of the other warehouse
died, having mortgaged his estate, and soon after both warehouses were consumed by fire, and nothing was left of the
wall but its foundation.

The plaintiff then rebuilt her warehouse, and placed the
wall next the other lot upon its original foundation equally
upon both lots, but without any agreement in respect to its
construction with the other owner. The lot adjoining this
warehouse was sold, and the defendant built a store upon it,
using this wall for one side, and inserting the timbers of the

---

[1] Keteltas v. Penfold, 4 E. D. Smith, 122. See also Weyman v. Ringold, 1
Brad. 52, 61.

[2] Webster v. Stevens, 5 Duer, 553.

building in the same. The plaintiff then called on him to contribute a part of the expense of the wall. But the court held, that if the original wall had been built by the mutual agreement and at the joint expense of the proprietors of the two lots, each would have continued owner of the land on which the respective parts of it were built, and of course each owned one half of the wall in severalty. But neither would have had a right to pull down the wall without the other's consent, and to that extent the agreement upon which it was erected controlled the exclusive dominion which each would otherwise have had over the half of the wall, as well as over the soil on which it stood. But when the wall had been destroyed by the elements, there being no agreement to build a second wall, neither was under obligation to join with the other in doing so, and the law would imply no such obligation. By the common law, every man may build such buildings and in such manner as he pleases on his own land, nor is he bound to give his neighbor any use or advantage of his land for support, drip, or [*461] by the way *of any easement whatever. And if a stranger enters upon his unoccupied land, and sees fit to make erections or improvements on the same, he is not bound to make compensation therefor upon recovering possession of his premises. When, therefore, the defendant in this case made use of a wall standing on his own land, he was not thereby made chargeable for the expense of constructing the same.

There is, therefore, a marked distinction between the case of Campbell v. Mesier and the present, inasmuch as in the former the wall was a common one, built jointly, or presumed to have been so built, by both parties, whereas in the present case, though built upon the land of each proprietor, it was built wholly at the expense of one, and, so far as it stood upon the other's land, it was built without right.[1]

[1] Sherred v. Cisco, 4 Sandf. 480. See Orman v. Day, 5 Florid. 385, 392, affirming and sustaining Sherred v. Cisco, upon similar facts. See Partridge v. Gilbert, 15 N. Y. 601.

14. The case of Partridge *v.* Gilbert, cited above, is deserving attention, as one of the judges in that case, Denio, took occasion to refer to the foregoing cases of Campbell *v.* Mesier, and Sherred *v.* Cisco. In that case, the two buildings, having a common wall between them, were owned and erected by the same person. This wall rested upon the crown of an arch, beneath which was a passage-way, the legs of the arch standing one on one estate and the other upon the other, the centre line of the wall being the dividing line of the estates. The estates came by conveyances into two persons' hands, the centre line of the wall, by the description in the deeds, being the dividing line of the two. The buildings were occupied as stores, one in the possession of a tenant, the other in that of the owner. The wall being ruinous and unsafe, the owner of the latter store notified the tenant of the other store of his intention to take down and rebuild the wall. The tenant objected, but the owner proceeded to do so, leaving the tenant's store exposed, and for this and the injury to his business he sued the owner of the other store who had taken down the *wall. Two of the judges of the Court of Appeals [*462] gave opinions, and all concurred in the judgment.

They held that, the wall being ruinous and unsafe, the owner of the adjoining store had a right to take it down and rebuild it, and he might take it all down, for this purpose, unless he could make it safe by taking down and rebuilding only that part upon his own land. That though each party owned up to the centre line of the wall, each had an easement of support of his building upon the wall, which passed when the owner conveyed them as separate estates, and that this extended to the support of the legs of the arch, which stood one upon each parcel of the estate. Shankland, J. approved of the doctrine of Campbell *v.* Mesier, that in such a case the one causing the necessary repairs or restoration of the wall might have a remedy for contribution against the other party. And that the owner had the same right to

35

rebuild the entire wall as he had to repair it, if necessary to
its enjoyment.   Denio, J. held, that neither party could
have rightfully done anything, though upon his own land,
to weaken this wall, and cites Richards v. Rose.[1]   "In this
case we hold that the owner of the building occupied by the
plaintiffs was entitled to have it supported by the common
wall, while that wall remained in a condition to uphold it.
. . . . My view of the rights of these parties is this.   Each
had a title to the soil, to the division line, which was the
centre of the arch and wall, but this title was qualified by
the easement which each owner had of supporting his building by means of the common wall.   As the half of the wall
standing on the land of the owner would not alone afford the
requisite support, because the whole of the arch and the entire
thickness of the wall was required for that purpose, the law
gave him an interest, in the nature of an easement, in the
part of the wall standing on the land of the other
[*463] party.   This right existed as long as the wall *continued to be sufficient for that purpose, and the
respective buildings remained in a condition to need and to
enjoy that support."

The case of Dowling v. Hemmings was, in many respects,
like that of Partridge v. Gilbert.   The dividing wall of two
houses rested upon an arch, the legs of which rested one
upon each of the adjacent lots.   It was held, nevertheless,
to be a party wall with all the rights and incidents of such a
wall, after it had stood and been so used and enjoyed for
twenty years or more, and one of the parties having removed
the leg that rested upon his land, the wall fell, and he was
held liable for the injury thereby caused to the other party.[2]

In respect to the rights of the several parties to rebuild
the wall when it ceased to be sufficient, he refers to the cases
of Campbell v. Mesier, and Sherred v. Cisco, in the latter of
which it was held, that, if the buildings were destroyed by

[1] Richards v. Rose, 9 Exch. 218.
[2] Dowling v. Hemmings, 20 Md. 179.

fire, the parties were remitted to their original, unqualified title to the division line. " I do not perceive any solid distinction between a total destruction of the wall and buildings, and a state of things which would require the whole to be rebuilt from the foundation. In either case, there is great force in saying that the mutual easements have become inapplicable, and that each proprietor may build as he pleases upon his own land, without any obligation to accommodate the other. . . . . If the right of mutual support continues, by means of the original arrangement, or by prescription, it is for just such an easement as was originally conceded, or which has been established by long enjoyment. But in the changing condition of our cities and villages it must often happen, as it did actually happen in this case, that edifices of different dimensions, and an entirely different character, would be required. And it might happen, too, that the views of one of the proprietors as to the value and extent of the new buildings would essentially differ from those of the other, and the division wall which would suit one of them would be inapplicable to the objects of the other. If it were necessary to determine this point in this case, I should be strongly inclined to adopt the views of the late Judge Sanford, in delivering the opinion of the Superior Court in the case of Sherred v. Cisco, just cited." [1]

The doctrine stated in the above case, that the occupant of the store who was injured by taking down and *rebuilding the party wall had no cause of action [*464] thereby against the other proprietor, is in accordance with the French law, as stated by Pardessus.[2]

15. So far as the above cases sustain the doctrine that if two parties build a common wall between them, and erect houses on each side of the same, although each may be the owner of his half thereof in severalty, each has the easement of support by such wall so long as it stands, which the other

[1] Partridge v. Gilbert, 15 N. Y. 601.
[2] Pardessus, Traité des Servitudes, 251, ed. 1829.

may not weaken or destroy, it is confirmed by the case of Brown *v*. Windsor, although a cursory reading of that case might lead to an impression that one may acquire an easement in another's land by parol, under certain circumstances.[1]

16. In addition to the foregoing cases, reference may be had to those cited below, as bearing upon the remedy which one owner of a party wall may have against the other for an injury done to the same, or for recompense for expenses incurred in repairing the same, which are here alluded to, though not perhaps forming a part of the proper subject of easements.[2]

The case of Burlock *v*. Peck may be referred to also for another purpose, as illustrating the effect of an agreement in respect to party walls upon the successive owners of the respective estates. Peck owned two adjoining city lots, 69 and 71, and sold to H. the former, who was to have "the privilege of building a party wall twelve inches thick, extending six inches on each side of the line," the grantor in the deed agreeing to pay for said wall when used. H. erected a house on 69, and constructed the wall as above provided. H. sold to plaintiff's intestate. After this Peck sold 71 to the same H., who erected a house upon it, and used this party wall; and the administrator of the gran-[*465] tee of lot 69 brought an action to recover the *cost of half this wall against the administrator of Peck. The court held that by H.'s deed of Lot 69, the whole of the party wall passed, although six inches of it stood upon 71, the whole property in it was in him. When H. built upon 71, he appropriated, as he had a right to do, the wall to his use, and thereby gave the proprietor of No. 69 a right to recover for one half the cost of it under the covenant of Peck, as one running with the land.

17. Connected also with the subject of remedy of one of

---

[1] Brown *v*. Windsor, 1 Crompt. & J. 20; Dowling *v*. Hemmings, 20 Md. 179.
[2] Burlock *v*. Peck, 2 Duer, 90; Murley *v*. M'Dermott, 8 Adolph. & E. 138.

two owners of party walls against the other for acts injuriously affecting the same, may be cited the case of Phillips
v. Boardman, which related to two estates adjoining each
other, upon Washington Street, in Boston, between which
there was an ancient party wall twelve inches thick, used for
supporting the timbers of the respective houses. The owner
of one having taken down his, and being about to erect a
new building on the site of the old one, pared off four inches
from the old wall with a view to erect a new wall distinct
from the old one, twelve inches in thickness, occupying eight
inches upon his own land, and the four inches of the old
wall thus pared off. He had begun to erect such wall, occasionally extending his bricks two inches beyond the same,
so as to extend to the centre of the old wall, partly to aid in
the support of the new and partly to indicate the extent of
the limits of his line, and to prevent the owner of the remainder of the wall, if he took it down, ever joining it upon
his new wall. The adjacent owner applied for an injunction
to his erecting such wall. It was shown that the wall was
an ancient one, sufficient for such buildings as stood upon
the street, and that paring off four inches would essentially impair its strength, and that the new wall would not
afford any material aid or strength to the old one. The
court granted the injunction, because it being an ancient
party wall, both parties were jointly interested in it, and
neither of them can so deal with it as to diminish
its capacity for service, * without the consent of the [*466]
other; and if such new wall were enjoyed for twenty
years, the right to enjoy the whole wall as a party one would
be lost to the complainant.[1]

18. There were rules in the civil law, as there are in the
French code, the statutes of England, and in Pennsylvania,
regulating the rights of parties in respect to party walls between their estates, and the remedies to which either may
resort for compensation for their erection or repair, or for

1 Phillips v. Boardman, 4 Allen, 147.

injury done them. But these partake so much of a strictly local character, that, with the exception of the system in force in France, they are purposely omitted here.[1]

The rule of the civil law, whereby one may acquire by grant or prescription the right of having the beams of his house rest upon the wall of another house, though such wall is wholly built upon the land of the owner of the wall, has already been mentioned, and, as it would seem, the same easement may be gained at common law by long enjoyment.[2]

19. The cases, both in the English and American courts, have been so few in which the rights of parties in respect to party walls have been considered, that I have been induced by the importance of the subject to depart from the general rule adopted in reference to this work, and borrow somewhat freely from the French law, as throwing light upon some points not yet adjudicated upon by the common-law courts. But it should be remembered that, while, both by the civil and common law, if a structure becomes one answering to the character of a party wall, it must be made so by [*467] the *agreement, actual or presumed, of the parties to that effect; in France such agreement is not requisite. On the contrary, if one build the wall of his house upon the verge of his land, and his neighbor has occasion to build a house adjoining it, he may make use of this wall for the purpose, if of suitable dimensions, by reimbursing to the owner a fair ratable proportion of the value thereof, and of the land it occupies, so far as he uses the same. This is so in the cities, and is a rule based upon what is supposed to be a wise public policy. Nor will the age of the wall make any

---

[1] Code Nap., Arts. 655 – 661; Ayl. Pand. 309; Sherred v. Cisco, 4 Sandf. 480, 491; Dunlop, Laws of Penn. ed. 1847, c. 31, p. 39, Act of 1721; Purdon's Dig. 984, 985; Building Acts, 7 & 8 Vict. c. 84, §§ 20 - 27. See Woolr. Party Walls, *passim*; Evans v. Jane, 23 Penn. St. 34; Davids v. Harris, 9 Penn. St. 501. See 3 Kent, Comm. 438, note; *post*, sect. 19; La. Civ. Code, Art. 671; Graihle v. Hown, 1 La. Ann. 140. See as to Iowa, 3 Clark, 391.

[2] Ayl. Pand. 309; D. 8, 2, 36; Ibid. 8, 5, 14; 3 Kent, Comm. 437; 3 Burge, Col. & F. Law, 402; Ersk. Inst. B. 2, tit. 9, § 8.

difference, since prescription does not accrue against this right. The converse of the proposition, however, is not true, since the owner of the wall cannot compel the adjacent owner of land to become a joint owner in the structure.[1]

The proposition is broadly laid down in the Digest, that, where there is a party wall between two adjoining estates, neither party has a right to demolish or rebuild it at his pleasure, because he is not the sole owner or master of the structure.[2]

And whenever a house or estate is sold, whatever service belongs to it belongs to the alienee.[3]

In France, party walls, *murs mitoyens*, take their name from the combination of *moi* and *toi*, and include walls enclosing gardens and the like in cities and villages, as well as those between adjoining houses.[4]

In the erection of such walls, they should rest in equal parts upon the land of each owner, and there are sundry rules laid down in the Code and writers upon the subject for determining what walls come within this category.[5]

Toullier, in his Droit Civil Français, draws a plain *distinction between a party wall, *mur mitoyen*, and [*468] one in common, *mur commun*. In the latter, each party owns in each and every part of the wall, and neither can designate the part that belongs to him. Whereas, in the other, though constructed at a common expense, it stands upon land of which there is a several ownership, and the part that belongs to each may be defined by the line separating their lands. Nevertheless, as both parts are inseparable by the nature of their use, and form a seemingly entire thing, the wall in general terms is said to be common between the two neighbors.[6]

---

[1] 5 Duranton, Cours de Droit, Français, 342 ; 3 Toullier, Droit Civil Français, 134, 136 ; Inst. 2, 3, 4.

[2] D. 8, 2, 8.   [3] D. 8, 4, 12.

[4] Pardessus, Traité des Servitudes, ed. 1829, 217, 219, 221, 237.

[5] Ibid. 222, 238, 239, 242 ; Code Nap., Art. 654.

[6] 3 Toullier, Droit Civil Français, ed. 1824, 126.

Where a wall is party by agreement of the proprietors, their respective liabilities in regard to the same are regulated by the terms of their agreement. But, if no such agreement appears, the law presumes their rights and liabilities to be equal. This co-proprietorship creates, between those to whom it belongs, the same obligation as the law imposes upon all joint owners of property. Each is bound to watch over its safety and preservation with the same diligence as if the wall belonged to himself alone, and, moreover, he should personally avoid doing anything to damage or impair it. And each proprietor has a right of action against the other, to compel him to repair in whatever respect he may have wasted or impaired it.[1]

The Code Napoleon[2] provides, that the repairs and rebuilding of party walls are at the charge of all those who have a right in them, and in proportion to the right of each. This applies to cases where the wall is out of repair by reason of age or accident, which is not caused by the default of one of the proprietors. But it is not necessary that it [*469] *should be in ruins in order that one co-proprietor may compel another to join in its repair or reconstruction. It is enough that such repairs are apparently necessary; and if the parties do not agree upon the point of the repair being necessary, it becomes a question to be submitted to the judgment of experts, in a mode provided by law. Sometimes it is only necessary to reconstruct the wall partially, as where it leans from a perpendicular, or its materials are found to want sufficient cement or solidity in the upper part of it alone. In such cases a total reconstruction ought not to be required, and should only extend so far as the same is necessary. If the defect be in the lower part of the wall, it should be supplied by newly underpinning it.

[1] Pardessus, Traité des Servitudes, 248; 3 Toullier, Droit Civil Français, 128, 147.

[2] Code Nap., Art. 655; Pardessus, Traité des Servitudes, 249, 250, 251; 5 Duranton Cours de Droit Français, 327, 328, 370, 371; 3 Toullier, Droit Civil Français, 145, 147, 148.

In doing these, each proprietor should share equally in the inconveniences arising from the passage of the workman and the placing of their materials while doing the work, as well as in the expenses thereby occasioned. But, so far as it is necessary to remove anything, or place props and supports while executing the work, each party is to bear whatever part of this may particularly concern himself; and if either party has paintings or other ornaments upon his side of the wall which are thereby injured, he alone is to bear the loss, since he has to ascribe to his own imprudence the placing of ornaments upon a wall which the law has made a party one, and subject to be rebuilt.

So if one has a place of public amusement adjoining such wall, to which the public resort, and the same is a source of profit to him, and during the progress of such reconstruction he is deprived of this source of profit, he is without recompense or indemnity. It is one of the inconveniences incident to the nature of the property.

A different rule would be applied if the wall were taken down in order to favor a private enterprise of one of the proprietors. He must not only incur the whole expense of the work and its reconstruction, but must pay to his co-proprietor the damages thereby occasioned to him. If it is not *of sufficient thickness or of suitable material to [*470] serve the purposes for which it was erected, the expense of making it such and supplying the materials is a charge upon both parties. But, if it is made higher or thicker for the accommodation of one only of the proprietors, he must sustain the whole expense of this change.[1]

Either proprietor may raise the wall if he has occasion, though the other has not, provided it be of sufficient width and strength to sustain the addition. But, if it is not, the one desiring to raise it must make it competent and safe for such increase at his own expense, unless the wall at the time

---

[1] Pardessus, Traité des Servitudes, 251, 252 ; 3 Toullier, Droit Civil Français, 144 ; Evans v. Jayne, 23 Penn. St. 36 ; 3 Kent, Comm. 437.

be in such a condition as requires a present reconstruction. In the latter contingency the other proprietor may be held to contribute towards its reconstruction so far as to render it suitable for the purposes for which it was originally erected, if no increase were to be made in its height. If either wishes the wall to be made wider than its original thickness, he must make use of his own land for the purpose. But though thus widened, it still remains an entire party wall.

But unless such entire reconstruction be necessary, neither proprietor can cause it to be made against the consent of the other, even at his own expense, since such an operation always brings with it great inconvenience to the other party, for which he can recover no recompense.[1]

A like rule prevails in respect to building the wall deeper as in raising it higher. Either may do it, if he have occasion, by using like precautions in constructing the underwork of the wall not to injure his neighbor. He must so dig and build the under part of the wall, in respect to its solidity and strength, that the common wall above it shall not be endangered thereby ; nor can he call upon [*471] the other *party for indemnity for the expense of supporting the part which he has thus constructed. The part thus added belongs to him, and is to be repaired by him at his own sole expense.[2]

So far as either proprietor shall raise the wall above its original height, it will be for him to keep it in repair, at his own proper charge, unless the other party shall see fit to use it for the support of a building on his side. In that event it all becomes a party wall, and the latter must pay his share of its *cost*, together with that of the value of the land occupied, if it shall have been also widened, calculated upon certain prescribed principles of computation.

[1] Code Nap., Art. 659; Pardessus, Traité des Servitudes, 262, 263, 264; 5 Duranton, Cours de Droit Français, 368, 369; 3 Toullier, Droit Civil Français, 140, 142.
[2] Pardessus, Traité des Servitudes, 265 ; 3 Toullier, Droit Civil Français, 135.

The law also provides for settling questions between the parties, if the owner of the wall shall undertake to object to the adjacent owner availing himself of the benefit of it. And also for the judgment of experts, as to the mode and extent to which the owners upon one side and the other of party walls may use them in case of disputes between them.[1]

When a party wall between two houses has been rebuilt, all the servitudes belonging to the former one revive and continue in respect to the new wall or new house.[2]

Each proprietor may use the wall for the purposes for which it was erected and designed by the nature of its construction. This, however, is limited in its degree by what shall be for the interest of the other proprietor, so as not to deprive him of his equal rights. It is in a measure regulated by the Code, Art. 662, which prohibits either from making any recess in a party wall. And Pardessus considers this as preventing the construction of a safe, a niche, * a pipe, or a chimney flue in such a wall. [*472] But it does not prohibit making openings into the wall for supporting beams and joists, and the depth to which this may be done is fixed by law. So stones or bars of iron intended for strengthening or supporting the wall may be inserted into it.[3]

Either of the co-proprietors of a party wall may at any time discharge himself from liability to repair or rebuild it, provided he has not any building resting upon or supported by such wall, if he will abandon his right of property in the use of the same, and of the land on which it stands. It is not enough that he abandons the wall, he must abandon the

---

[1] Code Nap., Arts. 660, 662 ; Pardessus, Traité des Servitudes, 266, 267, 268 ; 5 Duranton, Cours de Droit Français, 377, 379 ; 3 Toullier, Droit Civil Français, 140, 142.

[2] 5 Duranton, Cours de Droit Français, 382 ; 3 Toullier, Droit Civil Français, 522.

[3] Pardessus, Traité des Servitudes, 256, 257, 258 ; 5 Duranton, Cours de Droit Français, 367, 379 ; 3 Toullier, Droit Civil Français, 138.

land also.[1] But he will not, by such abandonment, exonerate himself from responsibility on account of acts which he or those in his employ may have previously done to the wall. This is provided for by the Code, Art. 656, which is in these words: " Every joint owner of a party wall may exempt himself from contributing to its reparation and rebuilding by abandoning his right of partyship, provided such party wall does not support any building belonging to him."

On the other hand, the proprietor to whom the abandonment is made shall not be at liberty to suffer the wall to go to ruin in order to enjoy the benefit of the land and the materials of the wall, half of which still belong to the other proprietor.   The consequence is, that, if he abandon the use of the wall as a structure, the former co-proprietor may reclaim his 'land and his share of the materials of the wall.[2]

If one proprietor suffers the other to exercise exclusive control over the wall, as sole owner thereof, for thirty years, it will lose the character of a party wall by prescription.[3]

20. The principle upon which the laws of Pennsylvania, * in respect to party walls in the city of [*473] Philadelphia, are based, is so nearly in accordance with the doctrine of the French law above stated, that it is referred to again for purposes of illustration.   The statute provides for party walls between two estates being set out and regulated as to their thickness by surveyors, and that the foundations of these shall be laid equally upon the lands of the persons between whom such party wall is made ; " and the first builders shall be reimbursed one moiety of the charge of such party wall, or for so much thereof as the next builder shall have occasion to make use of, before such next builder shall any ways use or break into the said wall, the charge or value thereof to be set by the said regulators."

---

[1] Le Page Desgodets, 56, 57.

[2] Pardessus, Traité des Servitudes, 253, 254, 255 ; 5 Duranton, Cours, &c., 328, 341 ; 3 Toullier, Droit, &c., 149, 150, 151.

[3] Merlin, Repertoire de Jurisprudence, tit. *Mitoyennete.*

Provision is also made for having a survey made of any party wall against which one is about to build, to determine as to its sufficiency, with authority on the part of the regulators to direct the removal of any such wall if insufficient, and to regulate the width of the same, and no such wall may be less than nine inches in thickness.

A question arose under this law, in which Evans and Watson, having a party wall between their estate and that of Jayne, who was about to erect a store adjoining it, were notified to remove it by the regulators because of its insufficiency. From this order they appealed. The court say : " There can be no available objection to the principle upon which our law as to party walls is based. The law as to partition fences involves the same principle. It has constituted part of the law of France for ages, and is fully carried out in the Code Napoleon." The court then cite Article 659 : " The principle is no invasion of the absolute right of property, for that absolute involves a relative, in that it implies the right of each adjoiner, as against the other, to insist on a separation by a boundary more substantial than a mathematical line. This imaginary line is common, and so ought the real one to be, and it is only in the character of this that the difficulty lies which requires *legislation. And there is nothing more severe in [*474] submitting the question of the sufficiency of walls in a city to the city surveyor, than there is submitting the sufficiency of fences in the country to fence-viewers." And the appeal was accordingly disallowed.[1] They have in Iowa a law similar to that of Philadelphia, by which one of two adjacent owners is at liberty to place half the wall of his house upon the land of the adjacent owner, and when the latter comes to build upon his lot, he may use this as a party wall for supporting the timbers, &c., of his house, upon paying one half the value of the wall.[2]

---

[1] Purdon, Dig. 634, § 2, 11, 15; Evans v. Jayne, 23 Penn. St. 34; Ingles v. Bringhurst, 1 Dall. 341 ; 2 Bouv. Inst. 178.

[2] Zugenbuhler v. Gillim, 3 Iowa, 392.

SECTION IV.

EASEMENT OF SUPPORT OF SUBJACENT LAND.

1. Two freeholds in case of mines, surface and subjacent.
2. Right of support of upper freehold, one of property.
3. Analogy between support of adjacent and subjacent land.
4. Humphries v. Brogden. How mines must be worked.
5. Harris v. Ryding. What rights reserved with mines.
6. Where cause of action begins for impairing support.
7. Rowbotham v. Wilson. Effect of reserve of mines on support.
8. Support of houses gained by prescription against mines.
9. Rule as to surface support applies to public works.

1. THERE remains to be considered, as coming properly in connection with the doctrine of the support laterally of the soil or buildings of one man by those of another, how far the owner of the surface soil of the earth has a right to insist upon a support from beneath of his soil or buildings, as against excavations by the owner of the minerals below it in extracting the same. Numerous cases have arisen, of late, in the English courts, where such excavations have caused the surface of the earth to subside, and in some cases causing injury or destruction to buildings standing thereon.

These questions have arisen from what is now familiar law, that there may be two freeholds in the same body of earth measured superficially and perpendicularly down towards the centre of the earth, to which, theoretically, the unlimited ownership of the soil extends, viz. a free-
[*475] hold in *the superficial soil, and enough of that lying beneath it to support it, and a freehold in the mines underneath this, with a right of access to work the same, and extract the minerals there found.[1]

2. To this extent, the right of having the soil supported from below is a natural one, or, more properly, an incident to the ownership of the soil.[2] And in some cases the owner

---

[1] Wilkinson v. Proud, 11 Mees. & W. 33; Rowbotham v. Wilson, 8 Ellis & B. 123, 142; Zinc Co. v. Franklinite Co., 13 N. J. 341, 342.

[2] Rowbotham v. Wilson, 8 Ellis & B. 123, 152.

of such soil has a right of easement of support of buildings or other structures creating additional burdens thereon. Some of the cases involving these questions will be found below, and are referred to for purposes of illustration of the rules applicable in such cases.

3. It will be found that much aid may be derived in settling questions of the right of support against excavations for mining purposes from their analogy with the rules already stated in respect to the right of lateral support of soil and buildings.[1]

4. The case of Humphries v. Brogden, decided in 1850, has become a leading one upon this subject. It was for an injury to the plaintiff's soil by the defendants so working their mine beneath it as to cause it to settle and sink down. It was not found that the defendants had worked their mines carelessly, but, on the contrary, had done so carefully, according to the custom of the country. But they had failed to leave sufficient pillars and props to prevent the plaintiff's land from settling.

The Chief Justice, Campbell, refers to the cases above mentioned, relating to the lateral support of the soil of one man by that of another, and says: "*Pari ratione,* 'where there are separate freeholds, from the surface of the land and the minerals belonging to different owners, we are of opinion that the owner of the surface, while unencum-*bered by buildings, and in its natural state, is en- [*476] titled to have it supported by the subjacent mineral strata. Those strata may of course be removed by the owner of them, so that a sufficient support for the surface is left. But if the surface subsides, and is injured by the removal of these strata, although, on the supposition that the surface and the minerals belong to the same owner, the operation may not have been conducted negligently, nor contrary to the custom of the country, the owner of the surface may maintain an action against the owner of the minerals

---

[1] See *ante,* sect. 1.

for the damage sustained by the subsidence." He refers to the case of Harris v. Ryding,[1] and adds : " It seems to have been the unanimous opinion of the court, that there existed the natural easement of support for the upper soil from the soil beneath." It was held that the plaintiff was entitled to recover.

5. The case of Harris v. Ryding was decided in 1839. In that, the grantor of the mines sold the surface to the person under whom the plaintiff claimed, and in his deed reserved the mines with liberty to get them. Lord Abinger, C. B. says, that, if the owner had granted the surface, reserving the mines merely, he would have had no access through the surface, but must have reached them through other adits. And when he reserved the right of access, he did not thereby reserve the right to dig so as to destroy the surface, or to do anything in a manner unusual and improper, so as to prejudice the surface of the land. And as the case found that the defendant did not have sufficient support for the surface, the Chief Baron held that he was liable for the damage thereby occasioned. There were buildings, in this case, standing upon the surface, and one count in the [*477] declaration was for injury to these. But *the case turned wholly upon the point, in which all the court agreed, that, inasmuch as the defendants so worked their mines as not to leave a reasonable support for the surface, they were liable for the damages thereby occasioned.[2]

6. Where there has been a wrongful act of withdrawing the surface support by improper excavations for minerals, the surface owner is not obliged to wait until his land or

---

[1] Humphries v. Brogden, 12 Q. B. 739 ; Harris v. Ryding, 5 Mees. & W. 60. See Smart v. Morton, 5 Ellis & B. 30 ; per *Crowder*, J., Rowbotham v. Wilson, 8 Ellis & B. 154 ; per *Coleridge*, J., Bonomi v. Backhouse, Ellis, B. & E. 622, 639 ; Roberts v. Haines, 6 Ellis & B. 643 ; s. c., 7 Ellis & B. 625. See Dugdale v. Robertson, 3 Kay & John. 699.

[2] See Smart v. Morton, 5 Ellis & B. 30, 46, confirming the doctrine of the above cases. Rowbotham v. Wilson, 6 Ellis &. B 593, 602 ; Zinc Co. v. Franklinite Co. 13 N. J. 342.

buildings shall have actually cracked or subsided. The act is a violation of his right, and he may, in an action therefor, recover full compensation, including the probable damage to the fabric, and the Statute of Limitations begins to run from the time of such act done.[1]

7. In Rowbotham v. Wilson, Campbell, C. J. held, that though, in the absence of an express grant to that effect, the owner of minerals has no right so to work his mines as to withdraw the reasonable support required for the surface, yet the owner of both may so grant the surface as to secure to the owner of the mines a right to excavate the same, though by so doing he do not leave a sufficient support for the surface. Nor would the right of the surface owner, in this respect, be changed by his erecting thereon dwelling-houses which would be injured by such excavation, and that successive owners of the estate would be bound by the grant and its limitations.[2]

So where an enclosure act prohibited working a mine within a certain distance from buildings, the owner of the mine was held liable for injury done to buildings occasioned by working his mine, although he neither exceeded the limits of the act, nor worked his mine without using ordinary care in so doing. Neither excused him for failing to leave a sufficient support for the surface, a right to which is incident to the ownership thereof.[3]

The case came up again before the Exchequer Chamber in 1857. Watson, B. was of opinion " that the agreement or grant by which the owner of the mines was to be at liberty to work them without leaving a reasonable support was in effect a covenant not to sue on the part of the surface owner, and that this would not run with the *land, [*478] that such a right was not the subject-matter of a

---

[1] Nicklin v. Williams, 10 Exch. 259; Bonomi v. Backhouse, Ellis, B. & E. 622, 646; Wightman, J., contra, p. 637; 10 Law M. & R. 182; ante, p. *100.

[2] Rowbotham v. Wilson, 6 Ellis & B. 593.

[3] Haines v. Roberts, 7 E. & Black. 625.

grant, since, to be the subject-matter of a grant, it must be an easement to be imposed on the corporeal property of the grantor." He was therefore of opinion, that the plaintiff ought to recover.

Bramwell, B. was of opinion that the claim here made by the surface owner of a right of support of his premises was not that of an easement, because an easement is something additional to the ordinary rights of property. But he held that this right of support was something that he could convey away to the owner of the mines below, and, if he took his estate with such a right in the mine-owner below, he took it on the terms of its creation, and was bound thereby. He therefore was for confirming the judgment in the King's Bench.

Martin, B. was of opinion that the owner of land may grant the surface, subject to the quality or incident that he shall be at liberty to work the mine underneath, and not be responsible for any subsidence of the surface, and was therefore in favor of affirming the former judgment. Williams, J. was of the same opinion. Crowder, J. was of the same opinion. He admitted that a covenant not to sue would not run with land, but that the owner of land might release an easement or a right incident to an estate, and it would be binding upon those to whom that estate comes, and that here the owner of the surface took it subject to the same limited right of support as the original grantee under whom he held.

Cresswell, J. was of opinion that the judgment should be reversed, regarding the matter as a covenant on the part of the surface owner not to sue for an injury to his own property, and not a release of any easement or other right in the mines, or a grant of any interest in the land of the mine-owner, or a license to cause an injury to the surface, which would be personal to the licensee, and not grantable over. But the judgment of the King's Bench was
[*479] affirmed. *And when the case came before the House of Lords it was again confirmed.[1]

---

[1] Rowbotham v. Wilson, 8 H. of L. Cas. 248.

8. In Bonomi *v.* Backhouse, which was for an alleged injury to plaintiff's house and land by the working of defendant's mines, the house was an ancient one, and the judge, Wightman, remarked, " Where ancient buildings are standing upon the plaintiff's land, the defendant must take care not to use his own land in such manner as to injure them." [1]

And after an enjoyment of the support of the natural soil for a dwelling-house for twenty years, a mine-owner may not so work his mine as to injure the foundations thereof.[2] But if a house, though a modern one, be injured by a subsidence of the soil on which it stands, occasioned by excavations for minerals, he may, nevertheless, recover the damages thereby occasioned, unless the house was the cause of the subsidence.[3]

But if the owner of a house sues for an injury to the same, by weakening the support thereof, by excavating for minerals below it, he must state in his declaration the grounds upon which he is entitled to have his house supported by the land above the mines; and unless these are so stated, he will fail in his action.[4]

9. In Northeastern Railway Co. *v.* Elliot, the court held that the doctrine that the owner of a mine may not work it so as to take away the reasonable natural support of the surface, applies in cases where public works like a railway are constructed over it, and it is immaterial whether such company purchase, or take the land under its act of incorporation. But if such mine happened to be full of water when the road was constructed, whereby the surface was supported, as well as by props and ribs of coal left in the mines, the company could not complain that such water was afterwards pumped out, and the surface support thereby weakened, inasmuch as it was, from its nature, a mere tem-

[1] Bonomi *v.* Backhouse, Ellis, B. & E. 622, 836. See also Rowbotham *v.* Wilson, 8 H. of L. Cas. 348, 365, 367.

[2] Rogers *v.* Taylor, 2 Hurlst. & N. 828 ; Partridge *v.* Scott, 3 Mees. & W. 220.

[3] Strayan *v.* Knowles, 6 H. & Norm. 465 ; Brown *v.* Robins, 4 H. & Norm. 186.

[4] Hilton *v.* Whitehead, 12 Q. B. 734.

porary condition of the property.[1] Where one worked a mine in another's land, the shaft by which he reached it opening in a field in which the owner was accustomed to keep his cattle, the occupant of the mine was bound to keep the outlet of such shaft safely fenced so as to prevent the cattle, rightfully there, from falling into the shaft.[2]

[*480]   *SECTION V.

EASEMENT OF SUPPORT OF PARTS OF THE SAME HOUSE.

1. Separate freeholds may be had in the different parts of a house.
2. One owner may not impair the support of the part of another.
3. How far owners are to contribute towards repairs.
4. Owners in common contribute towards repairs. Doane v. Badger.
5. How far owners of one story contribute to support another.
6. Remedy in equity of the owner of one story against the owner of another.
7. Law of Scotland as to support of different stories.
8. Laws of France on same subject.
9. Laws of France as to houses falling by decay.
10. How one estate may protect itself from a privy on another.

1. WHILE the law is well settled, that there may be separate owners in freehold or inheritance of different parts of the same house, even though one of these be a single chamber therein,[3] the common law seems to be singularly deficient in definite rules in respect to the rights and obligations of the several owners, as to the extent and mode of using the parts of one tenement for the benefit of another, or how far the owner of either part is bound to repair the same, or to contribute to the repairs of other parts.

2. There are definite rules upon this subject in the Scotch and French laws which it is proposed to notice briefly, after considering how far the common law furnishes a guide in determining the rights of the respective parties.

___

[1] Northeastern R. W. Co. v. Elliot, 1 Johns. & H. 145.

[2] Williams v. Groncott, 4 B. & Smith, 149.

[3] Co. Litt. 48 b ; 1 Washb. Real Prop. 4 ; Rhodes v. M'Cormick, 4 Iowa, 375.

It is well settled, in the first place, that where there are different stories to the same house, each belonging to different owners, neither can do anything within his own story which shall impair the safety or enjoyment of that of the other owners. Thus it is said by Lord Campbell: "The books of reports abound with decisions restraining a man's acts upon and with his own property, where the necessary or probable consequence of such acts is to do damage to others. The case of common occurrence is where the upper *story of a house belongs to one man, and the lower [*481] to another. The owner of the upper story, without any express grant or enjoyment for any given time, has a right to the support of the lower story. . . . . If," he adds, "the owner of an entire house conveying away the lower story only, is, without any express reservation, entitled to the support of the lower story for the benefit of the upper story," &c., assuming this postulate as an undoubted rule of law, to which he refers for purposes of illustration.[1]

In the case last cited, Campbell, C. J. says: "If the owner of a house were to convey it to another by deed, reserving a lower story to himself, whatever powers he reserved for the enjoyment of this story, unless the right of support is renounced by the grantee of the superior stories, these powers must be considered as only meant to be exercised subject to this right being respected."

In Harris v. Ryding, which was a case involving the rights of surface owners as against the operations of subjacent mine-owners, Maule, J. says: "That right appears to me to be very analogous to that of a person having a room in a house over another man's room; yet his rights over his exclusive property are not unlimited, but are limited by the duty of so using it as not to do any damage to the property of another person."[2]

---

[1] Humphries v. Brogden, 12 Q. B. 739, 747. See also Smart v. Morton, 5 Ellis & B. 30, 47.

[2] Harris v. Ryding, 5 Mees. & W. 60, 76; Rhodes v. M'Cormick, 4 Iowa, 376.

In the case last cited, Parke, B. says: "It is very like the case of the grant of an upper room in a house with the reservation by the grantor of a lower room, he undertaking to do nothing which will derogate from the right to occupy the upper room; and if he were to remove the support of the upper room, he would be liable in an action of covenant, for a grantor is not entitled to defeat his own act by taking away the underpinnings from the upper room."

[*482]   *3. Neither of the above cases, however, reaches the question, how far the owner of one part is bound to contribute towards the repair or maintenance of any other part of the structure. If the notion of the French law is to be applied, so far as the walls or any other part of the house are necessary for the common benefit of the whole structure, they are to be considered in the nature of *party walls*, and each owner must contribute or aid in their support and repair. And this seems to be sustained by Kent, Ch., in Campbell *v.* Mesier.[1]

4. The same principle was applied in the case of Doane *v.* Badger, where the subject-matter of common property was a pump which was out of repair; and in illustrating the doctrine, the court refer to the case of a house: "If the two co-tenants tacitly agree or permit the house or its appurtenances to go to decay, neither can complain of the other until after a request and refusal to join in making repairs," clearly assuming, that if one joint owner of common property, after notice and demand of the other, cause necessary repairs to be made upon the same, he may have his remedy by action for his reimbursement.[2]

5. The point was incidentally discussed in Loring *v.* Bacon, where the plaintiff, who owned the upper story of a house, the roof of which required repairs, caused the same to be made, and then brought an action of *indebitatus assumpsit* for contribution against the defendant, who owned the lower

---

[1] Campbell *v.* Mesier, 4 Johns. Ch. 334.

[2] Doane *v.* Badger, 12 Mass. 65, 70.

story and cellar of the house. In giving an opinion in the case, the judge, Parsons, refers to a case from Keilwey,[1] where two of the judges were of opinion, that, if a man have a house underneath, and another have a house over it, the owner of the first house may compel the other to preserve the timbers of the house underneath ; and so may the owner of the house above compel the other to repair the timbers of his house below, and this by an action on the *case. But it is said : " Some of the bar were [*483] of opinion that the owner of the house underneath might suffer it to fall ; and yet all agreed that he could not pull it down to destroy the house above." And in Tenant *v.* Goldwin,[2] Lord Holt doubted the law of the above case.

The judge then proceeds : " But there, is unquestionably, a writ at common law, *de domo reparanda,*[3] in which A. is commanded to repair a certain house of his in N., which is in danger of falling, to the nuisance of the freehold of B., and which A. ought, and hath been used, to repair. This writ, Fitzherbert says, lies, when a man who has a house adjoining to the house of his neighbor suffers his house to lie in decay to the annoyance of his neighbor's house. And if the plaintiff recover he shall have his damages, and it shall be awarded that the defendant repair, &c. . . . . And there appears no reasonable cause of distinction in the cases, whether a house adjoin to another on one side or above or underneath it."

He then goes on to show why, if the case in Keilwey is law, the plaintiff in the case under consideration could not recover. And adds : " If the case in Keilwey is not law, then, upon analogy to the writ at common law, the plaintiff cannot compel the defendant to contribute to his expenses in repairing his own house. But, if his house be considered as adjoining to hers (the plaintiff's), she might have sued an

---

[1] Keilwey, 98 b, pl. 4.

[2] Tenant *v.* Goldwin, 6 Mod. 311 ; s. c., 2 Ld. Raym. 1089, 1093.

[3] Fitzh. N. B. 296.

action of the case against him if he had suffered his house to remain in decay to the annoyance of her house. . . . . We do not now decide on the authority due to the case in Keilwey, but, if an action on the case should come before us founded on that report, it will deserve a further and full consideration." [1]

6. The reasoning of the court in the above case of Loring *v.* Bacon, goes to sustain a liability of one part-owner [*484] of a * house to the other for neglecting to keep his own part in repair. But in Cheeseborough *v.* Green,[2] the court of Connecticut insisted that no action at law could be maintained by the owner of a lower story of a house against the owner of the upper one for neglecting to keep the roof of the same in repair, the only remedy being in equity. They also refer to the cases above cited from Keilwey, and Modern Reports, and seem to assume the law to be settled, that, for such neglect to repair the roof by the owner of the upper story, the owner of a lower one might have a complete remedy in equity.

To the above cases may be added one from a later volume of Modern Reports, *quantum valebat*, where it is said: "If a man has an upper room, an action lies against him by one that has an under room, to compel him to repair his roof; and so, where a man has a ground room, they over him may have an action to compel him to keep up and maintain his foundation." [3]

In giving the opinion of the court in a case in New York, the Judge, Rosekrans, uses this language: "The rule seems to be settled in England, that, where a house is divided into different floors or stories, each occupied by different owners, the proprietor of the ground floor is bound, by the nature and condition of his property, without any servitude, not only to bear the weight of the upper story, but to repair his

---

[1] Loring *v.* Bacon, 4 Mass. 575.

[2] Cheeseborough *v.* Green, 10 Conn. 318.

[3] Anonymous, 11 Mod. 7.

own property so that it may be able to bear such weight. The proprietor of the ground story is obliged to uphold it, for the support of the upper story." It however should be stated, that every case which he cites to support his position is one in relation to subjacent support of *land*, which has come to be well-settled law.[1]

7. This subject has been treated of here as a question of servitude at common law, if, for no other reason, because of the analogy there is between the support of one part of a dwelling-house by another, and that of land by what is adjacent or subjacent thereto.

The Scotch and French systems treat of it as embraced under the law of servitudes. The former prescribes minutely what each proprietor of the several stories of a house is required to do in supporting or maintaining the same. " Where a house is divided into different floors or stories, each door (floor?) belonging to a different owner, the proprietor of the ground floor is bound by the nature and condition of his property, without any servitude, not only to bear the weight of the upper story, but to repair his own property, in order that it may be capable of bearing that weight. As the roof * remains a common roof to the whole, [*485] and the area on which the house stands supports the whole, the proprietor of the ground story is obliged to uphold it for the support of the upper, and the owner of the upper must uphold it as a roof or cover to the lower. . . . . Where the property of the highest story is divided into separate garrets among different proprietors, each proprietor must uphold that part of the roof that covers his own garret."[2]

8. In the French law the subject is regulated by the Code,[3] by which : " Where the different stories of a house belong to different owners, if the writings relating to such property do

---

[1] Graves *v.* Berdan, 26 N. Y. 501.

[2] 3 Burge Col. & F. Laws, 404 ; Ersk. Inst., fol. ed., 357. See also Humphries *v.* Brogden, 12 Q. B. 739, 756.

[3] Code Nap., Art. 664. See Pardessus, Traité des Servitudes, 288, 290.

not regulate the custom of repairs and rebuildings, they shall be done as follows. The main walls and the roof are at the charge of all the owners, each one in proportion to the value of the story belonging to him. The proprietor of each story is at the expense of his own flooring. The proprietor of the first story makes the staircase which leads to it; the proprietor of the second story makes, beginning from where the former ended, the staircase leading to his, and so on."

This rule is based upon the above suggestion, that, while each is to do whatever is necessary within his own premises, so much of the structure as is for the common benefit of all the proprietors is made a common charge. And Toullier accordingly says, it is not only the principal walls of the house that become party (*mitoyens*), but also the roof, the stairs, the large beams, &c., and it was necessary to determine the manner of contributing to the several repairs which were common to the proprietors, which led to the adoption of the article of the code above cited.[1]

The proprietor of either story may do what he [*486] sees fit *within his own premises, provided he do nothing to prejudice the proprietors of the other stories, either in respect to the convenience or stability of the same. He may not, for example, place a forge therein, because of the inconvenience it would occasion to the proprietor above him. Nor may he change the flues of the chimneys or make new ones. And so with other changes or new structures which run through the parts of the house belonging to other proprietors.[2]

In several of the departments mentioned by Merlin, substantially the same rule prevails as to the support and repairs of houses as that given above as the Scotch law.[3]

Duranton refers to the position of M. Delvincourt, that,

---

[1] 3 Toullier, Droit Civil Français, 152; 5 Duranton, Cours De Droit Français, 384.

[2] Merlin, Repertoire de Jurisprudence, tit. *Batiment,* § 2.

[3] Ibid.

where there is no agreement, the several proprietors ought to contribute ratably to the repairs and reconstruction of the embankments, the arches and walls of the cellar of houses, and, in a word, of all the parts which are necessary to the stability of the edifice as a whole, or which serve for the convenience of the several tenants, such as wells, cess-pools (*fosses d'aisance*), and common passage-ways. But he differs from him in respect to arches in cellars. Such arches are not essential to sustaining the edifice, at least not generally, for the division walls which serve to support the several stories start from their foundations. The arches of the cellar are the flooring upon which the proprietor of the ground floor treads, and consequently they ought to remain at his charge, even though he may not be the proprietor of the cellar.[1]

If in a house divided as above supposed it shall be necessary to place props or supports, as, for example, while relaying the underpinning of the lower part of the same, in doing which it may require stays or supports for the upper parts thereof, a question has been made at whose *expense these props are to be provided. It might [*487] seem that it should be at the expense of the proprietor of the upper part, that being the part which is needed to be supported. But the custom of cities having imposed it upon the proprietor of the lower part of the house alone to sustain, at his own expense, the walls of the interior part, although they support the upper part of the house, it seems to be a necessary conclusion, that whatever occupies the place of these walls ought to be provided at the expense of the proprietor of the lower part. Consequently, the proprietor of the upper part of the house is not bound to contribute towards such support.[2]

In fixing the proportions of the joint expense of maintain-

---

[1] 5 Duranton, *supra*, 385, 386. See 3 Toullier, Droit Civil Français, 153. 1 Le Page Desgodets, 108 – 118.

[2] Merlin, *supra*, § 2.

ing the walls, &c., of houses, as stated in the above article of the code, among the several proprietors of the respective stories, regard is not had to what may have been incurred by way of embellishment or ornamentation by the proprietor thereof.[1]

If, in case a house be destroyed by fire or demolished on account of its age, one of the proprietors oppose the wishes of the others for rebuilding it, the latter may compel him to elect whether he will abandon his rights or contribute to its reconstruction, which will be apportioned upon each story according to the rules of law above stated. And the writer expresses an opinion, that in such case it ought not to be in the power of any one to change the nature of the ownership of the land into a common heritage, subject to be divided among the proprietors, for the proprietor of the ground floor or lower story ought not to be required to yield any part of the land, and the other proprietors have an interest to have their respective stories entire.[2]

[*488]   *9. The common-law doctrine of compelling a party to repair his house when it is ruinous by a writ *de domo reparanda*, was mentioned in the case of Loring *v.* Bacon,[3] above cited. By the French law, if a house is in such a ruinous condition as to threaten to fall, and the owner neglects to take it down or support it by sufficient props, he may be compelled by the police to do so, and his neighbor may also be authorized to make the demolition, or apply such necessary props at the expense of the delinquent proprietor.

10. Questions have arisen between the owners of adjacent estates, upon one of which an existing privy is in use, as to whether the owner of the privy or the owner of the other estate is to protect the latter from the effect of the same.

---

[1] 5 Duranton, *supra*, 387 ; 3 Toullier, *supra*, 153.

[2] 5 Duranton, *supra*, 388. For the effect upon a demise, of a destruction of the demised premises, see Winton *v.* Cornish, 5 Ohio, 477 ; Stockwell *v.* Hunter, 11 Metc. 448.

[3] Merlin, *supra*, § 3.

The rule, as stated in the case of Tenant *v.* Goldwin, seems to be this : If A has a privy upon his estate, which is separated from the house of B by a wall, and the wall belong to A, he is bound to keep the same in repair, and thus protect the estate of B. So if one own two houses, and there is a privy belonging to one, against which the other house is protected by a wall, and he sell the house and privy together, the purchaser will be bound to keep it in repair, and this duty will run with the estate. But if one erect a house with a privy adjoining a vacant estate, and the owner of the latter would dig a cellar and erect a house near the privy, it will be for him to erect a wall to protect his premises. And the same rule would apply if the owner of such house is also the owner of the vacant lot, and he sell the latter. If the purchaser would occupy it, he must protect himself, by works upon his own land, against the privy already standing upon the adjacent lot.[1]

[1] 2 Ld. Raym. 1089; s. c., 6 Mod. 313, 314; Holt, 500 s. c., Salk. 360, where the language of the court is, "an old privy," when speaking of one's digging a cellar, &c. near an existing privy, which may be regarded a material qualification of language reported in Lord Raymond.

In the French law, the Code prescribes rules regulating the distances at which one proprietor of an estate may construct cesspools and other causes of nuisance in reference to that of an adjacent owner. Thus, Art. 674 provides that, "He who digs a well or cesspool, near a party wall or not, is obliged to leave the distance prescribed by the regulations and usages particular to such things, or to do the work prescribed by the same regulations and usages to avoid nuisance to a neighbor." It is understood that this extends also to privies (*latrines*). There is also a duty imposed upon the owners of these to keep them cleaned out ; and if they shall fail to do so, the nearest neighboring owners may cause the same to be done at the expense of the owner of what causes the nuisance. 2 Fournel, Traité du Voisinage, 190; Code Nap., Art. 674, Barrett's ed.

[*490]   *1. THERE has long been recognized by the English common law, and now by the statute of 2 & 3
Will. 4, c. 71, a right, under certain circumstances, to enjoy,
in favor of one tenement, the light and air which naturally
reaches it in coming laterally from and across the land of an
adjacent proprietor. It is treated of as an easement in favor
of the one, and a servitude upon and over the other, though
it obviously wants many of the incidents of those easements

which are acquired by the adverse enjoyment, in some form, of a benefit in favor of one estate which injuriously affects another.

A question has sometimes been made, whether this right is a positive easement in favor of the estate which enjoys the benefit of the light, and which the adjacent owner may not impair, or a negative servitude imposed upon the adjacent land to which the owner is bound to submit.

2. In the civil law, among the negative services which might be imposed upon lands, one was, that the owner should not darken his neighbor's windows; another was, that he should not hinder his prospect by building or planting trees, and another, that he should not make any windows to overlook his neighbor, and in that way take away the privacy of his house. And it is said, if one has no service of this kind upon him, he may make as many windows as he pleases, but the other party may erect sheds against them, and so make them useless, unless the windows have been there time out of mind.[1]

3. Cresswell, J. seems to regard it rather as a negative servitude upon the land adjacent to the tenement, than a positive easement in favor of the tenement itself. " There are many cases in which the principle has been recognized, that one land-owner cannot, by altering the condition of his land, deprive the owner of the adjoining land of the *privilege of using his own as he might have done [*491] before. Thus he cannot, by building a house near the margin of his land, prevent his neighbor from building on his own land, although it may obstruct windows, unless, indeed, by lapse of time the adjoining land has become subject to a right analogous to what in the Roman law was called a servitude." [2]

4. This right of excluding the owner of vacant land from

---

[1] Ayl. Pand. 310 ; Wood, Inst. Civ. Law, 93 ; Inst. 2, 3, 1 ; D. 8, 2, 15 ; Ersk. Inst. B. 2, tit. 9, § 10.

[2] Smith v. Kenrick, 7 C. B. 515, 565.

building thereon, because a neighboring proprietor had enjoyed his own estate in such way as he saw fit, without in any manner injuriously affecting or interfering with the rights of the first, is admitted by most who have discussed it to be difficult if not impossible to sustain, upon any notion of prescription or grant known to the law. In the first place, such enjoyment is had upon the land of the one who claims it, and the subject-matter of such enjoyment is not anything which is the subject of grant from another, for light and air belong to no man except as they may be enjoyed upon, and in connection with, his own land or tenement. And in the next place, such enjoyment can in no sense be adverse to any one, since he thereby uses simply what is his own, and in no manner affects or interferes with the enjoyment of the same light and air by other persons, in such manner as they please. And the cases are uniform, that such adjacent owner may deprive his neighbor of the light coming laterally over his land, by the erection of a wall, for instance, upon his land within the period of prescription, although he may do it for the mere purpose of darkening his neighbor's windows. So far, therefore, as it prevails, this right, as it results from long enjoyment, may be deemed to exist rather by a positive rule of law than by the application of any of the ordinary principles of prescription, and is derived from a simple occupancy, without its being in any sense adverse in its enjoyment.[1]

[*492]   *And it is said, that, as a rule of law, it never became settled in Westminster Hall until 1786, in Darwin v. Upton, found in 2 Wms. Saund. 175 d, note.[2]

But in Calthorp's reports, published in 1661 (p. 3–8), it

[1] Moore v. Rawson, 3 Barnew. & C. 332, 340; Renshaw v. Bean, 18 Q. B. 112; Cox v. Matthews, 1 Ventr. 239; Chandler v. Thompson, 3 Campb. 80; per Bayley, J., Cross v. Lewis, 2 Barnew. & C. 686; Parker v. Foote, 19 Wend. 309, 317; Mahan v. Brown, 13 Wend. 261; Pickard v. Collins, 23 Barb. 444; Ray v. Lynes, 10 Ala. 63; Cherry v. Stein, 11 Md. 122; Tud. Lead. Cas. 123; 2 Washb. Real Prop. 61.
[2] Parker v. Foote, 19 Wend. 309, 317.

is shown that by the custom of London one might not erect a new house upon a vacant lot so as to obscure the windows of an ancient house, for the ancient house had, by the enjoyment, acquired an easement of light by prescription. If both were new houses no such custom obtained, nor did it, if the windows which are obscured be new ones. So if one built upon an old foundation, but no larger than the foundation itself, he would not be liable, if he built higher than the original building, and thereby obscured ancient windows which opened from the adjoining houses which had not been obscured by the original building. But no one could claim an easement of prospect by prescription.[1]

But the right to build upon an old foundation, so as to obscure ancient windows, is taken away by the Stat. of 2 and 3 Wm. 4, C. 71.[2]

5. There is a view, indeed, by which the so-called prescriptive right of light and air is sometimes sustained, which is more compatible with the general rules of law than by treating it as a thing gained by grant evidenced by adverse enjoyment, and that is as evidence on the part of the owner of the land over which it is claimed, that, for a sufficient consideration, he, or those under whom he claims, had covenanted or agreed not to use his land so as to interrupt the enjoyment of the buildings standing upon the adjacent lot. It is but carrying out what has already been shown to be a familiar rule of law, that, if one grant an estate to which certain apparent and continuous subjects of enjoyment belong, and are used therewith, like that of an aqueduct, lateral support by adjacent soil, and the like, he cannot afterwards derogate from the benefit of his own grant by interfering therewith. Upon the same principle, if one who has a house with windows looking upon his own vacant land sell the same, he may not erect upon his vacant land a structure which shall essentially deprive such house of the

[1] See Anon., Com. Rep. 273.
[2] Truscott v. Merch. Tailor's Co., 11 Exch. 855.

light through its windows. And if the length of enjoyment
is sufficient to raise a presumption that it was done under
some such actual or implied covenant or agreement, the
doctrine may be sustained without violating the ordinary
rules of prescription, as they have generally been understood.[1]

[*493]   *But how this right to light and air over another's
land may be considered as acquired by law is spoken
of by Patteson, J. as " a question of some nicety." [2]

6. Upon whatever ground the claim rests, it has long been
held in England that one may prescribe for the right of light
and air to come to his windows unobstructed across the land
of another, if enjoyed for twenty years, or the period of ordinary prescription.[3]

7. It may be stated, however, in respect to the civil-law
easement or servitude of a right of prospect, that it cannot
be acquired at common law, by any mere length of enjoyment.[4]

But a party may, by the terms of his grant, be estopped

---

[1] Moore v. Rawson, 3 Barnew. & C. 332, 340 ; Palmer v. Fletcher, 1 Lev.
122 ; Aldred's case, 9 Rep. 58 b ; Darwin v. Upton, cited, 3 T. R. 159 ; 2
Wms. Saund. 175 d, note ; Harbridge v. Warwick, 3 Exch. 522. But see Rowbotham v. Wilson, 8 Ellis & B. 143, per *Watson*, B. ; United States v. Appleton,
1 Sumn. 492, 501. See *Crompton*, J., Stokoe v. Singers, 8 Ellis & B. 31, 38. See
White v. Bass, 7 H. & Norm. 722.

[2] Blanchard v. Bridges, 4 Adolph. & E. 176.

[3] Cross v. Lewis, 2 Barnew. & C. 690 ; Aldred's case, 9 Rep. 58 b ; Renshaw
v. Bean, 18 Q. B. 112, 131 ;. Sury v. Pigott, Poph. 166. *Contra*, Bury v. Pope,
Cro. Eliz. 118 ; Lewis v. Price, 2 Wms. Saund. 175 a, note ; 3 Kent, Comm.
448.
Numerous cases have arisen in the English courts upon the acquisition of a
prescriptive right to easements, like light and air, under the provisions of the
statute of 2 & 3 Will. 4, c. 71, and the construction given to it by the courts,
among which is that of Flight v. Thomas, 8 Clark & F. 231, which are purposely
omitted in this work, as being matters of local statute law, except so far as they
may have served to illustrate some doctrine of the common law. See Ward v.
Robins, 15 Mees. & W. 237, 242 ; Wright v. Williams, 1 Mees. & W. 77 ; Plas-
terers' Co. v. Parish Clerks' Co., 6 Eng. L. & Eq. 481. See Cooper v. Hubbuck,
12 C. B. N. s. 456.

[4] Aldred's case, *supra ;* Com. Dig., *Action on the Case for a Nuisance,* C ;
Parker v. Foote, 19 Wend. 309 ; Calthorp's Rep. 5.

from afterwards obstructing the prospect which the grantee of the premises was to enjoy as an incident to his grant.[1]

8. And in order to acquire an easement of light over a parcel of land, by adverse enjoyment, the same must have been had while the servient estate was in the possession of the owner of the inheritance. No length of en-*joyment, as against a tenant, can bind the rights of [*494] a reversioner.[2]

9. In applying the doctrine above stated, that one may not derogate from his own grant, to the case of the enjoyment of lights belonging to dwelling-houses which have been the subjects of the grant, there is a series of cases, beginning with Palmer v. Fletcher, where it has been held by the English courts, that, if one having a house with windows to which the light comes over his adjacent land sell the house, neither he, nor any one claiming under him, can do anything upon the adjacent land to obstruct these.[3]

10. But if the vendor had sold the land, and reserved the house, he would not have thereby reserved the right of enjoyment of the lights, except by express terms of his deed.[4]

Nor would it make any difference in the application of this principle, that the grantor of the house had, previously, let it to his grantee by a lease which limited and restricted him from erecting a house on the leased premises, so as to obscure the lights upon the lessor's premises. The grantor, by his subsequent unqualified grant of the reversion to the lessee, abrogated this limitation and restriction in the lease.[5]

[1] Piggott v. Stratton, Johns. Ch. (Eng.) 341, 356, 357. See Attorney-General v. Doughty, 2 Ves. Sen. 453; Squire v. Campbell, 1 Mylne & C. 459.

[2] Shelf. R. P. Stat. 98; Baker v. Richardson, 4 Barnew. & Ald. 578; Daniel v. North, 11 East, 372.

[3] Palmer v. Fletcher, 1 Lev. 122; Cox v. Matthews, 1 Ventr. 237; Rosewell v. Pryor, 6 Mod. 116; s. c., Holt, 500; Tenant v. Goldwin, 6 Mod. 311; s. c., 2 Ld. Raym. 1089; Compton v. Richards, 1 Price, 27; Swansborough v. Coventry, 9 Bing. 305. Per Bayley, J., Canham v. Fisk, 2 Crompt. & J. 126; s. c., 2 Tyrw. 155; Shelf. R. Stat. 98; Robins v. Barnes, Hob. 131; United States v. Appleton, 1 Sumn. 492, 501; 2 Dane, Abr. 716; Com. Dig., Action on the Case for a Nuisance, A.

[4] Per Kelynge, Palmer v. Fletcher, supra; Tenant v. Goldwin, supra.

[5] White v. Bass, 7 H. & Norm. 722.

But where there were two subsisting tenements adjoining
each other, and the owner leased one of them, the lessee
would not have a right to obstruct the lights in the other
tenement as they existed at the time when the lease was
made, although the same were a recent erection, and there
were no stipulation in regard to the same in the lease.[1]

11. In the case of Swansborough v. Coventry, the building complained of had been erected, upon the site of an old
one which had been torn down, upon land purchased for
building purposes.   But the new building was higher
[*495] than *the old one, and it appeared that both estates
had been derived from the same vendor, and were
both sold at the same time.   The plaintiff's house was an
ancient one, and was conveyed with " all lights, easements,"
&c. ; and it was held that the defendant had no right to
erect a new building higher than the one formerly standing
upon his land, so as to obscure the ancient lights in the
plaintiff's house.[2]

12. In the case of Compton v. Richards the buildings and
lots in relation to which the question of the right of enjoyment of lights arose were parts of a general enterprise for
the erection of a range of buildings at Clifton, called the
Royal York Crescent.   The design having been abandoned,
the several lots and houses, so far as erected, were sold in
lots, with certain conditions stipulated in the sale.   The
plaintiff's lessor and the defendant bought adjoining lots,
and it was alleged that the defendant had raised the walls
of his house higher than were laid down in the plan and elevation of the same, as described and referred to in the conditions of sale.   It appeared that the spaces for the windows
alleged to be obstructed were actually opened in the walls
at the time of the sale.   The Chief Baron says : " This purchase must have been taken to have been subject to certain
conditions at the time of sale, and as these unfinished houses

1 Riviere v. Bower, Ry. & M. 24.
2 Swansborough v. Coventry, 9 Bing. 305.

were at that time so far built as that the openings which were intended to be supplied with windows were sufficiently visible as they then stood, we must recognize an implied condition that nothing would afterwards be done by which those windows might be obstructed.   And the purchasers must have taken subject to what then appeared." Wood, B. says: " When this house was granted to the plaintiff's lessor, he became grantee of everything necessary to its enjoyment, as much as if it had been said, at the time, that no one should obstruct the light which it then enjoyed." [1]

*13. This doctrine, that the rights of parties to [*496] the use of light, where claiming under the same grantor, and that these are governed by the state of the premises at the time of acquiring title to the same, is illustrated in the case of Coutts v. Gorham, where the owner of two estates, each of them ancient houses, leased one of them for twenty-one years to A. B., who assigned it to the defendant.   Defendant afterwards, and during the term, took a new lease from the owner for twenty-one years.   But between the making of the first and second leases the owner altered the windows in the other house, and let the same to the plaintiff, a few months before the defendant took his second lease.   The defendant obstructed these new windows in the tenement of the plaintiff, for which he brought an action.   It was held, that, by taking a new lease from the plaintiff's lessor, the defendant surrendered his first one, and that he took the premises as they then were, and had no right to obstruct the windows as they then existed in the plaintiff's tenement.[2]

14. The more ancient case of Robins v. Barnes is in accordance with the doctrine above stated.   In that case there was an ancient house, and an adjacent owner having erected a new one which obscured the windows of the former house, the owner thereof purchased the new house, and

[1] Compton v. Richards, 1 Price, 27, 36, 38.
[2] Coutts v. Gorham, 1 Mood. & M. 396.

then sold the ancient one. It was held, that by such unity of title and possession the easement of light and air once belonging to the ancient house was extinguished, and the purchaser therefore took the premises in the condition in which they were when the same were conveyed, without any such right of easement.[1]

15. Where an easement of light is acquired by enjoyment and user, the extent of such right is measured by the purposes and mode of such enjoyment. Thus where [*497] one had *acquired a right of light for a malt-house, and complained of the obstruction thereof, it was held that the question to be determined was, whether the defendant had obstructed the light so as not to have enough left for the use and enjoyment of a malt-house. For any excess beyond such obstruction he would not be liable, although the malt-house had been changed to a dwelling-house, and the enjoyment of more light was requisite to its convenient occupation.[2]

16. And in respect to the extent or degree to which the obstruction of one's light must be carried, in order to enable the party entitled to it to maintain an action for the injury, it is said by the courts that " there must be a substantial privation of light, sufficient to render the occupancy of the house uncomfortable, and to prevent the owner from carrying on his accustomed business on the premises as beneficially as he had formerly done." And it is for the jury to discriminate between practical inconvenience and a real injury to the enjoyment of the premises.[3]

17. The subject has thus far been treated of chiefly from the point of view of the English common law, with a brief allusion to English local statutes. This has been done in order to present, in something like a connected order, the rules which prevail in the American States upon the subject

---

[1] Robins v. Barnes, Hob. 131.

[2] Martin v. Goble, 1 Campb. 320.

[3] Back v. Stacey, 2 Carr. & P. 465 ; Parker v. Smith, 5 Carr. & P. 438 ; Pringle v. Wernham, 7 Carr. & P. 377 ; Wells v. Ody, 7 Carr. & P. 410.

of acquiring rights to light and air by mere length of enjoyment. These will generally be found to be at variance with
the English law. And even as to the effect to be given to
grants, in respect to the enjoyment of light and air, arising
from the condition and circumstances of the estates to which
they relate, the decisions will be found to be far from uniform, and some of them not very satisfactory.

The reasons generally assigned for adopting a different
rule in this country, as to prescriptive rights to light and
air, from that which prevails in England is, that the
latter *is not suited to the condition of a country [*498]
which is growing and changing so rapidly in all its
relations of property, as well as its value and modes of enjoyment. And in this is witnessed another illustration of
the influence of those silent agencies which are constantly at
work in a free community, in adapting and giving form and
consistency to the rules of its common law, to meet the wants
and condition of the body politic. And it seems proper, in
this light, to trace briefly the course of decisions in the several States, whereby the law has become settled, and to point
out some respects wherein the same differs in the different
States.

It will be found, it is believed, that in New York, Massachusetts, South Carolina, Maine, Maryland, Pennsylvania,
Alabama,[1] and Connecticut the doctrine of gaining a prescriptive right to light and air, by mere length of enjoyment,
has been discarded; while the English rule in this respect is
retained in Illinois, New Jersey, and Louisiana.

In the case of Mahan v. Brown,[2] the Chief Justice, and in
Banks v. American Tract Society,[3] the Chancellor of New
York, examine and discuss the point without settling it.
But in Parker v. Foote,[4] after a most elaborate examination

---

[1] Ward v. Neal, 37 Alab. 501 ; post, p. *505.
[2] Mahan v. Brown, 13 Wend. 261, 263.
[3] Banks v. Am. Tract Society, 4 Sandf. Ch. 438.
[4] Parker v. Foote, 19 Wend. 309.

of the subject, and also in Myers *v.* Gemmel,[1] the rule seems to be finally adopted and settled as above stated.

18. In Parker *v.* Foote the court, in showing the want of analogy between ordinary easements of ways, watercourses, and the like, where the enjoyment by which they are gained worked an injury to those against whom they are claimed, say: " But in the case of windows overlooking the land of another, the injury, if any, is merely ideal or imaginary. The light and air which they admit are not the subjects of property beyond the moment of actual occupancy, [*499] and for *overlooking one's privacy no action can be maintained. The party has no remedy but to build on the adjoining land opposite the offensive window. . . . . . In the case of lights, there is no adverse user, nor indeed any use whatever of another's property, and no foundation is laid for indulging any presumption against the rightful owner. . . . . There is, I think, no principle upon which the modern English doctrine on the subject of lights can be supported. It is an anomaly in the law. It may do well enough in England, but it cannot be applied in the growing cities and villages of this country without working the most mischievous consequences. It has never, I think, been deemed a part of our law, nor do I find that it has been adopted in any of the States." [2]

19. In Myers *v.* Gemmel the reasoning of the court in Parker *v.* Foote is approved, and it was further held, that, if one having a dwelling-house opening upon a vacant city lot lease the dwelling-house, he is not thereby prevented from erecting a house upon the vacant lot, although it occupy the whole space and darken the windows opening upon it in the house so leased. It was not held to be in derogation of his own grant, since the law attaches no right of enjoyment of light as an incident to the occupation of an estate, unless it exists in the form of a dedication to groups or collections of

---

[1] Myers *v.* Gemmel, 10 Barb. 537.

[2] See Radcliff *v.* Mayor, &c., 4 Comst. 195, 200.

houses partaking of the character of a public easement. Thus the court put the case of buildings built around a court, with an open space for light and air, with a common entrance to the same, and open for all the tenants of these houses, and express an opinion that it would be held that the owner who appropriated the space dedicated it for the benefit of all the tenants.[1]

In Banks v. American Tract Society, where the plaintiff was induced by the adjacent owner to remove a part of his building, so as to enjoy light for the same from an open *space between that and the building of the [*500] defendant, and the latter then began to erect a wall within this open space, which would darken the windows in the plaintiff's house, the Court of Chancery granted an injunction to restrain such erection.[2]

20. In Massachusetts it has not been till recently that the full determination of the question of prescriptive right to light was reached. In Story v. Odin, where the action was for an obstruction to the plaintiff's lights, the case turned upon the effect of a sale by one of a house adjoining an open space of land belonging to him, and over and across which it derived its light and air, the court say : " This grant being without any exception or reservation of a right to build on the adjacent ground, or to stop the lights in the building which they sold, it is clear the grantors themselves could not afterwards lawfully stop those lights, and thus defeat or impair their own grant. As they could not do this themselves, so neither could they convey a right to do it to a stranger," [3] and they refer to Palmer v. Fletcher and Roswell v. Pryor [4] with approbation.

In Atkins v. Chilson, where the point was made by the counsel, and referred to by the court, it was left wholly un-

[1] See also Palmer v. Wetmore, 2 Sandf. 316.

[2] Banks v. Am. Tract Society, 4 Sandf. Ch. 438, 470.

[3] Story v. Odin, 12 Mass. 157. See also Grant v. Chase, 17 Mass. 443 ; Thurston v. Hancock, 12 Mass. 221.

[4] Roswell v. Pryor, ante, pl. 9.

settled, as the case turned upon another question than the prescriptive right to enjoy light by one tenement over and across an adjacent one, though the court say, that up to that time (1844) " the tendency of our decisions has been the other way " from those of New York and Connecticut.[1]

In the Fifty Associates v. Tudor, the court, in reference to the question whether the owner of a city tenement having windows opening upon the land of another, and enjoying the light therefrom for twenty years, acquires [*501] *thereby an absolute right to the continued enjoyment of the same, say : " Upon the question, we think there has been no direct judicial decision in this Commonwealth. The general rule of the common law seems to have been in favor of the affirmative of the question." This was in 1856. But the court held, in that case, that the wall under consideration was not near enough to the window said to be obstructed, within the rule laid down in Back v. Stacey, above cited,[2] to constitute " a substantial privation of light," so that the main question remained still unsettled.[3]

In Collier v. Pierce the question referred only to how far one may acquire an easement of light from being the grantee of a tenement which, while in the possession of the grantor, enjoyed the benefit of light over the same grantor's other land. In that case, the parcels owned by the plaintiff and defendant respectively, were offered for sale at auction, in lots designated by metes and bounds, and were sold on the same day. The plaintiff's lot was bid off first, and his deed was prior in time. But no reference to light or air was expressed in the deeds. The court say, the sale was of the nature of a partition of the estate rather than of a grant by one proprietor of a part of his estate, retaining to himself another part. And inasmuch as the case did not find that the enjoyment of the light through the window in question

---

[1] Atkins v. Chilson, 7 Metc. 398, 403.

[2] Back v. Stacey, 2 Carr. & P. 465.

[3] Fifty Associates v. Tudor, 6 Gray, 255.

was necessary to the convenient enjoyment of the plaintiff's estate, the court held that the easement did not pass by construction. And they liken it, in principle, to the case of Johnson v. Jordan.[1]

But in Carrig v. Dee (in 1860) the court say that they " are of opinion that the plaintiff acquired no right to the use of air and light coming laterally to his windows over the vacant lot of the defendant, though continued for twenty *years before the statute (1852, c. 144) took [*502] effect. And that the window on hinges, swinging outwards over the defendant's land, did not constitute such adverse possessory use of the adjoining land as to make any difference in principle." [2]

The law may, therefore, be considered as now settled in Massachusetts, both as a common-law rule and as a statutory provision, adversely to any prescriptive claim to light and air as an easement. And the tendency of the cases seems to be, that no such right would pass by the mere grant of a dwelling-house having windows looking out upon the grantor's other land, unless such enjoyment of light should be so far necessary to the enjoyment of the house, that if the grantor were to build upon such vacant land he would virtually deprive the owner of the means of enjoying what he had sold him.

21. In Maine the question arose, and was decided in 1847. The court, in a full analysis of the cases more directly bearing upon the point, deny that the common law originally contained the principle upon which the modern English decisions rest. And it is now settled, that both the statute of that State and the common law there are alike adverse to the acquisition of an easement of light in favor of a tenement, by its having enjoyed it over and across another's land for more than twenty years.[3]

---

[1] Collier v. Pierce, 7 Gray, 18 ; Johnson v. Jordan, 2 Metc. 234.

[2] Carrig v. Dee, 14 Gray, 583.   See also Rogers v. Sawin, 10 Gray, 376 ; Paine v. Boston, 4 Allen, 169.

[3] Pierre v. Fernald, 26 Me. 436.

22. The statement of the law of Connecticut upon this point, as being adverse to a prescriptive right to light and air, is based upon the reasoning of the court in Ingraham v. Hutchinson, although it was not the point directly raised in the case. And the Statute of the State sustains that doctrine.[1]

23. In Maryland the question arose in the case of Cherry v. Stein. The court expressly adopt the reasoning [*503] in Parker *v. Foote, above cited, and deny that the English law, as to prescriptive right to light and air, prevails in Maryland. And as to the point that, if one owning a house whose windows open upon a vacant piece of land belonging to him sell the house without reservation, he would not be at liberty to build upon the vacant lot so as to obstruct the light of those windows, the court, without either affirming or disaffirming the proposition, say : " That principle is only applicable where the vendor of the house having the lights was, at the time of sale, not only owner thereof, but likewise owner of the adjacent vacant lot." And add : "Now it might be conceded that the doctrine of the cases referred to is the law of Maryland, and still it would not sustain the appellant's claim to have his lights protected by injunction." [2]

24. In one of the reported cases of the courts of South Carolina,[3] the doctrine of the English law as to prescriptive rights of light and air is assumed to be the law of that State. But in a subsequent and more fully considered case[4] the doctrine was discarded, and denied to be the law there.

In the case last cited the subject is examined at considerable length, and its analogies considered. And among them

[1] Ingraham v. Hutchinson, 2 Conn. 584 ; Stat. of Conn. Comp. 1854, tit. 29, c. 1, § 18, p. 636.

[2] Cherry v. Stein, 11 Md. 1, 24, overruling the doctrine in Wright v. Freeman, 5 Harr. & J. 477.

[3] M'Cready v. Thomson, Dudley, 131.

[4] Napier v. Bulwinkle, 5 Rich. 311.

the court remark: " The same distinctions would prevent the acquisition of an easement in the shade of a tree which stands on his neighbor's land near his boundary, or of an easement to have continued the protection against winds which a neighbor's forest, or a hill on his land, had long afforded to another's orchard." [1]

25. The subject has been repeatedly brought before the courts of Pennsylvania. But it will be necessary to refer to only two or three of these cases. In Hay v. Sterrett (1834) * Rogers, J. says: " The doctrine of the [*504] English books in respect to ancient lights is not very well understood in this country. . . . . I am not aware that any case has been ruled in this State in which the principle has been recognized. It should be introduced with caution." [2]

In Haverstick v. Sipe (1859), Lawrie, C. J. says: " It has never been considered in this State that a contract for the privilege of light and air over another man's ground could be implied from the fact that such a privilege has been long enjoyed." [3]

In Maynard v. Esher,[4] while the court assume the rule to be, that if a man sells a house with windows looking out upon his other vacant land, he would not be at liberty to build upon his other land so as to obstruct these, they limit the doctrine to cases where the grantor, at the time of sale, owns both estates. And they adopt the doctrine stated by the court in the case of Collier v. Pierce, above cited,[5] that where the two estates are conveyed at the same time to different purchasers, no easement in favor of one or servitude upon the other in respect to light and air passes with the estates. In that case, lots Nos. 6 and 7 were sold at the same auction. No. 6 was a vacant lot, adjoining No. 7, a

---

[1] Napier v. Bulwinkle, 5 Rich. 324.
[2] Hay v. Sterrett, 2 Watts, 331.
[3] Haverstick v. Sipe, 33 Penn. St. 368, 371.
[4] Maynard v. Esher, 17 Penn. St. 222, 226.
[5] Collier v. Pierce, 7 Gray. 18.

dwelling-house. No. 6 was bid off first, and sold " free of
encumbrances." The other lot was bid off within five minutes of the first, and the memorandum of the sale signed
immediately by the parties. The court held, that if the
sales were to be taken as simultaneous, neither lot would
be servient to the other. And if priority of sale affected the
question, it was in favor of the purchaser of No. 6.

26. So far, therefore, as weight of authority both English
and American goes, it would seem that, if one sell a house,
the light *necessary* for the reasonable enjoyment
[*505] whereof is *derived from and across adjoining land,
then belonging to the same owner, the easement of
light and air over such vacant lot would pass as incident to
the dwelling-house, *because necessary to the enjoyment thereof;* but that the law would not carry the doctrine to the se-
curing of such easement as a mere convenience to the granted
premises.[1]

27. The cases where the English doctrine of prescriptive
rights to light and air is sustained are Gerber *v.* Grabel in
Illinois,[2] Robeson *v.* Pittenger in New Jersey,[3] Durel *v.*
Boisblanc in Louisiana;[4] and to these may be added the
case of Ray *v.* Lynes in Alabama,[5] although now overruled.[6]

In Robeson *v.* Pittenger considerable stress is laid upon
the fact that the house was built by the owner of both
estates, that the windows had long enjoyed the light over
the vacant land, and that the house was first granted by the
original owner of the two estates.

In Ray *v.* Lynes the court, to an application for an injunction to placing a shop which partially obscured the light of
recent windows, say : " The foundation of this right is the

---

[1] See also Biddle *v.* Ash, 2 Ashm. 211, 222 ; Durel *v.* Boisblanc, 1 La. Ann.
407 ; Lampman *v.* Milkes, 21 N. Y. 505 ; Story *v.* Odin, 12 Mass. 157.

[2] Gerber *v.* Grabel, 16 Ill. 217.

[3] Robeson *v.* Pittenger, 1 Green, Ch. 57, 64.

[4] Durel *v.* Boisblanc, 1 La. Ann. 407.

[5] Ray *v.* Lynes, 10 Ala. 63.

[6] Ward *v.* Neal, 35 Ala. 602 ; s. c., 37 Ala. 501 ; *ante*, p. *498.

privation of an ancient privilege, so long enjoyed as to become a right. Such is not the fact here."

28. In United States v. Appleton, Story, J. recognizes the doctrine as in force, that if one owns a store or dwell-*ing-house whose doors or windows open upon his [*506] own land, and he sells the building, " there can be no doubt that the grant carries with it the right to the enjoyment of the light of those windows, and that the grantor cannot by building on his adjacent land entitle himself to obstruct the light or close up the windows. . . . . It is strictly a question what passes by the grant. . . . . Their grant carried by necessary implication a right to the door and window, and the passage as it had been, and as it then was, used. . . . . It is observable that in this case reliance is placed on the language of the grant, ' with all ways,' &c. But this is wholly unnecessary, for whatever are properly incidents and appurtenances of the grant will pass without the word ' appurtenances,' by mere operation of law." [1]

29. An instance was referred to, in another connection, in the case of Hills v. Miller, of an easement of light and prospect being gained by construction of the terms of a grant.[2] In that case plaintiff bought the land which Miller had purchased of one B. A lot of land in front of it was by agreement of B. to be always kept open, and he gave Miller a bond to that effect, of which Miller informed the plaintiff when he sold him the house-lot in question. It was held that this created an easement of light and prospect over this vacant lot, which run with all and every part of the land purchased of B., and it was not in Miller's power to release or affect the plaintiff's right to enjoy this easement.

30. Among the rights which are necessary to the enjoyment of tenements, and which it had been held may be ac-

---

[1] United States v. Appleton, 1 Sumn. 492, 502. See the general subject treated of, 3 Kent, Comm. 448. See Parker v. Nightingale, 6 Allen, 341, & Cases cited. See also ante, p. *63, pl. 44.

[2] Hills v. Miller, 3 Paige, 254, 257 ; Whitney v. Union Railway Co., 11 Gray, 359 ; 2 Washb. Real Prop. 33. See ante, pp. 90 – 97.

quired by long enjoyment in the nature of easements, is that
of the owner of a windmill to the use of the wind and air
over adjacent lands, and for an obstruction of this
[*507] *by the erection of walls or buildings upon the adjacent land an action will lie.[1]

  * 31. On the other hand the right freely to enjoy pure air
is an incident to property in houses designed for dwelling
or occupation by man. But a right to carry on a noisome
trade may be acquired by as long enjoyment as twenty
years, as against the proprietor of an estate thereby injuriously affected. And if one erect his house within the influence
of a tanyard upon the atmosphere, for instance, he cannot
complain that its occupation is thereby rendered unpleasant.[2]

  Questions have arisen as to what would be such a tainting
or corrupting the air by one man as to give another a right
of action therefor, on the ground of its creating a private
nuisance. In one case it was held that the erection of a
brewery upon adjacent land, and burning sea-coal therein,
was not a nuisance, but erecting and using a privy upon the
same was. The declaration averred that *horribiles vapores
et insalubres* arose from these. Doddridge, J. said, among
other things, " If a man is so tender-nosed that he cannot
endure sea-coal, he ought to let his messuage." [3]

  But in a recent case, the Vice-Chancellor enjoined a
neighboring owner of land from burning brick thereon
near a dwelling-house which had stood for many years,

---

  [1] Goodman v. Gore, 2 Rolle, Abr. 704. See Winch. 3. But this doctrine
is questioned, and overruled, by the late case of Webb v. Bird, 10 C. B. N. S.
269. See also 1 Am. Law Reg. N. S. 637 ; s. c., 13 C. B. N. s. 841.

  It is stated by Fournel that windmills were not subjects embraced within the
Roman law of servitudes. They were first known in France and England in
the eleventh century, having been brought thither by the Crusaders on their
return from the East. 2 Fournel, Traité du Voisinage, 222.

  [2] Bliss v. Hall, 5 Scott, 500 ; Dana v. Valentine, 5 Metc. 8, 14 ; Elliotson v.
Fretham, 2 Bing. N. C. 134 ; Commonwealth v. Upton, 6 Gray, 473 ; 3 Kent,
Comm. 448 ; Rex v. Cross, 2 Carr. & P. 483 ; Flight v. Thomas, 10 Adolph.
& E. 590 ; Rowbotham v. Wilson, 8 Ellis & B. 123, 143 ; Jones v. Powell,
Palm. 538.

  [3] Jones v. Powell, Palm. 536.

because * the smoke and vapor thereby occasioned [*508]
would be " materially interfering with the ordinary
comfort, physically, of human existence," and " not merely
according to elegant or dainty modes and habits of living." [1]

In the above case from Palmer, Doddridge, J. remarked,
that, if the brew-house was a noisome trade, still if it was an
ancient one, and the other party came to dwell near it, he
must be content with it as he found it.[2]

And although one may acquire a right to the enjoyment
of light and air in connection with an estate, it is always
subject to the reasonable enjoyment by others of their own
property. One man's fire, for instance, may make the air
of his neighbor less sweet and pure, but the latter cannot,
for that cause, complain. Nor could he, if his neighbor, by
planting a tree upon his own land, were somewhat to obscure his light, or obstruct his air and prospect. But one
would be liable for carrying on a manufacture so near another as to render the air thereby sensibly impure.[3]

It is not easy to draw the line between what trade or
business may be carried on upon one's premises which cause
inconvenience to another, and what may not be thus prosecuted. Thus in one case, the court held that it was not
actionable to burn brick upon one's own land, though the
smoke was offensive to a neighboring dwelling-house, if the
place was a proper one and convenient for the business.
" The common-law right," says Willis, J., " which every proprietor of a dwelling-house has to have the air uncontami-
nated and unpolluted, is subject to this qualification, that
such interference be in respect of a matter essential to the
business of life, and be conducted in a reasonable and proper
manner, and in a reasonable and proper place." [4] The case
of Hole v. Barlow was afterwards referred to with approba-

---

[1] Walter v. Selfe, 4 De Gex & S. 315, 322.

[2] Jones v. Powell, Palm. 538.

[3] Embrey v. Owen, 6 Exch. 353; Wood v. Waud, 3 Exch. 748, 781 ; 2
Washb. Real Prop. 64.

[4] Hole v. Barlow, 4 C. B. N. S. 334.

tion by the Barons of the Exchequer, in giving an opinion in Stockport Waterworks *v.* Potter, but it seems that the fact that the kiln complained of in that case was used for a temporary purpose, might have had some influence upon the minds of the court in holding that its use was not actionable. In the case last mentioned, the defendant had calico printing works upon a stream, into which he threw materials used in his dye works, which contained arsenic, and thereby poisoned the stream. This trade was a proper one in itself, and he carried it on in the accustomed manner, but there was no evidence as to its being a reasonable one or in a reasonable and proper place. But it was held, that he had no right so to carry it on as to poison those living below upon the stream, and had occasion to use the water. The case was decided upon the general policy of the trade being noisome and dangerous to the public health, and did not involve any question of prescriptive right to carry it on.[1]

32. One may also gain a negative easement, which was originally created by grant, such as that the adjacent owners should not carry on any offensive trade or trades of particular kinds, although the same may not be unlawful as being a public nuisance. Thus where an owner of several lots adjoining each other inserted a covenant in the deed of each of the purchasers of these lots, that the occupant should not carry on any offensive trade thereon, it was held that any one of these purchasers could have an injunction against any other owner of either of these lots who should undertake to carry on such kind of business thereon.[2] And the court, in another case, after referring to the above class of cases, add: " When, therefore, it appears, by [*509] * the fair interpretation of the words of the grant, that it was the intent of the parties to create or reserve a right, in the nature of a servitude or easement in the property granted, for the benefit of other land owned by the

1 Stockport Water Works *v.* Potter, 7 H. & Norm. 160.
2 Barrow *v.* Richard, 8 Paige, 351.

grantor, and originally forming, with the land conveyed, one parcel, such right shall be deemed appurtenant to the land of the grantor, and binding on that conveyed to the grantee, and the right and burden thus created will respectively pass to, and be binding on, all subsequent grantees of the respective parcels of land." [1]

SECTION VII.

MISCELLANEOUS EASEMENTS AND SERVITUDES.

1. Easement to pile logs, &c. for the use of a mill.
2. Easement of placing boxes, &c. in using a store.
3. Custom of turning teams on land in ploughing.
4. Easement of drying clothes in another's yard.
5. Prescriptive right to dockage and wharf.
6. Easement of carrying away iron ore, &c.
7. Easement of taking sea-weed on a beach.
8. Right to throw rubbish in a stream.
9. Reservation of grass and herbage, a servitude.
10. Easement of a right of common.
11. How far common of cutting timber, &c. is apportionable.
12. Possession of the two estates suspends easement of common.
13. Easement of a town to dig stone on another's land.
14. Easement of a town to use parish buildings.
15. Right to lay gas-pipe an easement in a gas company.
16. Servitude of maintaining fences to land.
17. Pew rights and burial rights, how far easements.

1. Among the easements which have been recognized by the courts of common law, as known to and governed by its rules, is that of piling logs and lumber for the accommodation of a saw-mill, on land to be used as a yard for such mill.[2]

*2. So is that of placing boxes or bales of mer- [*510] chandise, for the purpose of drawing them into a store by a windlass over a way. And the same is true of

---

[1] Whitney v. Union Railway Co., 11 Gray, 359 ; 2 Washb. Real Prop. 33. See also Hills v. Miller, 3 Paige, 254, 257 ; *ante*, p. *63, pl. 44.

[2] Gurney v. Ford, 2 Allen, 576 ; Pollard v. Barnes, 2 Cush. 191.

a right to swing shutters of a store, and the like, over a way.[1]

3. So adjoining owners of unenclosed lands may acquire, by custom, a right to turn their teams, in ploughing, upon each other's land, the same being a reasonable and useful custom.[2]

4. So one may have an easement to hang clothes to dry in another's yard, or use a neighboring wall to support a clothes-line for that purpose.[3]

5. So one may acquire a prescriptive right of dockage upon another's land, or of bringing vessels up to a wharf and laying them along the side of the same.[4]

One may gain a right to maintain a wharf below low-water mark by prescription against the Commonwealth, but the owner could not thereby acquire any exclusive rights beyond the limits of the wharf itself.[5]

6. So one may have an easement to dig and carry away the iron ore in a certain parcel of land. Such a right is an incorporeal hereditament, and can only be erected by grant or reservation in a deed.[6] The distinction and limitation as to this right, as adopted by the courts of Iowa, seem to be this. If one by parol license grant a mine to another, who goes on and works it, and expends money in structures, &c., for carrying it on, and in excavations, and be expelled without notice and compensation for such expenditures, he may recover possession of the mine by a writ of ejectment. If the grant be of a privilege to dig ore, it is regarded as an incorporeal hereditament, and ejectment would not lie.[7] But if there be an open mine upon premises in possession of a ten-

---

[1] Richardson v. Pond, 15 Gray. See also United States v. Appleton, 1 Sumn. 492; O'Linda v. Lothrop, 21 Pick. 292, 297.

[2] Jones v. Percival, 5 Pick. 485; Pain v. Patrick, 3 Mod. 289, 294.

[3] Drewell v. Towler, 3 Barnew. & Ad. 735.

[4] Sargent v. Ballard, 9 Pick. 251.

[5] Gray v. Bartlett, 20. Pick. 186.

[6] Arnold v. Stevens, 24 Pick. 109.

[7] Beatty v. Gregory, 17 Iowa, 116; Bush v. Sullivan, 3 Green (Iowa) 344.

ant, he would have a right to work it, whether he be tenant for life, years, or a single year.[1]

7. One may have a right to take sea-weed upon a particular beach, provided he can claim it as appurtenant to a part of an estate once embracing the beach. If such is granted as appurtenant to an estate, it cannot, however, be separated from the land to which it is appurtenant so as to become a right in gross, under which one may gather such weed for purposes of sale. Such conveyance of the right to a stranger would either be a void grant, or extinguish the right. But no change in the beach itself, so long as one remains, can affect the right to the sea-weed accumulating upon it which one has acquired as an easement. On the other hand, it is not requisite that the owner of the land to which the right is appurtenant should exercise it solely in reference to *expenditure or use upon that particular land. He [*511] may when it is gathered, use it upon that or other land, or may sell it to others.[2]

Ordinarily the sea-weed which is thrown upon the flats, islands, or mainland bordering upon the sea belongs to the owner of the land.[3] But the right to take it may be acquired by prescription, or otherwise, as an incorporeal hereditament.[4] But whether it can be gained in gross, irrespective of the ownership of any estate to which it is appurtenant, does not seem to be well settled. In one case[5] the court say such a right may be personal, and a man may claim it by long continued enjoyment by himself and his ancestors or grantors, while, in the case of Phillips v. Rhodes (sup.), the court express doubt if it can be acquired as a personal one, independent of a que estate. And the case of Weekly v. Wildman is referred to, where Treby, C. J. says of a right of common : " Although a right of common sans

---

[1] Freer v. Stotenbur, 36 Barb. 641.

[2] Phillips v. Rhodes, 7 Metc. 322.

[3] Emans v. Turnbull, 2 John. 313 ; Hill v. Lord, 48 Maine, 96 ; Phillips v. Rhodes, 7 Met. 323.

[4] Hill v. Lord, sup.   [5] Hill v. Lord, sup.

nombre may be granted at this day, yet such grantee cannot grant it over.[1] But the case of Goodrich *v.* Burbank[2] may perhaps be thought to favor the idea of an independent property in such an easement as that of taking sea-weed.

8. So one may acquire a right by prescription to throw the washings of sand and rubble made in working a tin-mine into a stream running through another's land, though he thereby cause the water to overflow the other's land.[3]

9. A reservation in a grant of land of the " grass, herbage, feeding, and pasturage," gives the grantor, and all persons representing him, a right to enter with their cattle and depasture the land as a servitude or easement created by the acceptance of the deed containing such reservation.[4] But it seems that one may not prescribe for the exclusive use of the herbage upon another's land as appurtenant to his own land.[5]

10. A right of common in another's land is also treated as an easement.[6]

But so far as this doctrine is applicable to this country, it is not believed to be necessary to do anything more than briefly notice the general rules in respect to the more familiar kinds of common.

In New York, lands may, by statute, be suffered to lie common by any one who chooses not to fence them, but it does not create a common-law right of common in the same in favor of third persons.[7]

In Illinois there are lands granted as commons to towns, hamlets, and villages, and by law always to remain common to the inhabitants of such town or village. Lands, accordingly, granted by the French government and confirmed by

---

[1] Weekly *v.* Wildman, 1 Ld. Raym. 407.

[2] *Ante,* p. *11, pl. 12 *a.*

[3] Carlyon *v.* Lovering, 1 Hurlst. & N. 784.

[4] Rose *v.* Bunn, 21 N. Y. 275.

[5] Donnell *v.* Clark, 19 Me. 174, 182.

[6] Per *Watson,* B., Rowbotham *v.* Wilson, 8 Ellis & B. 143; Thomas *v.* Marshfield, 10 Pick. 364; Livingston *v.* Ten Broeck, 16 Johns. 14, 25.

[7] Perkins *v.* Perkins, 44 Barb. 134.

the U. States to the inhabitants of the village of C, were held to be for the use and enjoyment of such only as were inhabitants of that village, and could not be conveyed to others.   By village was to be understood a small assemblage of houses occupied by artisans and the like.[1]

But it was held in Missouri, that commons belonging to towns in that State, might be lost to the public by an adverse possession in an individual inhabitant sufficiently protracted.[2]

In Thomas v. Marshfield the question arose upon a claim for compensation for taking certain land for public use. The court say : " There seems to be no doubt that a right of common of pasture is such a title in the land as may sustain a claim for compensation under the statute.   A commoner is not the absolute owner of the soil, but he has a special and limited interest in it. . . . . He (the plaintiff in that case) relies on two titles : first, a title by prescription to a right of common as appurtenant to his farm ; second, a title by grant," &c.

*A common, it is said, imports a privilege to take   [*512] a profit in common with many.   The common known in this country, it is believed, would come under the class of what is appurtenant, and has its origin in grant.   And of course the extent of the right, the character and number of animals to be fed, and the like, must be regulated by the terms of the grant or the right acquired by prescription. The commoner has no interest in the soil where he takes his common.   And if he purchases the land in which he has common, it will operate as an extinguishment of the right as being any longer appurtenant to the other estate.[3]

11.   A question arose in Livingston v. Ten Broeck, whether a common of " cutting and hewing timber for building " could be apportioned by alienation of a part of the land to which it is appurtenant ; and it was held that it could be.

---

[1] Hebert v. Lavalle, 27 Ill. 448.

[2] Funkhouser v. Langkopf, 26 Mo. 453.

[3] Com. Dig., *Common*, A, C, H, L.

But in that case Livingston granted a certain farm to Wessels, with a privilege of grazing his cattle, and of cutting and hewing of timber for building or firewood on the manor, and the defendant held title under Wessels. The owner of the granted premises, to which the common belonged, conveyed a part of them to the owner of the manor, out of which the common is claimed, so that there was a unity of title to a part of the two estates in him, and the question was if such conveyance did not extinguish the right altogether, on the ground that the party having this right could not, by releasing a part of the land, throw an increased burden upon the remaining part of the land. The court held that it operated to extinguish the right altogether. " There would be an extinguishment of the right of common in part, by the unity of title in one and the same person to part of the land entitled to common, and a part of the land out of which common is to be taken, and then the principle applies, that if common appurtenant be *extinct* in part, it is entirely gone." The question turned, it will be [*513] *perceived, upon the distinction between conveying a part of the right of common by conveying a part of the estate to which it belonged, and extinguishing it altogether.[1]

12. And upon the same principle, if the one having a right of common appurtenant take a lease of a part of the estate out of which he has the right of common, all his common shall be suspended during the term.[2]

But where a right of common has been extinguished by unity of possession, it may be revived, if a grant be made of the estate which had previously enjoyed it, " with all common therewith used or enjoyed." But it is in the nature of a new grant.[3]

---

[1] Livingston v. Ten Broeck, 16 Johns. 14, 27 ; Tirringham's case, 4 Rep. 36 ; Rotherham v. Green, Cro. Eliz. 593 ; Com. Dig., *Common*, L ; Co. Litt. 122 a ; Wild's case, 8 Rep. 79.

[2] Wild's case, *supra ;* Com. Dig., *Common*, M.

[3] Com. Dig., *Common*, O ; Bradshaw v. Eyre, Cro. Eliz. 570.

13. A right of easement may be acquired by the inhabitants of a town to dig stones from a parcel of land for the use of such persons as belong to the town, as was the case in Worcester v. Green,[1] and Green v. Putnam,[2] where the proprietors of a township voted " that one hundred acres be left common for the use of the town for building-stones." It was held not to pass the fee, but merely the right to take the stones for building purposes, that interest being in the town as a corporation, in trust for the individual inhabitants.

There may, therefore, be a trust in an easement in lands in the same manner as in the freehold of the land itself.

14. So a town may, by adverse user, acquire a right of easement in a parish meeting-house, to hold public meetings therein. But if such meetings were held by permission of the parish, it would lay no foundation for such a claim.[3]

15. A right granted by charter to a gas company to lay *gas-pipes in the streets of a city is an ease-   [*514] ment, and not a mere license.[4]

16. There are rights in respect to fences which the owners of lands may acquire or be subject to by prescription, whereby one may become liable to support and maintain a division fence between the two parcels of land, or a particular part thereof. And this is regarded as an easement in favor of the one estate, and a servitude upon the other.[5]

But while there would probably be little diversity in applying the doctrine of prescription as to fences when once established, it is not clear that all courts would agree as to what amounted to such a prescription. Thus it seems, from the cases stated in Viner, that prescription arises in cases

[1] Worcester v. Green, 2 Pick. 425.
[2] Green v. Putman, 8 Cush. 21.
[3] Medford v. Pratt, 4 Pick. 222.
[4] Providence Gas Co. v. Thurber, 2 R. I. 15.
[5] Star v. Rookesby, Salk. 335 ; Boyle v. Tamlyn, 6 Barnew. & C. 329; Rust v. Low, 6 Mass. 90 ; Dyer, 295 b, pl. 19 ; Heath v. Ricker, 2 Me. 72 ; Sury v. Pigot, Poph. 166 ; 2 Dane, Abr. 658, 660 ; Binney v. Hull, 5 Pick. 503, 505 ; Thayer v. Arnold, 4 Metc. 589.

where one of two adjoining owners, and those under whom he claims, " have used to make it (the fence) time out of mind," or where the fence between two closes has time out of mind been repaired by the tenant of one of them.[1]

In Rust *v.* Low, *sup.*, the court recognize the doctrine of prescription in respect to maintaining fences, and speak of ancient assignments of fence viewers, and also ancient agreements made by the parties which may have once existed and are now lost by lapse of time, as among the grounds upon which such prescription may rest.   And in Binney *v.* Hull, *sup.*, the court rely upon the fact as establishing prescription, that the party and his ancestors had maintained the fence in question for fifty-six years, at the commencement of which period it was an old fence, carrying back the obligation beyond the time of memory.   In Adams *v.* Van Alstyne, the court hold that there may be a valid prescription in such cases.   " Nor do I doubt," says the Judge, " that when such a prescription is established, it fastens itself upon the land charged with the burden and in favor of the tenements benefited by it.   It is the usual case of a servitude in lands, the law concerning which has been adopted by the common law from the civil law, and every part of the premises charged with the burden called the servient tenement, is as much bound as the whole of the original premises were, and every part of the dominant tenement is entitled to claim the benefit of the charge against the premises bound."   But under the facts of that case, the prescription was not established.   The facts were, that from time immemorial there had been a fence between the farms of L. and H., the western half had been supported by H. and his predecessors, and the eastern half by L. and his predecessors.   Upon the death of H., his farm was divided between his two heirs, the west half going to one and the east to the other.   The plaintiff claimed under L., and the defendant under one of those heirs, and the question was if the successors of L. and H. were bound,

[1] Viner Ab. Fences E. p. 164, 166 ; 2 Dane. Abr. 660.

by prescription, to maintain the parts of the fence which their predecessors had done. But the court held that, as each of the original proprietors was bound to maintain half of the division fence, their acts in so doing were to be regarded as having been done by mutual arrangement and not under any adverse claim, nor any acquiescence by either in any encroachment by the other, and when new owners came into possession of one of the farms, a new arrangement or division became necessary, since there was no ground of prescription of grant or covenant that the particular half of the fence should be perpetually supported by either of the adjacent owners.[1]

A similar doctrine was maintained by the court of Connecticut, as to the effect to be given to a long-continued custom or usage of two adjacent proprietors as to keeping a division fence between their lands in repair. If done by mutual agreement, it does not run with the land like a covenant to bind third parties who neither knew nor concurred in the same. It does not sustain a prescription.[2]

But if a grantor, in terms, when granting land by deed, covenant for himself, his heirs and assigns, to fence the premises, it would be a covenant which runs with the estate, and binds successive owners.[3]

Where one is bound to build and maintain a fence between his own and an adjoining lot of land, he may place one half of it, if of reasonable dimensions, upon his neighbor's land.[4]

At common law, whenever there was a prescription to fence, it was enforced by a writ of *curia claudenda*, sued out by him in whose favor it existed, against him who was charged with the support of such fence, in which he could recover damages for his failure to make or maintain the same. But when bound by prescription to fence his close,

<hr />

[1] Adams v. Van Alstyne, 25 N. Y. 232, 237.
[2] Wright v. Wright, 21 Con. 242.
[3] Easter v. L. M. R. R., 14 Ohio St. 48.
[4] Newell v. Hill, 2 Metc. 180.

the owner was not required to do this against any cattle but those which were rightfully in the adjoining close.[1]

And in this connection the case of Rose v. Bunn may be referred to, where it was held that, if one grant another land, reserving the right of pasturage upon the land, and afterwards the grantee cultivates any part of it for the growth of a crop of grain, it is incumbent upon the one who sows the grain to protect his crop by fences against the cattle of the one who owns the right of pasturage.[2]

[*515]   *17. Rights of burial in churchyards, and pew rights in churches, although acquired by deed of a particular lot, or pew, are only easements in land belonging to the religious society which owns the church and churchyard. It is an easement in, and not a title to, a freehold, and is to be understood as granted and taken subject, with compensation of course, to such changes as the altered circumstances of the congregation or the neighborhood may render necessary.

In all these cases supposed, the general property in the house and land is in some society or body politic, and the doctrine as to burial rights does not apply to cases where the grave is in a separate independent cemetery.[3]

And yet the interest of a pew-holder is of such a character that he may have trespass *qu. cl.* against any one who shall enter the same against the consent of the owner, on any of those occasions for which pews are designed to be used. But this may probably be referred to the character of the property in them which has been given by the statutes of the State in which the question arose.[4]

---

[1] Rust v. Low, *supra* ; 2 Dane, Abr. 658, 660.

[2] Rose v. Bunn, 21 N. Y. 279.

The subject of fences is also regulated by statute in England, and in the several States of this country ; but for obvious reasons these, as well as the cases arising under them, have been purposely omitted in this work.

[3] Richards v. Dutch Church, 32 Barb. 42 ; Gay v. Baker, 17 Mass. 435 ; Daniel v. Wood, 1 Pick. 102 ; Bryan v. Whistler, 8 Barnew. & C. 288 ; Downey v. Dee, Cro. Jac. 605.

[4] Jackson v. Rounseville, 5 Metc. 127.

OF LOSS OR EXTINGUISHMENT OF EASEMENTS, ETC.

SECTION I.

EFFECT OF THE UNITY OF THE TWO ESTATES.

1. As easements may be acquired by actual or constructive grant in various forms, as has been shown, so they may be surrendered, lost, or extinguished by actual or constructive release. Among these would be a release in terms by deed by the owner of the dominant to the owner of the servient estate. It is hardly necessary to illustrate this proposition by decided cases. But there are often such relations in the

ownership of the two estates as will have the same
[*517] effect as *a direct release, which may require a word
of explanation. Such would be the effect of a union
of ownership of the two estates in one person. So while
there are various acts of ownership which serve as evidence
of title to an easement, after long repetition, there are acts
and omissions on the part of the owner of the dominant
estate which are deemed to be evidence of the servitude
upon the servient estate having been released or surrendered
to the owner thereof.[1]

2. To give something like a classification of the modes by
which easements may be lost or extinguished by acts of the
owners of the two estates, the effect of the unity of these in
one person will first be considered.

As no one can be said to use one part of his own estate
adversely to another part, the proposition is universally true,
that if the owner of one of the estates, whether dominant or
servient, becomes the owner of the other, the servitude which
one owes to the other is merged in such ownership, and
thereby extinguished.

This mode of losing or extinguishing an easement is
known to the French law under the name of *Confusion*,
which they borrowed from the language of the civil law.[2]

3. But the proposition thus far assumes that both estates
become united in title and possession in one man, whereby
each has alike all the incidents of a common ownership.
And this might and would be true to a limited extent, if the
possession only of the two estates were united in the same
person. So long as such possession should continue united,
the easement in favor of the one and the servitude upon the
other would be suspended, inasmuch as the occupant has a
paramount right to enjoy them in such manner as he pleases.
But when such possession terminates, as, for instance, by the
expiration of a term of years, or of a life for which the ten-

1 Pardessus, Traité des Servitudes, 411.
2 Ibid. ; 3 Burge, Col. & F. Laws, 445 ; D. 8. 6, 1.

ant may have held the estates, the incidents of easement and *servitude belonging to them at once re-   [*518]
vive. The unity of title and possession of the two
estates, therefore, which operates an extinguishment of an
easement in the one upon or over the other, can only have
that effect where the same proprietor has a permanent estate
in both tenements not liable to be defeated by the perform-
ance of a condition, or the determination of a determinable
fee by the happening of some event beyond his control, and
where the estates cannot be again disjoined by operation of
law.[1]

4. But where there is a union of an absolute title to and
possession of the dominant and servient estates in the same
person, it operates to extinguish any such easement absolutely and forever, for the single reason that no man can
have an easement in his own land.[2]

5. In the case above cited of Ritger v. Parker, J. G. conveyed one of the parcels to M. G. in mortgage, in 1836,
who took possession under the same to foreclose it, in
1841, and in 1842 conveyed it to Parker. The other parcel
was conveyed to J. G. in 1839, who mortgaged it to M. G.
in 1839, and possession to foreclose was taken at the same
time with that under the other mortgage in 1841. The
same was foreclosed by M. G. in 1844, who conveyed the
estate to the plaintiff. It will be perceived that J. G. held
an equity of redemption in both parcels, from 1839 to 1844,
and that M. G. held mortgages upon both parcels, from

---

[1] Ritger v. Parker, 8 Cush. 145; Canham v. Fisk, 2 Crompt. & J. 126;
Thomas v. Thomas, 2 Crompt. M. & R. 34, and reporter's note; Tyler v. Hammond, 11 Pick. 193, 220; James v. Plant, 4 Adolph. & E. 749; Hazard v. Robinson, 3 Mason, 272; Keiffer v. Imhoff, 26 Penn. St. 438, 443; Woolr. Ways,
74; Pardessus, Traité des Servitudes, 442; Manning v. Smith, 6 Conn. 289,
291; Pearce v. M'Clenaghan, 5 Rich. 178.

[2] Hancock v. Wentworth, 5 Metc. 446; Gayetty v. Bethune, 14 Mass. 53, 55;
Grant v. Chase, 17 Mass. 443; Canham v. Fisk, 2 Crompt. & J. 126; Robins
v. Barnes, Hob. 131; Hazard v. Robinson, 3 Mason, 272; Sury v. Pigot, Poph.
166; Packer v. Welstead, 2 Sid. 39; Keiffer v. Imhoff, 26 Penn. St. 438, 442;
Lalaure, Traité des Servitudes Réelles, 63; Atwater v. Bodfish, 11 Gray, 152.

1839 to 1842, when she assigned one of them to the defendant Parker. And it was contended that here was
[*519] *such a unity of title and possession, as to extingush
an easement of way that had existed in favor of one
parcel over the other. But the court held otherwise. So
long as M. G. held them, they were both defeasible estates,
and defeasible upon different conditions. One might have
been redeemed and the other foreclosed, and redemption or
foreclosure of either would have effected an entire separation
of the two, each retaining its own incidents. And when
actually foreclosed, one estate belonged to one man and the
other to another.

When a mortgagor or the assignee redeems, he regains the
estate just as it existed when he made the mortgage. The
operation of the mortgage is defeated by force of the condition, and he takes the estate with all the incidents and benefits, and subject to the servitudes to which it was subject
when the mortgage was made. And no lease, change, or
encumbrance made by the mortgagee can be set up against
the claims of the mortgagor. The estate is restored unchanged.

So if the mortgage is foreclosed, the estate which was conditional and defeasible in its creation becomes absolute, and
the incidents, privileges, and covenants attached to it, unchanged by anything which the mortgagor or any other
person may have done in the mean time, remain attached to
it as if the original conveyance had been absolute. M. G.
then never had, at any one time, an unconditional, indefeasible interest in the then two estates. She held mortgages on
both at the same time, after having entered on both for condition broken, but before foreclosure. This was not the
unity required to constitute a merger. Before foreclosure,
she conveyed one of the estates to the defendant. It is clear
that, at the time of the foreclosure, the estates were held by
different owners in fee.[1]

---

[1] See Ballard v. Ballardvale Co., 5 Gray, 471; Curtis v. Francis, 9 Cush.
427, 457; Pardessus, Traité des Servitudes, 445.

*6. So if the title to one of the estates fail in the [*520]
hands of the joint owner of the two, the easement of
the one in the other revives upon the failure of such title.[1]

7. In Hinchliffe *v.* Kinnoul, which has already been noticed in another connection, the ancestor of Earl G. made a
lease in 1728 of open and unoccupied land, which expired
in 1824.   Upon this parcel many houses had been built by
various sub-lessees, and, by the terms of the lease, Earl G.
would then have had the entire lands, houses, &c., and if,
in the mean time, any easements had been acquired in favor
of one of these parcels upon or over another, the same, upon
such union of title and possession, would have been, at the
time of such union, extinguished.

The plaintiff held one of these messuages, and the defendant the adjoining one, and over this the plaintiff claimed
easements of passage of a *coal-shute* and of a watercourse.

The titles of these two messuages were as follows.   Mrs.
Forrester held the plaintiff's by a lease which was to have
expired in 1822.   In 1799 she let the same to Mrs. Hinchliffe for a term ending in 1820, with the appurtenances
thereto belonging.   Of course the immediate reversion of
Mrs. Hinchliffe's term was in Mrs. Forrester, the remote one
in Earl G.

The other messuage came to Hampden by a lease in 1793,
to expire in 1824, subject, as above stated, to Earl G.'s reversion, to whom all the leases would fall in, in 1824.

In this state of the ownership, Earl G., in 1819, let the
plaintiff's messuage to him for fifty-seven years, to hold from
and after 1824, the plaintiff having been in possession of the
premises under an under-lessee of the original lessee for
some years before 1819.   And in 1822 Earl G. made a lease
of the defendant's messuage to Hampden for sixty-one years,
to commence in 1824, both said leases, of course, being of
reversionary interests on the part of Earl G.

*One question made in the case was, whether [*521]

---

[1] Tyler *v.* Hammond, 11 Pick. 193, 290 ; Pardessus, *supra,* 446.

the unity of title to both messuages in 1824 in Earl G., under whom both parties claimed, did not extinguish the right of easement which one messuage had acquired in the other ? But the court held that there was no such unity of possession as would operate upon the right of easement. Earl G. had only a reversionary right to the premises when he made the leases in question. And it was further held, that the easements mentioned, being necessary to the enjoyment of the plaintiff's messuage, and something which Earl G. could then grant, his lease of the messuage passed these easements as incident or appurtenant to the messuage of the plaintiff, because they were in existence and necessary to its enjoyment. And, as to the supposed unity, the court say : "In consequence of Earl G.'s reversionary lease of the messuage in 1819, the right to the possession of both properties was severed, and there could be no unity of possession of both the messuage and the passage in him ; and if so, it is obvious that he could not, by his subsequent grant, derogate from a former valid grant which he had already made." The facts of the case are numerous and complicated, and it is not easy to present the points settled in it in a simple and intelligible form. But it will serve the present purpose to state that in substance the court held, that, as by long enjoyment the tenant of one messuage had acquired an easement in the adjoining messuage while in the occupancy of another tenant, which easement was necessary to the enjoyment of the first messuage, the mere ownership of both messuages *in reversion* by one and the same man did not create a unity of title and possession to the two in him, so but that when he leased them separately, to take effect at a future time, when his reversion fell in, he leased them in the state they were then in, with the easement appurtenant to one and the servitude upon the other.[1]

[*522]   *8. Although there is no limitation to the proposition that, because no man can have an easement

---

[1] Hinchliffe *v.* Kinnoul, 5 Bing. N. C. 1.

for one parcel of his land in or over another, whenever two estates which have been dominant and servient in other persons' hands become his by a joint absolute ownership and possession, all easements and servitudes previously existing between them are thereby extinguished ; it will hereafter appear that the effect of again separating the ownership of these estates in reviving these easements varies essentially according to the nature and character of these easements. In some cases the law, in order to give effect to a grant, restores the former easement to the estate granted, while in others this can only be done by express terms in the deed.

And whether an easement shall revive or not upon the alienation of one of the estates, may depend upon the act of the owner while holding both. If, for instance, the former easement consisted of an artificial trench of water, or of pipes for an aqueduct, by which water is conducted over or from one parcel to the other for the benefit of the latter, and the owner while in possession of both were to fill up the trench or cut off the aqueduct, and were then to convey what had been the dominant estate, by itself, it would, in order to revive the former easement, be necessary to grant it in express terms.[1]

And the same principle would apply if, while two estates were in the ownership of the same person, and they consisted of mills upon the same stream, the owner were to so arrange the operation of the two as to increase the power of the one by flowing back water upon the other, whereby the power of the latter was partially destroyed, and he should then sell the upper estate by itself, the original easement which it had enjoyed would not be restored thereby beyond its then existing condition.[2]

[1] Nicholas v. Chamberlain, Cro. Jac. 121 ; Sury v. Pigot, Poph. 166 ; ante, 313.
[2] Hazard v. Robinson, 3 Mason, 272.

*SECTION II.

EFFECT OF CONVEYING ONE OF TWO ESTATES IN REVIVING
FORMER EASEMENTS.

1. THOUGH the law intended to be considered under this head must obviously have many analogies with the general subject discussed in a former part of this work, the effect of dividing heritages in creating easements or servitudes in one part in favor of the other, there seemed to be a propriety in treating, as a separate topic, the case of two estates in respect to which easements may have once existed, but which have subsequently been extinguished by a union of the two in the same ownership and possession. The question in such case arises as to the effect of a conveyance of one of these estates by such owner, retaining the other himself, or of a separate conveyance of each estate to two different owners. Do the easements or servitudes in such a case revive thereby, as they had existed in relation to each estate before they had been extinguished by unity of title and possession, or by what line and limit is the rule determined in regard to such easements reviving upon the conveyance of one or both of the estates?

2. So far as the easements come within what are called *natural*, like the flow of water in a natural stream from one to the other, or that class which grows out of locality, like the discharge of rain or surface water from a higher upon a

lower field, they would revive in respect to each other,
the *moment the ownership and possession of the   [*524]
two parcels had passed to different hands, because,
as has been heretofore shown, they exist *jure naturæ*, and
are incidents of property in the several parcels.[1]

3. The same would be true of such easements as are
necessary to the enjoyment of the one parcel or the other,
as in the case of ways; though by making the new grant in
such a case, it is rather the creation of a new right of way
by implication, than the reviving of a former one, and ways
thus created are appurtenant only so long as the necessity
continues.[2]

4. This subject, it will be perceived, assumes two things:
first, that the owner has done nothing while holding both
estates to destroy the existence of what was once an easement, like cutting off the pipe of an aqueduct, for instance;
and, second, that, in making his conveyance of the one or
the other estate, he makes no specific reference in his deed
to what is claimed as the easement.   From this arises the
question which is now under consideration, What must be
the situation of the two estates, and what the character of
the easement, to have a simple conveyance of the one estate
or the other revive and pass it, or reserve it as an appurtenant to the dominant estate?

5. In the first place, in order to pass with an estate, the
easement, in the case supposed, must be an *apparent* one.
Among the cases illustrative of this, that of Seibert v. Levan
may be referred to, where the owner of two closes, upon one
of which he had a mill, and upon the other the dam and
pond of water by which it was operated, conveyed the latter,
it was held that his grantee took it subject to the servitude
of the dam and right of flowing a pond for the use of the
dam.[3]

---

[1] Dunklee v. Wilton R. R. Co., 4 Foster, 489, 497; Sury v. Pigot, Poph. 166.
[2] Grant v. Chase, 17 Mass. 443, 448; Jenk. Cent. case, 37; Pomfret v. Ricroft, 1 Wms. Saund. 323, n. 6.
[3] Seibert v. Levan, 8 Penn. St. 383, 387.

[*525]   *Another would be the case of two mills upon the same stream belonging to the same owner, so arranged that the water of the pond of the lower mill flows back upon the wheel of the upper one, if he were to convey the upper mill, describing the premises as so much land with a mill and privilege, the purchaser would take it subject to the effect of the lower works upon its operation.[1]

The same principle has been extended to cases of lights, air, gutters, eaves' drip, and the overhanging of the eaves of a house upon the adjoining estate, where one or both these adjoining estates are conveyed by a common owner, though in the matter of light and air it should be remembered, the common law does not prevail in several of the United States.[2]

So the doctrine has been applied to the case of one parcel of land drained through another by an artificial ditch, cut from the former through the latter, to a canal into which the water was discharged. These two parcels had come to the same owner by different purchasers, and of course, while held by him, this right of drain became extinct as an easement. But upon his conveying the first-mentioned parcel separately, it was held that the right of drain as an easement revived, and passed as appurtenant to the parcel thus conveyed.[3]

A like principle is also said to apply to the case of a way, not strictly of necessity, but which has been used from one parcel across another to a church or a mill and the like, both parcels having been owned by the same person. If he should convey the intermediate close, there would be at once an easement of way from the other close to the church [*526]   *or mill, across it, without any words of grant conveying the same in terms.[4]

---

[1] Cary v. Daniels, 8 Metc. 466, 480, 482; Hazard v. Robinson, 3 Mason, 172.

[2] Robins v. Barnes, Hob. 131; ante, p. 44; Nicholas v. Chamberlain, Cro. Jac. 121; ante, p. 392.

[3] Ferguson v. Witsell, 5 Rich. 280. See Shaw v. Ethridge, 3 Jones (Law), 300; Dodd v. Burchell, 1 H. & Colt. 121.

[4] Seibert v. Levan, 8 Penn. St. 383; Sury v. Pigot, per Doddridge, J., Poph.

6. It may be stated here that the same rule applies as to reviving an easement by conveying one of the estates, whether the parcel conveyed be the dominant or servient estate. If it be the dominant, the easement over the other passes as appurtenant to it. If it be the servient, the easement is created in favor of the dominant remaining in the grantor's hands, by way of reservation. The authorities upon this point are Seibert *v.* Levan, above cited, and Dunklee *v.* Wilton Railroad,[1] controverting if not overruling the doctrine of Burr *v.* Mills [2] and Preble *v.* Reed,[3] which make a distinction between an easement being raised by a grant of the dominant estate, and the case of a reservation by the grantor of the dominant estate.

The language of Jewett, C. J. in French *v.* Carhart, may probably be taken as a sound principle, that a " reservation should be construed in the same way as a grant by the owner of the soil of a like privilege. . . . . The sound and reasonable rule is, that whatever is necessary to the fair enjoyment of the thing granted or excepted, is incidentally granted or excepted." [4]

7. It should be remembered, moreover, that in giving effect to a deed of one of two parcels, in respect to a way, for instance, nothing results from a general clause granting therewith all ways *appurtenant* to the granted premises. When the two estates came to be united in the same ownership and possession, the way was thereby extinguished, and of course ceased to be any longer appurtenant, and could only be made so again by express grant. It was accordingly *held, in James *v.* Plant, that, " where [*527] there is a unity of seizin of the land and of the way

---

166, 172; Jordan *v.* Atwood, Owen, 121 ; 1 Rolle, Abr. 936 ; Woolr. Ways, 71 ; Phillips *v.* Phillips, 48 Penn. 178, 186 ; 1 Jenk. Cent. case, 37 ; Leonard *v.* Leonard, 2 Allen, 543.

[1] Dunklee *v.* Wilton R. R. Co., 4 Foster, 489.

[2] Burr *v.* Mills, 21 Wend. 292.

[3] Preble *v.* Reed, 17 Me. 169. See also *ante*, p. 36 ; Guy *v.* Browne, F. Moore, 644 ; Nicholas *v.* Chamberlain, Cro. Jac. 121.

[4] French *v.* Carhart, 1 Comst. 103, 104.

over the land, in one and the same person, the right of way
is either extinguished or suspended, according to the duration of the respective estates in the land and the way ; and
after such extinguishment, or during such suspension of the
right, the way cannot pass as an appurtenant, under the
ordinary legal sense of that word." [1]

The same doctrine was applied to the case of an aqueduct
from one parcel to another, the ownership of both estates
having come to the same person, who subsequently conveyed
the estate for whose benefit the aqueduct was designed,
" with all appurtenances." [2]

The last-mentioned case is cited to sustain the effect to be
given to the word *appurtenances* in a grant in passing artificial easements with one of two estates, where the easement
had been extinguished by unity of seizin ; for it is not clear,
to say the least, that the right of aqueduct in that case would
not have passed as being an apparent continuous ease or benefit which one part of the joint estate had in the other at the
time of the conveyance, upon the principle of other cases
already cited.

The doctrine that an easement, extinguished by unity of
seizin of the estates, may not pass with one of them as an
appurtenant, was held to apply in the case of a right of
common.[3]

And the rule, as laid down in the Digest upon the subject,
is explicit in its terms : " Si quis ædes quæ suis ædibus ser-
virent, cum emisset, traditas sibi accepit, confusa sublataque
servitus est : et si rursus vendere vult, nominatim impo-
nenda servitus est ; alioquin liberæ veniunt." [4]

[*528]   *8. But while the cases last cited serve to show
that certain rights, though formerly united with an
estate, will not, after becoming extinguished by unity of the

---

[1] James v. Plant, 4 Adolph. & E. 749.

[2] Manning v. Smith, 6 Conn. 289.

[3] Clements v. Lambert, 1 Taunt. 208.

[4] D. 8, 2, 30. See 3 Burge, Col. & F. Law, 446 ; Pardessus, Traité des
Servitudes, 446.

two estates, revive or pass under the term *appurtenant*, they
do not bear upon the main point intended to be illustrated
in this part of the general subject, — what will pass as an
ease or benefit with one estate in or over another as an incident to the grant, although no reference be made to the
same in the deed of such estate.

That such would be the effect in the case of certain *apparent* easements has already been shown. And that this is
true, but that unless the same was thus apparent it would
not pass, seems to be settled in Glave *v.* Harding, where
Pollock, C. B. says: "It cannot be denied, that if a man
builds a house, and there is actually a way used or obviously and manifestly intended to be used by the occupiers
of the house, the mere lease of the house would carry with
it the right to use the way as forming part of its construction." Which ruling was thus modified by Bramwell, B., in
these words: "It (the lease) did not grant the right in
terms, and the only way in which it could grant it was, that
the condition of the premises at the time when the lease was
granted showed that it was intended that the right of way
should be exercised, upon the principle of law I have ad-
verted to, that, by the devolution of the tenements originally
held in one ownership, a right of way to a particular door or
gate would, as an apparent and continuous easement, pass
to the owners and occupiers of both of them. But I think
the way in question was not a continuous and apparent easement within that principle of law, and therefore I arrive at
the conclusion that there was no evidence of the right of
way alleged in this case."

The subject of grant in this instance was a single house
in a block, sold when partly finished, which had openings in
the walls, but whether for doors or windows was not apparent, in which respect it differed materially from the
* case of Compton *v.* Richards,[1] and consequently it [*529]
could not be claimed that there was an apparent ex-

---

[1] Compton *v.* Richards, 1 Price, 27.

isting way from the street to any particular opening, as a door. And the judgment of the court went upon the ground that " the right is not granted in terms, nor by implication, as a continuous and apparent easement; therefore it was not granted at all." [1]

In the case of White *v.* Bass, a question as to an implied servitude of light and air over a part of the granted premises for the benefit of another part, arose in this way. A house and parcel of land adjoining belonged to one owner who leased the land upon a long term, and in it restricted the tenant from building so as to obstruct the light of the lessor's house according to a prescribed plan. He afterwards sold the reversionary right to the leased premises by an absolute and unqualified deed. The house, afterwards, was conveyed, and came to the plaintiff, and the other premises to the defendant, who begun to erect a building to obstruct the light of the plaintiff's house. In answer to an action growing out of this, the court held that there was no servitude of light in favor of the plaintiff's house. The effect of the grant of the reversion to the lessee was, to extinguish his obligation as to the mode of using the premises under the lease, and therefore it stood as if, owning the house and land, he had sold the land reserving the house, in which case he could not claim for his house an easement over the granted land in derogation of his own grant. And one of the Barons, in comparing it to the case of a way where, if it is one of necessity, the law might reserve it to a grantor over the granted premises, limits it to cases like ways of necessity.[2]

The case of Pyer *v.* Carter,[3] which was decided in accordance with the doctrine of the foregoing cases, was that of a drain from one house running under and through an adjacent one; and the right to maintain it was held to pass

---

[1] Glave *v.* Harding, 3 Hurlst. & N. 937, 944.

[2] White *v.* Bass, 7 H. & Norm. 722.

[3] Pyer *v.* Carter, 1 Hurlst. & N. 916; *ante,* p. 62, *et seq.*

with the first-mentioned house, being an easement continuous and apparent in its character.

9. And yet it seems that, in order to have such easement revive and pass as appurtenant to one of the estates, it should be to a certain extent necessary to the enjoyment of it. The extent of this necessity, however, does not seem to be well settled. The decided cases clearly do not come within the rule of necessity which carries a right of way in the grant of premises; for there no degree of inconvenience raises a right to such a way, provided it be not actually necessary, nor does the easement exist any longer than the necessity continues. There is a distinction between *continuous* enjoyments, like drains, and *discontinuous*, like rights of way, and the court say : " We do not think, on the severance of two tenements, any right to all ways, which during the unity of possession have been used and enjoyed in part, passes to the owner of the dissevered tenement, unless there be something in the conveyance to show an intention to create the right to use the ways *de novo*." [1]

In a former part of this work it was said, " The test seems to be, whether what is claimed is reasonably necessary to the enjoyment of the part granted" : [2] and this is justified by the language of Jewett, C. J., in French *v.* Carhart.[3] It does not depend upon whether another easement of the kind can be obtained at an inconsiderable expense or not, provided such an easement as is then existing is necessary for the reasonable enjoyment of what
*is granted. And the cases of Pyer *v.* Carter, above   [*530]
cited, and Johnson *v.* Jordan,[4] when examined in the
light of the facts of each case, go to confirm this position.

10. The case of Dunklee *v.* Wilton Railroad, though be-

[1] Pearson *v.* Spencer, 1 B. & Smith, 583 ; S. C. 3 B. & Smith, 761. See Dodd *v.* Burchell, 1 H. & Colt. 118, 120 ; *ante*, p. *44.

[2] *Ante*, p. *61. See also pp. *36, *54.

[3] French *v.* Carhart, 1 Comst. 104.

[4] Johnson *v.* Jordan, 2 Metc. 234, 242. See also 2 Fournel, Traité du Voisinage, 403, 404.

fore cited, has been purposely reserved until now, because, though covering many of the points before stated, and referring with much apparent research to most if not all the cases hereinbefore enumerated, it assumes to place the rule of law applicable to such cases upon an original ground.

" Our next position is," says Bell, J., " that property conveyed passes in its existing state subject to all existing easements and burdens of a similar nature, in favor of the other lands of the grantor which are apparent, and which result naturally from the relative situation of the land, and from the nature, construction, and intended use of the buildings, mills, &c., upon it, and their situation and connection with other property as they were usually enjoyed at the time of the conveyance. We propose to advert to the authorities upon this point more at length, because, though there is a series of decisions for several centuries back, all, as we regard them, tending to support the above position, few if any of them are distinctly placed upon this broad ground, while many of them rest upon the once fashionable refinement of unity of possession, revivor, and extinguishment." [1]

If, as the cases all seem to show, the union of two estates in one owner extinguishes whatever easement the one has in or over the other, and if that ease or benefit be of a character so apparent, continuous, and necessary to one of these estates as to raise, in the eye of the law, a reasonable presumption that, upon a sale of such estate, both vendor and vendee must have understood and expected, in the [*531] absence of any language to the contrary, that the *vendee was to have the advantage and benefit thereof, and in consequence of this the law holds that such ease or benefit becomes again appurtenant to such estate, it is not easy to see why giving this effect to " unity of possession, revivor, and extinguishment," should be regarded as a " *once fashionable refinement.*"

The facts of the case were briefly these. The plaintiff, by

[1] Dunklee v. Wilton R. R., 4 Foster, 489, 496.

purchase, became the owner of a parcel of land below his mill, through which by an artificial race-way the water was discharged from his mill into the stream below. This state of things had continued some thirteen years, during which time the original channel through this land had grown up to grass and bushes, and had become filled up, and in some parts difficult to trace. In this state of things the plaintiff conveyed a parcel of land covering this race-way and the old channel at their intersection, by deed with covenants of warranty, and the question was, if by so doing he had lost the right to use this race-way through the granted premises. The court held that he had not; and in stating the grounds upon which the case was rested, there is a principle laid down applicable to this class of easements, which, so long as confined to these cases, seems to be well sustained by reason and authority, that, as the owner of an estate " has the right, by virtue of his ownership, to make any disposition of the property which he pleases, it seems to follow that, if he does make any change in the property, those who claim under him, and derive their titles from him, must take the property in the state it is in at the time, precisely as if it had been its natural state, and no other had ever existed." But it still seems to be limited, in the matter of easements, to such only as are apparent; and in the case to which the doctrine was applied it was not only an apparent, but a continuous one, and *necessary* to the enjoyment of the principle estate, which the grantor retained when he granted the servient tenement.

*SECTION III.

OF CHANGES IN ESTATES AFFECTING RIGHTS OF EASEMENT.

1. Way lost by destroying the dominant tenement.
2. Rights of private way not lost by a public dedication.
3. Easement lost by its purpose ceasing.
4. Chase v. Sutton Manufacturing Company. When change of purposes of flowing destroys the right.
5. Effect on a way of destroying the intermediate estate.
6. Easements destroyed by act of God or that of the law.
7. Locating a public way does not destroy an existing private one.
8. Private right of drain not affected by creating a public one.
9. Effect of destruction of the two tenements on party walls.

1 ANOTHER mode of extinguishing easements is by such a change in the condition of the estates, in reference to which such easements have existed, as to render the use and enjoyment thereof no longer of any practical utility or avail. Thus where one had a right of way across an open space of land to certain outhouses, and these were removed, and the land on which they stood was laid out as a highway, it was held that the right of way was thereby extinguished.[1]

So where the owner of a defined way stood by and saw the purchaser of the servient estate erect a house across the way, so as effectually to stop it, and made no objection, it was held to work an estoppel to any claim of right to remove the building for the purpose of opening the way.[2]

So where one, owning a barn, had a right of way of necessity to the same over the land of another, and suffered his barn to go wholly to decay, it was held that the right of way thereby became extinct.[3]

---

[1] Hancock v. Wentworth, 5 Metc. 446 ; 2 Fournel, Traité du Voisinage, 405.
The French law is thus stated : " Les servitudes cessent lorsque les choses se trouvent en tel état qu'on ne peut plus en user, comme si le fonds dominant et le fonds servant viennent à périr. . . . . Mais les servitudes revivent si les choses sont rétablies de manière qu'on puisse en user." 3 Toullier, Droit Civil Fran- çais, 522. See Lalaure, Traité des Servitudes, 84 ; Pardessus, Traité des Ser- vitudes, 437.

[2] Arnold v. Connman, 50 Penn. 361.

[3] Gayetty v. Bethune, 14 Mass. 49 ; ante, p. 167.

2. But one does not lose an easement of way as a private right by the owner of the servient estate dedicating it to the public use.[1]

3. And it is stated, as a general proposition, that, "If an *easement for a particular purpose is grant- [*533] ed, when that purpose no longer exists, there is an end of the easement." The cases in which this doctrine has been applied have been chiefly, though not always, those of public easements ; as, for instance, the right of maintaining a public canal across the land of an individual. In one case such a company had a sluice from below the plaintiff's mill, which they applied, not only for the purposes of their canal, but also for working a mill. When the water was kept down, it did not impede the plaintiff's wheel, but when the canal was full, it did. The canal was discontinued by act of Parliament, and a railroad substituted therefor ; but the latter was to retain the easements which had been acquired by the canal. Under this the company continued to use the sluice, and to keep up the water to the injury of the plaintiff's wheel. It was held, that, being a use for a different purpose than that for which the sluice was constructed in connection with the canal, the right thus to keep up the water did not pass to the railroad.[2]

4. In Chase v. Sutton Manufacturing Company, a canal company was authorized to flow lands, &c. of individuals, paying damages for the same. The plaintiff recovered damages for flowing his land, under proceedings for that purpose against the company. The company were, by their charter, authorized to erect mills and other works on the reservoirs, &c. of the company, and the plaintiff's land was flowed by a pond raised for a reservoir, and also used for carrying a mill, now belonging to the defendants. And it was held that the damages recovered by him covered as well the flowing for

---

[1] Regina v. Chorley, 12 Q. B. 515.

[2] National Manure Co. v. Donald, 4 Hurlst. & N. 8, 19. See Gayetty v. Bethune, 14 Mass. 49 ; M'Donald v. Lindall, 3 Rawle, 492 ; 2 Fournel, Traité du Voisinage, 406.

the purposes of a canal reservoir as for the purposes of the mill.

The canal was subsequently abandoned and filled up, and the bed of it was sold to a railroad, under authority granted [*534] by the legislature. The act authorized the canal company *to sell their entire property, or any part thereof, and to vest a good title to the same in the purchaser. It further authorized the dams erected by the canal company to be kept up by the mill-owners thereon for their benefit. In the sale of their road-bed to the railroad company, the canal company reserved the land, dam, and waters retained by them on the river. The court held, that the damages recovered by the plaintiff were for a permanent easement to flow his land, as well for mill purposes as for the canal ; that it was competent for the legislature to authorize the canal company to sell the right to keep up the dam for mill purposes, although the canal was discontinued ; and that, having once recovered damages for such flowing, he could not recover these a second time of the defendant for continuing to flow the land for the purposes of his mill. But the whole reasoning of the case goes upon the assumption, that, if the easement had been acquired for the canal only, and the canal had been discontinued, the easement would have been lost, unless saved by the act of the legislature.[1]

5. So where there was a right of way from a piece of upland through a dock to deep water, and a street was laid out between such parcel and the deep water, and by its construction filled up the dock, cutting off communication between the upland and the water, it was held that the right of way was thereby extinguished, or at least suspended, and if, while so suspended, the owner of the estate grant it to another, the easement of way would not pass with it.[2]

Where a right of way was by its terms limited as a servi-

[1] Chase v. Sutton Mg. Co., 4 Cush. 152.
[2] Mussey v. Proprietor Union Wharf, 41 Me. 34.

tude to a garden connected with a dwelling-house in the country, it was held that it could not be extended to the use of the house, if separated from the garden.[1]

6. The general doctrine is stated to be : " Where a right, title, or interest is destroyed or taken away by the act of *God, operation of law, or act of the party, it [*535] is called an *extinguishment*," and an " easement is one of the rights which may be extinguished or destroyed." [2]

But an easement, by custom, of taking water from a well is not extinguished by an act of enclosure of the common in which it is situate, although those acts of enclosure are laws of the land.[3]

7. But the mere location of a public way over a private one does not deprive the owner of ·the latter of his rights as such owner in the same, against any one who should obstruct it.[4]

8. Nor would the construction of a public drain from the land of one who has hitherto enjoyed a private right of drain, affect this right, although the private drain may cease to be necessary to the enjoyment of the land.[5]

9. A question of a somewhat peculiar character, as to how far an easement may be lost without any act of either party, has arisen in respect to *party walls*. It was held in one case, that if the buildings, in respect to which there was a mutual easement of a party wall, were destroyed by fire, the easement would be extinguished, neither party could require the other to help rebuild the wall, and, if one built the wall upon his own land, the other could not claim any right to use it.[6]

And in a case where the wall had become so ruinous as to require to be taken down, Denio, J. was inclined to hold the

[1] 3 Toullier, Droit Civil Français, 496.

[2] Hancock v. Wentworth, 5 Metc. 446, 451 ; 1 Rolle, Abr. 934, 935.

[3] Race v. Ward, 7 E. & Black, 384.

[4] Allen v. Ormond, 8 East, 4 ; Woolr. Ways, 73 ; per *Patteson*, J., Duncan v. Louch, 6 Q. B. 904, 915.

[5] Hastings v. Livermore, 7 Gray, 194.

[6] Sherred v. Cisco, 4 Sandf. 480.

40

easement of party wall extinguished in the same way as if destroyed by fire;[1] though in Campbell v. Mesier,[2] Chancellor Kent had held that, if a party wall needs repair, one of the parties can, after request made, proceed to make the repairs, and call upon the other party for contribution.

M. Toullier states the general rule of law to be substantially as follows. Servitudes cease when the subjects [*536] of *them happen to be in that condition that they cannot be used. As if the dominant and servient estates go to ruin, or they are submerged, or the house which owes the servitude and that to which it is due are burned or demolished.

It would be the same if the cause of the servitude should cease, as, for example, if a spring where I have a right to draw water becomes dry, I should not only lose the right of drawing water, I should lose the right of passing over the neighboring tenement, because the right of passage was only accessory to the right of drawing water, and that which is accessory cannot subsist when the principal right is lost.

But servitudes revive when the estates are so restored that the servitude can be again used, unless a space of time shall have then elapsed sufficient to raise a presumption that such servitude has been extinguished. Thus when one reconstructs a party wall, or a house which has been demolished or destroyed by fire, the servitudes both active and passive are continued in respect to the new wall or new house, under certain limitations similar to that above stated.[3]

---

[1] Partridge v. Gilbert, 15 N. Y. 601, 615.

[2] Campbell v. Mesier, 4 Johns. Ch. 334; 2 Fournel, Traité du Voisinage, 236; 5 Duranton, Cours de Droit Français, ed. 1834, 382; Code Nap., Art. 665.

[3] 3 Toullier, Droit Civil Français, 522.

SECTION IV.

OF ACTS OF OWNERS OF EASEMENTS AFFECTING RIGHTS TO THE SAME.

1. Acts to have effect upon easements must be so intended.
2. No parol release affects a right of easement.
3. Abusing an easement does not destroy the right.
4. Effect of wrongfully increasing the extent of an easement.
5. One may not alter the condition of dominant or servient estate.
6. Luttrell's case. Change of mode of enjoyment.
7. If one change lights, the other may stop them.
8. Light limited to the prescriptive quantity enjoyed.
9. Enlarging a window does not destroy the original right.
10. Same subject.

*1. In considering what acts of the owner of an [*537] easement, or of the estate in or over which it exists, will operate to extinguish the same, it may be somewhat difficult to classify them. But it may be stated, generally, that the act must be such as indicates an intention to extinguish the easement, or it must be something which enhances the burden upon the servient estate, to the injury of the same, against the consent of the owner thereof.

2. A mere parol release of an easement, or an agreement not to exercise the same, would of itself be of no avail.[1]

3. Nor does one having an easement in another's land lose it by merely abusing it, or using it for purposes for which he has no right to exercise it. Thus if one having a right of way for certain purposes across another's land use it for other and different purposes, he would, as to such use, be a trespasser. But it would not justify the owner in stopping the way altogether.[2]

4. But if, in the first place, the owner of the easement materially change the condition of the estate to which the same belongs, so as thereby to increase the burden of the

---

[1] Dyer v. Sanford, 9 Metc. 395 ; Liggins v. Inge, 7 Bing. 682.
[2] Mendell v. Delano, 7 Metc. 176.

servitude upon the servient estate, and the enjoyment of the excess cannot be separated from that of the original right, it may operate to destroy or extinguish the right of easement altogether.[1]

This subject has been somewhat considered in its relation to easements of water, and it may be necessary to repeat some things that are there said in order to apply them to the general doctrine of easements.

5. The language of Jervis, C. J., in Wood v. Copper Miners' Co., is : " In the case of an easement, you cannot alter the condition of either the dominant or servient tenement."[2]

[*538]   * And where one had an easement of a drain which the land-owner was bound to keep in repair, and he wrongfully increased the quantity of water which he had a right to discharge through the same, he thereby lost the right to require the other party to keep the same cleansed for his accommodation.[3]

6. One of the leading cases upon this subject is Luttrell's. In that case the plaintiff, having two old fulling-mills, tore them down and erected two corn-mills upon the same privilege, and the question was whether by such a change the owner lost the prescriptive right to the use of the water in the manner in which he had enjoyed it, in respect to his former mills. Various cases are referred to in the discussion of the point raised, illustrating acts that will and such as will not operate to extinguish an existing easement. It was held that the change did not affect the prescriptive right, " provided always that no prejudice may thereby arise either by diverting or stopping of the water, as it was before."

" So if a man have estovers, either by grant or prescription, to his house, although he alter the rooms and chambers of his house, as to make a parlor where it was the hall, or the hall where the parlor was, and the like alterations of

---

1 Jones v. Tapling, 11 C. B. N. s. 283.

2 Wood v. Copper Miner's Co., 14 C. B. 428, 446.

3 Sharpe v. Hancock, 7 Mann. & G. 354.

qualities, and not of the house itself, and without making
new chimneys, by which no prejudice doth accrue to the
owner of the wood, it is not destroying of the prescription.
And although he build new chimneys or maketh a new addition to his old house, by that he shall not lose his prescription, but he cannot imply or spend any of the estovers in the
new chimneys, or in the part newly added.   The same law
of conduits and water-pipes and the like." It was held, in
this case, that the alteration being of the *quality*, and not of
the *substance* of the tenement, and it being without any prejudice in the *water-course to the owner   [*539]
thereof, did not affect the prescriptive right belonging to the mill.[1]

In Luttrell's case, the court refer to the case of an easement of light belonging to a house, the owner of which
changes it.   The cases upon this point will be found to be
numerous, and in respect to some of them a difficulty exists
in drawing a precise and definite rule which may apply to
other cases.   Thus it is said in Luttrell's case : " So if a man
have an old window to his hall, and afterwards he turn the
hall to a parlor, or any other use, yet it is not lawful for his
neighbor to stop it, for he shall prescribe to have the light in
such part of his house." [2]

7. In accordance with what has been stated, it was held
in Garritt *v.* Sharp, that if one, having an easement of light
over another's estate, alter his premises so that the enjoyment of the light will be more disadvantageous to the servient tenement than that which he before had, the latter may
stop the same.[3]

8. And an easement of light cannot be carried beyond the
enjoyment of access of light through the same aperture, or
one of the same dimensions, and in the same position, as it

[1] Luttrell's case, 4 Rep. 86 – 89. See Allan *v.* Gomme, 11 Adolph. & E.
759 ; M'Donald *v.* Bear River Co., 13 Cal. 220.

[2] Luttrell's case, 4 Rep. 87 a.

[3] Garritt *v.* Sharp, 3 Adolph. & E. 325 ; Jones *v.* Tapling, 11 C. B. N. s. 283.
See *post*, pl. 10.

had been used and enjoyed at the time when the consent or grant, which prescription implies, was given. Therefore, where one had an ancient window in his wall, and carried out the wall several feet in the form of a bow, and in it inserted three windows instead of the original one, but not occupying the same place as the former one, it was held that the change prevented his claiming for these the prescriptive right of light which belonged to the former window.[1]

[*540]   *9. It is, however, stated in one case to be law, that, by merely enlarging a window in one's house, he does not lose the right to enjoy the original space of access of light, though he cannot claim a right to any easement outside of such space. But the owner of the adjacent estate may obstruct all except the original extent of the aperture.[2]

10. The subject had been agitated and variously decided by the English courts as to the effect upon an easement of light which any one had in favor of a dwelling-house, if he were to enlarge his ancient windows, and how far an adjacent owner could, for that cause, stop any portion of this ancient light in his attempt to exercise what seems to be conceded as a right by all authorities, to stop or darken the newly enlarged portions of the windows. Among the cases involving this question were Renshaw v. Bean,[3] Hutchinson v. Copestake,[4] Bincks v. Park,[5] and Jones v. Tapling,[6] in its earlier stages. But the question was finally settled in the House of Lords, where the doctrine laid down in the two first cases was overruled, and the irreconcilable differences of opinion between the judges in the other cases were obviated. In the final decision of the case it was held, that, inasmuch as it was doing no wrong on the part of the owner

---

[1] Blanchard v. Bridges, 4 Adolph. & E. 176; Hutchinson v. Copestake, 9 C. B. N. s. 863; Cherrington v. Abney Mil', 2 Vern. 646.

[2] Chandler v. Thompson, 3 Campb. 80.

[3] Renshaw v. Bean, 18 Q. B. 112.

[4] Hutchinson v. Copestake, 9 C. B. N. s. 863.

[5] Binckes v. Park, 11 C. B. N. s. 324.

[6] Jones v. Tapling, 11 C. B. N. s. 283; 12 C. B. N. s. 826; ante, pl. 7.

of the house to enlarge his windows, he lost, thereby, no right of enjoying his prescriptive easement of light, so that if, in attempting to stop or obstruct the enlarged capacity of these windows, the adjacent owner interfered with the extent of the ancient lights, he was a tort feasor, and liable in damages for so doing.[1]

And in another case it is said, "It has been held that where a party enlarges an ancient window, the owner of the adjoining land cannot obstruct any part of the light which ought to pass through the space occupied by an ancient window."[2]

*SECTION V.   [*542]

EFFECT OF ABANDONING AN EASEMENT.

1. An act of abandonment requires intent.
2. Stokoe v. Singers. Stopping light not an abandonment.
3. Lovell v. Smith. Substituting a way not an abandonment.
4. Loss of easement of light by ceasing to occupy.
5. Taylor v. Hampton. What amounts to an abandonment.
6. Corning v. Gould. Doctrine applied to ways.
7. Partridge v. Gilbert. Stopping a way defeating the right.
8. Rebuilding house with new windows, loss of ancient light.
9. Length of time not necessary to work abandonment.
10. Changing wheel of a mill may affect the easement.
11. Change of premises not affecting natural easements.
12. Difference in effect of act of God and of owner on easements.
13. What owner must do, if suspended by act of God.
14. Effect of removal of mill by one, and a new one by another.
15. Acts done by owner on dominant estate affecting easement.

1. THE owner of an easement may destroy his right to the same by actually abandoning the right as well as the enjoyment, especially if a third party become interested in the servient estate after such act of abandonment; and

it would *operate unjustly upon him if the exercise [*543] of the easement were resumed in favor of the dominant estate.   It is not easy to define, in all cases, what would

---

[1] Jones v. Tapling, 13 C. B. N. S. 876.

[2] Thomas v. Thomas, 2 Cromp. M. & R. 34, 40.

be such act of abandonment as would destroy a right of easement, and each case seems to be a matter for a jury to determine.   But nothing short of an intention so to abandon the right would operate to that effect, unless other persons have been led by such acts to treat the servient estate as if free of the servitude, and the same could not be resumed without doing an injury to their rights in respect to the same.   And in this it is not intended to embrace questions which may arise from a mere non-user of an easement.

2. The case of Stokoe *v*. Singers (in 1857) presents several of the points above referred to.   In that case there was, in 1837, an ancient warehouse with windows on both sides. In that year the owner blocked up the windows on one side of the house, on the *inside* thereof, with rubble and plaster. The bars remained on the *outside*, so that one there could see that there had been windows there.   The windows remained in this state till 1856.   The defendant, having become the owner of the land next to the side of the warehouse on which the windows had thus been stopped, was preparing to build a house thereon which would effectually darken the windows, and actually erected a board on his own land which stopped them, and for this an action was brought before the twenty years expired from the stopping of the windows by the plaintiff in 1837.   The judge who tried the case instructed the jury that the right to light and air " might be lost by abandonment, and that closing the windows, with the intention of never opening them again, would be an abandonment destroying the right, but that closing them for a temporary purpose would not be so. . . . . Though the person entitled to the right might not really have abandoned his right, yet if he manifested such an appearance of having abandoned it as to induce the owner of the adjoining land to alter his position, in the reasonable belief [*544] *that the right was abandoned, there would be a preclusion, as against him, from claiming the right." He left it to the jury, whether they believed that the plain-

tiff's predecessor blocked up the windows with the intention of abandoning them forever, and told them, unless he did, the right was not gone. In the course of the discussion of the case, Earle, J. says : " In Moore v. Rawson it seems to be said, that an intention to abandon it permanently destroys it, unless a contrary intention be manifested within a reasonable time, which is not defined. I should feel inclined to say, that the intention permanently to abandon it would destroy it as soon as it was communicated to the owners of the servient tenement, without lapse of time." Lord Campbell, C. J. : " I doubt whether the communication of that intention destroys the right until the communication is acted upon. Then it certainly does." The final judgment by Earle, J. was : " Taking the whole summing up together, it seems to us the true points were left by the judge to the jury. We consider the jury to have found that the plaintiff's predecessor did not so close up his lights as to lead the defendant to incur expense or loss, on the reasonable belief that they had been permanently abandoned, nor so as to manifest an intention of permanently abandoning the right of using them." [1]

In Perkins v. Dunham the same rule was applied as in the above case, that the question of abandonment was one for the jury.[2]

3. In Lovell v. Smith there was an attempt to establish an abandonment of a way under the following facts. The owner of a right of way across the land of another made a parol agreement with him to substitute another way across the same land and to give up the one he had. He accordingly made use of the new way for some years, less than twenty, and the question arose whether he had not thereby *abandoned the first way and lost it. But [*545] the court held that he had not, for that such was not his intention ; that he merely intended to substitute one for the other, and as he had not enjoyed the new one the

---

[1] Stokoe v. Singers, 8 Ellis & B. 31 –39.
[2] Perkins v. Dunham, 3 Strobh. 224.

requisite time to acquire it by prescription, the owner of the servient estate might, at his election, revoke the license by which he used it, and leave him without any way if his first right was lost. To work an abandonment of a right of way acquired by prescription, there must be a release by deed, or evidence from which a jury may presume a release.[1]

4. But in case of light, the right to which was acquired by occupancy, the same ceases when the person who acquired it discontinues the occupancy.[2]

5. What shall be an act of abandonment of an easement in any given case depends, of course, upon the nature of the property and the easement. In Taylor v. Hampton, the easement in question was a prescriptive right of flowing back water upon another's land for the use of a mill. The owner of the mill to which this right belonged, removed it up the stream, and established it upon a new spot, and ceased to flow the former land. The owner of this land then converted it into a rice-field, and cultivated it, and subsequently sold it. And it was held that the mill-owner could not afterwards resume the occupancy of the land by replacing his mill, and flowing it again.[3]

In Hale v. Oldroyd the owner of three closes had an ancient pond for their accommodation, which was supplied by water through a ditch in another's land. He dug a pond in each of the closes as a substitute for the general one, and enjoyed the same for twenty years, the old pond having, in the mean time become filled up with rubbish. But upon a trial for diverting this water, his title to the three [*546] ponds *by prescription having failed, he was allowed to make good his original right to fill the ancient pond, not having lost his right by abandonment, as he did not intend to abandon the right to the water.[4]

---

[1] Lovell v. Smith, 3 C. B. N. s. 120; Wright v. Freeman, 5 Harr. & J. 467 478. *Contra*, Pope v. Devereaux, 5 Gray, 409.

[2] Per *Littledale*, J., Moore v. Rawson, 3 Barnew. & C. 332, 341.

[3] Taylor v. Hampton, 4 M'Cord. 96.

[4] Hale v. Oldroyd, 14 Mees. & W. 789.

6. The case of Corning *v.* Gould illustrates many of the positions above taken, as they apply to ways. In that case, there was a way between the plaintiff's premises and defendant's, the centre line of which was the dividing line between the estates. The plaintiff built upon a part of the way next his estate, and run a fence along the middle of it, leaving the other half within the enclosure of the adjacent estate. This was less than twenty years before the action brought. In that state the owner of the other estate sold it to the defendant, who proceeded to occupy the part of the way inside of the fence next to his estate. It was held that the plaintiff had, by his act, abandoned and lost the easement, since his actions showed an intent to do so on his part, and this was followed by the act of the party owning on the other side of the line, constituting a joint abandonment by both, and the defendant purchased the estate in this condition.[1]

7. So in Partridge *v.* Gilbert, where a passage over two adjoining estates through an arch in the dividing line of the estates was stopped by the parties converting the arch into a solid wall, the easement of way was mutually abandoned.[2]

8. In a leading case upon this subject, where the easement claimed was that of light and air, the owner of the building to which it was appurtenant tore it down, and erected another with a blank wall, and suffered the same to remain in that situation for seventeen years. A question having arisen whether the house had, by this, lost this easement, the court held that it was incumbent upon the owner to show that, at the time when he erected the *blank wall, and apparently abandoned the use of [*547] the windows that gave the light and air, it was not a permanent, but a temporary abandonment, and that he intended to resume the enjoyment within a reasonable time.

---

[1] Corning *v.* Gould, 16 Wend. 531, 538; Pardessus, Traité des Servitudes 478.

[2] Partridge *v.* Gilbert, 15 N. Y. 601.

By building the blank wall, he may have induced another person to become the purchaser of the adjoining ground for building purposes, and it would be most unjust that he should afterwards prevent such person from carrying those purposes into effect. And it was held that the plaintiff could not recover for an obstruction to the light of windows opened in this blank wall.[1]

In Lawrence v. Obee the same doctrine was applied, except that, in that case, the window had been bricked up, and remained so for twenty years, which was held to be an abandonment. And an adjacent owner, having constructed a privy upon his premises, which was not a nuisance so long as the window remained closed, was held not liable for such erection, although, when the first owner reopened his window, it became a nuisance to the first-mentioned house.[2]

9. Although, as will be seen, an abandonment is sometimes inferred from a non-user for twenty years, it seems to depend less upon the duration of the time than the acts which accompany the ceasing to use the easement, for its effect upon the right. The length of time that this is continued is one of the elements from which the intention to abandon or retain the right is inferred. It is not therefore necessary to have ceased to use a private way the whole term of twenty years in order to lose it. And among the illustrations given to this effect, is that of a way to a malthouse through a gate leading from a lane, and the owner were to tear down the malt-house, and erect a wall where the gate was. It would authorize the inference that [*548] the * way had been effectually abandoned. The cesser to use, coupled with any act clearly indicative of an intention to abandon the right, would have the same effect as a release, without any reference to the time during

---

[1] Moore v. Rawson, 3 Barnew. & C. 332 ; Dyer v. Sanford, 9 Metc. 395. See Ballard v. Butler, 30 Me. 94.

[2] Lawrence v. Obee, 3 Campb. 514.

which such cesser has continued.   And in the same case, it was held that the owner of the servient estate, over which the dominant estate had a right of way, could not affect the right of the latter by dedicating the way to the public use.[1]

But Lord Campbell, in Stokoe v. Singers, said the case of Regina v. Chorley was " an authority that an abandonment is effectual if communicated and acted upon.   It goes no further." [2]

In Crain v. Fox, one having a right of way to a house across another's close, took down the house, and, after twelve years, enclosed the way and cultivated it.   It was held that he had abandoned it as an easement.[3]

10. In one case, a party having acquired a right to the use of water for operating a mill with a low wheel, changed the use, so as to employ a larger wheel and greater head of water, and continued this long enough to acquire a right to the same.   He then voluntarily discontinued the use of the larger wheel, and resumed that of the smaller one, and it was held that he thereby abandoned the right to maintain the increased head of water.[4]

11. But this would not apply to the case of an interruption of the natural flow of a stream of water through one's premises.   As where one who had enjoyed the waters of a natural stream, flowing, in a particular channel, through his land for nineteen years, sued for an obstruction to the same above his premises, it was held to be no defence, that, prior to that time the stream had been obstructed for a time, or that the course of the stream had been changed
* above the plaintiff's land, by the act of the plain-   [*549] tiff himself.[5]

12. In the above-cited case of Taylor v. Hampton, the

[1] Regina v. Chorley, 12 Q. B. 515 ; Pope v. Devereux, 5 Gray, 409.

[2] Stokoe v. Singers, 8 Ellis & B. 31, 37.

[3] Crain v. Fox, 16 Barb. 184.

[4] Drewett v. Sheard, 7 Carr. & P. 465.

[5] Hall v. Swift, 4 Bing. N. C. 381.   See Patteson, J., in Carr v. Foster, 3 Q. B. 581, 585.

judge thus discriminates between the effect of the act of the party owning the easement and the act of God in destroying or interrupting the same. " Where a right is suspended by the act of God, as by the drying up of a spring, it will revive again if the spring chance to flow. But if it be suspended by the act of the party, as by building a house or a wall, it would not be restored, even though the obstacle should be removed by a stroke from heaven." [1]

13. But it would seem that, if the enjoyment of the easement was suspended by the act of God, and might be restored by the owner thereof, but he fail to do so within a reasonable time, and in the mean time another party is suffered to go on and enjoy an easement upon his own land, which he could only do upon the assumption that the first was abandoned, it would have the effect to defeat the original easement altogether. Thus where one had, by user, acquired the right to divert water from a stream for the working of a mill, but the mill was carried away, and the channel filled up by which the water of the stream had been diverted, and it remained so for forty-five years, during which time a mill below had enjoyed the use of the natural stream, it was held that the owner of the original mill-site could not, by erecting a new mill thereon, and opening the old channel, have a right to divert the water into its former channel. The lower mill had, by this period of enjoyment, acquired the right to the natural flow of the stream, which the former mill-owner might not disturb.[2]

14. And the case put by Tindal, C. J., in Liggins [*550] v. Inge, *is this : " Suppose a person who formerly had a mill upon a stream should pull it down and remove the works, with the intention never to return, could it be held that the owner of other land adjoining the stream

---

[1] Taylor v. Hampton, 4 McCord, 96. See Corning v. Gould, 16 Wend. 531, 541.

[2] Thomas v. Hill, 31 Me. 252. See *ante*, sect. 3, pl. 9; Dunklee v. Wilton R. R., 4 Foster, 489.

might not erect a mill and employ the water so relinquished? or that he could be compellable to pull down his mill, if the former mill-owner should afterwards change his determina-tion, and wish to rebuild his own?" The question would be for the jury, whether he had completely abandoned the use of the stream or not.[1]

15. And the court in Dyer v. Sanford say : " It may well be maintained, upon the authorities, that the owner of a dominant tenement may make such changes in the use and condition of his own estate as in fact to renounce the ease-ment itself. And this may be relied on by the owner of the servient tenement as evidence of abandonment." [2]

SECTION VI.

EFFECT OF NON-USER OF EASEMENTS.

1. Must be an adverse user to have non-user an abandonment.
2. No length of non-user bars a right granted by deed.
3. What acts on servient estate defeat a non-used right.
4. Doe v. Butler.   What presumption arises from non-user.
5. Effect of non-user of a right gained by prescription.
6. Grounds and extent of presumption from non-user.
7. Twenty years non-user, if explained, no abandonment.
8. What necessary to have non-user operate an abandonment.
9. Hatch v. Dwight.   Case of a mill; same subject.
10. Williams v. Nelson.   Non-user of right to flow lands.
11. Non-user of right to flow under Massachusetts mill laws.
12. Farrar v. Cooper.   Non-user with acts of abandonment.
13. Shields v. Arndt.   Right lost by non-user extinguished.
14. When one is bound to inquire if the other has abandoned.

1. IN some cases an abandonment of an easement is in-ferred from a non-user of the right.   But though this is * true, under certain circumstances, it is be- [*551] lieved never to apply unless the non-user shall have been of as long duration as the period that is required in order to gain the easement by user, and rarely, if ever, un-

---

[1] Liggins v. Inge, 7 Bing. 682.
[2] Dyer v. Sanford, 9 Metc. 395, 401.

less there has been, besides, such a use by the owner of the premises in or over which the easement has been enjoyed, as to indicate a claim of right which is adverse to the enjoyment of the easement. Here, as in the case of acts of abandonment, the non-user must be of such a character and duration as to show an intent to abandon the easement, or it must have induced another to expend money upon the supposition of such abandonment, which is known and acquiesced in by the one who might otherwise claim it, and where to enforce the right of easement would work injustice upon an innocent party.[1]

And even a public easement in a highway may be lost by non-user. The law in such cases presumes an extinguishment by abandonment for a long time. But an encroachment upon a highway will not destroy the easement in the part thus encroached upon, if for a less period of time than twenty-one years.[2] Very strong evidence must generally be given of abandonment, yet such evidence need be made much less strong when the owner has allowed any other person to assert rights which will be seriously and irremediably damnified by the reassertion of the right of easement. This language was applied to a case where the non-user had continued twenty-five years.[3]

And an adverse enjoyment of the servient estate, though presumptive evidence, in some cases, of an extinguishment of the easement in or over the same, is always subject to be rebutted by evidence.[4]

2. In the first place, if the easement has been acquired by deed, no length of time of mere non-user will operate to impair or defeat the right. Nothing short of a use by the owner of the premises over which it was granted, which is adverse to the enjoyment of such easement by the owner

---

[1] See 2 Fournel, Traité du Voisinage, 406; Crossley, v. Lightowler, L. R. 3 Eq. 292, 294.

[2] Fox v. Hart, 11 Ohio, 416. See State v. Alstead, 18 N. H. 65.

[3] Crossley v. Lightowler, L. R. 3 Eq. 294.

[4] Hoffman v. Savage, 15 Mass. 130.

thereof, for the space of time long enough to create a prescriptive right, will destroy the right granted.[1]

Thus where the owner of an aqueduct through another's land discontinued the use of it, and the owner of the land took up the logs, and did other acts inconsistent with a further use of the aqueduct, and this was continued for thirty years, it was held that the right was, thereby, lost, although originally acquired by express grants, these acts being adverse to the right of easement and acquiesced in by the owner thereof.[2]

In the case of Arnold v. Stevens the easement granted was the right to dig ore in the grantor's land, which had remained unused for forty years, but there had been no *adverse enjoyment of the premises, and it was [*552] held to be no abandonment of the right.[3]

In Butz v. Ihrie there was a grant of land, excepting and reserving a right to raise the water of a stream running through the same to a certain height by means of a dam, to be erected in a certain locality. This right had remained unused for over thirty years, and it was contended by the land-owner that the right had been abandoned and lost. The court held that, inasmuch as the terms of the reservation did not require the right to be exercised at once, no mere lapse of time during which it was not exercised could be deemed evidence of an abandonment, and that the law of limitation did not apply so as to run against such right, until some default, negligence, or acquiescence was shown, or might be fairly presumed in the owner. "The time of limitation may begin to run as soon as the laches exists, but not before."[4]

---

[1] Bannor v. Angier, 2 Allen, 128; Jennison v. Walker, 15 Gray; Arnold v. Stevens, 24 Pick. 106, 113, 114; White v. Crawford, 10 Mass. 183; Jewett v. Jewett, 16 Barb. 150; Farrar v. Cooper, 34 Me. 394, 400; Smiles v. Hastings, 24 Barb. 44; 3 Kent, Comm. 359; Ang. Watercourses, § 252; Nitzell v. Paschall, 3 Rawle, 76; French v. Braintree Co., 23 Pick. 222.

[2] Jennison v. Walker, 11 Gray, 425.

[3] See also 2 Evans, Pothier, Oblig. 137.

[4] Butz v. Ihrie, 1 Rawle, 218, 222. See Nitzell v. Paschall, 3 Rawle, 76, 82.

The case of Yeakle *v.* Nace was that of an easement of a way, and confirms the doctrine above stated.

3. It was held, that, though such easement might be lost by an enjoyment or occupation of the servient estate, adversely to the right claimed, it must be such as indicates a denial of the right on the part of the owner of the land. Otherwise, a mere non-user of a privilege in land granted or reserved, where there is nothing in the grant to show that it was to be exercised immediately, would not deprive one of his right.

The facts to which this doctrine was applied were as follow. One granted a house and lot, adjoining another lot belonging to the grantor, with a right of a passage-way between the lots of four feet in width, reserving to himself a right to build over and under this passage-way. It was held that a mere non-exercise of the right thus to build would [*553] not * operate to defeat the same, though continued for ever so long a time. But if the grantee in such a case were to build over the passage-way, and occupy it thus for twenty-one years, it would destroy the right reserved to the grantor, by such adverse occupation and enjoyment by the grantee. In that case, the same grantor sold eleven lots to different purchasers, lying by the side of each other, with a right of way across the rear ends of each of these lots, twenty feet in width from one street to another. The purchaser of the outside lot, next to one of these streets, enclosed his lot, including the twenty feet in width in the rear, and kept it so enclosed and cultivated for thirty years ; and it was held that the owners of the other lots, by acquiescing in this enclosure, had lost the right of way over and across the lot so enclosed.[1]

A mere obstruction, however, of an easement, a way for instance, caused by the owner of the servient estate, for less than twenty years, though yielded to by the owner of the easement, would not bar the right any more than a mere

[1] Yeakle *v.* Nace, 2 Whart. 123.

non-user of it for that length of time. An obstruction to its use cannot be said to be an adverse possession of an ease. ment, since an easement is not capable of actual possession apart from its enjoyment.[1]

So in regard to the effect of an interruption of the right of way. It must have been acquiesced in by the owner of the easement to be affected by it. " If the right be once established by clear and distinct evidence of enjoyment, it can be defeated only by distinct evidence of interruptions acquiesced in." [2]

4. So that the doctrine stated in Doe. v. Butler applies to cases of incorporeal hereditaments in the case of a mere non-user. " The rule of presumption is, *ut res rite acta est*, and is applied whenever the possession of the party is *rightful, to invest the possession with a legal title. [*554] Such a presumption will be made when it is necessary to clothe a rightful possession with a legal title, but the court must first see that there is nothing but the form of a conveyance wanting. But this presumption in favor of a grant against written evidence of title can never arise from the mere neglect of the owner to assert his right, where there has been no adverse title or enjoyment by those in whose favor the grant is to be presumed, for the obvious reason that the presumption of the person showing title, which arises from the delay in asserting his title, is equally balanced by the like presumption arising from the same delay on the part of the supposed grantee." [3]

5. In respect to the effect to be given to a mere non-user of an easement which has been acquired by adverse user or prescription, although the language of some of the cases would imply that if continued for twenty years it would be, of itself, an abandonment, it is believed that such non-user is in no case anything more than evidence of an intent to

---

[1] Bowen v. Team, 6 Rich. 298, 305 ; 2 Smith, Lead. Cas., 5th Am. ed. 211.

[2] Harvie v. Rogers, 3 Bligh, N. s. 440, 447.

[3] Doe v. Butler, 3 Wend. 149, 153.

abandon the right; that it never applies when the period of
such non-user is less than the period of limitation, and is
open to explanation and to be controlled by evidence that
the owner of the easement did not intend to abandon it while
omitting to use it.[1]

A case is mentioned by Mr. Evans, in his edition of Pothier
on Obligations, where the court held that a cesser to use a
watercourse was an extinguishment of such right, although
no act had in the mean time been done by the owners of the
adjacent land adverse to the right. But the editor contends
that such inference ought not to have been drawn, because,
among other reasons, no inconsistent or adverse enjoyment
had been acquired in the mean time.[2]

6. So it is laid down in Hillary v. Walker, by
[*555] Erskine *Ch.: "The presumption in courts of law
from length of time stands upon a clear principle.
It resolves itself into this, that a man will naturally enjoy
what belongs to him. As to incorporeal hereditaments, 1st,
rights of way not enjoyed for a number of years, though a
convenience, if not a necessity for the enjoyment, has existed,
the court directs the jury to presume either that it never did
exist, or that it was surrendered, upon this plain reason, the
absence of any cause why a man possessed of a right that is
convenient or necessary for him should in no instance have
enjoyed it. So as to the use of water and light, and whenever a party has been long out of possession of an incorporeal
hereditament, the question has always been determined in
that manner."[3]

The language of Abbot, C. J., in Doe v. Hilder, on this
subject, is this: "The long enjoyment of a right of way by
A to his house or close over the land of B, which is a prejudice to the land, may most reasonably be accounted for by
supposing a grant of such right by the owner of the land.

[1] Pardessus, Traité des Servitudes, 458; Crossley v. Lightowler, L. R. 3 Eq.
292.
[2] Prescott v. Phillips, 2 Evans, Pothier, Oblig. 136.
[3] Hillary v. Walker, 12 Ves. 239, 265.

And if such right appear to have existed in ancient times, a long forbearance to exercise it, which must be inconvenient and prejudicial to the owner of the house or close, may most reasonably be accounted for by supposing a release of the right. In the first of these cases, therefore, a grant, in the latter a release, of the right is presumed." [1]

This seems to put it on the true ground, as a matter of evidence, and not a conclusive presumption.[2]

7. Thus it was held in Ward v. Ward, that "the presumption of abandonment cannot be made from the mere fact of non-user. There must be other circumstances in the case to raise that presumption. The right is acquired by adverse enjoyment. The non-user, therefore, must be the consequence of something which is adverse to the user." *And in that case the presumption was [*556] effectually met by showing that the owner of the close, for which the right of way was claimed, had had a more convenient and easy access to it in some other way during the time of the cesser to use the way.[3]

8. The language of the court in Corning v. Gould[4] upon the subject is this: "Abandonment is a simple non-user of an easement, and in order to make out an effectual answer to the claim upon that ground, I find it perfectly well settled that the enjoyment, nay, all acts of enjoyment, must have totally ceased for the same length of time that was necessary to create the original presumption." And the cases cited below not only sustain this position, but that non-user for a longer period of time than necessary to acquire a right is only evidence of an abandonment, where the right has been gained by user. There must be an adverse enjoyment by some party adversely interested for twenty years, to give a non-user the effect of evidence. Such non-user must be

---

[1] Doe v. Hilder, 2 Barnew. & Ald. 782, 791.
[2] See Eldridge v. Knott, Cowp. 214.
[3] Ward v. Ward, 7 Exch. 838.
[4] Corning v. Gould, 16 Wend. 531, 535.

accompanied by acts or declarations indicating an intent to abandon the right, and the non-user must have continued for twenty years, or other persons have been induced, by such acts or declarations of abandonment, to expend money upon the premises over which the easement once existed.[1]

9. In Hatch v. Dwight, the easement was the use of water by a mill, which was obstructed by the owner of a lower mill. The court say: " If a site once occu-
[*557] pied *had been abandoned by the owner, evidently with an intent to leave it unoccupied, it would be unreasonable that others, owning above or below, should be prevented from making a profitable use of their sites from fear of being exposed to an action for damages by their neighbor. Questions of this kind, however, are proper for the consideration of a jury."

And it is said by Coke: " The title being once gained by prescription or custom, cannot be lost by interruption of possession for ten or twenty years, but by interruption of the right." [2]

10. In Williams v. Nelson, mill-owners had acquired a prescriptive right to flow certain lands of another without payment of damages therefor. They took down their mill and removed it, carrying away all the valuable parts thereof except the wheel, which they did not afterwards use in rebuilding the mill. Some of the owners of the mill had moreover declared, and one of them had done this in the presence of the owner of the land, that the mill would not again be put in operation. The premises continued in this

---

[1] Hatch v. Dwight, 17 Mass. 289 ; Emerson v. Wiley, 10 Pick. 310; Williams v. Nelson, 23 Pick. 141, 147 ; French v. Braintree Mg. Co., 23 Pick. 216 ; White v. Crawford, 10 Mass. 183; Arnold v. Stevens, 24 Pick. 106 ; Regina v. Chorley, 12 Q. B. 515 ; Jewett v. Jewett, 16 Barb. 150 ; Wright v. Freeman, 5 Harr. & J. 467, 476 ; Hurd v. Curtis, 7 Metc. 94, 115 ; Pillsbury v. Moore, 44 Me. 154 ; Townsend v. M'Donald, 2 Kern, 381 ; Dyer v. Depui, 5 Whart. 584 ; Perkins v. Dunham, 3 Strobh. 224 ; Farrar v. Cooper, 34 Me. 394, 400 ; Nitzell v. Paschall, 3 Rawle, 76, 82 ; Hall v. Swift, 6 Scott, 167 ; Miller v. Garlock, 8 Barb. 153 ; Crossley v. Lightowler, L. R. 3 Eq. 293.

[2] Co. Litt. 114 b.

position nine years, and the owner of the land had in the mean time cultivated and improved his meadow, cutting the brush thereon, and turning some parts into English grass. But the court held it was not an abandonment, and that they were justified in resuming the occupation of the mill, and overflowing the land, without thereby being liable to damages for such flowing.[1]

11. But it would seem, that if the right of the mill-owners to flow the land had been acquired under the mill acts of Massachusetts by paying annual damages therefor, and they had removed the mill, and given notice to the land-owner of their intention not to flow the land any *longer, it might operate to extinguish the privilege [*558] and remit the land-owner to his original rights.[2]

12. And the case of Farrar v. Cooper affirms the doctrine above stated, that, if the owner of an upper mill-privilege abandon the use of it, he may lose the same, if he so acts towards the owner of a lower privilege, proposing to occupy the same, as to give him reasonable ground to suppose the privilege had been abandoned, and he proceeds to occupy the lower one accordingly. Thus where the owner of an upper privilege ceased to use it, and joined with other owners, of which he was one, in occupying a lower privilege, it was held to be such an abandonment that he could not afterwards resume the occupation of the first to the injury of the second.[3]

13. The case of Shields v. Arndt is referred to in this connection, as presenting some of the foregoing propositions in a somewhat peculiar light, but illustrating how, though a mere non-user of an easement may not operate as the loss of the same, yet if it results from an adverse enjoyment of the land-owner over which it is claimed, and this is continued for twenty years, the effect is to extinguish it, as if it never had

---

[1] See Hurd v. Curtis, supra; Dyer v. Depui, 5 Whart. 584, 597 ; Mowry v. Sheldon, 2 R. I. 369, 378.

[2] French v. Braintree Mg. Co., supra; Liggins v. Inge, 7 Bing. 682. See Baird v. Hunter, 12 Pick. 556 ; Hunt v. Whitney, 4 Metc. 603.

[3] Farrar v. Cooper, 34 Me. 394, 400 ; Mowry v. Sheldon, 2 R. I. 369.

existed. Thus where one owning land upon a stream, below
that of another, suffered the upper owner to divert the entire water of the stream from his land, so that for twenty
years none ran to the land of the lower owner, and then the
upper owner turned the water so that it ran again upon the
lower owner's land, and continued to do so for a time less
than twenty years, it was held that the upper owner might
again divert it upon his own land, and that the lower owner
would be without remedy for such diversion.[1]

14. In the case of Mowry v. Sheldon, above cited,
[*559] the *language of the court bears upon the inference
that may be drawn from a mere discontinuance of
the use of a mill-privilege, and how far that depends upon
the intent with which it is done, namely: "It is said, that,
leaving the dam not only unoccupied for such a length of
time (nine years), but so injured as not to pond the water,
and taking the gate out of the bulkhead, were calculated to
mislead the owner below, who might go on and erect his
dam in the belief that the privilege was abandoned. We
think, in such a case, it is the duty of the owner below, before he attempts to flow out the privilege above, to inquire
of the owner thereof. If the owner of the upper privilege
acts in good faith with the actual intent to repair the dam,
and occupy it or sell to some one who will, we do not think
he ought to lose his privilege." [2]

[1] Shields v. Arndt, 3 Green, Ch. 234.
[2] Mowry v. Sheldon, 2 R. I. 369, 378.

SECTION VII.

EFFECT OF AN EXECUTED LICENSE UPON AN EASEMENT.

1. Effect of acts done on dominant and servient estates.
2. Acts on dominant estate which destroy easements.
3. Acts done by license on servient estate.
4. If act done destroys easement, it is irrevocable.
5. Liggins v. Inge.   Case of act done on servient estate.
6. Morse v. Copeland.   Easement destroyed by an executed license.
7. Dyer v. Sanford.   Act on servient estate destroying easement.

1. In some of the cases which have been referred to, the rulings of the courts might have been sustained upon what has now become well-settled law, that, if the owner of the dominant estate do acts thereon which permanently prevent his enjoying an easement, the same is extinguished : or, if he authorize the owner of the servient estate to do upon the same that which prevents the dominant estate from
any *longer enjoying the easement, the effect will be   [*560]
to extinguish it.

2. In respect to the first part of the proposition, it has been heretofore illustrated by referring to the case of light and air, where the owner of a dominant estate had erected a permanent blank wall in place of the one through which the light and air had been enjoyed ; and it is only necessary to repeat the doctrine in this connection.[1]

3. But the other part of the proposition requires a more extended explanation, in order to distinguish between the cases of a license to do acts on the land of the licenser and similar acts on that of the licensee.   If one licenses another to do an act upon the licenser's land, he may, at common law, revoke it, so far as it remains unexecuted, at his pleasure, with very rare, if any, exceptions.[2]

[1] Dyer v. Sanford, 9 Metc. 395; Moore v. Rawson, 3 Barnew. & C. 332; Lavillebeuvre v. Cosgrove, 13 La. Ann. 323 ; La. Civ. Code, § 779.

[2] Hewlins v. Shippam, 5 Barnew. & C. 221.

4. And consequently, if the act so licensed to be done affects the enjoyment of the land, or any easement connected therewith, when the same is revoked the right to the easement revives with full vigor. But if the act be to be done on the licensee's land, and the effect thereof is to impair or destroy an easement belonging to land of the licenser, the latter cannot himself restore what has been changed on the other's land, nor can his revocation of the license affect what has already actually been accomplished; and it would be sufficient that the license was by parol, and not in writing.

This position will be found illustrated by the cases which are cited below.[1]

[*561]   *5. In Liggins v. Inge, the plaintiff's ancestor, a mill-owner, by parol, licensed or authorized the defendant to lower the bank of the stream within his own land, and to raise a weir in the stream there, whereby the water of the stream was diverted. This the defendant did at his own expense, and, after the same had continued in that state for five years, the mill-owner called on the defendant to restore the bank to its original state, which he refused to do. The court held, that, when the mill-owner authorized this diversion to be made, he thereby signified his relinquishment of a right to so much of the water; and after he had done this by words or acts, and suffered other persons to act upon the faith of such relinquishment, and to incur expense in doing the very act to which his consent was given, it was too late to retract such consent, or to throw on those other persons the burden of restoring matters to their former state and condition. " There is nothing unreasonable

---

[1] Liggins v. Inge, 7 Bing. 682 ; Winter v. Brockwell, 8 East, 308 ; Morse v. Copeland, 2 Gray, 302 ; Elliott v. Rhett, 5 Rich. 405, 418, 419; Dyer v. Sanford, 9 Metc. 395.   See also Addison v. Hack, 2 Gill, 221 ; 3 Toullier, Droit Civil Français, 506 ; 3 Burge, Col. & F. Law, 445 ; ante, p. 394.

Lalaure states the law thus : " Si je vous devois un droit de chemin à travers mon champ, et que vous me permissiez de bâtir sur le chemin ; ou d'enclorre le champ, alors vous perdriez la servitude." Traité des Servitudes, 80. See D. 8, 6, 8.

in holding that a right which is gained by occupancy should be lost by abandonment." The court put the following case by way of illustration: "Suppose A authorizes B, by express license, to build a house on B's own land close adjoining to some of the windows of A's house, so as to intercept part of the light, could he afterwards compel B to pull down the house again, simply by giving notice that he countermanded the license?"

The act authorized to be done in Winter *v.* Brockwell was for the owner of the servient estate to place a skylight thereon, adjoining the dominant estate, the effect of which was to prevent the light and air coming to the latter, as it had previously done; and it was held not to be revocable, after it had been executed.

6. The case of Morse *v.* Copeland was in many respects like that of Liggins *v.* Inge; and a similar doctrine was sustained in it. The plaintiff owned a mill and a right to flow the defendant's land. He gave the defendant oral permission to erect a dam on his own land, which excluded *the water of the plaintiff's pond from a [*562] portion of the land previously flowed, which dam he erected. The plaintiff also gave the defendant license to cut a trench from the part of the land thus cut off by the dam, across the plaintiff's land, and thereby to drain the water from that part of the defendant's land, which trench the defendant also constructed. A few years after this, the plaintiff revoked these licenses, and insisted upon having the dam removed and the ditch filled up. But the court held, that, as to the executed license under which the defendant had erected a dam on his own land, it was not revocable; but as to that which related to a ditch across the plaintiff's land, it might be revoked, and, in an action for keeping up the dam and ditch, judgment was rendered in accordance with this ruling.

7. The same doctrine is again repeated in Dyer *v.* Sanford, which related to an obstruction of an easement of light and

air, by an erection by the owner of the servient estate upon
his own land, by the license and permission of the owner of
the dominant estate. " It results from the consideration
that a license when executed is not revocable, and if the
obstruction be permanent in its nature, it does, *de facto*,
terminate the enjoyment of the easement. But the license
is for the specific act only, and if, when executed, it is of
such a nature as, *de facto*, to destroy the easement, but is
only temporary in its nature, or limited in its terms, then,
as the easement is not released when the obstruction, erected
in pursuance of such specific license, is removed, the owner
of the servient tenement cannot erect another obstruction
of the same or of a different kind without a new license."
But this statement of the law is accompanied by the remark : " We think there is a distinction between an executed license to impede or obstruct an easement of this
description, and an abandonment of the easement." So
that it seems that, whether the execution of the license is a
suspension merely, or a practical destruction of the
[*563] right of *easement, depends upon the nature and
effect of the act licensed to be done. And further-
more, such license, or the act done under it, can extend no
further than the right and interest of the licenser in the
estate, since the tenant of a term cannot bind the reversioner
by acts done by him while in possession of the premises as a
termor. Thus it is said in the case cited : " The license in
question, and the acts done under it, could not operate as a
release, because not in writing, nor as an abandonment,
because E. T. (the licenser) was not the owner of the inheritance, and had at most a right of dower in the premises,
and the occupation as guardian of her children, or otherwise." [1]

So if the act be to be done on a third person's estate by
the licensee, and the license be executed, it cannot be revoked.
Thus, one owning an aqueduct which extended across the

[1] Dyer *v.* Sanford, 9 Metc. 395.

land of a neighboring proprietor to his own, granted to a third person a right to draw water from it to be taken at a point within the grantor's land. He then gave the grantee of this right a license, by parol, to draw the water from the aqueduct at a point in the land of the adjacent owner, before it had reached the land of the grantor. The licensee having done as he was licensed to do, it was held that the licenser could not afterwards revoke the license.[1]

[1] Curtis *v.* Noonan, 10 Allen, 406.

*CHAPTER VI.

REPAIRS OF EASEMENTS AND REMEDY FOR INJURIES.

SECTION I.

REPAIRS OF EASEMENTS.

1. As a general proposition, whoever has an easement, like a right of way, for instance, in or over another's land, is the one to keep it in repair. He may not call upon the land-owner to make such repairs, unless bound to do so by covenant or prescription. And if a private way becomes founderous or impassable, the owner of the way has no right, in consequence thereof, to go upon other parts of the land over which it lies, unless the owner of the land is bound to make the repairs. Having such easement carries with it the right to make all necessary repairs at all reasonable times.[1]

[1] Com. Dig., *Chimin.* D. 6; Pomfret *v.* Ricroft, 1 Saund. 322; Duncan *v.* Louch, 6 Q. B. 904; Taylor *v.* Whitehead, Dougl. 745, 748; Garrard *v.* Cooke, 2 Bos. & P. N. R. 109; Prescott *v.* White, 21 Pick. 341; Peter *v.* Daniel, 5 C.

But if the way be over or across a watercourse, he has no right so to repair or maintain it as to obstruct the flow of the stream, and if he does, to the injury of the land above, he would be liable in damages.[1]

*2. Where one granted a lot of land having a [*565] well upon it, and, in his deed, reserved to himself, and to his heirs and assigns who might occupy a certain dwelling-house, "the right to take water freely from the well, &c., or from any other well which may be sunk there," it was held that the grantee was not bound to keep the well in repair, or to preserve its existence.[2]

But if the owner of the servient estate covenant to keep the easement in repair, he is not exonerated from the burden by the dominant one having actually repaired it himself, in one case for forty years.[3]

3. The grant of a right to build a dam and flow the grantor's land carries the right to erect and repair the dam and cleanse the pond, as occasion may require.[4]

The grantee of a way is the party who is to make as well as repair it.[5]

So where one granted to another the right to enjoy a certain strip of land, to be used as a way in connection with certain houses from a public highway, it was held to pass a right to lay down a flagstone, within this space, in front of one of those houses, for the accommodation thereof, it being a suitable mode of repairing the same, so that it should not be wet and dirty.[6]

B. 568; Prescott v. Williams, 5 Metc. 429; Doane v. Badger, 12 Mass. 65, 70; Jones v. Percival, 5 Pick. 485; Miller v. Bristol, 12 Pick. 550; 2 Fournel, Traité du Voisinage, 358; Liford's case, 11 Rep. 46, 52; Bullard v. Harrison, 4 Maule & S. 387, 393; Rider v. Smith, 3 T. R. 766; Com. Dig., Chimin, D. 6; Ayl. Pand. 307; Williams v. Safford, 7 Barb. 309; Robins v. Jones, C. B. 26 Law Rep. 291; Gillis v. Nelson, 16 Louis. An. 279.

[1] Haynes v. Burlington, 38 Verm. 360.
[2] Ballard v. Butler, 30 Me. 94.
[3] Holmes v. Buckley, 1 Eq. Cas. Abr. 27.
[4] Frailey v. Waters, 7 Penn. St. 221.
[5] Osborn v. Wise, 7 Carr. & P. 761.
[6] Gerrard v. Cooke, 2 Bos. & P. N. R. 109.

But where one had acquired a prescriptive right of way, by long-continued use and enjoyment, it was held that he did not thereby acquire a right to dig ditches in the [*566] servient *estate for the purpose of repairing the way, unless he had gained this right by use and enjoyment, as he had that of the way itself.[1]

M. Fournel states the French law upon the subject of the right to do acts upon the freehold of the servient tenement, by the way of repairing a way or an aqueduct, as being much more restricted than what might be done in the original construction of such way. He quotes the civil law: *Aliud est enim reficere, longe aliud facere.*[2]

4. In Liford's case, it is said : " The law giveth power to him who ought to repair a bridge to enter into the land, and to him who hath a conduit within the land of another to enter the land and mend it when cause requireth, as it was resolved in 9 Ed. IV. 35," where it was held that the right to scour and amend a trench was incident to a grant of a right to dig it in another's land for the purpose of drawing water through the same ;[3] and the same doctrine is sustained in Peter *v.* Daniel.[4]

5. The law upon the subject is thus stated by Mr. Burge:[5] " With the exception of the servitude *onus ferendi,* where the owner of the servient tenement is bound to repair that which is used for the support, the owner of the dominant tenement is bound to keep in repair the way or other means by which he uses the servitude. Thus the person entitled to a servitude of drain must at his own expense cleanse and repair it. So the dominant of a road must keep it in order for his own use, and any stipulation to the contrary imposes

---

[1] Capers *v.* M'Kee, 1 Strobh. 164.

[2] 2 Fournel, Traité du Voisinage, 362 ; 5 Duranton, Cours de Droit Français, 626 ; D. 43, 19, 3, 15.

[3] Liford's case, 11 Rep. 46, 52.

[4] Peter *v.* Daniel, 5 C. B. 568 ; 3 Toullier, Droit Civil Français, 508 ; D. 8, 4, 11, 1.

[5] 3 Burge, Col. & F. Law, 443.

a personal obligation superadded to the servitude. The owner of the dominant has the right, as a part of the *servitude, to perform at his own expense all [*567] such works as are necessary for preserving and making use of the servitude, and so he is entitled to have access to make the necessary repairs. The owner of the servient estate can do nothing to diminish the use or convenience of the servitude to the owner of the dominant. Nor can the owner of the dominant enlarge his use so as to increase the burden on the servient, unless, in so far as such change of use may be necessary in order to make the servitude effectual."

Though for the doctrine above stated Mr. Burge has chiefly cited authorities from the civil and Scotch law, it is apprehended that the rules here laid down are equally established as a part of the common law. One or two citations may be added to those above given, sustaining the views expressed by him. Thus Duranton, after saying that the owner of the dominant estate may do whatever is necessary to his enjoying a servitude upon another's tenement, adds, that this must be at his own charge, and not at that of the owner of the servient estate, since it is of the very nature of a servitude that he who has the right to it is the one to act, while the other is only to suffer and not to do.[1]

And, by the Scotch law, the servitude *onus ferendi* does not, as it did by the civil law, impose upon the servient estate the burden of maintaining the wall at his charge.[2]

6. Where the easement is of a character that a want of repair injuriously affects the owner of the servient land, it becomes not only the right but the duty of the owner of the easement to cause all necessary repairs to be made. As, for instance, if one has an aqueduct by pipes or a gutter across

[1] 5 Duranton, Cours de Droit Français, 619, 620; 3 Toullier, Droit Civil Français, 501; Ayl. Pand. 307, 309; Gillis *v.* Nelson, 16 La. An. 275.
[2] 3 Burge, Col. & F. Law, 404.

the land of another, he is bound to keep these in repair, so that the owner of the land shall not be damaged by the want of such repair.[1]

[*568]   *7. For the law relative to the repairs of party walls reference may be had to a former part of the work in which the subject is treated of.[2]

8. It may be observed, as a well-settled rule of the civil law, which would doubtless be regarded as a part of the common law, that, if a house, a wall, a water-spout, or anything of that kind with which or by which a servitude exists or is enjoyed, is destroyed, and the same is afterwards, within the period of prescription, reconstructed or restored, whatever may have been the servitudes connected therewith, they are, by such restoration, revived.[3]

SECTION II.

REMEDY AT LAW FOR INJURIES TO EASEMENTS.

1. Action lies for an injury to a right, though no damage.
2. Owner of easement not affected by suit between others.
3. Distinction in remedy for injury to private and public easement.
4. Action for injury to easement, Case and not Trespass.
5. When actions for such injury are local.
6. Any one in possession may have the action.
7. Right of easement not triable in ejectment.
8. Right of easement no bar to a real action.
9. When one liable for *continuing* a nuisance.
10. Norton *v.* Volentine.   Continuing nuisance to natural easement.
11. When notice necessary to sustain action for nuisance.
12. After easement destroyed, alienee of the estate not liable.
13. Lessor liable for nuisance on the demised estate.
14. Grantor with warranty, when liable for nuisance.
15. One who erects nuisance on a third person's land liable.
16. Of justifying under a right of easement for a trespass.

1. ALTHOUGH it is not proposed to dwell at any length

---

[1] Egremont *v.* Pulman, Mood. & M. 404 ; Bell *v.* Twentyman, 1 Q. B. 766.
[2] *Ante*, chap. 4, sect. 3, pp. *459, *472.
[3] Toullier, Droit Civil Français, 522 ; D. 8, 2, 20, 2.

upon the forms of pleading or rules of evidence applicable to
an alleged violation of a right of easement, there seems to
be an obvious propriety in treating briefly of the
remedy *which the law has provided to secure to [*569]
one the enjoyment of such a right, or an adequate
redress for being unlawfully deprived thereof. These remedies are either in equity or at common law, and may be considered separately.

Though it is, generally, true that, in order to maintain
an action at law for the recovery of damages, something
amounting to an actual loss or injury must be shown to
have been sustained on the part of the plaintiff, it is now
settled, as an elementary principle, that one having an incorporeal hereditament, like an easement, may maintain an
action to vindicate his claim to the same, if he can show a
violation of his right to enjoy it, although he may be unable
to show any actual damage or loss occasioned thereby. The
law, in order to protect him from a repetition of such acts
as might, in time, defeat or impair his right, will presume
damages to have resulted therefrom, and, by a rendition of a
judgment therefor, establish his right and protect it from interruption.[1] A writer in the Law Magazine and Review examines two or three leading English decisions upon the subject of when an action must, and when it may be maintained
for an injury to a *right*, and whether it must be brought
when the act is done which causes the damage, or it may be
delayed until the damage has actually been caused. This
bears, too, upon the question of the action being barred by
the statute of limitations.

The writer cites Nicklin *v.* Williams[2] and Bonomi *v.*
Backhouse,[3] both of which, it is said, were overruled in the

[1] *Ante,* p. *229, and cases cited. See also Ashby *v.* White, 2 Lord Raym.
938 ; Woodman *v.* Tufts, 9 N. H. 88 ; Northam *v.* Hurley, 1 Ellis & B. 665,
673 ; Tillotson *v.* Smith, 32 N. H. 90, where defendant turned a new stream into
an old one ; Smith L. Cas., 5th Am. ed. 105 *et seq.*

[2] Nicklin *v.* Williams, 10 Exch. 259.

[3] Bonomi *v.* Backhouse, E. B. & El. 622.

Court of Exchequer Chamber, revising the former cases,[1] whereby it was established, that it is the doing of damage to the owner of the surface by excavating for minerals under it by one who owns them, that gives the right of action, and not the excavation that may do such damage, if it has not yet actually caused it. And he adds, "This very important question is thus now settled upon true principles of justice, and, we may add, of expediency. It is better, both for owners of surface land and owners of mines, that the cause of action should accrue upon the happening of actual damage rather than upon an imaginary injury to a right."[2]

But it is still true, that an action will lie for a violation of a *right*, although no actual damage has been done. The rule given in this respect is, " whenever an act injures another's right, and would be evidence in future in favor of the wrong doer, an action may be maintained for an invasion of the right, without proof of any specific damage." [3]

2. Another circumstance, in connection with the vindication of rights of easements by actions at law, which has already been referred to, is that the claimant of such right would not be affected by any judgment which might be rendered in a real action brought by a stranger against the owner of the servient estate, to recover possession of the same.[4]

3. There is a clear and well-sustained distinction between a right to maintain an action for an infringement of one's right to use a private, and that of using a public way. In the latter, in order to maintain a personal action, the plaintiff must show special damages sustained by himself [*570] in *order to recover. In the former, he only need show the violation of a right.[5]

---

[1] Bonomi v. Backhouse, E. & B. & El. 646.

[2] 10 Law M. & R. 182.

[3] E. & B. & El. p. 657; Mellor v. Spateman, 1 Wms. Saund. 346 b ; 96 Eng. C. L. Rep. 659 note.

[4] Hancock v. Wentworth, 5 Metc. 446.

[5] Atkins v. Bordman, 2 Metc. 456, 469; Greasly v. Codling, 2 Bing. 263;

4. Where the action is to recover consequential damages for interfering with the plaintiff's right of easement, and not for an act done upon his own land, the form of the action is case, and trespass will not lie.[1]

5. If it be for obstructing a watercourse, it is local in its nature.[2] But where the act complained of is done in one county, but the injurious consequences thereof are felt in another, as, for instance, if one erect a dam in A, which flows back upon another's mill in B, the mill-owner may bring his action in the latter county.[3] So where the plaintiff's fishery in A was injured by a dam in B, it was held that the plaintiff might sue in either county, if either of the parties lived there.[4] If there are owners of a water-power upon opposite sides of a stream, the thread of the stream being the boundary line between their lands, they are tenants in common thereof, and if either draws or diverts more than his undivided half of the water, to the injury of his co-tenant, he would be liable to an action by the other owner therefor. But questions of difficulty have arisen as to the nature and form of the remedy in such case, and as to acquiring prescriptive rights by adverse enjoyment, where this dividing line is also the boundary line of two States, the period of prescription being different in different States. Thus in one case such stream divided Connecticut and Rhode Island, the time of prescription in the first State being fifteen years, and that in the other twenty years. The owner upon the Rhode Island side diverted the water from the upper of two dams on the stream, and did not return it again into the stream till it had passed by the lower of these dams.

In respect to the jurisdiction which should take cognizance

Hartshorn v. South Reading, 3 Allen, 501 ; Nash v. Peden, 1 Speers, 17 ; Sedgw. Damages, 141, et seq.

[1] Com. Dig., Action upon the Case for a Nuisance, A ; Baer v. Martin, 8 Blackf. 317.

[2] Mersey & Irwell Nav. Co. v. Douglass, 2 East, 497.

[3] Thompson v. Crocker, 9 Pick. 59 ; Sutton v. Clarke, 6 Taunt. 29 ; Worster v. Winnipiseogee Lake Co., 5 Fost. 525.

[4] Barden v. Crocker, 10 Pick. 383.

of this injury, the court held that an injury to an easement
by acts done in one State, may be sued for in that State,
though the principal estate be in another, as for obstructing
a way in A, which is appurtenant to an estate in B. In this
case, therefore, as the owner on the Connecticut side was injured by the act done by the other party on the Rhode Island
side, the former may bring his action in Rhode Island for the
injury thereby done. If, for instance, the owner on the Connecticut side instead of this were to obtain an injunction
against the owner upon the other side in the courts of that
State in respect to the canal by which he diverts the water,
it would be inoperative, and could not be enforced in Rhode
Island, it being a proceeding *quasi in rem*.

And it seems that one who is injured by such an act may
have his action, either where the act is done, or the consequential injury is suffered at his election. Nor could the
defendant to a suit in Rhode Island avail himself of the statute of limitation of Connecticut. The action, in this respect,
would be governed by the statute of the State in which the
action was prosecuted. So, in the courts of Rhode Island, the
parties would be governed as to what acts would give a prescriptive right by the law of Rhode Island, as, for instance, if
a mere occupation of a water privilege would give a prescriptive right to the enjoyment of it in Connecticut, it would not
justify the act done in Rhode Island, where, to gain such
right, requires that it should be by an adverse occupation
and enjoyment.[1]

6. Any one in possession of the premises to which an
easement belongs may have an action for an obstruction or
disturbance of enjoyment of the same.[2] Thus a tenant at
will may have such an action for disturbance of a right of
way or drain.[3] And if the same be an injury to the inheri-

[1] Stillman v. White Rock Co., 3 W. & Min. 538; Thompson v. Crocker, 9
Pick. 61; 3 Lion, 141; Borden v. Crocker, 10 Pick. 383; Bulwer's case, 7 Co.
1. See Rundle v. Delaware &c. Canal, 1 Wallace, Jr. 275; Farnum v. Blackstone
Canal, 1 Sum. 46.
[2] 3 Stephen, N. P. 2366; Com. Dig., *Action upon the Case for a Nuisance*, B.
[3] Foley v. Wyeth, 2 Allen, 135; Hastings v. Livermore, 7 Gray, 194.

tance, an action will also lie in favor of a reversioner.[1] What would constitute such an injury is considered, among many others, in the cases cited below.[2]

*7. An action of ejectment will not lie against [*571] one claiming an easement in a parcel of land, to try his right to enjoy the same.[3]

8. But the owner in fee of land may maintain a writ of entry to establish his title to the freehold against one having a prescriptive right of way over the same.[4]

9. In respect to who is liable to be sued on account of a nuisance to a private easement, the rule at common-law is thus stated : " An action of the case lies against him who erects a nuisance, and against him who continues a nuisance erected by another. The occupant, as well as the owner of the place, suppose a house or mill, erected to the nuisance of another, is liable in an action of the case, which may be brought by successive owners and occupants of the place where the injury is sustained. In short, the continuance, and every use of that which is in its erection and use a nuisance, is a new nuisance, for which the party injured has a remedy for his damages. And although, after judgment, and damages recovered in an action for erecting a nuisance, another action is not to be maintained for the *erection*, yet another action will lie for the continuance of the same nuisance." [5] And a party aggrieved may sue the one creating or the one continuing a nuisance, at his election.[6]

10. A similar doctrine is maintained in Norton *v.* Volen-

---

[1] Hastings *v.* Livermore, 7 Gray, 194; Com. Dig., *Action upon the Case for a Nuisance*, B ; Kidgill *v.* Moor, 9 C. B. 364; Metropolitan Association, &c. *v.* Petch, 5 C. B. N. S. 504 ; Tinsman *v.* Belvidere, &c. R. R. Co., 1 Dutch. 255 ; Brown *v.* Bowen, 30 N. Y. 519.

[2] Baxter *v.* Taylor, 4 Barnew. & Ad. 72; Tucker *v.* Newman, 11 Adolph. & E. 40 ; Shadwell *v.* Hutchinson, 3 Carr. & P. 615; Dobson *v.* Blackmore, 9 Q. B. 991 ; Sedgw. Damages, 139 *et seq.*

[3] Child *v.* Chappell, 6 Seld. 246, 251 ; Wilklow *v.* Lane, 37 Barb. 244 ; Caldwell *v.* Fulton, 31 Penn. 483 ; Clement *v.* Youngman, 40 Penn. 341.

[4] Morgan *v.* Moore, 3 Gray, 319.

[5] Staple *v.* Spring, 10 Mass. 72, 74 ; Sedgw. Damages, 144.

[6] Eastman *v.* Company, &c. 44 N. H. 158, 159.

tine, whereby a purchaser of an estate upon which there is a subsisting nuisance affecting an easement upon an adjoining estate, was held liable for continuing the same, without any previous notice or request to remove it. The subject-matter, however, of the injury there, was an interruption of the natural flow of a stream by means of the nuisance complained of.[1]

[*572]   *11. The rule would doubtless be uniform in respect to the liability of any purchaser or occupant of an estate, for continuing a nuisance thereon, which had been erected by a previous owner or occupant.[2] But there are cases where it has been held, that, before such purchaser can be made liable, he must be notified, and requested to abate or remove the nuisance. The rule, as laid down in Penruddock's case,[3] is a general one, that such purchaser would not be liable for simply continuing a structure which causes a nuisance, until after notice and request to remove it. And such seems to be recognized as law in the cases of Johnson v. Lewis,[4] Pillsbury v. Moore,[5] Plumer v. Harper,[6] and Woodman v. Tufts.[7] And the case of Norton v. Volentine, under its circumstances, can hardly be considered as opposed to these cases, for the judge, in giving the opinion, says : "If it were necessary to decide this case upon this point, I am not at present prepared to go the length of the old cases, nor that in Connecticut, still less am I prepared to say they are not well founded.[8]

In Michigan, however, the court doubt if it is necessary to notify the purchaser of what constitutes an existing nuisance

[1] Norton v. Volentine, 14 Vt. 239.

[2] Sedgw. Damages, 145 ; 2 Hilliard, Torts, 90 ; Brady v. Weeks, 3 Barb. 157 ; Bemis v. Clark, 11 Pick. 452, 485.

[3] Penruddock's case, 5 Rep. 101.   [4] Johnson v. Lewis, 13 Conn. 303.

[5] Pillsbury v. Moore, 44 Me. 154.

[6] Plumer v. Harper, 3 N. H. 88. See also Carleton v. Redington, 1 Fost. 291 ; Eastman v. Company, 44 N. H. 156 ; Snow v. Cowles, 2 Foster, 296.

[7] Woodman v. Tufts, 9 N. H. 88.

[8] Norton v. Volentine, 14 Vt. 239, 245. See also Salmon v. Bensley, Ry. & M. 189, that notice to one tenant binds his successor.

to another, before he would be liable to an action for continuing it. But they hold that if such notice had been given, and then the owner of the land affected by the nuisance were to convey it to a third party, it would not be necessary for him to give a new notice before bringing his action for such continuance of the nuisance.[1]

So if the party who creates the nuisance continues it after the owner of the land which is injured by it has conveyed it to a third person, such purchaser has no occasion to notify him of its being a nuisance before commencing an action for continuing it.[2]

But it was held in Maryland, that if one buys land affected by a nuisance, he must give notice to the party maintaining it, before he can bring his action for continuing it.[3]

And the reader will find a collection of American cases upon the subject in a note to the case of Todd v. Flight.[4]

12. But where the owner of the servient estate destroys the subject-matter of the easement, as, for instance, fills up the well from which the dominant drew water, or builds buildings over it so that it cannot be reached, and then conveys it to a stranger, the latter would not be liable to the owner of the dominant estate for the loss of the easement. It is gone before he becomes the owner.[5]

*13. If the owner of an estate erect a nuisance [*573] thereon to the injury of a neighboring estate, and demise it in that condition, he will still continue liable if the nuisance is continued by his tenant.[6]

14. The same rule would apply if the vendor conveyed the premises with covenants of warranty; he would be liable

---

[1] Caldwell v. Gale, 11 Mich. 77.

[2] Eastman v. Company, 44 N. H. 157 ; Curtice v. Thompson, 19 N. H. 471.

[3] Pickett v. Condon, 18 Md. 417.

[4] Todd v. Flight, 9 C. B. N. S., Am. ed. 377, 390.

[5] Ballard v. Butler, 30 Me. 94.

[6] Fish v. Dodge, 4 Denio, 311 ; Rosewell v. Prior, 1 Lord Raym. 713. See Todd v. Flight, 9 C. B. N. S. 377, and note to Am. ed. ; Sedgw. Damages, 145.

for a continuance of the nuisance subsequently to the conveyance.[1]

15. And one who erects a nuisance to another's estate would be liable for a continuance of the same, though the erection were upon land not belonging to the defendant, and he could not abate or remove the same without being a trespasser.[2]

16. While the owner of an easement may have an action against the owner of an adjacent estate for a disturbance thereof created upon his own premises, it often occurs that one undertakes to justify acts which would otherwise be unlawful, as injuriously affecting another's possession, on the ground that he had a right to do so under and by virtue of a right of easement. And where, to an action for such injury, the defendant justifies in his plea, great particularity and precision are required in stating, for instance, the right of way under which the defendant alleges a right to enter upon the close of the plaintiff.

Illustrations of this are found in Wright v. Rattray[3] and Slowman v. West.[4] In the first of these it was held, that, if the way be claimed by prescription, it must be set out in the same manner as if it had been by grant. Thus, if one justify, under a right of way from A over B and C [*574] *to D, he would not sustain his plea of a right of way over B, by showing a prescriptive right of way from A to C, which does not extend to D. But had he set up a claim of a way from A over B *towards* D, whether this would have amounted to a justification or not, is left doubtful. In the other, Doddridge, J. puts this case: "If a man have a right of way from his house to the church, and the close next his house, over which the way leads, is his own, he cannot prescribe that he has a right of way *from* his

---

1 Waggoner v. Jermaine, 3 Denio, 306, explaining Blunt v. Aikin, 15 Wend. 522 ; Sedgw. Damages, 145 ; 2 Hilliard, Torts, 91.

2 Thompson v. Gibson, 7 Mees. & W 456 ; Smith v. Elliott, 9 Penn. St. 345.

3 Wright v. Rattray, 1 East, 377.

4 Slowman v. West, Palm. 387.

house to the church, because he cannot prescribe for a way over his own land."

And the more recent case of Colchester v. Roberts is equally definite and precise in the application of these rules. The action was trepass *qu. cl.* The defendant pleaded a right of way from a highway over the plaintiff's close, to his house, by having enjoyed the same for twenty years. The plaintiff replied, that such enjoyment had been by plaintiff's leave and license. On the trial it was proved that the defendant owned a close, R, to reach which he had to go from his house over the plaintiff's close and across a highway to the same. The plaintiff showed that the defendant had had leave and license to go from his house to the highway, and thence where he pleased, without going to his close R. But it was held that the replication did not meet the defendant's plea, for he might have a right of way to his close A, whereby he might go to and cross the highway, and another to the highway, and not to go to his close R, but to some other place on the highway, or to which the highway leads, and that the latter way, by license, was no answer to the right set up to go to R by passing to and across the highway. The general right of way *to* the road and thence to all other places included a right to go to R. The traverse, therefore, by the replication, would include the right of going to the highway, and thence to R, and as the case finds the defendant had the last-mentioned *way, and as he [*575] had it without leave and license of the plaintiff, the replication was not sustained.[1]

So where defendant to an action of trespass pleaded a right of way on foot and with horses, cattle, carts, wagons, and other carriages, for the convenient occupation of his close K, the jury found he only had a right to cart wood and timber over plaintiff's close. It was held that the plaintiff was entitled to a general verdict, for it was not averred

---

[1] Colchester v. Roberts, 4 Mees. & W. 769.

in the plea that he was using the way to carry wood or timber on the occasion charged in the declaration.[1]

SECTION III.

REMEDY IN EQUITY FOR INJURIES TO EASEMENTS.

1. Where a bill in equity for an injunction lies.
2. To what class of injuries this applies.
3. Where courts restrain public nuisances.
4. Injunction not granted to individuals for public nuisance.
5. Granting injunction a discretionary power.
6. Power of courts of equity over nuisances.
7. Cases where this power has been applied.
8. Barrow v. Richard. Equity interposes where the law cannot.
9, 10. Where equity interposes, though title doubtful.
11. Where equity will not interpose till right settled at law.
12. Statute proceedings for abating private nuisances.

1. BESIDES his remedy by action at common law, the owner of an easement may, as a general proposition, not only seek redress for an infringement of his right to the same through a court of equity, but may prevent the same, when threatened, by an application to that court for an injunction to that effect. If the title of the plaintiff, in such case, is in controversy, the court will not ordinarily [*576] *interpose by way of injunction until the same has been established at law, unless the injury to be done by the threatened act is of a nature to require immediate interference in order to prevent great and permanent mischief.

The language of Story, in his Equity Jurisprudence, upon the subject is this: " In regard to private nuisances, the interference of courts of equity, by way of injunction, is undoubtedly founded upon the ground of restraining irreparable mischief, or of suppressing oppressive and interminable

---

[1] Higham v. Rabett, 5 Bing. N. C. 622. See Knight v. Woore, 3 Bing. N. C. 3.

litigation, or of preventing multiplicity of suits. It is not every case which will furnish a right of action against a party for a nuisance which will justify the interposition of courts of equity to redress the injury or remove the annoyance. But there must be such an injury as from its nature is not susceptible of being adequately compensated by damages at law, or such as, from its continuance •or permanent mischief, must occasion a constantly recurring grievance which cannot be otherwise prevented but by an injunction. A mere diminution of the value of property by the nuisance, without irreparable mischief, will not furnish any foundation for equitable relief. On the other hand, where the injury is irreparable, as where loss of health, loss of trade, destruction of the means of subsistence, or permanent ruin to property may or will ensue from the wrongful act of erection ; in every such case courts of equity will interfere by injunction in furtherance of justice and the violated rights of the party. Thus, for example, where a party builds so near the house of another as to darken his windows, against the clear rights of the latter, either by contract or by ancient possession, courts of equity will interfere by injunction to prevent the nuisance, as well as to remedy it, if already done, although an action for damages would lie at law, for the latter can, in no just sense, be deemed an adequate relief in such a case." [1]

And equity often interposes to protect easements and enforce their enjoyment where there is no adequate remedy at law, by reason of the want of privity between the owners of the estates alleged to be dominant and servient to each other. And this is, especially, true of that class of easements which have been called equitable.[2]

*2. Among the cases mentioned as those where [*577]

---

[1] 2 Story, Eq. Jurisp., Redfield's ed., §§ 925, 926 ; 1 Fonbl. Eq., Laussat's ed., 3, note.

[2] Parker v. Nightingale, 6 Allen, 341 ; Gibert v. Peteler, 38 Barb. 513 ; Brouwer v. Jones, 23 Barb. 153 ; Hubbell v. Warren, 8 Allen, 173 ; Tallmadge v. East River Bank, 26 N. Y. 105. Ante, p. *63, and cases cited.

courts of equity will interpose for the protection of parties, are obstructions to watercourses, the diversion of streams from mills, and pulling down of the banks of rivers, and thereby exposing adjacent lands to inundation, or adjacent mills to destruction, and digging in one's soil so as to endanger a neighbor's buildings. So where easements or servitudes are annexed to private estates.[1]

3. They can interpose in case of public nuisances, where courts of law cannot, to restrain and prevent them when threatened, or if they are in progress, as well as to abate those already existing.[2]

4. But though a bill in equity will lie to restrain a permanent and continuous injury to a private easement, courts will not in that manner aid an individual to sustain his right to enjoy a public easement, when the injury of which he complains affects the whole community.[3]

In Rhea v. Forsyth the court say : " Where the plaintiff's right has not been established at law, or is not clear, but is questioned on every ground on which he puts it, not only by the answer of the defendant, but by proofs in the cause, he is not entitled to remedy by injunction."[4]

5. But whether the court will exercise this power of granting an injunction in any given case or not, is within the sound discretion of the court, and it will be withheld if it will operate oppressively or inequitably, or contrary to the real justice of the case. Thus, where the owner of a building encouraged the owner of adjoining land to build [*578] thereon, * the court will not stop the work on the ground that it is likely to do an injury to the premises of the other party.[5]

---

[1] 2 Story, Eq. Jurisp., Redfield's ed., §§ 927, 927 a; Bardwell v. Ames, 22 Pick. 332, 353 ; Stevens v. Stevens, 11 Metc. 251.

[2] 2 Story, Eq. Jurisp., Redfield's ed. §§ 924, 924 a. See 2 Green, Ch. 139, note.

[3] Hartshorn v. South Reading, 3 Allen, 501 ; Brainard v. Conn. Riv. R. R. Co., 7 Cush. 506.

[4] Rhea v. Forsyth, 36 Penn. St. 503, 507 ; King v. M'Cully, 38 Penn. St. 76 ; Coe v. Lake Co., 37 N. H. 254.

[5] 2 Story, Eq. Jur., § 959 a ; 1 Fonbl. Eq., Laussat's ed. 49, note ; Williams

6. In a note to Fonblanque's Equity, just cited, it is said: "In cases of private nuisance, chancery has a concurrent jurisdiction with courts of law.[1] It can order them to be abated, as well as restrain them from being erected. On motion, the court will sometimes order a thing going on to be stayed. But it will never order it to be pulled down, without first hearing the opposite party.[2] But the cases in which chancery has interfered by injunction to prevent or remove a private nuisance are those in which the nuisance has been erected to the prejudice or annoyance of a right which the other party had long previously enjoyed. It must be a strong and mischievous case of pressing necessity, or the right must have been previously established at law."[3] In the case of Earle v. De Hart the Chancellor says: "The complainant is entitled to have the obstruction removed. There is no reason why the court should not exercise a power to abate as well as prevent the erection of nuisances, in clear cases."

So equity may interpose and abate a dam which causes an injury to another's land, if erected or maintained without right.[4] Or it may suppress a nuisance like the corrupting of the waters of a stream, at the prayer of an injured party.[5]

7. The case of Van Bergen v. Van Bergen was that of a mill, where the plaintiff alleged that the defendant flowed back water to interrupt its use. But the court refused to grant an injunction, first, because the plaintiff had an ade-

v. Jersey, 1 Craig & P. 91. See Short v. Taylor & Anonymous, 2 Eq. Cas. Abr. 522.

[1] Gardner v. Village of Newburgh, 2 Johns. Ch. 162; Van Bergen v. Van Bergen, Ibid. 272.

[2] Van Bergen v. Van Bergen, supra; Earle v. De Hart, 1 Beasl. 280, 287; Hammond v. Fuller, 1 Paige, 197. See cases collected, 2 Green, Ch. 136, note.

[3] Van Bergen v. Van Bergen, 3 Johns. Ch. 282; Reid v. Gifford, 6 Johns. Ch. 19. See Wood v. Sutcliff, 8 Eng. L. & Eq. 217; Burden v. Stein, 27 Ala. 104; Corning v. Lowerre, 6 Johns. Ch. 439; Back v. Stacy, 2 Russ. 121.

[4] Ackerman v. Horicon Co., 16 Wisc. 154; Sheldon v. Rockwell, 9 Wisc. 166; Ang. W. C. §§ 444, 445.

[5] Holsman v. Boiling Spring Co., 1 M'Cart. 342. See Lewis v. Stein, 16 Ala. 214.

quate remedy at law; and his right, moreover, at law was in dispute. And it appeared, besides, that the plaintiff actually erected his mill after the defendant had erected [*579] the * dam complained of, and he ought to settle his legal rights in respect to the same before the court could properly be called on to interpose to prevent the defendant in the use of his dam.[1]

In Burwell v. Hobson the defendant undertook to build a dike and embankment along the margin of a stream, the effect of which would be to throw the water thereof upon the land of the plaintiff on the opposite side of the stream, and the court granted the injunction prayed for.[2]

Where one had an easement to lay logs, &c. upon another's land as a mill-yard, and the owner of the land obstructed the use of the same by placing gravel upon the land, the court granted an injunction, and decreed. damages to the plaintiff for the injuries thereby sustained.[3]

So where one in mining dug so near another's dwelling-house as to endanger the same by weakening its lateral support by the natural soil, the court restrained any further excavation by injunction.[4]

So courts of equity will restrain one mill-owner from unlawfully obstructing the mill-privilege of another.[5]

In Corning v. Lowerre, above cited, the injury complained of and enjoined was the building of a house upon a street, which materially injured the plaintiffs, as owners of lots adjoining the same upon the street.[6]

And in Attorney-General v. Nichol, the court held that they would interpose to prevent one man from obstructing the light of another, where, from the circumstances of en-

1 See Simpson v. Justice, 8 Ired. Eq. 115.
2 Burwell v. Hobson 12 Gratt. 322, 332.
3 Gurney v. Ford, 2 Allen, 576; Richardson v. Pond, 15 Gray.
4 Hunt v. Peake, Johns. Ch. (Eng.) 705.
5 Crittenden v. Field, 8 Gray, 621; Bemis v. Upham, 13 Pick. 169; Ballou v. Hopkinton, 4 Gray, 324; Hill v. Sayles, 12 Cush. 454.
6 Corning v. Lowerre, 6 Johns. Ch. 439. See.Hills v. Miller, 3 Paige, 254.

joyment, usage, or interest, some contract can be implied that the adverse party should not build upon the premises on which he has erected the obstruction, if the *consequences of the act of obstruction appear to [*580] be such as should not only be redressed, but prevented. But they will not do this upon every degree of darkening one's lights and windows, though ancient, nor in every case where an action upon the case could be sustained.[1]

8. On the other hand, equity will sometimes interpose to prevent the doing of an act injurious to the plaintiff's estate, although he would be without remedy for the injury by an action at common law. Thus in the case of Barrow v. Richard, where M., having a large parcel of land in a city, cut it up into building-lots, and sold them to sundry individuals, taking a covenant in the deed of each that no offensive trade should be carried on in the premises. The plaintiff was one of these purchasers, and the defendant another. The defendant having begun to carry on such a business, it was held that, upon the plaintiff's complaint, the court would enjoin him, although the plaintiff could not maintain an action upon the covenant into which the defendant had entered with the vendor.[2]

9. But in Biddle v. Ash the court refused to restrain one from building so as to stop the plaintiff's lights, because the title was doubtful and in controversy, though they held that, if the plaintiff were to make out a case of clear right by contract or ancient possession, they would enjoin against the erection of any nuisance which should darken his lights or interfere with his right of way.[3]

10. Accordingly the court, in Robeson v. Pittenger,[4] granted an injunction against building a wall which dark-

[1] Attorney-General v. Nichol, 16 Ves. 338.
[2] Barrow v. Richard, 8 Paige, 351 ; Trustees, &c. of Watertown v. Cowen, 4 Paige, 510, 514 ; Bedford v. Trustees of British Museum, 2 Mylne & K. 552. See ante, p. *63, *576.
[3] Biddle v. Ash, 2 Ashm. 211.
[4] Robeson v. Pittenger, 1 Green, Ch. 57.

ened the lights of the plaintiff. And in Shields *v.* Arndt [1]
they granted a like injunction, to prevent the diver-
[*581] sion of *the water of a stream, and that without
first having the title of the party to do so tried at
law, the right claimed by the plaintiff having been long
enjoyed. They recognize, however, the ordinary rule to be,
to have questions of doubtful title settled at law before
equity will interpose by way of injunction.

11. But if the injury be a reversionary one, and is not in
its nature irreparable, or can be compensated in damages,
the court will not grant an injunction. Nor will they where
the plaintiff's title is doubtful, and there is no danger of
irreparable mischief therefrom, until after an issue of fact
tried at law.[2]

12. In Massachusetts there is provision made by statute
that, after a judgment upon proceedings at common law for
the recovery of damages for a private nuisance, the court
may issue a warrant to an officer, authorizing him to abate
and remove the nuisance, at the expense of the defendant.
And in this the statute is little more than carrying out the
principle of the common law.[3]

In South Carolina there is a statute authorizing certain
authorities to cause dams or embankments to be abated,
which one may erect upon his own land, across streams,
which prevent the natural flow of the water in the same, to
the injury of another's land, above such dam, unless the
owner of such dam or embankment shall have made an
artificial drain on his own land, and kept the same in repair,
suitable to draw off such water into the natural stream.
These regulations have reference to the culture of rice-
swamps in that State.[4]

---

[1] Shields *v.* Arndt, 3 Green, Ch. 234, 245, 246.

[2] Ingraham *v.* Dunnell, 5 Metc. 118 ; Dana *v.* Valentine, 5 Metc. 8.

[3] Mass. Gen. St., c. 139 ; Stevens *v.* Stevens, 11 Metc. 251 ; Baten's case, 9
Rep. 55. See Bemis *v.* Clark, 11 Pick. 452.

[4] Brisbane *v.* O'Neall, 3 Strobh. 348.

*SECTION IV.   [*582]

REMEDY BY ABATEMENT FOR INJURIES TO EASEMENTS.

1. General right of party injured to abate a nuisance.
2. Care in one abating not to exceed his right to do so.
3. Greenslade v. Halliday.   Case of exceeding this right.
4. One having the right may do it effectually.
5. Abating a mill-dam in part, though spoiling the privilege.
6. One may not injure third parties to protect his own estate.
7. Within what time the right of abatement is to be exercised.
8. Of the effect of danger to the peace in abating a nuisance.
9. Abatement no bar to an action for the nuisance.

1. In cases of violation of a right like that of an easement, by the wrongful acts of another in erecting upon his own land that which causes such injury, the party whose right is thereby invaded is not obliged to seek his redress by a suit at law, or proceedings in equity, but may vindicate the same by his own act, by entering upon the land of such wrong-doer; and *abating*, as it is called, the cause of such injury.   The language of Coke is : " Note, reader, there are two ways to redress a nuisance, — one by action ; and that is to recover damages, and have judgment that the nuisance shall be removed, cast down, or abated, as the case requireth ; or the party grieved may enter and abate the nuisance himself, as it appeareth by 17 Edw. III. 44 and 9 Edw. IV. 35." [1]

2. But the party exercising this right of abating a nuisance to his property must be careful not to exceed the right by doing more than he is justified to do.   Thus, one *injured in his property by another raising his dam [*583] higher than he had a right to do, and thereby flowing

[1] Baten's case, 9 Rep. 55 ; Perry v. Fitzhowe, 8 Q. B. 757 ; Penruddock's case, 5 Rep. 101 ; Great Falls Co. v. Worster, 15 N. H. 412; Adams v. Barney, 25 Vt. 225 ; Amick v. Tharp, 13 Gratt. 564, 567 ; Rex v. Rosewell, 2 Salk. 459; *ante*, chap. 3, sect. 5, pl. 14 ; 2 Rolle, Abr., *Nuisance*, S ; Raikes v. Townsend, 2 Smith, 9 ; Com. Dig., *Action on the Case for a Nuisance*, D. 4 ; Rhea v. Forsyth, 37 Penn. St. 503.

back water upon the same, may enter upon the premises of
the owner of the dam, and abate the same to its proper
height. But he may not abate it altogether, nor beyond
what is necessary to reduce the flowing to its proper limits ;
and the same rule applies to all cases of abating nuisances
by the party's own act.[1]

3. Thus, in Greenslade v. Halliday, one had a right to
divert the water of a stream for the purpose of irrigating his
land, by placing loose stones or a board across the stream.
He drove stakes in the stream to support the board more
firmly than it had been previously done, but which he had no
right to do ; and another, who was interested in the water,
entered upon the premises, and removed the stakes and the
board ; and it was held that he was liable for the removal
of the board, though he might have removed the stakes.

So in Dyer v. Depui, one having erected a house so high
as to obstruct the ancient windows of another, it was held
that the latter might abate so much of the house as obstructed his lights, but could not destroy the entire house.[2]

But the party will not be justified in abating by his own
act an erection upon his neighbor's land, until he shall have
actually been injured by it. It is not enough that he
apprehends the structure will injure him, or that the one
erecting it intends to use it so as to injure him
[*584]   *in the enjoyment of his estate. He must wait until
it has begun to injure him before he can enter upon
his neighbor's land to abate it.[3]

[1] Dyer v. Depui, 5 Whart. 584; Heath v. Williams, 25 Me. 209 ; Jewell
v. Gardiner, 12 Mass. 311 ; Hodges v. Raymond, 9 Mass. 316 ; Greenslade v.
Halliday, 6 Bing. 379 ; Colburn v. Richards, 13 Mass. 420 ; Gates v. Blincoe,
2 Dana, 158 ; Prescott v. Williams, 5 Metc. 429 ; Prescott v. White, 21 Pick.
341 ; Rex v. Pappineau, Strange, 686 ; Perry v. Fitzhowe, 8 Q. B. 757 ; James
v. Hayward, W. Jones, 221, 222 ; Rex v. Rosewell, 2 Salk. 459 ; Mason v.
Cæsar, 2 Mod. 65 ; Davies v. Williams, 16 Q. B. 546 ; Moffett v. Brewer, 1
Green, Iowa, 348 ; Elliot v. Fitchburg R. R. Co., 10 Cush. 191 ; Wright v.
Moore, 38 Ala. 599.

[2] See also Rex v. Pappineau, supra.

[3] Norris v. Baker, 1 Rolle, 393 ; Jones v. Powell, Palm. 536.

Though if his neighbor erects his house with eaves projecting over his land, he need not wait till the rain shall have actually fallen upon his neighbor's roof, and been thereby thrown upon his land, before he may abate the part that projects over his land.[1]

4. But if one having a right of easement in another's premises unlawfully extends the use of the same, or uses it in connection with rights not belonging to them, the owner of the tenement may stop the excess of such use ; and if he cannot do this without stopping its use altogether, he may do so, until a separation of the lawful from the unlawful use can be made, and the illegal part is stopped by itself.[2]

So if the branches of a tree growing in one's land extend beyond the line of the same, and over his neighbor's land, the latter may cut them off so far as they extend over his land.[3]

5. And this doctrine of the right of abating a nuisance by one's own act was applied in the case of two owners of a mill-privilege divided by the thread of the stream, where one of them erected a dam across the entire stream. It was held that the owner of the land upon the other side of the thread of the stream might abate so much of the dam as stood upon his land.[4]

If in abating the dam upon his own land he do no more than is necessary to remove it, but the effect is to have the whole water of the pond escape, and the other part of the *dam to fall, he would not be responsible for [*585] these consequences. And it is said: " So if one erects a wall upon his own land and the land of his neighbor, and the neighbor pulls down the wall upon his land, and thereupon all the wall falleth down, this is lawful." [5]

[1] Penruddock's case, 5 Rep. 101.

[2] Elliott v. Rhett, 5 Rich. 405, 421. See ante, as to lights, p. *540.

[3] 3 Sharsw. Black. Comm. 5, and cases cited.

[4] Adams v. Barney, 25 Vt. 225 ; Merritt v. Parker, Coxe, 460 ; Ang. Watercourses, § 332.

[5] Wigford v. Gill, Cro. Eliz. 269.

6. Upon the same principle, one may protect his property against being overflowed by the unlawful act of another, by erecting embankments along the stream, provided by so doing he does not injure the land of a third party, who took no part in causing such overflowing. "But," says Daniel, J., in Amick v. Tharp, "The circumstances which justify a resort to counter works, which must result in damage to the property of the wrong-doer, are by no means clearly defined." In that case, the city had turned the course of a spring on to the defendant's land, which he stopped, and thereby caused the water to set back upon the plaintiff's land ; and for this the defendant was held liable.[1]

7. The court in Iowa held, in the case of Moffit v. Brewer, that, in order to justify one in going upon another's land to abate a nuisance, he must do it within a reasonable time after the nuisance was created, or began to operate as a nuisance upon him ; and if he forebore to exercise the right within such reasonable time, his only remedy would be by a resort to legal proceedings, though they add, upon the point, "We have very little law before us."[2]

'8. And in Perry v. Fitzhowe the court held, that, if a dwelling-house constitutes a nuisance to a commoner, though he might abate it if unoccupied, he might not do so while actually occupied by a family, because of the almost [*586] *necessary risk of life and breach of the peace. And it would seem, moreover, that, if the nuisance complained of had been erected by another person than the occupant thereof, the party thereby injured should give notice to the owner, and request him to abate it, before he might actually proceed to abate it himself.[3]

[1] Amick v. Tharp, 13 Gratt. 567.

[2] Moffit v. Brewer, 1 Green, Iowa, 348, 351. See Bract., fol. 233, § 1.

The language of Bracton is : "Ea vero quæ sic levata sunt ad nocumentum injuriosum, vel prostrata vel demollita statim et recenter flagrante maleficio (sicut aliis disseysinis) demolliri possunt et prosterni vel relevari et reparari si quereus ad hoc sufficiat."

[3] Perry v. Fitzhowe, 8 Q. B. 757, 776 ; Davies v. Williams, 16 Q. B. 546, 556 ; Jones v. Williams, 11 Mees. & W. 176, 182.

SECT. 4.]   REMEDY BY ABATEMENT FOR INJURIES.   679

The rules upon this subject, as stated by writers upon the French and civil law, may be briefly alluded to in this connection, as they throw light upon some parts of the common law.

The French and civil law apply the doctrine of prescription to the case of losing, in the same way as in gaining, a servitude, with the exception that, by the Code Napoleon, thirty years is the uniform period which will operate to extinguish a servitude by non-user. Extinguishment in such a case rests upon a presumed abandonment of the right. But this presumption may be met by showing that the cesser to use was the result of obstacles thrown in the way of such use without the fault of the owner, which had rendered the enjoyment of the right impossible. By the Roman law, if the enjoyment of a servitude were suspended by obstacles which the owner thereof could not prevent, it revived again, and became re-established, when the premises were restored to their former condition. And Lalaure, a French writer of high authority, illustrates the proposition by supposing three tenements. The first acquires, by grant from the third, an easement of view in favor of his tenement over and across that of the third, there being nothing at the time upon the intermediate estate to prevent the owner of the first enjoying this right of prospect across the third. The owner of the second estate then erects upon the same a house so high as wholly to obstruct the view of the first in the direction of the third, whereupon the third erects a *house upon his estate; and this state of things [*587] continues for thirty-one years, when the intermediate house is destroyed by fire. The owner of the first then insists upon his right of servitude of prospect over the third estate. The question raised is, whether this right has not been lost by cesser of enjoyment for thirty years. Lalaure and Domat insist that it was not lost, the obstacle which prevented such enjoyment having been interposed by the act of a third party, which the owner

could not control.   But M. Toullier maintains that it was
laches on the part of the first owner in not having obtained
command of the second tenement, so as to enjoy what he
had purchased of the third, and that if he allowed this to
continue for the term of thirty years, he would lose the
right by prescription.[1]

Abandonment is to be presumed where the owner of
a right has neglected to use it while at liberty to do so.
And if the servitude be a discontinuous one, like that of
a way or a right to draw water, the time from which prescription runs is from the last act of user done under it.   If
the servitude be a continuous one, like that of eaves'
drip or of prospect, the time of prescription runs from the
doing of some act which conflicts with the right of servitude.[2]

Where the interruption of the enjoyment of a right of
servitude is caused by the act of God, and the capacity of
enjoyment is again restored, that the right will revive is a
doctrine both of the Roman and French laws.   Thus, where
a spring, from which the dominant estate drew water in
the servient land, became dry, and after a lapse of years
began to flow again, prescription would not bar the right
during this suspension.   So where the servient estate
across which was the servitude became inundated by the
waters of the sea, and submerged, and after a course of
years the waters receded again, the same principle was
applied.[3]

[*588]   *On the other hand, if one own a house with a
servitude of prospect or right of view belonging to
it, and the same is burned, and the owner of the adjacent
estate build thereon so as to obscure this view, and after
thirty years the first owner rebuilds his house, the servitude

[1] 3 Toullier, Droit Civil Français, 524, 526, 533 ; Lalaure, Traité des Servitudes, 71, 72 ; Domat, B. 1, tit. 12, § 6, Art. 4.
[2] 3 Toullier, Droit Civil Français, 528, 529.
[3] Ibid. 530 – 532.

belonging to the first will have been lost. His forbearing to do what he might have done is a presumed abandonment of the right.[1]

In respect to what acts one must do in order to retain his right of servitude, and prevent it being barred by a presumed abandonment, several rules have been applied. In the first place, if he does more than he has a right to do under the servitude, and it is of the same character in matter and manner with what he has a right to do, it will save the servitude, upon the ground that the greater always contains the less. Thus if one has a right of footway, and passes in a carriage, or has a right to water five cattle, and drives ten to the spring to drink, he will thereby save the right so far as it lawfully belongs to him. On the other hand, if the servitude is in its nature separable into what is greater or less in its parts, and one, possessed of the greater, use only the less, for the period of prescription, he will lose the excess over and beyond what he has during that time exercised and enjoyed. If one has a right to draw water from another's well at all times, both in the day and night, and forbears to use it during the night for thirty years, he may still retain the servitude of drawing during the day, but lose it for other periods.[2]

The mode of using a right of servitude often becomes essential in determining how far one has retained it. The civil law is thus stated : " Itaque differentia est inter aliud facere et plus facere, qui aliud facit, servitutem amittit non utendo, qui plus facit, servitutem non amittit." This applies where the servitude is not apparent and continuous, and the same *is exercised in a manner different [*589] from what one has a right to do. In such case, he loses his right by lapse of time. He did not do what he had a right to do, but something else. But if the servitude be apparent and continuous, and one to whom it belongs exer-

[1] 3 Toullier, Droit Civil Français, 535.
[2] Ibid. 535, 536, 538 ; Domat, B. 1, tit. 12, § 6, Art. 5.

cises it for thirty years, but in part only, he loses the right beyond the use thus made. But if he uses and enjoys more than he has a right to, for thirty years, he acquires thereby a servitude to the whole extent of his enjoyment.[1]

It may be added, that it is not necessary that the owner of the servitude should himself do the acts requisite to retain it by user. If, for instance, it be a right of way, it would be sufficient if it were used by a workman, a friend, or even a stranger in making a visit to the owner of the servitude.[2]

And it may be further remarked, that the same rule applies as to successive owners of the dominant or servient estate, in respect to losing, as in acquiring, easements. The period of prescription which has run against, or in favor of a former owner, will be added to that of his vendee or successor, in completing the requisite period to gain or lose the servitude.[3]

But in Davies v. Williams, above cited, it was held that, after notice and demand of the tenant to remove the house, the owner of the right of common, with which the house unlawfully interfered, might pull it down, although the family of the tenant were actually in it at the time. But the case affirms the necessity of a demand and notice to the tenant to remove the house, before proceeding to abate it.

The court had previously, in Burling v. Reed, taken occasion to limit and modify the doctrine of Perry v. Fitzhowe, in which case the plaintiff owned the house, by saying, that

if the party in the house did not own it, and was
[*590] a stranger, *his being in the house was no reason
why the owner of it might not do what he liked
with it.[4]

The question of how far the grantee of the estate that is injured may avail himself of his right of abating a nuisance

---

[1] 3 Toullier, &c., 536 – 539.

[2] Pardessus, Traité des Servitudes, 451, 465.

[3] Pardessus, Traité des Servitudes, 451, 465 ; 3 Toullier, Droit Civil Français, 542 ; Domat, B. 1 tit. 12, § 6, Art. 8.

[4] Burling v. Reed, 11 Q. B. 904.

upon the land of another which was erected by the grantor of the latter estate, is settled in Penruddock's case, where it was held that in such a case the owner of the former estate must notify the owner of the latter to remove it, unless it be immediately dangerous to life and health ; and if he do not remove it, the former may proceed to abate it himself in the same manner as his grantor might have done against the grantor of the other estate, and that he need not wait, before so doing, till he shall have actually suffered prejudice by the erection which causes the nuisance.[1]

In the case of Salmon v. Bensley the court held, that an action would lie against a tenant for continuing a nuisance, if his immediate predecessor had been notified to remove it. " I am," says Abbott, C. J., " of opinion that a notice of this nature, delivered at the premises to which it relates, to the occupier for the time being, will bind the subsequent occupier. And that a person who takes premises upon which a nuisance exists, and continues it, takes them subject to all the restrictions imposed upon his predecessors by the receipt of such a notice." [2]

9. The abatement of a nuisance, moreover, does not operate as a bar to an action for the recovery of damages occasioned thereby prior to such abatement.[3]

The law on this subject may be summed up in the language of Blackstone : " A fourth species of remedy by the mere act of the party injured is the abatement or removal of nuisances. Whatever annoys or does damage to another is a nuisance ; and such nuisance may be abated, that is, * taken away or removed by the party ag- [*591] grieved thereby, so as he commits no riot in the doing of it. If a house or wall is erected so near to mine that it stops my ancient lights, which is a private nuisance, I may enter my neighbor's land and peaceably pull it down.

---

[1] Penruddock's case, 5 Rep. 101 ; Jones v. Williams, 11 Mees. & W. 176.
[2] Salmon v. Bensley, Ry. & M. 189.
[3] Call v. Buttrick, 4 Cush. 345.

And the reason why the law allows this private and summary method of doing one's self justice is because injuries of this kind, which obstruct or annoy such things as are of daily convenience and use, require an immediate remedy, and cannot wait for the slow progress of the ordinary forms of justice." [1]

[1] 3 Black. Com. 5.

www.ingramcontent.com/pod-product-compliance
Lightning Source LLC
Chambersburg PA
CBHW021541210326
41599CB00010B/275